C0-BVI-581

INDIANA HISTORICAL COLLECTIONS

THE act of the Indiana General Assembly signed by Governor Ralston on March 8, 1915, creating the Indiana Historical Commission, assigned to that body as one of its duties to collect and publish documentary and other materials on the history of Indiana. The law provides that these volumes should be printed and bound at the expense of the State and be made available to the public. Copies are offered at practically the cost of printing the volumes, the proceeds to go into the State treasury for the use of the Historical Commission in producing other volumes. One copy is to be furnished at the expense of the Commission to each public library, college and Normal School in the State.

Two hundred copies are to be furnished to the Indiana State Library and two hundred copies to the Historical Survey of Indiana University, for purposes of exchange with other states for similar publications. Of the $25,000 appropriated to the Commission for Centennial purposes, $5,000 were permitted to be used for historical publications.

FORT WAYNE PRINTING COMPANY
CONTRACTORS FOR STATE PRINTING AND BINDING
1916

INDIANA HISTORICAL COLLECTIONS

INDIANA AS SEEN BY EARLY TRAVELERS

A Collection of Reprints from Books of Travel, Letters and Diaries Prior to 1830

SELECTED AND EDITED BY

HARLOW LINDLEY

Director Department of Indiana History and Archives
Indiana State Library
Secretary Indiana Historical Commission

$1.50

PUBLISHED BY THE
INDIANA HISTORICAL COMMISSION
INDIANAPOLIS
1916

Indiana Historical Collections

INTRODUCTION

Many of the first books relating to Indiana were written by travelers whose aim was to tell the Old World what the New World was like. During the first half century following the Revolutionary War many travelers came from Europe to visit the New Republic and to explore the frontiers of America, and during the early decades of the nineteenth century many travelers from the Atlantic Coast states made trips into the interior to learn of the possibilities in the newer regions.

After a lapse of a century these descriptions are of much interest from an historical point of view. Personal estimates of the region vary and opinions were obviously warped in many cases but these descriptions reflect conditions about which we could today secure information in no other way. These books are now out of print and are not available for most people. Because of the growing demand for this material it has been deemed wise to issue a volume reprinting the material which concerns Indiana previous to 1830, in as near the original form as possible. Spelling, punctuation and capitalization have been followed. In some instances repetitions will be noticed, but it seemed best in most cases to give the full account as originally prepared by the author. Practically all of David Thomas' *Travels through the Western Country in the Summer of 1816*, with his additional notices, has been reprinted, since this Diary was written just one hundred years ago, portraying conditions here just as Indiana became a State, and also because of the particular value of this individual journal.

The object of this volume has been to make available to the people of the State and others interested in Indiana history, material which could not be procured easily otherwise. The original editions can be found in the Indiana State Library.

Included in the volume are four contributions which never before have appeared in print—the Journal of Thomas Scattergood Teas, Letters of William Pelham, Personal Reminiscences of Charles F. Coffin, and Diary and Recollections of Victor Colin Duclos. The Pelham letters have been made possible by Miss

Caroline Creese Pelham, of New Harmony, Indiana, a great granddaughter of William Pelham.

The Editor wishes to acknowledge the assistance given him by Miss Esther U. McNitt, Dr. John W. Oliver and Mr. Henry S. Miller, of the Department of Indiana History and Archives, Indiana State Library, and Dr. Walter C. Woodward, Director of the Indiana Historical Commission.

HARLOW LINDLEY.

Earlham College,
October 9, 1916.

CONTENTS

From *A Topographical Description of Virginia, Pennsylvania, Maryland, and North Carolina*, by Thomas Hutchins [1778], pp. 26-30.

HUTCHINS, THOMAS.

The first and only civil geographer of the United States and the originator of the land platting survey system was Thomas Hutchins. He was born in New Jersey in 1730, and after spending several years in the military service, he became interested in exploring the interior of the United States. The intimate knowledge gained, fitted him for laying out roads and making such topographical surveys as Congress desired. Hence in 1782 he was appointed official Geographer of the United States. For the next fifteen years he was busy surveying new lands, locating boundaries between states and collecting such scientific data as requested by the United States government. He was recognized as one of the foremost scientific men in the country, and his geographical works formed the basis for that famous American Geography of Jedidiah Morse.

The *Wabash*, is a beautiful River, with high and upright banks, less subject to overflow, than any other River (*the Ohio excepted*) in this part of *America*. It discharges itself into the *Ohio*, one thousand and twenty-two miles *below Fort Pitt*, in latitude 37° 41′.—At its mouth, it is 270 yards wide; Is navigable to *Ouiatanon* (412 miles) in the Spring, Summer, and Autumn, with Battoes or Barges, drawing about three feet water. From thence, on account of a rocky bottom, and shoal water, large canoes are chiefly employed, except when the River is swelled with Rains, at which time, it may be ascended with boats, such as I have just described, (197 miles further) to the *Miami* carrying-place, which is nine miles from the *Miami* village,[1] and this is situated on a River of the same name,[2] that runs into the south-south-west part of Lake *Erie*.—The Stream of the *Wabash*, is generally gentle to Fort *Ouiatanon*, and no where obstructed with Falls, but is by several *Rapids*, both above and below that Fort, some of which are pretty considerable. There is also a part of the River for about three miles, and 30 miles from the *carrying-place*, where the Channel is so narrow, that it is necessary to make use of setting poles, instead of oars. The land on this River is remarkably fertile, and several parts of it are natural meadows, of great extent, covered with fine long grass.—The timber is large, and high, and in such variety, that almost all the different kinds growing upon the *Ohio*, and its branches (but with a greater proportion of black and

1. Later Fort Wayne.
2. Maumee River.

white mulberry-trees) may be found here.—A silver mine has been discovered about 28 miles above *Ouiatanon*, on the northern side of the *Wabash*, and probably others may be found hereafter. The *Wabash* abounds with Salt Springs, and any quantity of salt may be made from them, in the manner now done at the *Saline* in the *Illinois* country:—the hills are replenished with the best coal, and there is plenty of *Lime* and *Free Stone*, *Blue*, *Yellow and White Clay, for Glass Works and Pottery.* Two *French* settlements are established on the *Wabash*, called *Post Vincient* and *Ouiatanon;* the first is 150 miles, and the other 262 miles from its mouth. The former is on the eastern side of the River, and consists of 60 settlers and their families. They raise Indian Corn,—Wheat; and Tobacco of an extraordinary good quality;—superior, it is said, to that produced in *Virginia*. They have a fine breed of horses (brought originally by the *Indians* from the *Spanish* settlements on the western side of the River *Missisippi*) and large stocks of Swine, and Black Cattle. The settlers deal with the natives for Furrs and Deer skins, to the amount of about 5000 *l*. annually. Hemp of a good texture grows spontaneously in the low lands of the *Wabash*, as do Grapes in the greatest abundance, having a black, *thin* skin, and of which the inhabitants in the Autumn, make a sufficient quantity (for their own consumption) of *well-tasted Red-Wine*. Hops large and good, are found in many places, and the lands are particularly adapted to the culture of Rice. All European fruits:—Apples, Peaches, Pears, Cherrys, Currants, Goosberrys, Melons, & thrive well, both here, and in the country bordering on the River *Ohio*.

Ouiatanon is a small stockaded fort on the western side of the *Wabash*, in which about a dozen families reside. The neighbouring Indians are the *Kickapoos*, *Musquitons*, *Pyankishaws*, *and a principle part of the Ouiatanons*. The whole of these tribes consists, it is supposed, of about one thousand warriors. The fertility of soil, and diversity of timber in this country, are the same as in the vicinity of *Post Vincient*. The annual amount of Skins and Furrs, obtained at *Ouiatanon* is about 8000 *l*. By the River *Wabash*, the inhabitants of Detroit move to the southern parts of *Ohio*, and the *Illinois* country. Their rout is by the *Miami River* to a carrying-place, which, as before stated, is nine miles to the *Wabash*, when this River is raised with Freshes; but at other seasons, the distance is from 18 to 30 miles including the portage. The whole of the latter is through a level country. Carts are usually employed in transporting boats and merchandise, from the *Miami* to the *Wabash* River.

From *A Topographical Description of the Western Territory of North America*, by George Imlay [1793], pp. 66-67, 81, 93-97, 113, 137-38, 402-13, 427.

Imlay, George.

George Imlay was a captain in the American army during the Revolutionary war, and later appointed commissioner for laying out lands in the "Back Settlements." Taking advantage of the opportunity, he spent considerable time in making a topographical study of the region. He describes with considerable interest the soil, climate, natural history, population, agriculture, manners and customs of the people. By supplying a few maps and a table of distances he presented a very readable and somewhat valuable book for that day—1793.

Immediately in the fork[1] the land is flat, and liable to overflow; but as you advance on either river the banks rise, and the country expanding, displays a luxuriant soil for a long distance above the Wabash on the Ohio side, and quite to the Illinois on the Mississippi side, which is about two hundred and thirty miles above its junction with the Ohio, and twenty above the mouth of Missouri. This country lies nearly in the same parallel of latitude of Kentucky. From the mouth of the Wabash* the bottoms on the Ohio are extensive and extremely fertile, as is the country from thence to Post St. Vincent; but towards the rapids of the Ohio, and beyond the bottoms of this river, the country is considerably broken, and the soil in some places light and indifferent. After leaving Post St. Vincent, in the route to the Illinois country, you soon fall into those extensive plains which have been described in such glowing colours by Hutchins. . . .

The country lying between the Miami, Wabash, the Ohio, and the same hills, I would put into another State; and the country lying between the Wabash, Ohio, Mississippi, and Illinois rivers, I would establish into a fifth State. . . .

Here is found all the variety of soil and climate necessary to the culture of every kind of grain, fibrous plants, cotton, fruits, vegetables, and all sorts of provisions. The upper settle-

*The Wabash is nearly 300 yards wide at its mouth, and except some inconsiderable rapids, it is navigable upwards of 400 miles.

1. Formed by the Ohio and Mississippi Rivers.

ments on the Ohio produce chiefly wheat, oats, barley, rye, Indian corn or maze, hemp and flax. The fruits are apples, pears, cherries, peaches, plums, strawberries, rasberries, currants, gooseberries, and grapes; of culinary plants and vegetables, there are turnips, potatoes, carrots, parsnips, cymbiline or squash, cucumbers, pease, beans, asparagus, cabbages, brocoli, celery and sallads; besides which there are melons and herbs of every sort. The provision consists of beef, pork, mutton, veal, and a variety of poultry, such as ducks, Muscovy ducks, turkeys, geese, dunghill fowls, and pigeons. The superfluous provisions are sold to the emigrants, who are continually passing through those settlements, in their route to the different districts of country, and which I have enumerated. Some considerable quantities of spirits distilled from rye, and likewise cyder, are sent down the river to a market, in those infant settlements where the inhabitants have not had time to bring orchards to any perfection, or have not a superfluity of grain to distil into spirits. The beef, pork, and flour are disposed of in the same way. The flax and hemp are packed on horses and sent across the mountain to the inland towns of Pennsylvania and Maryland, and (as I hinted in a former letter) in a few years, when grazing forms the principal object of those settlers, they will always find a market for their cattle at Philadelphia, Baltimore, and Alexandria.

These settlements might produce a considerable quantity of sugar, but hitherto what they have made has served for little more than home consumption, as every part of the back country from lat. 42° to 36° and upon the Mississippi, as far north as lat. 45°, produces an abundance of the sugar maple-tree as would be equal to furnish sugar for the inhabitants of the whole earth; and to send it to any of the market towns on the Atlantic is too far to be profitable, until the canals of the Potowmac shall have been finished. That country produces also all the pot-herbs which are common in Europe: several kinds of nuts grow in the forests, such as chestnuts, hickory, and black walnuts. The mountains, hills, and uninhabited parts abound in deer, wild turkeys, and a species of grouse, called by the Americans promiscuously partridge or pheasant. There is an abundance of wild fowl, as indeed is the case in every part of the western country: to enumerate these could prove for you neither amusement or instruction.

Linen and woolen cloths, leather, and hats, for home consumption, are manufactured with considerable success. The two first articles are only made in families for their own use; but the latter are made by men of profession in that business, and are of a quality that would not disgrace the mechanics of Europe. Blacksmiths' work of all sorts, even to making fire arms, is done there; as is also cabinet work, wheel-wright, mill-wright, house carpentry, joinery, shoe-making, etc., etc., in short, all the trades, immediately necessary to the promotion of the comforts of new settlements, are to be found here.

After passing to the southward of lat. 40 deg. the climate becomes favourable to the culture of tobacco. It will, no doubt, grow farther to the north; but neither its flavour is so aromatic, or the crop so certain or productive. Indeed, the farther south tobacco grows, generally the finer its quality; hence it is, that the saegars of Cuba are so much admired for their peculiar scent, and the Oroonookoo for its mildness. However, this is of little consequence to any country, as it is certain no cultivation is so pernicious to the soil, and of so little real advantage to the cultivator. It continually impoverishes the land; and every additional season, instead of producing riches to an estate, tends to beggar it: every vestige of its growth is misery and devastation, and no soil, but one as prolific as that of the Nile, would be capable of producing it for any length of time, according to the system which has been pursued in Virginia and Maryland. However, the whole of the Ohio and Mississippi country below lat. 40 deg. is perhaps better adapted to produce tobacco in quantity than any other country upon the face of the globe. . . .

There are also portages into the waters of Lake Erie from the Wabash, Great Miami, Muskingum, and Allegany, from 2 to 16 miles.* . . .

Copper mines have been discovered in several places, but the mine on the Wabash is, perhaps, the richest vein of native copper in the bowels of the whole earth; and no doubt will render all the others of little or no value. Sulphur is found in several places in abundance; and nitre is made from earth which is collected from caves and other places to which the wet has not penetrated. The making this salt, in this country, is so common, that many of the settlers manufacture their own gunpowder. . . .

Extract from a letter written by a member of the expedition against the Indians in 1791:

"General Scott, at the head of 800 Kentucky Volunteers, marched from opposite the mouth of the Kentucky River, about the

*Some of these have been noticed in a note in a preceding part of this work.

beginning of June, the course he steered was about north 20° west, and in about fifteen days he struck and surprized the lower Weaucteneau towns on the Wabash River, and the pararie adjoining; but unfortunately the river at that time was not fordable, or the Kickapoo Town on the north-west side, with the Indians who escaped in their canoes from the Weau Town on the south, must have fallen completely into our hands; however, about 20 warriors were killed in the Weau villages, and in the river crossing the Wabash, and 47 of their Squaws and children taken prisoners.

"Immediately after the engagement, a council of war was called, when it was determined, that Wilkinson should cross the Wabash under cover of the night, with a detachment of four hundred men, and endeavour to surprise the town of Kathtippacamunck, which was situated upon the north side of that river, at the mouth of Rippacanoe creek, and about twenty miles above the Lower Weau towns. This expedition was conducted with so much caution and celerity, that Wilkinson arrived at the margin of the pararie, within a mile, and to the west of the town, about an hour before the break of day; whilst a detachment was taking a circuit through the pararie to co-operate with the main body on a given signal; day appeared, and the volunteers rushed into the town with an impetuosity not to be resisted. The detachment in advance reached the Rippacanoe Creek the very moment the last of the Indians were crossing, when a very brisk fire took place between the detachment and the Indians on the opposite side, in which several of their warriors were killed, and two of our men wounded.

"This town, which contained about 120 houses, 80 of which were shingle roofed, was immediately burnt and levelled with the ground; the best houses belonged to French traders, whose gardens and improvements round the town were truly delightful, and, every thing considered, not a little wonderful; there was a tavern, with cellars, bar, public, and private rooms; and the whole marked a considerable share of order, and no small degree of civilization.

"Wilkinson returned with his detachment, after destroying the town, and joined the main army about seven in the evening; and the day following our little army were put in motion with their prisoners; and steering about south, in twelve days reached the Rapids of the Ohio, with the loss only of two men, who unfortunately were drowned in crossing Main White River.

"The success of this expedition encouraged Government to set another on foot, under the command of General Wilkinson;

which was destined to operate against the same tribes of Indians; whose main town, near the mouth of Ell River, on the Wabash, had not been attacked in the first excursion; and accordingly, on the first of August following, the general, at the head of 500 mounted volunteers, marched from Fort Washington, north 16° west, steering, as it were, for the Manmic villages on the Picaway Fork of the Manmic (or Miami of the lake) and St. Mary's River—This movement was intended as a feint, and the Indians, who afterwards fell upon our trail, were completely deceived; nor did we change our course, until by the capture of a Delaware Indian, we ascertained that we were within 30 miles of the principal of the Manmic villages, and having marched down our northing, at the very time we received the information, shifted our course to due west, and at the distance of 180 miles from Fort Washington we struck the Wabash within two miles and a half of Longuille, or, as the Indians call it, Kenapacomaqua—It was about 4 P. M. when we reached that river, and crossing it immediately, we marched in four columns across the neck of land, formed by the junction of the Wabash and Ell Rivers: passing several Indian war posts that had been fresh painted, we arrived completely concealed on the south bank of Ell River, and directly opposite the town of Kenapacomaqua.

"The surprize of this town was so very complete, that before we received orders to cross the river and rush upon the town, we observed several children playing on the tops of the houses, and could distinguish the hilarity and merriment that seemed to crown the festivity of the villagers, for it was in the season of the green corn dance.

"The want of day-light, and a morass, that nearly encircled the town, prevented us from suddenly attacking, which enabled several of the Indians to escape; and in some measure obscured the brilliancy of the enterprize, by limiting the number of warriors killed to eleven, and capturing forty Squaws and their children, after burning all the houses, and destroying about 200 acres of corn; which was then in the milk, and in that stage when the Indians prepare it for Zossomanony. This success was atchieved with the loss of two men, who were killed.

"About four o'clock in the afternoon we mounted our prisoners, and took a west and by north course toward the Little Kickapoo Town, which the general hoped to surprize on his way to the Great Kickapoo Town, in the pararie, on the waters of the Illinois River; but the difficulties we encountered in this march, through these almost boundless pararies, were such, that upon our arrival at the Little Kickapoo Town, we found one half the horses in the army non-effective, and unlikely to reach the Ohio, by the nearest course we could take; which consideration induced the general to relinquish the enterprize against the Great Kickapoo Town; and, accordingly, after destroying about 200 acres of corn at Kathtippacanunck, Kickapoo, and the lower Weauctenau towns, we gained General Scot's return tract, and on the 21st of August, after a circuitous march of 486 miles, arrived with our prisoners at Louisville.

"In the course of this march, I had an opportunity of observing the general face of the country through which we passed.—Between Fort Washington, at the crossing of the Great Miami, where at present there is a considerable settlement under the protection of Fort Hamilton, a fine body of land is found, but which is very indifferently watered. The situation of Fort Hamilton is well chosen, as advantageous for defence, as pleasing to the eye; it stands on a narrow neck of land, commanding the Miami on N.W. and a pararie and sheet of water on the N.E. about a mile wide, and two miles and a half long; from this pararie an abundant supply of forage may be got for the use of the army by repeated movings [mowings] of a very fine natural grass, from the month of June till the end of September. After passing the Miami River hills, on the west side, the country in places is broken, though, generally speaking, from thence to the limits of our march, toward the Manmic villages the face of it is agreeably varied with hills and dales; well watered, and the timber mostly such as indicates a strong and durable soil. Between the Manmic trace and our west line of march toward Kenapacomaqua, there are a number of beech swamps, which will require draining before they will admit of settlements being formed—there are however delightfully pleasant and fertile situations on the Balemut and Salamine Rivers, which are only inferior to the woody plains of Kentucky in extent and climate. The pararie, in which was situated Kenapacomaqua, on the north bank of Ell River, is chiefly a morass, and produces little else, other than hazel, sallow, a species of dwarf poplar, and a very coarse, but luxuriant grass; the latter of which covers mostly the whole surface of the earth.—The same kind of pararie extends, with little alteration, until you approach Kathtippacanunck, when the whole country gradually assumes a more pleasing and valuable appearance.

"On our line of march from Kenapacomaqua to Kathtippacanunck (the distance of which from the traverses we were obliged to make to avoid impassable morasses, was sixty miles), in several places, the prospect was only bounded by the natural horizon, the uniformity of which was here and there broken by the distant looming of a grove on the edge of the plane, which strongly resembled the projecting points of a coach clothed with wood, and seen by mariners at a distance from the shore.

"The situation of the late town of Kathtippacanunck was well chosen for beauty and convenience; it stood in the bosom of a delightful surrounding country on a very rich bottom, extending east and west, on the Wabash River about two miles; the bottom about half a mile wide, bounded on the east by Tippacanoe, and westward by a beautiful rising ground, skirted and clothed with thin woods—from the upper bank you command a view of the Wabash River, which is terminated by a towering growth of wood to the south, and Tippacanoe Creek to the East—the country in the rear from the upper bank spreads into a level pararie of firm, strong land, of an excellent quality, interspersed with copses, naked groves of trees, and high mounds of earth of a regular and conical form, all of which conspire to relieve the eye, and cheer the scene with a most agreeable variety. The top of this bank, which is level with the plane of the pararie, and about two hundred feet perpendicular from the bottom in which the town stood, forms an angle about 60°, and about midway there issues from its side two living fountains, which have hitherto constantly supplied the town with water.

"The country between Kathtippacanunck and the Little Kickapoo town is beautiful beyond description. The numerous breaks, and intermixture of woodland and plains, give the whole an air of the most perfect taste; for nature here, in a propitious hour and in a benignant mood, seems to have designed to prove, in beautifying, how far she excels our utmost efforts, and the most laboured improvements of art.

"Between the Little Kickapoo town and the lower Weausteneau towns, the land is of the first-rate quality—at the edge of the wood lands, and before you descend into the river bottoms, one of the most charming prospects the imagination can form, displays itself in all the variegated pride of the most captivating beauty. From this place, through the glades and vistas of the groves in the bottom, you catch a view of the meandering river, which silently steals through this smiling country, as if pregnant with its charms, and, as if it was hurrying to communicate its joys to less happy streams. The bottoms of the Wabash on the opposite side are confined by a bluff bank nearly two hundred feet, which interrupts the prospect, and runs parrallel with the river—from the top of this bank a plain is seen stretching out to the east and west as far as the eye can reach, without tree or bush, covered with a most luxuriant herbage, and in every respect assuming the appearance of a highly improved and cultivated meadow. The plain is terminated on the south by a distant prospect of the rising woodlands, which, with a misty bloom, and in all that azure beauty, so peculiar to these fair regions, here appears in all its ætherial lustre; and seems finally lost in combining with the clouds.

"The Briares extend about twenty-five miles south of the Wabash, from thence the country gradually breaks into hills and valleys, and until we reached the waters of White River, we found the soil tolerably good. There it is very much broken, the bottoms of the rivers are narrow, and subject to frequent and violent inundations.

"There is some tolerable good land on Rocky River, but as we approached the waters of the Blue River, the country again opens into plains, in which are interspersed clumps of scrubby oak, dwarf laurel, plumb, and hazel, that extend to Indian Creek, when the country again improves, and though it is rather broken, it continued to improve until we reached the Rapids of the Ohio." ...The country within the Wabash, the Indian line before described, the Pennsylvania line, and the Ohio, contains, on a loose estimate, about 55,000 square miles, or 35 millions of acres.

During the British government, great numbers of persons had formed themselves into companies under different names, such as the Ohio, the Wabache, the Illinois, the Mississippi, or Vandalia companies, and had covered, with their applications, a great part of this territory. Some of them had obtained orders on certain conditions, which, having never been fulfilled, their titles were never completed by grants. Others were only in a state of negociation, when the British authority was discontinued.

From *A view of the soil and climate of the United States of America*, by C. F. Volney [1804], pp. 24-25, 70-71, 121, 124, 331-37, 352-55.

VOLNEY, CONSTANTIN FRANÇOIS CHASSEBOENF.

C. F. Volney was a Frenchman who first gained distinction by publishing an account of his travels in Syria and Egypt. In 1796 he came to America and made a study chiefly of its physical conditions, its surface and climate. A few remarks were added upon the character of the aboriginal tribes. The writer was somewhat prejudiced and his descriptions smack strongly of conceit. Yet, unassisted as he was, he presents as nearly a scientific review of conditions as was possible for any one observer.

...I traversed one hundred and twenty miles of this forest, from Louisville, near the rapids of Ohio, to Vincennes, on the Wabash, without lighting on a hut, and, what surprised me still more, without hearing the voice of a bird, though in the month of July. This forest ends just before you reach the Wabash, and from thence to the Mississippi, a distance of eighty miles, all is prairie or meadow. Here commences the *American Tartary*, bearing, in all respects, a strong resemblance to the Asiatic. Though warm and sultry in the southern quarter, the air becomes chill, and the soil unkindly, as you go northward. Beyond the 48th degree of north latitude, the waters are frozen six months in the year, the ground is overshadowed by deep woods, or drowned in swamps, and intersected by rivers, which, in a course of three thousand miles have not fifty miles of interruption or *portages*. In all these features, we recognize a likeness to the ancient Tartary, which would be entire and complete, could we see its natives metamorphosed into horsemen. This transformation has, within the last twenty-five or thirty years, taken place, in some degree, among the Nehesawey or Noudowessey Indians, who are mounted upon Spanish horses, stolen in the plains north of Mexico. In half a century, these New Tartars will probably become formidable neighbours to the people of the United States, and the settlers beyond the Mississippi will encounter difficulties totally unknown to their ancestors.

...On my return from Vincennes, on the Wabash, I was first struck by the position of a ridge of hills, situated below *Silver Creek*, about five miles from the *rapids*. This ridge, vaguely denominated, by the Canadians, *the Banks*, stretches from north to south, across the *basin* of the Ohio. It compels the stream to change its course from east to west, in search of an outlet, which presents itself at its conflux with the Salt River. It may be said to require the accession of that river, in order to force a way through the rampart before it. The rapid but smooth declivity of these *banks* may be descended in a quarter of an hour. Compared with other heights, their elevation may be stated at 400 feet. The summit is too thickly studded with trees to permit us to trace the lateral course of this chain with the eye. We may discover, however, that it stretches far to the north and south, and that it shuts up the entire basin of the Ohio.

Viewed from this summit, the general appearance of this vale tended strongly to confirm all my previous opinions respecting the existence of an ancient lake. Other circumstances likewise lent their aid to this conclusion; for from this ridge to the *White River*, eight miles from Vincennes, the whole surface is roughened by hills, frequently steep and lofty. They are high and precipitous near the Blue River, and on both sides of the White River. They take a course, in general, transverse to the Ohio.

...Wheat is not grown at Vincennes. The products chiefly attended to are maize, tobacco, and cotton, all which have been deemed congenial to a hot climate.

...The Wabash is usually frozen in winter, but only for five, ten, or fifteen days. In Kentucky, and throughout the vale of the Ohio, the snow remains from three days to ten, and even in January they experience hot sultry days, when the mercury rises to 66 and 72, with the wind at south or south-west, and a clear sky. The spring is ushered in with showers, blown from the north-east and north-west, and the heats become great and permanent within forty days after the equinox. For sixty or seventy days ensuing the summer solstice, they prevail with the greatest intensity, the thermometer ranging between 90 and 95. This period is tempestuous, storms almost daily occurring on the Ohio, and these storms rather aggravate than moderate the heat. Rain is sometimes brought by the south and south-west winds, and sometimes is formed by the vapours rising copiously from the river and the immense forest that overshadows all the country. The rain, which descends in torrents, gives only momentary relief to the parched soil, and the heat of the ensuing day obliging it to reascend, it forms heavy morning mists, which afterwards become clouds, and thus continually renews the electrical process. The river water is at the temperature of 64 or 66. After a night of dead calm, a breeze is called up from the west or south-west, between eight and ten in the morning, which dies away about four in the afternoon.

. . . Louisville (Kentucky) has about a hundred houses, and is two miles above the falls, more properly the *rapids*, of the Ohio, which I passed over in a boat. I waited here eight hours, till a caravan was collected of four or five horsemen, necessary to travel upwards of 100 miles of woods and meadows, so desart as not to contain a solitary hut.

After a hasty march of three days, we reached (August 2, 1796) Vincennes, on the Wabash. The eye is at first presented with an irregular savannah, eight miles in length by three in breadth, skirted by eternal forests, and sprinkled with a few trees, and abundance of umbelliferous plants, three or four feet high. Maize, tobacco, wheat, barley, squashes, and even cotton, grow in the fields around the village, which contains about fifty houses, whose cheerful white relieves the eye, after the tedious dusk and green of the woods.

These houses are placed along the left bank of the Wabash, here about two hundred feet wide, and falling, when the waters are low, twenty feet below the scite of the town. The bank of the river is sloping towards the savannah, which is a few feet lower: this slope is occasioned by the periodical floods. Each house, as is customary in Canada, stands alone, and is surrounded by a court and garden, fenced with poles. I was delighted by the sight of peach trees loaded with fruit, but was sorry to notice the thorn apple, which is found in all the cultivated places from beyond Gallipolis. Adjoining the village and river is a space, enclosed by a ditch eight feet wide, and by sharp stakes six feet high. This is called the fort, and is a sufficient safeguard against surprises from Indians.

I had letters to a principal man of the place, by birth a Dutchman, but who spoke good French. I was accommodated at his house, in the kindest and most hospitable manner, for ten days. The day after my arrival a court was held, to which I repaired, to make my remarks on the scene. On entering, I was surprised to observe the audience divided into races of men, in persons and feature widely differing from each other. The fair or light brown hair, ruddy complexion, round face, and plump body, indicative of health and ease, of one set, were forcibly contrasted with the emaciated frame, and meagre tawny visage of the other: the dress, likewise, of the latter denoted their indigence. I soon discovered that the former were new settlers from the neighbouring states, whose lands had been reclaimed five or six years before, while the latter were French, of sixty years standing in the district. The latter, three or four excepted, knew nothing of English, while the former were almost as ignorant of French. I had acquired, in the course of a year, a sufficient knowledge of English to converse with them, and was thus enabled to hear the tales of both parties.

The French, in a querulous tone recounted the losses and hardships they had suffered, especially since the last Indian war, in 1788. Between that period and the peace of 1763, when England obtained Canada, and Spain Louisiana, they enjoyed tranquillity and happiness, under the protection of Spain. Unmolested and sequestered in the heart of the wilderness, fifty leagues from the nearest post on the Mississippi, without taxes, and in friendship with the Indians, they passed their lives in hunting, fishing, trading in furs, and raising a few esculents and a little corn for their families. Many of them had inter-married with the Indians, whose amity was by these ties secured and strengthened, and their numbers amounted to three hundred persons.

During the revolutionary war, their remote situation exempted them from all its evils, till, in 1782, they were visited by a detachment from Kentucky, who plundered and insulted them, and killed or drove off the cattle which formed their chief wealth.

The peace of 1783 gave them to the United States, under whose benign government they began to breathe again; but unluckily an Indian war commenced in 1788, and siding with the whites, as duty and discretion enjoined, they were annoyed by the savages, whose animosity was embittered by the remembrance of their ancient friendship and alliance. Their cattle were killed, their village closely beset, and, for several years, they could not carry the plough or hoe a musket shot from their huts.

Military service was added to their other hardships; but, in 1792, the compassion of the federal government gave four hundred acres of land to every one who paid the capitation, and a hundred more to every one who served in the militia. This domain, so ample to a diligent husbandman, was of little value to the hunting Frenchmen, who soon bartered away their invaluable ground for about 30 cents an acre, which was paid to them in goods, on which an exorbitant profit was charged. This land was of the best quality; it sold as early as 1796, at two dollars an acre, and I may venture to say is now worth at least ten. Thus, for the most part, reduced again to their gardens, or the little homestead which was indispensable to their subsistence, they had nothing to live on but their fruit, potatoes, maize, and now and then a little game; and, on this fare, no wonder they became as lean as Arabs.*

They complain that they were cheated and robbed, and, especially that their rights were continually violated by the courts, in which two judges only out of five were Frenchmen, who knew little of the laws or language of the English. Their ignorance, indeed, was profound. Nobody ever opened a school among them, till it was done by the abbe R. a polite, well educated, and liberal minded missionary, banished hither by the French revolution. Out of nine of the French, scarcely six could read or write, whereas nine-tenths of the Americans, or emigrants from the east, could do both. Their dialect is by no means, as I had been previously assured, a vulgar or provincial *brogue*, but pretty good French, intermixed with many military terms and phrases, all these settlements having been originally made by soldiers. The primitive stock of Canada was the regiment of Carignon. I could not fix with accuracy the date of the first settlement of Vincennes; and, notwithstanding the homage paid by some learned men to tradition, I could trace out but few events of the war of 1757, though some of the old men lived before that period. I was only able to form a conjecture that it was planted about 1735.

These statements were confirmed, for the most part, by the new settlers. They only placed the same facts in a different point of view. They told me that the Canadians, for by that name the French of the western colonies are known among them, had only themselves to blame for all the hardships they complained of. We must allow, say they, that they are a kind, hospitable, sociable set, but then for idleness and ignorance, they beat the Indians themselves. They know nothing at all of civil or domestic affairs: their women neither sow, nor spin, nor make butter, but pass their time in gossipping and tattle, while all at home is dirt and disorder. The men take to nothing but hunting, fishing, roaming in the woods, and loitering in the sun. They do not lay up, as we do, for winter, or provide for a rainy day. They cannot cure pork or venison, make sour crout or spruce beer, or distil spirits from apples or rye, all needful arts to the farmer. If they trade, they try by exorbitant charges to make much out of a little; for *little*

*This implies that hunger or spare diet makes them lean, but this is evidently absurd. They cannot want plenty of the best food, and are probably greater eaters than their sleek and jolly neighbors. Their thinness must be owing to their constitution or their activity.—Trans.

is generally their *all*, and what they get they throw away upon the Indian girls, in toys and baubles. Their time is wasted too in trifling stories of their insignificant adventures, and journies *to town* to see their friends.*

When the peace of 1793 incorporated them with the United States, their first demand was a *commanding* officer, and hard it was to make them comprehend the nature of elective or municipal government.—Even now they have nobody fit to govern the rest. They will not learn English, and it is not worth while for us to learn the language of eighty or ninety people, who may leave us to-morrow for Louisiana. Indeed they would be wise in doing so, for their indolence will never be a match for our industry.

...My stay at Vincennes afforded me some knowledge of the Indians, who were there assembled to barter away the produce of their red hunt. There were four or five hundred of them, men, women, and children, of various tribes, as the Weeaws, Payories, Sawkies, Pyankishaws, and Miamis, all living near the head of the Wabash. This was the first opportunity I had of observing, at my leisure, a people who have already become rare east of the Allegheny. It was, to me, a new and most whimsical sight. Bodies almost naked, tanned by the sun and air, shining with grease and soot; head uncovered; hair coarse, black, and straight; a face smeared with red, blue, and black paint, in patches of all forms and sizes; one nostril bored to admit a ring of silver or copper; ear-rings, with three rows of drops, down to the shoulders, and passing through holes that would admit a finger; a little square apron before, and another behind, fastened by the same string; the legs and thighs sometimes bare, and sometimes covered with cloth hose; socks of smoke-dried leather; sometimes a shirt, with short loose sleeves, and flowing loosely on the thighs, of variegated or striped cloth; over this a blanket, or a square piece of cloth, drawn over one shoulder, and fastened under the other, or under the chin. On solemn occasions, or for war, their hair is braided with flowers, feathers, or bones. The warriors have their wrists adorned with broad metal rings, like our dog collars, and a circle round their heads, of buckles or beads. They carry in their hand a pipe, knife or tomahawk, and a little looking-glass, which they examine with as much attention and complacency as any European coquet. The females are a little more covered about the loins. They carry one or two children behind them in a sort of

*Thus they speak of New Orleans, as if it were a walk of half an hour, though it is fifteen hundred miles down the river.

bag, the ends of which are tied upon their forehead. In this respect they have a strong resemblance to our gypsies.

The men and women roamed all day about the town, merely to get rum, for which they eagerly exchanged their peltry, their toys, their clothes, and at length, when they had parted with their all, they offered their prayers and entreaties, never ceasing to drink till they had lost their senses. Hence arise ridiculous scenes. They will hold the cup with both hands, like monkies, burst into unmeaning laughter, and gargle their beloved cup, to enjoy the taste of it the longer; hand about the liquor with clamorous invitations, bawl aloud at each other, though close together, seize their wives, and pour the liquor down their throats, and, in short, display all the freaks of vulgar drunkenness. Sometimes tragical scenes ensue: they become mad or stupid, and falling in the dust or mud, lie a senseless log till next day. We found them in the streets by dozens in the morning, wallowing in the filth with the pigs. It was rare for a day to pass without a deadly quarrel, by which about ten men lose their lives yearly. A savage once stabbed his wife, in four places, with a knife, a few paces from me. A similar event took place a fortnight before, and five such the preceding year. For this, vengeance is either immediately taken, or deferred to a future opportunity by the relations of the slain, which affords fresh cause for bloodshed and treachery. I at first conceived the design of spending a few months among them, as I had done among the Bedwins; but I was satisfied with this sample, and those the best acquainted with them assured me, that there was no Arabian hospitality among them: that all was anarchy and disorder. The greatest chief could not strike or punish the meanest warrior, even in the field, and at home nobody obeyed him but his own wife and children. They dwell separately, in mistrust, jealousy, and eternal animosity. With them, what they want they have a right to, and what they have strength enough to seize is their own. Besides, as they scarcely made provision for themselves, a stranger would run the risk of being starved.

I chiefly regretted, on abandoning my scheme, the loss of an opportunity for gaining some knowledge of their language, and forming a vocabulary: a scheme the importance of which, with respect to a people who want all other monuments, I have elsewhere insisted on.* The missionary R., whom I have already

*See my Lectures upon History, Lecture V.

mentioned, having failed in all his efforts to this purpose, left me no hopes of succeeding. Some of the people of Vincennes are acquainted with the Indian dialects, but their pronunciation is so bad, and their ignorance of all grammatical distinctions so great, that they could afford him no aid.

From *Travels in America performed in* 1806, *for the purpose of exploring the rivers Allegheny, Monongahela, Ohio and Mississippi, and ascertaining the produce and condition of the banks and vicinity*, by Thomas Ashe, Esq. [1808], pp. 232-33, 246-49.

ASHE, THOMAS.

Thomas Ashe was an Englishman, and like many of his kind, came to America for the purpose of travel and exploration. He arrived here in 1806, came west, explored the Allegheny, Monongahela, Ohio and Mississippi Rivers. His sole view was "to examine in a satisfactory manner this new and interesting country."

While rather plain spoken about conditions as they existed here, yet his description does not smack of undue criticism. His letters, published in 1808, were read with interest by emigrants and antiquarians.

Fourteen miles from the North Bend, and twenty-one from Cincinnati, I passed the mouth of the great Miami; on the right-hand shore from it is the Western boundary of the Ohio State, and the Eastern commencement of the Indiana territory, which, in a short time, and with the increase of population, will receive the title of a State and become the brightest star in the galaxy of the Union. The land is for a great part richly wooded, fertile, and applicable to all the purposes of agriculture and extensive and productive improvement. The territory is upwards of six hundred miles square, and is thus copiously watered; on the north by the Lakes; on the south by the Ohio; and on the west by the Mississippi. Through it also runs, generally in a south course, the Wabash, the Illinois, and variety of creeks and streams. . .

Mouth of the Wabash, Indiana Territory.
September, 1806.

PREVIOUSLY to leaving Louisville, I crossed the river and visited the town of Jefferson, which is also seated about two miles above the falls. It is yet very small, but the inhabitants appear determined to add to its character and opulence, being now employed in forming a canal, by which navigators may avoid all dangers, and proceed down the river at all seasons of the year. I surveyed the line of the canal, and think it much more practicable than that marked off on the opposite shore. I entertain no doubt of the commerce of the river being adequate to the support of both undertakings, and that the proprietors will be hereafter amply remunerated.

I descended the falls by the shore, and once more enjoyed their grandeur, though from a different point of view. I then crossed over to my boat, which lay at Clarksville, a small settlement lying near the eddy formed by the recoiling flood. It is as yet a village of no importance, however, if it forms the mouth of the intended canal its rise is certain. Twenty-five miles from Louisville, I passed the mouth of Salt River on the Kentucky shore. All I could learn respecting it, was, that it received its name from the number of salines on its banks, which impregnate its waters, when in a low state, and fifty-seven miles farther down I put into Blue River on the Indiana side, which takes its name from its colour being of a fine azure.

In the whole run to the Wabash of two hundred and seventy-two miles, effected in six days, and I made little or no stop, and met with no event to be called interesting. I very strongly perceived that occurances capable of affording information and anecdote were ceasing. Above the falls, the banks of the river are enlivened by plantations, towns, and villages; below, nothing is seen but the state of nature, broken at vast distances, of from twenty to thirty miles, with wretched huts, the residence of solitude and misfortune. Most of the settlers on the lower parts were criminals who either escaped from, or were apprehensive of, public justice. On descending the river, they fix on some inviting spot without ever looking after the proprietor of the soil, erect a log-hut, plant a little corn, make salt at a neighbouring saline; coffee from the wild pea; and extract sugar from the maple tree. In time they extend their labours, and embrace all the necessaries of life. Some do more—from living in habits of industry they lose the practise of vice, and learn the consequence of virtue; while unhappily, some others pursue their former crimes, and live by the means of murder and the plunder of various boats.

The aspect and banks of the river in the late run I have made, are nearly similar to those above the falls, and from below Pittsburg. The banks are formed of a chain of mountains; some rising up and above the rest; and some are so low, interwoven, and contrasted, that they form an agreeable diversity of hills and dales. From several points of view, the opposite bank looks like an immense amphitheatre, which has all the charms that can be produced by an infinite variety of the most sumptuous trees and shrubs, reflecting uncommon beauties on each other, and on the bosom of their favourite flood. Twenty miles below Blue River I crossed the mouth of another river on the same side. I believe it has not been named. The navigation of the three last rivers I have mentioned, is very trifling. Their waters are low, and broken by rocks and rapids.

About ninety miles below the Blue River, and eight hundred and thirty-nine from Pittsburg, is Yellow-bank Creek; so called from the banks changing its general colour and quality of a black mould to a bright yellow clay. In the space of eight miles below this creek, I passed a chain of islands, six in number, which added much to the effect and beauty of the water, and gave more variety of the general scene. The islands were richly wooded, as are all others on the river. Between a creek called Hacden's and the Yellow-bank, which maintains its colour for the distance of a mile, the low lands commence. The high hills, which up the river are uniformly to be met with, now entirely disappear, and there is nothing to be seen on either hand but an extensive level country. It is remarkable, that the hills should subside on each shore exactly at equal distances down, and in a similar distinction and manner twenty-five miles from the Yellow-bank. I crossed the mouth of Green River on the Kentucky shore. It is the fine water which I mentioned in my last. It is navigated by a bateaux at one season, and by flat bottomed boats through the year. The lands are healthy, and inhabited by a stout race of people. Nearer the Ohio it is subject to inundation, is sickly, and thinly settled. Lower down, twenty-five miles more, I came to a place called the Red Bank, in consequence of its varying from the general colour, and assuming a deep red. I could not learn that any mineral or any ore had ever been discovered in the Red or Yellow-bank. This colour would encourage a belief that they contain something analagous to its distinction from that of the common and adjoining soil. The United States should order such appearances to be analized and explored. At the Red Bank, which is included in a grant by Congress to one Henderson, of two hundred thousand acres—a town is laid off. Owing to a remarkable bend in the river, though the distance from the mouth of Green River to Henderson by water is twenty-five miles, yet by land it is only about seven. Henderson consists of about twenty houses, and inhabited by a people whose doom is fixed. I never saw the same number of persons look so languid, emaciated and sick. The whole settlement was attacked in the spring by the ague, which subsided in a nervous fever, and is now followed by a violent and wasting flux.

I left Henderson with the commisseration due to the sufferings of its inhabitants, and after a run of fifteen miles, came in view of

Diamond Island, which is by far the finest in the river, and perhaps the most beautiful in the world. It is higher than the adjoining main land, containing twenty-thousand acres; and is of the exact form of a diamond, whose angles point directly up and down, and to each side of the expanded river. The shades, views, and perspective of an island so situated, clothed with aromatic shrubs, crowned with timber, surrounded by water, bounded by an extensive and delightful country, are too numerous, varied, and sublime, to come under the controul of written description.

I visited the island in several directions, and found established on it a few French families, who live nearly in the original Indian state and bestow very little labour on the ground. They have planted a few peech-orchards which thrive well, as do every other exotic introduced. Native grapes abound, and I tasted wine expressed from them, which was as good as any inferior Bourdeaux. Fish are innumerable in the water, and swans, ducks, and geese reside eight months in the year around the island. It also abounds with game of every description, and is often visited by herds of deer, which swim from the main land to enjoy its fragrant herbage and luxuriant pasture.

The Wabash enters on the Indiana or N.W. side. It is nine hundred and forty-nine miles from Pittsburg, and is one of the most considerable rivers between that town and the mouth of the Ohio. It is very beautiful, four hundred yards wide at its mouth, and three hundred at St. Vineconne's, which is one hundred miles above the mouth in a direct line. Within this space there are two small rapids which give very little obstruction to the navigation. In the spring and autumn it is passable for bateaux, drawing three feet water; four hundred and twelve miles to Ouiatona, a small French settlement on the west side of the river; and for large canoes it is navigable for one hundred and ninety-seven miles further, to the Miami carrying-place, which is nine miles from the Miami village. This village stands on Miami River,[1] which empties into the S.W. part of Lake Erie. The communication between Detroit and the Illinois and Indiana country, is up Miami River to Miami village; thence, by land, nine miles through a level country to the Wabash, and through the various branches of the Wabash to the respective places of distinction.

A silver mine has been discovered about twenty-eight miles above Ouiatonan, and salt-springs, lime, free-stone, blue, yellow and white clay, are found in abundance on this river's banks.

1. Now called Maumee.

From *Travels in the United States of America, in the years 1806, 1807, 1809, 1810* and *1811*, by John Melish [1812], Vol. II, pp. 150-57.

MELISH, JOHN.

Mr. Melish was an English merchant who early became interested in the business possibilities offered in the United States. As early as 1798, when on a trip to the West Indies, he began taking note of the natural and geographic conditions peculiar to America. A few years later he made an extensive trip through the Atlantic Coast states, going as far south as Georgia, and kept careful notes of his travels. Becoming financially interested in an American business undertaking, he studied the American institutions in great detail. On all of his journeys 1806-1807; 1808-1809, he kept a careful diary. He was especially interested in the prospective lines of communication; the political and economic views of the settlers; their attitude toward Great Britain, etc. Several maps were charted, and published along with his travels, 1812.

LOUISVILLE, being the principal port of the western part of the state of Kentucky, is a market for the purchase of all kinds of produce, and the quantity that is annually shipped down the river is immense. A few of the articles, with the prices at the time that I was there, may be noticed. Flour and meal have been quoted. Wheat was 62½ cents per bushel; corn 50; rye 42; oats 25; hemp 4 dollars 50 cents per cwt.; tobacco 2 dollars. Horses 25 to 100 dollars; cows 10 to 15 dollars; sheep 1 dollar 25 cents to 5 dollars; *negroes* about 400 dollars; cotton bagging 31¼ cents per yard.

As to the state of society I cannot say much. The place is composed of people from all quarters, who are principally engaged in commerce; and a great number of the traders on the Ohio are constantly at this place, whose example will be nothing in favour of the young; and slavery is against society everywhere. There are several schools, but none of them are under public patronage; and education seems to be but indifferently attended to. Upon the whole, I must say, that the state of public morals admits of considerable improvement here; but, indeed, I saw Louisville at a season, when a number of the most respectable people were out of the place. Those with whom I had business were gentlemen, and I hope there are a sufficient number of them to check the progress of *gaming* and *drinking*, and to teach the young and the thoughtless, that mankind, without virtue and industry, cannot be happy.

JEFFERSONVILLE is situated on the opposite side of the river, a little above Louisville, and is the capital of Clark county, in the Indiana territory. It was laid out in 1802, and now contains about 200 inhabitants, among whom are some useful mechanics. The United States have a land office at this place, but the principal objects of my inquiry being more to the eastward, I did not visit it. There is a good landing at Jeffersonville, and, as the best passage is through what is called the Indian Shute, it is probable that this place will materially interfere with the trade of Louisville, unless it be prevented by a plan to be hereafter noticed, in which case, each side will have its own share of the valuable commerce of this river; which, as it is yearly encreasing, cannot fail to convert both sides of the Ohio here into great settlements.

CLARKSVILLE, a small village, is situated at the foot of the falls on the Indiana side, as is SHIPPINGPORT, on the Kentucky side; and both answer for re-shipping produce after vessels pass the falls.

THE FALLS, or rather RAPIDS OF THE OHIO, are occasioned by a ledge of rocks, which stretches quite across the river; and through which it has forced a passage by several channels. The descent is only 22 feet in the course of two miles, and in high water is only to be perceived in the encreased velocity of the current, when the largest vessels pass over it in safety. When I was there, the water was low, and I observed three different passages, of which that on the Indiana side, called *Indian Shute*, is said to be the best; the middle one next best; the one on the Kentucky side cannot be passed, except when the water is pretty full. But when the water is very low, they are all attended with danger, 'ess or more, of which we saw an instance in a boat that came down the river along with us. Her cargo was unloaded at Louisville, and she proceeded down the river; but, on taking the stream, she struck on the rocks, and lay there a wreck, when I came away. Good pilots have been appointed to carry vessels over the falls.

On visiting this place, a question immediately occurs: Why is a canal not cut here, which would remove the only obstruction to the trade of this fine river? It appears that the subject has been long in contemplation, and a company was incorporated by the legislature of Kentucky to carry it into effect. The ground has been surveyed, and no impediment has been suggested to the execution of the plan, except that there is a danger of the locks being injured by the freshets in the river, which, however, can be guarded against. But sufficient funds have not yet been raised, and it is said that an opinion prevails here, that the execution of a canal would hurt the trade of Louisville. As to funds, there should be no lack, for this is an object of *national utility*, in which the rich states of Kentucky, Virginia, Pennsylvania, and Ohio are particularly interested. No very great sum can be wanted to cut a canal, with only 22 feet fall, the distance of two miles, in a situation where stones are plenty; and if it is found that individuals would not wish to embark their capital in it, there is no question but the United States, and the individual states noticed, would fill up the subscription, were the matter judiciously laid before them. As to the supposition that it would hurt the trade of Louisville, if it exists, it is founded on very narrow policy, and is just as correct an idea, as that a good turnpike road leading through a town, will hurt the trade of that town. A free communication through a country is favourable to every portion of that country; and were a canal cut upon the Kentucky side here, it would not only counter-balance the benefit arising to the other side from the Indian Shute, but would be productive of advantages to Louisville, that at present cannot be estimated. The mills alone that might be erected, and set in motion, by a judicious application of the water, would be of more intrinsic value than a gold mine.

The following table, exhibiting the commerce on the Ohio, is extracted from the Pittsburg Navigator, and shows the importance of this place, and the vast utility of a canal.

Commerce of the Ohio from November 24, 1810, to January 24, 1811.

In these two months 197 flat-boats, and 14 keel-boats descended the falls of the Ohio, carrying

18,611 bbls. flour
520 bbls. pork
2,373 bbls. whisky
3,759 bbls. apples
1,085 bbls. cyder
721 bbls. cyder royal
43 bbls. cyder—wine
323 bbls. peach-brandy
46 bbls. cherry-bounce
17 bbls. vinegar
143 bbls. porter
62 bbls. beans
67 bbls. onions
20 bbls. ginseng
200 groce bottled porter
260 gallons Seneca oil
1,526 lbs. butter
180 lbs. tallow
64,750 lbs. lard
6,300 lbs. beef
4,433 lbs. cheese
681,900 lbs. pork in bulk
4,609 lbs. bacon
59 lbs. soap
300 lbs. feathers
400 lbs. hemp
1,484 lbs. thread
154,000 lbs. rope-yarn
20,784 lbs. bale-rope
27,700 yards bagging
4,619 yards tow-cloth
479 coils tarred rope
500 bushels oats
1,700 bushels corn
216 bushels potatoes
817 hams venison
14,390 tame fowls
155 horses
286 slaves
18,000 ft. cherry plank
279,300 ft. pine plank

Also, a large quantity of potter's ware, ironmongery, cabinet-work, shoes, boots, and saddlery; the amount of which could not be correctly ascertained.

The country round Louisville is rich, but it is not well drained nor cultivated, and is consequently subject to fever and ague in the fall. There are a great many ponds in the neighbourhood of the town; at one of them, I observed a rope-walk erecting and the people were draining the pond, by sinking a deep well, and letting the water run into it, which answered the purpose remarkably well. It would appear hence, that the water filtrates to the river below ground, and perhaps this plan might be generally adopted. I am persuaded that nothing but draining is wanted to render Louisville quite healthy, and one of the most agreeable situations on the Ohio river.

BEING now at the *ne-plus-ultra* of my journey to the westward. I shall here take a brief view of the western territories.

INDIANA TERRITORY.

Is situated between north latitude 37° 47′ and 41° 50′; and west longitude 7° 40′ and 10° 45′. Its greatest length is 284 miles, and its breadth 155. Its area is 39,000 square miles; or 24,960,000 acres.

The face of the country is hilly, not mountainous, and the scenery is said to be rich and variegated, abounding with plains and large prairies.

The principal river is the WABASH, which is said to be a beautiful stream, 280 yards broad at its outlet, and navigable upwards of 220 miles. It rises near the boundary line between the state of Ohio and the Indiana Territory, about 100 miles from lake Erie, where there is a portage of only eight miles between it and the Miami of the lakes. Its course is nearly south-west, and the distance it runs, including its windings, is not less than 500 miles. A great many tributary streams flow into it, the chief of which is *White river*, upwards of 200 miles long. *Tippacanoe* river, near which are the largest settlements of Indians in the territory, falls into the Wabash; and it is near the outlet of that river where the *Prophet* is at present collecting his forces.

The soil is said to be generally rich and fertile.

The climate is delightful, except in the neighbourhood of marshes, chiefly confined to the lower parts of the territory.

The settlements commenced about 12 or 14 years ago, and have made considerable progress, though they have been retarded by the settlement of the fertile and beautiful state of Ohio, which is situated between this and the old states.

The greater part of the territory is yet subject to Indian claims. Where they have been extinguished, and the white settlements have been made, it is divided into four counties, and 22 townships, the greater part of which are on the Ohio; and some few on the Wabash and White-water river. The inhabitants amounted by the census of 1800, to 5,641; they now amount to 24,520 being an increase of 18,879 in 10 years.

The principal town is VINCENNES, on the Wabash. It is an old settlement, and the inhabitants are mostly of French extraction; they amounted, by last census, to 670. The greater part of the others have been noticed.

The agriculture of the territory is nearly the same as that of the state of Ohio. Every kind of grain, grass, and fruit comes to maturity, and towards the southern part of it considerable crops of cotton are raised, though only for domestic use.

As the inhabitants make nearly all their clothing, they have little external trade. What little they have is down the river to New Orleans.

This, in common with the other territories, is under the immediate controul of the government of the United States. It has a certain form of government prescribed by a special ordinance of congress, by which the religious and political rights of the members of the community are guaranteed. In this ordinance it is declared: That no person demeaning himself in a peaceable and orderly manner shall ever be molested on account of his religion. The inhabitants shall always be entitled to the benefits of the writ of habeas corpus, and the trial by jury. All offenses shall be bailable, unless they are capital. Fines shall be moderate. Religion, morality, and knowledge, being necessary to good government and the happiness of mankind, schools and the means of education shall for ever be encouraged. Good faith shall always be observed to the Indians, and their lands shall never be taken from them without their consent. The navigable waters leading into the Mississippi and St. Lawrence, and the carrying places between the same, shall be common highways, and for ever free, as well to the inhabitants of the said territories as to the citizens of the United States, and those of any other states that may be admitted into the confederacy, without any tax, impost, or duty therefor. Whenever any of the territories shall have 60,000 free inhabitants they shall be erected into a state, to be admitted, by its delegates, into the congress of the United States, on an equal footing with the original states. Slavery was originally prohibited, but the law has been relaxed in favour of the new-settlers who have slaves, and there are now 237 slaves in this territory.

From *Travels in the interior of America in the years 1809, 1810 and 1811; including a description of upper Louisiana, together with the states of Ohio, Kentucky, Indiana and Tennessee, with the Illinois and western territories*, by John Bradbury, [Liverpool, 1817], pp. 307-10.

BRADBURY, JOHN.

John Bradbury, a member of the Liverpool Philosophical Society, and later, of the New York Philosophical and Literary Societies, came to the United States in 1809, for the purpose of making a botanical study of the recently acquired Louisiana Territory. He was encouraged in this work by President Jefferson and established his headquarters in St. Louis. For three years, 1809, 1810 and 1811, he was engaged in this work. His results were not published until 1817, due to loss of health which he suffered from the trip, and the war that occurred between the United States and Great Britain.

The work represents an earnest attempt on the part of the author, and stands as one of the best scientific studies of the early days.

The more northerly parts of the states of Ohio and Indiana, together with the whole of the Illinois and western territories, including an area of about 128,130,000 acres, comprehends that part which, in the beginning of this article, has been noticed as possessing a different character in its natural state. The original state of the region already spoken of was that of a continued forest, not convertible into a state fit for cultivation without great pains and labour. This region is an assemblage of woodland and prairie or savannas intermixed; the portions of each varying in extent, but the aggregate area of the prairies exceeding that of the woodland in the proportion of three or four to one. The soil of this part is inferior to none in North America, or perhaps in the world. In a state of nature, these prairies are covered with a luxuriant growth of grass and herbaceous plants, affording a most abundant supply of food for the stock of the new settler; and it is worthy of notice, that any part of these prairies, when constantly fed on by cattle, becomes covered with white clover and the much esteemed blue grass (*Poa compressa*) as frequent pasturing seems to give those plants a predominance over all others.

In the geological formation, this country also differs in some degree from the one entirely covered with wood in its natural state. The surface is much more level, and the strata more regular and undisturbed. In general the order of the strata is sand lying on sand-stone, afterwards lime-stone, beneath which is argillaceous schist lying on coal. For the settler who is not habitually accustomed to the felling of trees, and who has the courage to fix himself on wild land, this is by much the best part of the United States, excepting Upper Louisiana. If he places his house at the edge of one of these prairies, it furnishes him food for any number of cattle he may choose to keep. The woodland affords him the materials necessary for his house, his fire, and fences, and with a single yoke of oxen, he can in general immediately reduce any part of his prairie land to a state of tillage. Had this portion of the country been placed at no greater distance from the Alleghanies than the woody region, it would undoubtedly have been the first settled; but being situated from 500 to 1,000 miles beyond those mountains, and separated from them by one of the most fertile countries in the world, the consequence is, that emigrants are so well satisfied with what advantages a first view of the country presents, that they are anxious to sit down as soon as possible. Another reason why this portion of the wild lands has not been more rapidly settled, is the total indifference of the American farmer to the present or future value of coal. This arises in part from his prejudice against the use of it for fuel, but more from his want of knowledge of its vast importance to other countries, and a consequent want of foresight. The farmer who is possessed of 500 acres of land, expects that in time it will probably be divided into ten properties or farms by his posterity, each of which must be supplied with timber for fuel and fences: he wishes, therefore, that the land unreclaimed may remain covered with timber, as a reserve for posterity, although perhaps he has an excellent bed of coal at no great distance beneath the surface.

Nothing so strongly indicates the superiority of the western country, as the vast emigrations to it from the eastern and southern states. In passing through the upper parts of Virginia, I observed a great number of farms that had been abandoned, on many of which good houses had been erected, and fine apple and peach orchards had been planted. On enquiring the reason, I was always informed that the owners had gone to the western country. From the New England states the emigrations are still more numerous. They mostly cross the Hudson river betwixt Albany and Newburg, and must pass through Cayuga in their way to Pittsburg. I was informed by an inhabitant of Cayuga, in April, 1816, that more than 15,000 waggons had passed over the bridge at that place within the last eighteen months, containing emigrants to the western country.

From *A topographical description of the Indiana territory*, from Jervasse Cutler's Book of travels, Boston, 1812.

Cutler, Jervasse.

Major Jervasse Cutler was a son of the famous Reverend Manassah Cutler. Through his father, who was one of the three directors of the Ohio Land Company, he became interested in the western country. He first entered the northwest territory in 1788. He experienced all the dangers and hardships of a frontiersman; later entered military life, received the appointment of major, and was later stationed at New Orleans. In 1812 he prepared and published a Topographical Description of the State of Ohio, Indiana Territory, etc. It combines his own observations, with the reports gathered from other travellers.

This part[1] of the northwestern country was constituted a territorial government, by an act of Congress, passed the 7th day of May, 1800, and was bounded eastwardly by the following line of separation; viz. "All that part of the territory of the United States, northwest of the Ohio river which lies westward of a line beginning at the Ohio, opposite to the mouth of the Kentucky river, and running thence to fort Recovery, and thence north until it shall intersect the territorial line between the United States and Canada, shall, for the purpose of temporary government, constitute a separate territory, and be called the Indiana Territory. And Saint Vincennes, on the Wabash river, shall be the seat of the government." Only the eastern boundary is named in the act, and the Indian claim of a large portion of the Territory is not extinguished. The whole tract, agreeable to this line, is bounded south by the Ohio, west by the Mississippi, and north by the line between the United States and Canada, which makes the extent of this Territory considerably greater than the State of Ohio.

The general face of the country approaches to a level, but some parts of it are hilly. It has a number of large, navigable rivers meandering through it to the Ohio and Mississippi, and many smaller streams, some of which run into the lakes.

The Wabash is a large river, rising near the head waters of the river St. Joseph, and the Miami[2] at the lakes, and running in a southwesterly direction empties into the Ohio, about four hundred and seventy miles below the Great Miami river. It is four hundred yards wide at the mouth, and navigable for keel boats, about

1. Indiana Territory.
2. Maumee.

four hundred miles, to Ouiatan, an ancient French village; and from this village, with small craft, to a portage on a south branch, which forms a communication with the Miami that runs into Lake Erie. This portage is eight miles, and comes to the Miami near Fort Wayne.

From a north branch, by a short portage, a communication is made with the river St. Joseph, running into Lake Michigan. The Wabash is replenished with numerous tributary streams, and has generally, a gentle current above Saint Vincennes. Below are several rapids. Those which principally obstruct the navigation are between Saint Vincennes and White river, called the great Rapids. Near the village Ouiatan, it is said a silver mine has been discovered, which it is apprehended will prove valuable. About forty miles below the village comes in the river Vermillion Jaune. On this river is the residence of the much famed Indian prophet. The town in which he lives is large for an Indian village, and has received the name of Prophet's town. Much of the land on the Wabash is rich and well timbered, but towards the head waters there is less timber, and very fertile and extensive prairies. A white and blue clay of an excellent quality is said to abound on this river. There are many salt springs, and plenty of lime and free stone.

Saint Vincennes is a handsome town, about an hundred miles from the mouth of the river, situated on the east bank, upon a beautiful, level, and rich spot of ground. It is the largest town in the Territory, and is made the seat of government. This was an ancient French Fortress, called Post Saint Vincennes. Since the American revolution the town has been repaired and enlarged, and is now a very thriving place, but the inhabitants still are mostly French. There are more than an hundred houses, some of which are built of free stone, in a handsome style, a considerable number of merchantile stores, a post office and printing office. Here, a profitable trade is carried on in furs and peltry. The situation is healthy, the winters mild, and the rich and highly cultivated lands around it are delightful.

About forty miles from Saint Vincennes, in a southwesterly direction, is the Great Saline, so called, where salt, in large quantities is made. It is situated in hilly land, on a stream of water which flows into the Ohio. The land is still owned by the government of the United States, but rented to those who carry on the salt works, and who are said to obligate themselves to make, at least, a certain quantity annually, and are not permitted to sell it for more than at a stipulated price. The waters in this Saline are said to have double the strength of those at the great salt springs on the Scioto river.

The land on the Indiana side, bordering on the Ohio river, from the Great Miami nearly to the Mississippi, a distance of about six hundred miles, is generally hilly and broken, but some excellent bottoms, of different extent, are interspersed. From a small distance above fort Massai and down to the mouth of the Ohio, the land gradually becomes level, forming a rich and delightful prairie. In this distance, there are many small streams, but no considerable river, excepting the Wabash, which falls into the Ohio.

But on the opposite side, within a less distance three large, navigable rivers, besides numerous smaller streams, contribute their waters to the Ohio. The first is Kentucky river, which comes in about seventy miles following the bends of the river below the Great Miami, is ninety yards wide at its mouth, and the same width, when the water is high, eighty miles above. It is navigable for loaded boats, at a high stage of the water, two hundred miles. The second is the Cumberland, or Shawnee river, which falls into the Ohio about five hundred miles below the Kentucky river, and four hundred miles below the Rapids, and is three hundred yards wide at its mouth. There being no obstructions, and having a fine gentle current, ships of four hundred tons can descend in times of floods from the distance of about four hundred miles into the Ohio. The third is the Tennessee, or Cherokee river, which enters the Ohio, about twelve miles below the Cumberland; and is five hundred yards wide at its mouth. This is the largest river that empties into the Ohio. It is computed to be navigable for boats one thousand miles, and will admit vessels of considerable burden as far as the Muscle Shoals, which is two hundred and fifty miles from its mouth.

On the Indiana side of the Ohio, there are only some scattering settlements, excepting Jeffersonville, and Clarksville, two small villages, at the Rapids, one hundred and fifty miles below the Great Miami. Jeffersonville is situated in the bend of the river, on a high bank, just above the Rapids, where pilots are taken off for conducting vessels over them. It is a post town, but contains only a small number of inhabitants, and probably will never be a thriving place. Clarksville is another small village immediately below the Rapids, and opposite the elbow at Shippingport. In time it may become a place of considerable business. On the opposite bank, about midway between these two villages and opposite the Rapids, is Louisville, which is much larger, and bids fair to become a flourishing town. It is situated on an elevated plain, and contains about one hundred and fifty houses, a printing and a post office. It is a port of entry, and has a considerable number of mercantile stores, and several ware houses for storing goods. Shippingport is on the same side, at the foot of the falls. Here, boats generally make a landing after passing the Rapids. Ship building was begun and was carried on with considerable spirit here, until it received a check by the late embargo law. Having an excellent harbour, the situation appears eligible for prosecuting this business to advantage.

The Rapids are occasioned by a ledge of rocks extending entirely across the river, and is the most dangerous place for navigation, in the whole extent of the Ohio river. The distance over them is about two miles, and the descent from a level above is twenty-two feet and a half. When the water is high the fall is only perceived by an increased velocity of the vessel, which is computed to be at the rate of about ten or twelve miles an hour. When the water is low, a large portion of the rocks are seen and it is then that the passage becomes dangerous. There are three channels. One is on the North side, called Indian Schute, and is the main channel, but not passable when the water is high; another is near the middle of the river and called the Middle Schute, and is safe and easy in all heights of water above the middle stage. The third is on the south side, called the Kentucky Schute, and is only passable when the water is high. Immediately above the falls, in the mouth of the Beargrass creek, is a good harbour, having twelve feet of water in the lowest stage of the river. At the foot of the falls is another harbour, called Rock Harbour, with water sufficient, at all times, for vessels of any burden. These two harbours are of the greatest importance to those who have occasion to navigate this dangerous passage.

Opening a channel for the passage of ships by the Rapids has been seriously contemplated; which would be of immense advantage to the trade of the Ohio. That it is practicable cannot be doubted. The only difficulty seems to be to raise a fund sufficient for the purpose. It has been principally proposed to open the canal on the Kentucky side, to commence below the Beargrass creek, and enter the river below Shippingport, a distance of about one mile and three quarters; and that it should be sufficient for ships of four hundred tons. The ground through which it would pass is a stiff clay, down to within about three feet of the floor of the canals which then is a rock. The average depth of the canal is computed at about twenty-one feet, in order to admit a column of water three feet by twenty-four, at the lowest stage of the river.

In the Ohio Navigator a very accurate description is given of the Rapids, with an excellent map of the falls. From this description the account of them here given, is principally taken. To this very valuable work, the writer is indebted to many observations respecting the Ohio and Mississippi rivers, and for much information in regard to the country bordering upon them.

In passing down the Ohio, about forty miles below the Wabash, a curious cave is seen in a high bank, on the Indiana side.[3] Its mouth opens to the river, and when the water is high it nearly flows into it. The entrance is an arch in a rock about twenty-five feet high in the centre, eighty feet wide at the base, and extending back from the opening one hundred and eighty feet. The mouth is darkened by several large trees growing before it, which gives it a gloomy and solemn appearance. Passengers usually visit it, and have engraved on the sides within the mouth, a great number of names, dates and other inscriptions. Indian superstition and other fabulous stories reported respecting this cave do not merit a repetition.

---

3. Indiana territory included all of Illinois at that time, the division being made in 1809.

From *Travels through the western country in the Summer of 1816*, by David Thomas [1819], pp. 110-87, 189-206, 207-33, 240-41.

THOMAS, DAVID.

An American pomologist, florist, and writer on agricultural subjects was born in Pennsylvania in 1776. He later removed to New York State and there became interested in engineering and exploration. In 1816, he. in company with Jonathan Swan—a merchant of Aurora—made a journey through the Wabash region in the New Purchase. When the "Travels" were published in 1817, Dewitt Clinton of New York was so attracted by them that he offered Mr. Thomas the position of chief engineer on the Erie Canal, for the district west of Rochester. As a florist and pomologist Mr. Thomas had few equals in the United States. He was a very important contributor to the Genesee Farmer, and did much to advance the science of farming in his day.

At *Meek's Ferry*, below Lohary Island, we crossed the Ohio River, and landed in Indiana. We went down the flats half a mile, and stopped at the house of a man, from the state of New-York, who treated us to ripe morella cherries. The trees were large, and grew in two fine rows, which he assured us had only been planted five years. On my remarking the great height of the sandy flats, on which his house stood, he pointed to a mark on the wall, about four feet above the first floor, and observed, that the river had been there; and that they had taken refuge on the neighbouring hills. It is said that the difference between high and low water mark, sometimes equal sixty feet perpendicular; and our observations tend to give credence to this statement. The volume of water which pours down the channel at such times, must therefore be immense.

Our path now led through bars into a vineyard of one or two acres, and the vines appeared thrifty. This road is only travelled by horsemen. The rank vegetation of the river flats crowded so close as sometimes to brush both sides of us as we rode along; and indeed everything conspired to remind us of being in a new country. After a traverse of three or four miles we came to the *Rising Sun*.

This village, of forty or fifty houses, is built on an easy slope that fronts the Ohio. We recollect no situation more pleasant. The buildings are not first-rate, but the town only claims, as it were, the date of yesterday. A floating grist-mill was anchored in the river, near the shore; and the float-boards of the water-wheel were turned by the current.

On leaving the river, we ascended the hills, the soil of which is very fertile, and the vegetation uncommonly fine. We had gazed at the majestic beech of this country, three feet in diameter, with branches of a great size;—we had seen the honey locust, the black walnut and the horse chestnut* of equal magnitude;—and here we saw, with surprise, the black locust almost a rival in stature, with grape-vines, like cables, hanging from the tops of the trees in every direction.

6 *mo.* 30.—I have avoided remarks on our treatment, except where gratitude required us to treasure the remembrance. When our fare has been *slim*, and our bills high, we have passed on quietly, in the hope of something better. Occurrences of this kind are but trifles of a moment; and my only motive, for departing in one instance from this practice, is to give some information which the untravelled reader may wish to acquire.

It does not appear that any regular tavern is kept on these hills; and as the chief part of the inhabitants have arrived since the war, at evening, we were induced to abide at the first place where food for our horses could be procured. Our host and his family were very civil and attentive; but on awakening from the first sound sleep, we despaired of all further repose. The *bugs* ran riot. Our friend D. S. who through condescension had taken the floor in the evening, with a saddle under his head, escaped the disturbance; but we were kept in a state of continual activity. Though greatly fatigued by travelling, we saw, through the chinks between the logs, the slow approach of the dawn with impatience, and long before sunrise resumed our journey.

Our road led for several miles over high, level land, apparently cold and wet;—timbered with beech, white oak, &c. and soon becoming covered with briars† where the fields are neglected. The aspect of things is discouraging to new settlers. What their progress will be, is uncertain; for though the soil is moderately fertile, and well adapted to grass, all the improvements are very recent and scattering.

It is remarkable, that on descending from the tops of the hills, the soil becomes excellent. The fact is, that near the summit level, the superstratum is clay; but not more than twenty or thirty feet

*This is called "the sweet buck-eye," to distinguish it from the kind which we first noticed on the Ohio. Dr. Drake has shewn these to be specifically distinct, and has named the former Æ. *maxima*. "It frequently arrives to the height of one hundred feet, and the diameter of four."

†*Rubus villosus*, or blackberry.

below it, there is limestone in horizontal strata. In the side of every declivity, at that depth, this rock appears; and by decomposing, imparts to the soil beneath it, a dressing of marl. These constitute a mixture of elementary earths which cause perpetual fertility.

This country, including much of that above Cincinnati, and all that we saw of Kentucky, is more destitute* of durable water than any other region that we have traversed.

Plants, whose features are new to me, appear almost every day. Some occupy but a small region, while others are extensively scattered. The idea, that *every district marked by small differences of soil and climate, has plants and animals peculiar*, presents itself at an early date to the naturalist. To-day, I first observed the southern Aralia (*A. spinosa*) and some are twelve feet high. No shrubbery should be without these singular and beautiful plants.

The *buffalo*, or *wild clover*, grows abundantly among the bushes, on the fertile though narrow flats of a small brook, down which the road winds. It appears to vegetate earlier than the white clover; or at least, the seed is sooner ripe.

The Columbo root (*Frasera Walteri*) which abounds between the Sciota and the Miami, is a large *tetrandrous*† plant four or five feet in height. As a bitter tonic, I am told that it is much used by physicians in this country; and some consider it equal in efficacy to the imported. I first noticed it on the oak plains, west of the Genesee River; and it is also found on the hills round Short Creek; but we have seen none since we passed Cincinnati.

Half a mile east of Indian Kentucky, we saw stones of the gun fllint kind, in the road. The surface is chalky, orange, or red. These form between the limestone, a regular stratum which spreads

*Dr. Drake, in noticing that part of Kentucky which is adjacent to Cincinnati, remarks, that "wells cannot be dug on account of the limestone rocks, which, except in the valley of the Ohio, are everywhere found at the depth of a few feet." Water was very scarce, when we were at Boone Court House; and of this place he adds that "it is not likely to be of any consequence, as in summer and autumn, water, even for domestic use, cannot be had within the distance of two miles."

It is evident that the Ohio River never wore these rocks away after the petrifaction was complete.

†Dr. Drake says that Professor Barton proposed to call it *Frasera verticillata*, and he has adopted the alteration. The name is very appropriate. It is founded on one of the most striking features of the plant; for *whorls* of five leaves, a few inches apart, surround the purple stalk, in some individuals to the height of six feet.

The former specific names are exceptionable. *Walteri* only refers to a book; and *Carolinensis* to one small district in which this vegetable is indigenous. Botanists, perhaps, have not sufficiently considered the impropriety of imposing such names on species which are scattered over extensive regions.

over a large tract of country. Like the strata in Washington county, it is visible in both sides of every little valley that we crossed. The texture is excellent; and these give fire with the steel equal to the imported flints; but the cracks, or lines of division, are numerous. Though these stones are silicious, the singularity of their situation, induced the celebrated SAUSSURE to ask, if calcareous earth, in any circumstances, can be transmuted into flint? Certainly not; but silex in solution appears to displace a large* portion of that earth, and to combine with the residue so silently as even in many cases to preserve the original form† of the stone. In vegetable petrifactions this earth is so accurately insinuated, that the sap vessels remain visible; and even the colouring matter of the wood is retained, as we observe in the Irish hone.

Notwithstanding its hardness, much of this earth is annually held in solution to supply the demands of vegetation;‡ and Professor Davy has even shewn that the hollow stalked grasses derive firmness from this essential ingredient.

As we approached the banks of *Indian Kentucky*, hearing shrill screams over our heads, we looked up, and first saw the parroquet. These birds, which are about the size of wild pigeons, are sometimes seen on the Miami.§

This *Creek* now scarcely flows, though it has a channel wide enough for a heavy mill stream. Indeed, most of those through this country are very shallow,—bottomed on horizontal lime rock; and in some places, this stone has been whirled up by the water into heaps. The cavities thus formed are now ponds. It is remarkable that where horizontal rocks lie near the surface, the streams diminish greatly in drowths, whether these strata are calcareous or aluminous.

The north-west side of the Ohio was a wilderness after the adjacent parts of Virginia and Kentucky were settled; and the streams of these states were consequently named before many on the opposite side of the river were known to the white people. To

*Wiegleb found gun-flint 80 per cent of silica.

†De Cazozy and Macquart have observed the transition of the Gypsum of Cracovia to the state of calcedony.—Dorthes has proved that the quartz in cockscombs at Passy owed its origin [shape] to plaster. CHAPTAL.

‡It was long since discovered that silica (the earth of flints) was contained in vegetables: but it was commonly considered extraneous or accidental until professor Davy showed that many plants, without it, could not "support a healthy vegetation". From parcels of the following kinds of *Corn*, weighing two pounds each, SCHROEDER obtained of this earth the annexed number of grains respectively:—Wheat, 13.2; Rye, 15.6; Barley, 66.7; Oats, 144.2; and from the same quantity of rye-straw 152 grains.

§Drake says on the Sciota.

such creeks with the word *Indian* prefixed, the appellation of the southern branches are transferred; and thus we have Indian Short Creek, Indian Wheeling, and Indian Kentucky, which denote that Virginia Short Creek, Virginia Wheeling, and Kentucky River, join the Ohio in those respective neighbourhoods.

On ascending the hill from this creek, we travelled several miles on a winding ridge, in many places only about the width of a turnpike, with gulphs on each side awfully profound. I estimate these hills at 500 or 600 feet above the Ohio River; and on all parts below the limestone strata, which appears on their sides, the soil is extremely fertile.

This country, in general, is wretchedly cultivated; very little wheat appears, and corn constitutes their staff of life. But even this is greatly neglected; and wherever moderate marks of industry were observed, we felt pleasure from the novelty. We have never before seen so much difference in the growth of corn; some being scarcely six inches high, and some four or five feet.

On the hill side which bounds the flats on the Ohio above *Madison*, I saw for the first time, a horse stripping bark. I had long since understood, that such practices prevailed in new parts of our south-western states, where these animals receive no food from their owners in winter; but we think it remarkable that bark should be preferred to grass. The nettle tree, (*Celtis occidentalis*) here called hack-berry, which grows in abundance over all these hills, is the favorite; though sugar-maple and some others do not escape. He had stripped the butt to the height of three feet.

We had not seen the *Ohio* since we left *Rising Sun*, until we arrived on these flats, though we have chiefly kept within a few miles. *Vevay*, noted for its vineyards and *Swiss* inhabitants, is situate on the banks of the river, but our road led to the right.

This morning the sun shone faintly through the thickening veil of clouds, and soon disappeared. Moderate rain without wind succeeded; and having travelled through it a long time, just before sunset, as the sky was brightening in the west, we arrived at Madison, wet and fatigued. Here we met the members of the CONVENTION, who had come from the eastern part of the state, now on their return home. *Corydon*, the seat of government, is forty miles below this village, which place they left this morning.

36 miles.

7 *mo.* 1.—MADISON is the seat of justice for *Jefferson* county. It is situate on an upper flat of the Ohio, and back, a few hundred yards from the river. It consists of sixty or seventy houses, the

principal number of which appear new. Indeed the larger part of the improvements which we have seen in this territory is of very recent date. Many of these houses are small and of hewn logs.

The jail is about twelve feet square, of the same materials; and, in aspect as well as in strength, forms a great contrast to those gloomy piles which older communities have erected in their own defence. With surprise we had also remarked one of similar appearance at *Boone Court-house*, in *Kentucky;* and though these buildings neither shine much in topographical description, nor add to the beauty of these villages, yet posterity, from such specimens will learn with interest the simplicity of new founded empires; for in a few years these will be only *remembered.*

From the great number of small houses, and an apparent want of regularity in the streets, the aspect of this village is not imposing. With these impressions my companion asked one of the convention how long this *little town* had been laid out? Whether the dignity of the ex-member was offended by such approach,—or whether he thought his country undervalued,—I leave for his biographers to determine; but assuming all the majesty of repulsive greatness, he exclaimed "I hope you don't call this a *little town.*" It is true my friend had seen some cities, if not characters rather greater, but we think this a thriving place, and from its situation on the river, will rapidly augment in wealth and population.

We were pleased, however, with the affability and politeness of some of the gentlemen; and M. from *Wayne county,* informed me that a cave, near Corydon, contains a great quantity of Glauber's salt, amongst which nitre is intermixed. It is in high repute as a cathartic medicine. The quarter section, which includes the cave, has been lately secured by an individual.

It has long since been ascertained that abundance of *nitre* is found in the limestone caves of this country, but it appears to be mixed in unusual portions, not only with this sulphate of soda, but also with the common salt. Hams, cured with that from Kenhawa, requires no particular application of nitre; and in redness and in flavor resemble those in New-York, where an ounce of this mineral is appropriated to each.

This morning I noticed on a hand bill "the best *qualified* cut nails" advertised. This expression is a good match for that of "a well *faculized* person," so common in the eastern part of New-York state. No doubt both phrases are very convenient to those who are unused to better language.

The peach trees, near this town were finely loaded with fruit, but those on the hills have been more injured by frost.

The laborious operation of ascending the heights from the river, we performed, four miles west of Madison, but we believe the hills are not so high as those in the neighborhood of Pittsburgh. However, since we arrived in this territory, we have been compelled to trace many a long line, greatly diverging from the plane of the horizon.

On reaching the summit, we travelled one or more miles over wet clayey land, similar to what we noticed yesterday on the heights. This plain gradually slopes at last, towards the *Muskakituck* branch of the *White River*, which we crossed nine miles west of Madison, there flowing to the north-west. It is a common mill stream in size, bordered by handsome flats, and apparently comes from the Ohio, which is only four miles distant. I am assured that it heads within two or three miles of that river; and probably some of its branches have a greater proximity, but the circuit cannot be less than three hundred miles before its waters effect a junction.

Oats are in blossom, but wheat and rye are almost fit for the sickle.

The sides of the road where the soil is calcareous, are nearly destitute of grass. It has been a dry season, but we have no cause to believe that these vegetables ever obtained possession. We cannot solely refer this deficiency to climate, though its appearance is remarkable.

Eleven miles west of Madison, we passed through a land of swales or drains, in the bottom of which limestone lies under a shallow coat of earth. Beneath this rock the water finds a subterranean passage. In some places the arch is broken; the cavity of the rock then appears four or five feet deep; and the stream along the bottom, alternately brightens into day, and glides beneath the vault, sheltered from the vicissitudes of this upper world. In some of these *sinks* or broken arches, no water was visible.

New Lexington is seventeen miles west of Madison. It consists of forty houses, a few of which are handsome brick or frame buildings; but a great proportion are scattered back from the road, formed of hewn logs with a *cobbed* roof, one story high and one room on a floor. On their appearance I can pass no encomiums, though the whole has very recently sprung from the woods.*

At this place the sign of the *Lexington Bank* was displayed by nine swindlers; several of them are now imprisoned.

We were told that salt was manufactured near this place from water completely saturated with that mineral, but which is very limited in quantity. In order to obtain a better supply, a shaft was sunk about one hundred feet. At this depth brine appeared, similar in quality to what was procured before, and some of it was driven up to the surface by a wind which roared through caverns in the rocks. However, the water soon subsided; and though the proprietors have penetrated to the depth of more than seven hundred feet, the labour has not been crowned with success. The last two hundred feet cost $1,500. The boring was performed by machinery moved by a horse. The salt which is made here, sells for two dollars a bushel, but the quantity is not equal to the demand.

Near this village we met a large drove of cattle, some of which we were told came from the *Missouri*. The great population and consequent demand for beef in Baltimore and in the cities to the northeast, not only attract the drovers from a vast distance, which would bring them on this line, but the ruggedness of the mountains in Virginia appears to turn the principal current of travelling as high up as Brownsville on the Monongahela.

Another branch of the *Muskakituck* flows on the north east side of this village.

At the *Pigeon Roost*, eight miles from Lexington, twenty-three women and children were massacred in the late war. It appears that the settlement was composed of several families near akin, who resided in houses contiguous to each other. The men who had given some offence to the Indians, were then all absent in the militia near Louisville, except one old man. On the last of the week, about two hours before sun set, while the women were ironing their clothes and the children were playing round the doors, the savages rushed to the attack. In this awful extremity, the old man endeavoured to protect them, till his gun-lock was broken by a ball. He then escaped, but the rest all perished. No part of this frontier, during the war exhibited such a scene of slaughter.

Adjacent to New Lexington on the west, we saw the last of the

*Predicting from past movements, in a few years these villages will not be recognized from my descriptions; and these sketches, though imperfect, will then interest by shewing the march of improvement.

limestone; and five miles further on our road, clay slate is uncovered by a brook which flows to the northwest. The soil, through a space of twenty miles from this village to the Knobs, like the level country over which we have passed, is a loam inclining to a stiff clay, and moderately fertile. The timber is large,—chiefly beech intermixed with oak, poplar,* and sweet gum;† but to us the country is not inviting. There is scarcely one clearing of older date than last season. These are scattering, and in places we traversed intervals of forest five miles wide. At the brook that runs northerly at the foot of the Knobs, a soft clay slate appears in the bank, and no stone in all this distance was observable on the soil.

We were informed at New-Lexington, that we should find no accommodations for our horses east of the *Knobs*. It was then past twelve o'clock, and we departed at the close of a heavy shower, on a brisker gait than we had usually travelled. But the uncertainty of lodgings, distant thunder in the west, dark clouds that concealed the sun, and the thick branches of a tall forest, conspired to begloom our path.

My nerves had thrilled at the name of the *Knobs;* for these are supposed by the celebrated VOLNEY to constitute the west bank of a vast lake, which once covered all the upper country of the Ohio, and from which waters, successively were deposited, the sand, the shells, and the vegetables which have stratified that region with sand rocks, lime-stone and coal. We were therefore about to enter a scene peculiarly interesting. But these heights would interest without the aid of philosophy. As we approached the summit, the prospect assumed the features of sublimity. From the north, northerly round to the southeast, the line of the horizon was as smooth as if ruled by a pencil; but wild mountain heads projected in the opposite direction. This landscape though obscured by the rain, was rendered more awfully grand by the thunder and lightning which now flashed and rolled over us.

These heights are several hundred feet above the country to the eastward. Observing some rocks not far below the summit, I alighted in the shower to examine them. I was induced to do this because their formation must have a powerful bearing on the theory of that writer, for whose talents I had conceived much respect, and who has been styled "a genius of the first order in physical geography." These rocks were of two kinds, calcareous

*Tulip poplar.
†Liquidambar styraciflua.

and silicious; and as both are of the secondary class, the inference is conclusively hostile to his hypothesis.

The sides of these hills are deeply gullied, and the peninsulated points appear like ribs attached to the vertebrae. Some stand separate, or detached from the main mass, conically shaped; and high up the sides of one, a horizontal stratum of rock projects, which has the appearance of limestone. The wearing of water on these piles in some distant age, must therefore have been very extraordinary.

Chestnut grows near the base, and chestnut-oak on the peaks; but as we leave these, and advance westward where the soil is less exposed to the wasting action of winds and rains, the timber becomes nearly as thrifty as on the plains below; and papaw and spice-wood, as usual, constitute the principal underbrush.

In the channel of a brook which flows southerly one or two miles west of the ascent, we saw many chrystallized stones, varying much in size and nearly spherical in the general form, though the surface is protuberant and irregular. These are usually hollow, break easily, and small chrystals cover the internal surface. I arrange them with the most recent secondary class of stones, as in one, a lump of limestone composed of shells, was found embedded.

In the cabinet of specimens in mineralogy at Pittsburgh, if my recollection is distinct, there is a broken shell of this kind, which had been a prolate spheroid, twelve or fifteen inches long, eight or ten inches wide, and less than an inch in thickness. One part of the cavity is apparently coated with verdigrise. I have seen none here equal to that specimen in size.

This day we travelled nearly forty miles, and about dark arrived at our lodgings, excessively fatigued. This was occasioned by our hurrying over the last twenty-three miles, without stopping to procure refreshment.

On asking for supper we were told that the water in the well, on account of the rain was unfit for use. As we did not comprehend the reason why a moderate shower should be so injurious, I only notice the fact at present, and add that butter-milk ill supplied the place of more stimulating food which our exhausted condition required.

7 *mo.* 2.—THIS house was fortified during the war, and several familes occupied it as a garrison. Log houses like this are readily converted into such fortifications by taking off the upper part down to the joists, and then building it up again with logs two or three feet longer. Such projections on every side are intended to

give the besieged an opportunity to fire down on the enemy, if he should attempt to force the door, or set fire to the building; but we are told that no instance of Indians making such attack is known. We had observed houses of this description, soon after our landing in the state, and we have noticed more or less every day since.

This fortress had an appendage (and I believe it is generally so, when neighbours unite together) consisting of a picket fence which encloses the yard and extends the limits of safety. The construction is as follows;—Planks three or four inches thick and twelve or fifteen feet long are placed edge to edge in a trench which has been previously dug, and the earth then rammed closely round them. These are difficult to scale, and impenetrable to small arms.

Cooped up in such lodgments, our frontier citizens have generally weathered the storm of war; and when necessity compelled them to venture out, the men have gone armed in a body. On my remarking how unhappily they must have lived in such times of alarm, our host replied, "We enjoyed ourselves much better than you imagine, perhaps as well as we do now,—we were so kind and friendly to one another." These words of the old man were impressive; and I rode on reflecting, from how much real pleasure we are debarred by the jarring interests of this world.

Our progress this morning was unusually slow, in consequence of the excess of yesterday; and our horses convinced us that they were suffering from sore feet. The circumstance in itself is a trifle, and will cease to interest us as soon as they recover; but the *lesson* ought not to be forgotten. At Circleville, we saw men from Dutchess county (N.Y.) who had been under the necessity of changing horses, once or twice, on the road; and another such a day's ride would compel us to a similar measure. He who wishes to avoid being left to the mercy of strangers (if mercy there be) should preserve an easy and regular gait through the day; and at whatever time his hackney shews unequivocal symptoms of fatigue, stop. In this exhausted condition, a small excess is hurtful, and a repitition often ruinous. A horse of common constitution, accidents excepted, will perform the circuit of the United States, if well fed and moderately used.

Salem, where we stopped to breakfast, is a new village of thirty or forty houses. A small but handsome brick court-house for *Washington county*, built on arches, is one of the principal ornaments of the place.

One mile and a half north-easterly from this village, a monthly meeting is held by a number of *Friends* who are settled in this vicinity.

At breakfast I was exposed to the infection of an eruptive fever, which, however, to me has never been a subject of much alarm; but my friend J.S. shewed such anxiety that I left the house with half a meal. To have a disease of such uncertain termination in a strange land, is not desirable; but the bearing of one event on another, and consequently, what will finally be best, is not given us to know.

The uncertain tenure of our lives, at all times, ought also to mitigate our apprehensions of apparent danger. We walk in the midst of deaths; and with the dawn of each day the possibility returns, that those connexions which are inexpressibly dear to us will be dissolved before night.

On the west side of this village, *Blue River*, which is here a small mill-stream, flows in a southerly direction. The banks contain horizontal strata of limestone, which is literally *composed* of shells.

The country westward of *the Knobs*, (or rather the summit level) though not hilly, is varied in surface; and has a looser soil than the low district to the east. Ferruginous sandstone, the stalagmites before noticed, excellent gun flints, and abundance of limestone are found. The two first kinds, in places, considerably encumber the soil. The flint varies much in colour; lumps three or four inches in diameter are embedded in the lime-rocks; and this sort in texture resembles the imported flint.

We noticed many wells which were dug, in the bottom of *limestone sinks;* and generally the inhabitants obtain durable water with little labour. It is worthy of remark, that this elevated region preserves the same singular feature as the country round New-Lexington, which is several hundred feet below it; for, in no other district that I have seen would it be advisable to dig for water in a sink.

Many of the settlers in this quarter are Carolinians; and some told us (probably with a reference to their native land) that "this is a miserably cold country."

Our host, where we fed our horses, had been bitten by a *copper-head* some months ago, and was scarcely recovered. It was said, when we were in the state of Ohio, that the poison of this reptile, lingers a long time in the system, and eventually proves destructive to the constitution. The evil appears magnified;

but the opinion is common, that these are not less dangerous than the rattle snake; and we know they are much more difficult to exterminate. The dry hills of the Ohio country seem to be their favorite residence. We think however, that snakes are less numerous, even now, than on the eastern side of the mountains.

About 5 o'clock we arrived at J. LINDLEY'S[1] for whom I had an introductory letter. His kind invitation to stay with him a day, we willingly accepted.

This distinguished Friend removed from North Carolina about five years ago; and with a few others fixed his abode in the wilderness. During the late war, this little community formed the frontier; but its members appear not to have suffered either from fear or injury. He has frequently explored the lands beyond the borders of the settlement in the time of that commotion, and never considered either himself or his companions in danger. Indeed there was small cause. No instance of Indian hostility towards this society is known; so firm and inviolate has been the peace which the ancestors of these savages established with WILLIAM PENN, and so faithfully is the memory of his virtues transmitted from sire to son.

The wilderness, however, has now become thickly populated; and a monthly meeting is held a half a mile from his house; but we learn that no other meeting of *Friends* is established further westward. 26 miles.

7 *mo.* 3.—We admired the refreshing coolness of last evening. We are assured that in summer, the heat of the day like what we experience is rarely oppressive; and seldom protracted beyond sunset. On the eastern side of the mountains, in this latitude, it is often uncomfortable till midnight.

In our country, the rainy clouds in their approach, seldom vary from between the west and south-west points; but the lower currents of the atmosphere frequently carry the scud in every direction. Here we are told that both rain and snow arrive chiefly from the south-west; and that winds from the east of north or south are seldom known.

This statement supports the opinion that we have passed beyond the influence of the great Lakes. Winds are often deflected for [from] their original courses by the sinuosities of the shore; and from this cause we sometimes find them blow in opposite directions.

---

1. Near the present site of Paoli.

The surface of the land in this neighbourhood is uneven; but the elevations scarcely merit the name of hills; and much of it appears to be *cellared*. This feature is strong and perhaps peculiar to the western country. Nearly all the brooks are more or less subterranean. In places, the arch is broken for small distances, and the stream visible; but *Lost River*, to the north of this place, wholly disappears for seven miles; and though this NATURAL BRIDGE is destitute of the sublime scenery of *Cedar Creek* it stands unrivalled in width.

Many of the brooks may be traced by a line of sinks. These in heavy rains become ponds, in consequence of the narrowness of the channel* through the rocks—into some of which the current boils from below, while others receive the torrents that collect on the land; and in all, the water not undergoing the process of filtration,—partakes of all the impurities of the surface. To this cause I ascribe the state of the well which we noticed in the evening after we ascended *the Knobs*.

But we have reason to suspect that this water, even when limpid is prejudicial to the health of strangers. In us, it uniformly induced a sense of weight in the stomach, and others have made similar complaints. We discontinued its use.

It is probable that the *Salt Petre caves*† in Kentucky are on the same level with those near New-Lexington; but these around us, as I have remarked, are in a different stratum, notwithstanding the sameness of appearance. We are informed that one cavern in that state has been explored for ten miles; and without dismissing all doubts of this statement, we may be allowed to remark that *Lost River* proves that some in this vicinity are surprisingly extensive. I observed a sink of one or two acres which was only a few feet in depth, and evidently occasioned by the falling of the cavern roof.

We rarely observe any natural cavity in the land which would hold water except in two cases. The first consists of the basins of lakes, which are generally on a large scale, and formed either by the irregular projection of primitive rocks, or by the unequal deposition of alluvial matter. The second case comprises those cavities of small extent which were produced by a depression of

*Our friend, who has a mill on a large spring, finds great difficulty in forming a pond, on account of fissures in the limestone that surrounds it.

†Cramer in noticing Harden's Creek in that state, 112 miles by water below Louisville, and southeasterly from this place, remarks that "*Sinking Creek*, a branch of that stream, after heading in three springs and running several miles, sinks, and runs about four or five miles under ground before it appears again."

the friable earth. Of these we observe that their formation belongs to a period since "the dry land appeared;" and such are chiefly confined to districts that embosom limestone. Perhaps the only exception to making this remark general, will be found, where primitive rocks loosened by some convulsion of nature, have promiscuously fallen together and then been covered by earth.

The cavities of calcareous regions belong to two classes. The first will embrace depressions of the surface where the earth has sunk into caverns, through small apertures in the roof, and hence assuming the shape of a funnel. These appear wherever limestone in great quantities is present, without any regard to the primitive or secondary formation. The second class obtains where the earth over beds of gypsum has gradually settled. The solution of that salt in five hundred times its weight of cold water, removes all obscurity from this point; but the cause of caverns in common limestone is more difficult to elucidate.

It is not probable that this earth remained in its pulverulent form while the masses around it hardened into rock; and that afterwards it was removed by water. United with different acids, however, it varies exceedingly in its degrees of solubility. Though carbonic acid renders it an insoluble precipitate in water, yet the same agent in excess completes its solution; and vegetable matter fermenting in confined situations might furnish the supply.

The nitric and muriatic acids combining with lime also preserve it in solution; and by displacing the carbonic acid may have taken possession in latter periods. Neither should the combination of sulphuric acid be overlooked. Perhaps all these agents, in different places, have assisted in forming the caverns which abound in this rock; and some circumstances render it probable that the process of excavation is continued.

The *hard water*, so common in limestone districts, proves that the rocks through which these currents flow are wasting by solution. The impregnating material is chiefly plaster; but nitrates and muriates of lime, which only exist in a liquid state, are sometimes discovered: and perhaps have been recently formed. The carbonic acid which is found disengaged in the earth under the name of *damp*, and which is also emitted by some fountains, supports this idea; but without such decomposition, clearly shows that water with this addition may become a solvent of limestone.

This view will be less imperfect, when we consider that *new sinks* frequently appear in such regions. The earth on those spots had been settled and compact for thousands of years; and its sudden depression evinces a recent breach in the cavern roof.

It will be obvious that the depth of the cavern will greatly assist in determining the *figure of the sink*. In the lower parts of Pennsylvania, where the quantity of earth over the aperture is very considerable, it generally assumes the form of an inverted cone. Here where the cavern is near the surface, the longitudinal breaches in the roof are more apparent, and that figure is rarely observed.

The limestone in this neighbourhood is composed of small shells which differ from all that I have noticed to the eastward. One stone, from the minuteness of these remains, resembled a mass of mustard seed.—The cement was ochre.

Half-Moon Spring,* which we visited this morning, is a curiosity. The *aperture* of the fountain is thirty feet deep, and three rods in diameter; but the *basin* is more extensive. The name is derived from its semi-circular figure. Uniting with the current of J. Lindley's mill spring, half a mile to the northward, it forms *Lick Creek*, a beautiful stream.

The *Section* [or square mile] that includes this fountain is public property; being *Lot No.* 16, which *in each township throughout the territory, is appropriated for the use of schools.* Leases of such lands have been granted only for short periods; and in consequence its value for water works, probably will long remain unrealized. Though the fall of its current is small, yet by raising *a curb*, it might doubtless be converted into a valuable mill seat; and the firm and level surface round it would favor such an undertaking.

East of New-Lexington we had found limestone in the bottom of swales, which formed an arch for *subterranean brooks*. The late heavy rain has unfolded the cause of this singular appearance. As soon as the cavity is filled, the surplus water bursts from the sink-holes, forming ponds where the sink is deep, but flowing over where the sides are low. Thus we have a double brook; and the upper current, sweeping away the leaves has also channelled out the land.

Coal is found two miles from J. Lindley's, but of its quantity and quality but little can be said at present. Salt springs† of

*This spring is forty miles west of Louisville.

†On the map in range 1 west, Township 6 north, the reader may find marked a *Salt Lick*. J. Lindley, to whose kindness I am indebted for much valuable information, says in his letter of 2 mo. 2, 1818, that they are at work at this lick; and that the prospect is encouraging.

value, on the New Purchase, north of this place, have been partially examined; but as the Government of the United States reserve the lands which include such, if known before the sale, individuals who explore, deem it prudent to be silent on these subjects. After the sales much more may be learned of the fossil treasures of this country.

The inhabitants of this neighbourhood preserve much simplicity of dress, and like members of the same family, feel an interest in each others welfare, in the inverse ratio of the parade exhibited. Such manners are characteristic of new settlements; and notwithstanding the privations to which this period is subject, those who have risen to independence not unfrequently recall in memory these days as the happiest in life.

Apparel, however, should vary with the state of society. To wear that of which we are neither proud nor ashamed is the best rule that can be given; and who departs from this maxim has a mind directed to improper objects.

Our horses had been put to pasture where the grass was chiefly *timothy*, yet *salivation* was induced. The cause of this disease has been hitherto unexplained, though it would be difficult to enumerate all the opinions on this subject. Several of these, however, are absolute crudities; and much objection will attend the best that have been assigned.

It appears that thirty years ago, this malady was unknown in the United States. Near Philadelphia, it was first observed about the time that clover and plaster were generally introduced; and to these it was naturally ascribed. To this theory the present case will completely fix a negative; and in our county where horses suffer much from this disease, plastered clover, in fields recently *laid down*, does not induce it. On the reverse, in white clover pastures, which have never received a sprinkle of that manure, the salivation has been distressing.

By some, the *Lobelia inflata* or wild tobacco, has been charged as the cause; by others, the *Euphorbia maculata*, or spotted spurge; but both plants are indigenous, and must have occupied the old fields near the sea coast almost a century before this disease was known. Others have spoken of the venom of spiders. The question, where were they forty years ago? will instantly occur; neither would this hypothesis explain why the grass of one field will salivate profusely, while *that* in another field not two yards distant, may be eaten with impunity. Nor can we learn why these plants or animals should be more venomous after a shower; yet this phenomenon is very observable. If it be said that the insects have sheltered in the grass, we should reflect that a better shelter might often be found across the fence, and that the insects would venture forth on the return of fair weather; but for several days much acrimony is apparent.

The same objection will arise against ascribing it to *dews*. We have not been able to discover why these should not descend alike on the adjoining fields where a single fence constitutes all the partition; yet I have noticed at *Cayuga*, that horses in new fields are generally exempt; and the same remark applies to meadows annually mowed.

In the afternoon we visited T. Lindley, whose interesting family we shall remember. It is now the middle of wheat harvest, and only this concern deprives us of his company to the Wabash. He has appropriated a field of several acres to the culture of tobacco, and the prospect is encouraging.

Lands partially improved rate at twelve dollars an acre.

Sugar maple is found throughout all the Ohio country; and from it *sugar* is generally made in quantities sufficient for home consumption. We have seen little of this article from New-Orleans since we left Pittsburgh. There the retail price is from twenty-three to twenty-five cents a pound.

It appears that *Kanhawa Salt*, with few exceptions, supplies at least all the country above the falls of Ohio. Near the river the current price has been six dollars a barrel. In the manufacture much slovenliness is evident, and we presume that no pains are taken to separate the ochreous matter which floats in the water, for the whole mass is tinged of a dirty red. The snow-white salt of Montezuma is obtained from water equally impure.

The *parroquet* commits depredations on the wheat in harvest, but it is a bird of uncommon beauty. The head is red, the neck yellow, and the body a light green.

In the evening we returned with J. L. to our former lodgings.

In this neighbourhood an earth resembling *bole* is employed as a red dye for cotton. It is squeezed through a linen bag into an alkaline solution; and requires the same time as indigo to perfect the colour.

The trees, in this neighbourhood, are chiefly *beech* and *sugar-maple;* but the quantity of timber to the acre, varies considerably in different places. The *papaw* forms the underbrush, and by closely shading the ground with its broad leaves, nearly excludes the herbage.

Iron ore is found in many parts of this country. It is mentioned that two furnaces* will soon be erected, at the respective distances of eight and sixteen miles west of this place.

7 *mo.* 4.—ABOUT nine o'clock this morning, we took leave of our kind friends, and proceeded on our journey. Three or four miles west of J. Lindley's, the land is hilly; and near the summit, a *reddish sand rock* overlays the *limestone.* It may be noticed, though such appearances are not uncommon, that on the hills above the limestone level, there are no *sinks;* but on descending the western side to that level, these depressions are visible. Strata, however, are not so regular in this district as towards Pittsburgh.

After a ride of ten miles, we arrived at the *French Licks.* This place is a reservation, lately owned by the United States, but now transferred to Indiana. I oberved three *sulphur springs,*† one of which was more strongly impregnated than any that I have seen. We thought these waters were slightly tinctured with salt and iron.

From the base of a high bank of limestone that bounds this vale on the west, a large spring of fresh water breaks forth, and flows eastward between the other fountains. As we paused on the north bank of this stream, our hourses immediately strained down their heads, and began to lick the ground. We now perceived that the stones had a whitish coat, like frost; and which, on tasting, we discovered to be *common salt,* apparently free from impurities. This recalled the remark of H. DAVY, that "rock salt almost always occurs with red sandstone and gypsum." The sandstone, in its proper colour, is found on the spot; and though we have no proof of the presence of gypsum, sulphur springs‡ in New-York are one of its indications.

The celebrated SAUSSURE had previously enquired, why salt mines§ are found near mountains of gypsum? Perhaps the answer to be given, will be, that both are confined to regions of secondary formation. No strata of gypsum are known of an older date than

*J. Lindley, in a letter of 2 mo. 2, 1818, says, "The furnaces talked of when thou wast here, have not been built."

†Several others are found in the adjoining woods. On our return I filled a bottle with this water, which at that time was limpid; but in a few hours it became milky and the fetid smell was lost. It is well known to the chemists that hydrogen is a solvent of sulphur, and that the appearance here noticed, results from the escape of that gas. The mineral no longer soluble, floats in the water.

‡Though sulphurated hydrogen is not a constituent of gypsum, it abounds in all the best *plaster stone* of Cayuga. Water, in which this mineral is diffused, soon becomes sulphurous.

§"To examine the reason of the singular connexion observed between mines of salt, or salt springs, and mountains of gypsum." See his AGENDA.

limestone which contains shells; and in this remark salt may be included.

The coincidence, however, is curious; and prevails in our country as well as on the eastern side of the Atlantic. Saussure could not have been acquainted with this fact when he wrote; but the western district of New-York is now equally famous for its salt springs and its quarries of plaster.

Such springs are properly ascribed to water which has fallen in rain, and which by soaking through saline earth, or by flowing over salt rocks, is gradually wasting the mine. Indeed, it is probable that in regions of secondary formation, many fountains, now perfectly sweet, were originally brackish. This opinion is strongly supported by the fact, that the salt springs of the present day, have been commonly found to ooze through coverings of mud, in low, marshy situations without any visible outlet; and though Onondaga may furnish an exception, yet it is well known that subterranean waters, sometimes acquire new outlets by earthquakes.

This place is the favorite residence of the parroquet, flocks of which were continually flying round. These birds seem to delight in screaming.

We observed that the stream from these *Licks* soon becomes of a pale whitish blue, like a mixture of milk and water; and we had previously noticed, that Lick creek, and its other branches had acquired the same colour. To these appearances, probably, we owe the names of White water, White river, Blue river, &c.

Westward, the country is still more rough and hilly, and much of the soil is encumbered by sand rocks. This district resembles the roughest of the sandstone region north of Pittsburgh. Fine springs issue from the hills; and once more we enjoyed the luxury of pure cold water.

Near the top of a hill two miles westward, over which our road led, the inhabitants procure *whetstones*, which, it is said, are *equal* in quality to the *Turkey oil-stone*. The grit is extremely fine and sharp.

From the position of this quarry, on the top of a high ridge, I conjectured that the sand had not been deposited by water, but collected by the wind, previous to its petrification; but whether the horizontal arrangement will form a sufficient objection to this view, must be left undetermined.

Six miles west of the Lick, the land is less rugged, and some tracts are handsome.

We came to *Lick creek*, ten miles west of these Licks. Swelled by the late rains, it was too deep to ford, though only three or four rods wide, and we passed it in a ferry boat. At this place it flows to the north-west.

As the last gleamings of day were departing, we arrived at Schultz's near the *Driftwood Branch of White River*.

Though we have been several days on the frontiers, we find some change of manners at every remove. Tonight our horses, with many others, were turned loose, in a yard, to a great trough, bountifully replenished with Indian corn; and though oats is far better adapted to their habits, and though their treatment has always been a subject of solicitude, we felt much satisfaction in effecting our escape from the dark shades of a thick forest.

26 miles.

7 *mo.* 5.—THIS tavern is a recent establishment. The proprietor formerly from Pennsylvania, but latterly from Seneca County in New-York, has adopted the eastern mode of clearing land, and at once lays it open to the day. The pleasantness of the prospect, the safety of the cattle and the excellence of the crop,—which now promises to exceed by one half every other that we have seen in the country,—will strongly recommend this method to his neighbours; but we fear there will be more admirers than imitators.

At this place, we saw *the under jaw of a Mammoth*, in which the teeth remain. Though large, it is not one of the largest. It was found in the channel of the river nearly opposite to the house.

Since the discovery of the Mammoth, on the coast of Siberia, in the year 1808, conjecture respecting its figure is confined within narrow limits; while the place of its abode is involved in much obscurity. The situation in which it had lain, cased in ice, for thousands of years, shews that it floated thither. This inference is clear and regular; and perhaps the best evidence, that these quadrupeds belonged to our continent, is not furnished by the circumstance that their remains have been discovered at the Big bone Lick, but that there were strong inducements for them to frequent it.

Currents of water have swept over this country in a period comparatively recent; and the establishment of this fact has a tendency to weaken our faith in the opinion that New-York was once the residence of this creature. The bones discovered near Springfield, N. J., by my ingenious friend C. KINSEY, under a covering of six feet of solid earth, shew at least that great changes have taken place in the surface, since the deposition of these remains; and perhaps it will be difficult to account for this inhumation* in any way so plausibly as by a reference to that deluge, which has left its traces throughout our land long since the existence of air-breathing animals.

Corn, on the west branch of White River, now sells at twenty-five cents a bushel.

About sunrise we resumed our journey. Weakened by disease, I was indulged with a walk to the river, while my companions were preparing the horses, whither they were soon to follow.

Last evening we had heard the noise of *falls* at the distance of a mile or two over the hills; and on approaching, I found the water to pitch down about four feet over a level sand rock, extending straight across the river. The thick woods on the opposite shore, the clear sky, the smooth expanse of water, the foam of the cascade, and the unbroken quiet, formed one of the sweetest scenes of solitude.

Avoiding the force of the stream, small fish in great numbers had come in close with the shore; and eager to ascend the little currents from ledge to ledge, were so crowded together that I could take them up by hand-fulls.

On these banks I first saw the red trumpet flower† growing indigenously.

Yesterday we were joined by a genteel Kentuckian, who was also proceeding to Vincennes. He was from Shelbyville; and had attempted to travel the upper road, which leads more directly west from Cincinnati. That route, however, he found to be impassable from the quantities of fallen timber and under-brush; and after advancing nearly forty miles was compelled to retrace his steps.

Our company arriving, we forded the river a few rods above the falls. The level sand rock is uncovered two thirds of the distance over, except by water; and the remaining third seems

*Large bones (probably of this creature) have been found near the great western canal in the town of Manlius. One of the contractors in a letter to me of 5 mo. 15, 1818, says, "For the embankment across a swamp, I have taken earth from a small hill. At a depth varying from eight to twelve feet, we found *muscle shells* in abundance, with bones of some large animal. One half of a tooth weighed 2 lbs. 6 oz."

Dr. Drake remarks, that "on the upper table on which Cincinnati is built, a joint of the back bone of one of these species was found at the depth of twelve feet from the surface."

We have no reason to believe that these remains, in either case, would be buried at such depths in the common order of nature.

†Bignonia radicans. On our return I found this plant in Madison County, (Ohio) but the size was diminutive.

paved with muscle shells of a large size. The breadth of this beautiful stream we estimated at 150 yards. The upland adjoining it is good, and the hills retiring, admit flats of moderate extent, which are thickly timbered.

After ascending the hill, which may be 100 feet high, we passed through open oak woods into an extensive plain or *prairie*. Here such are called *barrens*, but improperly, for the soil is very fertile.

These openings present a striking contrast to the eastern parts of the continent, which were shaded by forests; and the cause has become a subject of general speculation. The thrifty growth of timber, which is found through this country in many places, proves, that though the woodlands decrease as we advance westward, the cause ought not to be attributed to climate. Indeed we have never seen, to the eastward, more timber on the same extent of ground than many tracts in this vicinity exhibit, if we except groves of white pine. Our search must therefore be confined to the soil, and to circumstances entirely incidental.

To me it is evident that the immediate causes of these wastes are fire and inundation; but the *predisponent* cause (if physicians will allow the expression) is either an impenetrable hard-pan, or a level rock. At page 98 I have noticed the wet prairies. The same rock, extending under the drier parts, confines the roots, and intercepts the supply of moisture that sub-soils generally contribute. The trees, thus stunted admit amongst them a luxuriant herbage; in autumn it is speedily dried by the sun and wind, and the underbrush perishes in the annual conflagration. Near the borders sufficient evidence of this was often before us in the stools of oak, with shoots from one to six feet in height, which were blasted by recent fires.

These tracts are generally situate near the height of land. On the bordering ridges, the timber attains a moderate size, and the adjoining declivities also produces it of the usual height; but trees, encircled by these wastes, are uniformly stunted.

In all the wells which we saw in these plains, a hard slate rock was found at the depth of a few feet.

The soil is various. Clay is not uncommon; in some places sand predominates; but a fertile loam will give the general character.

These lands may be subdued at a small expence. Near all that we have seen, materials for fencing, at present may easily be procured, and a strong team, with a good plough, would readily overturn the tea plant and the hazle. I saw not one stone on the surface.

Water may be procured in wells of a moderate depth; but in some, the quality is injured by foreign matters. In one, copperas is so abundant as greatly to discolour clothes in washing; and the proprietor assured me it would make a good dye.

Several habitations have been lately erected; but we saw no improvement which induced us to believe that the occupants had much capital.

Over these plains I saw the dodder (*Cuscuta*) for many yards round, entangling the herbage. This singular vegetable germinates in the soil, and ascending a few inches, takes hold of the first plant it can reach. The root then perishes, and it becomes *parasitic.* On breaking the stem, I have observed the pith to contract, which brought the epidermis together and closed the wound. What I broke to-day, however, was rigid; and perhaps this contraction only happens at an earlier period of its growth. It is extremely injurious to flax. This circumstance has claimed some attention of the farmer; and strange as it may seem, some have believed that the dust of flour mixed with flaxseed in a bag would infallibly produce it.

In the more clayey parts of these prairies, we saw heaps of earth as large as a bushel, which are inhabited by a little animal of the mole kind. We found none of the proprietors abroad, and we were not prepared for invasion. Their name, in this quarter, is gopher.*

As we were descending from the prairie, I observed a halt in the front of our company; and on riding forward, found our Kentucky friend engaged in destroying a large rattle-snake. This was the first venomous reptile we had seen on the journey, except two that lay dead in the road. I believe we have not seen half a dozen snakes of any kind.

Having travelled sixteen miles we took breakfast at Liverpool, [now *Washington*] a village of three houses. Our landlord was from Kentucky; and it appears that state has furnished much of the population of this district.

Here the peach-trees were loaded with fruit. We had previously observed that west of the Knobs, the frosts had not been injurious; but fruit trees between these points are scarce.

*Perhaps *gauffre*. "Only two species [of *Diplostoma*] are known as yet, and they have been discovered and ascertained by Mr. Bradbury. Both are found in the Missouri Territory. They burrow under ground and live on roots; and are called *gauffre* by the French settlers." C. F. RAFINESQUE.

Throughout all this western country, it is the fashion amongst the middle or lower classes to salute us by the name of "*stranger.*" The term may often be strictly proper, and it is seldom, if ever, accompanied by rudeness; yet the practice is so ungraceful, that we shall enter our protest against it, the authority of Walter Scott to the contrary notwithstanding.

A good tract of woodland extends three miles to *the West Fork of White River.* This stream in size and appearance resembles the other branches. Rapids of equal height, also are formed by a sand rock which occupies the whole bottom of the river, and at both places the direction is straight across. On this rock we forded.

No hills appear between Schultz's and Vincennes, excepting those that bound the flats on the rivers. It is seventeen miles from the West Fork to that turn, and much of the eastern part of that distance is prairie. Several miles east of the Wabash, we entered woodlands with a more diversified surface.

Observing a plumb tree, filled with large red flowers twelve feet high, I turned from the road to take a fairer view, and with surprise beheld a rose bush resting its vine-like stem on the branches to that height. The blossoms are in clusters; and as the colour varies with age the appearance is beautiful. I have seen this shrub almost every day since we crossed the Sciota, and believe it might be trained to the height of twenty feet.

Two miles from Vincennes we descended into the prairie that spreads round that town. Here the prospect over level land became extensive; low hills appeared in the horizon, while in the intermediate ground, the academy, rising above the range of buildings, imparted a cast of grandeur to the scene. Backward on our left, two mounds of extraordinary size, rose from the hill at the edge of the prairie. These seem to overlook the country, and resembled in this respect the monuments of the ancient Greeks.

> Around both urns we pil'd a noble tomb,
> ....that all
> Who live, and who shall yet be born, may view
> Thy record, even from the distant waves.
>
> COWPER'S HOMER.

These remains of antiquity shew that this plain has been the seat of wealth and power; and though it is now only the frontier town of a new race, it will probably long retain a superiority over the towns and cities of this country.

After sun set we took lodgings in this ancient capital of *the West.* 36 miles.

7 *mo.* 6.—VINCENNES stands on the east bank of the Wabash, a beautiful river, 300 yards in breadth. The site is a sandy plain resting on gravel. No flat, subject to inundation, intervenes; and a margin of rounded stones gradually slopes to the water.

This town embraces a great extent of ground; but large gardens, near most of the houses, leave it but small claims to compactness. It is decorated with a few good buildings of frame and brick; but there are many of logs and plaster, on which we can bestow no commendations.

Every valuable or elegant improvement is recent; for although this place has been settled almost a century by the French, we have remarked that the mode of business first adopted by new settlers, long continues to operate; and the history of this town may be cited as an example. A few hunters associated with Indians were the first white inhabitants; and though after the lapse of a few years several Canadian families arrived; and though they retained much of the national politeness, it appears that the cabin bounded their views in architecture, and corn purchased of the natives has frequently preserved their existence.

This primitive indolence, though lessened in appearance by the influx of a northern population, is still conspicuous; and I suspect in some measure contagious. Several enclosures are filled with Jimson* as high as the fences; and without this notice, a view of the town would be incomplete.

But perhaps a traveller never commits greater injustice than in generalizing his remarks; for the meritorious and the unworthy will be found in all districts, and in all communities. Neither am I unapprised that in reviewing these inhabitants, there are many considerations to soften the severity of criticism.

The precepts of charity require that man should be judged by his own moral principles. And, the point at which he stops in one state of society, may be censurable, while in another state, to have advanced to that point, may be merit of the first degree.

Separated from the civilized world by immense forests, this people were estranged to its comforts, its ambition, and, doubtless, to much of its crime. Avarice had small opportunity to amass treasure, and the love of splendour could be very partially gratified. If, then, we consider that the two main-springs of action in civilized society were wanting, we shall cease to wonder at this result.

*i. e. Jamestown weed, the thorn apple (*Dalura stramonium.*)

But in addition, they were a conquered people. The British kept a garrison in their town for a number of years; and since the Anglo-Americans arrived, they have often been exposed to Indian hostilities. Indeed when we consider the paralizing effects of such a state, and that partially it has continued till the present time, our censures should be sparingly pronounced.

At the time of determining the streets, no correct idea could have been formed, of the increase of population and of consequence that await this town. A want of sufficient room in some has accordingly been the result; but this inconvenience, in a few years, will be more sensibly felt. Paving has not been commenced; and though the soil is sandy, these avenues are occasionally incommoded by mud. The houses are built on different squares, but are more extended along the river. The number we should estimate between 200 and 300.

This plain is very fertile. Although the sand is clear or white, the "finely divided matter" is so abundant as to give a black colour to the mass. In such gardens as are well cultivated, the vegetation is luxuriant. Drouths are slightly felt. The soil is so absorbent, and the loose substratum admits the ascent of moisture so freely, that though rain has been withheld eleven weeks, we saw small traces of such extreme.

Modern geographers have assigned *fine grass* to this plain. Such an idea is easily acquired by inference; because a rich soil, like this to the north east would produce fine grass,—but the error is striking. Indeed, sufficient proof might be educed to shew that on this spot none ever vegetated. The herbage chiefly consists of perennial weeds with spaces of *naked earth* between, which coarse wild grass, probably once occupied.

On the bank of the river I found several petrifactions. One of these in grit and colour resembled the white part of the Irish hone. The tree that gave it shape had been six inches in diameter, and this fragment contained one fifth of the circumference. The bark had been removed. The surface left by that covering retained its smoothness; and the different annual growths were distinctly visible.

About ten o'clock we commenced our journey up the river towards Fort Harrison. Near the town I counted seven small mounds. Adjoining these a bank and ditch remain which once belonged to a small fortress or store house, probably erected since the arrival of Europeans. All this bank of the river is beyond the reach of inundation.

We soon passed into woodland. *Fort Knox* once stood on this bank, two miles above the town; but the site is now only discoverable by excavations, remnants of old chimnies, and hewn timber scattered over the ground. The soil, though dry and gravelly, produced, wherever the trees had been thinned by the axe, briars* of luxuriant growth; and the blackberry was now ripe.

From a bank a little further up the river, a thick stratum of sandstone projects. It contains mica, like that at Pittsburgh which is formed into grindstones.

Yesterday, seven miles east of Vincennes, I noticed *mica slate*, and at that town several waggon loads of this stone were lying in a heap; but I could not learn whence it was brought. From its appearance on the south shore of Lake Erie, and in all the principal ridges of the Allegany, it is probable that the secondary strata, throughout the Ohio country, rest on this rock; but whether it projects in places through these strata,—or whether the small quantities which I observed were brought by the great northern deluge from the ridge that divides the waters of the Ohio and St. Lawrence—can only be determined by the position of these masses.

The stems of the *Trumpet-flower* at White River were diminutive; but here these plants had climbed up many of the trees to the tops; and the large reddish blossoms extending beyond the branches, presented objects uncommonly novel and beautiful.

[A just medium between cool reserve and colloquial freedom, in recording travels, is a *desideratum*. It is true, our interest in the welfare of the traveller increases as he unfolds his pleasures and his sufferings; but still there is an insipid triteness, and a minuteness of detail that we wish not to hear. We care not whether he loves fat meat or lean; carries a cane, or walks with his hands in his pockets. Such facts are of no value. It must be confessed, however, that the temptation to egotistic prolixity is great; and, ware of this danger, I should be deterred from retaining the folowing paragraph, did it not convey instruction which ought not to be withheld.]

Since we ascended the Knobs, my health had been gradually declining. My stomach was the seat of the disease. Paroxysms of that distressing sensation, which physicians have denominated *anxiety*, had daily increased; and my friend J. S. had marked the change with silent apprehension. On descending into the *first flats* of the river, it returned with violence, and I entreated my

*Rubus villosus.

companions to prepare an emetic without delay; but the proposal was rejected, for the air was replete with putrid vapour, the sky overcast, and the ground wet with the late rain. In this comfortless extremity, without the means of preparation, I applied dry pearlash to my tongue till the skin was abraded, taking it rather in agony than with hope. The relief, however, was sudden: the *fomes* of fever was neutralized, and my recovery seemed like enchantment.

[Repeated doses of this alkali in a few days completed the cure; and since, I have frequently witnessed its efficacy on others. Its action is chiefly chemical. In acidity of the first passages it is invaluable; in dysentery it has ranked as a specific; and though no medicine deserve this encomium, yet it has speedily afforded relief in numerous cases of that dreadful disease.

A lump, the size of a hazelnut, dissolved in half a gill of water, is a small dose for an adult; but when there is much acid, more pearlash will be necessary to neutralize it; and in such cases twice that quantity may be taken with safety, if the solution be sufficiently diluted.]

Eight miles above Vincennes, we passed from the woodland flats into the south end of the prairie that extends up to Shakertown. Old driftwood and weeds encumbered the soil, which was black and very fertile; but we could not believe that human beings could frequent it in summer and enjoy health; yet we saw huts that were inhabited on the border towards the river.

As we advanced, the prospect became more inviting; and we discovered what we had not before learned, that *these celebrated prairies are the upper or second flats on the river*. The surface is undulated; and at once we assent to the opinion, that it owes its form to some preternatural deluge. The back channel, or *bayou*, through which the water flows when the currents of the creeks are checked by the river floods, unquestionably had the same origin. The level part of this channel is several rods wide, and in many places it was covered by standing water; yet we saw no spot that appeared miry, and the cattle, which were feeding in considerable numbers, passed over without difficulty. The sides of the bayou slope so gradually, that except in the lines of driftwood no traces of inundation are visible.

The advantages that these *natural canals* afford in times of flood have not been overlooked; and boats often pass up the country at the distance of one or two miles from the river.

The path, which in places scarcely served to direct us, led along the eastern side of the bayou; and after riding a few miles, we gained a beautiful ridge on which we stopped to refresh our horses. Hard wild grass scarcely one foot high, thinly scattered among weeds, constituted the pasturage. Were we to judge only from this appearance we should not fix the estimate of its fertility very high; but Indian corn of a most luxuriant growth, as high as the fences, presented a remarkable contrast; and the looseness and blackness of the soil on that eminence, which for ages has been above the river floods, excited our admiration.

To the west, the land rises from the bayou for a considerable distance; and the summit, crowned with trees, hid the river from our view. On the east side of this prairie, several farms appear which were probably located for the convenience of timber, as we saw none where the proprietors had ventured far out into the plain. This tract is from one to three miles wide, and ten or twelve miles in length; and the novelty, beauty, and extent of the prospect had a very sensible effect on our spirits.

The wind met us, on entering this prairie, and continued so regular as to remind me of the current from a fanning-mill. Like the clouds that move in the superior regions of the atmosphere, it was exempt from the flaws and whirls that prevail amongst hills and vallies.

Shakertown, the residence of the Shakers, consists of eight or ten houses of hewn logs, situate on a ridge west of the bayou, eighteen miles above Vincennes. The site is moderately elevated. As we approached, the blackness of the soil, and the luxuriance of vegetation, was peculiarly attractive; but much water was standing on the low grounds to the east; and a mill-pond on *Busseron Creek*, of considerable extent to the west, must suffuse the whole village with unwholesome exhalations. In addition, the first flats of the Wabash, extending one mile west from the creek, are frequently overflowed by the river.

The number of inhabitants is estimated at two hundred, who live in four families.

Pondering on the evils of this mortal life, some have doubted whether it was given in wrath or in mercy;* and though we are not authorised to assert, that this sect has been influenced by darksided views of our nature, yet marriage is prohibited. From dancing, as an act of devotion, their name is derived. Like several other sects, they conform to great plainness in apparel, but their garb is peculiar. In language they are also very distinguishable.

*Jefferson's Notes.

It appears that all complimentary phrases are discarded; but they never use the second person singular in conversation, or say *yes* or *no*, substituting for the latter terms *yea* and *nay;* and tho' I contend with no man about his religious principles,—believing that in every nation he that worketh righteousness is accepted, —yet I could not resist the impression, that they had mistaken the antiquated style of King James the first for the original language of the Scriptures.

In their dealings they are esteemed as very honest and exemplary. Until within a few months they entertained travellers without any compensation; but the influx has become so great that they have found it necessary to depart from that practice.

The *estate* at this place consists of about 1,300 acres. The *mills,* which they have erected, are a great accommodation to this part of the country, and to these they have added *carding machines.*

A field of sixty acres of *wheat* on the north side of this village, has just been reapt, and put up in shock. The crop is excellent.

Indigo and *cotton,* to the extent of a few acres, are cultivated; and the plants appeared in a thriving state. The products* are wholly designed for home consumption. It is not pretended that these articles would afford a profit on exportation; but it is deemed economical to raise a sufficiency for this numerous family. The price of Tennessee cotton would be enhanced by the carriage hither, and the profits of this cotton would be reduced by its transportation to a market. The same reasoning will apply to the indigo with this additional circumstance: it is only macerated, and the fabrics to be coloured are then introduced. Much labour in preparing it is consequently saved.

These people settled here before the late war; but after their estate was ravaged by the troops who went with Hopkins on his expedition, they sought refuge amongst their own sect in Ohio and in Kentucky, and only returned last summer. They have a fine young *orchard* of grafted apple trees; and their *nursery* is considered as the best in the country.

Their *neat cattle* are numerous. Their flock of *sheep* consists of some hundreds, and a shepherd with his dog and gun is employed as a guard.

Sweet potatoes grow remarkably well in this black sand.

The *common potatoe* flourishes most in a rich soil, watered by frequent showers; but though the late drouth has been unfavour-

*About 150 lbs. of clean cotton is produced on an acre.

able, the appearance of this plant is much finer than some of our travellers had induced us to expect.

Water is procured from a *well* between twenty and thirty feet deep. In digging they found the sand coarser as they descended, until it terminated in gravel so loose, that to prevent the sides from falling, it became necessary to work in the hollow trunk of a buttonwood,* which they introduced; and which settling as the gravel was removed, ensured their safety, and now forms the wall of the well. It ought to be repeated, however, that wood soaking in water always injures the quality.

The extensive flat, between Busseron Creek and the River, abounds with the *Pecan*,† a species of hickory. The nut is superior in delicacy of flavour, and the shell is so soft as to yield to common teeth. The Indians, as well as the white inhabitants, have gathered it in great quantities; a market is found for it in every considerable village of this country; and at the falls of the Ohio, the current price has been four dollars a bushel, or twenty-five cents a quart.

On our arrival, we found a young man of genteel appearance, from Kentucky. His intention had been to explore the country up the river, but he concluded to direct his course to the Missouri, giving it as a reason that *farmers in this territory must perform their own labour.*

After procuring some refreshment, we resumed our journey,—turning eastward, and nearly at right angles to the river, intending to visit M. Hoggatt, to whom we had been directed by our friends at Lick Creek. He resides on a farm belonging to the Shakers, at the distance of seven miles.

The configuration of this district is so different from the regions to the east, only excepting some small tracts near the borders of the Sciota, that we seem to have arrived in a new world. Whereever the surface of the ground has been broken, *the blackness* and *depth of the soil* excite our admiration. Neither is there any thing delusive in this appearance, for *the growth of the crops* fully equals any expectation we could form.

Three miles from Shakertown, we passed a field which contained the harvest of two seasons. Last autumn the Indian corn had been cut near the ground, and put into well banded shocks. Wheat was then sown amongst them; it had produced a fine crop,

*Platanus occidentalis. The sycamore.

†Pronounced Pek-kawn.

and this was now also standing in shocks,—a clear inference that provisions are plenty.

Plants which are not found in the eastern parts of the United States are very numerous; perhaps three fourths of the herbage is of this description. I noticed three species of *Helianthus?* one of which is a remarkable plant. It grows six feet high with a disk nearly three inches in diameter, and the leaves much resemble the fern. Observing it first near the Sciota, before the stalk had arisen, I even believed it to be one of this curious assemblage. Nature, like water poured on a plain, though spreading into varieties in every direction, is partial to particular forms; and perhaps this partiality is evinced in nothing more than in *fern leaves.*

A small though beautiful species of *Hollyhock* is scattered over the prairie. Its blossoms are a fine red. At first sight, I considered it an exotic; but it may be a native, for it is found in the wildest situations among the groves.

From this prairie we ascended a ridge,—not steep, and of a moderate elevation,—thinly shaded by small trees. The sand continues, but a diminution of fertility is immediately discernible, though the district eastward may be called a tract of good land. It is composed of some ridges of that description with intervening vales. Beyond, the prospect opened into a clayey prairie of great extent, which is nearly destitute of Inhabitants.

We shall not be surprised if many situations in this district prove unhealthy. The streams have low banks and in heavy rains, spread wide through the vallies, but the water may be easily led off, whenever it shall be undertaken with spirit, and in such business the scraper would be eminently useful.

As we advanced across the prairie, we saw horses, neat cattle and swine, scattered over it in considerable numbers, and moving about in different directions. Though we had seen much of such openings, our relish of the novelty was unsated; and these feelings were not diminished, when we saw across this great but uncultivated plain,—on the remote border of the civilized world, and where only log cabins have appeared legitimate—a spacious brick mansion in front of the woodlands. This evinces a spirit of improvement highly commendable.

In several places *the land was gullied*, and afforded an opportunity to observe that the black soil is nearly two feet deep; and that it rests on a substratum of yellowish clay. If this part was more remote from the sandy prairies, it would rank higher in the estimation of farmers.

In the evening we arrived at our intended lodgings, where we met a cordial welcome. Hospitality is a strong characteristic of southern manners; and our friend, to an enlightened mind, has added the sympathies acquired by travel.

This, and two other families who live adjacent, constitute all of the society of *Friends* now known to be residents near this river. 25 miles.

7 *mo.* 7.—LAST night we had a heavy storm. In the evening the wind and scud were easterly, but the approach of thunder and lightning from the west, proved that the upper currents of the atmosphere move from that quarter. This morning was overcast, with an east wind,—evincing that counter currents similar to those on the east side of the Allegany Mountains prevail even here.

Our friend has resided between two and three years on this farm. On his first removal from North Carolina, he fixed his abode at Blue River; but came hither to explore *the lands of the New Purchase* previous to the sale. These lands have excited much attention, but various circumstances have conspired to prevent the surveys from being completed.

It will be recollected, that the expedition to *Tippecanoe* resulted from the dissatisfaction of the Indians, to the treaty in which their title to this tract became extinguished; that hostilities on their part commenced in the spring of 1812; and that after the defeat of Proctor, and the death of Tecumseh at Moravian town in upper Canada, the Indians sued for peace. The treaty that followed, however, did not restore tranquillity. A Potawattamie chief, reposing confidence in that arrangement, proceeded to Vincennes; but the next morning he was found dead in the street, into which he had been dragged, and his skull fractured apparently by clubs. On this occasion it was remarked, that though Indians often kill each other, their weapons are the knife and the tomahawk. The perpetrators of this outrage remained undiscovered. The chief was buried with the honours of war; but the light in which the Indians viewed the transaction was soon disclosed by the murder of several white settlers. After this retaliation, though hostilities were discontinued, yet perfect cordiality was not restored till the treaty at Fort Harrison in the present season. One of the surveyors who had been deterred by these unfavourable circumstances from fulfilling his contract, is now out with a company.

These last acts of violence happened since our friend arrived at this place, and several of his neighbours were sufferers. The case of one young man is too extraordinary to be omitted. Riding out to hunt cattle, he passed near Indians in ambush, who shot him through the body, and he fell from his horse. As the savages advanced to scalp him, he recovered from the shock; ran with his utmost speed, warmly pursued; and in the moment of extremity when his strength and breath failed him, his horse, which had loitered behind, came up on full gallop and allowed him to remount. He effected his escape, recovered from his wound, and is now living.

This farm consists of 1,000 acres. The soil contains little sand, and is consequently more favourable to some crops than the Prairies near the river. We are told that *timothy* flourishes; but a *drowth*, the longest known in many years, which only ceased a few days ago,—and *the army worm*, which has ravaged the meadows,—prevent us from forming a proper judgment from our own observation. By the same creature, the corn has perished twice this season.

These animals, which have committed similar depredations in the eastern part of Ohio, bear some resemblance to the grub-worm; and are regarded as periodical. The name is derived from their moving by myriads in one direction. Some fields and meadows have been saved by deep furrows, in which logs were constantly drawn by horses, so long as these devourers continued to approach. In this manner thousands on thousands have been destroyed.

Wood, for fuel and for fences, is an object of such importance to the farmer, that none is yet found willing to forego that convenience, and to seat himself out in the prairie. On this account, a stranger is liable to err in judging of the population, for we find the eastern border of this tract thickly inhabited.

To satisfy the *claims of the old French settlers*, the United States directed to be set apart, all the lands bounded on the west by the Wabash River; on the south by the White River; on the east by the West branch; and on the north by the north bounds of the Old Purchase. Four hundred acres was assigned to each person entitled to a donation. The land has never been surveyed by order of the government, consequently it has never been regularly performed; and the *maps* of this territory within these boundaries are generally blank.

All lands held in this quarter are therefore under French* grants. In locating, it was necessary to begin at the general boundary, or at some corner of lands, the lines of which would lead thither; but no course was given, and the claimant settled the point with his surveyor as he deemed most to his interest. These claims have been the source of considerable speculation; but the principal part is now located; and it is expected there will be a large surplus of land, soon to be surveyed by the United States.

Many of these tracts will be destitute of timber fences. In some parts of the *Grand Prairie*, which extends from the Wabash towards the Mississippi, we are informed that ditches are advantageously constructed. The sods are placed on the edges in two parallel rows, with the turf outward; the loose earth from both trenches is employed for filling; and the strong roots of the wild grass on vegetating, bind the parts firmly together.

It appears that this prairie has not been ravaged by fire for some years; and in various parts, but more especially near the eastern border, shrubs and young trees begin to shade the soil. Their scattered situations, with the injuries received from cattle, give them a stunted aspect. From these circumstances it will be difficult to judge what quality of timber this prairie would produce; but where it terminates on the east in a stately wood of honey locust, sugar maple, blue and white ash, I can perceive no change of soil. Neither have I discovered any marks of an impervious subsoil; and must ascribe the destruction of the ancient forest, with the wastes below Meadville, to conflagration.

This opinion may be explained by a few observations. Near some part of every prairie that we have seen, whether clayey or sandy, there are trees of diminutive size; and though not always distant from each other, the sun and air has such access that the dampness which prevails in forests, is generally unknown. The leaves and herbage, consequently become highly combustible; and the flame driven by brisk winds, will enlarge the boundaries of the prairie. Several instances of this have been before us. The small timber has been destroyed, and many large trees have been partly burnt. The cause why this prairie extends close to the tall wood on the east, will doubtless be found in these circumstances; for though *windfalls* would let in the sun and air, and be attended by a similar diminution of moisture, we recollect no such tracts in the Western Country.

The *Columbo Root* grows here in great abundance.

*I have since learned that some militia claims were located in this tract. The residue is directed to be sold on the 1st of 9th mo. 1818.

In winter when hay and corn have been scarce, some farmers in this district have driven their cattle towards the White River. The woods shelter them from the winds; and abound with grass, bearing the name of that season, which is evergreen, two or three feet in height, and extremely nutritious. In spring, the droves return home literally fat. This advantage, however will be temporary.

Every district, marked by small differences of soil and climate, has plants and animals peculiar. This remark which occurred at P. 113, is well exemplified by these wastes, and we have already learned the names of several new quadrupeds.

The *prairie wolf* is half the size of the common wolf, and it is believed to be *specifically* distinct. It is confined to the prairies, and burrows in the sandy earth. The colour is grey. The legs are short, flat, broad, and stronger in proportion than the common wolf. It has not been known to injure domestic animals; but when sheep are more generally introduced, it will doubtless acquire new habits.

Its motion is slow; and when discovered out in the prairie far from its burrow, is easily run down by horsemen. One was pursued, and so much exhausted in a mile, that the men leapt from their horses, and dispatched it with clubs.

The *gopher* has been mentioned.

The *prairie squirrel* in size and colour nearly resembles the grey squirrel, but the legs are shorter. It is only found in these districts and burrows like the prairie wolf.

It was suggested by some men of observation that, as these creatures are only found in the prairies, such land must have been in this state since the creation. But I cannot perceive that this conclusion is necessarily implied. We have no facts to shew that land destitute of timber is essential to their existence; we only know that their manners at present are best adapted to such scenes. Indeed we have strong reasons for doubting the correctness of this inference. We have no evidence of original prairies, except those that were formed by excess of moisture. We have no evidence of dry prairies, before conflagrations became regular: in other words, before the arrival of human beings on this continent. The persimmon, the tea plant, and every other tree that can bear the annual bearing, shoot up in abundance; and if such were undisturbed by fire, by cattle and by culture, these wastes in fifty years would be shaded by forests,—not lofty indeed, but such as sand resting on gravel would nourish and support.

The grey squirrel, the ground squirrel, and the flying squirrel, are found native, but do not appear to be numerous. To this list should be added the fox squirrel of the southern states.

The deer, the elk, the wolf, and the bear, inhabit the woods. The panther has been rarely discovered, but the wild cat is numerous.

In the brown rabbit, which has frequently bounded across our path, I recognized an old acquaintance, and with it associated the remembrance of early days. This quadruped appears to be very numerous.

7 *mo.* 8.—THE weather of both yesterday and to-day, has been unfavourable to travelling, as showers have been frequent, though the wind and scud are from the east. This circumstance, with the unaffected kindness of our friends, has induced us to remain stationary.

At Vincennes I observed a curious fly-flapper. The construction is simple, and in hot weather the fresh air that attends its motion, is scarcely less agreeable than relief from these troublesome insects. Its position is over the centre of the table.

Two strips of lath three feet long, with a hole in the lower end of each to receive a gudgeon, are first prepared. A broad board with a gudgeon so placed in each end, that one edge shall always preponderate, is then connected with the strips. To that edge a piece of linen one foot wide is fastened; and a handle, eighteen inches long, projects from the opposite edge. The upper ends of the laths are then nailed at the ceiling, and a small cord attached to the handle communicates motion to the instrument.

A joint in the laths near the ceiling would afford the convenience of elevating or removing it at pleasure.

The privileges granted to the Canadian Volunteers have occasioned severe strictures on the general government; and in travelling one hundred and fifty miles, we have conversed with but few persons who have not expressed dissatisfaction. We are told that the whole of the New Purchase, excepting fractions* and public

*A *fraction* is a tract of land where rivers or oblique boundaries have prevented the *section* from being completed. It may consist of any quantity less than a section.

The law of Congress which authorized these donations, directed that the Canadian claimants should locate by sections and quarter sections. Fractions not having been mentioned, and as many of these are very valuable, and include nearly all the lands adjoining the river, the Register of the Land Office with propriety reserved them till the day of the public sale.

Lot number sixteen in every township, as in other parts of this territory, is appropriated for the use of schools. A tract has also been reserved round Fort Harrison. We knew of no other reservation, though possibly some may be made on account of minerals.

reservations, is spread before them; more than three months have been allowed them to locate their claims without interruption; and to select the most valuable lots and mill seats, from three millions of acres of the best land, ever offered for sale by the United States.

It has been the policy of governments, however, to reward such persons as from principles of attachment have come over from the enemy; and in the present case, they were native citizens of the United States. Many of them left all their possessions behind. Perhaps those who scan the measures of government with candour, would have been satisfied, if the actual sufferers had been put in possession of property so generously bestowed. But a transfer of claims was inconsiderately permitted; certain expence met them in the onset; the office for adjusting their claims, was three hundred miles from the place where the principal number resided; many difficulties had arisen at the end of this long journey; and as cash to the necessitous is tempting, very few will receive one fifth of the value of these donations.

No blame can attach to those who have purchased in a fair market; but some idea of this speculation may be formed from one statement. The right of a private for three hundred and twenty acres, was bought for one hundred and seventeen dollars and fifty cents, and was sold for five thousand dollars. The choicest lots near Fort Harrison have been estimated at fifteen dollars an acre.

A small cotton wood tree stands opposite to the window where I am writing, dark excrescences on its branches like those which appear on this species in the western parts of New-York. It is well known that these blemishes are produced by the irritation of insects;—first by a puncture when the egg is deposited, and afterwards by the growth and motion of the worm. To procure this food, the *parroquets* have been busily employed, at times, through the day; but though they have become so familiar; and though they excel all the birds of this country in beauty of plumage,—their scream is so discordant, and their fierceness of disposition so apparent, as to preclude every sensation of attachment.

These birds build their nests in hollow trees. The strength of their necks is remarkable; and we are assured that when both wings and feet are tied they can climb trees by striking their bills into the bark.

Birds are not so numerous in the Ohio country as in New-York and Pennsylvania. The *prairie hen*, probably a species of the genus *Tetrao*, is a native. The *tetrao tympanus*, or drumming pheasant of Pennsylvania, called the partridge in New-York is also an inhabitant. The partridge of Pennsylvania called the quail in New-York is very numerous. But this confusion of names is to be regretted; and in both states the application is improper; for the pheasant of Europe belongs to the same genus as our dunghill fowls, and the partridge of England is a distinct species from all those of that name in our country.

The *large black bird* (Gracula purpurea), frequents the principal streams; and small brownish black-birds, probably of the same species as those that infest the marshes of the Seneca river, are very numerous, and equally predatory.

The *meadow lark*, the *kildee*, and the *land plover* inhabit the prairies. The last has been called the *rain bird*, from its notes being more frequently heard in the calm that precedes changes of the atmosphere. But the mildness of the air may inspire its song, and the stillness allow it to hover more easily over the fields where it loves to wander. From elevations in the air where it is scarcely visible, its note is heard to a great distance like a long shrill sigh. Who hears it in youth will hardly outlive the recollection.

We had been taught to expect that *turkies** were very numerous, but we have been disappointed, for certainly we have not seen half a dozen full grown in all the Western Country.

The *turkey buzzard*, or carrion vulture, is gregarious, but we have seen no large flocks. It is less shy than any other undomesticated bird of its size. When searching for food, it moves in circles so elevated as almost to elude the sight. There is reason to believe that the effluvia of dead bodies, by being specifically lighter than common air, is arranged at a certain height in the atmosphere. On reaching this stratum they more readily discover whence the stream ascends.

The *red headed woodpecker* is seen, but not in such destructive numbers as at Cayuga.

The *little yellow bird* sometimes moves in flocks, and complaint is made of its devouring flax-seed.

To the foregoing list of the birds of this country, may be added the *crane*, the *crow*, the *blue-jay*, and the *red winged starling*.

We learn that *mountain rice* is cultivated by one person, and it has succeeded well. The product varies from thirty to sixty

*At that time, it appears that these fowls were hatching or secreted with their young. In the ADDITIONAL NOTICES, a different account will be given.

bushels to the acre in the rough; but it may diminish to one third of these quantities by hulling. This is the best sort; but it requires more attention and culture than the water rice, as the hoe must be introduced to destroy the weeds, which amongst the latter, the process of flooding completely effects. The latter kind would also grow in this climate, if the land could be regularly laid under water.

Our friend has a handsome little *nursery* of thrifty apple-trees which he raised from *suckers** procured in his neighbours' orchards. He intends to transplant them when he locates a farm. In new countries, where it is difficult to obtain young trees, the emigrant would do well to adopt this method.

7 *mo.* 9.—M. H. having agreed to attend us in exploring the lands up the river, and as maps are necessary, and the creeks unusually swelled by the late rains,—which would retard if not prevent our progress in that direction,—this morning, he and I departed for Vincennes. Our course was south by west, and the distance twenty miles.

This road being back from the river, presented some new objects. Having passed the beautiful wood which I mentioned, including an extensive sugar camp, the trees as we advanced appeared of less and less magnitude, till our path led through oaks of small stature into the prairie.

As the surface of the land is moderately undulated, these openings are interrupted at small distances by *plains*, which differ from the prairies in being dry ground, and in supporting flat-topped oaks thirty or forty feet high, between which are interspersed oak stools. The growth of former years having perished by the annual burning, the young shoots of this season have sprung up in abundance. These are chiefly the white oak, the swamp white oak, and the true black jack.

To the annual conflagrations may be ascribed in part, the scarcity of *snakes* in this district; but the deficiency of hills and quarries to afford them shelter in winter, must remain as the principal cause.

Of these reptiles are enumerated the rattlesnake and the viper. Some garter snakes are found; and I learn that the water snake

*Although it is a current opinion amongst nursery men, that suckers produce suckers in abundance, the emigrant may dismiss all apprehensions on this subject. I have a considerable number of trees, budded on such stocks, several of which now bear apples; and from none of them have I perceived a sucker. I do not assert that these are more exempt than seedling stocks, and nurseries on a large scale could not be conveniently supplied in this manner; but no farmer should be discouraged from raising his own trees.

and black racer will complete the list. The copper head, so common through the wooded country to the eastward, is said to be unknown.

At the end of seven miles we came to *Marie's Creek*. The channel was nearly filled by muddy water, and with difficulty we forded. It is a lazy stream scarcely two rods wide.

During the late war, a neighbouring hunter having started a deer, near the banks of this creek, cautiously approached the root of an old tree, and was earnestly looking through a thick underbrush for his game, when he descried two Indians passing in file at a small distance. Instinctively he shrunk back—raised his rifle, but paused—it was a perilous moment. He knew not their numbers; and as he was undiscovered, he determined to be still. In a few minutes he heard the report of a gun; and my friend pointed down the stream to the spot, where at that instant, they killed and scalped a young man who was gathering grapes. A short time before, in full health, he had left his father's dwelling.

The rage and anguish of the parent was excessive. We soon passed by his house; and the most melancholy reflections arose on my mind. *War*, at best, is a dismal picture. Famine, slaughter and rapine, crowd the pages of its history; but the keen anguish that invades the domestic circle is unnoticed. To his country, a soldier, or a citizen has perished; to his family, a father, a husband, a son, or a brother.

South of the creek, oak, not very thrifty, constitutes the principal timber. This tract extends within seven or eight miles of Vincennes; and with the more open lands to the north, forms a border to the Shakertown prairie. The soil is but moderately fertile. The inhabitants are few, scattered, and in some places we passed on for miles without seeing a house.

Below, the country is more inviting. Beech, sugar maple, honey locust and some black walnut, forms a tall forest; and a luxuriant growth of herbage overspreads the ground. This woodland extends to the river,—separating the Vincennes prairie from that of Shakertown,—retains a great degree of moisture, like the beech and maple lands to the eastward,—and appears well adapted to the cultivation of grasses. The soil is a strong clayey loam.

Lands partially improved, in this district, rate from twelve to fourteen dollars an acre.

In Vincennes, N. EWING and J. BADOLLET of the *Land-Office*, for whom I had introductory letters, received me with frankness. The former is a native of Lancaster county, Pennsylvania;

and the latter of Geneva, in Europe. The friendship of their old neighbour, the celebrated A. GALLATIN, procured them these appointments about nine years ago; and the high rank which they deservedly hold in public estimation, proves the wisdom of his choice.

In the evening, having acceded to the kind invitation of N.E. to go to his house, which is four miles southeasterly from Vincennes, we took the opportunity to ride to the top of the second mound before noted, and which is near the side of the road. The prospect was extensive and delightful. Excepting a ridge of moderate elevation up the river, where the woodland extends over into the Illinois Territory, there is nothing within the range of the eye that merits the name of a hill.

This *pyramid* was the largest I had ever approached. We estimated the diameter at one hundred and fifty feet, and probably it will exceed forty in height on the west side. As it stands on the slope of the hill, the acclivity on the east side is much less; and though steep, we ascended it on horseback.

We observe the same singularity of construction as in those to the eastward. The surface is sand, which the adjoining hills may have furnished; but the interior part is clay, and notwithstanding the greatness of the labour, it must have been brought from a distance. In it, human bones have been discovered. We therefore suppose it was not raised in one age; and the transportation of the latter material, probably, formed a part of the funeral ceremonies.

At the distance of a furlong to the south, a mound of equal magnitude appears nearly in a right line with the two which I have noticed. All these are separated from the prairie by a swamp that lies along the base of the hill.

This swamp or bog resembles nothing that we have seen in the western country. A pole may be thrust perpendicularly downwards to the depth of twenty feet; and as it extends to the borders of the White River, twenty miles below, our intelligent friend conjectures that it was an ancient channel of the Wabash.

In adopting this opinion, however, I refer to a period before the formation of the sandy prairies. The vast quantities of sand and gravel that overwhelmed the river plains, appears to have filled this channel north-easterly from Vincennes, for a considerable distance downwards; and to have turned the river to the southwest; but I consider this deluge to have been long anterior to the mounds.

Our road now led through a country variegated by low hills, chiefly shaded with oak. The soil near the prairies is sandy; but as we receded we found it inclining to a clayey loam; and beech, &c. appears through the woods.

The mansion of our friend is of brick, handsomely situated on a ridge which commands a pleasant prospect of his farm. His daily practice is to ride to Vincennes, and in the evening to return. This exercise doubtless contributes to health; and the bustle of a town contrasted with this charming but sequestered spot, must increase the relish for domestic enjoyment.

7 *mo.* 10.—THE antiquities of this country interest every intelligent mind; and curiosity seems more awake because history has shed no light on the subject. N. E. informed me, that nine miles above its mouth, the Wabash is wearing away a bank which contains great quantities of the bones of different quadrupeds, and hence it is termed *the Bone Bank.* At the same place, under a covering of clay and sand twelve feet deep, vessels of various kinds are found stratified with ashes. Some of these are large and shaped like a Dutch stew-pot; others are spherical bottles with long necks. Like the fragments found in other parts of the western country, these contain pounded muscle shells. The cement, however, has become very feeble; the parts crumble at the touch, and in every flood the river effects some removal.

Though the ordinance of Congress, under which all the governments north west of the Ohio were organized, expressly declares that no persons, except in punishment for crimes, shall be held in bondage; and though that ordinance has remained unrepealed; yet *slaves* were considered to be so convenient, that the territorial legislature authorized their introduction. For this purpose, indentures were employed. The negro was directed to sign an article, binding himself to serve his master for some specified term of years; refusal could avail nothing, and compliance was termed *voluntary servitude.* I learn, however, from various sources, that it is now generally understood that these *articles* must be declared nugatory whenever a legal investigation shall be made.

In this affair originated a powerful opposition; and for several years past, the territory has been divided into two active parties. Those who were opposed to this innovation, however, soon became the majority; and the members of the late Convention, acting agreeably to the directions of Congress, put the question at rest forever, by excluding the principle of slavery from the state constitution.

After breakfast we returned to Vincennes. The hills that border the prairie on the east, are chiefly composed of sand; and the inequalities of the surface, which are very considerable, show the violent agitation of the deluge that whirled it hither.

Having procured the necessary maps by the very liberal accommodation of the Register, we continued our journey.

We had been invited by B. PARKE, a distinguished citizen, to visit him on our return. This we now performed with much satisfaction. He resided in a spacious brick building, erected by the late Governor Harrison, situate at the north end of the town, and which adds much to the appearance of the place. The ground in front is level; but the slope towards the river is easy, and admits of delightful gardens. At this time the *tomatoes* were full grown and abundant; and the *black morella,* which loaded the branches furnished an agreeable repast; but the *Chickasaw plumbs,* with one solitary exception, had all ripened and disappeared. This fruit is delicious, and the tree a great bearer, but suckers appear to spring up around it as far as the roots extend.

Here I discovered that the *worm* which *destroys the inner bark round the root of the peach tree,* is an active inhabitant; and that the *Curculio* destroys much of the fruit.

In conformity to an engagement made last evening, we travelled seven miles further to J. M. M'Donald's, a friendly, hospitable man, where we abode for the night. He has been much in the service of the United States as a surveyor; and was employed to run the *West Bounds* of this territory; north from Vincennes, when it was first discovered that the Wabash River, for more than forty miles, meanders on or west of that meridian.

In his field he pointed out to me a grass, of which I had heard much, known through all the western country by the name of *nimble Will.* It is much esteemed for pasture, especially in Kentucky. I cannot give very strong testimony, however, in its favour, as I have always seen it thin on the ground. In the western parts of New-York, where it also grows indigenously, it scarcely withstands the encroachment of other grasses.

We have been led to believe from seeing so many persons who had marched to Tippecanoe, that the whole military strength of this district was engaged in that expedition. Amongst these our hospitable friend may be numbered.

7 *mo.* 11.—WE departed about sunrise, and soon passed into the same road that we traversed two days ago.

Marie's Creek, which has been dignified with the appellation of *a river* on some maps, was now reduced to a light mill-stream; and I think it would be easy to jump across it with a pole. Not far below the surface, sand rock in horizontal strata appeared in the south bank.

About 9 o'clock we arrived, and found my old companions in anxious waiting. In our absence they had explored the country in the neighbourhood of Shakertown, and had returned yesterday, expecting to meet us.

At 2 o'clock in the afternoon, accompanied by our kind friend M. H. we commenced our journey for *Fort Harrison.* Our road led northwesterly through prairies principally composed of clay, though very fertile, and interspersed with fine farms. It is remarkable that though some parts of these tracts are wet, and now, even covered with water; yet the bog or quagmire is unknown, and there is no danger of being swamped.

Near *Busseron Creek* we passed through a fine tract of woodland, as level and as fertile as the prairie.

At the end of seven miles, we crossed that creek at *a mill* below which, the water had laid bare a slaty rock in horizontal strata.

We then passed through *barrens* (so called), which produced corn of uncommon luxuriance. The prospect soon became more interesting. To the left spread an undulated plain of dark fertile sand, thinly timbered by oaks without underbrush; and on our right the scene was variegated with lawns and groves. The low ground is wet prairie, or that kind which is occasioned by the collection and subsequent evaporation of water. Every little knoll of only two feet in height supports a grove. These are termed *islands* by the inhabitants, and not improperly, as floods must frequently surround them.

At the distance of three miles we came out into the *Gill Prairie,* where the extent and beauty of the scene, and the luxuriance of the corn excited our admiration, but the driftwood was deposited in lines, above the level of no inconsiderable part of this fine tract. Indeed we have seen none except the Vincennes prairie that is free from *bayous.* These in times of flood, convert the parts adjoining the river literally into islands; and nearly all communication with the back settlements must be intercepted. In places the channel is excavated, forming when the current subsides, shallow ponds or marshes. These, however, are not miry, and the cattle pass over without inconvenience. This bayou, ten miles in length, receives its waters from *Turtle Creek.*

We were now within the limits of the *New Purchase,* and consequently none of the few inhabitants who have fixed here can have titles to the land except through the intervention of Canadian claimants. A cabin and a few acres of corn, constitute the principal improvements.

At Turtle Creek, the woodland commences. Immediately we observed the irregularities of the surface to be greatly increased; and a clayey loam, which the river alluvions have never reached, producing beech and sugar maple, indicated a total change of soil.

Of the trees in this country we make the general remark, that the trunk, and more especially the branches, are larger than those of the same kinds to the eastward, and stand from each other at greater distances.

From a bluff two miles above Turtle Creek, we had a most charming prospect of *La Motte Prairie,* west of the river in the Illinois Territory; and the beams of the sun, nearly setting, imparted a yellow tinge to the distant woods that encircle this plain. The bluff is upwards of one hundred feet high, and the river flows at its base. The ground declines to the east; the regularity of the descent is remarkably beautiful; and the herbage, like that throughout all this tract of woodland, is very luxuriant.

One man and his family have fixed their residence on this interesting spot, and have cleared a small farm. *Possession* has been deemed of so much consequence in many parts of the United States, and such indulgence has been granted to those persons who have formed the *frontier* in time of war, that even now these settlers anticipate important advantages. Among neighbours, who fear to do each other wrong, such hopes might be realized; but amongst speculators, who will be found here on the day of sale, from all parts of the Union, we can hardly believe that their little claims will obtain much respect.

Our route still led through woodlands. We had five miles further to travel, and the approach of evening induced us to mend our pace; but it became dark before we arrived at *Tarman's,* where we lodged. 20 miles this afternoon.

7 *mo.* 12.—THIS person, with his family, resided here before the late war. A small *prairie* of 200 or 300 acres, known by his name, and bordered by thick woods, except towards the river, chiefly contains the improvements. Last spring they removed from the prairie to a new cabin in the woodlands, near the road. The upper story of this building projects for the purpose of defence;

and may serve as a memorial, of the apprehensions which overspread the white settlers, before the late treaty with the Indians at Fort Harrison.

A short time before the approach of those persons who came with HOPKINS, this family, fearful of the Indians, abandoned their dwelling and retired down the river. In the hurry of removal many articles were necessarily left behind. When the band arrived they wasted everything that could be found; and the sons told me that their hogs and neat cattle were wantonly shot down, and left untouched where they fell.

Near the edge of this prairie, I observed some small *mounds*. These are the first I have noticed above the Vincennes Prairie.

I have mentioned the wood house of the eastern states, and the spring house of the middle states, but omitted to notice in its proper place *the smoke house* of Virginia. At least by some, the erroneous opinion has been adopted, that pork cannot be preserved in pickle during the summer heat of this climate. Whether the prevalence of this notion has caused the southern farmer to convert his pork into *bacon;* or whether custom has rendered the flavour most agreeable I leave undetermined; but certain it is that the smoke house is considered an appendage of great value. Our host faithfully practises this branch of rural economy; and in an open log building, we saw nearly one thousand weight of ham, flitch, and shoulder, which was undergoing this process. We presumed that the animals had been recently killed.

Several springs appear in the north side of the bank on which this dwelling is situate. The subsoil is principally sand or sand stone; and throughout this western country, as in other places, we remark that wherever water comes filtered through this substance, the quality is excellent.

After breakfast we continued our journey. Several families have fixed their abode one or two miles further north; and so much confidence has been felt in the right of possession that *a saw mill* has been erected in the present season on a small creek. We should be gratified hereafter to learn, that such industry and enterprize have been respected.

In this neighbourhood we passed *a coal mine*, which has been recently opened, though the work has been but partially performed. The stratum is laid bare to the depth of four or five feet. As the excavation is made in the channel of a small brook, the torrent, by removing the loose earth, doubtless led to this discovery. All the strata of this fossil that we have seen in the western country has appeared near the surface; and it would not surprise me, if it should be brought forth in a thousand places where the shovel and the pickaxe have never yet been employed.

Last evening between Turtle Creek and the Bluff, we travelled some distance on the first flats of the River; and in our progress through twelve miles of woods this morning, the same thing occurred. These flats, like the uplands adjoining on the east, are well sheltered with thrifty timber. Overshadowed by woods for such a length of way, we almost forgot our proximity to natural meadows; and so different are these two kinds of land, that a stranger would as soon expect to find a prairie in the forests of New-York.

In these woods our intelligent friend pointed out to us the ground, on which the escort and drivers of some provision waggons, intended for the relief of Fort Harrison, were attacked during the late war. The Indians lay in ambush on both sides of a bank over which the road led, and when the waggons gained that position, commenced their fire. Only two of the poor fellows escaped. The foremost driver cut loose one of his horses, and after a precipitate flight of more than twenty miles, reached Fort Harrison. The other was a private who concealed himself under the side of a log. From this insecure retreat, continually expecting death, and sometimes almost trodden over, he beheld with horror the butchery of his comrades. After all was *still*, the Indians discharged their guns into the casks of liquor, and cut the waggons to pieces.

Prairies (I am told) are seldom found opposite on both sides of the river. The Wabash has closely traced the west side of this forest; and directly over in the Illinois Territory, the valley is occupied by *Union* and *Walnut Creek Prairies*. From these facts it appears, that the same irregularity, prevails in regard to hills and table land, that I have noticed in the eastern part of the Ohio country.

The pecan is only found on the first flats, and appears to be confined within the limits of common floods. It is a stately tree. We saw some three feet in diameter, and nearly one hundred feet in height. The leaf consists of fifteen leaflets: fourteen in pairs, and one terminal.

I have often been surprised at the confused ideas that botanists have exhibited, when treating of this vegetable, and of the species with which it is allied. Though *the outer shells of the walnuts have no determinate opening* like the hickories; and though *the inner shells are perforated* while that of the latter is smooth—yet one *genus* has been made to include them; and so much has that ESSENTIAL CHARACTER, and even *specific differences* been overlooked, that *the butternut*, *the shell bark*, and *the pecan*, have been arranged as only varieties of the same species. We believe no two *genera* of the same NATURAL ASSEMBLAGE* are more distinct.

The timber of the first flats comprises, in addition to the *pecan*, the *bitternut*, the *river nut*, and the *shell bark hickory*. The *butternut*, and, in some places, the *black walnut*. At the river, the *water maple;* where it is swampy, the *red maple;* and in the drier parts, the *ash-leaved*, and the *sugar maple*. To these should be added, the *button wood* or *sycamore*, the *ash*, the *elm*, and the *cotton wood*. The last tree sometimes attains a diameter of four feet, and preserves its thickness of trunk to a remarkable height.

The soil of these flats is remarkably fertile; but mud, left on the herbage by the freshets, causes much of it to putrify; and the exhalations are very offensive.

A channel, which receives the surplus water of many thousand square miles, must be very unequally supplied; and during heavy rains it is evident, that

> . . . innumerable streams
> Tumultuous roar; and far above its banks
> The river lift . . .

Accordingly, near the northern border of this great tract of woodland, the *flood marks* on the trees were higher than we could reach on horseback.

These marks consist of annular spaces on the bark from which the moss has been removed. We conjecture this happens during floods in the latter part of winter. The ice, forming in the night, encloses the moss; and as the thaw commences at the tree, when the water subsides, the moss will be torn off by the ice in its fall.

On entering *the Prairie* we found it a low strip of land; and like the south end of the Shakertown Prairie, entirely within the reach of common floods. Whenever the river rises over its banks the road must therefore be impassable. This tract, five miles long, and averaging about one mile in width, is bounded on the north by *the narrows*, where the woodlands from the river and from the hills,

*Since writing the above I have observed with much satisfaction, in a late periodical work that C. S. RAFINESQUE, an accurate and distinguished naturalist, has placed the *hickories* in a new genus, *Hiccorius*. Of the old genus *Juglans* eleven species were enumerated, and a majority of these were *hickories*.

approach within ten rods. A heavy current sweeps through in times of flood.

This Prairie is considered to be of small value from its being so subject to inundation; and no inhabitants are found near its borders. Its name is derived from *Prairie Creek*, a light stream which flows through it from the eastward. A small mound appears on its north bank.

Our friend in leading us towards the woods near the north east corner, directed our attention to the dry ground on which we were riding. In a few minutes we came to a fine brook which has its sources in the hills; but which on reaching the plain is immediately lost in the sand over which we had passed. We found several cases of this kind, but observed one serious inconvenience:—as these currents have never formed a channel to the river, the water in heavy rains, spreads over the prairie, and in some places coats the herbage with mud.

These hills are about one hundred feet higher than the prairies.

Leaving that stream we travelled to the north along the hill side, through the woods, and soon came out into *Honey Creek Prairie*. We were delighted with the prospect. As we traversed this extensive tract, we contrasted the granite hills in the east with this soil which requires no manure; and nothing but moderate culture to produce an overwhelming plenty*; we thought of the thousands who had toiled and pined on barrens, while this land for ages had been a range for wild beasts; and indulged, in fancy, a view of farm houses on the numerous and elegant sites that have emerged from this plain.

We explored this Prairie about noon, in clear sunshine. The weather was warm, but not sultry. We found the most inconvenience from the green-headed horse fly, which were numerous and active. Excepting this instance, we have suffered very little from such insects; and indeed much less than we expected. It is an erroneous notion that warm climates produce them in greatest abundance;—the sultry summers of northern regions have a full share; and perhaps in no country are they more distressing than in Lapland.

It having become necessary to procure some refreshment, our experienced guide led us into the woodland on the east; and after

*We are assured that when corn (maize) is very excellent, the whole crop is rarely harvested. After securing what is deemed sufficient, the live stock is turned into the field in the winter to consume the remainder. We do not believe, however, that this practice will be of long continuance.

ascending the hill, directed our course to a new cabin, which was occupied by two families. On entering we were furnished with seats, but the beds were all spread on the floor. In one corner a woman lay in a burning fever. She complained of much pain in her side, and many involuntary moans escaped while her husband supported her head. They were strangers,—young,—probably indigent; and no physician could be found nearer than Fort Harrison.

It was a case of real distress, and the circumstances were discouraging. However, we left medicine with directions.

This family were lately from the state of Ohio. They had arrived in a boat, fixed their residence on the prairie, and drank the warm water from a brook. Apprehensive of disease, they had only left the borders of the river within a few days past, and were received into this cabin as tenants.

[We were much gratified to learn in three or four days that she was likely to recover. Unquestionably many of these emigrants suffer from want of suitable food, and of medicine, and from the want of comfortable lodgings, and of proper attendance.]

The summit of this hill appears to be an extensive tract of table land. The soil is fertile, and produces thrifty timber, but contains little sand except in knolls. This remark will apply to the country in general; and as it perfectly accords with what I have observed in the western parts of New-York; and as some rocks of *granite* are also scattered here, doubtless this land has been overwhelmed by the same deluge. I allude not to inundations produced by extraordinary rains, but to a preternatural flood which swept over the highest hills, and which, to my view, was occasioned by *exterior attraction.*

In descending from the hill, the prospect through the trees had the brightness of a great lake in calm weather. The low angle at which the sky appears across the prairie, was the cause of this optical deception.

Through this prairie, on the sloping sides of the ridgy knolls, we frequently observed irregular hollows, several rods in diameter, and a few feet in depth, which would hold water, had the soil been clayey and compact. The origin ought not to be ascribed to a depression of the surface, but to the unequal deposition of sand and gravel in the time of that extraordinary flood. The sides are neither so steep, nor the depth so great but the plough may readily pass through, and we feel confident that wheat would flourish in the bottom. The *Ceanothus americanus*, or tea plant, which only grows on dry banks to the eastward, and which also appears on the driest parts of this land, is found in that situation; so loose and so little retentive of water, is the soil. Indeed we are assured that within an hour or two after heavy rains, the ploughman may resume his labour without inconvenience.

This species of Ceanothus is completely naturalized to the prairies. Burnt down to the ground every season it has relinquished the habit of a shrub; and conforming to the vicisitudes of its situation, the same stalks that grew this spring to the height of six or eight inches, are now loaded with flowers.

We now directed our course to the westward; and at the distance of two or three miles, passed into the woods that shelter *Honey creek*. It is worthy of remark that wherever the streams overflow and deposit a clayey sediment, we find thrifty timber; and indeed the dry land adjoining,—which is the same as the prairie soil—commonly retains more or less oak. This fact I consider as an additional proof that these wastes are occasioned by fire. As it can only approach from one side, the chance for the flame to be driven through the trees, is considerably diminished.

As a continuation of the first remark, it may be noticed, that bayous rarely (if ever) deposit any sediment; and in the lower parts of the prairies that are overflowed by the river, we observed the naked sand.

Honey creek is a considerable mill stream. The *prairie* to which it gives a name is computed to be eight miles long, and from one to five wide; but I suspect the latter estimate is large. It is a beautiful tract of land. By the creek it is separated on the north from the *Terre Haute** (i.e. High land) *Prairie;* and on the west or north west, from the *Little Prairie.*

On crossing this creek we passed ten or fifteen rods (as we had done on the opposite shore) through a thrifty wood of *beech, sugar maple, white* and *blue oak, black walnut, honey locust*, and *nettle tree;* and then came out into the *Little Prairie.* This contains about eight hundred acres. On it, our friend had made some improvements; and this was our chief motive in departing from the direct road to Fort Harrison. It is separated from the Terre Haute Prairie by woodland which extends from the river to Honey creek, joining it some distance above where we forded. The timber on the drier parts of this strip is chiefly *black oak.* The ravages of fire amongst it has been very considerable; and in this part, the prairie, was visibly gaining on the woods.

*Vulgarly pronounced Tar Holt.

We now passed along through the western part of the *Terre Haute Prairie;* and in the calm evening of one of the finest days in summer, the shadows of the oaks lengthening over the plain. Novelty still lent its charms; and even after we arrived at our lodgings, four miles south of the fort, we were delighted with the prospect of lawns and of distant woods.

This establishment, is not a tavern, but travellers are occassionally entertained. The house was erected in the present season. A few acres of corn are enclosed; but the proprietor of those improvements has no claim to the soil but the *right of possession.* This site which is about fifty feet above the prairie to the eastward, commands one of the most extensive prospects that we have seen in the country.

Notwithstanding its elevation, and its proximity to the woods that shelter it on the west, we observed the same *black sand* that appeared in other parts of these singular tracts; and where a small excavation has been made for a cellar, I perceived no change at a less depth than two feet. In some of the lower parts of the prairies, I learn that it is even found at the depth of five feet.

7 *mo.* 13.—EARLY this morning we resumed our journey. A few families live near our landlord, but two miles to the north there is a very considerable encampment. Many of these emigrants are from the state of New-York. It is said that *fevers* are prevalent amongst them; and last night a man from the neighbourhood of Genesee river, died. We stopt a few minutes to visit *N. Kirk,* lately from the state of Ohio, with whom our companion D. S. was acquainted. His wife has an intermittent fever.

These notices may seem minute, but the apology will be obvious and ample. The *report* of a traveller which may influence the emigrant, ought to embrace "the truth and the whole truth;" and the profit and the peril, the bane and the antidote should be set in order before him.

I observed the *Columbo* growing near the borders of these woods, with stalks about six feet in height.

Beyond this encampment to the north, we passed a field containing two hundred acres of corn, which made a very fine appearance, and is the principal crop. The enclosing of this tract with oak rails, was the labour of a company; and each man occupies land in proportion to the length of fence he erected. The whole has been lately covered by a *Canadian claim;* and though in strictness these occupants might be considered as intruders, their case has excited sympathy and called forth some expressions of dissatisfaction with the claimant.

The cabins along the road, from these improvements to the Fort, are numerous; the immediate vicinity of this station has assumed the aspect of a considerable village, and once more we were surrounded by "the busy hum of men."

Fort Harrison stands within a few rods of the river, on a bank which, though not steep, is beyond the reach of floods. It is garrisoned by a detachment from the army of the United States. It was built in the autumn of 1811, by the late governor *Harrison* and the troops under his command, who halted for that purpose on their march to *Tippecanoe.*

The pernicious effects of spirituous liquors were sadly exemplified a few weeks ago near this place. After the treaty, whiskey was liberally dealt out to the Indians; and in the frenzy of intoxication, one killed his fellow. To terminate this feud, and to prevent retaliation, it became necessary by their custom, that the murderer should be dispatched by his own brother, and the horrid task was accordingly performed.

About 10 o'clock we resumed our traverse of the country. Directing our course to the northeast through the prairies, we crossed over high broad ridges which might be laid into beautiful farms. The fertility of these lands has been noticed. Such elevations we would expect to be exempt from mud in all seasons, nor do we believe that any unwholesome exhalation would approach.

At the distance of one mile and a half, we came to *Otter Creek* which is a fine mill stream. One mile above the ford is an excellent mill seat, which has just been located by R. Markle, and which he intended soon to occupy.

This prairie is thirteen miles long. The surface declines to the eastward, and becomes so low near the creek, that the water flows thro' in times of flood, forming a bayou which communicates with Honey creek. From the ford, the course of Otter creek is nearly north-west, and just before its junction with the river, the Terre Haute Prairie terminates.

Agreeably to previous observation, Otter creek is sheltered by woodland, and the trees appear on each side as far as the clayey sediment extends.

Spring Creek Prairie lies to the north of this stream. It is about four miles from north to south, and nearly two from east to west. We have seen no tract of this extent equally delightful.

One glance takes in the whole opening; and the eye, undazzled by distant prospects that fade into ether, rests with pleasure on woods distinctly visible.

The woods on the northern boundary, chiefly consist of beech, sugar maple and oak, spread over *uplands*, which terminate the prairies on the east side of the river. Along the south border of this tract, *Spring Creek*, a light mill stream, meanders. Its sources are among the hills, and being fed by durable fountains, it suffers less diminution in summer, than many of the larger streams to the south.

We believe that this prairie will be salubrious. From the exhalations of the river, it is sheltered by high lands on the west, which are crowned with oak. No streams sink into its sands. These, with the soakings of the country to the eastward, are intercepted by *Lost Run*, which flows southerly towards Otter Creek; and it appears that no bayou in times of flood, divides it.

The latter circumstance merits consideration. The surface of this prairie, like that of Terre Haute, slopes from the sides towards the middle, and exhibits a depression throughout its whole length. This is in the same line with the bayou from Otter Creek; and if Spring Creek, instead of its short course, formed a channel for the surplus water of a large district, it would doubtless pass through. Indeed I am not convinced that this does not happen, in extraordinary floods.

On the north side of this stream, we traversed the open woods along the base of the hill. This, we were told, was the route of the army to Tippecanoe; and we saw *timothy* of fine growth, probably from seed which was scattered at that time.

On the banks of a small brook of pure water, which flows from the hill, we took our noontide repast. We were then six or eight miles beyond the limits of the civilized world; and no white settlers of any description, are known above Fort Harrison.

Gun flints, similar to those which we noticed near Indian Kentucky, are found in the channels of the brook. I have seen none which give more fire with steel.

In moist places, the common wild nettle (*Urtica divaricata*) occupies much of the soil. Its sting, which was doubtless designed for a defence, is severe to horses; and one of our hacknies was so irritable as to lie down under the rider.

On the west side of Spring Creek, where it turns north, we found an opening of many acres. Beyond it, towards the river, the land is a sandy plain, above the reach of floods, and thinly covered with oak of moderate size. We consider this an eligible site for a village. The Wabash flows at its base; the descent to the water is short and easy; and the communication with the country, will probably be at all times uninterrupted.*

Near this plain, the *strawberry plant* grows in abundance; but the season for gathering the fruit, in this climate, had long since past.

Some idea of the fertility of the woodlands that surround these prairies, may be obtained from the growth of the *Ambrosia trifida*, which we frequently observed. In no other region have I seen it, except on the first flats of rivers.

This day's journey was productive of much satisfaction. We had proposed to encamp; but unprovided with *punk*,† and unsuccessful in all our attempts to kindle fire, we were compelled to return to our former lodgings, more than ten miles from the district in which we wished to spend to-morrow. No traveller in new countries should be destitute of a tinder-box.

7 *mo.* 14.—FROM our lodgings, the prospect of this great prairie is delightful. The night was cool, and the morning dripping with dew. The sun at rising, was obscured by a dense cloud of fog which settled near the border of the prairie; and on enquiry, we learned that a brook‡ flowed from the hills at that place, and was lost in the sands.

We now proceeded eastward across the Prairie. Knolls or ridges of several acres, lying in a north and south direction, appear through these wastes; and evince a commotion to which we cannot conceive any river flood to be subject. In the bayou towards the middle of this tract, our horses waded through much standing water.

Near the eastern border of the Prairie we saw a field of corn, the seed of which had been dropt in every third or fourth furrow, and the sod consequently turned down upon it. We consider it a strong proof of the lightness and warmth of the soil. From seed corn treated in such manner in our cool and moist climate, no return could be expected. One precaution, however, is necessary. The inverted soil must be rolled or trodden closely down; for if

*The following remark appeared in a Vincennes newspaper, in 1817. "It should not be *forgotten* by those who *know*, nor should it *remain untold* to those who do not know, that there are few places on the Wabash, where high land approaches it so as to afford at all seasons of the year, easy access to the river."

†Punk is a fungus, which extends its sponge like fibres through the decaying wood. The *maples* and *hickories* are the only trees in which we have seen it perfect.

‡Lost Creek, for which see the map.

the *plumule* unfolds within the cavity, it will be unable to pierce the soil, and must perish.

Crops, in the first season that the prairies are ploughed, exhibit but little of that luxuriance of vegetation, which in succeeding years is so remarkable. This is imputed to the hardness of the wild grass roots, which consist chiefly of the *woody fibre*, absorb even when buried a part of the nutriment contained in the soil, and yield very slowly to decay.

Several families have erected huts in the edge of the woodlands. The inducement has been the convenience of timber and fire wood, a supply of water, and land adjoining ready cleared. But we consider the situation unhealthy. The brooks that descend from the hills, having no channel or outlet to the river, spread, when swelled by heavy rains, and deposit all the impurities that were whirled along by the torrent. The herbage had been coated with mud, and the smell at this time was very offensive.

Changing our course to the north, we crossed Otter Creek at the old ford, and bearing to the east side of Spring Creek Prairie, we passed through groves and thickets that form its border in that direction. This tract is very little elevated above the prairie, and from its soil and productions, belongs to the class of *barrens*. We saw some openings of several acres, moist, and which might form productive meadows. These spaces were beautifully chequered with the meadow sweet, a species of *Spirea* which is herbaceous.

At the distance of two or three miles from Spring Creek Prairie, we came to a rectangular opening of thirty or forty acres which greatly resembled an old field. It is enclosed by black oaks of good size. The surface is handsomely level, and the soil has marks of fertility; but near the north west corner, where a tree had torn up the subsoil, I found a whitish sand, with scarcely any traces of that black fertilizing matter, which so strongly marks the river prairies.

We had intended to visit *Raccoon Creek*, the mouth of which forms one point in the north bounds of the *New Purchase*, being desirous to see the extensive forests of black walnut, which are on the upper parts of that stream; but there was a prospect of rain, and the day was too far advanced. It was therefore determined to explore the lands adjacent to Spring Creek. For this purpose, directing our course westwardly through moist prairies, which are separated by thin groves of stunted oak, we came to *Lost Run*. At this time I judged its current to be as heavy as

Spring Creek; but its channel indicated a stream of inferior magnitude; and our intelligent friend informed us, that in severe drowths it ceases to flow. Its banks were thickly covered with pea-vine, as it is here called; but I think it nearer allied to the bean. The aspect of this plant is pleasing, the blossom blue, and the vegetation luxuriant.

Near the north east corner of Spring Creek Prairie, we found a grove of sugar maple on land that declines towards the Creek. Wherever this tree flourishes, the soil is favorable to the production of *timothy;* and, in all places that we have seen, contains no inconsiderable portion of clay. Here a farm might be located that would embrace sandy prairie, fine meadows, a durable stream, good timber, and an extensive sugar camp.

In the woods on the south bank of Spring Creek, we found the remains of wigwams, erected by the Indians, on their hunting expeditions. Some were evidently designed as winter habitations. Of these, dry leaves interlaced with small poles, formed the walls; and the work displayed much skill and neatness.

We have seen no serpent in travelling four days, except a small garter snake, which was coiled on a leaf two feet from the ground.

In traversing such delightful regions, the mind acquires a degree of cheerfulness that rarely attends it in the deep gloom of the forest. But on reverting to the long toils and privations that beset the inhabitant of the wilderness,—and on contrasting the lightness of labour to possess these ancient abodes—a feeling more intense must pervade the patriot. The dark days of his country are past. In fancy, must he view the current of population breaking from the mountains, full, broad, resistless; and the vast and long deserted plains of the Mississippi, fill with life, with intellect, and with elegance.

END OF THE DIARY.

ADDITIONAL NOTICES OF THE WESTERN COUNTRY.

"THE *State of Indiana* is bounded on the north by a parallel of latitude, ten miles north of the southern extremity of Lake Michigan; on the south by the Ohio river; on the east by a meridian passing through the mouth of the Great Miami; and on the west by the Vincennes meridian, until, in coming south, it intersects the Wabash, and then by that river to its confluence with the Ohio."

OF the first settlement made at Vincennes by the French, it is difficult to find two accounts that agree. The old French *records* were destroyed by fire; and all that has descended to us on this subject, appears to be traditional. Two of my correspondents have furnished the subjoined paragraphs. Both accounts are too interesting to be omitted; and the difference of the dates shows the uncertainty of the reports in circulation at Vincennes, though I think the chronology of the first should be preferred.

"About the year 1690 the French traders first visited Vincennes, at that time a town of the Piankeshaw Indians, called Cippecaughke. Of these the former obtained wives, and raised families.

"In the year 1734 several French families emigrated from Canada and settled at this place. The first governor, or commandant, was M. St. Vincent, after whom the town is now called. In the year 1763 the country was ceded to the British who held it till the year 1778, when the fort was taken by the American Gen. George Clark. The United States confirmed the French in their possessions; and a donation of a tract of country round *the Post*, was made to the inhabitants."

"About the year 1702, a party of French from Canada, descended the Wabash river, and established *posts* in several places on its banks. The party was commanded by Capt. St. Vincennes who made this his principal place of deposit, which went for a long time by no other name than *the Post.*

"The French of this place, took an active part on our side in the war that separated us from Great Britian; but not until they saw an adequate force to assist them in maintaining their standing. In *Ramsay's Life of Washington*, it is stated, that a Spanish merchant of this place, gave information to the Americans, of the situation and strength of the British forces that were stationed here, and that Col. Clark easily obtained possession by his directions. This Spanish merchant, as he is there called, is the venerable Col. Vigo, who resides about three miles south east of Vincennes. He is an ornament to the country and a warm friend to our government."

"In the Indian wars that ended in 1794, the people of this place, though not active, defended themselves against the Indians. The latter, however, were not very hostile towards the French, but killed the Anglo-Americans without mercy wherever they could be found.

"In our last war, the French were as much engaged against the Indians as any other inhabitants of the frontier."

Vincennes, from its antiquity, and from having long been the capital of the Western Country, merits a more particular description than could be included in the Diary. The manuscripts that now lie before me on this subject are voluminous; part of which have been supplied by my correspondents, and part have been procured from other sources.

In the following account of the houses in this town, I place the fullest confidence, as the writer was so obliging as to examine every part of it, on receiving my request for information.

"There are eight brick houses, ninety-three frame houses, and one hundred and fifty French houses—in all, two hundred and fifty-one. These are exclusive of barns, stables, and old uninhabited houses, which I think are equal to the number of French houses, and make the whole number of buildings about four hundred. On the commons east of the town, there are many cellars and old chimney places, which lead me to suppose that Vincennes has decreased in the number of buildings."

Some idea of the *commerce*, *manufactures*, and *importance* of this place, may be obtained from the following List, which is dated 1st of 1 mo. 1818.

18 Store of Merchandise, (*a*)
6 Taverns, (*b*)
4 Groceries
4 Black-Smiths' Shops
2 Gun Smiths' shops
3 Shoemakers' shops
3 Saddlers' shops
4 Tailors' shops
2 Cabinet Makers
3 Hat Factories
1 Silver Smith
1 Tin Factory
1 Chair Maker
1 Tobacconist
1 Tannery
1 Apothecary
2 Printing Offices, (*c*)
7 Lawyers
7 Physicians
1 Limner
Chapel
Academy, (*e*)
Post Office
Bank, (*f*)
U. S. Land Office
Court House (*g*)
Jail, (*h*)
2 Market Houses, and a Livery Stable.

(*a*) This note will comprise all my remarks on the commerce of the Wabash.

We learned at Vincennes that the merchants only accepted cash in pay for goods. At that time, the surplus productions of the soil were too small to have formed any regular channel to distant markets. I am not able to state that it is even now accomplished, but all kinds of *produce* are in brisk demand for cash. The chief part of these purchases are doubtless to supply the immediate wants of the new settlers; but cash has been offered for large quantities of grain at several places near the river.

In the 2d month, 1818, the following prices were current:

	$	Cents.
Wheat, per bushel, was	1	
Corn, per bushel, was		50
Potatoes, per bushel, was		37½ to 50
Pork, per cwt	4	50
Beef, per cwt	3 to 4	

The reader will recollect, that in 1816, Corn was only 25 cents, and a considerable advance in price, has therefore taken place.

In the prices of *Dry Goods*, there is not much difference between Vincennes and some of the stores in Cayuga county. In respect to *Groceries* on the Ohio River, as well as on the Wabash, the following retail prices are current:

	$	
Coffee, per pound		37½
When scarce		50
New Orleans sugar, per pound		25
Loaf sugar, per pound (on the Ohio river)		37½
Loaf sugar, per pound (at Vincennes)		50
Young Hyson, per pound	1	50
Brandy, per gallon	6	
Madeira Wine, per gallon, first quality (at Vincennes)	8	
Common Rum, per gallon	4	
Iron, per pound, retail		16
Ham, per pound, retail		25

Together with *Salmon* and *Herring*, *Shad* are sometimes brought from New Orleans, and retailed at 25 cents a pound, or 62½ cents each. *Mackerel* 25 cents a piece. *White fish* are brought from the neighbourhood of Detroit.

Since *the Kanhawa works have been monopolized*, salt* has greatly advanced in price along the Ohio. When we were at Vincennes; it was said that a large quantity could be bought at $5, but $6 was the common price. Now it is sold at $10 a barrel, and

*Salt at Cincinnati, in 12 mo. 1818, was selling at $3 per bushel of 50 lbs.; and at Vevay, it was sold for $3.50. Salt is sold according to the marks made on the barrels at the Kanhawa works; and on account of the leakage of the brine, a loss of weight is commonly sustained.

retailed from $2, to $2.50 a bushel. Salt from the Salines near *Shawnee Town,* at $1.50 a bushel. Last autumn at Fort Harrison, it was sold for $15 a barrel,—a scarcity having been occasioned by unusual floods in the river

Common *boards* sell at $1.50 per 100 feet. Plank at $2.

The amount of *merchandise* in Vincennes two years ago, was estimated at one hundred thousand dollars.

The merchants of that town procure New Orleans goods at Louisville.

Beer and *Porter* are brought from the breweries in Cincinnati.

The current charge for transportation of goods from Pittsburgh* to Vincennes is............*per cwt.* $1 00
When boats are scarce............ 1 25
From Vincennes to Pittsburgh............ 3 00
From Vincennes to New Orleans............ 1 00
To Vincennes from New Orleans............ 4 00

(*b*) An innkeeper, in a Vincennes paper of "Feb. 6, 1818," offers to accommodate his customers on the following terms, viz.:

"Breakfast	$0 25
Dinner	25
Supper	25
Lodging	12½
Horse to corn and hay one night	37½
One horse feed	12½

This agrees well with our experience of *tavern bills,* though in some places the charges were higher. For instance, a horse at oats and hay one night was 50 cents. But oats are scarce in Indiana, and horses are fed on corn, which is shovelled out to them without measure. The common practice is to charge 12½ cents for *a feed;* that is, as much as the horse can consume, be it more or less.

In some good houses in the state of Ohio, the fixed price was 75 cents for every thing that a traveller needs for one night, including his horse. But in that state, sometimes we meet with extortioners.

(*c*) The following *Newspapers* were published in Indiana in 2d *mo.* 1818. These were all *weekly.*

*The transportation from Pittsburgh to Louisville is from 40 to 50 cents per cwt. when the amount of freight is considerable.

"The Western Sun	Vincennes	E. Stout, Editor
Indiana Centinel	Vincennes	S. Dillworth.
Indiana Register	Vevay	J. F. Dufour.
Indiana Republican	Madison	J. Lodge.
Dearborn Gazette	Lawrenceburg	B. Brown.
Indiana Gazette	Corydon	A. Brandon.
Indiana Herald	Corydon	R. W. Nelson.
Plain Dealer	Brookville	B. F. Morris.

"The above offices, except the Western Sun, have all been established since the constitution of this state was formed."

N.B.—We learn that the Herald is discontinued at Corydon, and the INDIANIAN, by the same editor, is now published at Jeffersonville.

(*d*) "This was built by the French Roman Catholics, and in their own style. It is sixty-six feet in length, about twenty-two feet wide, and nine feet from the ground to the eaves. It has a kind of steeple, about eight feet high, with a small bell."

"The Roman Catholics, at present, have no pastor, and no other religious society is established. Itinerants of all sorts preach here occasionally, and have nearly the same audience."

(*e*) "The *Academy* stands east of the town. It can be seen a considerable distance in every direction, and makes a very handsome appearance. It was erected in 1807. The walls are brick; the length is sixty-five feet the width forty-four feet, and the height three stories. It was designed for eighteen rooms. Ten thousand dollars have been expended, and it stands unfinished. The fund consists of land, twenty-five miles south of this place. The Legislature authorized the sale of a part of this tract, and appointed twenty-one trustees to govern the Institution;" but the hopes of its founders have not been realized. "Only a common school has been kept in it. [March 24, 1817."]

"Two large *Schools* are now kept in this town."

"A *Library* was established in 1817, which now consists of more than 700 volumes. The annual contribution is two dollars on each share."

(*f*) This institution was chartered on the 10th of September, 1814, and the capital has been increased to $1,500,000. Nathaniel Ewing, President; Isaac Blackford, Cashier.

A power is vested in the Directors to establish branches, so as not to exceed one to every three counties; and one has lately been located at Brookville.

On the "29th of November, 1817, a dividend was declared by

the Directors at the rate of twelve per cent. per annum, for the last six months on amount of stock paid in."

The charter of the Farmers' and Mechanics' Bank of *Madison*, also bears the date of September 10, 1814. The capital is $500,000, John Paul, President, and John Sering, Cashier. A branch has been fixed at Lawrenceburgh, Thomas Porter, Cashier.

(*g*) "This is a brick building, forty by fifty feet, and two stories high. It is very handsome and commodious."

(*h*) The jail is built of logs.

(*i*) The livery stable is of brick, and very large.

"Above the town, though within sight, they are building a *steam grist mill* and saw mill. The latter is so far completed, as to have commenced sawing timber for itself and the grist mill, on the 1st of January, 1818."

Vincennes is situate one hundred and twenty miles by the road, north-west of *Louisville;* one hundred and seventy east of *St. Louis* by the present route; three hundred miles south south-west of *Chicago;* and one hundred and sixty miles northeast of *Kaskaskias.*

The number of *Inhabitants* at Vincennes has been estimated at from 1,500 to 2,000.

"Unimproved *lots* of half an acre, on the principal streets, sell from five hundred to one thousand dollars. In the back streets, the prices of lots are from fifty to one hundred dollars." 7 *mo.* 1817.

To their former intercourse with the Indians, we trace a singular practice in this town. "As soon as it becomes dark every store is shut up." My correspondent adds, that "though licentiousness and dissipation prevail, they also rigidly abstain from opening them on the sabbath."

Climate is always an interesting subject to the geographical enquirer; and all my correspondents, aware of this circumstance, have been minute in their remarks. "Accurate observations on the thermometer have been made and registered by Judge PARKE," of whom my obliging friend J. B. BENNETT, procured the following statement. It will be perceived that an account of one month has been inadvertently omitted.

EXTREMES OF FARENHEIT'S THERMOMETER.

	Deg.	Deg.
"December, 1816	17 lowest	61 highest
January, 1817	11 below zero	60
February	5 below zero	66
March	18	70
April	39	83
June	52	88
July	58	95
August	53½	95
September	40	93
October	23	80
November	24	70
December	2	66
January, 1818	5 below zero	59
February (to the 12th)	16 below zero	40"

As *the seasons* are infinitely irregular, I deem it best to give the views of my correspondents separate and entire. The difference in their statements, may be reconciled by considering that some have drawn conclusions from a long series of observations; and that others have been guided by a few recent facts. A considerable difference of temperature is also observable, between the black sandy prairies, and the clayey woodlands.

"The *winds* in summer prevail most from south and west; in the winter from the north and east.* East winds generally produce falling weather. West winds are common with a clear sky.

"The *Summer* is generally dry, especially in the month of August. At such times vegetation is checked, particularly in sandy soils, and the streams diminish considerably. Wells, however, seldom or never fail at Vincennes.

"In winter, the atmosphere is generally clear and cold. The *Snows* are seldom more than three inches deep, and are commonly melted by sunshine. *Sleighing* sometimes continues for two or three weeks.

"*Spring* is attended by much wet and cloudy weather. Vegetation commences about the 20th of March. The *peach* blossoms

*I do not consider this to be incompatible with the statement which I received at Lick Creek. The direction of winds thro' the vallies of large streams and over elevated plains, in the same neighbourhood, is often very different; and this circumstance deserves the attention of all those who study METEOROLOGY. The following extract from Cook's last Voyage, will place this subject in a clear and proper point of view:—

the last of that month. *Grass* is abundant after the first of April, but young cattle do well in the river bottoms during the whole winter. The *strawberry* ripens the last week in April. *Wheat harvest* commences from the 20th to the 30th of June. *Vernal frosts* have been noticed as late as the first of May, and the earliest *autumnal frosts* about the first of November. To this, however, there are some exceptions. July 18, 1817."*

"The *depth of our snows* for the last ten years, has not exceeded six inches. The *thickness of the ice*, in the Wabash, is sometimes ten or twelve inches. *Ploughing* may be commenced by the tenth of March, and carried on with very little subsequent interruption from frost or snow. *Strawberries* ripen about the 15th of May. *White frosts* are sometimes seen in the early part of April, and have been known on the 23d of October. March 30, 1817."

"*Winter* generally sets in about the first of January, and breaks up about the first of March. Last winter the *thickness of the ice* in the Wabash, was eight inches; and this winter [1818] about the same. The *snow* at Princeton has been four inches deep; at Vincennes eight inches deep for five weeks, and at Fort Harrison twelve inches deep."

"*Wheat harvest* is generally about the last of June or first of July. *Strawberries* ripen about the middle of May. In backward seasons, *common fruit trees* are in full bloom about the middle of April, but often earlier. *Vernal frosts* are all over by the first of May, tho' last spring was an exception. *Autumnal frosts* at Vincennes commonly begin about the first of November. Last fall I saw beans, tobacco, and other tender vegetables, unhurt by frosts on the 4th of November; but in the vicinity of Fort Harrison, frosts appear in September. The *snows* at this place are very light. Eight inches has been the deepest which has fallen in many years. Last winter there was little; but we had *sleet*, which made good sleighing for four or five days.

"I have seen more serene weather, during this winter, than in ten winters in your country."

*"Before we had got up one anchor [in *Awatska Bay*] so violent a gale sprung up from the *northeast*, that we thought proper to moor again, supposing from the position of the entrance of the bay, that the current of wind would in all probability set up the channel. The pinnace was dispatched to examine the passage, and returned with intelligence, that the wind blew violently from the *southeast*, with a great swell setting into the bay."

"On the 7th of November I left *Corydon,* and arrived on the 13th. On our way, the snow fell about three inches deep. *The weather* from that time till the 20th, was cold, when it became mild, and continued so till the 10th of January. On the morning of the 18th, the *mercury* stood eleven degrees below zero; the Wabash River closed, and has remained so ever since. [10th February, 1817.]

"The *snow* has not at any time fallen more than three inches, and but three times in all. There is a peculiarity in this climate, and the absence of turbulent winds is remarkable. The old settlers agree, that there has been less snow than usual; but that the cold has continued longer than at almost any time within their recollection. Yet there has not been five days that a northern man would be uncomfortable at work with his coat off.

"The farmer may be well employed the whole autumn and winter. Prairie lands, in particular, may be broken up with the plough from the first of March until the first of November, and most of his laborious business may be performed in temperate seasons.

"I am told that a great portion of the year is warmer than in the vicinity of Philadelphia, but the nights in summer are much cooler. The mercury is seldom above 94 degrees, although it has been at 98. Wild greens are sometimes procured the first week in March. Peas with common attention are fit for use by the 15th of May, but with care may be produced much earlier."—W.P.B.

I learned, while in that country, that the snow in eight years had not at any time exceeded five inches in depth. In the remarkable snow of 3 mo. 31, 1807, it was about eleven inches; but in Scipio it was two feet.

Except when walking at noon day, we were seldom disagreeably warm, although we wore boots, with coat, vest and pantaloons of fulled cloth; neither did we find one night in which a blanket was uncomfortable, unless in apartments heated by the afternoon sun.

These observations include a period of ten days near the Wabash river; but we were told that on the prairies it was sometimes very hot;* and indeed this has been sufficiently indicated by the thermometer.

*M. Birkbeck, however, says "the heat of this climate is not so oppressive as I expected. I have been using strong exercise through three of the hottest days that have been experienced in four years. On one of these days, I walked with my gun in the Prairie, and traveled on horseback the other two, without great inconvenience. The only sultry night I have experienced proved the prelude to a thunder storm".

Near Salem, on the high *table land* at the sources of Blue River, I was assured, that in the winter of 1815-16, the *sleighing* continued for six weeks, though in part of that time the depth of the snow did not exceed one and a half inches. In Cayuga county, steady cold for such a period would be very remarkable: but the south winds, which often occur within the vicinity of the lakes, dissolve snows of common depth in a few hours. It appears that Indiana is exempt from these sweeping gales, and that the snows are melted by sunshine.

As a *test* to these remarks, I give the following extracts from Dr. Drake's excellent "*Picture of Cincinnati.*" This town it should be recollected, is situate in a deep reverberating valley of the Ohio; that part of the waters of this river arrive from the south, while those of the Wabash come from the regions of steady cold in winter; and though Vincennes is one third of a degree further south, probably the temperature is not higher than at Cincinnati.

The dates of his CALENDAR of FLORA "are the mean terms of several years observations." From this list I can give only a few items, but the whole of his remarks deserve attention.

March 5.	Commons becoming green.
April 8.	Peach tree in full flower.
April 18.	Lilac tree in full flower.
April 20.	Apple tree in full flower.
April 24.	Dogwood tree in full flower.
May 9.	Flowering locust in full bloom.
June 4.	Cherries beginning to ripen.
June 4.	Raspberries beginning to ripen.

From 1806 to 1813 inclusive, the lowest extreme of Farenheit was eleven degrees below 0, and the highest ninety-eight degrees.

"The greatest degree of cold ever observed at this place was on the 8th of January, 1797; when, according to Governor Sargent, the mercury fell to eighteen degrees below zero."

"The quantity of snow which falls at Cincinnati is inconsiderable. The deepest that has occurred was perhaps ten inches; but four is about the ordinary depth, and many are not more than two or three. The ground seldom remains covered longer than two or three days."

"The latest veneral [vernal] frosts are generally at the close of the first week in May.

"In general, the last of September is the earliest period at which white frost is perceptible in the valley of the Ohio."

The Ohio Countries have been considered much warmer, in the same parallels, than the Atlantic states." This opinion, Dr. Drake has controverted with much ability; and his independence on this occasion, entitles him to the respect of every friend to natural science. He admits a difference of temperature, but deems this to consist more in the distribution than in the absolute quantity of heat.

I am inclined to believe, however, that this difference of distribution is in favour of the Western Country. Observations made near Schuylkill and in Cincinnati, at sunrise and at 2 P.M. though averaging the same, will give very unequal views of those climates In the south-eastern part of Pennsylvania, the approach of evening is often attended by an uncomfortable heat which is frequently protracted until midnight, while on the western side of the mountains a refreshing coolness prevails. Here then, are several hours, of which we have no account, and which would, in summer, considerably affect the thermometrical register. If vegetation is equally advanced at Cincinnati under a lower temperature, the inference is clear that spring is milder than on the western [eastern] side of the mountains.

In addition to our own observations on the coolness at evening, I select the following notices:

"The dew, in the woody vallies of this country, is so copious in the summer and early autumn, as to be felt before sunset. In the night it sprinkles from the trees like drops of rain; but in more elevated and open situations, its quantity is much less." DRAKE.

"Melting, oppressive, sultry nights are unknown here. A cool breeze always renders the night refreshing." BIRKBECK'S Notes at Cincinnati.

"The nights are more comfortable than they are even in Virginia," CRAMER, on the Climate of Mobile.

The *water* of the Wabash forms a good lather with soap. At Pittsburgh, for washing, the river water was good, but it becomes harder in its descent. At Cincinnati an increase of lime was evident; and near the mouth of the Wabash, the water of the Ohio was *hard*.

The reader may observe that limestone is scarce above Pittsburgh, but in parts of Ohio, Kentucky, and Indiana the quantity is immense. It appears, that in this stone there is always more or less gypsum.

The *Wabash* has a gentle current, except at the *Rapids*, twenty-three miles below Vincennes. This obstruction, however, is not very difficult, as flat bottomed scows eleven feet wide, have readily ascended. "In dry seasons, it is necessary to lighten boats."

"The *Rapids* are occasioned by flat rocks, which extend across the river and might easily be removed."

"*Steam* boats* may navigate this river from four to six months in the year."

The *distance* from Vincennes to the mouth, has been variously represented. It was formerly estimated at one hundred and fifty miles, and in some instances the computation has been reduced to one hundred. It appears to be about one hundred and twenty. Boats frequently go up in six days, but ten days are more commonly required.

The *south wind* which prevails in spring, and which greatly facilitates the ascent of boats, often becomes a head wind in consequence of the winding channel of the river.

"The Wabash is boatable about four hundred and fifty miles. Perogues have been taken out of this river into the Miami of the Lake. In low water the portage is nine miles. This communication is not so much used now as formerly."

Neither the Ohio nor the Wabash can be ascended in times of full flood by common boats. The advantage which has been taken of the bayous on the latter river, has been noticed.

My friend, D. STEER, observed that the navigation of White River must be difficult on account of its crookedness, as a boat, without great exertions and continual care, will cross the current and run a-ground. The Wabash is also remarkable for its serpentine course, and from Vincennes to Fort Harrison, which is

*"It is expected that a steam boat will be in complete operation on the Wabash, next spring or summer." Letter of 6 mo. 16, 1818.

only reckoned seventy miles by land, it is computed to be one hundred and fifty by water.

"The Wabash is four hundred yards wide at its mouth, three hundred at Vincennes, and two hundred at Fort Harrison. It is fordable in many places."

To avoid accompanying boats in the tardy ascent of this river, many travellers land at *Evansville** which is situate at the mouth of Great Pigeon Creek, and proceed to Vincennes by land. The distance is fifty-six miles. The road is tolerably good in summer, and much used; but after the autumnal rains, quicksands are frequent in *the barrens* through this country.

Princeton stands on the road between these towns, and is twenty-eight miles from each. It is four miles south of the Potoka river on a handsome elevation. The following list was made in 1 mo. 1818.

"Brick houses, three; frame houses, ten; log houses eighty. Total ninety-three. Six stores of merchandise; three taverns; three lawyers; two physicians. There is also a court house, jail, clerk's office, recorder's office, post office, and the following mechanics' shops: blacksmiths, two; cabinet makers, one; gunsmiths, one; shoemakers, two; taylor, one; saddlers, two; hatters, one; tannery, one; chairmaker, one."

"The inhabitants are principally *Kentuckians*."

"Instances of *longevity* are frequent. There are now living in Vincennes four Frenchmen, who were at the defeat of General Braddock, and who have lived here between fifty and sixty years. There are, also, two French women between eighty and ninety years old. One person by the name of Mills, died on the Wabash, aged one hundred and fifteen years." 3 mo. 30, 1817.

"A soldier who was with the troops that defeated general Braddock, now resides here. He is a stout healthy man, and able to labour, though near one hundred years old. He has always been temperate." July 1817.

This is not used to invalidate the first statement. Another account says, "last year there were four Frenchmen at Vincennes, who were in Braddock's defeat, and two this year." 1818.

*The mouth of Great Pigeon forms one of the best harbours between Pittsburgh and New Orleans.

The *army worm* is periodical. The cut worm and the caterpillar are annual, but their depredations are inconsiderable. The weevil is unknown on the Wabash."

The correctness of Thomas Jefferson's opinion, that the *Bee* is not a native of our continent, has been questioned. I have therefore been particular in my inquiries, and the following statement will be read with interest.

"It appears that the time has been, when the bee was not known in our country. The old French settlers saw none; and toward the Mississippi, it has not been more than twenty or twenty-five years since it was first discovered. J. M'Donald informs me, that in the Military bounty lands above the junction of the Illinois with the Mississippi, which he surveyed last winter, the bee has not been seen more than fifteen years."

Another correspondent says, "Bees are very plenty in the woods; and as the Indians here call them "white people's flies", it is believed they are not natives.

"Great quantities of honey have been found in the woods above Fort Harrison. One man found twelve bee-trees in less than half a day." 6 mo. 16. 1818.

Pine grows up the Wabash, and on the knobs of the Ohio and Silver Creek." It appears, however, to be a scarce article, and even window-sash is made of black walnut.

"*Red cedar*, of good quality, is found up the Wabash."

"I have seen neither the chestnut nor cucumber tree in this country."

Wherever the fire ceases to ravage, wild fruits soon become abundant. The plumb, the crab apple, and the persimmon trees appear in the borders of the Prairies; and the grape-vine should be included in this remark. Near M. Hoggatt's, we judged that a hogshead of hazel nuts might be readily collected. A correspondent confirms these observations.

"This country produces grapes in the greatest abundance. I came down the Wabash eight miles by water. The shores are lined with willows, many eight or nine inches in diameter, and the whole appear to be loaded with grape vines. Hazel nuts are equally plenty. The same may be said of the black walnut and hickory nut, and of the latter there are several kinds. These afford food in abundance for hogs, and they live through the winter in the woods without any other sustenance."—"It is not uncommon for a farmer to kill one hundred hogs and receive six hundred dollars for them, without giving them one ear of corn. I know one man, who sold pork this winter [1818] to the amount of one thousand dollars, without one dollar's cost for food."

"The *Pecan* in the middle is about the size of a white oak acorn, but much longer, and terminates at each end in a point. I think these are more delicious than the small shell bark.

"The *Persimmon* [near Vincennes] is quite plenty. It grows on a large shrub, or small tree. The fruit is about the size of a small peach, and is very delicious. The green fruit is remarkably astringent; and if eaten, affects the mouth so much, that for some time the person is almost incapable of speaking.

"The *papaw* is another fruit which is unknown in New York. I have seen some trees of these twenty or twenty-five feet in height. The fruit is cylindrical, and larger than a turkey egg, ripens late in autumn, and then becomes yellow. The seeds like those of the persimmon, resemble gourd seed. The scent and flavour are too luscious to be agreeable to those who are unused to this fruit; but the disgust soon abates, and we find it highly delicious."

With these fruits, I have been familiar from infancy, but have preferred the language of my correspondent.

"Wherever a high piece of land appears on one side of the River, the opposite shore is low and sunken; and from Raccoon Creek, fifteen miles above Fort Harrison to the mouth of the river, I believe there is no exception to this remark.

"There is one inconvenience attending this country, exclusive of the overflowing of the Wabash. All its tributary streams after a heavy shower of rain, rise above the banks; and overflow the low land adjoining, which on all, is of considerable extent. In time of high water, it is one of the most difficult countries to travel through, I ever saw. I have known it for more than four weeks at one time, that no person could get away from Union Prairie, without swimming his horse, or going in a boat."

"The *Buffalo* has totally abandoned our country, but the *Elk* still remains in many places."

"*Raccoons* are in great plenty, and very destructive to corn.

"The *Pole Cat* or *Skunk* are very numerous through out the country, as well on prairie as on wood land.

"The *Opossum* also inhabits this country in great numbers. Some are as white as snow, and others of a light grey, resembling in colour the grey rabbit.

"The *Porcupine* has been seen in this country, but is very scarce.

"The *Prairie Wolf* is numerous. In size, it is a medium between the red fox and the common grey wolf. The colour is grey. Its ears are sharp and erect like those of the fox. Unless several are in company, it is not destructive to sheep; but it destroys lambs and young pigs. On Christmas day, 1816, thirteen were killed on Fort Harrison Prairie without firing a gun. During the same winter, there were about thirty killed on Union Prairie, by running them down with dogs and horses. It is very resolute when attacked and unable to escape; no dog alone is able to subdue it. In the summer season it is not to be seen; but in winter it frequents the prairies in great numbers.

"The *grey* and the *black wolf* are also natives. Whether these are different species or not, I must leave undetermined."

"I find no *black squirrels* in this country, but it abounds with *grey ones* hardly so large as the black squirrel with you."

"The *Pelican*, so common on the Mississippi, also frequents this river, but not in great numbers. I saw the head of one which had been taken near Vincennes. From the point of the bill, which is from seven to ten inches long, a pouch or loose skin extends to the breast, which would contain about ten quarts."

"The *Swan* is sometimes seen on this river."

The *Crow* appears in great numbers, and are very destructive to corn."

"A bird inhabits this country, called the *sandy hill Crane*. Its size is remarkable. When full grown and standing erect (for its legs and neck are very long) it is between five and six feet in height. The colour is nearly that of iron rust. I have seen large flocks on the prairies. It is very wild and noisy. When slightly wounded, no dog can approach it with impunity."

"The *Prairie Hen* is rarely seen in summer; but in winter, it is more numerous on the prairies than quails are in the state of New York. The size is nearly that of the common domestic hen. It is spotted like the guinea fowl, but the colour is browner, like the pheasant. The tail is shorter and does not spread like that of the pheasant. The difference between the cock and the hen is not greater than in those of the quail; the male is a little larger, and the stripes on the side of the head are a little brighter than those of the female. It can fly much farther, and with more apparent ease, than either the quail or pheasant. As an article of food, I think it inferior to the dung-hill fowl. It lays about twenty eggs, and brings forth its young in the early part of summer. Though its common food is procured in the woods, it is fond of corn and grain."

"The *Robin* and the *red headed Woodpecker* are numerous."

"On the approach of any large bird the *Parroquets* immediately commence flying round and round in flocks, screaming most hideously. In this way, they escape the hawk."

"The *Hen Hawk* is not very numerous."

"*Wild Turkies* abound in this country. *Wild geese* and *ducks* are also plenty. I have never seen a *loon* in these waters."

"The Wabash abounds with fish of many kinds; which, in the months of April, May and June, may be readily caught with the hook and line."

The *Gar* or *Bill fish* is more than two feet in length. It is quite slim. The bill is about six inches long, tapering to a point. Its scales are very close, thick, and hard."

"The strength of this fish is great. In a small Creek which flows into the Wabash, I discovered a considerable number, and caught several in my hands; but was absolutely unable to hold one."

There are three kinds of *Cat-fish:* the Mississippi cat, the mud cat, and the bull head. Some of the first have weighed one hundred and twenty pounds. The mud cat is covered with clouded spots, and is a very homely fish. The head is very wide and flat. Some have weighed one hundred pounds.

"The real *sturgeon* is found in the Wabash, though the size is not large. These have been taken from twenty to sixty pounds weight.

"The *shovel fish* or *flat nose* is another species of sturgeon. It weighs about twenty pounds.

"The *pond pike* is taken in ponds from one to three feet long, but very slim. It is an excellent fish.

"The *river pike* is large and highly esteemed, but scarce.

"The *drum* or *white perch* weighs from one to thirty pounds. It is shaped like the sun fish.

"The *black perch* or *bass* is excellent, and weighs from one to seven pounds.

"The *streaked bass* is scarce.

"The *Buffalo fish* is of the *sucker* kind, and very common. Weight from two to thirty pounds.

"The *rock Mullet* is sometimes seen three feet long. It is slim, and weighs from ten to fifteen pounds.

"The *red horse* is also of the sucker kind. It is large and bony, weighing from five to fifteen pounds.

"The *Jack pike* or *pickerel* is an excellent fish, and weighs from six to twenty pounds."

In another communication, I found the *silver-sides* noticed without any description. "It weighs from three to six pounds."

The *eel* is frequently taken in the Wabash, and weighs from one to three pounds. I was told that no fish was found in these waters of a good quality for pickling; and the facts, that mackerel are brought over the mountains from Philadelphia, and white fish from Detroit, tend to confirm that statement.

"The *fresh water clam* or *muscle* is so plenty, as to be gathered and burnt for lime. Twenty years ago, I am told, no other kind of lime was procured."

"*Craw fish*, which resembles the *lobster*, is very common in the low lands of this country. It is a size larger than the common crab. It works in the ground, and throws up heaps of earth about six inches high, and hollow within. These little mounds are very numerous, and the surface of the ground resembles a honey comb."

"The *Ground Mole* of this country is nearly as large as the common rat. It is very injurious in gardens. It moves along at the depth of two or three inches under ground, raising a considerable ridge; and not only loosens the roots of vegetables, but devours them. It is remarkable how fast these little animals can force their way through the earth."

"*Horned cattle* are subject to the *murrain*, which sometimes has been very destructive. It may be prevented by care, and cured by proper applications."

"In the old settled parts of this country, but little fodder is saved; the wood pastures are exhausted; and the cattle in spring, become poor, get sickly and die."

"The most common *diseases* are fevers and agues, with some liver complaints. The dysentery is very little known. In my opinion, diseases yield sooner to medicine than in more northern climates."

"The prevailing diseases of this country are *bilious*, which sometimes terminate in malignant typhus. It is quite rare to hear of sickness from November until some time in the summer."

"A list of the *prevailing diseases* in this country is subjoined.

"Typhus, gravior et minor—Bilious, intermittent and remittent fevers. Pleurisy is frequent in spring. Rheumatism and consumption are very rare, compared with New-York. A wet spring followed by drowth is an unfavourable indication."

From my DIARY of 7 mo. 15. I copy the following paragraphs.

'It ought not to be concealed that at present in this country, there are many sick people; and we believe that there are many situations, some of which have been noticed, that may properly be denominated *sickly;* but we could not, with any propriety, extend this remark to the country in general. We know of no person who is sick near this river, but who would have been sick, probably, with the same exposure in any part of the United States. The manner of removing hither, is such, that our surprise is rather excited that so few are diseased. Many are cooped up during the heat of summer for six weeks, exposed to the powerful reflection of the sun from the water, while the roof over their heads is heated like an oven. In addition, they have the smell of bilge water, and the exhalations from the muddy shores. Their daily drink is supplied by the river; its warmth relaxes the tone of the stomach; and the putrid particles which float through it, operate unresisted.

'On landing, their situation is not much better. Huts insufficient to shelter them from storms, or from the chilling damps of the night, become their homes; and bad water, with provisions not well chosen, and to which the constitution is not habituated, combine to derange to system. When this event happens, and fevers prevail, *the occasional cause* is not removed, and in many cases no proper medicine is administered. Such have been the circumstances of many emigrants from the eastward, and especially of those who were indigent.'

These paragraphs explain the causes of disease which in that summer so remarkably prevailed near the Wabash. Of the sick, the chief part were new comers. In 1815 the same observation was made; and from the population of Vincennes, and of the district immediately around it, which was estimated at three thousand, "twenty-five persons died, but nineteen of that number were strangers."

In the first settling of Cayuga county, it was remarked that emigrants from the eastward, were more sickly than those who crossed the mountains from the south. The causes of disease could be clearly traced to the marshes of the Seneca river, which was the common thoroughfare in summer, before the present turnpike road was completed.

From what I have observed, a change of climate (where it chiefly consists of a change of temperature) has but a slight influence on a healthy constitution; and this will appear rational when we consider, that the heat of summer in high latitudes, is frequently as great and as oppressive as is regions far to the south.

But a change of climate is often attended by other changes of greater importance. Excessive and unaccustomed fatigue, uncomfortable lodgings, and inferior diet, are only part of the vicissitudes to which travellers in new countries are exposed,

The danger to this class is sometimes increased by inquietude of mind, which prompts the convalescent to exertions beyond his strength; and a relapse in fevers is frequently fatal.

Having thus brought the danger into view, some remarks on the best means to avoid it, may not be inappropriate.

In the spring of 1817 the late S. R. BROWN, desired my opinion on the question, whether a residence in Indiana would be favourable to the health of emigrants from higher latitudes? A paper was accordingly prepared under the disadvantages of great haste and much indisposition, and without any corrections, published in his WESTERN GAZETTEER. The advice which it contains, however, I am persuaded is of importance; and having apprised him that that view of the subject was intended for this work, I shall proceed with the transcription, altering, where I deem it proper. Much of this is intended for emigrants from the eastern states.

Descend the river after the commencement of autumnal frosts. The effect of these in neutralizing or preventing putrid exhalations has been frequently observed; and the smell from the shores after a flood, in warm weather, is very offensive.

Avoid going in a vessel with a leaky roof. A crowded boat is an inconvenient place to dry wet clothes; and the expense of being comfortably sheltered, will frequently be less than the damage in furniture, without considering the probable loss of health. To bend thin boards for a cover is customary, but not sufficient. I have seen no roof of that kind which would be a shelter from a driving shower of rain. A sick woman said to me near the Wabash, "I ascribe my sickness, in great measure, to one dismal night that I endured on the river. The rain poured through every part of the roof, and to sit on the bed with my children under an umbrella was our only refuge".

If, however, to descend in spring is unavoidable, start as soon as the river is clear of ice. Make no delay; for not only health, but life may depend on a timely escape from the effluvia of those shores.

If the river be low, and by this or other unavoidable delays, warm weather should surround the emigrant on the river, guard against a heated roof overhead. Boards nailed on the inside, or an awning on the outside, will be important auxiliaries to comfort and to health.

At such times, no river water should be used without filtering. This operation may be expeditiously performed in a vessel like an upright churn with two bottoms. These are three or four inches apart; and the upper, in which many small holes are bored, receives in the center, a tube one inch in diameter, extending above the vessel, and communicating with the cavity between the bottoms. After spreading a cloth on the upper bottom, fill the vessel upward with well washed sand, and from above let in water downward through the tube. In a short time it will rise through the sand, divested of its impurities, and run over at an ear in sufficient quantities for every culinary purpose. In a few days the apparatus may need cleansing. As the filth will be chiefly below, a hole opened in the lower bottom will allow it to pass off. See Melish's Travels, vol. 1. p. 159.

If the water have not an agreeable coolness, cider or strong beer should be mixed with it for drink, as the warmth without some stimulant will relax the tone of the stomach, and predispose the system to disease.

But beware of spiritous liquors. If such, however, are taken, let the quantity be cautiously regulated. Every excess debilitates; and to think of escaping disease, by keeping always in a state of excitement, is desperate folly. When fevers attack such subjects it is commonly fatal. Some men who travel much, and who have neither moral nor religious scruples to dissuade them, totally abstain from *spirits* in unhealthy situations. Rich wholesome* food, guards the stomach much better from infection, nor would I omit in the list of such articles, well cured ham and strong coffee.

Travellers should never change their diet for the worse. The fatiuges [fatigues] of mind and body, in most cases, require that it should be for the better. To live comfortably is true economy. Any additional expense in provisions would form but a small item in a doctor's bill, without taking into view the loss of time, of comfort, or of the expenses of nursing. To lay in a good stock of wholesome provisions should therefore, by no means, be neglected.

On landing, let one of the first objects be to provide a comfortable habitation. Water from brooks should be filtered, but during summer no dependance ought to be placed on this supply. If springs are not convenient, dig wells. Much of the sickness of new countries is induced by bad water.

Let no temptation prevail on the emigrant to go fishing in

*In a medical author I find the following interesting remark: "The predisposing cause of intermittents, is clearly debility, with penury of blood; because the robust, and such as have a generous diet, are most free from this disease."

warm weather. Of the smell of the shores I have spoken. To be wet is imprudent; and to be exposed to the chilling damps of the night, greatly increases the danger. But fresh fish* are unwholesome, except for a slight change of diet. We know of no new settlement that has been healthy, where the inhabitants live chiefly on fresh fish. If, however, fish must be eaten, buy them; any price is cheaper than health; and if fishing must be done, do it in cloudy weather; but at night be comfortably sheltered.

Let no fertility of the river flats be an inducement to cultivate them, until naturalized to the climate; or more properly, recovered from the fatigues attending emigration, for composure of mind is as important as refreshment to the body. When the body is debilitated either by labour or fasting, it is more susceptible of infection, and these exhalations after floods are putrid. Land of an inferior quality, in a dry airy situation will yield greater *neat profits*.

Delay in taking medicine, is often fatal. The patient ought not to wait till he is *down sick*, but if the stomach is disordered, which is the case at the commencement of all fevers, a glass of pearl ash and water may afford relief. The quantity is stated at page 147. If this should prove insufficient, take an emetic, or small doses of emetic tartar, only to nauseate. Should this produce an intermission, with a moist skin and clean tongue, take peruvian bark, or those of dogwood, (*box-wood*) willow, or oak, which have been found eminently useful.

Of alkaline medicines, perhaps pear lash is the best. Its good effect in *cholera morbus*, *diarrhoea*, &c. have been often experienced; and it is always an excellent preventive. It sweetens the stomach and promotes digestion.

I have one caution more for the emigrant. The water, in places, throughout all the Ohio country, is saturated with sulphate of lime. This, like the sulphates of soda and magnesia, is cathartic; and in one ounce doses, is an active medicine. Inconvenience to grown persons from these waters, however, is rarely experienced; but on small children the effect is considerable, and

*"The Roman Catholics, who, during forty days Lent, rigourously abstain from flesh, but indulge freely in a fish diet, are said to be less nourished by it, and to become sensibly thinner and weaker, as HALLER, indeed, tells us he had himself experienced.

"The disorders of the system, the herpetic, leprous and scorbutic eruptions to which the *ichthyophagi* are said to be more especially liable, show, we think with other observations, that fish is neither so easily digested nor assimilated to the human system as flesh.

"Sea fish are more flourishing than those which inhabit the rivers and fresh waters." Edin. Encycl. Art. Aliment.

to those just weaned it has often proved fatal, by inducing diarrhoea,* which exhausts the patient, for no medicine can give permanent relief while the *occasional cause* is unremoved. This is easily done by refusing water and giving milk. If the disease is far advanced, paregoric may be necessary to diminish the irritability.

From the same cause, the waters in many parts of the Western District of New-York, produce a similar effect. I discovered the benefit of this practice in one of my children, who seemed wasting to a skeleton; and have since witnessed much of its good effects on others.

The beautiful bluff above *Turtle Creek*, noticed at page 170, now called *Merom*, has become the seat of justice for Sullivan county; and was selected by commissioners appointed under an act of the Legislature. The agent, who was authorized to sell the lots, makes the following remarks in his advertisement:

"It is situate on the east bank of the River, thirty-five miles above Vincennes, on that elevated ground known by the name of *The Bluff*, the highest bank of the Wabash from its mouth to the north† line of the state. The river washes the base of this high land one mile. Freestone [sandstone] and a quality [quantity] of [impure] limestone, appear in the bank in great abundance. Springs in every direction around the town are discovered.

"From the most elevated point of the bluff, the eye can be gratified with the charming view of *La Motte Prairie*, immediately below in front; and with *Ellison and Union Prairies* on the right and left; the whole stretching along the river a distance of not less than thirty miles, and all now rapidly settling. In the rear

*Children accustomed to take all their food in a liquid form, retain after weaning an eagerness for liquids; and as water is generally at hand, it is substituted for the mild aliment of which they have been deprived. When either the sulphate of lime or of magnesia, is held in solution, these substances operate actively on the delicate fibre and the peristaltic motion is greatly increased. In proportion to the loss of moisture thus sustained by the system, will be the thirst. With every draught fresh causes of irritation succeed,—the motion of the *lacteals* become inverted— and emaciation and debility rapidly ensue.

†It should have been written *east line of the State.* In no part of its course does the Wabash approach the north line of the state.

of this beautiful site, is a flourishing settlement of twenty or thirty farmers, three miles east of the town."

Gill's Prairie, south three miles, has at present a handsome population of industrious farmers.

"A mile and a half from the town, a mill will soon be erected on Turtle Creek by *a** Mr. Bennett.—June 27, 1817."

It is with much satisfaction, that we perceive a new name for a new town or village. Hitherto when the *importations* from Europe or Asia have been insufficient, it has become necessary to borrow from our neighbours, to a degree that is absolutely humiliating; and perhaps in no part of the United States is this practice carried to the same excess as in *Ohio*. The following list of names is copied from *Kilbourn's Gazetteer* of that state, published in 1817.

6 towns or villages of the name of Fairfield.
5 towns or villages of the name of Franklin.
5 towns or villages of the name of Goshen.
10 towns or villages of the name of Green.
7 towns or villages of the name of Harrison.
7 towns or villages of the name of Jackson.
11 towns or villages of the name of Jefferson.
6 towns or villages of the name of Liberty.
14 towns or villages of the name of Madison.
5 towns or villages of the name of Milford.
5 towns or villages of the name of Oxford.
5 towns or villages of the name of Pleasant.
5 towns or villages of the name of Richland.
7 towns or villages of the name of Salem.
10 towns or villages of the name of Springfield.
17 towns or villages of the name of Union.
11 towns or villages of the name of Washington.
12 towns or villages of the name of Wayne.

To persons who find it necessary for them to impose a name, we would suggest, that any thing is more tolerable than the repetitions that now assail us.

Rapp's congregation are settled at *Harmony*, fifty miles below Vincennes. The cultivation of the vine has engaged their atten-

*We object to employing the indefinite article in this manner. Though it may seem discourteous to attack in an individual, what fashion has sanctioned, yet we mean no personal rebuke—entering our protest in general terms against a custom, which in our ears has always been harsh, unnecessary and ungraceful. If the writer means in this manner to guard against mistaking one person for another, it must at least be conceded, that the attempt is awkward and insufficient; and as it is understood for a hint that the individual so noticed is obscure, we suggest whether its discontinuance would not be an advancement in good manners.

tion; but the manufacture of *cloth, nails,* &c. with the production of grain has claimed a share. *A steam Mill* has been erected.

"We have a *law* which requires every military and civil officer to take an oath or affirmation to suppress *duelling* in every shape and form." It will be well if this oath be not considered as words without meaning, for on the opposite side of the Ohio, this atrocious practice is quite in fashion.

"Forty dollars may be collected by a Justice of the Peace."

I noticed the following *vegetables* growing indigenously, near the Wabash, between Vincennes and Fort Harrison; but am aware that this list gives a very imperfect view of the BOTANY of that District.

Acer saccharinum........................sugar maple.
Acer glaucum............................river maple.
Acer negundo............................ash leaved maple.
Acer rubum..............................soft or red flowering maple.
Ascelepias decumbens....................butterfly weed.
Asclepias syriaca.......................silk weed, Indian hemp.
Asclepias...............................milk weed and others.
Annona triloba..........................papaw.
Arum dracontium.........................many leaved Indian turnip.
Asarum canadense........................wild ginger.
Aralia spinosa..........................angelica tree.
Aralia racemosa.........................spikenard.
Ambrosia trifida...
Ambrosia artimisifolia..................hog or bitter weed.
Adiantum pedatum........................maiden hair.
Bignonia radicans.......................red trumpet flower.
Corylus americana.......................common hazel.
Corylus cornuta.........................horned.
Celtis occidentalis.....................nettle tree or hackberry.
Cercis canadensis.......................fish blossom, or Judas tree.
Carex, many species.....................sedge.
Cassia marylandica......................wild senna.
Ceanothus americanus....................Jersey tea plant.
Cephalanthus occidentalis...............button flower.
Convallaria multiflora..................Solomon's seal.
Convolvulus panduratus..................wild potatoe.
Carduus, several species................thistle.
Carpinus americana......................horn beam.
Circea lutetiana?.......................Enchanter's night shade.
Collinsonia canadensis..................horse weed.
Dyospyros virginiana....................persimmon.
Dirca palustris.........................leather wood.

*Æsculus flava** .... stinking buckeye.
Evonymus americanus .... spindle tree.
Fragaria virginiana .... strawberry.
Fagus ferruginea .... beech.
Fraxinus .... ash—white and blue.
Frasera verticillata .... Columbo root.
Guilandina dioica .... Kentucky coffee tree.
Gleditsia triacanthos .... honey locust.
Monosperma? .... (almost without spines.)
Galium, several species .... goose grass.
Helianthus, several species .... Sunflower.
Hedera quinquefolia .... poison ivy.
Hydrangea arborescens.* ....
Impatiens .... touch-me-not.
Iris virginica .... blue flag.
Juglans pecan ...... } Hiccorius of RAFINESQUE ...... pecan.
Juglans squamosa .. } ...... shell bark.
Juglans ovata ...... } ...... bitter nut.
Juglans .... } ...... upland pig nut.
Juglans cinerea .... black walnut.
Juglans nigra .... butter nut, or white walnut.
Jeffersonia diphylla .... two leaved Jeffersonia.
Laurus sassafras .... sassafras.
Laurus benzoin .... spice wood.
Liquidambar styraciflua .... sweet gum.
Liriodendron tulipifera .... tulip poplar, white wood.
Lobelia inflata ....
Monardo .... wild mint.
Morus rubra .... mulberry.
Nyssa iutegrifolia .... gum-tree—pepperidge.
Platanus occidentalis .... button wood.
Populus angulata .... cotton wood.
Pyrus coronaria .... crab apple.
Potentilla, two species .... cinquefoil.
Podophyllum peltatum .... mandrake, May apple.
Polygonum, various species ....
Panax quinquefolium .... ginseng.
Prunus .... wild plumb.
Quercus nigra .... black oak.
Quercus alba .... white oak.
Quercus rubra .... red oak.
Quercus prinos v. *palustris* .... swamp chestnut oak.
Quercus phellos .... willow leaved.
Quercus triloba .... true black jack.
Quercus discolor .... swamp white oak.
Quercus .... spanish oak.
Robinia pseud-acacia .... black locust.
Robinia? .... (in the swamp east of Vincennes.)

*This is not abundant. The wood is of small value. Cattle have been poisoned by the fruit.

*Rubus villosus**........................black berry.
Rubus occidentalis.......................black raspberry.
Rhus glabrum...........................smooth sumach.
Rhus typhinum..........................stag's horn.
Rhus radicans...........................poison vine.
Rhus.................................another.
Smilax rotundifolia......................green briar.
Smilax................................herbaceous.
Spirea salicafolia........................willow leaved spirea.
Spirea herbaceous........................meadow sweet.
Salix conifera...........................cone bearing willow.
Salix nigra.............................black.
Salix trislis............................shrub.
Salix?................................(with linear leaves near Fort Harrison.)
Scandix, two species.....................cicely.
Solanum carolinense†.....................horse nettle, or Irish plumb.
Tilia americana.........................basswood, or linden.
Ulmus................................red elm.
Ulmus................................white elm.
Urtica divaricata........................common nettle.
Urtica pumila...........................stingless.
Urtica................................another.
Vitis, two species........................grape vine.
Vitis vulpina...........................fox grape not observed.
Verbena, several species...................vervain.

DR. DRAKE mentions the *Catalpa* in Indiana as far north as Cincinnati, but I did not observe it.

A plant, which I conjecture to be a species of *Plantago,* abounds in the channels of small streams west of Loghary. It is of a larger growth than the *P. major*. I have not seen it as far west as Madison; but on our return I observed it in the state of Ohio, between Xenia and Columbus.

A new species of *Viburnum* also grows along these streams. It resembles the *V. dentatum;* but the bark is scaly like the *Spirea opulifolia*, and has no suckers like the arrow wood.

The Potoka discharges its waters into the Wabash, one mile below the mouth of White river. It is navigable for boats. Where

*One of these shrubs had grown up near the branches of a crab tree, which prevented the stalk from bending until it had attained the height of twelve feet. When I observed it, it was finely loaded with ripe fruit.

†This vegetable grows in the clayey prairies east of Shakertown. Whether a native, or not it is uncertain. It is scantilly armed with spines, and when it takes possession of a piece of ground, on account of its deep penetrating roots, is removed with difficulty.

the road from Princeton to Vincennes, crosses this stream, the current is dull and deep; but there is a mill-seat just below which is formed by considerable rapids.

'*Coal* is found thirty miles below Fort Harrison, in the banks of a small brook. This *mine* we viewed as we went up the river. On the White river, and its branches this fossil is abundant. It is also found in the neighbourhood of Fort Harrison. *Limestone* appears in considerable quantities in the bank of a small creek which empties into the Wabash three miles below that Fort, and in several places further up the river.' Diary of 7 mo. 1816.

"Limestone is found near *Princeton*. It also appears below *York*, on fraction No. 17, of Township 8, north Range 11 west. *Coal* is found west, directly opposite to Fort Harrison, under a bank six feet high. It has also been found under limestone, in the Illinois Territory on the line between townships No. 8 and 9, north range, 12 west. 1818."

I have no doubt that coal, limestone, and sandstone will be found plentifully in the high woodlands in every part of that country, when proper search shall be made. In such soils we have never seen the friable earth very deep, and solid rock unquestionably forms the foundation of the hills.

"Last autumn, [1817,] the Indians brought twenty-eight pounds of *copper* to Fort Harrison, in one lump. The metal is so pure, that without any refining, it has answered all the purposes of imported copper. It is supposed that the Indians found it about thirty miles above the mouth of *Raccoon creek*, in Indiana." My friend J. BENNETT, from whom I received this account, has kindly furnished me with a specimen, and no doubt can exist of its excellence. Its malleability I have well ascertained.

But though it should be proved that they found it at the place designated, there would be much uncertainty at present, whether the discovery is of much importance; that is, whether the metal is a native of the rocky strata which underlay the country, or whether, like the granite, it has been scattered on the surface. When the numerous facts which shew that the granite arrived from the north are considered,—and also, the resemblance of this copper to that on the south shore of lake Superior,—a conjecture, assigning both to the same origin, would be plausible.

All the best *lands* near the Wabash river which had not been reserved by government, or located by Canadian claimants, were sold at auction in the 9 mo. 1816. Much land of the second or third quality, (and no inconsiderable part of these kinds is very fertile) remained, however, for entry at two dollars an acre payable within four years, by instalments. One fourth within two years, and the remainder in two equal annual payments. This condition is the rule; and eight per cent interest is added to all payments after such become due, and eight per cent discount is allowed for prompt pay. Thus lands paid for at the time of entry, only cost one dollar and sixty three cents an acre.

To accommodate persons who may be unprepared to make a payment in full—or who may wish to secure a lot while they attempt further discoveries,—lands are permitted to be entered for a certain number of days. This privilege, however, has been frequently abused. Entries have been made for the sum of sixteen dollars, (one twentieth of the purchase money,)—which confers the right to remove within forty days, every valuable timber tree from the premises; and if no other purchaser appears, the term is even lengthened to 90 days.

Last winter (1817-18) from five to ten dollars was the price of Prairie Lands, and from two to five the price of Wood Lands.

The fertility of *the sandy prairies* near the river is very remarkable. If lime is a constituent of this soil, the portion must be inconsiderable, as acids produce no effervescence. Neither is the vegetable matter in much quantity. The finer parts diminish but little in the fire, and are changed from black to a reddish brown. Hence the fertilizing principle is a mineral earth.

The idea of *soils perpetually fertile,* was not original with H. Davy, though to him we owe the first scientific view of the subject. Vegetable matter soon dissipates, but the primitive earths are imperishable; and if my conjecture is correct, these prairies will be sources of abundance through distant ages. A field was pointed out to me, which had recently been enclosed from the commons of Vincennes, and which produced corn of extraordinary luxuriance. From the nakedness of this ground it is evident that a vegetable soil would soon become sterile.

One of my correspondents remarks, "We have a prairie below

this place, which has been in cultivation seventy or eighty years, and now produces well."

Lord KAIMS mentions a field near the Clyde, in Scotland, which had annually produced a crop for 101 years, and still retained its fertility. The subjoined extract is from the EDINBURGH ENCYCLOPEDIA. "The lands of *St. Jago,* [Chili] though constantly cultivated for two centuries and a half, without receiving any artificial manure, have suffered no diminution in their amazing produce."

Some of the great Bottom of the Mississippi, between Kaskaskia and Illinois, "has been in cultivation 120 years, and still no deterioration has yet manifested itself." BROWN'S WESTERN GAZETTEER.

"I have lately visited Fort Harrison, passing upwards from Vincennes on the Illinois side of the river. After traversing a rich tract of *woodland* four miles, I went five miles through an *arm of the Grand Prairie.* Much of this is too low. Fine *woodland,* three miles wide, separates this from *Ellison Prairie,* which is a rich tract, seven miles long, and averaging three miles in width. Good *Woodland,* but not of the first quality, then extends thirteen miles to *La Motte Prairie.* This is an extraordinary tract, and is eight or nine miles long. I then passed through *woodland* of a good quality ten miles to *Union Prairie,* on which *York village* is located. Here I crossed the river to the Indiana side.

"*Fort Harrison Prairie* is a most delightful tract. It contains, perhaps, 22,000 acres, including the woodland lying between it and the Wabash. This woodland is very fine, and on an inclined plane from the prairie to the bank of the river—which is generally from twenty to thirty feet high for several miles. The woodland on the east of this prairie is an elevated tract with a rich soil. Springs and brooks flowing from it, are numerous.

"This prairie is bounded on the north by Otter Creek, on which Major Markle is building mills." [W. P. B.] These have since been completed. The construction, it is said, is uncommonly excellent; and that the saw mills are capable of sawing 6,000 feet of boards in one day.

"The soil of the *prairies* is excellent for both corn and wheat. Of the latter, the crops vary from twenty to forty bushels an acre; and of the former, from fifty to one hundred bushels. Major Markle for rent alone, besides what he raised himself, has more than 3, 700 bushels of corn." 11 mo. 1817.

The country will be more healthy when *levees* shall be raised across the *bayous*, and longitudinal ditches cut in particular places. The expense of forming a bank six feet high at Otter Creek, would not be a work of extraordinary magnitude for an individual; and a prairie thirteen miles in length would be exempted from inundation. At Honey Creek, the same remark may be made in respect to the construction.

Of the practicability of such measures, we were well convinced, when we were near the Wabash; but on our return, at *Franklinton,* we saw a levee which had been raised to that height by the *scraper,* and which has completely rescued a valuable tract from the river floods.

I have noted that *ponds* appear in places through the bayous. The small streams which are lost in the sands, probably after heavy rains supply the water; and the expense of a small canal, which would render the lowest parts of these tracts arable, would be a slight tax for the neighbouring inhabitants. Indeed the proprietors themselves, would be reimbursed in one or two seasons for such expenditure.

If the bayou from *Otter Creek* were closed, the stream which sweeps through *Honey Creek Prairie* would be less formidable. Where two such currents form a junction, the narrow and winding channel, already dammed by the river, is insufficient to discharge the accumulating waters; the torrent at every creek receives an accession of force, and spreads the inundation still wider in its progress to the south.

A Post office has lately been established at Honey Creek, two and a half miles south of the old ford on that stream, in Range 9 West, Township 11 North, Section 25.—Name, *Hoggatt's*—M. HOGGATT, Post Master.

Cant phrases, the true marks of a defective education, are common in the Western Country.

A considerable number is expressed by *a smart chance;* and our hostess at Madison said, there was "a smart chance of yankees" in that village.

Rolling is a term which may be frequently heard in conversations relative to lands. We are not to understand by this word, *a turning round*, but *a diversified surface*.

Slashes, means flat clayey land which retains water on the surface, after showers. From this comes the adjective, *slashy*. It is in common use, and, like the word *chore* [corruption of *chare*] in the eastern states, is almost an *indispensable*.

Balance is another word which is *twisted* from its proper meaning. This is made to imply the remainder. "The balance (unappropriated residue of land) will be sold at auction."

The *Cane*, which once overspreads a large part of Kentucky, is nearly destroyed; but it grows abundantly on the Wabash, and extends from the mouth of that river almost to Vincennes.

The *iron-weed*, which I first saw above Pittsburgh, extends on clayey lands all the way to the Wabash. It is a pernicious plant in meadows.

The wet Prairies abound with the fern-leaved *Helianthus*, and on our return, we saw thousands of these blossoms turned to the sun.

N. EWING had six kinds of *exotic grapes* in his garden, which flourish; and though receiving little attention, were finely loaded with fruit. That climate is congenial to the vine. Indeed we believe this culture will become very profitable. At Harmony, fifty miles below Vincennes, we understood that twelve acres had already been planted as a vineyard.

Various kinds of *esculent vegetables* are taken to Vincennes by the SHAKERS, nearly two weeks earlier than such can be raised in the wood-lands round that town.

Six miles west of the French Licks, we saw the semblance of a *corn-stalk*, of very remote antiquity, which was found in that neighbourhood. It appeared that the cavity of this plant (once occupied by the pith) was filled with sand, which became cemented by ferruginous matter. The impressions of the nerves were very distinct. It had been nearly two feet in length, and was raised out of the earth by the root of a falling tree.

The district from the Knobs to the east branch of White river, is high *table land;* and apparently composed of strata, which were deposited on this part, after the general surface of the Ohio country was formed. There is some reason to believe, however, that parts of this great bank were removed before the commencement of petrification. The *White river* flows round it on the north. When we ascended these *heights* on the east, we were in constant expectation, during our progress for some miles, of descending on the western side; so different is this tract from any we had ever traversed. On our return we particularly noticed the ascent and descent of every little ridge, and could discover no general inclination of the surface. No plain, barren, or prairie, is found within its limits.

We are assured that the Knobs do not appear south of the Ohio. The sides are surprisingly irregular. On a north course from Salem Meeting-house, within three miles, the *descent* appears; but on an east course, the distance to the *edge* is computed at ten miles. From the latter spot, beyond the winding of that vale to the westward, these hills extend to the north-east till the eye is bewildered with the prospect in the distant horizon.

In this district, *petrifactions* are numerous. In the channel of a brook I found the semblance of a perennial rooted herb, in which the different annual growths were exhibited. It was five inches long by one inch in thickness. The *bark* of the root appears to have been the *mould,* as the internal part was hollow, or filled with chrystals. The *rattles* of a snake, remarkably large, had also been converted into stone.

The *stalagmites,* or dumpling stone, which was noticed in the DIARY, appears confined to this region. We observed it near the border, but not on the plains below.

From the singularity of its figure, from its cavity, and from the numerous petrifactions in this vicinity, I could scarcely resist the impression that the fruit of some species of *Cucurbita* had been the model. Other considerations, however, would be unfavourable;

and it must be confessed that nature has performed many operations in Mineralogy, which continue secrets. . . . .

...In the eastern parts of Indiana, much of the grain for bread is ground in *horse mills.* I have learned that the proprietor of the mill finds horses; and takes for *toll,* one fourth of the wheat, and one sixth of the corn or other grain, if not bolted. The floating mills on the Ohio river, take one sixth of the *wheat* and one eighth of the *corn.*

...*Notes of a Journey from Fort Harrison to Fort Wayne.*

45 miles, a small village of the Miamis, on the waters of Eel river.

25 do. the second Indian town, also on Eel river.

50 do. to Pipe Creek. Many small creeks water this district, but Pipe Creek is a considerable stream, and famous for its mill seats. Much of these lands are low and wet.

8 do. above Pipe Creek is the Massasinaway town of Indiana. It is at the junction of this river with the Wabash.

50 do. continuing up the Wabash.

13 do. across from the Lower Portage to Fort Wayne. Here are some irregular hills, and some marshes.

191 miles, total distance.

...The right pronunciation of *names* is as necessary as the right pronunciation of *words;* and believing that many of our untravelled readers would receive it favourably, we have bestowed some attention on this subject. There have been omissions, however, which we will supply in this place.

Wau-bash is the common pronunciation on that river; but in this country we frequently hear the uncouth sound of *Way-bosh.*

Vincennes is pronounced *Vin-cenz* by the most respectable persons in that place.

Pa-ra-rah is a common pronunciation; but it is too great a barbarism to be tolerated. By placing the letters in this manner, *prai-rie,* the proper sounds cannot be mistaken.

In *Levee,* (an embankment) the accent is sometimes placed on the last syllable. It should be *lev-e.*

From *The Western Gazetteer; or Emigrant's Directory*, by Samuel R. Brown [1817], pp. 37-80.

Brown, Samuel R.

This work, like several others of a similar nature, resulted from a demand on the part of emigrants for a History and Guide of the western Country. It appeared 1817, and illustrates the ambitious efforts of a publisher to furnish detailed information on every section of the region lying between the Allegheny and Rocky Mountains, the Lakes and the Gulf. In the space of three hundred and sixty pages, the territory, water courses, routes of travel and climatic conditions comprised within one thousand millions of acres are reviewed in detail.

The work contains fewer errors than might be expected in such a gigantic undertaking. An excellent map accompanies the notes.

INDIANA.

Is bounded west by the Wabash river, from its mouth to 40 miles above Vincennes, and thence by a meridian line to the parallel of the south end of lake Michigan, (supposed to be in N. lat. 41, 50.) which divides it from Illinois territory. Its northern limit is the above parallel, which separates it from the Michigan territory. A meridian line running from the mouth of the Big Miami, until it intersects the aforesaid parallel of the south end of lake Michigan, divides it from the state of Ohio, on the east. The Ohio river forms its sourthern boundary. Length, from north to south, 284 miles; breadth, from east to west, 155 miles—contains 39,000 square miles, or 24,960,000 acres. Its form would be that of a paralellogram, were the course of the Ohio due west.

RIVERS, LAKES.

The Ohio washes the southern border of Indiana, from the mouth of the Big Miami, to that of the Wabash, a distance, measuring its windings, of 472 miles—all the streams which intersect this extensive line of coast, are comparitively short; for the southern fork of White river, having its source within a few miles of the Ohio boundary line, runs nearly parallel with Ohio, at the distance of from forty to sixty miles. The principal of these enter the Ohio in the order named:

Tanner's Creek—Two miles below Lawrenceburgh, thirty miles long; thirty yards wide at its mouth—heads in the Flat woods to the south of Brookville.

Loughery's Creek—Fifty yards wide at its mouth, and forty

miles long, is the next stream worthy of mention, below the Big Miami, from which it is distant eleven miles.

Indian Creek—Sometimes called Indian Kentucky, and by the Swiss *Venoge*, after a small river in the Pays de Vaud (Switzerland) constitutes the southern limit of the Swiss settlement, eight miles below the mouth of the Kentucky river. It rises in the hills near the south fork of White River, 45 miles north east of Vevay.

Wyandot creek, heads in the range of hills extending in a transverse direction, from near the mouth of Blue river, to the Muddy fork of White River, and falls into the Ohio about equidistant from the falls and Blue river.

Big Blue River, heads still further north; but near the south fork of White river. After running fifty miles southwest, it inclines to the east of south, and enters the Ohio 32 miles below the mouth of Salt river, from the south. Its name indicates the colour of its water, which is of a clear blueish cast; but in quality pure and healthful.

Little Blue River empties into the Ohio 13 miles below the mouth of Big Blue River—it is about forty yards wide at its mouth—its course is from north east to south west. Ten miles below is Sinking creek, fifty yards wide at its mouth.

Anderson's river, sixty miles farther down, is the most considerable stream between Blue river and the Wabash. Below this, are Pegion and Beaver creeks. In addition to the preceding creeks and rivers, a large number of respectable creeks and runs also enter the Ohio, at different points between the Miami and the Wabash, so that that part of Indiana, lying between White river and the Ohio, may be pronounced *well watered*. It is the character of most of the foregoing streams, to possess a brisk current and pure water; the consequence is, an abundance of convenient mill seats, and a salubrious and healthful climate.

The *Wabash* waters the central and western parts of the state. The main branch of this fine river, heads two miles east of old fort St. Mary's and intersects the portage road between Loramie creek and the river St. Mary's, in Darke County, Ohio. There are three other branches, all winding through a rich and extensive country. The first, called *Little river*, heads seven miles south of fort Wayne, and enters the Wabash, about eighty miles below the St. Mary's portage. The second is the Massasinway, which heads in Darke county, Ohio, about half way between forts Greenville and Recovery, and unites with the others, 5 miles below the mouth of Little river. The third is *Eel river*, which issues from several lakes and ponds, eighteen miles west of fort Wayne; it enters the Wabash, eight miles below the mouth of the Massissinway. From the entrance of Eel river, the general course of the Wabash is about ten degrees south of west, to the mouth of Rejoicing river, (85 miles) where it takes a southern direction, to the mouth of Rocky river (forty miles)—here it inclines to the west, to the mouth of the Mascontin, (thirty-six miles)—where it pursues a south eastern course, to Vincennes, (fifty miles)—from this town to the Ohio, its general course is south, (one hundred miles). It is three hundred yards wide at its mouth, and enters the Ohio at right angles. Its length, from its mouth to its extreme source, exceeds five hundred miles. It is nevigable for keel boats, about four hundred miles, to Ouitanon, where there are rapids. From this village small boats can go to within six miles of St. Mary's river; ten of fort Wayne; and eight of the St. Josephs of the Miami-of-the-lakes. Its current is generally gentle above Vincennes—below this town there are several rapids; but not of sufficient magnitude to prevent boats from ascending. The principal rapids are between Deche and White rivers, ten miles below Vincennes.

The tributary waters, which enter from the left bank of the Wabash, and which are called rivers, are:

1. The *Petoka*, from the north east, comes in twenty miles below Vincennes; it heads a few miles south east of the Muddy fork of White river, with which it runs parallel, at the distance of 10 or 12 miles. It is about seventy-five miles in length, and meanders through extensive rich bottoms.

2. *White River* enters four miles above the Petoka, and sixteen below Vincennes. This is an important river, as it reaches nearly across the state in a diagonal direction, watering a vast body of rich land—thirty-five miles from its mouth there is a junction of the two principal forks—the North or Drift wood Branch, interlocks with the north fork of *Whitewater*, and with the branches of Stillwater, a tributary of the Big Miami. The south or Muddy fork heads between the branches of the west fork of *Whitewater*. The country between the two main forks of Whiteriver is watered by the Teakettle branch, which unites with the north fork, twenty miles above the junction of the two principal forks.

3. Deche river, unites with the Wabash, about half way between Vincennes and the mouth of Whiteriver—it comes from

the north east—is a crooked, short stream, but receives several creeks.

4. *Little river*, called by the French *Le Petite Reviere*, winds its devious course, from the north east, among wide spreading bottoms, and enters its estuary a little above Vincennes. Between this river and the Wabash lies an alluvion of several thousand acres, uniformly bottom, of exhaustless fertility.

5. The *St. Marie*, from north east, enters eighteen miles above Vincennes, and is about fifty miles long.

6. *Rocky river*, sixty miles further up, comes in from the east, and interweaves its branches with those of the Main fork of White river. It is one hundred yards wide at its mouth, and has several large forks.

7. *Petite*, or *Little* river, is the only *river* entering from the left, for seventy miles above Rocky river. It comes from the south east, and heads near the sources of Rocky river.

8. *Pomme* river comes in from the south east—forty miles higher up, and twenty miles below the mouth of Massissinway. It rises near the Ohio boundary, a little to the north of the head branches of Whitewater. Besides the rivers above enumerated, which water the left bank of the Wabash, there are an immense number of creeks and runs, affording, in most places a sufficient supply of water. But there are pretty extensive districts between the *Little* and *Rocky* rivers, where water cannot be readily procured.

The right or north west bank of the Wabash, receives a greater number of rivers than the left. Crossing this noble stream, at the mouth of Pomme river, and descending upon its right shore, the first considerable water that obstructs our progress, is *Richard's creek*, from the north west—ten miles below. Ten miles farther enters Rock river, from the north west—its banks are high, and the country around it broken.

Eight miles farther down, is the *Tippacanoe*, rendered famous by the battle upon its banks, between the Americans and Indians, in Nov. 1811. This river heads about thirty miles to the West of fort Wayne. Several of its branches issue from lakes, swamps, and ponds, some of which have *double outlets*, running into the St. Josephs of the Miami-of-the-Lakes. Upon this stream, and on the Wabash, above and below its junction, are Indian villages, and extensive fields. Two Indian roads, leave these towns for the northern lakes—one ascends the right bank of the Wabash, to Ouitanan and fort Wayne; the other ascends the Tippacanoe, and crosses the head branches of the Illinois, to the St. Joseph of lake Michigan.

From the mouth of Tippecanoe, we successively pass Pine, and Redwood creeks; Rejoicing, or Vermillion Jaune, Little Vermillion, Erabliere, Duchat and Brouette rivers, at the distance of from ten to fifteen miles from each other, and all coming from the west or north west; mostly small, and having their heads in the Illinois territory.

Whitewater, rises near the eastern boundary line, twelve miles west of fort Greenville, and nearly parallel with this line, at the distance of from six to ten miles, and watering in its progress, twenty-two townships, in Wayne, Franklin, and Dearborn counties. At Brookville, thirty miles from its entrance into the Miami, it receives the West fork, which heads into the Flat woods, thirty miles west of that village, and interlocks with the branches of White river. This beautiful little river waters nearly one million of acres of fine land, and owes its name to the unusual transparency of its water. A fish or a pebble can be seen at the depth of twenty feet. It is sufficiently cool for drinking during summer. The inhabitants living upon its banks, contend that its water is less buoyant than that of any other river; and endeavored to dissuade me from bathing in it. I nevertheless, swam several times across the stream, where it was one hundred yards wide; and, although an experienced swimmer, was not a little fatigued by the exercise. But I ascribed the effect to the *coldness* rather than to any extraordinary buoyancy of the water.

One of the eastern branches of this river, heads six miles east of the state line, in the State of Ohio; and Greenville creek, a tributary of the Stillwater fork of the Big Miami, heads about the same distance within the state of Indiana.

The north eastern part of the state is watered by the St. Josephs of the Miami-of-the-lakes, and its tributaries—this river heads about sixty miles to the north west of fort Wayne, and forms a junction with the St. Mary's, just above this post. Panther's creek, from the south, is its largest fork. Its remote branches interlock with those of the rivers Raisin, Black, St. Josephs of lake Michigan, and Eel river.

That part of the state bordering on the Michigan territory, is liberally watered by the head branches of the river Raisin, (of lake Erie;) the numerous forks of Black river, (of lake Michigan;) and the St. Josephs of lake Michigan—the latter heads near, and interlocks with the branches of Eel river; and pursues a serpentine course, seventy miles, through the northern part of Indiana.

The river Chemin, Big and Little Kennomic, all of which fall into Lake Michigan; the Theakaki, Kickapoo, and a part of the chief branch of the Illinois, all wind through the north western section of the state; and all, except the last, are entirely within its boundaries; the three first run from south to north; the latter south and south west. Besides, the country is chequered by numerous creeks. The Vermillion of the Illinois rises in Indiana, near the sources of Tippacanoe.

The northern half of the state is a country of lakes—38 of which, from two to ten miles in length, are delineated on the latest maps; but the actual number probably exceeds one hundred—many of these, however, are mere ponds, less than one mile in length. Some have *two distinct outlets;* one running into the northern lakes; the other into the Mississippi.

The phenomenon of waters with double outlets, is not uncommon. The great Ganges, the greater Burrumpooter, and the great river of Ava, all rise and issue from the same fountain—so do the Rhine and the Rhone; the Suir, the Nore, and the Barrow, in Ireland, spring from the same well—and after traversing a vast range of country, in three opposite directions, re-unite and form one basin, in Waterford Harbor; there are two rivers in the Isthmus of Panama, whose head waters are not farther apart than the Ouisconsin and Fox river; one stretches into the southern ocean; the other into the Mexican sea.

The greater part of these lakes, are situated between the head waters of the two St. Josephs, Black river, Raisin, Tippacanoe, and Eel rivers.

ASPECT OF THE COUNTRY.

A range of hills, called the knobs, extends from the falls of the Ohio, to the Wabash, nearly in a south western direction, which, in many places, produces a broken and uneven surface. North of these hills, lie the Flat woods, seventy miles wide and reaching nearly to the Ouitanan country. Bordering all the principal streams, except the Ohio, there are strips of bottom and prairie land; both together are from three to six miles in width. Between the Wabash and lake Michigan, the country is mostly champaign, abounding alternately, with wood lands, prairies, lakes, and swamps.

A range of hills run parallel with the Ohio, from the mouth

of the Big Miami, to Blue river, alternately approaching to within a few rods, and receding to the distance of two miles, but broken at short intervals by numerous creeks. Immediately below Blue river, the hills disappear, and the horizon presents nothing to view but an immense tract of level land, covered with a heavy growth of timber.

That part of the state lying west of the Ohio boundary line, north of the head branches of White river, east and south of the Wabash, has been described by the conductors of expeditions against the Indians, as a "country containing much good land; but intersected at the distance of four or six miles, with long, narrow swamps, boggy and mirey, the soil of which is a stiff blue clay."

North of the Wabash, between Tippacanoe and Ouitanan, the banks of the streams are high, abrupt, and broken—and the land well timbered, except on the prairies.

Between the Plein and Theakaki, the country is flat, wet, and swampy, interspersed with prairies of an inferior quality of soil.

In going from the Ohio to the Wabash, say from Clark's ville or Madison to Vincennes, you ascend from two to three hundred feet before you find yourself at the top of the *last* bank of the Ohio. You have then before you a strip of country, twenty miles wide, tolerably level, except where gullied by the actions of streams. This brings you at the foot of the "*Knobs*," which are at least 500 feet higher than the land in your rear; after this you pass no very tedious hills, until you find yourself within three miles of Vincennes. In travelling from this place to the Ohio, you are not sensible of *ascending* to the height at which you find yourself, on the summit of the "*Knobs*," from which you have a boundless prospect to the east. You can distinctly trace, with the eye, at the distance of twenty miles, the deep, serpentine vale of the Ohio, and the positions of New-Lexington, Corydon, and Louisville, in Kentucky.

PRAIRIES.

There are two kinds of these meadows—the *river* and *upland* prairies: the first are found upon the margins of rivers, and are *bottoms* destitute of timber; most of these exhibit vestiges of former cultivation. The last are plains, from thirty to one hundred feet higher than the alluvial bottoms; and are far more numerous and extensive; but are indeterminate in size and figure—since some are not larger than a common field, while others expand beyond the reach of the eye, or the limits of the horizon. They are usually bounded by groves of lofty forest trees; and not unfrequently adorned with "islands," or copses of small trees, affording an agreeable shade for man and beast. In spring and summer they are covered with a luxuriant growth of grass, and fragrant flowers, from six to eight feet high, through which it is very fatiguing to force one's way with any degree of celerity. The soil of these plains is often as deep and as fertile as the best bottoms. The prairies bordering the Wabash, are particularly rich—wells have been sunk in them, where the vegetable soil was *twenty-two feet deep,* under which was a stratum of fine white sand, containing horizontal lines, plainly indicating to the geologist, the gradual subsidence of water. Yet the ordinary depth is from two to five feet.

The several expeditions against the Indians, during the late war, enabled many of our officers, to become extensively acquainted with the geography of the Indiana and Michigan territories.

An officer, who conducted several expeditions against the Indians, and who was at the Putawatomie villages, on the St. Joseph's of lake Michigan, writes to me as follows:

"The country [between fort Wayne and the St. Joseph's of lake Michigan] in every direction, is beautiful, presenting a fine prospect. There are no hills to be seen; a champaign country, the greater part prairie, affording inexhaustible grazing, and presenting the most delightful natural meadows, and the grass cured would be almost equal to our hay; there are also, vast forests of valuable timber, and the soil exceedingly rich. The rivers have their sources in swamps, and sometimes form delightful inland lakes. It is not unfrequent to see two opposite streams supplied by the same water or lake, one running into the waters of the Mississippi, and the other into the northern lakes. Neither China nor Holland ever had such natural advantages for inland water communications."

Another officer, who had opportunities of seeing and exploring the country between the Wabash and lake Michigan, describes it as a country, "admirably calculated for the convenience of inland navigation. The sources of the rivers are invariably in swamps or lakes, and the country around them perfectly level. A trifling expence would open a navigable communication between Eel river, and a branch of the Little St. Joseph's; the two St. Joseph's; the Raisin of lake Erie, and the Lenoir (Black river) of lake Michigan. Small lakes are discovered in every part of this extensive and romantic country. We found them covered with ducks, and other water fowls. For the diversion of fishing, we had no leisure; consequently, I am not able to inform you whether they abound with fish, but presume they do, as many of their outlets empty into the tributaries of the great lakes.

"The country around the head branches of Eel river, Panther's creek, and St. Joseph's, (of the Miami)[1] is generally low and swampy; and too wet for cultivation. But even in that quarter there are many beautiful situations. The timber is oak, hickory, black walnut, beach, sugar maple, elm, and honey locust. The wood lands line the water courses; but branch out frequently into the prairies.

"The immense prairies on the south bank of the St. Josephs, (of lake Michigan) afforded us many rich, beautiful, and picturesque views. They are from one to ten miles wide; and of unequal lengths. They are as level as lakes; and in point of fertility, not inferior to the lands around Lexington, Ken. or the best bottoms of the Ohio.

We crossed two, whose southern limits were not descernable to the naked eye; they were doubtless capacious enough to form two or three townships each; and perfectly dry, being at least one hundred feet above the river bottoms. These natural meadows are covered with a tall grass; and are separated by strips of woods, containing oak, maple, locust, lyn, poplar, plum, ash, and crab-apple. In these wood lands, we generally meet with creeks, runs or springs; but *never* in the open prairies, unless in wet and rainy seasons, when the waters form temporary sluggish brooks, whereever there is sufficient descent for the purpose.

"The St. Josephs [of lake Michigan] is a charming river, and navigable to within a short distance of the river of the same name. Its current is brisk, and at the upper villages, one hundred yards wide. The Indians have cleared large fields upon its banks: several Canadian French families reside with them. Their manners and habits of life are semi-savage.

"All the rivers in the interior of Indiana and Michigan, have spacious bottoms, and they uniformly wander from the line of their courses, so that in making fifty miles progress, in a direct line, they water one hundred miles of territory by their sinuosities. By these frequent bends, the length of *river coast*, and the

---

1. Maumee.

quantity of bottom land is nearly doubled, which amply compensates for extra toil and expence of navigation."

Mr. D. Buck, of Auburn, (N. Y.) who assisted in the survey of twenty-two townships, six miles square each, writes to his correspondent as follows:

I have seen a great deal of excellent land; the prairies on the Wabash in the vicinity of fort Harrison, exceed every thing for richness of soil and beauty of situation, I ever beheld. The prairies are from one to five miles wide, bordering on the river, and from one to twelve in length; the streams which run into the Wabash, divide one prairie from another; on these streams are strips of woods from half a mile to a mile wide, the timber of which is excellent; the soil of the prairies is a black vegetable mould, intermixed with fine sand, and sometimes gravel. In choosing a situation for a farm, it is important so to locate a tract, as to have half prairie and half wood land; by which means you will have a plantation cleared to your hand.

The new purchase contains one hundred and twenty townships, or 2,765,040, acres. The lands sell very high in the neighborhood of Fort Harrison, for it is the most delightful situation for a town on the Wabash—the soil is the richest of any in the state. This will undoubtedly become the seat of a new county, and that at no remote period. The fort is garrisoned by one hundred and fifty riflemen, of the regular army, under the command of Major Morgan. There are six families living in log cabins, near the fort, who improve congress lands. They have been here five years. Wherever they have cultivated the ground, it produces abundantly. Besides these, there are several Indian traders—Great numbers of Indians resort hither to sell their peltries. The tribes who frequent this place and reside on the Wabash, are the Kickapoos, Miamis, Putawatomies, Shawanœse, Weaws, and Delawares. They encamp in the woods convenient to water, where they build wigwams. We came across a great many while surveying in the wilderness—they appeared friendly, and offered us honey and venison. Our business has principally been near the Indian boundary line, sixty miles from any white settlements. The woods abound with deer, bears, wolves, and wild turkies. About three-eighths of the land we surveyed is excellent for most kinds of produce; the remainder is good for grazing, but too hilly, flat, or wet, for grain.

The lands on White river are well watered with springs and brooks. You can hardly find a quarter section without water;

the country in this quarter is, in many places, hilly and broken, and in some parts stony. Limestone is most predominant; but there are quarries of free stone. Although the country is well watered, good mill seats are scarce. There can be a sufficiency of small mills for the accommodation of the inhabitants. Steam mills, without doubt, will be in operation as soon as the country is sufficiently settled for the purpose of flouring for exportation.

"There are some excellent tracts of land in Indiana and Illinois—corn is raised pretty easy; and stock with little attention, and in some places with little or no fodder. This country is full of prairies; some of which are excellent land. The timber around them consists principally oak, of which the inhabitants make most of their rails, and sometimes draw them three miles. These prairies are destitute of water; but it can be obtained by digging twenty or thirty feet. Wheat grows stout; but the grain is not so plump as it is in the state of New York."

"It is difficult building in Knox county, and always will be, on account of the scarcity of mill seats. Horse mills are common; the miller takes one eighth part of the grain for toll; customers finding their own horses."

He further states, that the two branches of Whiteriver are navigable with boats in high water for the distance of 130 miles; that coal mines are numerous near the Wabash. Iron ore is found on Whiteriver. That wheat yields the inhabitants, who are neat farmers, 68 lbs. a bushel, and never gets winter-killed or smutty; the only difficulty they experience in its culture is, that the land in many places is too rich until it has been improved. Apple trees bear every year. Peaches some years do exceedingly well; so do cherries, currents, and most kinds of fruit. Wheat is 75 cents a bushel; flour $3 a hundred—delivered at Fort Harrison four; corn 25 cents a bushel—pork $4—beef $4; butter and cheese from 12½ to 25 cents; honey 50 cents per gallon. Maple sugar 25 cents. European goods exorbitantly high.

Reptiles and venomous serpents are not numerous. A few rattle snakes and some copperheads comprise all that are dangerous.

The banks of the Wabash are in many places, subject to be overflowed in high water. When the Ohio is at full height its waters set back and inundate the bottoms of the Wabash to the distance of four or five miles.

Mr. Buck, who descended this river in March, 1816, says, "I came down the river at the highest stage of water; the banks were completely overflowed almost all the way. The prairies extending to the river appeared like small seas; and in many places, it was with difficulty that we could keep our boat from running into the woods. The distance from Fort Harrison to Vincennes by water, is 120 miles; by land only 65. Below the fort the river is very crooked to its mouth; above, as far as the Indian title is extinguished, it is quite strait in a north and south direction. The breadth of the river (at Vincennes) is from 40 to 70 rods. It overflows its banks every spring, except at a few places where there are handsome situations for towns. It inundates a considerable extent of country opposite Vincennes. The floods do not last long; nor are they dangerous, if people will use a little precaution in removing their stock and swine.

"The winters are mild, compared with those of the northern states. By all accounts, last winter was uncommonly severe for this country. There were three or four weeks of freezing weather, during which the snow was from six to nine inches deep. The Wabash was frozen over so that it was crossed in many places upon the ice with safety. I think that autumnal frosts are earlier here than in the western counties of New York; but the weather is very fine till Christmas; then changeable until about the middle of February, when winter ›reaks up, and spring soon commences. Peaches are in blossom by the first of March, and by the 10th of April, the forests are "clad in green." The flowering shrubs and trees are in full bloom some days before the leaves get their growth, which gives the woods a very beautiful appearance."

"Salt, at and above Vincennes is two dollars a bushel, though considerable quantities are made at the U. S. Saline 30 miles below the mouth of the Wabash, in the Illinois territory, where it is sold for one dollar a bushel. The chief supply comes from the salt wor s on the Great Kenhaway.—There have been salt wells sunk, (by boring) near the Ohio, to the depth of 500 feet, where the water is said to be very strong. There are likewise salt springs on the Indian lands, not far from the northern boundary of the new purchase."

POPULATION, COUNTIES, VILLAGES.

Population of Indiana in November, 1815.

Counties.	No. of Inhabitants.
Wayne	6,290
Franklin	7,970
Dearborn	4,426
Jefferson	4,093

Counties.	No. of Inhabitants.
Washington	6,606
Harrison	6,769
Gibson	5,330
Knox	6,800
Switzerland	3,500
Clark	7,000
Posey	3,000
Perry	3,000
Warwick	3,000
Total	68,784

DEARBORN COUNTY,

Is bounded east by the state of Ohio, south by the Ohio river, west by Switzerland county, and north by Franklin county. It is well watered by Tanner's Hougelane's and Loughery's creeks, Whitewater and the head branches of Indian Kentucky. The south part of this county is broken; the north end level, being in the Flat Woods. The Ohio bottoms are low but fertile. The timber in the middle and northern parts is oak, hickory, poplar, and sugar maple.

Lawrenceburgh—Stands on the bank of the Ohio, two miles below the mouth of the Big Miami. It has not flourished for several years past, owing, principally to its being subject to inundation, when the Ohio is high. A new town called Edinburgh, half a mile from the river, on a more elevated situation promises to eclypse it.

Rising Sun—Is delightfully situated on the second bank of the Ohio, with a gradual descent to the river. It contains thirty or forty houses, and is half way between Vevay and Lawrenceburgh. It has a post office, and a floating mill anchored abreast of the town. It has had a very rapid growth, and will probably become a place of considerable trade.

FRANKLIN,

Has the state of Ohio on the east, Dearborn county south and Indian lands west and north. It is one of the best counties in the state, and was established about four years ago. It is principally watered by Whitewater and its branches, upon which there is some of the best bottom lands in the western country and has been the centre of an ancient population, as is proved by the great number of mounds and fortifications, to be seen on the bottoms and hills. There are no prairies in this county. Both sides of Whitewater, from its mouth, to Brookville, are tolerably well settled. Here are some of the finest farms to be met with in the western country. A number of mills have been erected. The upland is pretty level, and the principal timber white oak, hickory and black walnut. The oak trees are remarkably tall and handsome; and well suited either for rails, staves, or square timber. The soil is free from stones, and easily cleared and ploughed; producing fine crops of wheat and corn. In July last, I saw several cornfields, which in the preceding March, were in a state of nature with the trees and brushwood all growing.

Yet the corn looked as flourishing as it did upon the bottoms. In the woods, on the bottoms of Whitewater, I discovered several *natural wells*, formed in a most singular manner. They were from ten to fifteen feet deep, substantially curbed, being nothing more nor less than parts of the upright trunks of the largest sycamores, which has been hollowed out by the hand of time. To explain: When these trees were in their infancy, their roots spread near the surface of the ground; but in the course of time, successive inundations and the annual decay of a luxuriant vegetation, have formed a stratum of the richest soil, from ten to fifteen feet deep, over the roots of these venerable trees. At length these vegetable Mathusalems die, and are prostrated by the winds of heaven, and where once stood a tree of giant growth, now yawns a well scooped out by nature's hand.

Genseng grows in the bottoms to a perfection and size, I never before witnessed; and so thick, where the hogs have not thinned it, that one could dig a bushel in a very short time. Upon the spurs of the hills, and the poorest soil, is found the wild columbo root, and is easily procured in any quantity. There are two villages in this county—Brookville and Harrison.

Brookville—Is pleasantly situated in the forks of Whitewater, thirty miles north of Lawrenceburgh and the Ohio river; twenty miles south of Salisbury[2]—about forty-two north west of Cincinnati, and twenty-five from Hamilton, "It was laid out in the year 1811; but no improvements were made until the succeeding year, and then but partially; owing to the unsettled state of the frontiers, and its vicinity to the Indian boundary, being not more than fifteen miles. The late war completely checked the emigration to the country, and consequently the town ceased to improve.

2. The county seat of Wayne county at that time.

At the close of the war, there was not more than ten or twelve dwelling houses in the place; but since that period, its rapid accession of wealth and population has been unexampled in the western country.

"There are now in the town upwards of eighty buildings, exclusive of shops, stables, and out houses, the greater number of which were built during the last season. The buildings are generally frame, and a great part of them handsomely painted. There are within the precints of the town, one grist mill and two saw mills, two fulling mills, three carding machines, one printing office,* one silversmith, two saddlers, two cabinet makers, one hatter, two taylors, four boot and shoemakers, two tanners and curriers, one chairmaker, one cooper, five taverns and seven stores. There are also a jail, a market house, and a handsome brick court house nearly finished.

"The ground on which the town stands, is composed of a rich and sandy loam, covering a thin stratum of clay, underneath which is a great body of gravel and pebbles—consequently the streets are but seldom muddy, and continue so but for a short time. The public square and a great part of the town stands on a beautiful level, that is elevated between eighty feet above the level of the river: and, in short, the situation of the town, the cleanlines of the streets, the purity of the waters, and the aspect of the country around, all combine to render it one of the most healthy and agreeable situations in the western country.

"There are, perhaps, few places that possess equal advantages, or that present a more flattering prospect of future wealth and importance than this. As a situation for manufactories, it is unequalled; the two branches of Whitewater affording a continued succession of the best sites for the erection of water works, from their junction almost to their sources, and many valuable situations may be found below the town, on the main river.

"The country watered by this stream is inferior to none. Along the river and all its tributary streams, are extensive and fertile bottoms, bounded by hills of various heights; and immediately from the top of these, commences a level and rich country, timbered with poplar, walnut, beech, sugar tree, oak, ash, hickory, elm, buckeye, &c. and a variety of shrubs and underbrush. The

*At this press is published a respectable and well conducted weekly Journal, entitled "*The Plain Dealer*," edited by B. F. MORRIS, Esq. to whose pen and the politeness of N. D. GALLION, Post Master, I am indebted for the above interesting and correct account of Brookville, and which I have preferred to my own.

soil of this land is peculiarly adapted to the culture of small grain, and for grazing. The last harvest produced several crops of wheat, in the neighborhood of this place that weighed from sixty-five to sixty-eight pounds per bushel; and the best crops of grass I have ever seen, are produced without the aid of manure. Corn, oats, rye, flax, hemp, sweet and Irish potatoes, &c. &c. are produced in abundance.

"During the last season, 1816, many successful experiments were made in rearing tobacco, and the soil has been pronounced by good judges, to be as congenial to its growth, as the best lands in the state of Virginia, Kentucky, or the Carolinas. As an evidence of the fertility of the country, corn and oats are selling at twenty-five, rye at forty, and wheat at seventy-five cents per bushel, beef at three and a half, and pork at four cents per pound. The country is well supplied with good water, from a great number of springs, and water may also be obtained in almost any place by digging to a moderate depth.

"Another source from which this town must eventually derive great importance, is the ease and small expence with which the navigation of Whitewater, from the junction of the forks, can be so far improved as to carry out into the Ohio, all articles that may be raised for exportation.

"To the north and north west of this place, is an extensive and fertile country, that is fast growing into importance; and in wealth and population, will soon be inferior to but few districts on the waters of the Ohio; and, owing to the geographical situation of the country, all the intercourse of the inhabitants with the Ohio river, must be through this place."

I was at Brookville in July last, on business, and was highly pleased with the amenity of its situation, and the industry, intelligence, and healthful appearance of the inhabitants.—The road from thence to Harrison, was very fine.

Harrison.—This village is situated on the north side of Whitewater, eight miles from its mouth, eighteen north east [south-east] of Brookville, and in the centre of a large tract of some of the best land in the state. More than one half of the village stands on the Ohio side of the state line. There are about thirty-five houses, mostly new. A considerable number of the inhabitants are from the state of New York. Mr. Looker, from Saratoga county, Mr. Crane, from Schenectady, and Mr. Allen, the post master, from New Jersey, own the surrounding lands. They have all very fine and valuable farms, worth from forty to sixty dollars an acre. The settlement was commenced about sixteen years ago. The bottoms are here from one to two miles wide; the soil remarkably deep and rich, and the woods free from brushwood. The trees are of a moderate growth, but straight and thrifty. The traces of ancient population cover the earth in every direction. On the bottoms are a great number of mounds, very unequal in point of age and size. The small ones are from two to four feet above the surface, and the growth of timber upon them small, not being over one hundred years old; while the others are from ten to thirty feet high, and frequently contain trees of the largest diameters. Besides, the bones found in the small ones will bear removal, and exposure to the air, while those in the large ones are rarely capable of sustaining their own weight; and are often found in a decomposed or powdered state. There is a large mound in Mr. Allen's field, about twenty feet high, sixty feet in diameter at the base, which contains a greater proportion of bones, than any one I ever before examined, as almost every shovel full of dirt would contain several fragments of a human skeleton. When on Whitewater, I obtained the assistance of several of the inhabitants, for the purpose of making a thorough examination of the internal structure of these monuments of the ancient populousness of the country. We examined from fifteen to twenty. In some, whose height were from ten to fifteen feet, we could not find more than four or five skeletons. In *one*, not the least appearance of a human bone was to be found. Others were so full of bones, as to warrent the belief, that they originally contained at least one hundred dead bodies; children of different ages, and the full grown, appeared to have been piled together promiscuously. We found several scull, leg and thigh bones, which plainly indicated, that their possessors were men of gigantic stature. The scull of one skeleton was one fourth of an inch thick; and the teeth remarkably even, sound and handsome, all firmly planted. The fore teeth were very deep, and not so wide as those of the generality of white people. Indeed, there seemed a great degree of regularity in the form of the teeth, in all the mounds. In the progress of our researches, we obtained ample testimony, that these masses of earth were formed by a *savage people*. Yet, doubtless possessing a greater degree of civilization than the present race of Indians. We discovered a piece of glass weighing five ounces, resembling the bottom of a tumbler, but concave; several *stone axes*, with grooves near their heads to receive a withe, which unquestionably served as helves; arrows formed from flint, almost exactly similar to those in use among the present Indians; several pieces of earthen ware; some appeared to be parts of vessels holding six or eight gallons; others were obviously fragments of jugs jars, and cups; some were plain, while others were curiously ornamented with figures of birds and beasts, drawn while the clay or material of which they were made was soft and before the process of glazing was performed. The *glazier's art* appears to have been well understood by the potters who manufactured this aboriginal *crockery*. The smaller vessels were made of pounded or pulverized muscle shells, mixed with an earthen or flinty substance, and the large ones of clay and sand. There was no appearance of *iron;* one of the sculls was found pierced by an arrow, which was still sticking in it, driven about half way through before its force was spent. It was about six inches long. The subjects of this mound were doubtless killed in battle, and hastily buried. In digging to the bottom of them we invariably came to a stratum of ashes, from six inches to two feet thick, which rests on the original earth. These ashes contain coals, fragments of brands, and pieces of *calcined bones*. From the quantity of ashes and bones, and the appearance of the earth underneath, it is evident that large fires must have been kept burning for several days previous to commencing the mound, and that a considerable number of human victims must have been sacrificed, by burning, on the spot! Prisoners of war were no doubt selected for this horrid purpose. Perhaps the custom of the age rendered it a signal honor, for the chieftains and most active worriors to be interred, by way of triumph, on the ashes of their enemies, whom they had vanquished in war. If this was not the case, the mystery can only be solved by supposing that the fanaticism of the priests and prophets excited their besotted followers to voluntary self-devotion. The soil of the mounds is always different from that of the immediately surrounding earth being uniformly of a soft vegetable mould or loam, and containing no stones or other hard substances, to "press upon the dead and disturb their repose."

Almost every building lot in Harrison village contains a small mound; and some as many as three. On the neighboring hills, north east of the town, are a number of the remains of stone houses. They were covered with soil, brush, and full grown trees. We cleared away the earth, roots and rubbish from one of them, and found it to have been anciently occupied as a dwelling. It was about twelve feet square; the walls had fallen nearly to the foundation. They appeared to have been built of rough stones, like our stone walls. Not the least trace of any iron tools having been employed to smooth the face of them, could be perceived. At one end of the building, we came to a regular hearth, containing ashes and coals; before which we found the bones of eight persons of different ages, from a small child to the heads of the family. The positions of their skeletons clearly indicated, that their deaths were sudden and simultaneous. They were probably asleep, with their feet towards the fire, when destroyed by an enemy, an earthquake, or pestilence.

WAYNE.

This county is bounded on the east by the state of Ohio, on the south by the county of Franklin, on the west and north by *Indian lands*. It is watered by the north fork of White-water, the head brooks of the north fork of Whiteriver, sources of Rocky river, Massissinway, and main branch of the Wabash. It is very extensive, of a level surface, well timbered, contains fine lands, and has been settled ten years. Its products are, Indian corn, wheat, rye, oats, and tobacco.

Salisbury.—Lies thirty miles north of Brookville; contains about thirty five houses, two stores and two taverns. It is at present the seat of justice for Wayne county; but Centerville, a new village, being more central, threatens to become its competitor for that privilege.

SWITZERLAND,

Is bounded west by Jefferson, south by the Ohio river, north in part by Indian lands, and east by Dearborn county. Its surface is, in some places, broken by the Ohio and Silver creek hills, which, however, are of a pretty good soil. It is watered by Venoge and Plum creeks, and several small runs; some running into the Ohio, and others into Whiteriver.

New Switzerland.—The settlement of New Switzerland was commenced by a few emigrants, from the Pays de Vaud, in the spring of 1805. It extends from about three quarters of a mile above the mouth of Plum creek, down the river to the mouth of Indian creek, now called Venoge; a distance of about four miles and a half, fronting the river, and originally extended back far enough to cover 3,700 acres of land; about half of which was purchased under a law in favor of J. J. Dufour, and his associates, upon a credit of twelve years. Subsequent purchases have been made on the usual terms, excepting an extension of credit, in order to encourage the cultivation of the vine. There has been a gradual accession of numbers to this interesting colony. As early as 1810, they had eight acres of vineyard, from which they made 2,400 gallons of wine, which, in its crude state, was thought by good judges, to be superior to the claret of Bordeaux. A part of this wine was made out of the Madeira grape. They have now greatly augmented the quantity of their vineyard grounds, which, when bearing, present to the eye of the observer the most interesting agricultural prospect, perhaps, ever witnessed in the United States. The principal proprietors of the vineyards, are the Messrs. Dufours, Bettens, Morerod, Siebenthal. Mr. J. J. Dufour arrived from Switzerland in September last, with a large number of emigrants. The Swiss speak the French language in its purity; and are a temperate, industrious and polished people, fond of music and dancing, and warmly attached to the United States. They are rapidly extending their vineyards; they also cultivate Indian corn, wheat, potatoes, hemp, flax, and other articles necessary to farmers—but in quantities barely sufficient for domestic use. Some of their women manufacture *straw hats.* They are made quite different from the common straw bonnets, by tying the straws together, instead of plaiting and sewing the plaits. They are sold in great numbers in the neighboring settlements, and in the Mississippi and Indiana territories.

Vevay.—Half a mile above the upper vineyards, was laid out in 1813, but was a forest in 1814, till the first of February, when the first house was built.

During the same year forty four others, four stores, and two taverns were erected, and the village selected as a suitable place for the seat of justice for Switzerland county. There are at present eighty-four dwelling houses, besides thirty four mechanics' shops, of different professions. The court house, jail, and school house are of brick. A brick market house and church are building. It has eight stores, three taverns, two lawyers, two physicians, and a printing office printing a weekly newspaper, called the *Indiana Register.* There is a library of 300 volumes; and a literary society in which are several persons of genius, science, and literature.

This delightful village is situated on the second bank of the Ohio, twenty-five feet above high water mark, and is nearly equidistant from Cincinnati, Lexington, and Louisville, or forty five miles from each. The view of the Ohio is extensive, being eight miles. The country in the rear is broken but fertile. The climate is mild, and the sweet potatoe is cultivated with success. Cotton would doubtless do well. There are several roads which diverge from the settlement. Three mails arrive weekly.

JEFFERSON,

Is bounded on the east by Switzerland county, on the south by the river Ohio, on the west by the county of Clark, on the north by Indian lands. It contains a great proportion of excellent land. It is watered by several small creeks running into the Ohio, and by the Mescatitak, a branch of the south fork of Whiteriver, which heads within five miles of the Ohio river.

New Lexington.—This flourishing town is famous for having produced the pretended monied institution, called "The Lexington Indiana Manufacturing Company," which has exploded. It is situated in a rich settlement, sixteen miles nearly west of Madison, and five miles east of the Knobs; and contains about forty houses, some of them handsome, brick and frame, and others built with hewn logs, in the true western style. There is a post-office, and printing establishment, in which is printed the "*Western Eagle.*" The surface of the surrounding country is for several miles, sufficiently *rolling* to give the water of the creeks and runs a brisk motion. The stones towards the Ohio are calcareous: to the west and north west, clayey slate. The soil is very productive. In the vicinity of this place, the enterprising General M'Farland has, with astonishing preseverance, dug to the depth of nearly five hundred feet, in quest of salt water. His exertions have been crowned with success, inasmuch as the water exceeds in strength any salt water in the western country, and affords from three to four bushels of salt, to the hundred gallons of water.

Madison.—This is the seat of justice for the county, and is situated on the upper bank of the Ohio, thirty miles below Vevay, contains sixty or seventy houses, mostly small and new. The banking institution, called the "Farmers' and Mechanics' Bank," is established here.

CLARK,

Is bounded east by Jefferson county, south by the Ohio river, west by the counties of Harrison and Washington, north by the county of Jackson and Indian lands. It is watered by several creeks running into the Ohio, such as Silver creek, Cane run, &c. and several brooks falling into the Mescatitak branch of the south fork of Whiteriver. Its surface is considerably broken in the central parts of the county. Hickory and oak are the prevailing timber. It is thought that this country contains many valuable minerals; some have been discovered; copperas is found in the high banks of Silver creek, about two miles from its mouth. A medicinal spring, near Jeffersonville, has been much frequented—its waters are strongly impregnated with sulphur and iron. The reed cane grows on the flats.

Charleston—The seat of justice for Clark county, is situated in the centre of a rich and thriving settlement, thirty-two miles south of west from Madison, two miles from the Ohio river, and fourteen from the falls. This village, like many others in the western country, has sprung up suddenly by the magical influence of American enterprize, excited into action by a concurrence of favorable circumstances.

Jeffersonville—Stands on the bank of the Ohio, nearly opposite Louisville, and a little above the falls. It contains about one hundred and thirty houses, brick, frame and hewn logs. The bank of the river is high, which affords a fine view of Louisville, the falls, and the opposite hills. Just below the town is a fine eddy for boats. A post-office, and a land-office, for the sale of the United States' lands, are established, and it promises to become a place of wealth, elegance and extensive business. The most eligible boat channel is on the Indiana side of the Ohio.

Clarksville—Lies at the lower end of the falls; and, although commenced as early as 1783, does not contain above forty houses, most of them old and decayed. It has a safe capacious harbor for boats.

New Albany—A short distance below Clarksville, has been puffed throughout the Union; but has not yet realized the anticipations of the proprietors.

HARRISON,

Is bounded east by Clark county, south by the Ohio, west by the new county of Perry, and north by Washington. Its principal stream is Blue river, which is navigable for boats about forty miles. Gen. Harrison owns a large tract of land upon this river, and has erected a grist and saw mill, about eight miles from its mouth, on a durable spring brook, running into it. On both banks of this river are large quantities of oak and locust timber. Gen. H. had it in contemplation, shortly before the commencement of the late war, to establish a ship yard at its mouth, where there is a convenient situation for building and launching vessels.

Corydon—The seat of justice for Harrison county, is situated twenty-five miles nearly west from Jeffersonville, and ten miles from the Ohio river. It was commenced in 1809, and is the seat of government for the state. The selection of this place by the legislature, as the seat of government for the period of eight years, has excited great dissatisfaction in other parts of the state. It has rapidly encreased since the meeting of the state convention, in July, 1816. The *Indiana Gazette* is printed in this village.

WASHINGTON

County is bounded on the east by Clark county, on the south by the county of Harrison, on the west by the county of Orange, and on the north by the county of Jackson. It is watered by the south fork of Whiteriver—is moderately hilly, and was established in 1814.

Salem—Is the only village deserving notice; and is situated thirty-four miles north of Corydon, and twenty-five nearly west from Jeffersonville, on the Vincennes road.

JACKSON

Lies west of Clark and Jefferson counties, north of Washington, east of Orange, and south of the Indian country. It is watered by Whiteriver and its tributary creeks, and was set off in 1815. *Brownstown* is the seat of justice; and is situated twenty-five miles east of north from Salem.

ORANGE

County is bounded by the counties of Washington and Jackson on the east; by Harrison and Perry on the south; by the county of Knox on the west; and by Indian lands on the north. It has a rich soil, and is well watered by Whiteriver and Petoka. A gentleman, who surveyed several townships in the county, declares it to be equal in point of fertility of soil, and excellence of water, to any county in the state. "The surface is agreeably undulating. The timber on the hills consist of black walnut, oak, hickory, ash, sugar maple; on the low grounds, basswood, pawpaw, honey locust, buckeye and spicewood; besides, grape vines, and a variety of shrubs. We occasionally met with rattlesnakes and copperheads on the uplands, but never in the bottoms. The most common game are deer and bear. There is a coal-mine a little below the forks of Whiteriver; besides, we met with frequent signs of minerals; and the needle often refused to settle. The bottoms of Whiteriver are nearly as wide as those of the Wabash, and contain evidence of having been formerly inhabited by Indians, as the remains of their cabins and corn-hills are yet visible. The new village of Paoli is the county seat. It is forty miles nearly east of Vincennes; and thirty north of west from Salem."

KNOX.

This county is bounded by Orange on the east; by the county of Gibson on the south; by the Wabash river on the west; and by Indian lands on the north. This is the oldest and most populous county in the state. It is watered by the Deche, Whiteriver, Wabash, Littleriver, St. Marie, Busseron, Raccoon and Ambush creeks. It has upwards of 200,000 acres of the best prairie and bottom land, and is rapidly encreasing in inhabitants and improvements.

Vincennes.—The seat of justice for Knox county, stands on the east bank of the Wabash, one hundred miles from its junction with the Ohio, in a direct line, but nearly two hundred by the courses of the river; and one hundred and twenty west of the falls of Ohio. It contains about one hundred houses, most of which are small and scattering; some have a neat and handsome aspect, while others are built in an uncouth manner, having a frame skeleton filled up with mud and stick walls, similar to some of the old German houses on the Hudson and Mohawk rivers. The best buildings are a brick tavern, jail, and academy. The latter, which is an honor to the state, stands in the public square, and is under the direction of the Rev. Mr. Scott, a presbyterian minister, a gentleman of letters; yet, hitherto, his pupils have not been numerous. He teaches the ancient languages, mathematics, &c. The meeting house, a plain building, stands on the prairie, one mile from the town. The plan of the town is handsomely designed; the streets are wide and cross each other at right angles. Almost every house has a garden in its rear, with high, substantial picket fences to prevent the thefts of the Indians. General Harrison is one of the principal proprietors of the soil. The common field near the town contains nearly 5,000 acres, of excellent prairie soil, which has been cultivated for more than half a century, and yet retains its pristine fertility. The United States have a land office for the disposal of the public lands; and formerly kept a small garrison, in a little stockade near the bank of the river, for the protection of the inhabitants. The Governor of the territory resided, and the territorial legislature convened here. The place has possessed many political advantages. "The bank of Vincennes" enjoys a good character, and its paper has already attained an extensive circulation. It has recently become a state bank. There is also a printing office, which issues a paper, called the "*Western Sun*", edited by Mr. E. Stout. This village was settled nearly one hundred years ago, by the French, who mostly came from Lower Canada. Buried in the centre of an immense wilderness, unprotected, and without intercourse with the civilized world, these colonists gradually approximated to the savage state. Many of the males intermarried with the Indians, whose amity was by these ties secured and strengthened, and their numbers amounted to three hundred persons.

"During the revolutionary war, their remote situation exempted them from all its evils, till, in 1782, they were visited by a detachment from Kentucky, who plundered and insulted them, and killed or drove off the cattle which formed their chief wealth.

"The peace of 1783, gave them to the United States, under whose benign government they began to breathe again; but unluckily an Indian war commenced in 1788, and siding with the whites, as duty and discretion enjoined, they were annoyed by the savages, whose animosity was embittered by the remembrance of their ancient friendship and alliance. Their cattle were killed, their village closely beset, and, for several years, they could not carry the plough or hoe a musket shot from their huts.

"Military service was added to their other hardships; but, in 1792, the compassion of the federal government gave four hundred acres of land to every one who paid the capitation, and one hundred more to every one who served in the militia. This domain, so ample to a diligent husbandman, was of little value to the hunting Frenchmen, who soon bartered away their invaluable ground for about 30 cents an acre, which was paid to them in goods, on which an exorbitant profit was charged. This land was of the best quality; it sold, as early as 1796, at two dollars an acre, and I may venture to say is now worth at least ten. Thus, for the most part, reduced again to their gardens, or the little homestead which was indispensable to their subsistence, they had nothing to live on but their fruit, potatoes, maize, and now and then a little game; and, on this fare, no wonder they became as lean as Arabs.

"Their ignorance, indeed, was profound. Nobody ever opened a school among them, till it was done by the abbe R. a polite, well educated, and liberal minded missionary, banished hither by the French revolution. Out of nine of the French, scarcely six could read or write, whereas nine-tenths of the Americans, or emigrants from the east, could do both. Their dialect is by no means, as I had been previously assured, a vulgar or provincial brogue, but pretty good French, intermixed with many military terms and phrases, all the settlements having been originally made by soldiers. The primitive stock of Canada was the regiment of Carignon."*

The country around Vincennes in every direction, being well adapted to settlements and cultivation, what is there to prevent this place from equalling, in a very few years, in numbers, wealth, and refinement, the fine towns of Lexington, Louisville and Cincinnati. Building lots in Vincennes sell at from fifty to one thousand dollars a lot. There are two roads leading to the Ohio; one to fort Harrison; one to Princeton; and one to Kaskaskia.

A new village has feen laid out at *Terre Haute*, three miles below fort Harrison. This situation, for beauty of prospect, is exceeded by none in the state.

PRICES AND SALES OF PUBLIC LANDS.

Congress lands, after the auction sales are closed, sell invariably for $2 an acre. For a quarter section, $80 are to be paid down —the same sum in two years; and the remainder in annual payments, without interest, if punctually made. Those who pay in advance, are entitled to a discount of eight per cent.

Harrison's Purchase, containing upwards of 3,000,000 acres, lying between Whiteriver, the Wabash, and Rocky river, was opened for sale at auction, at Jeffersonville, in Sept. last, and altho' the Canadian volunteers had previously selected their donation lots, numerous tracts were sold at from $4 to $30 an acre. A fractional section on the Wabash, below fort Harrison, sold for $32.18, and several others from $20 to $30. Speculators from all quarters attended the sales.

The Canadian volunteers deserved the munificence of the United States, for they freely shed their blood under our banners, upon the Niagara frontier, under the intrepid Wilcocks, Delapierre, and Markle. But unfortunately the cup of generosity was upset before it reached their mouths. We gave them the choice of the

*See Volney's View of the Soil and Climate of the United States, pages 334 and 335.

best lands in the United States, merely to enrich the Mammon of speculation. Most of these brave men have blindly or necessitously parted with their lands for a song.

ANTIQUITIES.

On the hills, two miles east of the town, are three large mounds; and others are frequently met with on the prairies and upland, from Whiteriver to the head of the Wabash. They are in every respect similar to those in Franklin county, already described.

The French have a tradition, that an exterminating battle was fought in the beginning of the last century, on the ground where fort Harrison now stands, between the Indians living on the Mississippi, and those of the Wabash. The bone of contention was the lands lying between those rivers, which both parties claimed. There were about 1,000 warriors on each side. The condition of the fight was, that the victors should possess the lands in dispute. The grandeur of the prize was peculiarly calculated to inflame the ardor of savage minds. The contest commenced about sunrise. Both parties fought desperately. The Wabash warriors came off conquerors, having *seven* men left alive at sunset, and their adversaries but *five*. The mounds are still to be seen where it is said the slain were buried.

GIBSON.

This county is bounded by the counties of Warwick and Orange on the east, the county of Posey on the south, the Wabash river on the west, and the county of Knox on the north. It is watered by several creeks and runs, falling into the Petoka and Wabash. About one half of this county has a fertile and highly favorable soil; and the greater part of the other half would be pronounced good, in any of the Atlantic states.

Princeton—Is the county seat; it lies thirty-five miles nearly south of Vincennes. It has a post-office; and has had a rapid growth, considering the newness of the surrounding settlements.

Harmony.—This village is situated on the Wabash, half a day's ride below Princeton, and is settled by the *Harmonists*, from Butler county, Pennsylvania. They are under the direction of the Rev. George Rapp; and hold their property in community. They have a very extensive establishment for the manufacturing of wool. Their *Merino* cloth is not surpassed by any in America. They also cultivate the vine; and are distinguished for their temperance, industry and skill in many of the mechanical professions.

POSEY,

Is situated south of Gibson, bounded on the east by the county of Warwick, on the south and west by the Ohio and Wabash rivers. It contains rich and extensive prairies; but the banks of the Wabash are in many places subject to inundation, both from its own floods, and those of the Ohio, which sets up the Wabash several miles.

WARWICK.

This county is situated east of the county of Posey, bounded on the east by the county of Perry, on the south by the Ohio river, on the west by the county of Posey, and on the north by the counties of Orange and Knox. It is a level and rich county, watered by several large creeks running into the Ohio, such as Beaver, Pigeon, &c. It is nevertheless but indifferently watered, owing to the early drying up of the streams. The prairies are numerous, but mostly inferior, in point of soil, to those bordering the Wabash. The prevailing timber being oak, the range for hogs is excellent.

PERRY,

Is bounded east by Harrison, north by Orange and Washington, west by Warwick, and south by the Ohio river. It is watered by the little river Anderson, and by creeks and runs falling into the Ohio. It was established in 1615. [1815].

INDIANS.

These consist of Mascontins, Piankashaws, Kickapoos, Delawares, Miamis, Shawanœse, Weeaws, Ouitanans, Eel-rivers, Hurons, and Pottawattamies.

The *Mascontins* and *Piankashaws* reside on the rivers falling into the right bank of the Wabash, between Vincennes and Tippacanoe. Their numbers are given at 1,000 souls. Hutchins affirms that they, together with the Kickapoos, could raise 1,000 *warriors*.

The *Kickapoos* reside on the west side of the Wabash, above Tippacanoe, and on the head waters of the Illinois. They have several large villages, and can raise 400 warriors.

The *Delawares* reside on the head waters of Whiteriver, in a village surrounded by large open prairies. I have no data for stating their numbers with accuracy; they are not numerous.

The *Miamis* inhabit the upper Wabash, Massissinway, Miami-of-the-lakes, and Little St. Josephs—mostly within one or two day's travel of fort Wayne. General Harrison burnt four of their towns at the forks of the Wabash, in September, 1813. They are the proprietors of excellent lands, and cultivate large quantities of Indian corn. They are reduced to about 1,100 souls.

The *Shawanœse* live on and near the banks of Tippacanoe, Ponce Passu creek, and the Wabash river. They were formerly a very formidable and warlike tribe; but have been reduced by their frequent wars, to about 400 warriors. They have fine lands, and raise an abundance of corn. Their country was invaded by General Wilkinson, in 1791, who destroyed their principal town, near the mouth of Tippacanoe, called *Kathtippecamunk.* "It contained one hundred and twenty houses, eighty of which were shingle roofed. The best houses belonged to the French traders. The gardens and improvements around were delightful. There was a tavern, with cellars, bar, public and private rooms; and the whole marked no small degree of order and civilization." Not far from the ruins of this town stands the celebrated Prophet's town, destroyed by General Harrison, in Nov. 1811, but since rebuilt. Above [below] Tippacanoe is the old French post of Ouitanan, situated on the north [south] side of the Wabash, in the centre of the Indian country. This place is as old as Vincennes.

Several half civilized French inhabitants reside here as well as at L'Anguille, on Eelriver. They raise corn, and trade with the Indians.

The *Hurons* reside in a small village, ten or fifteen miles south east of Ouitanan. There are only ten or twelve families of them. The *Eelrivers* and *Weeaws* are bands of the Miamis; and reside on the Wabash and Eelriver. They can collect about 100 warriors.

A part of the *Winnebagoes* occupy a village on Ponce Passu creek, seven miles east of the Prophet's town, which contains from forty-five to fifty houses, several of which are fifty feet long; others reside on the branches of Plein and Fox rivers, and frequent Chicago.

The *Pottawattamies* are the most numerous tribe in the state. They reside on the Elkhart branch of the St. Josephs, where they have five villages, one of which is situated in an immense prairie, sixty miles west of fort Wayne. The course of this branch is north west. The balance of this tribe live on the St. Josephs, Chicago, Kennomic, and Theakaki rivers.

The best proof of the excellence of the land on the Upper Wabash, is the circumstance of its being the scene of a numerous

Indian population. These sagacious children of nature are good judges of land. Indeed, they are rarely, if ever, found on a barren soil.

EXTENT OF NAVIGABLE WATERS.

	Miles
The Ohio river washes the southern boundary of Indiana, for the distance of	472
Wabash, navigable	470
Whiteriver, and its forks	160
Petoka	30
Blueriver	40
White River	40
Rocky River	45
Panne	30
Massissinway	45
Eel, and Little rivers	60
Western tributaries of the Wabash	330
St. Joseph of Miami and Panther's Creek	75
Elkhart and part of St. Joseph of L. Mich	100
Great and Little Kennomic	120
Chemin River	40
Chicago and Kickapoo	80
Theakaki, and parts of Fox, Plein and Illinois	300
Southern coast of Lake Michigan	50
Total	2,487

The foregoing estimate does not embrace streams boatable less than thirty miles; besides, several of those named are navigable for canoes and small boats many miles further than the given distances annexed.

The distance from Chicago, to New Orleans, by water, is 1,680 miles—to Buffalo, about 800. The surplus products of three fourths of the state will find their way to the New Orleans market.

VIEW OF PORTAGES.

All the streams in the northern parts of the state, which empty into the Wabash and Illinois, have their branches interwoven with many of the rivers running into lakes Erie and Michigan. Indeed, as before observed, they not unfrequently issue from the same marsh, prairie, pond, or lake. There are upwards of twenty portages near the Michigan frontier, only two of which have hitherto been used by the whites. The first of these is between the St. Marys and the Littleriver branch of the Wabash, and is nine miles long. The road which is good in dry seasons, leaves the St. Marys near Fort Wayne, where teams are kept for the transportation of boats and merchandize. It was by this route that the French, while in possession of Canada, passed from the lakes to their posts on the Wabash. From the levelness of the intervening country, a canal could be easily opened, uniting the two streams. The second is the short portage between the Chicago and the Kickapoo branch of the Illinois, rendered important by the inundations, which at certain seasons cover the intermediate prairie, from which the two opposite streams flow. By this means nature has herself opened a navigable communication between the Great Lakes and the Mississippi; and it is a fact, however difficult it may be of belief to many, that boats not unfrequently pass from Lake Michigan into the Illinois, and in some instances without being subjected to the necessity of having their lading taken out. I have never been on this portage, and therefore cannot speak from personal knowledge, yet the fact has reached me through so many authentic channels, that I have no doubt of its truth. Gen. P. B. Porter, whose geographical knowledge of the countries bordering the lakes, is excelled by that of no gentleman in the western country, has given his corroborative testimony in his speech on internal navigation delivered on the floor of congress in 1810. Lieutenant Hamilton of the United States army, a meritorious officer, whose services have not been adequately requited, informed a friend of mine living at Detroit, that he had passed with a laden boat, and met with no obstructions on the portage, except from the grass, through which, however, the men easily forced the boat. But, in order to multiply proof and remove every doubt, I consulted the Hon. N. POPE, the Territorial Delegate in congress from Illinois, who in answer to my enquiries stated, that "at high water boats pass out of Lake Michigan into the Illinois river, and so *vice versa*, without landing. A canal uniting them is deemed practicable at a small expense," &c. When on the upper lakes, I frequently met with voyageurs who had assisted in navigating boats across this portage.

This morass is not the only one possessing two distinct outlets, I have myself witnessed this phenomenon in several instances; but never where there was water sufficient to float a laden boat. Let us hear what the justly celebrated Volney, says on this interesting subject.

"During the vernal floods, the north branch of the Great Miami mixes its waters with the southern branch of the *Miami of the Lake*. The carrying place, or *portage*, of a league, which separates their heads, disappears beneath the flood, and we can pass in canoes from the Ohio to Lake Erie, as I myself witnessed in 1796.

"At Loremier's Fort, or store, an eastern branch of the Wabash serves as a simple canal to connect the two Miamis; and the same Wabash, by a northern branch, communicates, above Fort Wayne, in the time of inundation, with the Miami of Lake Erie.

"In the winter of 1792-3, two boats (*perogues*) were detached from Detroit, by a mercantile house, from whom I received the information, which passed, without interruption, from the Huron river,* which enters Lake Erie, into *Grand River*, which falls into Lake Michigan, by means of the rise at the heads of the two streams.

"The Muskingum, which flows into the Ohio, communicates, at its cources, through some small lakes, with the Cayahoga, belonging to Lake Erie."

There is a portage of four miles between the St. Joseph's of Lake Michigan, and the Theakaki; of two miles between the Theakaki and the Great Kennomic; of half a mile between the Great and Little Kennomic; of four miles between the Chemin and Little Kennomic; and of three miles between the west fork of Chicago and Plein; besides numerous ones between the head branches of the two St. Josephs; Black, Raisin and Eel rivers, which vary in length according to the dryness or moisture of the season. There is a short portage between the St. Marys and the main branch of the Wabash, over which, in times of inundation, the Indians pass with their light perogues.

MISCELLANEOUS.

Chicago is a small river, which forks sixteen miles from the lake, into the east and west branches. Sloops of forty tons burthen can enter its harbor. Six miles from the lake its current becomes brisk, and continues so as far as the portage. Fort Dearborn famous for the murder of its garrison in September 1815, [1812] by the Pottawattamies, stood upon its left bank near the lake shore. The Indians have relinquished to the United States a tract of land six miles square, at the mouth of this river. The fort has been lately re-occupied.

The Great Kennomic.—This river rises twenty or thirty miles S. of lake Michigan, and running a N. W. course approaches

*The river Huron mentioned by Volney, enters Lake Erie six miles below Malden. There are two other rivers of this name; one falls into Lake Erie twelve miles below Sandusky Bay, and the other into Lake St. Clair.

within two or three miles of that lake. Thence winding to the S. W. and north, it forms a curviture nearly similar to the end of the lake, and parallel with it, keeping at the distance of 8 or 9 miles. It thence turns suddenly to the S. E. E. and N. E. in a contrary but parallel direction to its former course, and empties into the lake 30 miles east of Chicago. It expands behind the sand hills near its mouth, and forms a spacious bay. It affords to the Indians an inexhaustible supply of fish, and an ample range for fowling and trapping. Its banks are low, and its current gentle.

Population.—I have recently received several letters from gentlemen residing in Indiana, which concur in stating that the population has doubled since May 1815. In other words, it now amounts to 128,000 souls, a rapidity of increase altogether unprecedented.

Price of Improved Lands.—Farms containing a log house and fifteen or twenty acres, sell as high as eight or ten dollars; in some instances the necessities or rambling dispositions of the inhabitants induce them to dispose of their plantations at a trifling advance upon the original price.

Falls of the Ohio.—An improvement of the navigation of the falls is about to be attempted by a canal round the rapids. The legislature have incorporated a company with a capital of $1,000,000. When this enterprize is accomplished, ship building will probably re-commence with vigor.

It was the difficulties encountered in getting vessels over these rapids, which chiefly contributed to discourage this important business above the falls.

The Wabash.—The rapids at Ouitanan are impassable for boats; but the navigation is so good between Vincennes and this place, that Gen. Hopkins in his expedition to Tippecanoe in 1813, conveyed his baggage and stores in large keels, of thirty tons burthen. General Harrison in his expedition against the Prophet, was accompanied in his march through the wilderness by a caravan of *waggons!* They were enabled to proceed with tolerable speed by keeping in the prairies to the west of the woodlands bordering the Wabash.

Washington County.—In addition to the streams mentioned in page 66, is watered by Blueriver, which rises in the eastern part of the county, and pursuing a S. E. course, passes through Harrison county twelve miles south-west of Corydon.

Climate.—From the latitude of Ouitanan, (40 20) to the borders of the Ohio, the climate of Indiana may be pronounced mild.

North of the head branches of the Wabash, the north and northwest winds are formidable enemies to human comfort, and the winters severe and rigorous; though snow is rarely known to fall so deep as it does in the northern counties of New-York. The southern shore of Lake Michigan, and the vast prairies in the direction of the Wabash have little to protect them from the rage of the brumal winds.

The Reed Cane.—This plant grows south of the ridge of hills extending from the falls of the Ohio to those of the Wabash above the mouth of Whiteriver. It is sometimes found as far north as the mouth of the Big Miami. Cotton, the vines of Spain, the silk worm, and the sweet potatoe will flourish wherever the reed cane grows, except, the first, which does not grow to perfection beyond 31 degrees of north latitude. Rice and Indigo, I think would do well between Blueriver and the Wabash, though I have never seen either cultivated, or heard that the inhabitants have yet made the trial. I have seen these plants growing luxuriantly in Overton county, Tennessee, which is a high broken country, near the Kentucky boundary line, in latitude 36 35. The mouth of the Wabash is in 37 50.

The state will doubtless produce cotton sufficient for its own consumption. It is already raised in considerable quantities at Vincennes, Princeton, Harmony, and in the settlements below the mouth of Anderson. The Wabash will at no very remote period, serve as a canal to supply with cotton, a part of the market on the northern lakes.

Game.—The forests of Indiana are abundantly stocked with game. Great numbers of deer are annually destroyed by the inhabitants. In travelling seven miles through the woods of Dearborn county, I counted two bears, three deer, and upwards of one hundred turkies; more that half of the latter, however, were young ones, just beginning to fly. I will here relate an adventure which may serve to throw some light on the natural history of the deer. In the course of the day, I missed my way and wandered several miles in the wilderness, in my endeavors to regain the path I started a fawn, which I soon caught, in consequence of its becoming entangled in the herbage. It bleated and appeared greatly frightened. Conceiving myself to be near a settlement and unwilling to destroy it, I resolved to carry it to the first house; but after travelling half a mile its dam made her appearance, and seemed by her piteous demonstrations, plainly to reproach me for my cruelty; upon which I gave the fawn its liberty. But I was not a little surprised, to find it so much attached to me during our transient acquaintance, that it absolutely refused to leave me. I pushed it from me and pursued my course; but soon found it at my heels, apparently as docile as a pet lamb, and was compelled to frighten it before it would turn from me. Relating this fact to some old hunters, they assured me that such is the docility of fawns, that they can be as effectually tamed in an hour, as a year.

Deer, it is said, are the mortal enemies of rattlesnakes; and often kill them designedly by jumping on them. They can scent them at considerable distance; and when pursued by dogs will avoid those which may happen to lie in their way, by suddenly inclining to the right or left. It is also reported that the turkey buzzard has the power of killing the rattlesnake by its intolerable stench—which it most powerfully emits by a violent fluttering in the air a little above the snake's head.

Farmers are greatly annoyed by the smaller animals, such as squirrels, moles and mice; for nature is as prolific in animal as vegetable productions. The mole is particularly troublesome to cornfields while the seed is coming up, and injurious to meadows, as it bores the earth in every direction.

Minerals.—The surface of Indiana is too champaign to be rich in mines of gold or silver. It is, nevertheless, stated that a silver mine has been discovered near Ouitanan. Iron ore is found in many counties, probably in sufficient quantities for domestic use. Chalybeate springs are plentiful. The water between Whiteriver and New Lexington is in some places impregnated with copperas to such a degree, that linen washed in it turns black; and a few of the inhabitants have been induced to abandon their habitations in consequence of the supposed unwholesomeness of their wells.

Indian Claims.—Near two-thirds of this state belongs to the Indians. Their title is extinguished in the eastern part, from Fort Wayne to the river Ohio, on an average of about twenty-five miles wide, on the margin of the Ohio and up the Wabash and western line to a point N. W. of Fort Harrison, and from thence eastwardly to the eastern purchase, about thirty-five miles from the Ohio. Notwithstanding the greater extent of soil purchased from the Indians in the west, a meridian equidistant from the eastern and western boundary would pretty fairly divide the population; but the western section will populate fastest, owing to the extent of recently purchased lands.

From *Notes on a journey in America from the coast of Virginia to the territory of Illinois*, by Morris Birkbeck [1818], pp. 81-118.

BIRKBECK, MORRIS.

Morris Birkbeck, a Quaker farmer of education and ability, decided in 1817 to leave England and make a new home for himself and his family somewhere in America.

In the spring of 1817 he joined his friend George Flower in Richmond, Virginia, and they proceeded westward through Pennsylvania, Ohio, Indiana and Illinois, finally locating and establishing a colony in what is now Edwards County. In 1818 his "Notes on a journey in America, from the coast of Virginia to the territory of Illinois" was published. The Edinburgh Review speaks of this book as "one of the most interesting and instructive books that have appeared in years." His description of Indiana is found on pp. 91-118 of the Dublin edition of 1818.

Mr. Birkbeck was drowned in 1825. He was one of the leaders against the attempt to introduce slavery into the new state of Illinois.

June 22 [1817]. As we approach the Little Miami river the country becomes more broken, much more fertile, and better settled. After crossing this rapid and clear stream we had a pleasant ride to Lebanon, which is not a mountain of cedars, but a valley, so beautiful and fertile, that it seemed, on its first opening on our view, enriched as it was by the tints of evening, rather a region of fancy than a real backwood scene.

Lebanon is itself one of those wonders which are the natural growth of these backwoods. In fourteen years, from two or three cabins of half-savage hunters, it has grown to be the residence of a thousand persons, with habits and looks no way differing from their brethren of the east. Before we entered the town we heard the supper bells of the taverns and arrived just in time to take our seats at the table, among just such a set as I should have expected to meet at the ordinary in Richmond; travellers like ourselves, with a number of store-keepers, lawyers, and doctors;—men who board at the taverns, and make up a standing company for the daily public table.

This morning we made our escape from this busy scene, in defiance of the threatening rain. A crowded tavern in an American town, though managed as is that we have just quitted, with great attention and civility, is a place from which you are always willing to depart. After all, the wonder is, that so many comforts are provided for you at so early a period.

Cincinnati, like most American towns, stands too low; it is

built on the banks of the Ohio, and the lower part is not out of the reach of spring-floods.

As if "life was not more than meat, and the body than raiment," every consideration of health and enjoyment yields to views of mercantile convenience. Short-sighted and narrow economy! by which the lives of thousands are shortened, and the comfort of all sacrificed to mistaken notions of private interest.

Cincinnati is, however, a most thriving place, and backed as it is already by a great population and a most fruitful country, bids fair to be one of the first cities of the west. We are told, and we cannot doubt the fact, that the chief of what we see is the work of four years. The hundreds of commodious, well-finished brick houses, the spacious and busy markets, the substantial public buildings, the thousands of prosperous, well-dressed, industrious inhabitants; the numerous waggons and drays, the gay carriages and elegant females;—the shoals of craft on the river, the busy stir prevailing every where; houses building, boats building, paving and levelling streets; the numbers of country people constantly coming and going; with the spacious taverns, crowded with travellers from a distance.

All this is so much more than I could comprehend, from a description of a new town, just risen from the woods, that I despair of conveying an adequate idea of it to my English friends. It is enchantment, and Liberty is the fair enchantress.

I was assured by a respectable gentleman, one of the first settlers, and now a man of wealth and influence, that he remembers when there was only one poor cabin where this noble town now stands. The county of Hamilton is something under the regular dimensions of twenty miles square, and it already contains 30,000 inhabitants. Twenty years ago the vast region comprising the states of Ohio and Indiana, and the territory of Illinois and Michigan, onlycounted 30,000 inhabitants:—the same number that are now living, and living happily, in the little county of Hamilton, in which stands Cincinnati.

Why do not the governments of Europe afford such an asylum, in their vast and gloomy forests, for their increasing myriads of paupers? This would be an object worthy a convention of sovereigns, if sovereigns were really the fathers of their people: but jealous as they are of emigration to America, this simple and sure mode of preventing it will never occur to them.

Land is rising rapidly in price in all well-settled neighborhoods. Fifty dollars per acre for improved land is spoken of familiarly: I have been asked thirty for a large tract, without improvements, on the Great Miami, fifty miles from Cincinnati, and similar prices in other quarters. An estate of a thousand acres, partially cleared, is spoken of, on the road to Louisville, at twenty dollars. Many offers occur, all at a very great advance of price. It now becomes a question, whether to fix in this comparatively populous state of Ohio, or join the vast tide of emigration that is flowing farther west, where we may obtain lands of equal value at the government price of two dollars per acre, and enjoy the advantage of choice of situation.

Though I feel some temptation to linger here, where society is attaining a maturity truly astonishing, when we consider its early date, I cannot be satisfied without seeing that remoter country, before we fix in this, still enquiring and observing as we proceed. If we leave behind us eligible situations, it is like securing a retreat, to which we may return with good prospects, if we think it advisable.

The probability is, that, in those more remote regions, the accumulation of settlers will shortly render land as valuable as it is here at present; and, in the interim, this accession of inhabitants will create a demand for the produce of the new country, equal to the supply. It is possible too, that we may find ourselves in as good society there as here. Well-educated persons are not rare amongst the emigrants who are moving farther west; for the spirit of emigration has reached a class somewhat higher in the scale of society than formerly. Some too may be aiming at the same point with ourselves; and others, if we prosper, will be likely to follow our example.

We are also less reluctant at extending our views westward, on considering that the time is fast approaching when the grand intercourse with Europe will not be, as at present, through eastern America, but through the great rivers which communicate by the Mississippi with the ocean, at New Orleans. In this view we approximate to Europe, as we proceed to the west.

The upward navigation of these streams is already coming under the controul of steam, an invention which promises to be of incalculable importance to this new world.

Such is the reasoning which impels us still forward; and in a few days we propose setting out to explore the state of Indiana, and probably the Illinois. With so long a journey before us, we are not comfortable under the prospect of separation. Our plan had been to lodge our main party at Cincinnati, until we had fixed on our final abode; but this was before our prospects had taken so wide a range. We now talk of Vincennes, as we did before of this place, and I trust we shall shortly be again under weigh.

June 27. Cincinnati.—All are alive here as soon as the day breaks. The stores are open, the markets thronged, and business is in full career by five o'clock in the morning; and nine o'clock is the common hour for retiring to rest.

As yet I have felt nothing oppressive in the heat of this climate. Melting, oppressive, sultry nights, succeeding broiling days, and forbidding rest, which are said to wear out the frames of the languid inhabitants of the eastern cities, are unknown here. A cool breeze always renders the night refreshing, and generally moderates the heat of the day.

June 28. The numerous creeks in this country, which are apt to be swelled suddenly by heavy rains, render travelling perplexing, and even perilous to strangers, in a showery season like the present. On my way this morning from an excursion of about fifteen miles, to view an estate, a man who was mowing at some distance from the road, hailed me with the common, but to us quaint appellation of "stranger":—I stopped to learn his wishes. "Are you going to ride the creek?" "I know of no creek," said I; "but I am going to Cincinnati."—"I guess it will swim your horse." "How must I avoid it?" "Turn on your left, and go up to the mill, and you will find a bridge." Now if this kind man had rested on his scythe, and detained the "stranger" a few minutes, to learn his country, his name, and the object of his journey, as he probably would had he been nearer to the road, he would but have evinced another trait of the friendly character of these good Americans.

In this land of plenty, young people first marry, and then look out for the means of a livelihood without fear, or cause for it. The ceremony of marriage is performed in a simple family way, in my opinion more delicate, and corresponding to the nature of the contract, than the glaring publicity adopted by some, or the secrecy, not so respectable, affected by others.

The near relations assemble at the house of the bride's parents. The minister or magistrate is in attendance, and when the candidates make their appearance, he asks them severally the usual questions, and having called on the company to declare if there be any objections, he confirms the union by a short religious formula; —the bridegroom salutes the bride, and the ceremony is over. Tea and refreshments follow. Next day the bridegroom holds his levée, his numerous friends (and sympathy makes them numerous on these happy occasions,) pour in to offer their congratulations Abundance of refreshments of the most substantial kind are placed on side-tables, which are taken, not as a formal meal, but as they walk up and down the apartments, in cheerful conversation. This running-meal continues from noon till the close of the evening, the bride never making her appearance on the occasion; an example of delicacy worthy the imitation of more refined societies.

June 28. Cincinnati. The Merino mania seems to have prevailed in America to a degree exceeding its highest pitch in England. In Kentucky, where even the negroes would no more eat mutton than they would horseflesh, there were great Merino breeders. There was and is, I believe, a sheep society here, to encourage the growth of fine wool, on land as rich as the deepest, fattest vallies of our island, and in a country still overwhelmed with timber of the heaviest growth. As strange and incomprehensible an infatuation this, and as inconsistent with plain common sense, as the determined rejection of the fine-woolled race by the English breeders of short-wooled sheep; but that there should ever have been a rage for sheep of any kind in any part of this country that I have seen, must be owing to general ignorance of the constitution and habits of this animal. There is not a district, scarcely a spot that I have travelled over, where a flock of fine-woolled sheep could be kept with any prospect of advantage, provided there were even a market for the carcase. Yet by the ragged remains of the Merino family, which may be recognized in many places, I perceive that the attempt has been very general. Mutton is almost as abhorrent to an American palate, or fancy, as the flesh of swine to an Israelite; and the state of the manufactures does not give great encouragement to the growth of wool of any kind; of Merino wool less, perhaps, than any other. Mutton is sold in the markets of Philadephia at about half the price of beef; and the Kentuckian, who would have given a thousand dollars for a Merino ram, would dine upon dry bread rather than taste his own mutton! A few sheep on every farm, to supply coarse wool for domestic manufacture, seems to be all that ought at present to be attempted, in any part of America that I have yet seen.

I have heard that in the western part of Virginia sheep are judiciously treated, and kept to advantage, and that there exists in that country no prejudice against the meat: also that the north-eastern states have good sheep pastures, and a *moderate* dislike of mutton: to these, of course, my remarks on sheep husbandry are not applicable. Deep woods are not the proper abodes of sheep.

When America shall have cleared away her forests, and opened her uplands to the breezes, they will soon be covered with fine turf, and flocks will be seen ranging over them here, as in other parts of the world. Anticipation often retards improvement, by giving birth to prejudice.

There are about two thousand people regularly employed as boatmen on the Ohio, and they are proverbially ferocious and abandoned in their habits, though with many exceptions, as I have good grounds for believing. People who settle along the line of this grand navigation generally possess or acquire similar habits; and thus profligacy of manners seems inseparable from the population on the banks of these great rivers. It is remarked, indeed, every where, that inland navigators are worse than sailors.

This forms a material objection to a residence on the Ohio, outweighing all the beauty and local advantages of such a situation.

July 6. We are now at the town of Madison, on our way through the State of Indiana towards Vincennes. This place is on the banks of the Ohio, about seventy-five miles from Cincinnati.

Our road has been mostly from three to six miles from the river, passing over fertile hills and alluvial bottoms.

The whole is appropriated; but although settlements multiply daily, many large intervals remain between the clearings.

Indiana is evidently newer than the state of Ohio; and if I mistake not, the character of the settlers is different, and superior to that of the first settlers in Ohio, who were generally very indigent people: those who are now fixing themselves in Indiana bring with them habits of comfort, and the means of procuring the conveniences of life; I observe this in the construction of their cabins and the neatness surrounding them, and especially in their well-stocked gardens, so frequent here and so rare in the state of Ohio, where their earlier and longer settlement would have afforded them better opportunities of making this great provision for domestic comfort.

I have also had the pleasure of seeing many families of healthy children; and from my own continued observation, confirmed by the testimony of every competent evidence that has fallen in my way, I repeat, with still more confidence, that the diseases so alarming to all emigrants, and which have been fatal to so many, are not attached to the climate, but to local situation. Repetitions will be excused on this important subject. Hills on a dry soil are healthy, after some progress has been made in clearing; for deep and close woods are not salubrious either to new comers or old settlers. The neighbourhood of overflowing streams, and all wet, marshy soils, are productive of agues and bilious fevers in the autumn.

Such is the influx of strangers into this state, that the industry of the settlers is severely taxed to provide food for themselves, and a superfluity for new comers: and thus it is probable there will be a market for all the spare produce, for a series of years, owing to the accession of strangers, as well as the rapid internal growth of population. This is a favourable condition of a new colony, which has not been calculated on by those who take a distant view of the subject. This year Kentucky has sent a supply in aid of this hungry infant state.

July 7. I have good authority for contradicting a supposition that I have met with in England, respecting the inhabitants of Indiania,—that they are lawless, semi-barbarous vagabonds, dangerous to live among. On the contrary, the laws are respected, and are effectual; and the manners of the people are kind and gentle to each other, and to strangers.

An unsettled country, lying contigious to one that is settled, is always a place of retreat for rude and even abandoned characters, who find the regulations of society intolerable; and such, no doubt, had taken up their unfixed abode in Indiana. These people retire, with the wolves, from the regular colonists, keeping always to the outside of civilized settlements. They rely for their subsistence on their rifle, and a scanty cultivation of corn, and live in great poverty and privation, a degree only short of the savage state of Indians.

Of the present settlers, as I have passed along from house to house, I could not avoid receiving a most favourable impression. I would willingly remain among them, but pre-occupation sends us still forward in the steps of the roaming hunters I have just described, some of whom we shall probably dislodge when we make our settlement, which, like theirs, will probably be in the confines of society.

As to the inhabitants of towns, the Americans are much alike, as far as we have had an opportunity of judging. We look in vain for any striking difference in the general deportment and appearance of the great bulk of Americans, from Norfolk on the eastern coast, to the town of Madison in Indiana. The same good-looking, well-dressed (not what we call gentlemanly) men appear every where. Nine out of ten, native Americans, are tall and long-limbed, approaching, or even exceeding six feet; in pantaloons and Wellington boots, either marching up and down with their hands in their pockets, or seated on chairs poised on the hind-feet, and the backs rested against the walls. If a hundred Americans of any class were to seat themselves, ninety-nine would shuffle their chairs to the true distance, and then throw themselves back against the nearest prop. The women exhibit a great similarity of tall, relaxed forms, with consistent dress and demeanour; and are not remarkable for sprightliness of manners. Intellectual culture has not yet made much progress among the generality of either sex where I have travelled; but the men have greatly the advantage in the means of acquiring information, from their habits of travelling, and intercourse with strangers:—sources of improvement from which the other sex is unhappily too much secluded.

Lexington. This town is only three years old. Madison dates its origin two years farther back. Yet, much as has been done during this short period, and much as there remains to do, we see in every village and town, as we pass along, groups of young able-bodied men, who seem to be as perfectly at leisure as the loungers of ancient Europe. This love of idleness where labour is so profitable and effective, is a strange affection. I have no notion of life as a pleasurable thing, except where connected with action. Rest is certainly a delightful sensation, but it implies previous labour: there is no rest for the indolent, any more than for the wicked: "They yawn and stretch, but find no rest."—I suspect that indolence is the epidemic evil of the Americans. If you enquire of hale young fellows, why they remain in this listless state—"We live in freedom," they say, "we need not work like the English." Thus they consider it their privilege to do nothing. But the trees of the forest are still more highly privileged in this sort of passive existence, this living to do nothing; for they are fed and exercised without any toil at *all;* the trees, "*sua si bona norint,*" did they but know their bliss, might be objects of envy to many a tall young American.

July 12. Hawkins's Tavern, sixteen miles east of Vincennes. On traversing the state of Indiana to this place, I retain the same idea as to the character of the settlers that struck me on our entrance. They are an order of colonists somewhat higher than the first settlers of their sister state. There remains, however, a considerable number of backwoods' men, somewhat savage in character, and who look on new comers as intruders. The accommodation for travellers will soon be greatly superior to those in the Ohio state, as are those of the Ohio to the taverns of Pennsylvania, west of the mountains.

The country, from the town of Madison to the Camp Tavern, is not interesting, and great part of it is but of medium quality. At the latter place commences a broken country, approaching to mountainous, which, if well watered, would form a fine grazing district; but the little streams are now dried up, notwithstanding the late copious rains. This beautiful country continues as far as Sholt's Tavern, on White River, thirty-six miles east of Vincennes. Most of this hilly distict is unentered, and remains open to the public at two dollars per acre.

Our rear party, consisting of one of the ladies, a servant boy, and myself, were benighted, in consequence of accidental detention at the foot of one of these rugged hills; and, without being well provided, were compelled to make our first experiment of "camping out."

A traveller in the woods should always carry flint, steel, tinder, and matches; a few biscuits, a half-pint phial of spirits, and a tin cup; a large knife or tomahawk; then with his two blankets, and his great coat and umbrella, he need not be uneasy should any unforeseen delay require his sleeping under a tree.

Our party having separated, the important articles of tinder and matches were in the baggage of the division which had proceeded, and as the night was rainy and exceedingly dark, we were for some time under some anxiety lest we should have been deprived of the comfort and security of a fire. Fortunately, my powder-flask was in my saddle-bags, and we succeeded in supplying the place of tinder by moistening a piece of paper and rubbing it with gun-powder. We placed our touch-paper on an old cambric handkerchief, as the most readily combustible article in our stores. On this we scattered gunpowder pretty copiously, and our flint and steel soon enabled us to raise a flame, and colecting dry wood, we made a noble fire. There was a mattrass for the lady, a bearskin for myself, and the load of the packhorse as a pallet for the boy. Thus, by means of great coats and blankets and our umbrellas spread over our heads, we made our quarters comfortable, and placing ourselves to the leeward of the fire, with our feet towards it, we lay more at ease than in the generality of taverns. Our horses fared rather worse, but we took care to tie them where they could browse a little, and occasionally shifted their quarters. We had a few biscuits, a small bottle of spirits, and a phial of oil: with the latter we contrived, by twisting some twine very hard, and dipping it in the oil, to make torches; and after several fruitless attempts we succeeded in finding water; we also collected plenty of dry wood. "Camping out" when the tents are pitched by daylight, and the party is ready furnished with the articles which we were obliged to supply by expedients, is quite pleaasnt in fine weather: my companion was exceedingly ill, which was, in fact, the cause of our being benighted; and never was the night's charge of a sick friend undertaken with more dismal forebodings, especially during our ineffectual efforts to obtain fire, the first blaze of which was unspeakably delightful; after this the rain ceased, and the invalid passed the night in safety; so that the morning found us more comfortable than we could have anticipated.

It has struck me as we have passed along from one poor hut to another among the rude inhabitants of this infant state, that travellers in general, who judge by comparison, are not qualified to form a fair estimate of these lonely settlers. Let a stranger make his way through England in a course remote from the great roads, and going to no inns, take such entertainment only as he might find in the cottages of labourers, he would have as much cause to complain of the rudeness of the people, and far more of their drunkenness and profligacy than in these back woods, although in England the poor are a part of a society where institutions are matured by the experience of two thousand years. The bulk of the inhabitants of this vast wilderness may be fairly considered as of the class of the lowest English peasantry, or just emerging from it: but in their manners and morals, and especially in their knowledge and proud independence of mind, they exhibit a contrast so striking, that he must indeed be a *petit maitre* traveller, or ill-informed of the character and circumstances of his poor countrymen, or deficient in good and manly sentiment, who would not rejoice to transplant, into these boundless regions of freedom, the millions whom he has left behind him grovelling in ignorance and want.

Vincennes, July 13. This town is scattered over a plain lying some feet lower than the banks of the Wabash:—a situation seemingly unfavourable to health; and in fact agues and bilious fevers are frequent in the autumn.

The road from Sholt's Tavern to this place, thirty-six miles, is partly across "barrens," that is, land of middling quality, thinly set with timber, or covered with long grass and shrubby underwood; generally level and dry, and gaudy with marigolds, sunflowers, martagon lilies, and many other brilliant flowers; small "prairies," which are grass lands, free from underwood, and generally somewhat marshy, and rich bottom land: on the whole, the country is tame, poorly watered, and not desirable as a place of settlement; but it is pleasant to travel over from its varied character.

Vincennes exhibits a motley assemblage of inhabitants as well as visitors. The inhabitants are Americans, French, Canadians, Negroes; the visitors, among whom our party is conspicuous as English, (who are seldom seen in these parts,) Americans from various states, and Indians of various nations,—Shawnees, Delawares, and Miamies, who live about a hundred miles to the northward, and who are come here to trade for skins. The Indians are encamped in considerable numbers round the town, and are continually riding in to the stores and the whiskey shops. Their horses and accoutrements are generally mean, and their persons disagreeable. Their faces are painted in various ways, which mostly gives a ferocity to their aspects.

One of them, a Shawnee, whom we met a few miles east of Vincennes, had his eyes, or rather his eyelids and surrounding parts, daubed with vermillion, looking hideous enough at a distance, but on a nearer view, he has good features, and is a fine, stout, fierce looking man, well remembered at Vincennes for the trouble he gave during the late war. This man exhibits a respectable beard, enough for a Germanized British officer of dragoons. Some of them are well dressed and good-looking people: one young man in particular, of the Miami nation, had a clear light blue cotton vest with sleeves, and his head ornamented with black feathers.

They all wear pantaloons, or rather long mocassions of buckskin, covering the foot and leg and reaching half way up the thigh, which is bare; a covering of cloth, passing between the thighs and hanging behind, like an apron, of a foot square. Their complexion is various, some dark, others not so swarthy as myself; but I saw none of the copper colour which I had imagined to be their universal distinctive mark. They are addicted to spirits, and often intoxicated, but even then generally civil and good humoured. The Indians are said to be partial to the French traders, thinking them fairer than the English or Americans. They use much action in their discourse, and laugh immoderately. Their hair is straight and black, and their eyes dark. The women are, many of them, decently dressed and good-looking; they ride sometimes like the men, but side-saddles are not uncommon among them. Few of them of either sex speak English; but many of the people here speak a variety of the Indian languages.

In the interior of Illinois the Indians are said sometimes to be troublesome, by giving abusive language to travellers, and stealing their horses when they encamp in the woods; but they never commit personal outrage.—Watchful dogs, and a rifle, are the best security; but I believe we shall have no reason to fear interruption in the quarter to which we are going.

At this remote place we find ourselves in a comfortable tavern, and surrounded by genteel and agreeable people. Our company at supper was about thirty.

The health of our party has been a source of some anxiety, increasing as the summer advances; and yet we have entirely escaped the diseases to which the country, or climate, or both, are said to be liable; but our approach to the Wabash has not been without some painful forebodings.

We have remarked, *en passant*, that people generally speak favourably of their own country, and exaggerate every objection or evil, when speaking of those to which we are going: thus it may be that the accounts we have received of the unhealthiness of this river and its vicinity, have been too deeply coloured. We are accordingly greatly relieved by the information we have received here on this subject. The Wabash has not overflowed its banks this summer, and no apprehensions are now entertained as to the sickly season of August and September.

July 18. Princeton.—We, in Great Britian, are so circumscribed in our movements that miles with us seem equal to tens in America. I believe that travellers here will start on an expedition of three thousand miles by boats, on horseback, or on foot, with as little deliberation or anxiety as we should set out on a journey of three hundred.

Five hundred persons every summer pass down the Ohio from Cincinnati to New Orleans, as traders or boatmen, and return on foot. By water the distance is seventeen hundred miles, and the walk back a thousand. Many go down to New Orleans from Pittsburg, which adds five hundred miles to the distance by water, and three hundred by land. The store-keepers (country shopkeepers we should call them) of these western towns visit the eastern ports of Baltimore, New York and Philadelphia, once a year, to lay in their stock of goods; an evidence, it might seem, of want of confidence in the merchants of those places; but the great variety of articles, and the risk attending their carriage to so great a distance by land and water, render it necessary that the store-keepers should attend both to their purchase and conveyance.

I think the time is at hand when these periodical transmontane journeys are to give place to expeditions down the Ohio and Mississippi to New Orleans. The vast and increasing produce of these states in grain, flour, cotton, sugar, tobacco, peltry, timber, &c. &c. which finds a ready vent at New Orleans, will be returned through the same channel, in the manufactures of Europe and the luxuries of the east, to supply the growing demands of this western world. How rapidly this demand actually increases it is utterly impossible to estimate; but some idea of it may be formed from a general view of the cause and manners of its gowth. In round numbers there are probably half a million of inhabitants in Ohio, Indiana and Illinois. Immigration (if I may be allowed to borrow a new but good word,) and births, will probably double this number in about six years; and in the mean time, the prosperous circumstances of almost every family are daily creating new wants, and awakening fresh necessities.

On any spot where a few settlers cluster together, attracted by ancient neighbourhood, or by the goodness of the soil, or vicinity to a mill, or by whatever cause, some enterprising proprietor finds in his section what he deems a good scite for a town: he has it surveyed and laid out in lots, which he sells, or offers for sale by auction.

The new town then assumes the name of its founder:—a store-keeper builds a little framed store, and sends for a few cases of goods; and then a tavern starts up, which becomes the residence of a doctor and a lawyer, and the boarding-house of the store-keeper, as well as the resort of the weary traveller: soon follow a blacksmith and other handicraftsmen in useful succession: a school-master, who is also the minister of religion, becomes an important accession to this rising community. Thus the town proceeds, if it proceeds at all, with accumulating force, until it becomes the metropolis of the neighborhood. Hundreds of these speculations may have failed, but hundreds prosper; and thus trade begins and thrives as population grows around these lucky spots; imports and exports maintaining their just proportion. One year ago the neighbourhood of this very town of Princetown was clad in "buckskin;" now the men appear at church in good blue cloth, and the women in fine calicoes and straw bonnets.

The town being fairly established, a cluster of inhabitants, small as it may be, acts as a stimulus on the cultivation of the neighbourhood: redundancy of supply is the consequence, and this demands a vent. Water mills, or in defect of water power, steam mills, rise on the nearest navigable stream, and thus an effectual and constant market is secured for the increasing surplus of produce. Such are the elements of that accumulating mass of commerce, in exports, and consequent imports, which will render the Mississippi the greatest thoroughfare in the world.

At Vincennes, the foundation is just laid of a large establishment of mills to be worked by steam. Water mills of great power are now building on the Wabash, near Harmony, and undertakings of a similar kind will be called for and executed all along this river, which, with its tributary rivers, several of which are also navigable from the east and the west, is the outlet of a very rich and thickly settling country, comprising the prime of Indiana and a valuable portion of the Illinois, over the space of about one hundred thousand square miles.

There is nothing in Vincennes, on its first appearance, to make a favourable impression on a stranger; but it improves on acquaintance, for it contains agreeable people; and there is a spirit of cleanliness, and even neatness in their houses and manner of living: there is also a strain of politeness, which marks the origin of this settlement in a way which is very flattering to the French.

It is a phenomenon in national character which I cannot explain, but the fact will not be disputed, that the urbanity of manners which distinguishes that nation from all others is never entirely lost; but that French politeness remains until every trace of French origin is obliterated. A Canadian Frenchman who, after having spent twenty years of his prime among the Indians, settles in the back woods of the United States, still retains a strong impression of French good breeding.

Is it by this attractive qualification that the French have obtained such sway among the Indians? I think it may be attributed with as much probability to their conciliating manner, as to superior integrity; though the latter has been the cause generally assigned.

This tenaciousness of national character, under all changes of climate and circumstances, of which the French afford many remarkable instances, is the more curious, as it is not universal among nations, though the Germans afford, I am told, examples equally strong. This country gives favourable opportunities for observation on this interesting subject.

What is it that distinguishes an Englishman from other men? or is there any mark of national character which neither time, climate, nor circumstance can obliterate? An anglo-American is not English, but a German is a German, and a Frenchman French, to the fourth, perhaps to the tenth generation.

The Americans have no central focus of fashion, or local standard of politeness; therefore remoteness can never be held as an apology for sordid dress or coarse demeanour. They are strangers to rural simplicity; the embarrassed air of an awkward rustic, so frequent in England, is rarely seen in the United States. This, no doubt, is the effect of political equality, the consciousness of which accompanies all their intercourse, and may be supposed to operate most powerfully on the manners of the lowest class: for high and low there are, and will be, even here, and in every society, from causes moral and physical, which no political regulations can or ought to controul.

In viewing the Americans, and sketching in a rude manner, as I pass along, their striking characteristics, I have seen a deformity so general that I cannot help esteeming it national, though I know it admits of very many individual exceptions. I have written it and then erased it, wishing to pass it by: but it wont do:—it is the truth, and to the truth I must adhere. Cleanliness in houses, and too often in person, is neglected to a degree which is very revolting to an Englishman.

America was bred in a cabin: this is not a reproach, for the origin is most honourable; but as she has exchanged her hovel of unhewn logs for a framed building, and that again for a mansion of brick, some of her cabin habits have been unconsciously retained. Many have already been quitted; and, one by one, they will all be cleared away, as I am told they are now in the cities of the eastern states.

There are, I believe, court-houses, which are also made use of as places of worship, in which filth of all kinds has been accumulating ever since they were built. What reverence can be felt for the majesty of religion, or of the laws, in such sites of abomination? The people who are content to assemble in them can scarcely respect each other.—Here is a bad public example. It is said, that to clean these places is the office of no one: but why is no person appointed? Might it not be inferred that a disregard to the decencies of life prevails through such a community?

July 19. We are at Princeton, in a log tavern, where neatness is as well observed as at many taverns in the city of Bath, or any city. The town will soon be three years old; the people belong to old America in dress and manners, and would not disgrace old England in the general decorum of their deportment.

But I lament here, as every where, the small acocunt that is had of time. Subsistence is secured so easily, and liberal pursuits being yet too rare to operate as a general stimulus to exertion, life is whiled away in a painful state of yawning lassitude.

July 20. The object of our pursuit, like the visions of fancy, has hitherto seemed to recede from our approach: we are, however, at length, arrived at the point where reality is likely to reward our labours.

Twenty or thirty miles west of this place, in the Illinois territory, is a large country where settlements are just now beginning, and where there is abundant choice of unentered lands of a description which will satisfy our wishes, if the statements of travellers and surveyors can be relied on, after great abatements.

This is a critical season of the year, and we feel some anxiety for the health of our party, consisting of ten individuals. July and the two succeeding months are trying to the constitutions of new comers, and this danger must be incurred by us; we hope, however, under circumstances of great mitigation. In the first place, the country is at present free from sickness, and the floods were too early in the spring to occasion any apprehensions of an unhealthy autumn to the inhabitants. In the next place, we have an opportunity of choice of situation for our temporary sojourn. Unfortunately this opportunity of choice is limited by the scarcity of houses, and the indifference evinced by settlers to the important object of health in the fixing their own habitations. The vicinity of rivers, from the advantages of navigation and machinery, as well as the fertility of soil, have generally suspended a proper solicitude about health.

Prince Town affords a situation for a temporary abode more encouraging than any place we have before visited in this neighbourhood; it stands on an elevated spot, in an uneven or rolling country, ten miles from the Wabash and two from the navigable stream of the Patok: but the country is very rich, and the timber vast in bulk and height, so that though healthy at present to its inhabitants, they can hardly encourage us with the hope of escaping the seasoning to which they say all new comers are subject. There is a very convenient house to be let for nine months, for which we are in treaty. This will accommodate us until our own be prepared for our reception in the spring, and may be rented, with a garden well stocked, for about £20. I think we shall engage it, and, should a sickly season come on, recede for a time into the high country, about a hundred miles back, returning here to winter when the danger is past.

As to travelling in the backwoods of America I think there is none so agreeable, after you have used yourself to repose in your own pallet, either on the floor of a cabin or under the canopy of the woods, with an umbrella over your head and a noble fire at your feet; you will then escape the only serious nuisance of American travelling, viz. hot rooms and swarming beds, exceeding instead of repairing the fatigues of the day. Some difficulties occur from ferries, awkward fords, and rude bridges, with occasional swamps; but such is the sagacity and surefootedness of the horses that accidents happen very rarely.

July 21. This is an efficient government. It seems that some irregularities exist, or are suspected in the proceedings of certain of the offices which are established for the sale of public lands. Whilst we were at Vincennes, a confidential individual from the federal city made his appearance at the land office there, with authority to inspect and examine on the spot. Last night the same gentleman lodged here, on his way to the land office of Shawnee Town, at which we propose to make our entries, where he is equally unexpected as he had been at Vincennes, and where his visit is somewhat *mal-a-propos* as to our convenience. One of the efficient officers, the register, had been left by us sick about seventy miles from Cincinnati; and the other, the receiver, passed this place for Vincennes yesterday, and fixed to return on Sunday, in order to proceed with me through the woods on Monday, on an exploring expedition to the Illinois. The republican delegate informed me immediately on his arrival, that he had left an absolute injunction for the instant return of the receiver to his office, expressing regret at deranging my plans, at the same time making ample amends by his own arrangement for my accommodation.

The effect produced at Vincennes under my observation, and the decided manner of this gentleman, convince me that this mode of treatment is fully as effectual as that by "motion for the production of papers and committees for their examination," by which deliberate procedure the inconvenience of suprize is politely obviated.

July 23. The small-pox is likely to be excluded from this state, vaccination being very generally adopted, and inoculation for the small-pox prohibited altogether,—not by law, but by common consent. If it should be known that an individual had undergone the operation, the inhabitants would compel him to withdraw entirely from society. If he lived in a town, he must absent himself, or he would be driven off.

Mental derangement is nearly unknown in these new countries. There is no instance of insanity at present in this State, which probably now contains 100,000 inhabitants. A middle-aged man, of liberal attainments and observation, who has lived much of his life in Kentucky, and has travelled a good deal over the western country, remarked, as an incident of extraordinary occurrence, that he once knew a lady afflicted with this malady.

The simple maxim, that a man has a right to do any thing but injure his neighbour, is very broadly adopted into the practical as well as political code of this country.

A good citizen is the common designation of respect; when a man speaks of his neighbour as a virtuous man—"he is a very good citizen."

Drunkenness is rare, and quarrelling rare in proportion. Personal resistance to personal aggression, or designed affront, holds a high place in the class of duties with the citizen of Indiana.

It seems that the Baptists (who are the prevailing sect in this country,) by their religious tenets, would restrain this summary mode of redressing injuries among the brethren of their church: a respectable but knotty member of that community was lately arraigned before their spiritual tribunal for supporting heterodox opinions on this subject. After hearing the arguments derived from the texts of scripture, which favour the doctrine of non-resistance, he rose, and with energy of action suited to his words, declared that he should not wish to live longer than he had the right to knock down the man who told him he lied.

July 24. Regretting, as I must, my perpetual separation from many with thom I was in habits of agreeable intercourse in old England, I am much at my ease on the score of society. We shall possess this one thing needful, which it was supposed the wilderness could not supply, in the families of our own establishment, and a circle of citizen neighbours, such as this little town affords already. There prevails so much good sense and useful knowledge, joined to a genuine warmth of friendly feeling, a disposition to promote the happiness of each other, that the man who is lonely among them is not formed for society. Such are the citizens of these new states, and my unaffected and well considered wish is to spend among them the remainder of my days.

The social compact here is not the confederacy of a few to reduce the many into subjection; but is, indeed and in truth, among these simple republicans, a combination of talents, moral and physical, by which the good of all is promoted in perfect accordance with individual interest. It is in fact a better, because a more simple state than was ever pourtrayed by an Utopian theorist.

But the people, like their fellow men, have their irregular and rude passions, and their gross propensities and follies, suited to their condition, as weeds to a particular soil; so that this, after all, is the real world, and no poetical Arcadia.

One agreeable fact, characteristic of these young associations, presses more and more upon my attention:—there is a great amount of social feeling, much real society in new countries, compared with the number of inhabitants. Their importance to each other on many interesting occasions creates kind sentiments. They have fellow-feeling in hope and fear, in difficulty and success, and they make ten-fold more of each other than the crowded inhabitants of populous countries.

July 25. Harmony. Yesterday we explored the country from this place to the Ohio, about eighteen miles, and returned to-day by a different route. There is a great breadth of valuable land vacant; not the extremely rich river-bottom land, but close cool sand of excellent quality. It is, however, not so well watered, nor so much varied in surface as is desirable; and we are so taken with the prairies we have seen, and with the accounts we have heard of those before us in the Illinois, that no "timbered" land can satisfy our present views.

We lodged last night in a cabin at a very new town, called Mount Vernon, on the banks of the Ohio. Here we found the people of a cast confirming my aversion to a settlement in the immediate vicinity of a large navigable river. Every hamlet is demoralized, and every plantation is liable to outrage within a short distance of such a thoroughfare.

Yet the view of that noble expanse was like the opening of bright day upon the gloom of night, to us who had been so long buried in deep forests. It is a feeling of confinement which begins to damp the spirits, from this complete exclusion of distant objects. To travel day after day among trees of a hundred feet high, without a glimpse of the surrounding country, is oppressive to a degree which those cannot conceive who have not experienced it; and it must depress the spirits of the solitary settler to pass years in this state. His visible horizon extends no farther than the tops of the trees which bound his plantation—perhaps, five hundred yards. Upwards he sees the sun, and sky, and stars; but around him an eternal forest, from which he can never hope to emerge:—not so in a thickly settled district; he cannot there enjoy any freedom of prospect, yet there is variety, and some scope for the imprisoned vision. In a hilly country a little more range of view may occasionally be obtained; and a river is a stream of light as well as of water, which feasts the eye with a delight inconceivable to the inhabitants of open countries.

Under these impressions a prairie country increases in attraction; and to-morrow we shall commence a round in the Illinois, which we hope will enable us to take some steps towards our final establishment.

July 26. Left Harmony after breakfast, and crossing the Wabash at the ferry, three miles below, we proceeded to the Big-Prairie, where, to our astonishment, we beheld a fertile plain of grass and arable, and some thousand acres covered with corn, more luxuriant than any we had before seen. The scene reminded us of some open well cultivated vale in Europe, surrounded by wooded uplands; and forgetting that we were, in fact, on the very frontiers, beyond which few settlers had penetrated, we were transported in idea to the fully peopled regions we had left so far behind us.

From *The Emigrant's Guide to the western and southwestern states and territories*, by William Darby [1818], pp. 213-217.

Darby, William.

Following our second war with England, there was a great rush of emigrants into the western and southwestern territories of the United States. This created quite a widespread demand for an emigrant's guide; and among those who first supplied the desired information was Mr. William Darby. He had been one of the surveyors in adjusting the Louisiana boundary, was familiar with the French and Spanish land claims, and perhaps was better qualified than any one else to publish a guide. His work appeared in 1817, and accompanied by maps, shows all the available roads, streams and routes to be followed by the emigrants.

THE STATE OF INDIANA, has the Illinois territory west, the state of Kentucky southeast, the state of Ohio, east, and the Michigan territory, and lake Michigan and the Northwest territory, north.

Extent, population, rivers, productions. This state covers an area of 36,640 square miles, equal to 23,449,600 American acres. More than one half of this surface remains yet in possession of the Indians. The southern and much most valuable part of the state is reclaimed, and is settling with emigrants from the northern and eastern states with great rapidity. The following statistical table exhibits the subdivisions of this state, and the population in 1810. This can afford but very defective document to give a correct idea of the present state of the country. There is no doubt but that the number of inhabitants have increased to near one hundred thousand at the present time.

STATISTICAL TABLE OF INDIANA.

Counties.	*Population* 1810.	*Chief Towns*
Clark	5,760	Jeffersonville.
Dearborn	7,310	Lawrenceburg.
Harrison	3,695	CORYDON.
Jefferson		
Knox	7,965	Vincennes.
	24,610	

Since the last census of 1810, the new counties of Washington, Switzerland, Jefferson, Wayne, Gibson, Posey, and Warwick, have been formed. The distributive population of the state of Indiana, at this time, as well as the aggregate amount, must differ essentially from the relative position and numbers found seven years past.

The rivers of the state of Indiana, are, Ohio, Wabash, Illinois, and Maumee.

Ohio river washes the state from the mouth of the Great Miami, to that of the Wabash, a distance, following the bends of the stream of three hundred and sixty-five miles. It is a curious fact, that in this long course, no stream, above the size of a large creek, falls into the Ohio from Indiana; White river branch of Wabash, having its head-streams within thirty miles of the bank of Ohio. There are few countries in the world can much exceed this part of the banks of the Ohio. The lands are varied, a considerable portion of the first quality, and but little that can be really considered unproductive. The settlements are in such quick progress as to render a description only necessarily correct for the moment.

Wabash river is strictly the principal stream of Indiana, from the surface of which it draws the far greater part of its waters. The head branches of Wabash is in the Indian country, of course very imperfectly explored. This river rises with the Maumee near Fort Wayne, and like the Illinois, flows to the west through Indiana, unto almost the west border of the state, where the river gradually curves to S. W. by S., which course it maintains to its junction with the Ohio. The entire length of the Wabash exceeds three hundred miles; it is a fine stream, without falls or extraordinary rapids. It was through the channel of the Wabash that the French of Canada first discovered the Ohio, to which they gave the name of *Belle Riviere*, or beautiful river, but considered the Wabash the main branch, and gave the united rivers its name. In many old maps of North America, the Ohio below the junction of the two streams, is called Wabash. The Tennessee was then very imperfectly known, and considered at one-fourth the size it was found to possess by subsequent discovery.

White River, the eastern branch of Wabash, is itself a stream of considerable importance, draining the heart, and far the finest part of the state of Indiana. About forty miles above its junction with the Wabash, White river divides into the north and south branches. North branch rises in the Indian country by a number of creeks, which, uniting near the Indian boundary line; forms a fine navigable river of about 180 miles in length; its course nearly

S. W. South branch rises in the same ridges with the White Water branch of the Great Miami; its course S. W. by W. 150 miles. Upon this latter river many of the most flourishing settlements in the state have been formed. The country it waters is amongst the most agreeable, healthy, and fertile in the Ohio valley.

Illinois river has its source in Indiana, but has been noticed when treating of the Illinois territory.

Maumee rises in fact in the state of Ohio, near Fort Loramie, but flowing N. W. enters the state of Indiana, turns west, encircles Fort Wayne, and turning N. E. again enters the state of Ohio, through which it flows to the place of its egress into Lake Erie.

The southern extremity of Lake Michigan penetrates the state of Indiana, and at or near its extreme south elongation, receives the Calumet, and not far north of its S. E. extension, the small river St. Joseph enters from the state of Indiana, but enters the Michigan lake in the Michigan territory.

The country is here but very imperfectly known; even the latitude of the southern extremity of Lake Michigan remains uncertain. When the French possessed Canada and Louisiana, their traders constantly passed by Chicago into Illinois, and by the Maumee into the Wabash, in their voyages. These passages are now again becoming frequented, and will, within the lapse of a few years, present the active transport of commercial wealth, and the daily intercourse of civilized men.

It may be doubted whether any state of the United States, all things duly considered, can present more advantages than Indiana. Intersected or bounded in all directions by navigable rivers or lakes, enjoying a temperate climate, and an immense variety of soil. Near two-thirds of its territorial surface is yet in the hands of the Indians, a temporary evil, that a short time will remedy. When all the extent comprised within the legal limits of this state are brought into a state of improvement, with one extremity upon the Ohio river, and the opposite upon Lake Michigan, with intersecting navigable streams, Indiana will be the real link that will unite the southern and northern parts of the United States. The connexion between the Canadian lakes and the Ohio and Mississippi rivers, is by no route so direct as through Michigan and Wabash, and by Lake Erie, Maumee and Wabash. The route by Lake Michigan and the Illinois river into the Mississippi is more circuitous than by that of the Wabash into either Lakes Michigan or Erie, and the route through Illinois has another irremediable disadvantage, that of being in a more northern latitude than the Wabash.

When the rivers are in a state of flood, loaded boats of considerable size pass from the head waters of Wabash into St. Mary river, the western branch of the Maumee; the same facility of passage exists between Maumee; the Chicago into the Illinois river.* These facts prove two things: first, the almost perfect level of the country, and secondly, the great ease with which canals can be formed, and the very limited expense of their construction.

In the present state of population, the communication by the Wabash and Miami of the Lakes into Lake Erie, must produce advantages of greatly more extensive benefit, than by Lake Michigan and Illinois river. Many years must elapse before either is opened. The country is yet wilderness, and the right of soil in the aboriginal inhabitants.

Like Illinois territory, the state of Indiana has no mountains; the latter is however more hilly than the former, particularly towards the Ohio river.

The southeastern extremity of Indiana, between White and Ohio rivers, is very broken. A ridge of hills commences above the junction of the Wabash and Ohio, which extending in a N. E. direction through Indiana, Ohio, Pennsylvania, is finally lost in the state of New-York. This ridge in Indiana separates the waters of Wabash from those of Ohio river; and in Ohio, Pennsylvania, and New-York, forms the demarkation between the streams which flow into the Canadian lakes from those which discharge their waters into the Ohio. No part of this ridge is very elevated; its component parts are limestone and schistose sandstone. It is barren of minerals except iron and coal.

Towns—Vilages—Schools.—Corydon, on the road from Louisville to Vincennes, is now the seat of government. This town is recent, but rapidly improving. The number of its houses or inhabitants we are unable to state, and it would not, if now accurately given, remain so one year.

Vincennes, upon the left bank of the Wabash, is the oldest and the largest town in the state; having been built by the French from Canada; most of the inhabitants are of French extraction. The site of the town is level, and when in its natural state, was an extensive prairie. The lands are fertile in a high degree. In a commercial point of view, the position of this town is very advantageous, and must advance rapidly. Standing upon the limit of two

*See Drake's Cincinnati, page 222 and 223. Volney, Paris edition, Vol. I. page 29.

territorial divisions, Vincennes cannot ever again become the seat of government, a loss more than compensated by a favourable situation for agriculture, and the transport of produce to New-Orleans, Pittsburg, and indeed to the entire western and southern parts of the United States.

Blackford, Harmony, Madison, Lawrenceburg, and Brookville, are all towns of this state. Being of recent formation, they are mostly small, and have nothing very worthy of notice to distinguish them from each other.

No good topographical or statistical account having been yet published upon this state, the data are not abundant respecting its towns or other artificial improvements.

The political institutions of this new state are honourable in a high degree to the framers; the constitution of the state provides every restraint against the encroachments of power, and the licentiousness of freedom, that human wisdom can perhaps foresee. Slavery is banished from the state, or rather it never was received within its borders. The inhabitants at this moment enjoy all that liberty, industry, and impartial administration of justice can bestow.

Colleges and schools can scarce be considered to exist as public institutions; private schools are numerous, and increasing with the population.

Productions—Staples.—Flour may be considered the principal artificial production and staple. Much of the land is well calculated to produce wheat. Mill streams abound. Rye is also extensively cultivated, and used as bread grain, to feed horses, and to supply the distillers. Maize is, next to wheat, the most valuable crop cultivated in Indiana. The fertile alluvion upon the rivers and many parts of the prairies are admirably adapted to the production of this excellent vegetable. The quantity made from an acre of land cannot be determined with any precision; but the production is generally abundant. In all the new settlements in the Ohio and Mississippi valley, maize is the crop first resorted to for providing subsistence, and we believe it to be the only grain that in many places would have rendered settlement possible. The rapidity of its growth and the easy application of its farina to use, will always secure to maize a rank amongst the most precious vegetables yet cultivated by mankind.

Oats, barley, and buckwheat, are also reared; the former in great abundance as food for horses. Potatoes (Irish potatoes) are cultivated in plenty, as is a great variety of pulse. Pumpions, squashes, melons, and cucumbers are cultivated and may be produced in any assignable quantity.

In no country could artificial meadow be made to more advantage. This useful part of agriculture is almost always neglected in our new settlements, and only becomes an object of attention when the natural range is exhausted. The great body of the emigrants coming from places where artificial meadows are in use, their immense benefits are not to be learned by all.

For domestic consumption and exportation, are made large quantities of beef, pork, butter, lard, bacon, leather, whiskey, and peach brandy. With but little exception, Natchez and New Orleans are the outlets of the surplus produce of Indiana. A few articles are occasionally sent to Pittsburgh, but that commerce, never extensive, is on the decline. The attention of the inhabitants is drawn towards the natural channel, through which their wealth must circulate. Sugar, coffee, wines, and foreign ardent spirits, are brought from New Orleans, but of the former necessary, considerable quantity is made in the country from the sap of the sugar maple tree.

Dry goods, hardware, ironmongery, paper, and books, are mostly imported by the route of Pittsburgh. Some of all those articles, the two latter perhaps excepted, are also imported from New Orleans. Saddles, bridles, hats, boots, and shoes, are manufactured, in great part, in the state. This indeed is a trait that marks the whole western states, that the latter indispensable articles of domestic consumption are generally to be found at every new settlement, for prices not greatly advanced above that of the same objects in large commercial cities on the Atlantic coast.

The same observations may be made respecting cabinet, and all other kinds of household furniture. Tables, chairs, and bedsteads, are made in all the large towns in the valleys of Ohio and Mississippi, with all the requisite qualities of elegance and strength.

Except in Lexington, Kentucky, and Pittsburg, book printing is not yet done to any considerable extent west of the Aleghany. In these two latter places and in Cincinnati, Nashville, and some other places, book stores have been established to considerable extent, but a well assorted library could not be formed in any, or perhaps all those towns. Professional men, and indeed all men who are emigrating to the west, ought to carry with them such books as they may need. It is not without more difficulty than is commonly believed to exist, that a good selection of books can be made even in New-York or Philadelphia, much less in towns upon the Ohio or Mississippi waters.

From *Geographical sketches on the western country designed for Emigrants and settlers*, by E. Dana [1819], pp. 48-49, 107-32.

DANA, EDMUND.

Mr. Dana spent six years among the native Indians living in the region of the Great Lakes. His knowledge gained there won for him considerable reputation as a guide, and by 1816 he had been employed by more than thirteen hundred persons to select for them tracts of land on which they desired to make permanent settlements.

The knowledge acquired while performing this work and his personal observations qualified him to speak with some authority on many phases of the northwest country. His sketches were published in 1817.

In the state of Indiana, not far from Big Blue river, is a spacious cave, more than two miles in extent. The entrance is in the side of an elevated hill. Large quantities of Epsom salt, and salt petre, are found in this cave. Here numerous calcareous exudations are displayed in a variety of shapes, resembling artificial carvings. Bats inhabiting this cave are numerous, and it is necessary for an adventurer who would explore it, to preserve his torch or candle from extinguishment by those creatures, with a lantern. Within the tract called *the barrens*, expanding in divers directions several miles, there are various other large caves; on the bottoms of some of which flow streams of water, large enough to drive mills.

There is in the county of Orange, in this state, a large stream, called *Lost river;*—after flowing several miles on the surface, the whole current suddenly sinks into the earth, and is never seen or heard of more. Near a creek that joins the Ohio about a mile west of New-Albany, is a spring, so strongly impregnated with sulphurated hydrogen gas, as to produce combustion, by placing a torch or lighted candle a little above the water. About six miles northwest of Corydon, near the Big Blue river, just above the base of an elevated hill, bursts from amidst the rocks, a cold spring, which in the dryest seasons is copious enough to drive two pair of stones and a saw, in an elegant stone mill, built just by its mouth. There are many other springs of this description, cold as any well water, on which profitable mills are built, within this state. .

INDIANA.

INDIANA was admitted into the federal union, as a state, in the year 1816. It is bounded by the state of Illinois on the west, by a line on the Wabash from its mouth to 40 miles above Vincennes, and thence on a meridian line so far north as to include the southern extremity of lake Michigan 10 miles in depth, by a boundary line on the north drawn due east: east by the state of Ohio, by a meridian line, running from the mouth of the Big Miami: on the south by the Ohio river. Length from north to south, 284 miles; breadth from east to west 155; contains about 37,000 square miles; lays between 37° 45′ and 41° 52′ north latitude, and 7° 40′ and 10° west longitude.

Face of the Country, Soil, &c.—There are in Indiana no considerable heights of land, that (strictly speaking) can properly be denominated mountains. The river hills from 100 to 200 feet high, diverging from 30 to 600 rods from the Ohio, according to the width of the alluvial margin, commence within two miles east of the Great Miami, and extend in the direction of the river Ohio, within about twelve miles above the Falls, where they gradually merge in a valley, which extends about 25 miles below; where the same range of hills reappears, and extends in the course of the river, as it runs, from 60 to 70 miles below, where the hills disappear, and a region sometimes level, and sometimes waving, commences, which is expanded southwestwardly to the Wabash, and northwestwardly and northeastwardly, with rare exceptions, to the great western lakes.

On the borders of most of the streams are strips of rich bottom, and there are also praira lands, from one to five miles wide. Between the Wabash and lake Michigan, the country is generally level, abounding alternately with prairas and woodland, and occasionally large marshes, and several small lakes. Some of the prairas between fort Harrison and fort Meigs, are covered with red top and fowl meadow grasses.

Between the Ohio and White river, a range of knobs forms the high table lands that divide the head waters of some of the tributaries to the Ohio from those of the White river, commencing about 25 miles north from the Ohio, and 20 miles eastwardly from Salem, and pursuing a course southwestwardly, reaches that river 12 or 13 miles below the Falls, where they terminate. Most of this region is thickly covered with large forest trees.

North of the Wabash, between Tippecanoe and Ouitanon, a

French settlement, the banks of the streams are high, abrupt and broken, and the lands, except the prairas, covered with timber. Between the Plein and the Theakiki, (which are the head branches of the Illinois) the country is flat and wet, interspersed with prairas of an inferior soil. In this region, the swamps seem to furnish the head streams of rivers, and the lands appear to be too low and wet for cultivation.

There are two kinds of prairas, the *river* and the *upland;* the former are destitute of timber, and are said to exhibit vestiges of former cultivation; the latter are from 30 to 100 feet more elevated, and are more numerous and extensive. Some of them are not larger than a common field, others extending farther than the eye can reach. They are usually interspersed with some clumps of trees, and bounded by heavy timbered forests. In spring and summer, they are covered with a luxuriant growth of grass and fragrant flowers, from five to eight feet high. The soil of these plains is often as deep and fertile as the best bottoms. The prairas near the Wabash are remarkably rich, and almost inexhaustible by crops. By the digging of wells, the vegetable soil has been found 22 feet deep, bedded on white sand; their common depth is from two to five feet.

Among the lands purchased of the Indians in 1818, are 8,500,000 acres within the state of Indiana. This new purchase is bounded on the south by a line drawn 18 miles above fort Harrison, at the Wabash, on the old Indian boundary—thence along on the east side of the Wabash to the forks of White river, and from thence to fort Wayne.

The acquisition of this new purchase, which is now surveying, and will soon be exposed for sale, will greatly contribute to increase the population and promote the prosperity of the state of Indiana.

The quality of the soil, for so large a tract in a body, will bear a comparison to any, perhaps, within the United States. Indeed, it has been esteemed, by intelligent men, who have often traversed it, in all directions, in point of rural scenery, a copious supply of pure water, fertility of soil and security to health, equal to any part of the western country. The greater part is covered with a beautiful growth of forest trees, not unlike those common to bottoms and uplands of the first quality in the state of Ohio; except on considerable portions of fine prairas, which in the centre and to the northwest in various places, are spread out extensively. The surface in this part of the tract is delightfully variegated by gentle undulations.

At the northeast, although the lands will make valuable plantations, the surface over a considerable part, approaches, too near, perhaps, a perfect champaign to embrace all the conveniences of the best agricultural situations. The soil is, however, strong and durable, well adpated to wheat and meadow grasses. The prevailing growth here is beech, although there be considerable sugar maple and other forest trees that indicate a rich soil. The infrequency of running streams, and the level surface in the northeast, cause a scarcity of good mill seats.

The lands bordering on the waters of the White river and its tributary streams are considered among those of the best quality, excepting a strip of about 30 miles by 15, laying near the west branch, which being low, marshy, and occasionally overflowed, is unfavorable to health. Much of this tract, not excepted, is delightfully situated, and the surface consisting of gentle undulations, supplied with good water, and variegated with numerous small, rich, dry prairas.

An extensive tract, bordering on the waters of the Tippacanoe and the two Vermillion and Eel rivers, are lands of superior quality, and not excelled for fertility by any in the state. The northern position of these lands, will afford a climate favorable to the health of emigrants not habituated to southern latitudes.

The productions of Indiana in corn, wheat, rye, barley, oats, beans, peas, Irish, sweet potatoes, and garden vegetables of every description, are abundant. In some parts of the state, where the soil consists of a sandy loam, certain species of the wine grape, particularly the grape of Good Hope, and cotton, have flourished. It is presumed that upland rice would succeed well in this soil, as it has been known to flourish within the state of Kentucky, in the same latitude. Farming is conducted on a large scale in the Wabash country for several miles around Vincennes and fort Harrison, where the soil is exceedingly productive. Within this region, single farmers have raised, in one year, from 4,000 to 10,000 bushels of corn, and various kinds of small grain. The soil in these places is of a deep, rich, dark gray, sandy loam, which is ploughed easily, and resists the effects of drought and drenching rains. It has proved so inexhaustible by cropping without manure, that the same corn fields have been planted for more than half a century in constant succession without a perceivable diminution of crops.

The population of Indiana has, perhaps, experienced a more rapid increase than any state in the union. At the census in 1810, it contained only 24,520 inhabitants, exclusive of Indians.

In the territorial census of 1815, the number returned to Congress, as a prerequisite to the formation of a state, was 67,784. At this period August, 1819, it is confidently believed, that 165,000 would not be an exaggerated estimate. Since the census of 1815, the number of counties have more than doubled, although until the late purchase in 1818, nearly two-thirds of the extent of territory was in the possession of the Indians.

The several counties to which the number of inhabitants is not annexed, have been formed since 1815—the other counties show, in the second column, the number of inhabitants they respectively contained, at that time—the third column presents the names of the towns in which are the seats of justice for the counties to which they are annexed.

Counties.	*Population.*	*Chief Towns.*
Clark	7,000	Charleston.
Crawford		Mount Sterling.
Dearborn	4,426	Lawrenceburgh.
Davies		Washington.
Dubois		
Franklin	7,970	Brookville.
Fayette		Connersville.
Floyd		New-Albany.
Gibson	5,330	Princeton.
Harrison	6,769	Corydon.
Jackson		Brownstown.
Jefferson	4,093	Madison.
Jennings		Vernon.
Knox	6,800	Vincennes.
Lawrence		Palestine.
Monroe		
Orange		Paoli.
Perry	3,000	Franklin.
Posey	3,000	Harmony.
Randolph		
Ripley		Versailles.
Spencer		Rockport.
Sullivan		Merom.
Switzerland	3,500	Vevay.
Vandeburgh		Evansville.
Warwick	6,606	Boonsborough.
Washington	3,000	Salem.
Wayne	6,290	Centreville.

Of the chief towns in this state, the progress of improvements and population, render an adequate description very difficult. We will, however, endeavour to give such sketches as will present to enquirers a tolerable view of the towns most considerable, and of the country surrounding them.

Salisbury, formerly the county seat of Wayne, situated on a head branch of Whitewater river, is but two miles eastwardly of Centreville, the latter place consisting of a few cabbins in the woods, where the courts are now holden. Concerning the seat of justice for this county, a great interest has been excited among the citizens; and on application to the legislature, commissioners have been appointed to designate the spot for a permanent establishment. Two expensive brick court houses, have already been erected, one at Salisbury, and the other at Centreville, not more than two miles apart. The land surrounding Salisbury and Centreville, and indeed, the whole county of Wayne, is one of the most valuable tracts for cultivation in the state. The surface in some parts is too flat and wet, but mostly gently waving, the soil strong and durable, covered with stately forest trees, finely watered by the head branches of the Whitewater, which furnishes divers valuable mill seats. Many of the settlers are from North Carolina, whose improvements have formed large and valuable plantations.

Brookville, the county seat of Franklin, stands upon a narrow elevated plain, in the forks of Whitewater. A considerable part of the town, however, is built on the margin of the East Fork, 65 or 70 feet lower than the upper bottom. The situation is pleasant and romantic, exhibiting the variegated prospect of the meanderings of the streams, and of hills topped with forest trees on either side, cultivated farms and water mills. This town, which did not contain 20 dwelling houses at the close of the late war, now, (1819) exceeds the number of one hundred, besides several stores, mechanic shops, &c. Within the limits of the town are two grist and two saw mills, three fulling mills, and three carding machines. There are a neat brick court house, a jail, and a market house. Distance from Cincinnati, north west, 42 miles. The county of Franklin contains excellent bottom lands on the margin of the two Whitewater forks; and the uplands are generally covered with a good soil, and well timbered.

Lawrenceburgh, the seat of justice for the county of Dearborn, stands on the west bank of the Ohio, 23 miles from Cincinnati, and two below the mouth of the Great Miami. The situation of this town is very pleasant, being on a spacious plain, which commands a view of the river, surrounded by extensve rich bottom lands. The spot occupied by the town, is the nearest convenient site on the Ohio west of the Miami. But it is subject to inundation by extraordinary freshets; the largest of which has covered Main, the highest street, four feet deep. But this street is now raised above the highest freshets, and the principal buildings are elevated above the street. On an average, the town is flooded not more than once in three or four years.—But as the inhabitants are familiar with the occurrence, they are prepared: they anchor their fences with little trouble, so as to secure them from floating; their upper rooms receive the contents of their cellars, their cattle and hogs are driven to high grounds; thus prepared they await the overflowing and the recession of the waters, as unconcerned as did the family of Noah the great deluge. The highest floods rarely continue more than eight or ten days. As no stagnant pools remain, the flooding of the town is followed by no injury to health, and by much less inconvenience to the inhabitants, than can be imagined by strangers. The preceding remarks apply only to Old Lawrenceburgh; for New-Lawrenceburgh, so called, within the limits of the same town, about 100 rods from the old settlement, is never overflowed. The latter is a handsome site, bounded by Tanner's creek on the west, which joins the Ohio a mile below, and is navigable to the new town.

It contains a number of large, elegant houses, built with brick, a large grist and saw mill, driven by four oxen, on an inclined plane wheel, a spacious cotton factory, driven by the same power, besides mechanic shops and other buildings, all erected within two years. This site, by itself, which is to be connected with the old town by a high street above the flooding waters, is spacious enough for a pretty large town. Lawrenceburgh, from its first settlement, till within two or three of the last years, has progressed very slowly. Nothing could have so long retarded the prosperity of this delightful situation, which nature seemed to have designed for a centre of much business, but the dreadful apprehensions which emigrants entertain of the evils of overflowing waters. It is the nearest point to the river for an immense tract of interior good land, and yet unsettled, in the most convenient outlet for the produce of the great Whitewater country, and is the natural place of deposite for staple commodities which float down the Big Miami. The evils contemplated from occasional overflowing, the old settlers have found more imaginary than real.

There is no place on the banks of the Ohio, perhaps, where better water is found or more perfect health enjoyed than at Lawrenceburgh. Nor is there any town in the state, we presume, which has flourished more within two or three of the last years; many neat brick houses and stores have lately been erected, both in the old and new town; some of which are nearly as spacious and elegant as any in the western country. Merchants and mechanics of various descriptions have met with encouragement. The town has, within 30 months, doubled its population, which, at this time (August 1819) may be estimated at about 700. Beside the Big Miami and Whitewater, seven considerable streams traverse the county of Dearborn, all emptying into the Ohio, within the county, which borders on that river not exceeding 17 miles. The most of these streams, including the Ohio, have spacious margins of bottom lands. The face of the country bordering on the Ohio, however, for some miles in width, has spread over it many abrupt hills, which as well as the vallies, are covered by a deep rich soil. But as we recede some distance back from the creeks, the surface becomes sufficiently level. In the northern part of the county are large tracts, of which the prevailing growth is oak of divers species. These lands, though the appearance be rather forbidding to a stranger, prove very productive in wheat, grass and most other crops, common to the country.

There appears a considerable propensity in the people of Dearborn county to the formation of towns, there being 12 or 13 already laid off. Our limits will permit us to notice some of the principal only.

Harrison is a pleasant little village on the Whitewater, about 14 miles northeast [south-east] of Lawrenceburgh; the main street being the boundary line between the states Indiana and Ohio. It would seem from the numerous tumuli and places of ancient sepulture, that this plain, centuries ago, was covered by the habitations of men.—The town which contains a considerable number of neat dwelling houses, is surrounded by a tract of excellent land, on which are many handsome plantations. *Hardensburgh*, on the west bank of the Great Miami, two miles from its mouth, occupies a handsome site, and contains about 50 houses, seven or eight of which are decent brick buildings.

Aurora, at the mouth of Hogan creek, on the west bank of that stream, four miles below Lawrenceburgh, and nine above Rising Sun, was laid off by 20 proprietors in 1818. About 40 frames, for dwelling houses and stores, were erected on donation lots, before any of the others were offered for sale. This town has a fine prospect of the meanderings of the creek and the river; and is accommodated with as good a harbor for boats, as any place between Pittsburgh and the Mississippi; a strong eddy from the Ohio putting into the creek, which exceeds 15 feet in depth at all stages of water.

Rising Sun, 13 miles below Lawrenceburgh, forms one of the most delightful situations on the banks of the Ohio.

It is surrounded by a spacious tract of rich bottom, and occupies a gentle, gradual descent, that commands a complete prospect of the river; between which and the front row of houses, is a broad street more than 150 rods in length. This town contains more than 100 houses, and affords employment for several traders, taverns, and a number of industrious mechanics.

Wilmington, a small village, stands on a high hill, about equidistant from the East and West Forks of Hogan.

Hanover is a little village two miles above the mouth of Laughry; the houses are mostly cabbins.

Hartford, about five or six miles from the Ohio, is a flourishing village on Laughry creek, containing 50 or 60 houses.

Vevay, the county seat of Switzerland, situated eight miles above the mouth of Kentucky river, on the Ohio, 45 below Cincinnati, is a pleasant flourishing town, containing 190 houses, a decent brick court house, a jail, printing office, a large distillery, several taverns and mechanic shops. A branch of the bank of Indiana is established here. It was commenced in 1814, within the tract granted by the United States, to about 30 Swiss families in 1804; who began their settlements, near the place where the town now stands, in the following year. This land was obtained from government on an extended credit, for the purpose of encouraging the cultivation of the grape vine; in which employment the Swiss have been more successful, it is presumed, than any attempt on a large scale, within the United States. In 1815, about 100 hogsheads of wine were produced from all the vineyards; some of which belonging to individuals, have singly grown grapes latterly, sufficient to make 1,000 gallons of wine. The Madeira and the Cape of Good Hope have flourished better than any other species which have been tried. The vines of each grow well, but the Cape being much less liable to be injured by early frost, is the least precarious and the most productive. This wine is wholesome, and not unpalatable. It is preserved through the summer months without distilled spirits, and grows better by age.

Madison, on the second bottom of the bank of the Ohio, is the county seat of Jefferson. This is one of the most beautiful and flourishing towns in the state; was commenced 1811; in February, 1819, contained 821 inhabitants, 123 dwelling houses, besides stores, mechanic shops, &c. Has a court house and jail, and a banking establishment. This town derives an importance from its central position, by standing in one of the most northerly bends of the Ohio; thereby presenting one of the nearest points of Ohio navigation to that extensive body of rich land, at and around the Delaware towns, which yet remains uncultivated. The town is, except on the river board, surrounded by rugged, high hills, which offer a steep and laborious ascent for a loaded team.

New-Lexington, 16 miles west of Madison, contains about 50 houses, and is in the vicinity of an extensive tract of good land.

New-London, 10 miles below Madison, on the Ohio, is formed by nature for one of the most pleasant situations on that river; presenting a gradual and gentle descent for 150 rods back from the river, the position of the ground affording a most excellent route for a good road to the back country, and exhibiting from a distance, a charming view of the broad expanse of the Ohio.

Charlestown, the county seat of Clark, is situated two miles from the Ohio, 29 miles south of west from Madison, and 14 miles above the Falls. It is one of the most flourishing and neatly built towns in the state; contains about 160 houses, chiefly of brick, a handsome court house, and is inhabited by an industrious class of citizens. There are numerous plantations around this town, consisting of good land, and better cultivated, perhaps, than any in the state. This tract is within the grant made by the state of Virginia, to the brave soldiers, who, under the celebrated general Clark, in the revolutionary war, by conquering the British troops and their savage allies, subjected the western country to the jurisdiction of the United States. A large portion of the Grant, so called, containing many thousand acres, is covered with a heavy growth of beech timber, considerably intermixed with sugar maple, and divers other species of trees.—The soil is very productive in fruit trees, wheat, and English grasses.

Jeffersonville stands just above the Falls, on the west bank of the Ohio. The noise, and the sight of the waters tumbling over the precipices below, together with a view of the town of Louisville, on the opposite shore, present a scenery at once variegated, romantic, picturesque and grand. The town is built on the second bottom, above the highest floods, affording a complete view of the river. The non-residence of the proprietors (of whom many are minors) of town lots and of the adjacent country, has hitherto much checked the prosperity of this delightful spot. Of the buildings, which are not very numerous, some are designed and executed in a neat and elegant style, particularly the mansion which was the resience of the late Gov. Posey. A land office, a post office and a printing office are established in this town.

A canal is projected, to commence a few rods east of Jeffersonville, at the mouth of a ravine, thence through the back lots of the town, terminating at an eddy, at the foot of the rapids, by the town of Clarksville. To effect this purpose, the legislature of Indiana, in January 1818, incorporated the Jeffersonville Ohio Canal Company, with a capital of $1,000,000; and granted them permission to raise $100,000 by lottery. In May, 1819, a survey and location having been previously made, the excavation was commenced, and continues to be prosecuted with spirit, and the fairest prospects of success. The extent of this canal will be 2¾ miles; the average depth 45 feet; width at top 100, and at bottom 50 feet. Except one-fourth of a mile at the upper end, there is a bed of rock to be cut through, 10 or 12 feet deep. The charter, which expires in 1899, requires that the canal should be completed before the end of the year 1824. The perpendicular height in the whole extent of the falls being about 23 feet, the canal is expected to furnish excellent mill seats, and a water power sufficient to drive machinery for very extensive manufacturing establishments.

In navigating the Ohio, the saving of time, expence, and waste of property, by means of a canal, to a great extent above the falls, is incalculable. It has been estimated, that Cincinnati alone, for several years past, has paid an extraordinary expence for transporting goods around the falls, exceeding $50,000. The several states bordering on the river above, are each interested in the success of this great undertaking, and it is presumed they will liberally contribute their aid to perfect it. The territory and population to be benefitted by this work, is so extensive, strong hopes have been entertained that some adequate provision will be made by the general government. Capital cannot, perhaps, at the present day, be vested in any public funds that will yield a more productive regular income, than in this establishment.

New-Albany, the seat of justice for Floyd county, is 4½ miles below Jeffersonville, on the bank of the Ohio, on an extensive plain of rich bottom lands. From the first settlement of this town, its progress was rather slow, until within two or three of the last years; since which period it has flourished greatly. The front street is more than three quarters of a mile in length; the number of houses, of which several are spacious and elegant, are supposed to exceed 150; a steam grist and saw mill, each of which perform extensive business, are a great advantage to the town and surrounding country. A spirit of enterprise and industry seems generally to animate the inhabitants, and to exhibit the appearance of a brisk, business-doing place. Floyd was erected into a county in the winter of 1818, out of the counties of Clark and Harrison.

Corydon, the seat of justice for the county of Harrison, is also the present capital of the state, the constitution having appointed it the seat of legislation until 1825. Distant from New Albany, northwest, 21 miles; from the nearest point of the Ohio, about 13—lays between the forks of Indian creek, at their junction—is surrounded by elevated ground, of gentle ascent—contains 8 or 10 neat buildings, beside many others which are ordinary; a spacious court house of stone, which is occupied by the legislature during their session. The supreme court is holden at this place, exclusively.

A few miles from the town, north, northeast and northwest, an extensive tract of land, called *the barrens*, commences, and spreads out in divers directions, in some points several miles—the surface commonly undulating—occasionally are deep sink holes, resembling half-filled wells—the growth is scattering, small oak shrubs, with here and there small clumps of oak trees, of a moderate size; a coarse, short, wild grass, grateful to cattle and sheep, overspreads the ground; the soil in some parts thin and sterile, but generally productive of good crops of corn, small grain, clover and timothy. The region of these barrens is remarkable for caverns, some of which are spacious, from five to fifty feet in height from the flooring; the bottom, roof and walls of flat limestone—the latter often as perpendicular as the walls of a room. It is not uncommon to find streams large enough to drive a mill briskly, pouring their waters over the bottoms of these caves. Small oaks, of a tolerable height, as thinly scattered as the apple trees in an orchard, usually commence at the termination of the *barrens*, and extend for a good distance, sometimes for the space of two or three miles. This description, it is conceived, will apply to most of the *barrens* in the state.

After the constitutional term expires, the seat of government will be removed from Corydon into the interior, probably on or near the West Fork of Whiteriver, within the late purchase—Congress having granted to the state four square miles, for a permanent seat of legislation, to be selected by the state from the public lands. Fixing the temporary seat of government at Corydon has not so much contributed to the prosperity of the town as was expected. Being without any water communication with the Ohio, one and the nearest of the great high ways of the west, Corydon is unfortunately located within that grade of distance from navigable water—where towns have never been known to flourish in this country—not so near as to enjoy the advantage of a river market, and not distant enough to obtain the country custom. The natural situation of the place, however, presents a scenery that attracts the attention of a stranger—a level bottom, encompassed by two fine never failing streams of water, and surrounded by high grounds, gradually rising like an amphitheatre.

Salem, the capital of Washington county, a new but flourishing town, 34 miles north of Corydon, and 25 north west of Jeffersonville, stands on a small branch of Blue river, and contains a decent court house, of brick, 80 or 90 houses, some of which are neat buildings. Around this town is an extensive tract of land, of a superior quality, covered with a thick growth of stately forest trees.

Brownstown, the seat of justice for the county of Jackson, 25 miles north of Salem, is situated near the eastern branch of White-river, on the eastern side, a short distance from the boundary line of the late purchase. The soil around Brownstown consists of a gray sandy loam; it is very friable, and not liable to bake and harden by the heat of the sun. This spot appears to be without the limits of the calcareous region—on a strip of land from two to five miles in width, and from eight to fifteen in length, scarcely any limestone are to be found. Within a mile of the town are large quantities of iron ore, the best which has been discovered in the state. This town was laid off in the midst of the forest, only three or four years ago, and the greater part of the houses are cabbins.

Paoli, the county seat of Orange, is about 70 miles eastwardly of Vincennes, and 40 northwest of Jeffersonville, near the centre of a large tract of valuable lands. The place where the town stands, but three or four years ago, was covered with large forest trees.

Fredonia, a post town in the county of Crawford, 42 miles below the Falls, is situated in the great *Horse-shoe bend*, on an elevated plain, commanding an extensive and romantic prospect of the Ohio. A convenient passage way is opened by nature, through the rocks, to the river; which is here very bold on the western shore, forming a fine eddy. Between the town and the river are a series of horizontal benches, terminating next the town in solid, perpendicular rock, where vines and fruit trees might be cultivated. There is a spring of good water near the centre of the town. In the ledges near the town, are abundance of good free stone. The town occupies as healthy a situation as any spot on the Ohio, and is so situated, in a great bend of the river, which projects so far to the north, at this place, as to cause it to be the nearest convenient accessible point of navigable waters for a great extent of country round. Its position, and the face of the country on each side of the river, for many miles, is favorable for much travel across from Kentucky and the southern states into the interior of Indiana. The town laying about the centre of Indiana, on the river, is supposed to be as near a point as any on the Ohio, to the spot which may be located for the permanent seat of government. It is believed that for 50 or 60 miles, no other spot on the river unites so many natural conveniences for a town. The settlement here was not commenced until the fall of 1818.

Levenworthville, about a mile below Blue river, is a new town in Crawford county, on the bank of the Ohio, containing a few houses.

Mount Sterling, the county seat for Crawford, is located in the woods, and contains a few cabbins; it is about eight miles northwest of Fredonia.

Washington, the seat of justice of Davies county, is situated 20 miles east of Vincennes, 4 miles from the north and 16 from the south fork of Whiteriver, in the centre of a large body of excellent land, lying within the forks of the river; its being thus intersected by those navigable streams, affords peculiar facilities for exporting the produce of the country, which is well supplied with many small streams of good water, and interspersed with several rich prairas.

Merom stands on a high bank of the Wabash, called the Bluffs, opposite Le Motte praira, in Illinois. The natural situation is very pleasant, near large bodies of stone coal. It is the seat of justice for Sullivan county, which consists of a beautiful, fertile, well watered tract of country, through which flows for a considerable extent, the waters of the Wabash. Here are spacious prairas of the first quality, and a number of very large, productive plantations. Among the prairas are included the Honey creek, Fort Harrison and Praira creek prairas, all which present a most delightful scenery; the surface admitting of excellent roads, at all seasons of the year, and the soil equal to any portion of the western country. These natural advantages have speedily produced an influx of population, and a degree of improvement, which has been rarely equalled in the west.

Terre Haute, within the same county, about two miles below fort Harrison, is delightfully situated on a high bank of the Wabash, with a gradual descent to the river, along which extends a skirt of woodland near a mile in width. It was laid out in 1816, and is rapidly increasing its population and extending its improvements.

Shakertown, settled by that industrious class of people called Shakers, lays at the lower end of the county, near the mouth of the Busseron, 15 miles above Vincennes.

Vincennes, the earliest settlement between Kaskaskia and Pittsburgh, is pleasantly situated on the west bank of the Wabash, being the seat of justice for the county of Knox, and formerly the seat of legislation for the territory of Indiana. It was settled by French emigrants in 1735, who in the remote recesses of a wilderness, isolated from the civilized world, formerly approximated in manner and appearance to the savage tribes around them, having scarcely any intercourse with other people—they have, however, since their acquaintance with the Americans, much improved their condition, and among them may now be found intelligent men, who have resumed much of that urbanity of manners peculiar to Frenchmen.

Vincennes, by the serpentine course of the Wabash, is distant from the mouth of that river 152 miles; while from Evansville, the nearest point of the Ohio, it is but 54. It is the most populous town in the state—and although long stationary, from causes not within its control, it is now, under the fostering care of a free government, by the accession of a class of intelligent and enterprising inhabitants, developing its natural resources, by a rapid increase of population, and an extension of various important branches of business. Wm. Fellows & Co. have built a large steam grist and saw mill, and are erecting the present year (1819) twelve spacious brick buildings. The town contains about 300 dwelling houses, a court house of brick, a jail, a spacious neat brick seminary, two places for public worship, one Presbyterian and one Roman Catholic, a public land office, a post office, a bank, and two printing offices.

Princeton, the seat of justice for the county of Gibson, 35 miles southerly from Vincennes, is a flourishing little town, very recently commenced. About one half of this county consists of a soil remarkably good; the residue is second rate. It is watered by the Wabash and White rivers, and some of their tributary streams.

Rockport, so named from its being situated upon a rock, which presents a high bold front on the Ohio, commands a romantic prospect of the river. This town, which is but just commenced, is the seat of justice for Spencer, one of the best counties in the state.

Evansville, stands on a bend in the Ohio, at the mouth of Big Pigeon creek, 54 miles south of Vincennes, and 45 miles above the mouth of the Wabash. It is the seat of justice for Vandeburgh county. This town is in the vicinity of a large tract of excellent land, and acquires an importance from being the nearest and most convenient landing for emigrants bound up the Wabash. This is considered among the best natural situations for mercantile business in the state.

Harmony, 54 miles below Vincennes, and 106 by water above the mouth of the Wabash, stands on the bank of that river, and is the capital of Posey, the southwestern county of the state. It was settled in 1814, by a religious sect of Germans, denominated Harmonists, now consisting of nearly 800 inhabitants. They were first established about 20 miles from Pittsburgh, whence they removed to this place, where they possess several thousand acres of good land, in a body; which is held in the name of Geo. Rapp, their head man and religious teacher, as he alleges, for the common use of the whole. These people are remarkable for the observance of the rules prescribed by their leader, whom they call father, and in whose name all purchases and sales are made; they are remarkable for their regularity, industry and skill in the mechanic arts—are cultivators of the grape vine, and manufacture several kinds of excellent cloths.

Rivers and principal streams.—The Great Miami, Ohio and Wabash rivers, which constitute a considerable portion of the boundary lines of Indiana, are to be found described in our preliminary remarks. The meanderings of the Ohio in passing the width of the state (in a right line but 155 miles) are reckoned 472 miles in extent.

Whitewater, flowing with a rapid current of pure water, generally over a sandy, pebbly bottom, draws its fountain from two chief branches; the east heading near Ohio western boundary, in that state, a few miles west of Greenville; the west takes its origin in the flat lands, 30 miles west of Brookville, just below which town the two branches form a junction, and after running about fifty miles in a southerly direction, empty into the Great Miami $4\frac{1}{2}$ miles in a right line from its confluence with the Ohio.

Next below, on the Ohio, in course as named, are Tanner's, Wilson's, Hogan's (the two main branches of which unite within one hundred rods from the mouth,) Laughry's, Arnold's and Grant's creeks, all within the county of Dearborn. Indian creek, the southern boundary of the Swiss settlement, is seven miles above the mouth of Kentucky river. Silver creek joins the Ohio a short distance below the Falls. Wyandot is equidistant from the Falls and Blue river.

The *Big Blue* river, after meandering 50 miles southwest, bends to the east of south, and empties into the Ohio, 32 miles below the mouth of Salt river.

Little Blue river finds its source in the hills which skirt the Ohio, and forming several cascades, the declivities of which furnish convenient mill seats, meets the Ohio about 12 miles below the mouth of Big Blue river. Ten miles below the former is Sinking creek.

Anderson's river, 60 miles further down, is the largest stream between Blue river and the Wabash. Piqua and Beaver creeks join the Ohio below. Many fine streams of water, affording convenient mill seats, intersect the country between White river and the Ohio.

The main branch of the *Wabash* heads two miles east of fort St. Mary's, in Dark county, Ohio. Of the three other branches, the one called *Little river* heads seven miles south of fort Wayne, and enters the Wabash 80 miles below St. Mary's portage. The east is the *Massissiniway*, heading equidistant from forts Greenville and Recovery, and reaches the Wabash 5 miles below the mouth of Little river. The third is Eel river, issuing from several lakes and ponds 18 miles west of Fort Wayne, and joins the Wabash eight miles below the mouth of the Massisinaway.

The whole range of country traversed by the water of the Wabash, is remarkable for its destitution of hills, and prominences.

Petoka, a small river, running a west course, about 75 miles through rich bottom, falls into the Wabash four miles below White river.

White River meanders nearly across the state southwestwardly, supplying with water and fertilizing a large body of good land, and joins the Wabash 16 miles below Vincennes; 35 miles above the mouth the two principal branches unite, called North or Driftwood-Fork, and the South or Muddy-Fork.

Deche River comes into the Wabash about half way between Vincennes and the mouth of White river, flowing from the north east; it is a rapid, short stream.

Little River, in a serpentine course from the northeast over wide spread bottoms, flows into the Wabash, a short distance above Vincennes. Between this and the *Deche*, a rich bottom expands to a great extent.

St. Marie flows from the north east 60 miles, joining the Wabash 18 miles above Vincennes.

Rocky River, 60 miles above St. Marie, interweaving its branches with those of the main fork of White river, directs its course to the Wabash—is 100 yards wide at its mouth, and branches into several forks.

The Pomme meets the Wabash about 100 miles above the Rocky river—rises near the eastern boundary of the state, not much north of the sources of Whitewater. Besides the above rivers, are a number of small streams, that water the country on the south-east branch of the Wabash. The other side, however, is more abundant in large water courses.

On the northwest side, 10 miles below the Pomme, is Richards creek; 10 miles still below is Rock river with high banks, flowing through a country rather broken.

Tippacanoe, comes in 8 miles below Rock river, on which was fought the bloody battle of November, 1811, with the savages. Near the confluence of this river with the Wabash, on both streams, are several Indian villages, with extensive cultivated fields.

Above the Tippacanoe are Pine and Redwood creeks; Rejoicing or Vermillion, Jaune, Little Vermillion, Erabliere, Duchet's, and Breuette rivers; at an interval of from eight to fifteen miles of each other; all flowing from the west or north west, mostly small, and heading in the state of Illinois. The rivers of Chanin, Big and Little Kemomic, which flow to lake Michigan; the Theakiki, Kickapoo, and a part of the chief branches of Illinois river, all meander through the north western part of the state; and all, except the last, entirely within its boundaries: the three first running from south to north; the latter, south and southwest. The Vermillion of Illinois rises in Indiana, near the sources of Tippacanoe. There are many smaller streams not enumerated. The borders of the Michigan lake, within the state, are well watered by the numerous forks of Black river and St. Joseph's, of lake Michigan; the latter heading near, and interlocking with the branches of Eel river, and pursuing a winding course 70 miles through the northern part of Indiana.

The northern half of the state is interspersed with a great number of lakes—38 of which, from two to ten miles in length, have been delineated on maps. The actual number is supposed to exceed 100. Some have two distinct out-lets; one running into the northern lakes, the other into the Mississippi. The greatest number of these lakes are between the head waters of the two St. Joseph's, Black, Raisin, Tippacanoe and Eel rivers.

From *A statistical, political and historical account of North America*, by D. B. Warden [1819], Vol. II., pp. 281-312.

WARDEN, DAVID BAILLIE.

David B. Warden, a French-Irish author, was born in Ireland in 1778. When twenty years of age, he came to America and soon gained recognition as a brilliant writer and antiquarian. In 1805 he was appointed Secretary to the United States Legation in Paris, and a few years later was appointed Consul. On two or three occasions he had some difficulty with the home government, and in 1814 was suspended from the consular service. He however, continued to reside in Paris, and turned his attention entirely to writing. Being an ardent antiquarian he undertook a survey of the United States. And his Statistical, Political and Historical Accounts of our country, published in 1819, affords one of the best available source books on the physical conditions of the United States.

INDIANA.

SITUATION AND BOUNDARIES.—The state of Indiana is situated between 37° 50′ and 42° 10′ of north latitude, and between 7° 40′ and 10° 45′ west longitude from Washington. It is bounded on the south by the river Ohio; north by the parallel of 42° 10′, which passes through Lake Michigan, ten miles beyond its southern extremity; east by the state of Ohio; and west by the Illinois territory, from which it is separated by the Wabash river from its mouth to Vincennes, and from Vincennes northward by a meridian line. Its form is pretty nearly a parallelogram; its length from north to south being about 284 miles, and its mean breadth about 155. Area, 39,000 square miles, or 24,960,000 acres.

Aspect of the Country, and Nature of the Soil.—The surface, from the falls of the Ohio to the Wabash, is broken and uneven, being traversed by a range of hills called the "*Knobs*," which rise to the height of 400 or 500 feet above their base. From this range is a level surface, called the "*Flat Woods*," seventy miles in breadth, extending to the Ouitanon country. Along all the principal streams, except the Ohio, there is a tract of rich alluvial soil, without timber, which terminates in meadow lands, rising from thirty to a hundred feet above the former, adorned with copses of beautiful shrubs, and bounded by lofty forests. In the summer season these meadows are covered with a luxuriant growth of herbage, from six to eight feet high. The common depth of the soil is from two to three feet; but along the Wabash, in forming wells, it was found to be twenty-two feet, and underneath a stratum of fine white sand was discovered. The lands on White river are hilly, broken, and in some parts stony; but exceedingly well watered. From the mouth of Big Miami to Blue river, a range of hills, intersected by streams, runs near to and parallel with the Ohio. Below Blue river, the country is level, and covered with heavy timber. Between the Wabash river and Lake Michigan, there is a champaign country, chiefly meadow, intersected by forests of fine trees, abounding in swamps, and inland lakes, the sources of numerous streams. From the south bank of the St. Joseph river extend rich meadow lands, from one to ten miles in breadth, and of variable length; the soil is dry, being at least 100 feet above high water. The soil around the sources of Eel river, Panther's creek, and St. Joseph of the Miami, and between the two extreme branches of the Wabash, is generally low and swampy, but interspersed with tracts of good soil. The overflowing of the rivers is very extensive; and, as most of them have a winding course, they water one-half more of the country, than if they ran in a straight line. General Harrison, who traversed this country in every direction, remarks, "that the finest country in all the western world is that which is bounded eastwardly by the counties of Wayne, Franklin, and part of Dearborn, Switzerland, and Jefferson; westward by the tract called the New Purchase; and extending northwardly some small distance beyond the Wabash. This tract, containing perhaps 10,000,000 of acres, is principally the property of the Miami tribe of Indians; part of it of the Miamis and Delawares. It includes all the head waters of the White river, and the branches of the Wabash which fall in from the south and southeast.*

Climate.—In all the high country the climate is particularly healthy; but in the low alluvial soil, formed of decaying vegetable substances, the air is unfriendly to health. The winter is milder, and much shorter, than in the northern states. The fine weather generally continues to Christmas, and spring commences about the middle of February. The peach blossoms about the 1st of March, and the woods are green by the 10th of April. But some winters are much colder. In that of 1815 the frost continued two or three weeks; the snow was from six to nine inches deep; and the ice of the Wabash, in many places, was strong enough to be passed over. Apple, cherry, and peach trees thrive well;

*Appendix to the Western Gazetteer, p. 358.

tobacco also thrives as well here as in Virginia. The vine and sweet potatoe are cultivated at New Switzerland and Vevay. Below Ouitanon, in latitude 40° 20′, the climate is mild. Above the sources of the Wabash, where the north and north-westerly winds prevail, the winters are much more severe. The reed cane grows as high up as the mouth of the Big Miami. Cotton is raised at Vincennes, Princeton, Harmony, and in the settlements below the mouth of Anderson; though it does not grow to perfection above the thirty-first degree of latitude.

Rivers.—This state is watered by the rivers Ohio and Wabash, and their numerous branches; the southern parts by the former, over a distance of 472 miles, following its course from the entrance of the Big Miami to that of the Wabash. The principal branches of the Ohio are—1. *Tanner's* creek, which rises in the flat woods to the south of Brookville; and running a course of thirty miles, falls in below Lawrenceburgh, where it is thirty yards wide. 2. *Loughery's* creek, forty miles in length, and fifty yards wide at its entrance, falls in eleven miles below the Big Miami. 3. *Indian* creek, called also Indian Kentucky, and by the Swiss, Venoge,* rises in the hills near the south fork of White river, forty-five miles north-east of Vevay, and falls in eight miles below the mouth of Kentucky river. It forms the southern limit of the Swiss settlement. 4. *Wyandot* creek issues from the hills which extend in a transverse direction from near the mouth of Blue river to the Muddy fork of White river, and joins the Ohio at about an equal distace between the falls and Blue river. 5. *Big Blue* river, so named from the colour of its waters, rises farther north, near the South fork of White river, runs fifty miles south-west, and then, taking a southern direction, enters the Ohio thirty-two miles below the mouth of Salt river. It is about fifty yards in breadth, and is navigable forty miles to a rift, which, if removed, would extend it farther ten or twelve miles.† 6. *Little Blue* river, forty yards wide, has its entrance thirteen miles below the former. 7. *Anderson's* river, which joins the Ohio sixty miles farther down, is the most considerable stream below Blue river and the Wabash. Besides these, there are several creeks, but none of great length. The current of all these streams is pretty rapid, and their waters are good. The *Wabash,* which waters the middle and western parts of the state, rises from two sources near the eastern boundary line, about 100 miles from Lake Erie, and runs across the state

*The name of a small river of Switzerland, in the Pays de Vaud.

†Schultz, Vol. I., p. 196.

in a south-western and southern course of above 500 miles, discharging its waters into the Ohio in latitude 37° 21′. The principal upper branch of the Wabash has its source two miles east of old Fort St. Mary's; another, called Little river, rises seven miles south of Fort Wayne, and enters about eighty miles below the St. Mary's Portage; a third, the Massassinway, rises in Darke county, state of Ohio; a fourth, Eel river, issues from several lakes and ponds eighteen miles west of Fort Wayne, and enters the Wabash eight miles below the mouth of the former, which unites five miles below the mouth of Little river. *White* river, the largest branch of the Wabash, is 200 miles in length. At the distance of thirty-five miles from its mouth, (sixteen miles below Vincennes,) it divides into two branches, which water the south-eastern parts of the state below the fortieth degree of latitude. The northern, called the Drift Wood branch, interlocks with the north fork of White water, and with the Still water of the Big Miami. The southern, known by the name of Muddy Fork, rises between the West fork of the White water. The Northern fork has a branch, called Teakettle, which extends from its junction, twenty miles above that of the two principal forks, across the intervening surface. During the period of high water, both the branches of the White river are boatable to the distance of 130 miles. The *Petoka* river has its source near that of the southern branch of White river, with which it runs parallel at the distance of ten or twelve miles; and, after a course of seventy-five, it joins the Wabash, twenty miles below Vincennes. *Decke* river, a short winding stream, which somes from the north-east, falls in about half way between Vincennes and White river. *Little* river, from the French name La Petite Rivière, comes also from the north-east, and enters a little above Vincennes. The *St. Marie*, from the same quarter, is fifty miles long, and enters eighteen miles above Vincennes; and, eighteen miles higher, is *Rocky* river, which is 100 yards wide at its mouth; it has several large branches. Another *Little* river, which comes from the south-east, from near the sources of Rocky river, is the only stream from this last which enters from the left, to the distance of seventy miles. *Pomme* river, which rises to the north of the head branches of White water, comes from the south-east, and falls in twenty miles below the mouth of Massassinway. *Richard's* creek, ten miles below on the right side, is a considerable stream; and about an equal distance farther south is *Rock* river, from the north-west, which passes through a broken country. Eight miles farther down is the *Tip-*

pacanoe, which has its source about twenty miles west of Fort Wayne. Several of its branches, issuing from lakes, swamps, and ponds, communicate with the St. Joseph's of the Miami of the lakes. Farther south are several streams coming from the west or north-west, running at the distance of from ten to fifteen miles from each other; the Pine and Red Wood creeks, Rejoicing, or Vermillion Jaune, Little Vermillion, Erabliere, Duchat, and Brouette. *White Water* river, so called from the transparency of its waters, runs across the southeastern parts of the state in its course to the Great Miami, and is said to water nearly a million of acres of fine land; it is more than 100 yards wide; its western branch interlocks with those of White river. The north-eastern parts of the state are watered by the St. Joseph's of the Miami of the lakes, which has its source about sixty miles north-west of Fort Wayne, above which it forms a junction with the St. Mary's; and its remote branches interramify with those of the Raisin and Black rivers, the St. Joseph of Lake Michigan, and Eel river. The borders adjoining the Michigan territory are watered by the head branches of the river Raison of Lake Erie, the branches of Black river, and the St. Joseph of Lake Michigan. The branches of the latter have a communication with those of Eel river. The north-western parts are watered by several streams flowing into Lake Michigan; the rivers Chemin, Big and Little Kennomic; the Theakiki, Kickapoo, and many smaller streams.

Chicago river, which runs into the south-western extremity of Lake Michigan, at the distance of sixteen miles from its mouth, divides into two branches. It forms a harbour, into which sloops of forty tons enter. The *Great Kennomic*, which also empties into Lake Michigan, thirty miles east of the former, has its source at the distance of twenty or thirty miles south of this lake; and runs first nearly westward, in a direction parallel to the shore of the lake; it then makes a doubling, and runs nearly eastward, after which it pursues a northern course, for a few miles, to the lake. Its outlet forms a spacious bay.

Lakes.—The upper parts of this state are diversified with a number of lakes, thirty-eight of which, delineated on the latest maps, are from two to ten miles in length; and the whole number is said to exceed a hundred. Some are found to have two outlets, into the lakes on one side, and into the Mississippi on the other. Most of these small lakes are situated between the sources of the two St. Josephs, Black River, Raisin, Tippacanoe, and Eel rivers.

Extent of Navigable Waters.—The Ohio river washes the southern boundary of Indiana, for the distance of 472 miles; the Wabash is navigable 470;* White river and its forks, 160; Petoka, 30; Blue river, 40; Whitewater, 40; Rocky river, 45; Pomme, 30; Massassinway, 45; Eel and Little rivers, 60; western tributaries of the Wabash, 330; St. Joseph's of the Miami and Panther's creek, 75; Elkhart and part of St. Joseph's of Lake Michigan, 100; Great and Little Kennomic, 120; Chemin river, 40; Chicago and Kickapoo, 80; Theakaki and parts of Fox, Plein, and Illinois, 300;† southern coast of Lake Michigan, 50. In all, 2,487.

A company, with a capital of a million of dollars, has been incorporated by the legislature, for the purpose of opening a canal along the falls, or rapids, of the Ohio, which, when executed, will be of great advantage

Minerals.—*Silver ore* is said to have been discovered at a place about twenty-eight miles above Ouitanon, on the northern side of the Wabash;‡ *copperas* on the high bank of Silver creek, about two miles from its mouth; *iron ore* on White river, and other places. Between White river and New Lexington, the wells are so impregnated with copperas, that they blacken linen; and being considered by the inhabitants as very unwholesome, several of them have on this account abandoned their habitations. A chalybeate spring, containing sulphur and iron, near Jeffersonville, is much frequented. *Coal.*—Mr. Hutchins states, "That the hills are replenished with the best coal; that there is plenty of swinestone and freestone; blue, yellow, and white clay, for glassworks

*The Wabash, at its mouth, is 300 yards wide; at Vincennes, 100 miles from its mouth, from forty to seventy rods, and it is navigable thence to the rapids of Ouitanon, for keel boats, or barges drawing three feet water, about 212 miles. Above this village small boats ascend nearly 200 miles farther, to within six miles of St. Mary's river, ten of Fort Wayne, and eight of the St. Joseph's, flowing into the Miami of the lakes. The banks of this beautiful river are high, and less subject to inundation than any other in this country, except the Ohio, though when the waters rise in March, its borders are partially overflowed from Fort Harrison to Vincennes, 120 miles by water, and 55 by land, and opposite this last place to the distance of four or five miles, which obliges the farmers to remove their cattle and swine. The rapids at Ouitanon are impassable for boats, but small vessels of thirty tons burden can navigate between this place and Vincennes.

†*Portages.*—In the northern parts of the state the Wabash and Illinois rivers are connected with Lakes Erie and Michigan, by numerous branches, which issue from sources near one another. Of twenty portages near the Michigan frontier, only two have been traversed by the white settlers. One extending nine miles, between near Fort Wayne on the St. Mary's and the Little river branch of the Wabash is a good route in dry seasons. It was by this channel the French passed from the lakes to their post on the Wabash River. The other portage, much shorter, extends between the Chicago and Kickapoo branch of the Illinois, and so level is the surface, that during the rise of their waters, boats pass between Lake Michigan and the Illinois River.

See Volney's account of this internal water communication between the lakes and waters of the Mississippi.

‡Hutchins, p. 28.

and pottery." There is a coal mine a little below the forks of White river.

Salt Springs.—Some valuable salt springs have been discovered on the Wabash river, and also on Salina creek, which are leased by the government of the United States to contractors, who are obliged not to receive more for salt than half a dollar a bushel at the works; but through the agency of private copartners, it is not sold at the storehouses for less than two dollars.* Near the town of New Lexington, at the depth of 520 feet, the salt wells give from three to four bushels of salt to the hundred gallons of water. These works are the property of General Macfarland. *Glauber's salt*, or sulphate of potash, has been lately found in a cave situated twelve miles from the Ohio river, and about the same distance west of New Albany. The quantity is so great as to promise an inexhaustible supply. *Epsom* salt (sulphate of magnesia) has been also found in a cave about thirty-five leagues from Louisville; and *saltpetre* exists in certain caves in the neighbourhood. A section of land of 160 acres, containing these treasures, was purchased† at two dollars an acre.

Forest Trees and Shrubs.—Mr. Hutchins remarks, that the timber on the Wabash river is large, high, and in such variety, that almost all the different kinds growing upon the Ohio, and its branches, (but with a greater proportion of black and white mulberry trees,) may be found here.‡ The natural meadows are intersected by narrow woods, containing oak, ash, maple, locust, poplar, plum, and the crab-apple tree. On the outside of these meadows oak abounds, and grows to a great size. The principal trees on the branches of White river are white oak, hickery, and black walnut. The hills of Whitewater river terminate in a level and rich country, thickly wooded with oak, walnut, beech, ash, elm, hickery, maple, sugar tree, &c. On Silver creek, Canerun, and other branches of the Ohio, and the south fork of White river, hickery and oak abound. The banks of Blue river are also covered with oak and locust; the neighbouring hills with black walnut, oak, hickery, ash, sugar maple; the low intervening grounds with bass-wood, papaw, honey-locust, buck-eye, and spice-wood, with the wild vine, and various shrubs. Along the borders of Whitewater river, ginseng grows to an uncommon size; on the poor soil of the spurs of the hills, the columbo root abounds. The

*Schultz, Vol. I., p. 199.

†—By Dr. Adams.

‡—Page 28.

cane grows to the south of the ridge of hills, which extend from the falls of the Ohio to those of the Wabash, above the mouth of White river, and in some places as far north as the mouth of the Big Miami. An extraordinary phenomenon is met with in this country in the woods along White river,—natural wells, from ten to fifteen feet deep, formed by the decay of the trunks and roots of large sycamore trees.

Animals.—The woods abound with deer. Bears and wolves are also numerous. Of the feathered race of game, wild turkeys, ducks, and pigeons, swarm in the woods, and on the waters of the northern parts. The rattlesnake and copperhead snake infest the woody country, but are seldom seen on the low lands. *Fishes.*—Of the fish which inhabit the rivers, we find no particular account. The Great Kennomic of Lake Michigan is said to furnish the Indians with an inexhaustible supply.*

Civil or Administrative Division of the State of Indiana, with the Population of each County and Chief Town in 1810, the year of the last Enumeration.

Counties.	*Population.*	*Chief Towns.*
Clarke	7,000	Jeffersonville.†
Dearborn	5,426	Lawrenceburgh.‡
Franklin	7,970	Brookville.§
Gibson	5,330	Princeton.
Harrison	6,769	Corydon.
Jefferson	4,093	Maddison.

*Western Gazetteer, p. 77.

†Jeffersonville, situated on the bank of the Ohio, a little above the falls, and nearly opposite Louisville, contained, in 1816, about 130 houses.

‡Lawrenceburgh, situated on the Ohio River, two miles below the mouth of the Big Miami, has not succeeded as was expected, owing to the annual inundation of the river. A new town has been laid out half a mile farther up on an elevated situation, and named Edinburgh. A place called "Rising Sun," in the same county of Dearborn, situated on an elevated bank of the Ohio, between Vevay and Lawrenceburgh, contains thirty or forty houses. Its growth has been rapid; and it will probably become a place of considerable trade.

§Brookville, in Franklin County, situated between the branches of White River, thirty miles north of Lawrenceburgh, was established in 1811; but being within fifteen miles of the Indian line of demarcation, it did not increase during the late war; since the peace, however, its growth has been very rapid. In 1816 it contained eighty dwelling-houses a grist mill, two saw mills, two fulling mills, three carding machines, and a printing office, besides a great number of workshops. The ground, elevated between seventy and eighty feet above the level of the river, is dry and pleasant, and is peculiarly favourable for the establishment of manufactures, the branches of the river affording fine situations for the erection of water machinery. Harrison village, in the same county, eight miles from the mouth of Whitewater, on the northern side, and eighteen northeast [southeast] of Brookville, commenced about the year 1800, and in 1816 contained thirty-five houses.

Counties.	*Population.*	*Chief Towns.*
Knox	6,800	Vincennes*
Switzerland	3,500	Vevey.†
Washington	6,606	Salem.
Wayne	6,290	Salisbury.
Orange	.....	
Posey	3,000	
Perry	3,000	
Warwick	3,000	
	68,784	

Population.—

In 1800 the population amounted to 4,875.
1810, 24,520 of whom 237 were slaves.
1815, 68,784

According to the numeration of 1810 there were 23,890 whites.
237 slaves.
393 fr. blacks.

24,520

Increase in 5 years............... 44,264.

The settlements extend chiefly along the Ohio, the branches of the Big Miami, the Wabash, and the Whitewater river. The most ancient and most populous part of the state is Knox county, on the east side of the Wabash river, and watered by several of its branches, the Decke, White river, Little river, St. Mary's, Busseron, Racoon, and Ambush creeks. It contains 20,000 acres of the best meadow and alluvial land.

Constitution.—Indiana was under a territorial government till 1816. Agreeably to an act of Congress, of 16th April that year, a convention was held at Corydon, on the 29th June, consisting of

*Vincennes, formerly St. Vincent, situated in Latitude 38° 51′ north, on the east side of the Wabash River, on a level and beautiful surface, nearly 200 miles from its junction with the Ohio, following its course, but 100 only in a straight line, contained in 1816 about 100 houses. The inhabitants raise Indian corn, wheat and tobacco of excellent quality. They have a fine breed of horses, (brought originally by the Indiana from the Spanish settlements on the western side of the river Mississippi.) and large herds of swine and black cattle. The settlers deal with the natives for furs and deer skins, to the amount of L. 5,000 annually. In 1817, steam mills upon an extensive scale were begun to be built. Ouitanon, a small stocked fort on the western side of the Wabash, traded with the neighbouring Indians to the amount of about L. 8,000 a year.—(Hutchins, p. 28, 31.)

†Vevay, situated on the bank of the Ohio, was laid out in 1813; and in 1816 the number of dwelling houses had incerased to eighty-four; the shops for mechanics to thirty-four; the stores to eight; the taverns to three. A court house, jail, and school house, were then building of brick materials. Vevay is seventy miles by water, and forty-five by land, below Cincinnati. New Switzerland, near the former, extending four miles along the Ohio from Indian creek or Venoge, was established in 1805 by emigrants from the Pays de Vaud, with the view of cultivating the vine. The vineyards are now very extensive, and the settlement is in a prosperous state.

forty-one delegates, chosen by all the male citizens of the state who were twenty-one years of age, had paid taxes, and resided a year in the territory. These delegates framed the constitution of the state.

The first article declares, that all power is inherent in the people, that all free governments are founded on their authority, and instituted for their peace, safety, and happiness; and that, for the advancement of these ends, they have, at all times, an unalienable and indefeasible right to alter or reform their government as they may deem proper; that all men have a natural right to worship God according to the dictates of their own consciences; that no man shall be compelled to attend any place of worship, or to maintain any ministry against his consent; that no preference shall be given by law to any religious sect; that no religious test shall be required as a qualification to any office of trust or profit; that elections shall be free and equal; the right of trial by jury inviolate in all civil cases where the value in controversy shall exceed the sum of twenty dollars, and in all criminal cases, except in petit misdemeanours, which shall be punishable by fine only, not exceeding three dollars, in such manner as the legislature may prescribe by law. All persons, their houses, papers, and effects, to be secure against unreasonable searches and seizures. The printing-presses to be free to every person. In all indictments for libels, the jury shall decide upon the law and the facts; that all courts shall be open; that no person arrested or confined in jail, shall be treated with unnecessary rigour; that all persons shall be bailable by sufficient sureties, unless for capital offences, when the proof is evident or the presumption great, and that excessive bail shall not be required. That the privilege of the right of *habeas corpus* shall not be suspended, unless in case of rebellion or invasion, nor then, unless the public safety require it. No *ex post facto* law, nor any law impairing the validity of contracts, shall ever be made, and no conviction shall work corruption of blood, nor forfeiture of estate. The people to have a right to assemble together in a peaceable manner, to consult for the public good, to instruct their representatives, and apply to the legislature for a redres of grievances. The people to have a right to bear arms for the defence of themselves and the state; the military to be kept in strict subordination to the civil power; no soldier to be quartered in any house without the consent of the owner, in time of peace. The legislature not to grant any title of nobility, or hereditary distinction, nor to create any office, the appointment to which shall be for a longer term than good behaviour.

Emigration from the state not to be prohibited. These rights are to remain for ever inviolable, and in order to guard against any encroachments thereon, are excepted out of the general powers of government.

The *legislative authority* is vested in a general assembly, consisting of a senate and house of representatives, both elected by the people. The number of representatives to be fixed by the general assembly, according to the number of white male inhabitants above twenty-one years of age in each county, and never to be less than twenty-five, nor greater than thirty-six, until the number of white male inhabitants, above twenty-one years of age, shall be 22,000; and after that takes place, in such ratio, that the whole number of representatives shall never be less than 36, nor exceed 100. An enumeration of the white male inhabitants, above the age of twenty-one years, to be made in the year 1820, and every subsequent term of five years. The representatives to be chosen annually by the qualified electors of each county respectively, on the first Monday of August. The qualifications of representatives are, to have attained the age of twenty-one years; to be a citizen of the United States, and an inhabitant of the state; to have resided within the limits of the county in which he is chosen, one year next preceding his election, and to have paid state or county taxes.

The *senators* to be chosen on the first Monday of August, for three years, by the qualified voters for representatives; to be divided into three classes, which are to be renewed in succession annually. The number of senators never to be less than one-third, nor more than one-half of the number of representatives. The qualifications of a senator are, 1. To have attained the age of twenty-five years. 2. To be a citizen of the United States, and to have resided two years, preceding the election, in the state, and the last twelve months in the county or district, unless absent on public business. 3. To have paid state or county tax. Two-thirds of each house constitute a quorum, but a smaller number may adjourn from day to day, and compel the attendance of absent members. The members of both houses to be privileged from arrest during the session of the general assembly, except in cases of treason, felony, or breach of the peace. Both houses to be open except in cases requiring secrecy. Bills may originate in either house, subject to alteration, amendment, or rejection in the other, except bills for raising revenue, which shall originate in the house of representatives. No person holding any office under the authority of the president of the United States, or of the state, except militia officers, are eligible to a seat in either branch of the general assembly, unless he resign his office previous to his election; nor can any member of either branch of the general assembly be eligible to any office during the time for which he is elected, the appointment of which is vested in the general assembly. An accurate statement of the receipts and expenditure of the public money to be published with the laws at every annual session of the general assembly. The governor and all civil officers of the state are liable to removal from office, on impeachment for, or conviction of treason, bribery, or other high crimes and misdemeanours; and to indictment, trial, judgment, and punishment, according to law. The general assembly meets on the first Monday in December.

The *governor* is chosen by the qualified electors, (on the first Monday in August, at the places where they respectively vote for representatives,) for the term of three years, and cannot hold this office longer than six years in any term of nine years. The qualifications are, 1. To be thirty years of age. 2. To have been a citizen of the United States ten years; and resided in the state five years next preceding his election, unless absent on public business. The salary of the governor neither to be increased nor diminished during the term for which he shall have been elected. He is commander-in-chief of the army and navy of the state, and of the militia, except when called into the service of the United States; but he is not to command in person, except advised so to do by a resolution of the general assembly. By and with the consent of the senate, he is authorized to appoint and commission all officers, the appointment of which is not otherwise directed by the constitution. He has power to fill up vacancies in offices, the appointment of which is vested in the governor and senate, or in the general assembly. To remit fines and forfeitures; grant reprieves and pardons, except in cases of impeachment; to convene the general assembly on extraordinary occasions; to approve and sign every bill, or to return it to the house with his objections for reconsideration. In case of death or resignation, his functions are exercised by the lieutenant-governor.

The secretary of state is chosen by the joint ballot of both houses of the general assembly, for the term of four years, and is commissioned by the governor. The treasurer and auditor for three years. A sheriff and coroner are elected in each county, by the qualified electors; they continue in office two years, and are not eligible more than four, in any term of six years.*

Judiciary.—The judicial power is vested in a supreme court, in circuit courts, and such other inferior courts as the general assembly may, from time to time, erect and establish. The supreme court to consist of three judges, any two of whom shall form a quorum, and shall have appellate jurisdiction only, co-extensive with the limits of the state. The general assembly may give to this court original jurisdiction in capital cases, and cases in chancery, where the president of the circuit court may be interested or prejudiced.

The circuit courts each to have a president, and two associate judges. The state to be divided into three circuits, but the number may be afterwards increased, and a president to be appointed and to preside in each. The president and associate judges, in their respective counties, to have common law and chancery jurisdiction, and also complete criminal jurisdiction, in all such cases as may be prescribed by law. The judges to hold their offices for the term of seven years. The judges of the supreme court are appointed by the governor, by and with the advice of the senate. The presidents of the circuit courts, by joint ballot of both branches of the general assembly. The associate judges of the circuit courts are elected by the qualified electors in the respective counties. The clerk of the supreme court is appointed by the court itself; those of the circuit court in the several counties are elected by the qualified electors. Justices of the peace are elected for five years by the qualified electors in each township.

Militia.—The militia consists of all free, able-bodied male

*The constitution may be revised, amended, or changed by a convention, to be held every twelfth year for that purpose, if a majority of the qualified electors, at the general election of governor, vote in favour of this measure, (Art. 8), Slavery or involuntary servitude can never be introduced into the state, except for the punishment of crimes, whereof the party shall have been duly convicted, and no indenture of any negro or mulatto hereafter made and executed, out of the bounds of this state, can be of any validity within the state.

By the 9th Article of the Constitution, the general assembly is authorized to grant lands for the support of seminaries and public schools; and, so soon as circumstances permit, they are to provide for a general system of education, ascending in a regular gradation from township schools to a state university, in which education shall be afforded gratis, and be open equally to all. The sums paid by the persons as an equivalent for militia duty, and also penal fines, are to be applied to the support of county seminaries. In laying off a new county, the general assembly is to reserve, at least, 10 per cent of the proceeds of the sale of town lots, in the seat of justice of such county, for the use of a public library therein.

Article 10th prohibits the incorporation of any other banks than the state bank and its branches.

persons, (negroes, mulattoes, and Indians excepted,) resident in the state, between the age of eighteen and forty-five years except such as are exempted by the laws of the state, or of the United States; those who are conscientiously averse to bearing arms, paying an equivalent. The captains and subalterns are elected by the companies; and the non-commissioned officers are appointed by the captains. Majors are elected by the battalions, and colonels by the regiments. Brigadier-generals are elected by the commissioned officers within the bounds of their respective brigades; and major-generals by the commissioned officers within the bounds of their respective divisions. The adjutants-general and quarter-masters-general are appointed by the governor; and also his aids-de-camp. Majors-general appoint their aids-de-camp, and all other division staff officers; brigadier-generals, their brigades-major; and colonels, their regimental staff officers. All militia officers are commissioned by the governor, and hold their commission during good behaviour, or till the age of sixty.

The seat of government is established at Corydon, in Harrison county, until the year 1825, and until removed by law. No person can hold more than one lucrative office at the same time, unless expressly permitted by the constitution. The following are the salaries fixed for the officers of government till the year 1819: The governor, 1,000 dollars; the secretary of state, 400; auditor of public accounts, 400; treasurer, 400; judges of the supreme court, 800 each; presidents of the circuit courts, 800. Members of the general assembly are allowed two dollars per day, during their attendance, and the same sum for every twenty-five miles they shall severally travel, in the usual route, to and from the assembly. After 1819, their pay is to be fixed by a new law.

Mounds.—A number of Mounds are seen from White river to the sources of the Wabash. Around Harrison village, in Franklin county, they are numerous, of very unequal size, and evidently formed at different and remote periods. On the largest, which are from ten to thirty feet high, trees are seen to grow of as great a size, and apparently as old, as any of the same species in the woods. The smaller mounds have no greater elevation than from two to five feet above the surface, and the trees which grow upon them are yet of small dimensions, indicating a growth of not more than 100 years. The bones which they inclose are still capable of supporting their own weight and of being removed, while those of the large mounds are so decomposed, that they are reduced to dust by the slightest touch. In a field, belonging to Mr. Allan, there is one sixty feet in diameter at the base, and twenty in height, full of the remains of human bones. Mr. Brown relates,* that, on the borders of White Water, he examined the interior structure of fifteen or twenty of these mounds, from ten to fifteen feet in height, and did not find more than four or five skeletons. In one none was found. Others were so full, that they probably contained the remains of a hundred skeletons.

Agriculture.—The soil is well adapted to maize, wheat, oats, rye, hemp, and tobacco. On the best lands the average produce of Indian corn is said to be from fifty to sixty bushels *per* acre; that of wheat about fifty, the bushel weighing fifty-eight pounds. In many places the land is too rich for this grain; which, though it does not become smutty, is not so good as in the state of New York. It is never killed, however, by the cold in winter.

The culture of the vine has been successfully introduced by a colony of Swiss emigrants, established at New Switzerland. In the year 1811, 2,700 gallons of wine were produced from a surface of twenty acres, and is found to be of a good quality. The grapes which have succeeded best are those from the Cape of Good Hope and the island of Madeira. Those of the country give wine of a tolerable good quality. Hutchins remarked, "that grapes, with a thin black skin, grow in the greatest abundance, of which the inhabitants in the interior make a sufficient quantity of well-tasted red wine for their own consumption." "That large and good hops are found in many places, and the lands are particularly adapted to the cultivation of rice. All European fruits, apples, peaches, pears, cherries, currants, gooseberries, melons, &c., thrive well. Cotton and the sweet potatoe are cultivated in the southern parts. The country is admirably fitted for rearing cattle and swine, having great abundance of acorns and roots on which they feed. The animals which are most injurious to agriculture in this prolific country are squirrels, moles, and mice. The mole is particularly so in meadows and corn fields, where the grain begins to shoot."

Finances.—According to the treasurer's report, the receipts into the treasury for the year 1817 amounted to 28,234 dollars 46 cents; the disbursements to 20,605 dollars 33 cents; balance 7,629 dollars 13 cents.

Price of Land.—In 1792 the French inhabitants of Vincennes gave their lands in exchange for goods, at the rate of thirty cents an acre. They were sold in 1796 at two dollars. The tract called

*Western Gazetteer, p. 57.

"Harrison's Purchase," situated between the White river, Wabash, and Rocky river, and containing upwards of 3,000,000 of acres, was sold from four to thirty dollars an acre, after the reservation of the most fertile parts, given as a donation to the officers who had served on the Niagara frontier. The lands of the settlement of New Switzerland were purchased at two dollars, in 1805; the lands of Harrison village, on the north side of White Water, are valued at between forty and sixty dollars an acre. In the town of Vincennes building lots sell at from 50 to 1,000 dollars a lot. The land offices in this state are, one at Vincennes, on the Wabash, the other at Jeffersonville, on the Ohio.

In general, improved lands, or farms of fifteen or twenty acres, with a log-house, can be purchased from eight to ten dollars an acre.*

The *manufactures*, in 1810, amounted to 196,532 dollars, besides doubtful articles, valued at 61,108 dollars.

Woolen, cotton, hempen and flaxen cloths	$159,052.00
Cotton and wool spun in mills	150.00
1,380 spinning wheels	
1,256 looms	
Nails, pounds 20,000	4,000.00
Leather tanned	9,300.00
28 distilleries	16,230.00
Wine from grapes, barrels 96	6,000.00
Gunpowder	1,800.00
33 flour mills	
14 saw mills	
Maple sugar, pounds 50,000	

The Harmonists, established at Harmoney, cultivate the vine, exercise various mechanical arts, and have an extensive wool manufactory. Their Merino cloth is excellent.

Commerce.—The external trade of this colony is carried on with New Orleans, and is yet very inconsiderable. Goods are brought from Canada, down the Wabash; from the eastermost states, down the Ohio; and from New Orleans, by the Mississippi and

*Prices at Brookville, in December 1817.—Beef 4 to 5 cents *per* pound; corn, 25 cents *per* bushel; wheat, 62 cents ditto; fowls, 1 dollar *per* dozen; eggs, 6½ cents ditto; pork, 3 to 4 cents *per* pound; butter 19 cents ditto.

Prices at Princetown, in August, 1817.—Wheat, 3s. 4½ d. sterling *per* Winchester bushel; 1s. 4d.; Indian corn, 11d.; hay, 35s. per ton; flour, 36s. *per* barrel, 196 lb. net; fowls, 4½d. each; eggs, ½d.; butter, 6d. *per* pound; meat, 2d.; a buck, 4s. 6d. without the skin; salt, 3s. 4d *per* bushel; tobacco, 3d. *per* pound; a good cow, 12 to 20 dollars; a two year old heifer, 6 dollars; ewes, 3 dollars a-head; a sow, 3 dollars, a stout horse for drawing, 60 dollars or upwards. Boarding in a tavern, 2 dollars *per* week. Travelling expences are very regular, amounting to a dollar *per* day for a man and horse. Birkbeck's Notes, p. 143.

up the Wabash. One branch of this last river forms a communication with the river St. Joseph, and another with the easternmost branch of the Miami of the Lakes, through which there is a passage to Lake Erie, with the exception of a short portage.

Forts.—Fort Harrison, situated on the Wabash river, has a garrison of 150 riflemen, of the regular army. *Fort Dearborn* stands upon the left bank of Chicago river, which empties itself into Lake Michigan, on the south-western extremity. Its garrison was destroyed, in September 1815, [August 15, 1812] by the Pottowatamie Indians, but has been since re-established. *Fort Wayne,* at the confluence of the St. Joseph's and St. Mary's river, near the north-eastern angle of the State.

Roads.—From Vincennes two roads lead to the Ohio, a third to Fort Harrison, a fourth to Princetown, and a fifth to Kaskaskia.

Newspapers.—At Brookville, "The Plain Dealer"; at Vevay, "The Indiana Register"; at Lexington, "The Western Eagle"; at Corydon, "The Indiana Gazette"; at Vincennes, "The Western Sun".

Manners and Character.—Indiana is but recently settled; but many of the settlers are of a respectable class, and their manners are more refined than could be expected in a place where society is but in its infancy. They are sober and industrious; drunkenness is rare, and quarrelling rare in proportion. They set a high value on the right of personal resistance to aggression. They possess great energy of character; and, though they respect the laws generally, do not hesitate sometimes to redress what they consider a public injury, by a more summary mode of proceeding. They are, however, friendly and obliging. Insanity is scarcely known, either in this or the other western states. The inhabitants of Vincennes, who are chiefly of French extraction, are neat and cleanly, and still retain strong traces of French good breeding.

Religion.—The number of Baptists, the denomination which prevails in Indiana, was stated in the general report of May 1817 to be 2,474; the number of churches, 67. We have not been able to ascertain the number belonging to other sects.

History.—When the French descended the Wabash, and established posts on its borders, it was inhabited by different Indian nations, the Kickapoos, Pyankashaws, Musquitons, Ouitanons, and others, whose warriors amounted to upwards of 1,200, and, according to French tradition, they were once far more numerous. It is said, that the country lying between the Wabash and

Mississippi being claimed by the Indians of both these rivers, it was mutually agreed, that it should become the prize of the victors, in an engagement between 1,000 warriors of each, who fought from the rising to the setting sun, when the former were declared conquerors, having seven men surviving, while the other had but five. The ground on which Fort Harrison stands was the theatre of this bloody scene; the bodies of the slain were inclosed in the neighbouring mounds. The French colonists, long after their first establishments in this country, lived on terms of friendship with the Indian proprietors of the soil; formed marriages with their women, joined in their hunting parties, and lived contented with the produce of the chace, of their cattle, and gardens. But, in the year 1782, a detachment of soldiers from Kentucky penetrated to their villages, plundered them, and carried off many of their cattle. The year following, peace ensued, and they came under the protection of the United States.

During the period of war with the Indians, which commenced in 1788, they suffered many vexations, and were obliged to perform military services of a severe nature.

By the treaty of Greenville, in 1795, the United States obtained six miles square at the mouth of Chicago river; the same quantity at the junction of the St. Mary's and St. Joseph's; one half of this extent at the head of the Little river branch of the Wabash, eight miles southwest of Fort Wayne; and six miles square at the Weeaw town (Ouitanon) on the river Wabash; other cessions were at the same time made without the limits of this state. For all which, the Pottawatamies were to receive, for their share of recompense, goods to the amount of 1,000 dollars; and the Kickapoos, Piankashaws, Weaws, and Elk river tribes, 500 each. In 1804, the Delawares and Piankashaws sold a large tract bordering on the Ohio; and, in 1805, another extensive tract was ceded by the Miami, Eel river, and Weeaw Indians, which, including a former cession around Vincennes in 1794, comprehended a tract of 130 miles in length, and fifty in breadth, extending from the Ohio river to the western limits. Another tract was ceded in 1809, by the Delawares, Pottowatamies, Miami, and Eel river tribes, including the south-western parts to above the fortieth degree of latitude. Notwithstanding these cessions, the contracting Indian parties were always hostile. In 1791, they were attacked by General Wilkinson, who destroyed the principal town of the Shawenese, near the mouth of the Tippacanoe, containing 120 houses. They were attacked on the 7th of November 1811, about 100 miles above Vincennes, by a detachment of American troops, under General Harrison, who destroyed the town of their celebrated Prophet. In September 1813, four of their towns, at the forks of the Wabash, were burnt by the same officer.

From *Narrative of Richard Lee Mason in the Pioneer west* [1819], pp. 33-39. Published by Chas. Fred Heartman, (by permission of the publisher).

Mason, Richard Lee.

Dr. Richard Lee Mason, a Marylander, who served with the "White Horseman" cavalry in the war of 1812, was awarded a large tract of bounty land near Alton, Illinois. In order to locate this, he made a journey from Pennsylvania to Illinois in 1819. He traveled through Pennsylvania, Ohio, Kentucky and Indiana. He was so well pleased with the "promised land" of the west that he sent for his family, moved to St. Louis, Mo., and took up a medical practice. Dr. Mason was a remarkably intelligent observer, as is evidenced by his journals.

Tuesday, Nov. 3.—Remained in Louisville Monday and part of today. Left Aleen's the 2d. Passed through Shipping Port, on the bank of the Ohio, two and one-half miles below Louisville. A very promising little village. Twelve or thirteen steamboats lying at this place aground, owing to the unusual drought. Curiosity induced me to go on board the largest steamboat in the world, lying at this place. She is called the United States, and is owned by a company of gentlemen. I have taken down her dimensions: Length of keel, 165 feet 8 inches; depth of hold, 11 feet 3 inches; breadth of beam and girder, 56 feet; length on deck, 176 feet 8 inches; breadth of beam without girder, 37 feet. This mammoth boat has eight boilers and elegant accommodations for a large number of passengers. Many of the steamships lying at this place are built on improved plans and are very handsome. We crossed the Ohio at a point where it is three-quarters of a mile wide. Passed through New Albany, Ind., a little village inhabited by tavern-keepers and mechanics. Traveled to Miller's, a distance of six miles over the knobs. Country very much broken. Some steep hills and sugar-loaf knobs. The woods being on fire, a scene truly sublime presented itself at night. The lands indifferent. Weather warm and dry. Passed many travelers bound to the west, and met three or four wagons with families returning from the promised land. Slept in a house without glass in the windows and no fastenings to the doors. The inhabitants imprudent and lazy beyond example. Supped on cabbage, turnips, pickles, beets, beefsteak made of pickled beef, rye coffee and sage tea. The people of Indiana differ widely from Kentuckians in habits, manners and even dialect. Whilst hospitality, politeness and good sense characterize Kentuckians, ignorance, impudence and laziness has stamped the Indianians.

Wednesday, Nov. 3, 1819.—Left Miller's tavern at 7 o'clock and arrived at Squire Chambers' at 6 o'clock, after traveling a distance of thirty-six miles. Passed a trifling village, Fredericksburg; also Greenville. A poor, barren, deserted country. For ten miles, stony, poor, mountainous and naked. Land a little better. Miserable huts, poor accommodations, cabin, taverns, and high charges. Crossed Blue river. Every man his own hostler and steward. Plenty of game—deer, turkeys, etc. Inhabitants generally possess a smaller share of politeness than any met with before.

Thursday, Nov. 4.—Left Squire Chambers' (who is only member of the assembly, by the by) at 7 o'clock a. m. Arrived at Lewis' at 6 o'clock, a distance of twenty-five miles. Passed a little village called Peola. The fact that this part of Indiana is a late purchase by the United States, accounts for its towns being so inconsiderable and being made up of log houses. The lands here are very fertile, the country mountainous and broken. Traveled twenty-five miles through woods and passed but four houses. With great difficulty obtained water for our horses. In the midst of one of those long and thick pieces of woods, we passed one of the most miserable huts ever seen—a house built out of slabs without a nail; the pieces merely laid against a log pen such as pigs are commonly kept in, a dirt floor, no chimney. Indeed, the covering would be a bad one in the heat of summer, and, unfortunately, the weather at this time is very severe for the season of the year. This small cabin contained a young and interesting female and her two shivering and almost starving children, all of whom were bareheaded and with their feet bare. There was a small bed, one blanket and a few potatoes. One cow and one pig (who appeared to share in their misfortunes) completed the family, except for the husband, who was absent in search of bread. Fortunately for the dear little children, we had in our carriage some bread, cheese, toddy, etc., which we divided with them with much heartfelt satisfaction. In this situation the woman was polite, smiled and appeared happy. She gave us water to drink, which had been refused to us by persons on the road several times during the day. What a lesson for many of the unhappy ladies that inhabit large cities, whose husbands are slaves to procure all the luxuries of life, a fine house, carpeted floors, elegant furniture, fine carriages and horses, gay and cheerful company, and a smooth brick pavement or marble to walk upon! Yet they are too often dissatisfied, and are sighing for that which cannot be obtained. Could they but contrast their situation with this ragged, suffering and delicate female, they would have just cause to be happy, and would be under the strong conviction that Providence does not interfere with the common affairs of this life. Traveled over excellent lands not taken up which could be cleared with very little labor.

Friday, Nov. 5.—Left Mr. Sears' at 7 o'clock, after having slept in a cabin with three wagons. My friend and self treated civilly by the family. The house not close enough to keep the cats and dogs out. Traveled over an extremely mountainous country to White river (east fork), where a town was laid out last May. Promising little place. Several houses building together, with the industrious appearance of saw and grist mills, give it the appearance of a place of business. Little town is called Hindoostan. In this part of the country the woods are large, the hills bold and lofty, and there is an abundance of bears, wolves, wildcats, panthers, etc. Thousands of acres of land of the first quality are unsettled and to be purchased at from $2.50 to $5 an acre. In crossing White river we had to descend a very steep precipice above the falls, in effecting which my friend, Dr. Hill, who happened to be driving our little carriage, was thrown headforemost into the river. Part of our baggage followed him, and the carriage was very near upsetting. However, we forded this elegant stream, which is 200 yards wide, without much difficulty. After halting a few minutes on the bank to examine our bruises and adjust our baggage, we proceeded on our journey. Traveled a distance of eighteen miles to the west branch of White river, which we forded without risk, the bottom being hard and rocky. Traveled over a fertile country four miles to Steenz, making a distance of thirty-four miles. At this dirty hovel, with one room and a loft, formed by placing boards about three inches apart, ten travelers slept. There were thirteen in family, besides two calves, making in all, with my friend and self, twenty-three whites, one negro and two calves.

Saturday, Nov. 6.—Supped on pumpkins, cabbages, rye coffee without sugar, bones of venison, salted pickles, etc.—all in the midst of crying children, dirt, filth and misery. The last entertainment made the first serious unfavorable impression on my mind relative to the west. Traveled six miles to breakfast and to entertain an idea of starving. No water, no food fit to eat, dusty roads and constantly enveloped in a cloud of smoke, owing to the woods and prairies being on fire for 100 miles. Breakfasted on sound provisions for a rarity and felt a little refreshed. This part of Indiana is rich and valuable. Corn and oats 50 cents a bushel. My good little horse being sick, my usual flow of spirits commenced a retreat. However, they were soon rallied again after a few long sighs for those that are dear and far from me. Arrived at Vincennes, on the Wabash, a bold and handsome river, the size of the Schuylkill. Vincennes, an ancient town, is small, ugly and meanly built, although beautifully situated. Its inhabitants are French, Americans, Indians—and, in short, persons from the four corners of the earth. Indian mounds or small round hills are common in this country. They are believed to be the work of art, and from bones and so forth which have been found in them are supposed to have been receptacles for the dead, when none but the footsteps of the savage was to be traced in these forests. We are now within a few miles of the Shakers and Harmonites, whom we intend to visit and give a correct account of. Very much revived this day, having lived well. Necessity is often the mother of invention. Yolk of egg, flour and water mixed is a good substitute for milk, and is often used in coffee in this country. Rye is frequently substituted for coffee and sage tea in place of the imperial.

Sunday, Nov. 7.—Left Vincennes at 7 o'clock. Crossed the meandering stream, Wabash, into Illinois.

From *Indiana Gazette*, *Corydon*, March 6, 1819, p. 2.

To the Editors of the Indiana Republican.

Vernon, Feb. 16, 1819.

Gentlemen.

Capt. Campbell and myself have just returned from an excursion made into the Delaware Lands, and should you consider the following sketch worth an insertion in your paper, for the amusement of your readers, the information of emigrants, and persons wishing to explore these lands, it will gratify some of your readers.

We travelled the new cut road from this place to Geneva, (on Sandy) a new town laid out on the old Indian boundary line, about 8 miles from this place in a N. W. direction, we then took a new cut road (opened to Flat Rock, sufficient for waggons) which bears nearly N. 45 W. The first stream we crossed after leaving Persors mill, on Sandy, is called little Sandy; the second, Leatherwood; the third Fallen Timber Creek; all appropriate names. We next passed a remarkable Beaver dam, in which the ingenuity of these animals is wonderfully exhibited. The 4th stream is flat creek, the 5th Deer Creek, 6th Crooked creek, all of which streams will answer for light machinery, and run to the S. W. the bottom is generally gravelly and water very clear.—We next came to a stream known by the name of Clifty, sufficient for any kind of water works, and about 10 miles distant in the new purchase. I think, without exaggeration, that every quarter section that may be laid out in this ten miles, will be fit for cultivation and will be settled; the lands are of a black, sandy quality, timbered with Black Ash and Beach, principally. The general face of that country is rather inclined to a plain, with the hollows rather wet. The lands on Clifty are very rich and well timbered on both sides of the stream, with Blue Ash, Walnut, Sugar Tree, Honey Locust, Beach, &c. &c.

After crossing this stream we came to a most beautiful walnut ridge about 1 and a half miles N. of Clifty. We next crossed Middle Creek; then Grassy Creek, then Tough Creek, Stillwater and Pleasant Run, all of which are small mill streams, running to the S. W. some of which have very muddy bottoms, and lie between Clifty and Flat Rock, at the distance of 7 miles; in this 7 miles the lands are principally very rich and level, the vallies rather wet, timbered principally with Oak, Black Ash, Walnut, Sugar Tree, Poplar, Hickory &c. until we came to the lands immediately on Flat Rock; these lands exhibit a scenery I never expected to see in Indiana; they resembled the rich lands on the two Elk horns in Kentucky, for richness and timber, and to appearances abound on both sides of the stream, which has a gravel bottom and is about 80 yards wide. On the north side of the creek we found only one stream (Sugar Creek) until we arrived at Driftwood (Blue River) about 8 miles in a S. W. direction from where we crossed Flat Rock, the lands between these two streams are level and very dry, timbered with White Oak, Black Oak, Walnut, Honey Locust, &c., underbrush, spicewood, dogwood and hazel. We found beautiful, rich and level lands on both sides of Driftwood, and well timbered; The river (by counting our horses steps was 180 yards) wide where we crossed it. I think there are very few springs in this country, but believe water may be had with very little labour. To sum up my views on the subject, I am of the opinion that if Jefferson county would make a good highway in the direction to this place, (individuals of this county have taken measures to make a good highway for our country without delay, suited to the direction, and Madison) that Madison would be the key on the Ohio river to one of the best tracts of country I have ever seen in this state, and a delay will speedily bring forward some other point, as the country is now settled. We met two families and teams on the road to this Eden.

Yours, With esteem,

JOHN VAWTER.

From *Indiana Gazette, Corydon,* March 2, 1820, pp. 1-2.

LETTER FROM CAPT. JAMES RILEY, TO THE EDITOR OF THE PHILADELPHIA UNION.

Fort Wayne, Indiana, November 24, 1819.

Having concluded my surveys for this season, and wishing to view the country between St. Mary's and Miami Rivers, to examine for myself the practicability of so uniting the Wabash with the Miami as to render intercourse by water safe and easy between the Ohio and Lake Erie, through the channel, &c. &c.; I set out yesterday, from Shane's Crossing, on the St. Mary's, and travelling thro' a district of good land, on or near the right bank of that river, forty miles, reached this place early in the evening; and early this morning I set off to look at the junction of the St. Joseph's and St. Mary's which forms the Miami river.

The St. Joseph's river rising in Michigan territory, runs southwesterly about 200 miles, receiving in its course several tributary streams; and the St. Mary's rising in Shelby county, Ohio, runs northwesterly more than 200 miles, including its meanderings—when forming a junction nearly from opposite points, the river turns suddenly south and assumes the name of Miami of the Lakes, or as pronounced by the French Maume; then turning gradually round again, these congregated waters flow off in a northeast direction about 200 miles, following the course of the river to the southwest end of Lake Erie.

Fort Wayne stands on a bluff just below the junction and on the right bank of the Miami; its situation is admirable, chosen by a general in whom were united the greatest personal courage and intrepidity; and the most consumate prudence and skill in conducting and supporting an army. Amidst forests and morasses, separated from the inhabited parts of the country by a dreary and extensive wilderness; surrounded on all sides by hosts of savage enemies, flushed by a recent and great victory over the unfortunate Gen. St. Clair.

The gigantic mind of General Wayne, created resources, as he went along, baffling the skill and cunning of his enemy, with astonishing industry and activity. He cut roads and marched his troops to the important points which he seized. With an unerring military eye, and profound judgment, he selected and fortified such posts, and such only as would inevitably secure his conquests, and afford the most sure protection to his army and our extensive frontier settlements. At every step in this country, every unprejudiced mind, will more and more admire the movements and achievements of the army conducted by this veteran, and truly wise and great General.

By occupying Fort Wayne, the communication between Lake Erie and the Ohio through the channel of the Maume and the Wabash, (which is the shortest and most direct water route from Buffalo to the Mississippi river) was cut off or completely commanded.

The Wabash River, which rises in Ohio, runs north past Fort Recovery, enters Indiana, about 10 miles from that post, and continuing its course northwestwardly, approaches Fort Wayne within 18 miles, when it turns more to the southwest, running diagonally across the state of Indiana, and receiving in its course numerous important tributary streams, until it reaches the line that separates Indiana from Illinois, in lat. 40; thence meandering into Illinois and back into Indiana in a southerly direction, discharges its waters into the Ohio river.

The Little Wabash rises in an elevated swamp prairie, 6 miles south of Fort Wayne, and joins the Wabash 18 miles from thence —thus in high stages of the water a portage of only six miles, carries merchandize from the head of the Maume, into the navigable waters of the Wabash, and vice versa; from whence floating with the current, it may either supply the interior wants of the country, or proceed to New Orleans or Lake Erie.

Through a part of the above mentioned swamp, which is very extensive, a canal might very easily be cut, six miles long, uniting the Wabash to the St. Mary's a little above its junction; and from what I saw and learned from others, it is my opinion that the swamp might afford water sufficient for purposes of canal navigation.

By the treatise of 1817 and '18 (mentioned in a former letter) lands in the state of Indiana, to the amount of from four to six millions of acres (lying principally on the left bank of the Wabash, and extending from the new line N. W. of Wayne, and South and West to former purchases) were ceded to the U. States.

These lands are charmingly situated in point of climate; their soil is mostly of the very first quality—the country is well watered and well timbered, and lying on and near the Wabash, enjoys immense advantages. Emigrants from the Northern and Eastern states, to this section of the country, as well as the new purchase in Ohio; will find it to be their interest and their comfort too, to go to Buffalo, and up the lake to Fort Meigs, 28 miles within the Maume Bay, and from thence up that river to the mouth of the Auglaze or Fort Wayne, and so on to their place of destination. Early in the spring of the year is the best time for emigration that way, as the streams are then full, and they will find an easy and sure navigation, even in its present unimpared state.

The country around Fort Wayne is very fertile; the situation is commanding and healthy, and here will rise a town of great importance, which must become an immense depot.

The Fort is now only a small stockade; no troops are stationed here and less than thirty dwelling houses, occupied by French and American families, form the whole settlement, but as soon as the land shall be surveyed and offered for sale, inhabitants will pour from all quarters into this future thoroughfare, between New York and the Mississippi, Missouri, &c. &c.

The unlooked for progress of that stupendous work, the New York Grand Canal, a work of the most momentous consequences to the people of the western country, and to the Union of the United States, whereby the countries bordering on the Lakes are to be bound by the strongest of all ties, interest, to the Atlantic states, electrifies the citizens of this country, who now behold themselves transported, as it were, with their rich possessions near the ocean, and already bless its proprietors and supporters.

From *An historical, topographical and descriptive view of the United States of America, and of upper and lower Canada*, by E. Mackenzie [1820], pp. 208-210.

MACKENZIE, ENEAS.

Unlike most of the other accounts, this work of Mr. Mackenzie's makes no attempt to force his own personal observations upon the reader, but simply presents in a well organized manner, the best historical and descriptive material that could be found concerning the New World. Mr. Mackenzie was by training a journalist and an historian. He had produced a history of Egypt; a history of Northumberland; a modern Geography, etc., and was in position to readily judge the value of authentic material. His work abounds with numerous letters written by people who were residents of America or who had visited here. These views are arranged in an interesting style, and the seven hundred and more pages contain one of the best accounts published during the first quarter of the last century.

INDIANA.

Situation and Extent. Indiana is situated between north lat. 37 deg. 47 min. and 41 deg. 50 min., and west long. 7 deg. 40 min. and 10 deg. 45 min. Its greatest length is 284 miles, and its breadth 155. Its area is 38,000 square miles, or 24,320,000 acres.

Natural Geography.—The face of the country is hilly, not mountainous; and the scenery is said to be rich and variegated, abounding with plains and large prairies.

The principal river is the Wabash, which is said to be a beautiful stream, 280 yards broad at its outlet, and navigable upwards of 220 miles. It rises near the boundary line between the state of Ohio and Indiana, about 100 miles from lake Erie, where there is a portage of only eight miles between it and the Miami of the lakes. Its course is nearly south-west, and the distance it runs, including its windings, is not less than 500 miles. A great many tributary streams flow into it, the chief of which is White river, upwards of 200 miles long. Tippacanoe river, near which are the largest settlements of Indians in the territory, falls into the Wabash; and it is near the outlet of that river where the Prophet is at present collecting his forces.

The soil is said to be generally rich and fertile. The climate is delightful, except in the neighbourhood of marshes, chiefly confined to the lower parts of the territory.

The settlements commenced about 22 or 23 years ago, and have made considerable progress, though they have been retarded by the settlement of the fertile and beautiful state of Ohio, which is situated between this and the old states. The greater part of the territory is yet subject to Indian claims. Where they have been extinguished, and the white settlements have been made, it is divided into four counties, and 22 townships, the greater part of which are on the Ohio; and some few on the Wabash and White-water river. The inhabitants amounted, by the census of 1800, to 5,641; they now amount to 86,734, being an increase of 81,093 in 17 years.

The agriculture of the territory is nearly the same as that of the state of Ohio. Every kind of grain, grass, and fruit comes to maturity; and towards the southern part of it considerable crops of cotton are raised, though only for domestic use.

Towns.—The principal town is *Vincennes*, on the Wabash. It is an old settlement, and the inhabitants are mostly of French extraction; they amounted, by last census, to 670.

Trade.—As the inhabitants make nearly all their own clothing, they have little external trade. What little they have is down the river to New Orleans.

Government.—The constitution or government in this new country is similar to that of the other neighbouring states,—excellent in theory, but too often vile and corrupt in practice. It declares, in pompous language, that all men are free; but if their skins be black, they are not included in this declaration, slaves being necessary for the ease and comfort of the freemen of Indiana.

We will now proceed to view the *Southern States* of the Union, agreeably to the arrangement we have adopted.

From *Journal of a tour to Fort Wayne and the adjacent country, in the year 1821*, by the Author.

TEAS, THOMAS SCATTERGOOD.

The author of this journal, which has never before been published, was born in Philadelphia, Pa., in 1796. He was well educated for his day and was a German and French scholar. He early developed an inclination to see the country and study nature at first hand. In his twentieth year he traveled on foot from Philadelphia to the Delaware Water Gap. He continued his tramp to New York City, which he describes as vastly inferior to Philadelphia in buildings and public spirit in general.

His next tramp was to Indiana by way of Niagara Falls, and the next year he traveled on foot from Philadelphia to Indiana by way of Pittsburgh.

"Brother Charles" Teas, mentioned at the beginning of this journal, lived eight miles north of Richmond, Indiana.

2nd day 7th month 9th, I sat off from my brother Charles completely equipped for a journey in the wilderness, and with three day's provisions—crossed the West fork of White-water, here about 2 yards wide, and came on 14 miles to the edge of the settlement—entered the wilderness at half past 12 o'clock—passed several dry channels of creeks, but not one running stream, till I reached the Massissiniway river. This stream is about 3 yards wide here, and very shallow. It flows about West—Soon after crossing it, I discovered a clearing, and finding a settler there, I put up with him; distance 30 miles—course due North—Here I was regaled with cold sour Indian bread and milk.

10th After passing the principal part of the night in continual warfare with myriads of fleas, I was compelled to retreat from the field, or rather bed of battle, about two hours before daybreak, and got a little sleep in a chair. A little before sunrise it began to rain, and continued pouring down till 7 o'clock, when having taken breakfast of the same delicate fare which constituted my supper, and paying 50 cents for what my host was pleased to call my "entertainment"; I departed, not much prepossessed in favour of the life of a frontier settler. The rain has made it very unpleasant travelling the soil being very mellow, the mud is ancle deep, and the dripping bushes soon wet me above the middle. The musquitoes and gnats are as numerous here as along the sea shore, and are very troublesome. About 8 'clock the sun shone out—hardly ever more welcome to me, arrived at the Wabash at 5 o'clock, P. M. This is a beautiful river, about 7 yards wide, flowing W. N. West.

Here I halted to rest, and by sitting in the smoke of a fire which I kindled, made out to keep off the musquitoes at the risk of suffocation. The remains of Indian hunting camps are numerous along the road. The principal game that are found here are deer—there are also plenty of wolves. Their tracks, and those of deer, are every where to be seen in the mud. I have not seen many bear tracks. After resting myself, I came on till sunset, and was looking out for a convenient place to encamp, when I discovered an opening ahead, and soon entered on a beautiful prairie, overgrown with high grass, and terminating in a thick wood. At the distance of about half a mile, I saw a cabin, and on reaching it was received with kindness. This prairie is about 40 miles long, and from $\frac{1}{4}$ to 15 miles wide. Its long grass, waving in the wind, bears some resemblance to the waves of the sea in a light breeze. Like most other prairies, the water on it is bad, and fevers and agues must be the companions of those who settle on it. The man at whose house I stopped, has four of his family sick. He dug a well 36 feet deep, in hopes of procuring good water, but has failed of success. The water is the most curious I ever saw. It is of a pale blue colour, strongly impregnated with sulphur, and has the smell of burnt gunpowder. He told me that it curdles milk almost instantaneously. Course to the Wabash due North, thence N. N. West—distance 30 miles.

11th Came on through a flat level country abounding in hiccory swamps, to the St. Mary's river, where I arrived at five o'clock. This is a handsome river, flowing about N. West with a slow current—it is about 25 yards wide—the road runs nearly parallel with it—three miles farther is the house of Robert Douglass, where I stopped. Course N. West, distance 15 miles. There was formerly an Indian village here—the ruins of 8 of the cabins are still visible. Douglas is building a raft of logs, to float down to Fort Wayne, and as he will be ready to start tomorrow, I accepted his invitation to accompany him.

12th While we were at breakfast, a Miami Indian and his family consisting of his wife and one small child, came to the house. They were on their way up the river. Douglas held a broken conversation with them in the few words of their language he knew. I accosted him in English and French, but he shook his head. They breakfasted with us, and after breakfast we all went down to the river. The Indian had left his canoe near our raft. It was made of hickory bark, stripped from a log in one piece, about ten feet long, the ends sewed up with filaments of bark, and the sides stiffened with ribs of wood sewed in the same manner. I was told that they would make a canoe in a couple of hours. The raft not being entirely finished, we set to work and by 12 o'clock were ready to get under way. The crew consisted ot Douglas, commander, two men, and myself, passenger. We proceeded slowly down, the river being low, for about half a mile, when Douglas sent the canoe (or long boat,) ahead to reconnoitre a ripple which was about half a mile farther, and it returned with a report that in consequence of the low stage of water, it would be impossible for us to pass it. There being no alternative but to wait for a rise of the river, we came too, and secured the raft to the shore, much to my satisfaction, as I had anticipated a tedious passage—returned to the house, and after taking in a supply of jerked venison, I sat off about 2 o'clock. About 6 miles further, I passed the remains of a large Indian hunting camp. About sunset, having found a convenient place to encamp, and collected materials for my fire, I found that I had lost my tinder box. This was a serious loss—for though I had tinder and flints, I had no steel; and to lie down without a fire, would have been almost certain death on account of the wolves. The only chance of safety was to climb a tree. While I was looking for a convenient one, I heard the report of a gun at some distance, and soon after, of 2 more: Supposing it to proceed from a hunting party of Indians, I pushed through the woods as rapidly as I could, and in about a quarter of a mile came to a clearing. Three or four young men (Indians,) were standing near the cabin, talking. As soon as they saw me, one of them gave a shout, and went into the cabin. Presently after, an elderly man came out, and on my accosting him, came to me, and shook hands, which banished the uneasy sensations I had felt at first for as I was alone and unarmed, their manner had given me some little alarm, though I still walked towards them and endeavored to conceal it. Finding that the elderly man spoke very broken English, I accosted him in French, which he spoke very fluently. He welcomed me to his house with such a friendly air, that I was soon at ease. I told him of the loss of my tinder box, and the predicament I was in, when I heard the firing. He said that it was his young men who had been out hunting, and congratulated me on the escape I had made. His name is La Fontaine; he is of French descent, and belongs to the Miami tribe. He has begun farming on a regular plan, after the manner of the whites. He has only been here since the 3rd month, and has erected a comfortable log cabin, with a bark one adjoining, and cleared 6 acres, which is in very fine looking corn—he has deadened about 30 acres more. His house is pleasantly situated on the West bank of the St. Mary's. His family consists of his wife, her sister, and a little boy, about 8 years old, whom he has adopted, having no children of his own. The young men I saw, are hired to assist him in farming. Our supper was served up in a curious style. The table was set with a tin bucket of young Hyson tea, in which a proper proportion of sugar and milk were mixed, a tin basin of fried vension, another of butter, a third of wheat cakes, two tin cups, and two knives. My host made an apology for the want of forks, that they had not got into the way of using them yet. The provisions were excellent. After spending a very agreeable evening with him, I retired to sleep, on a deer skin, with a blanket covering—distance today 12 miles, course N. West. La Fontaine informed me that the Miami tribe amounts at present to 1,800 souls, and that their number is nearly stationary, there being about the same number killed in their drunken quarrels, as are born. Thirty have been killed in their quarrels with each other, since the first of the 5th mo. last. Their pension is 18,400 dollars, which is equally divided between men, women, and children. They receive this annuity at Fort Wayne, and but a small part of it is taken from there—the principal part being expended for whiskey. The laws of the U. S. for preventing the introduction of liquors among the Indians, though very severe, are ineffectual. The evidence of an Indian, even if they would give it for the detection of smugglers of whiskey, will not be taken in law, and the country is as yet such a wilderness, that the chances of detection are few. A person might remain in the woods within five or six miles of Fort Wayne, for a year, without being discovered by any white settler. It has been the custom of the traders to bring whiskey in kegs and hide it in the woods about half a mile from the fort, a short time previous to the time of paying the annuity, and when the Indians come to the fort, to give information to such of the young men as the traders can confide in, that there is whiskey to be had at those places. These inform their comrades, and as soon as they receive their money, they go off in droves to the places appointed where they frequently buy it at two dollars a pint, till their money is gone, and then pawn their blankets, guns, bracelets, and other trinkets, till they are sometimes reduced to a state of nudity. In this manner the unprincipled traders evade the laws with impunity, and render all the efforts of the friends of civilization abortive.

13th After breakfasting with my hospitable host, I took leave of him, and proceeded on my journey. Four miles from his house, came to that of Rocheville, the principal chief of the Miamis. He has a very handsome farm, and lives in quite a genteel style. He was gone to Detroit, and neither his wife nor children speaking any language that I could understand, I made but short stay there, passed several Indian cabins, and entered on a large prairie which extended as far as I could see, crossed the St. Mary's, and soon after arrived at Fort Wayne. Distance 9 miles due West. The settlement at this place consisted of about 30 log cabins and two tolerably decent frame houses. It is situated on the Miami of Lake Erie, at the junction of the St. Joseph's and St. Mary's, which form the Miami. The inhabitants are nearly all French Canadians. The fort stands at the lower end of the village, and is composed of hewn log buildings about 35 feet high, and the intervals between them filled up with a double row of pickets, 20 feet high. It is about 60 yards square. There is no garrison kept here, and the barracks are occupied by the Indian Agent, the Baptist missionary, and some private families. There is a school for the Indian children in the fort, under the auspices of the Baptist Society. It is conducted on the Lancasterian system; the teacher's name is Montgomery. On my arrival, as the school was the principal object of curiosity, I waited on the missionary, whose name is McKoy, and requested him to accompany me to it, which he did; and during my stay in fort Wayne, treated me with an attention as unexpected as it was gratifying. There are about forty scholars. It is pleasing to see the order in which the school is kept, and the delight that the scholars seem to take in their studies. There were two boys of the Pottowattomie tribe, who had only been 2 weeks at school, who were spelling in words of four letters. As soon as they begin to learn their letters, they are furnished with a slate, and form letters on it in imitation of printed type. About half the scholars were writing, and many of them write a very good hand. Their improvement is such as to remove all doubts as to their capacity. After spending a very agreeable afternoon here, I returned to the tavern. There are considerable numbers of Indians here, of the Pottawattomies, Shawanees, Miami, Utawas, and Delaware tribes. Notwithstanding the efforts of the Indian Agent to prevent the traders from selling whiskey to them, they still contrive to do it; I have seen as many as fifty of them drunk during my short stay here. They assemble in groups of ten or twelve, men and women promiscuously, squat on the ground, and pass the canteen rapidly round, and sing, whoop, and halloo, all laughing and talking at once, with the most horrible contortions of the countenance; so that they reminded me of Milton's demons. It is not uncommon to see them entirely naked, except a strip of clothing a foot broad, about their middle. This evening six deserters, who had been taken and sent to Green Bay, and discharged after serving their time out, arrived here. They were miserable looking fellows—One of them came to the tavern, and offered to barter a roll of tobacco for whiskey, but was refused. They took up their quarters for the night in an empty cabin.

14th Spent the day in rambling through the woods round the town. I took care to procure a steel. There is an U. S. reserve of six miles square round the town, and the settlers are squatters, who pay no tax nor rent, and are liable to be ordered off at a minutes' warning. The village before the late war, was much larger than it is at present. The Indians destroyed all the houses except two which were near the fort, and which were burnt, by order of the commandant, to prevent the Indians from setting fire to them when the wind should set towards the fort, and burn it. Beyond the U. S. reserve, there are a number of reserves belonging to the Indians. The soil in the whole tract between here and Whitewater is very rich, and there is a rank growth of underwood —ginseng grows in abundance in the woods, and in the bottoms along the St. Marys, there is a great deal of sarsaparilla. There is much less beech timber here than farther south, and the principal timber is oak, white, black and red, and hiccory—there is no poplar. the other woods are the same with those along the Ohio, excepting the sycamore, of which I saw none. This part of the country possesses great commercial advantages, and when it becomes settled, will be a place of great business. The Grand Canal from N. York to Buffaloe will open a water course to the sea, and it is in contemplation to cut a canal from the St. Joseph's to the Little river, a branch of the Wabash; the distance from the nearest point of communication, (about ½ a mile from Fort Wayne) is 7½ miles, and the whole distance is through a prairie; so that the expense of cutting a canal will be trifling, and then there will be a water course either to New York or New Orleans. The only disadvantage that I observed in this county, (which, however is a great one,) is the scarcity of water. There is not at this time, a single running stream between here and the Whitewater, except the three rivers I mentioned. This inconvenience, however, will be less felt by those who settle along the rivers. I have never known what it was to suffer for water till I took this journey—the only water I could get was from waggon ruts which the rain had filled, and as it had not rained for several weeks, they were mostly dry. This water, where it was exposed to the sun, was generally covered with a green scum, and where it was shaded, was full of musquitoes—but necessity compelled me to drink it. The musquitoes are another great pest. I never saw them thicker along the sea shore than they are in the woods; and it is impossible to stop to rest without kindling a fire, and siiting in the smoke of it, at the risk of strangulation. The St. Mary's is navigable for perogues about 160 miles from Fort Wayne. The Fort is about 15 miles West of the Ohio line, in Randolph County. This is a fine country for raising stock. In the river bottoms, the grass grows very luxuriant and in the woods, there is an abundance of herbage of one kind or other, so that cattle will keep fat without feeding at home, with what they will find in the woods. There are some as fine looking cattle here as I ever saw.

15th. Sat off for Wapaughkonnetta, came 24 miles in a S. eastern course, and finding a settler, stopped at his house.—16th came on through a continued region of oak land, thickly wooded, to the St. Mary's river—crossed it at Shane's ferry—Anthony Shane is an Indian, who keeps a tavern here. He has a fine farm, and has laid out a town here, called Shanesville; there are three houses built, and one more begun. From here the country is settled about six miles. Soon after leaving Shane's, I entered on a beautiful prairie, thinly timbered with black and red oak which is scattered in groves over its whole extent. It is entirely clear of brush or underwood, and covered with long grass. The surface is not quite level, but gently undulating; and upon the whole it is the most beautiful land I ever saw. It extends from the St. Mary's river about ten miles. Came four miles from Shanesville to the house of—Dennison—distance 20 miles, Course S. East.

17th. Came 3 miles to twelve-mile-creek; crossed it, and entered the forest again. The timber here is principally beech—missed the Wapaughkonnetta trace, and came to Fort St. Mary's at the head of canoe navigation on that river. There has been no garrison kept here for several years, and the fort has gone to decay—a block house is the principal vestige of it remaining.—Near the fort is the tumulus of an Indian.—A wall is raised with saplings about 3 feet high, round it, covered with bark.—Crossed the St. Mary's here, and soon after struck an Indian trail which I supposed to lead to Wapaughkonnetta. After travelling along it about ten miles came to Pasheta's town, an Indian village of six or seven cabins, on the Au Glaize river—found an Indian who could speak a little English, and received directions from him for Wapaughkonnetta—crossed the Au Glaize, and two miles further came in sight of the town. The Indians are thickly settled in this part of the country. They are Shawanese—passed 4 more graves, covered like the first. Came to the house of Robert Broderick, U. States' blacksmith, where I was very hospitably received. The Indians here are about 500 in number, and receive 3,000 dollars per annum. This year's pension they requested in goods and it was accordingly forwarded last week in blankets, calicoes, broad cloths, &c. This evening Capt. Logan and his son came to Broderick's to have a chain mended. The son whose name is "Walk by the side of the Water," is the most perfect model of masculine beauty that I ever saw. He was very tastefully dressed in a costume not much unlike that of a Scotch Highlander. His father is a fat butcher looking man. After they had gone, I remarked to R. Broderick, that I thought the young man very beautiful. He replied that if I had seen him about three weeks before, with his clothes sprinkled with the blood of a man whom he had murdered, I might have thought differently. He had been commissioned by his father, who is one of the chiefs, to kill an Indian who had murdered another a few days before, and he accordingly went in quest of him, armed with a long knife. They met in the street, and "Walk" &c. informed the culprit that he was come to kill him; a piece of information which was in no wise agreeable to him. He attempted to make his escape, but the executioner soon overtook him and stabbed him in the neck, he fell, and was soon dispatched. Walk then came to Broderick's and shewed him the knife which was dripping with blood, gave him a full account of the murder with as much apparent concern as though he had been killing a cat. Distance today 27 miles. Course S. E. to Fort St. Mary's, thence due East. 18th Took a walk through the town. It is a tolerably large one, extending nearly a mile scattering. There are several French traders here. The society of Friends have erected a grist and saw mill on the Au Glaize at this place, and employ a person to attend them. A school is to be opened in the 9th month next. Just as we were sitting down to breakfast, a company of surveyors, accompanied by General Beasley arrived. They took breakfast with us, and after breakfast, I took leave of Brodericks, and returned to Fort St. Mary's, and thence to Dennisons. 27 miles. 19th. Came to Shanesville. Captain Shane shewed me a plot of the town. It is handsomely laid out, the streets six perches wide crossing each other at right angles, and intersected with alleys two perches wide. The lots on Main and Market Streets sell for 60 dollars. They are a quarter of an acre each. He also shewed me a copy of an act of Congress, granting him half a section of land (where he is settled), in consideration of his "valuable and honorable services during the late war." He commanded a company of Shawanese.

From here I took a blazed path, leading to Captain Riley's, but it being a new one, and but little travelled, I soon lost it, and concluded to follow the course of the river—a determination I soon had ample cause to repent—The river bottoms in general were from one to three hundred yards wide, and covered with grass from five to eight feet high, and so matted together, that it was extremely difficult to force my way through it. On the high grounds back of the river, the nettles grew about as high as my shoulders, and stung me almost beyond the power of endurance; and where there was no room for nettles, the vines and prickly bushes formed a thicket that at any other time I would have thought impenetrable. In order to get along here, I had to crawl on my hands and knees, and fairly push myself through them till wearied out with this way of getting along at the rate of a quarter of a mile per hour, I took to the river, and waded along its banks till they became so steep that the water came up to my armpits, and then took to the long grass, the nettles and thickets again.—Soon after, I crossed a fallen tree that I recollected having crossed about an hour before. By this time, I had wandered in so many different directions, that I was completely bewildered. The sun was about an hour high, and appeared to be in the east. I corrected that error with my compass, but owing to the difficulties of the ground, I could not carry it in my hand, and at last I could not tell when I saw the river, whether I was ascending or descending its banks. I now began to entertain serious fears of not being able to reach any house, and the alternative was, to perish in this execrable wilderness, as I had no provisions, nor any means of procuring them. The only living animals I saw, were deer, which were numerous in the long grass.—About sunset, as I was looking out for a place to encamp, being almost worn down with fatigue, and bleeding with scratches from the briers, I discovered the path! None but those who have been in a similar condition can form an idea of the joy I felt at being thus rescued from the most horrible death. As I knew that it would soon be too dark to see the path, I forgot my weariness, and pushed on as rapidly as the faintness of the tracks would allow, and after going about 2½ miles, saw Captain Riley's clearing, and a little after dusk arrived at his house. He received me very kindly, and when I told him the course I had come, he expressed great surprise that I should have reached his house at all—distance today 18 miles.—Course North, South, East, and West. Spent a very agreeable evening with the Captain and his family. 20th. After breakfast we sat off and came along as dim a road as the one I lost yesterday, but having had good cause to take more heed to my steps, I made out to keep it for about 8 miles, when I arrived at the house of Thomas Robinson, on the Wabash prairie. Course S. S. West. Here I struck the Richmond road, came about nine miles below the Wabash, and encamped—distance 25 miles. 21st. Came to the Massissiniway at ten o'clock. A few miles below, took Connor's trace (an Indian trader) by mistake, and came on 6 miles before I had discovered my error; but as the trace bore about S. S. W. I concluded to go on. This road leads to Greenville. I reached a settlement before dark—distance 30 miles.—22.—Came on about 30 miles, and arrived at my brother Charles' at 4 o'clock P. M. and thus ended my journey, having travelled 287 miles—and occupied two weeks very agreeably—

And so my paper being also nearly expended,
The account of my adventures shall be ended.

From *Memoirs of William Forster*, edited by Benjamin Seebohm.

Forster, William.

William Forster, a minister of the Society of Friends in England was born in 1784. He was recognized as a minister in 1805. He was a helper of Elizabeth Fry in her philanthropic work. In 1820 he was induced to undertake a mission to the United States in behalf of the Society of Friends in America. He spent five years in America traveling in New England, Canada, New York, New Jersey, Pennsylvania, Delaware, Maryland, Ohio, Indiana and Illinois. In 1821-1822 he spent several months in Indiana, chiefly among Friends in the newly settled districts.

He came to the United States again in 1853 in the interests of the anti-slavery movement and presented an address to the President of the United States and to the governors of a number of the States. He died in Tennessee in 1854 while on this mission.

11th mo. 29th [1821] At Lewis's Tavern, Shelby Raven, Indiana. ...This backwoods tavern consists of two log-houses, with a covered passage between them; each perhaps from fifteen to twenty feet square; the largest is our landlord's dwelling house for himself, his wife, and six children. How they dispose of several others members of the family it is difficult to imagine. The apartment which we inhabit just holds four beds; one of them is alloted to John and me; our companion and four other travellers will, I suppose, divide the other three between them. It is a most thoroughly disagreeable way of life. Our worthy host is a man of good understanding and established respectability, from Carolina. We were at their meeting yesterday, to which I found they had invited several of their neighbors. After a time of deep indwelling before the Lord, I was enlarged in consolation and invitation and counsel, to my own confirmation. I suppose the meeting does not consist of less than sixty or seventy families. We have now a long formidable journey on prospect, forty-six miles to Vincennes.

30th. Washington, Davies County.—Instead of the crowded cabin and noisy family of last night, we have a snug chamber to ourselves, a nice glowing hearth, and a neat chamber. We came eight miles to a late breakfast in Hindostan, a newly begun town of about twenty houses. Our road, so far, like that we travelled yesterday, was hilly, and the country but thinly inhabited. We ferried the river, which we were told is 400 yards in width; and, after ascending a hill, had a fine level road through a country comparatively open, and in some places wholly clear of large timber. We found the settlements much more numerous, and at intervals finely cultivated farms.

12th mo. 2nd. Vincennes.—We did not see our host till this morning. Por man! his history touched me; his wife died about four years ago, and has left him with ten children. Proprietor of 800 acres of land in that fine country, some of his children are covered with rags just hung over their shoulders, forming a spectacle that would have excited our compassion for the children of the poorest beggar at our door.

There is a great deal of travelling on the road. Some going out to Illinois and Missouri; and nearly as many returning to their former residences, discouraged by sickness, or disappointed in not finding the Elysium they had been seeking.

We appointed a meeting for the evening at the Court-house. On going to it, we found a considerable number of people assembled, who appeared very unsettled. I strove to be quiet, and, a small opening to service presenting, I rose with the tide, and was borne along on a gentle current of heavenly love, speaking of Christ and his salvation, warning and inviting the people, and, comforting the oppressed and penitent sinner with the hope of mercy and deliverance. I was afterwards engaged in prayer and intercession for the sincere and seeking believers, for the wordly and carnally minded, and the negligent and indifferent, and for the people at large in this place, that they might be turned from their iniquity, and seek to serve and fear the Lord.

The town is not so large, nor the houses so good, as some we have seen in the Western country. It was originally built and settled by a colony of French emigrants from Canada, above 100 years ago; and was, I suppose, one of the principal outposts on this side of the mountains for trading with the Indians. Latterly a number of Americans settled in among them; they have no place for worship but a Popish chapel; but the Methodists and Presbyterians occasionally use the Court-house for their meetings. The town stands on a large flat or sandy plain, which appears by nature uncongenial to the growth of timber. . . .

. . .I am sorry to say there are many slaves in the town—I suppose mostly such as were held under the territorial government; but the State Legislature had made provision for their freedom. We hear sad stories of kidnapping. I wish some active benevolent people could induce every person of colour to remove away form the river, as it gives wicked, unprincipled wretches the opportunity to get them into a boat, and carry them off to Orleans or Missouri, where they still fetch a high price. I have been pleading hard with a black man and his wife to get off for some settlement of Friends, with their five children; and I hope they will go. I hardly know anything that would make me more desperate than to be in the way of this abominable system of kidnapping; I cannot say, when once set on to rescue a poor creature, where I would stop. It is most shocking to think that they will betray one another, and sometimes the black women are the deepest in these schemes. A poor man told us that he never went to bed without having his arms in readiness for defence.

5th. Harmony, Posey County.—Believing I could not peacefully relinquish the prospect of visiting our friends to the west of the Wabash, we pursued our journey to the southward. Yesterday afternoon we had a meeting at the house of a widow Friend, in a little colony of emigrants from New York; some of them Friends, others more or less remotely connected with the Society.

After a wilderness journey, we arrived here just as the town clock struck five. This is an interesting village, a settlement of Germans who came into America upwards of sixteen years ago. They established themselves in the first instance on the waters of the Big Beaver, in Pennsylvania, and removed to this place about seven years ago. They have a fine estate of 25,000 acres—3,000 cleared and fenced, and from what we saw it was in a state of good cultivation. The village contains about 700 inhabitants; they appear an orderly, industrious, and sober people. There are some handsome brick dwellings and large wood houses in the village, a neat place of worship, and a commodious inn. It is difficult to form any correct opinion of the people on such very slight acquaintance, especially such as speak a strange language; but it is not too much to say there is nothing prepossessing in their appearance. It has to me more the appearance of a community devoted to temporal aggrandizement than to religious attainment. Their industry, neatness, and order, and especially their cleanliness, are great. It is difficult to ascertain their religious principles. They object to oaths and war, but are in the practice of paying a fine in lieu of personal service; community of goods and implicit submission to their elder or headman are enjoined.

Having crossed over into the State of Illinois, he continues his narrative.

6th. Albion.—We were ferried over the Wabash, about a quarter of a mile in width, by a man and two boys. I pleased myself with giving each of the lads a New Testament, and the poor man appearing anxious to posses the same treasure I did not hesitate to gratify him. The poor fellow, in the aboundings of his gratitude, offered to return the ferriage, which of course I did not accept. Our road was for the first few miles through a very extensive cane break. After traversing a more hospitable region, we came across two or three large prairies. Having been shut up in the woods for such a length of time, it was gratifying beyond description to enjoy the extent of prospect. We were heartily welcomed by the landlady at Albion, who turned out to be our cousin Morris Birkbeck's old servant. . . . .

Keeping near the Wabash they pursued their journey in Illinois to the north.

We got off early in the afternoon, and came about sixteen miles, most of the way a very lonely road, through a large extent of prairie. There being no inn on the road, we found more than common difficulty in obtaining accommodation for the night, but at length succeeded better than we had hoped for. One of the young men had brought home a fine fat buck the day before, and we had a nice broiled venison, both for supper and breakfast next morning. Our lodging was not quite so agreeable; my companion and I had a bed below stairs. In the same room was a poor woman, confined to her bed by sickness; our landlady was her companion for the night; another stranger slept on the floor, and our other friends up in the loft. The poor woman was very ill in the night, so that we had not a very comfortable time of rest. Being brought into feeling for the poor sick woman, I mentioned my wish to have the family collected, which was readily complied with; and I may confess with thankfulness that the opportunity was to my relief and comfort. With the hope of a quiet afternoon, and perhaps a meeting in the evening, we set off, intending to travel a stage of twelve miles. Instead of finding the distance to Laurenceville only twelve or fifteen miles, as we had been led to expect, from the time spent on the road we concluded it could not be less than twenty-one or twenty-two miles. When we got there, though the town is laid out for the county-seat, we found it so much in its infancy as to contain but one tavern, and that, with its rough exterior, affording but little hope of comfort. With the expectation of better fare farther on the road, we were easily induced to pursue our journey, intending to take up with such accommodation as we might meet with on the other side of the Embarras, which falls into the Wabash a few miles below Vincennes. We met with some detention at the ferry; but by the help of a crazy boat, and lazy, awkward ferry-men, got safe over. Here we had the vexation to find we had not come forward for much better fare; everything was so completely miserable, that after a little refreshment, for which we had to wait long, we determined to go on a few miles, and trust to the hospitality of some of the neighbouring farmers for a night's lodging. We found our way by the light of the full moon, to the house of a kind-hearted man, from the State of New York, who without much hesitation agreed to give us shelter for the night. Though lately a magistrate, and holding a large tract of fine land, he had but a small cabin; he readily gave us one bed, and made up another for our companions, on the floor; and the man and his wife and six children divided the other two among themselves. This was not very agreeable, but much more tolerable among strangers, than in the company of old acquaintance. I pleased myself with distributing some of our little store of books among their fine family; and with the expression of hearty good-will on both sides we took our seats in the waggon, soon after sun-rise, and reached the small town of Palestine, situated at the foot of La Motte Prairie, about mid-day. I took a short walk into the environs of the town: the scenery was novel and very striking; it had much the appearance of a large level common or green, of several miles in circumference, with settlements about every half-mile round the margin; and the adjacent woods, particularly towards the Wabash, contain large and very lofty timber, syca-more, hackberry, cotton-wood, &c.

Riding pretty nearly the length of this prairie, we came to another interval of wood, and then entered Union Pairie, and having a fine level road soon drove to the house of our friend Reuben Crow, eighty miles from Albion. After another cold and very wakeful night, we parted from our friends at Union, our host kindly accompanying us to the Wabash. Before we set off, we had an opportunity of retirement in the family; I was much engaged both on account of the father and children, and under the prevalence of Divine love it was a season of instruction and consolation. When we reached the river, we found the ice, which I suppose had been formed in the night, floating in large sheets. It wore a fearful aspect; and the ferryman not having all his men at hand, to reconcile us to the detention of two or three hours, said quite enough to make me think it would be hazardous crossing; but, taking the opportunity when the river was clearer than it had been for some time previous, we got through with safety.

Having now re-entered the State of Indiana they pursued their course to a small settlement of Friends on the eastern banks of the Wabash.

After two or three hours travelling, we met with a warm welcome from our friend Moses Hoggett, at his comfortable habitation on Honey Creek Prairie. Next day we had a meeting with Friends to some satisfaction and relief, and spent the afternoon and evening at the house of an agreeable, open-hearted friend on the banks of the Wabash. On Sixth-day, we had a bleak cold ride, about ten miles higher up the river, to Spring Creek.

We were guests to our friend Benjamin Bailey, and his worthy wife, who had not been previously visited by Friends. I think they did their very best to keep us warm; but, the cabin being without a window, we were obliged to have the door open for light, and the logs not being well plastered, it required some little watchfulness to suppress the rising of a murmer. We had a meeting with a few Friends in the neighbourhood in the evening, which, though not without some unpleasant interruption, was attended with sufficient feeling to satisfy us that we were pursuing the path of duty; and as there is a prospect of more Friends settling in the neighbourhood, I trust it will not be long before they are encouraged to hold a meeting among themselves. We parted from the dear friends in much love, early in the forenoon, and drove briskly along a fine road to Terre Haute, a small town and county-seat recently erected on a high bluff on the left bank of the Wabash. I wished to have had a meeting there; but, finding there was no suitable accommodation to be obtained, we come on without much delay to Moses Hoggett's. It was a fine clear winter's evening, and I took a pretty long walk on the prairie, to hunt for seeds. I met with many plants I had not seen before; and, had I been a few weeks earlier, I suppose I could have had a large collection of such as would have been very acceptable to many of my friends at home; however, I had gathered a few, which I intend to send to Philadelphia. These prairies would be a remarkably interesting field of research to some of our English botanists; and probably the time is not very distant when many of these plants will contribute much to the ornament of some of our gardens.

We were at a meeting again with Friends at Honey Creek, on First-day morning, when I was unusually enlarged in exercise for their help and preservation.

About noon, we got to our friend Joshua Dick's, on Turman's Creek, and in the evening had a meeting, about one mile distant, at Abner Hunt's, where we lodged. It is quite a new settlement of Friends, from the upper part of North Carolina; perhaps there may be fifty individuals, and it is but lately they have begun to hold a meeting. I was given up to labour in word and doctrine, as the way might be opened for me; and I trust that to some it was an opportunity of instruction, and the renewing of strength; the day closed in peace. We had now visited Friends very generally on the Wabash; their number is not large, and certainly, as to that which constitutes the life and power of religion, the Society must be considered to be in a low state. There is no friend acknowledged as a minister among them; and I had to fear that the dicipline is far from being supported in the authority of Truth, and that the attendance of meetings for worship was regarded by many Friends with great indifference.

"Feeling released from apprehension, by which he had been deeply exercised," that it might be required of him to extend his travels into the State of Missouri, he now proceeded to the "White River Settlement of Friends," in southern Indiana.

On Third-day morning we parted from our kind friend Moses Hoggett; we found him a sensible, well-informed man, and an agreeable companion. He is much interested in the prosperity of their rising colony, and has been in the office of a Circuit or District Judge. We got a tolerably comfortable inn that evening. The road being bad and slippery, we did not travel more than seventeen miles in the course of that day. We came to Carlisle next morning; and had hoped to have gone immediately to a small settlement of Friends, fifteen or twenty miles distant; but we were easily turned from our course, on hearing of the improbability of our being able to cross the river, as it was supposed to be frozen over, and yet not hard enough to bear our waggon. After some detention, we changed our course from east to north-east, and about three o'clock in the afternoon stopped at the cabin of very civil people, new settlers from Kentucky. It was well they did not turn us adrift, as we were twenty miles from the next house; and the weather being very cold, with a slight covering of snow on the ground, it would not have been the most pleasant night to have camped out for the first time. The people were very kind, and did their best; and we were too grateful for a shelter to murmur at accommodation to which we could hardly have submitted at the beginning of our Western tour. One of their children was very sick, and cried most piteously in the night. I endeavoured to think of something that might afford the poor child a little relief; and the parents were so thankful for a few articles of medicine that there was no making them take anything for our entertainment.

We had a pretty fair specimen of backwoods travelling the next day. The country was thinly wooded, undulating, and beautifully interspersed with prairies, and in some places the landscape was more picturesque than any I have seen, whilst entirely devoid of the aid of art. The prairies had much the appearance of large gentlemen's parks, with groups and groves of timber, situated as if planted to give the finest effect of scenery. We stopped to bait about one o'clock and made ourselves a fire in the woods for the first time. We enjoyed our dinner, but the country was too much frozen to afford us any water for ourselves or our horses. Early in the evening we reached the habitation of one of the most complete backwoodsmen we had met in our travels. He had been brought up among Friends in Georgia. He was a bachelor, and had his widowed sister and her family living with him. Everything was rough in the extreme. I had some serious conversation with the poor man next morning which I trust was well received. We then had five miles to the ferry, which we found had been kept open, and the water being low we were soon across, and travelling about six miles we reached the house of a Friend lately come into the woods. They showed us much kindness, and finding that if we pursued our journey more than two or three miles we could not get to any house that night, we were soon persuaded to stay and take up our quarters with them. It was a clean, agreeable, and well-ordered family; and, though we were crowded together within narrow limits, it was really more of a rest than we had met with for several days. We had an early breakfast the next morning, and an opportunity of retirement with the family to some comfort. They had bought land in the woods, expecting other Friends would follow them, and that they should have a meeting, but, as in some other instances that we met with, had been disappointed, and talked of moving. Such instances are much calculated to excite one's sympathy. Industrious, upright Friends in low circumstances, spending no small portion of their little property, and two or three years of the best of their strength, in settling themselves in a new country, and then when they have got a few acres of land under cultivation, and their buildings put up, have often to break up their establishment, and move again; but even that is far better than bringing up a family secluded from good society, and remote from meeting.

Early in the evening we reached the neighbourhood of Indian-creek, where our enjoyments were not superabundant. We had a very small meeting the next day; possibly there might be one or two to whom it is an opportunity of encouragement, and I thought that in great mercy I was permitted some access to the Source of good for my own help. Parting from our friends in that settlement, I believe in true love, we came on four or five miles to the house of a man who readily gave us shelter for the night; and it was well we had not occasion to ask for more, as the family were bare of meat of any description, and were then living on hominy, with plenty of fat pork. This was almost the only family we met with that was not abounding in the necessaries and ordinary comforts of life. We took to our lodging on the floor with pretty good heart; the man and his wife and eight or nine children, and their son and his wife, occupying the beds slung around the room.

On reaching the White River district the narrative proceeds:

After a journey through a hilly, broken country, we reached the habitation of a friend near White River meeting-house. They had but a small cabin, open and very cold; and, though they had begun a new house, capable of being made a comfortable habitation, in consequence of the sickness which had been general in that neighbourhood last fall, and with which they had been affected, they had made but little progress. Our meeting next day was to some comfort and relief. In the afternoon our friends kindly collected in a pretty strong party, and cut a way for us through the ice, about eight inches in thickness, so that we ferried over the east branch of White River, perhaps 100 or 150 yards in width. Early next morning we found ourselves at the home of our friend, Joseph Farlow, near Lick-creek; a meeting is lately settled just by his premises, of perhaps twenty-five families. We had a religious opportunity with them next forenoon, in which I was more enlarged than on some other occasions. That evening we visited a friend confined to the house in very great helplessness, and on Sixth-day had a meeting at a Friend's house on Lost River. It was small, and not to much relief; but not entirely in vain. On Seventh-day was the Monthly Meeting of Lick-creek, a large gathering of Friends. I ventured to speak on several subjects in the meeting for discipline. Friends showed us much love, and I trust there was a willingness at least to hear what was communicated. On First-day the meeting was large. I was poorly, and brought very low; but, in the riches of condescending mercy and goodness, was ultimately enlarged in much love. At the close was held their meeting for ministers and elders, which I attended, and in which I was not silent. On Second-day we had an agreeable ride through the woods to Mount Pleasant. On Third-day we were at a small and newly-settled meeting there.

It was late on Fourth-day when we reached the neighbourhood of Blue River Meeting. Nathan Trueblood gave us a kind welcome to his comfortable habitation, and next day accompanied us to a small meeting two or three miles from his house. It was an opportunity of profitable instruction to me, and possibly might be no less so to others. On Fifth-day we were at the week-day meeting at Blue River, in which I thought I was made sensible of the power of divine love, and spoke, I trust, to the encouragement of the afflicted, and such as were under depression; afterwards was held their Preparative Meeting, and the meeting of ministers and elders. In the latter I was much exercised, and ventured on some expression. Sixth-day was very cold; we walked to the little town of Salem, about two miles distant, where we had a meeting in the Court-house. I had gone through much discouragement about it; but I sought to be simple and resigned, and to move in what I believed to be the leadings of the Spirit. I was favoured to feel more relieved than could have been hoped for. Seventh-day we attended their Monthly Meeting. I was exercised under a concern to bring Friends into feeling for themselves and the low state of things among them; and in the meeting for discipline I was engaged to speak on different subjects. We went home with Matthew Coffin, an elderly friend, lately come with his wife and daughter from North Carolina.

I had requested public notice to be given of the meeting on First-day morning. It was a large gathering. I was much given up to labour honestly and faithfully in the work of the Gospel. I was exercised for the awakening of transgressors; and, having reason for fear that some of these had taken refuge in unbelief, it was no wonder if the terrors of the law, and the invitations of the Gospel, should be alike rejected. . . .

Turning now again to the north, they visited the meetings along the Driftwood, and then proceeded towards Richmond.

We parted from our friends at Blue River in much love, and on Second-day reached the house of Thomas Newby, near Driftwood Meeting-house, having forded the Muskaketah. After the meeting for worship, and their Preparative Meeting on Fourth-day, we went home with Jacob Morris and his wife, kind Friends. We had an open, heart-tendering opportunity the next morning, in which, under the sensible feeling of Divine love, consolation and encouragement were offered both to the friends and their daughters. Early in the evening we arrived at Thomas Newsome's, near Sandy-creek. There are four or five families in the neighbourhood recently emigrated from Carolina. We had a meeting with them in the evening, in which a door of utterance was opened. We set off soon after breakfast, and pursued our journey to a new settler's on the Flat Rock Creek. Being very remotely situated from other Friends, we appeared to be welcomed guests, and the dear woman did much to try to make us comfortable. They gave us a bed; but our companions, with two other visitors who came in the course of the evening, had their lodging on the floor. It is one of the great inconveniences attendant on an early settlement in the woods, that they are expected to take in all of every class who apply for accommodation. Some friends gave us an account of the number that had been housed on their cabin floors almost beyond credit.

On Seventh-day, having parted from our friends in love after a religious opportunity, we continued our journey, most of the way within sight of the waters of the Flat Rock. Our road was very much through the wilderness, sometimes five or six miles, or further, without seeing a house; but, considering that it is but about two years since the country was vacated by the Indians and offered for public sale, it far exceeded our expectation to find it so well inhabited, and in several places much improved, for the time they have had it in hand. I believe that nearly the whole of the State of Indiana has been purchased from the natives; and instead of holding reservations of land in their former territory, as in Ohio, New York, &c., with the exception of a few who form a small settlement somewhere in the centre of the State, they have accepted an annuity from Congress, and gone over the Mississippi. I do not pretend to much judgment in such things, but I think I have not seen in the course of my travels any country so well suited to support a large population as the interior of this State. Peach trees grow with astonishing rapidity, bearing fruit in three years. In the older settled parts of the country we found some good apple orchards; and they give a most tantalizing description of the size and richness of their water-melons. The country is undulating, with but few large hills, and not much that lies on a dead level; they have coals and salt, and iron.

We dined in the woods by a large fire, and that night were well accommodated at the habitation of a wealthy settler of German extraction, who has brought plenty of good things into the wilderness, and purchased not less than 1,000 acres of land. He was a zealous professor among the Baptists, and would not receive any remuneration for my accommodation, which I understand is not unfrequently the case with serious persons in America, especially when they know the traveller receives no pay for his ministry. It was First-day morning, and no small trial to me to turn out with the prospect of spending the day on the road; but unless we had made a halt in the woods—which, considering the weather, we could not, I believe, have done to any good purpose—I thought the time could not be spent more profitably than in our waggon; and having endeavoured to explain to our host the circumstances under which we were placed, and represented in pretty strong terms to our young friends how great a trial I felt it, my mind became more easy, and we had not an unpleasant day. Our lodging that night was not the most convenient; but, with our provision and many appliances, we did not suffer either for want of food or bedding. In the evening I read a few chapters to the family which I trust was well received.

Just about dark the next day we arrived in the neighbourhood of Milford[1] Meeting-house, and were hospitably entertained at John Bell's, whose father came from near Cockermouth. A meeting was appointed for the following day, and a large number attended, Friends and others. On Fourth-day we were at the week-day meeting at West Union. In the afternoon we came forward to West Grove,[2] and attended their usual week-day meeting next day.

We agreed that it might be safe for us to proceed thence direct for Richmond. I confess the attraction was very strong in that direction, as I was full of hope and expectation that I should find letters on my arrival. But there was not a single English letter for me. I endeavoured to bear up, but it was a disappointment deeply felt. We went that evening to the house of Jesse Williams; they were kind friends, and having some understanding of the

1. Near Milton, Ind.
2. Near Centerville, Ind.

comforts and refinements of civilized life, though for the present inhabiting but a poor cabin, we found it a place of true rest. The meeting at Chester was large; and, being in good measure enabled to cast off the burthen that I believed to have been brought upon me, I felt more relieved than at many other times.

We returned with our friends to their quiet habitation and went with them to their meeting at Whitewater, near Richmond on First-day morning. This is one of the largest meetings in the state, containing, I suppose, not less than 120 or 130 families, forty of whom live in Richmond, which is a thriving village, finely situated on a high bank above the Whitewater river. Apprehending it might be safest to express a little respecting a right exercise of the mind on such occasions, I uttered a few sentences; and my heart being made tender before the Lord, I had to rejoice in the grace of our blessed Saviour, and was enabled to offer a word for the consolation of some weary and tribulated pilgrims, seeking to gather Friends of the humbling power of Christ and the experience of his baptism, that thus the will and wisdom of the creature might be made to bow in subjection to his Spirit, and that he might be prepared individually to become subjects of that kingdom which is not of this world. In the afternoon we went with James Pegg to his quiet and peaceful cabin about two miles out of town. We spent a pleasant, and I trust not an unprofitable evening together; and on Second-day he accompanied us to a meeting appointed for us at Orange. It was much the exercise of my mind that the people might be drawn from outward expectations and dependence, to a deep feeling of their own state.

William Forster then spent some time visiting the numerous meetings of Friends in the eastern part of the State of Indiana.

From *A geographical description of the United States*, by John Melish [1822], pp. 347-356.

INDIANA.

Miles.

Length..250

Breadth..145

Area.

36,250 Sq. Miles.

23,200,000 Acres.

Situation.

Between 37° 47′ and 41° 43′ N.

Between 7° 45′ and 11° W.

Boundaries.—On the north, Lake Erie and Michigan territory; east, Ohio; south and south-east, Kentucky; and west, Illinois.

Face of the Country.—Indiana is pretty similar to Ohio. The country along the Ohio River has the appearance of being hilly and broken. In the interior, the country becomes flat, and in some places there are wet prairies. The upper country along the Wabash is agreeably uneven. Between that river and Lake Michigan, the country is mostly level, and abounds in prairies, small lakes, and swamps.

Rivers.—White Water River rises in Randolph county, near the head waters of the Wabash, and runs a south and south-east course, nearly 100 miles, receiving a number of branches in its progress, and falls into Miami River a little above its junction with the Ohio.

The great leading river in this state is the Wabash and its waters, but between these and the Ohio there are a number of lesser streams, from 30 to 50 miles long, all falling into the Ohio, which we shall merely notice as they lie from east to west. They have nearly one general character—they rise in the interior of the state, they run a southwardly course, they are generally favourable for mill seats, and have fertile banks.

Laughery Creek falls into the river six miles below the outlet of Miami River.

Indian Kentucky Creek, falls into the river a few miles above Madison.

Silver Creek falls in at the Falls of Ohio.

Indian Creek falls in 12 miles below Corydon, which is situated on its east bank.

Great Blue River falls in at the bend, seven miles below Indian Creek.

Anderson's Creek falls in at Troy.

Little Pigeon Creek falls in at Cyprus.

Great Pigeon Creek falls in at Evansville.

Wabash River is a large stream with numerous branches. The highest branch rises in the State of Ohio, and the head waters of the Miami and St. Mary's River interlock with it. Thence it runs a north-west course of about 60 miles, and receives the waters of Eel River from the northeast. Eel River rises near the Maumee River, and the streams may be connected by a short portage. From Eel River the Wabash runs nearly west about 30 miles, when the Mississinewa, a large stream from the south-east, falls into it. It then makes a bend of 15 miles and receives Tippecanoe Creek from the north.

The river now assumes a general south-west course, which it retains to the Ohio, distance above 300 miles. Seventy-five miles above the Ohio, it receives the waters of White River and Patoka River from the east.

White River is a large stream, with several branches. The west fork rises in the interior of the state, and runs a south-west course of more than 140 miles to where it meets the east fork. The east fork also rises in the interior of the state, about 40 miles south-east of the head of the west fork, and runs first a south, and then a west course, part of it very crooked, to the junction; the distance being more than 150 miles. In its progress it receives the waters of numerous streams, chiefly *Muskakituck River*, *Salt Creek*, and *Indian Creek*. From the junction this river runs 30 miles nearly a west course, to the Wabash, into which it falls 30 miles below Vincennes.

Patoka River rises near Fredericksburg and runs a west course of 80 miles to the Wabash River, into which it falls, two miles below White River.

The Wabash is navigable for large keel boats to Ouitanon, where there are rapids. Above Ouitanon it is navigable in all the branches nearly to their sources. Above Vincennes the current is generally gentle, below these are several rapids, but not of sufficient magnitude to prevent the navigation.

St. Joseph's River, of Lake Michigan, rises in this state, near the Wabash, and runs N. W. to the lake; and *Theakike* River, a branch of the Illinois, rises near St. Joseph's River. As the country has not been surveyed in this quarter, these streams are at present unimportant.

Geological Formation.—The geological formation of this state is wholly *secondary,* and its general elevation nearly the same as the state of Ohio. The elevation of Lake Michigan, in the N. W. corner, has been ascertained to be 589 feet. The S. E. corner is about 450, and the south-west about 330. The head waters of the Wabash are probably at an elevation of about 650 feet above the level of the dea.

Soil and Natural Productions.—Nearly the same as Ohio, but the southern part, being in a warmer latitude, is more favourable to such vegetable substance as require warmth. Vineyards have come to maturity at Vevay, and the grape flourishes when cultivated in all the lower part of the state. Cotton can also be raised.

Minerals and Mineral Waters.—Coal, iron, and salt are the chief minerals, and they are found in plenty. There is a medicinal spring near the falls of Ohio, which is strongly impregnated with sulphur and iron.

Climate.—Nearly the same as Ohio, except the southern part, which is a little warmer. At Jeffersonville, above the falls of Ohio, the mean heat of January was 47°, of July 80°, of December 37°; and of the whole year 60° 3′.

Historical View.—The general history of this part of the North West Territory of the United States is included in the article on Ohio, except as to a few local circumstances. About the year 1690 the French traders first visited this territory, and about the year 1702 they descended the Wabash, and established posts along its banks, the chief settlement being *Vincennes.* The settlers here were for a long time insulated from the rest of the world, and became gradually assimilated with the Indians, with whom they intermarried. In the revolutionary war they joined the cause of the United States; and at the peace they were confirmed in their possessions, and a tract of land around Vincennes was given to them by the United States government. After the peace the inhabitants suffered severely from the Indians, but peace was restored by the treaty of Greenville. Considerable purchases were made from the Indians up to 1811, but they still retained their power, and committed great depredations upon the people, in consequence of which a considerable force was sent against them, and being defeated in the close of that year, they sued for peace. During the late war with England, the Indians were again induced to renew hostilities, but were defeated at all points, and since the peace they have been very quiet, and have ceded the greater part of their lands to the United States.

In the year 1801, Indiana was erected into a territorial government. In 1815 the inhabitants petitioned Congress to be admitted into the Union, which being granted, a state constitution was formed in 1816; and in the same year Indiana became a state.

Population.—In 1800 the population of Indiana was only 5,641. In 1810 it was 24,520; in 1815, 68,784; and in 1820 it was 147,178, situated as in the following:

TOPOGRAPHICAL TABLE.

Counties.	*Whites.*	*Free Blacks.*	*Slaves.*	*Total.*
Clark	8,571	138	...	8,709
Crawford	2,583	...	...	2,583
Davies	3,400	32	...	3,432
Dearborn	11,396	72	...	11,468
Delaware	3,677	...	...	3,677
Dubois	1,160	8	...	1,168
Fayette	5,941	9	...	5,950
Floyd	2,707	69	...	2,776
Franklin	10,698	65	...	10,763
Gibson	3,801	45	30	3,876
Harrison	7,806	69	...	7,875
Jackson	3,974	36	...	4,010
Jefferson	7,926	112	...	8,038
Jennings	1,955	45	...	2,000
Knox	5,153	166	118	5,437
Lawrence	4,101	15	...	4,116
Martin	1,028	4	...	1,032
Monroe	2,671	8	...	2,679
Owen	827	10	1	838
Orange	5,272	96	...	5,368
Perry	2,314	15	1	2,330
Pike	1,465	4	3	1,472
Posey	4,044	6	11	4,061
Randolph	1,803	5	...	1,808
Ripley	1,820	2	...	1,822
Scott	2,328	...	6	2,334
Spencer	1,877	2	3	1,882
Sullivan	3,470	20	8	3,498
Switzerland	3,925	9	...	3,934
Vanderburgh	1,787	3	8	1,798
Vigo	3,364	26	...	3,390
Wabash	142	5	...	147
Warrick	1,742	6	1	1,749
Washington	8,980	59	...	9,039
Wayne	12,053	66	...	12,119
	145,761	1,227	190	147,178

Agriculture and Produce.—This being a new country, the chief employment is agriculture, and great improvements have been made in that branch. The soil and climate are both favourable, and the products are valuable and abundant. Wheat, Indian corn, oats, and rye, all flourish. Flax and hemp are cultivated. Potatoes, sweet potatoes, and other vegetables, are successfully raised. Cotton is cultivated in the lower part of the state, and vine dressing is brought to maturity. The number of persons employed in agriculture by the census of 1820 is 61,315.

Manufactures and Commerce.—The country is too new to have many manufacturing establishments upon a large scale, but they have been introduced, and are increasing. The *Harmonist Society*, who were originally settled in the state of Pennsylvania, have removed into this state, and settled on a portion of the land on the east side of the Wabash, which they have cultivated like a garden; and they have engaged largely in manufactures. This extraordinary society are about 800 in number, and hold all their property *in common*. They have regular office-bearers to conduct all the different branches of business carried on in the establishment, *agriculture, manufactures*, and *commerce;* and acting under a judicious and enlightened system, they have found manufacturing industry to be the most valuable part of their operations. It employs the greatest number of hands; it is most aided by machinery; and is more productive than any other. Settlers in the new countries would do well to take a lesson from this extraordinary people, who, in consequence of their simple but efficacious arrangements, good conduct, and industry, AND BY BEING INDEPENDENT WITHIN THEMSELVES FOR ALL THEIR MATERIAL WANTS, have accumulated more wealth, and probably experience more peace and happiness than any other 800 people, taken promiscuously, on the face of the earth.

When the census of 1810 was taken, Indiana was quite a new country, and the manufacturers were few, the amount being estimated at only $197,000. They have since greatly increased, and the number of persons employed in them is 3,229.

The principal commerce of Indiana centres at Vincennes and the falls of Ohio. The state exports wheat, grain, provisions, and tobacco, and imports groceries and dry goods. The number of persons employed in commerce is 429.

Chief Towns.—*Corydon*, situated on Pigeon Creek, 22 miles west from the falls of Ohio, is to be the seat of government until the year 1825. After which the government will be transferred to

Indianapolis, which has been recently laid out on the west fork of White River, near the central part of the state.

Vincennes is situated on the east bank of the Wabash, about 100 miles from its outlet, and is the largest town in the state, and a place of considerable trade.

The census does not give the population of any of the towns of Indiana, and we shall therefore merely notice them as they are situated on the respective waters, remarking that some of them are important.

On the Ohio and its waters. Lawrenceburg, at the outlet of the Miami; *Vevay,* the Swiss settlement; Madison, laid out in 1811, and now the second town in the state, in point of extent. Charleston, situated two miles west from the river, is the capital of Clark county. *Jeffersonville* is situated above the falls of Ohio, and is the seat of a land office. *New Albany* is below the falls, opposite to Shippingport. *Fredonia* is at the outlet of Big Blue River. *Washington* is opposite to Stephensport, in Kentucky. *Troy* is situated at the outlet of Anderson's Creek. *Rockport* is the capital of Spencer county, 16 miles below Troy. *Evansville* is situated on a bend of the river, at the outlet of Great Pigeon Creek, and here there is a road leading from the river to Princeton, and another to Harmony.

Towns on White Water River and its branches, Jacksonborough, Centerville, Salisbury, Richmond, Connersville, and *Brookville.*

On Laughery Creek. Ripley, Hartford, and *Wilmington.*

On Big Blue River. Salem, and *Fredericksburg.*

On Patoka Creek. Columbia, and *Princeton.* Princeton is a considerable thoroughfare, and place of some business.

On White River and its waters. Vernon, Browntown, Palestine, Hindostan, Greenwich, Orleans, Paoli, Washington, Petersburg, Russelville, and *Bloomington.*

On Wabash, Prophet's town, Clinton, Terre Haute, Miriam, and *Carlisle.*

Harmony is situated on the east side of the Wabash, 50 miles above its outlet, and is the seat of the Harmonist Society before mentioned. The country here is very rich, it is easy to raise all the necessaries of life, and by vesting surplus labour in manufactured articles, an industrious community must become wealthy and comfortable.

Roads, Canals, and Improvements.—The same regulation exists here as in Ohio as to the support of roads. Several roads have been made through the state, but they are indifferent. The national road, if extended, will pass through the central part of this state, in a southwest direction, probably touching at Indianapolis, and passing into the state of Illinois south of Terre Haute. It has been proposed to connect the navigation of the Wabash with St. Mary's River, a branch of the Maumee, and in a law of congress, appropriating a portion of the public lands for internal improvements, 100,000 acres were assigned to forward that object. It has also been proposed to make a canal round the falls of Ohio at Jeffersonville.

Government and Laws.—The constitution of Indiana was adopted in 1816, and *is Legislative, Executive,* and *Judiciary.* The *Legislative* branch consists of a Senate and House of Representatives. The senators are elected for three years, and must be 25 years of age; the representatives must be 21 years of age, and are elected annually. The legislature meet on the first Monday of December. The *Executive* is vested in a Governor and Lieutenant Governor, who are elected for three years, and are eligible six out of nine years. The *Judiciary* is composed of a supreme court and circuit courts. The judges of the supreme court are appointed by the governor for three years, and have appellate jurisdiction. The circuit courts are to be held in each county by one judge and two associates; the former to be appointed by the legislature for seven years, and the latter for the same period by the people. The elective franchise is vested in all free white males, of 21 years and upwards, who are citizens of the United States.

Education and Manners.—When Indiana was admitted into the union, the same law extended to it as to Ohio, regarding the support of schools; and an entire township consisting of 23,040 acres of land was appropriated for the support of a college, which is fixed at Vincennes. The manners of the people are pretty similar to those of Ohio.

From *An Excursion through the United States and Canada*, 1822-23, by an English gentleman, (Capt. Blaney) [1824], pp. 139-156, 243-253.

BLANEY, WILLIAM NEWNHAM.

Captain Blaney, after having spent several years in traveling throughout the continent of Europe, decided to make a tour of the United States. He left England in the summer of 1822, landed in New York made his way to Philadelphia, Baltimore, and then across the mountains into the Ohio valley. His stay in Indiana, although limited, was attended by some very marked observations. They have the ring of candor and genuineness in them not found in the average narrative. Only a few pages are here inserted, but they are full of interest and new facts are found on almost every page.

After the very hard frost, which came on just as I left Frankfort, there had been several days' rain, the usual commencement of winter in this part of the country. The roads in Indiana were almost impassable, even on horseback. The day after I crossed the river, the frost again set in; and the roads becoming worse, I could with difficulty proceed from eighteen to twenty miles between sun-rise and sun-set; having to walk a great part of the way, leading my horse by the bridle. The frost had followed the rain so immediately, that the drops were frozen on all the trees, which in the rays of the setting sun appeared loaded with diamonds, and as I rode through the forest, put me in mind of the gem-bearing trees in the beautiful tale of Aladdin.

At Greenville, a collection of straggling cabins, I stopped at a house kept by a Mr. Porter, a man from the New England States. This tavern, though small, was without exception the most clean and comfortable I had ever been in since I crossed the Alleghanies. Whenever indeed you stop at the house of a New Englander, you are certain to receive more attention, and to find every thing cleaner and of a better quality, than in a tavern kept by a Southern or Western man.

The Western Americans, and particularly those of Indiana, are more rough and unpolished in their manners than those of any country I ever travelled in.

Occasionally, after a long day's ride, when I have arrived cold and tired at the house where I intended to stop, I have dismounted, walked in, and upon finding the master, and perhaps one of his sons, seated by the fire, I have addressed him with,

"Sir, can I stay at your house to-night, and have some supper for myself and food for my horse?" and then he has just turned his head round, and without rising, has said, "I reckon you can." Upon further inquiry where I could put my horse, my host has replied, "There is a stable behind the house." I have then had to rub down and feed my own horse.

Those who have not tried this after riding all day, do not know how disagreeable it is. At the same time, I am certain that no kind of incivility was intended. All the people living in the same neighbourhood being nearly equal in point of wealth and education (with little enough of either), are not accustomed to show one another any attention, and therefore extend the same want of ceremony to the strangers who may chance to come to their houses. Besides, in these wild parts, there is often a distance of ten or fifteen miles between each cabin, even on the chief roads; and off the roads, a person might travel fifty miles without seeing any habitation whatsoever. A man, therefore, who receives a traveller in his house, and gives him a bed and food, considers with justice, that he confers a favour on his guest, even though he charge some trifle for his hospitality. For let any one imagine the alternative of either sleeping out in a cold night, without any thing to eat, or of staying in a log cabin, by a good blazing fire, with plenty of venison-steaks and corn-cake! Surely the traveller must acknowledge, that the paying about the value of eighteen-pence or two shillings, by no means cancels the obligation which he owes to the landlord.

In speaking of the houses at which I stopped, after crossing the Ohio, I make use of the word Tavern; but let not the English reader be misled by a word; for there is not one of these taverns that deserves to be compared to the common sort of our public houses. I have often laughed to see, fixed upon a miserable log cabin, a rough Sign, on which has been painted "Washington Hotel", or some such high sounding name, though the house probably contained only one, or at most only two rooms. Generally however, both in Illinois and Indiana, there is no Sign at all. A traveller enters without scruple any house near the road side, and breakfasts, or stays all night, even if the owner does not profess to keep a tavern: for every one is glad to have a stranger stop with him, as it gives him an opportunity of hearing some news, and also brings him in a dollar or so, if he chooses to accept any thing for his hospitality.

Owing to the great rise of the water, I found some difficulty in crossing Blue River, over which there was neither bridge nor ferry; and though swimming on horseback is not unpleasant in warm weather, I do not myself think it particularly agreeable during a hard frost. But I fortunately discovered some men with a canoe, in which I crossed over, taking off my saddle and saddle bags, and obliging my horse to swim.

Near this are some pretty extensive "Barrens." The Americans apply this term to those tracts of land, which, being covered with low shrubs and brushwood, much resemble what we call in England "Copses." The country beyond Blue River, is covered for the most part with thick forest. This grows upon a limestone formation; and in consequence, the whole country abounds with pits and caverns, some of which are of considerable magnitude. From these caverns great quantities of salt-petre have been obtained.

I now came to a large stream, called "Sinking River," which flows under ground for the distance of nearly ten miles. When there has been a very heavy fall of rain, and the water cannot find room to pass under ground, the overplus runs in a channel above, and joins the river again where it rises from the earth. This upper channel by no means follows the course of the subterraneous one.

The road passes over the upper channel, which is pretty deep, and which, in spite of the quantity of rain which had fallen only five or six days before, was, when I crossed it, nearly dry. . . .

A few miles from Mr. Byrom's, at a place called French Lick, is a very large pigeon roost. Several acres of timber are completely destroyed, the branches, even of the thickness of a man's body, being torn off by the myriads of pigeons that settle on them. Indeed, the first time I saw a flight of these birds, I really thought that all the pigeons in the world had assembled together, to make one common emigration. These pigeons do a great deal of mischief; for as they clear immense tracts of forest, of all the mast, acorns, &c. numbers of the hogs, which run at large in the woods, are in consequence starved to death.

When crossing a small stream, the day after leaving Byrom's, I saw a large flock of beautiful green and yellow parroquets. These were the first I had met with; and as they were very tame, and allowed me to come close to them, I got off my horse, and stopped a short time to admire them. I afterwards saw numbers of the same kind in the flats of the Wabash and Mississippi, for this beautiful bird apparently delights in the neighbourhood of streams.

Before arriving at Hindostan, a small village on the East Fork of White River, the country becomes very hilly; and being on that account thinly settled, abounds with game of all descriptions. Some idea may be formed of the abundance of it, from the price of venison at this place, and in the neighbourhood. A haunch will bring only 20 cents (about 1*s.* 9*d.* sterling), or the value of 25 cents, if the hunter will take powder, lead, or goods. The shop-keepers who buy the haunches, the only parts of the deer that are thought worth selling, cure and dry them much in the same manner as the Scotch do their mutton hams, and then send them for sale to Lousiville or New Orleans. These dried venison hams, as they are called, are very good eating.

The two young men who ferried me over the river, had just returned from a hunting excursion. They had only been out two days; and not to mention a great number of turkeys, had killed sixteen deer and two bears, besides wounding several others. The bear is much more esteemed than the deer; first, because his flesh sells at a higher price; and secondly, because his skin, if a fine large black one, is worth two or three dollars.

I was stopped for three days at the West Fork of White River, owing to the ice, which was of such a thickness, and came down the stream with such rapidity, that it was impossible for the ferry-boat to cross.

In these thinly settled countries, if a traveller be detained, or if he wish to stop a day or two to rest his horse, he can, if either a sportsman or a naturalist, find abundant amusement. Go to what house I might, the people were always ready to lend me a rifle, and were in general glad to accompany me when I went out hunting. Hence, in addition to the pleasure of the chase, I had, at the same time, an opportunity of becoming better acquainted with the manners of the Backwoodsmen, and with the difficulties and hardships which are undergone by all the first settlers of a new country. I found I had imbibed the most erroneous ideas, from seeing none of the inhabitants, but those who, living by the road side, were accustomed to receive money from travellers, and sometimes to charge as much for their coarse fare, and wretched accommodations, as would be paid in the Eastern States for the utmost comfort a tavern can afford. I therefore considered all the people a sordid and imposing set. But when I began to enter into the company of the Backwoodsmen, quite off the roads, and where a traveller was seldom or never seen, I found the character of the settlers quite different from what I had supposed. In general they were open hearted and hospitable, giving freely whatever they had, and often refusing any recompense. It is true they always treated me as their equal; but at the same time, there was a sort of real civility in their behaviour, which I have often looked for in vain elsewhere.

In the Backwoods, pork, or as they call it hogs-flesh, together with venison and hommony (boiled Indian corn), was my usual fare, and a blanket or two, on the floor of the cabin, my bed; but I was amply compensated for this want of luxuries by a degree of openness and hospitality, which indeed the most fastidious could not but have admired. Thus, on going away, my host has sometimes accompanied me four or five miles, in order to put me in the track leading to the road.

But notwithstanding the instances of good-heartedness, and simplicity of manners, which one meets with in these wild countries, yet few travellers are willing to quit the more frequented districts; and it is to this want of self-denial, that I should be disposed to attribute the erroneous accounts of the American character which have been given us. Some of our travellers moreover, are in the practice of detailing all the disagreeable scenes of low life, which they have witnessed at the taverns, and hence lead their readers to form a very incorrect idea of the whole people. If an American traveller in England were to do the same, he would have no difficulty, in proving us the most profligate, immoral, and cheating nation on the face of the earth.

After waiting in vain two days for the river to freeze over, so that I could pass on horseback, I at last hired two or three men, armed with poles, to assist in keeping off the cakes of ice; and thus succeeded in crossing, notwithstanding the width and rapidity of the river.

Between the White River and Vincennes is a large swamp, intersected by a small stream. Over this swamp, for the distance of two miles, is a piece of what the Western people very expressively term a "Corderoy Road," which is very common in these States, and is made wherever the ground is marshy.

A Corderoy Road consists of small trees, stripped of their boughs, and laid touching one another, without any covering of earth. As the marsh underneath is of various degrees of solidity, the whole road assumes a kind of undulating appearance. I found some of the logs a little apart from one another; and was therefore constantly afraid, that the animal that carried me would break his leg; but he was a Western horse, and by the manner in which he picked his way, showed that he knew the danger as well or better than I did. Any one crossing these logs in a wheeled carriage, must find the jolting truly formidable.

Vincennes is a small straggling place, situated on the bank of the Wabash, and is one of the oldest towns in the United States. It was founded by the French, the same year that William Penn founded Philadelphia; and was, for a long time, partly a French, and partly an Indian village. It once supplied all the neighbouring country for a very great distance around, with goods and merchandize; but is now declining, partly from having lost its superiority as a depôt for goods, and partly from the unhealthiness of its situation. I have scarcely been to a single spot on the western side of the Ohio, where, during the autumn of 1822, the people had not suffered from sickness.

The Wabash is a beautiful river, which, after a meandering course of about 600 miles, enters the Ohio in a stream about 400 yards wide, 140 miles from the confluence, of that river with the Mississippi. It may be considered as the largest tributary stream that joins the Ohio from the west. Its own principal tributaries are White River, Little Wabash, Embarrass, Big and Little Eel Rivers, Tree Creek, Ponce Passau, or Wildcat, Tippecanoe, and Massissiniway.

The Wabash flows through a rich and level country, which is well adapted to cultivation, and in which cotton has of late been raised successfully.

On the Wabash are the towns of Harmony, Vincennes, and Terre-haute, besides several others, which, having only been lately erected, contain as yet few inhabitants.

This river forms, for a considerable distance, the boundary between Indiana and Illinois. During the spring of the year, it is easily navigated by flat boats, as far as 450 miles from its junction with the Ohio; and craft drawing only two or three feet water, may ascend it as far as Vincennes at almost any season.

It is not till the traveller has crossed the Wabash, and advanced a considerable distance into the State of Illinois, that he can see any of the large "Prairies," of which there are many fertile ones on the west bank of the river. These Prairies, as their name denotes, are large open tracts of natural meadow, covered with luxuriant and rank grass, and destitute of trees or even shrubs.

There are no hills in them, though some have a gently undulating surface. . . .

I intended to have remained a few days at Vincennes, but the following circumstance drove me away the next morning.

A Missouri planter, attended by two slaves, a man and woman, was travelling to St. Louis, in a small wheeled carriage called a "Dearborn," and had stopped at Vincennes to rest his horses. Now the day before I arrived, both his slaves had run away. Trying to travel all night when nearly barefooted, the man had both his feet so severely frost bitten, that he could not proceed. Consequently he was overtaken by some people sent after him by his master, and was brought back to Vincennes the very evening after my arrival. When I got up early the next morning, I saw the poor old slave, who had passed the night in the kitchen, with a heavy chain padlocked round both his legs. A man from North Carolina, who had ridden in company with me from White River, where he had been delayed, came into the room at the same time I did; and, although a slave holder himself, was touched with compassion at seeing the miserable state of this old negro. Having procured the key, he took off one of the padlocks, and desired the unhappy being to come towards the fire, in order to warm his frost-bitten legs and feet, which were much swollen, and were no doubt very painful. The poor slave was so lame he could hardly move, but managed to come and sit down by the hearth. The Carolinian then said to him, "You have committed a great crime, as you must be well aware—how came you to do it?" The negro replied, "Master, I am an old man, upwards of sixty years of age, and I have been all my life in bondage. Several white men told me, that as this was a free State, if I could run away I should be free; and you know master! what a temptation that was. I thought if I could spend my few remaining days in freedom, I should die happy." But, replied the Carolinian, "You were a fool to run away; you know you are much better off as a slave, than if you were free." "Ah! master," said the poor old negro, "No one knows where the shoe pinches, but he who wears it."

Just at this time, in came the master of the slave, and after swearing a terrible oath that he would punish him, desired him to go and get ready the carriage. The poor old man answered that he was in too great pain even to stand upright. Upon this the brute, saying, "I will make you move, you old rascal," sent out for a "cowhide." Now the sort of whip called by this name is the most formidable one I ever saw. It is made of twisted strips of dried cow's skin; and from its weight, its elasticity, and the spiral form in which the thongs are twisted, must, when applied to the bare back, inflict the most intolerable torture.

The wife of the tavern keeper coming in, and hearing that the negro was going to be flogged, merely said, "I would rather it had not been on the Sabbath." For my part, I thought it signified very little upon what day of the week, such an atrocious act of wickedness was committed; so after trying in vain to obtain a relaxation of the punishment, I called for my horse, determined not to hear the cries of the suffering old man. Yet even when I had ridden far from the town, my imagination still pictured to me the horrors that were then being performed; and I should have thought myself deficient in human kindness, if I had not cursed from the bottom of my heart, every government, that, by tolerating slavery, could sanction a scene like this.

BIRKBECK'S SETTLEMENT.—EMIGRATION.

From Vincennes, I turned to the left, in order to cross White River, below the junction of its two Forks, and proceed through Princetown and Harmony, to Birkbeck's English settlement at Albion.

The road, or rather path, to the ferry on White River, runs chiefly through low flat Barrens, with here and there a patch of Prairie. Upon arriving at the bank, I found the ice running so thick, and in such very large cakes, that the boat could not cross. Some men with a drove of hogs had already waited there two days, and the ferryman said that I had very little chance of being able to cross for a day or two, and perhaps not for a week. I therefore determined to cross the country, in a westerly direction, so as to meet the Wabash just above its junction with White River.

Upon inquiring of the ferrymen, if there were any house in the neighbourhood at which I could stop, they informed me that there was only one, which belonged to a Scotch gentleman who had lately settled in this part of the country. "But although," said one of them, "I am certain he does not keep open house, yet perhaps as you are a stranger, he will allow you to stay there tonight."

As it was getting late I determined to lose no time, and accordingly, after a ride through the woods of about two miles, I found myself at the settlement.

The house, which was of a much better description than any I had lately seen, was situated on a gentle rise, overlooking the river, and surrounded with a large space of cleared land. I dismounted, and upon opening the door was delighted to see six or seven men in Highland bonnets, sitting round a blazing fire. I mentioned to the gentleman that I was a stranger, and should feel much obliged to him, for a night's lodging for myself and my horse; upon which he immediately, with the genuine hospitality I have so often experienced in his native land, said that I was welcome to stay there, and to partake of whatever his house afforded.

He had left Perthshire at the head of twenty of his countrymen, and had fixed himself on this spot; and although he had only been here eight months, had already put every thing into very good order.

My fare was sumptuous, compared to what it had been for some time past; and moreover I had a good bed to sleep in, with a pair of fine clean sheets.

I am particular in noticing this luxury, because it was only in two other places that I enjoyed it, during the whole of my travels, in the States of Indiana, Illinois, and Missouri. In general the beds were altogether without sheets; and the blankets had probably, since their manufacture, never experienced the renovating effects of a good washing. Sometimes indeed there would be one sheet, and occasionally two; but cleanliness in this particular I had almost despaired of.

Many of my countrymen, because they have not met with much comfort in these out of the way places, have, upon their return home, most unjustly and ridiculously imputed the same want of comfort to every part of the United States. But let us consider, that from Vincennes to Louisville is a distance of 120 miles, and that from thence to Washington, by the ordinary route up the Ohio river and through Wheeling is 731 miles: so that one of these delicate travellers would be equally entitled to abuse the whole of Great Britain, because he might meet with bad accommodation in the Orkneys. Moreover, woods are not cut down, and good inns established, in a day, nor even a year; and he who cannot put up with some inconvenience will do well to avoid travelling in a new country.*

This settlement is in a beautiful situation, surrounded by fertile

*In many places where I have met with execrable accommodation, future travellers will find good inns: for the whole country is so rapidly improving, that what is true of the Backwoods one year ceases to be so the next.

land; but alas! it has shared the fate of all the neighbourhood with regard to sickness; two of the emigrants having died, and several others being very ill. I went away in the morning, after receiving an invitation from my worthy host to repeat my visit if I should ever pass again in that direction.

The path from hence to the Wabash, lies through a thickly wooded country, abounding in game. I expected to have had much difficulty in crossing the river; for though there was a ferry boat, it had been drawn ashore and was frozen to the ground. Fortunately, however, I found a man going over in a flat boat with some cattle. The Wabash just above had closed up and frozen over, so that here, where the stream was very rapid, there was little or no floating ice.

I now crossed the Little Wabash, on which river Carmi is situated, and proceeded through a very thickly wooded country towards Harmony. The road, about four miles before arriving at this place, passes through the low grounds, or as they are called, "the Flats" of the Big Wabash. The lands of the river bottoms, or flats, throughout the whole of the United States, are always reckoned very rich and productive, and those of the Wabash are particularly so. They are covered with immensely large trees, between which grows, in amazing luxuriance, that noble vegetable the Cane (Arundinaria Macrosperma).

This beautiful and useful plant attains the height of from twenty to thirty feet. The fertile tracts, where it grows, are called Cane Brakes, and are always full of herds of cattle, who are very fond of its leaves, which remain green all the winter.

The low grounds of the Wabash would be thickly settled, and soon covered with a swarming population; but during a month or two in the Autumn, Fevers and Agues seem to stalk about here, seeking whom they may destroy. Indeed the countenances of the few settlers bespeak how often they have been attacked by these diseases. Where the ground has been cleared for any considerable space, the sickness does not prevail to such an extent. This is the case with the settlement of Harmony; but, even there, the inhabitants had in the autumn suffered a great deal.

The trees growing immediately on the banks of the Wabash, must, from their immense size, astonish every one. The Plane, with its long white arms, and the Tulip-tree (Liriodendron Tulipifera) called by the Americans the Poplar, attain to an enormous magnitude throughout the whole of the Western States.

There is a ferry which conveys the traveller directly over the

Wabash to Harmony. This pretty little town contains numerous well built, three-storied, brick houses, placed in regular streets, with a small railed garden to each, all conveying a great idea of comfort, particularly to a man travelling in the Backwoods. There are two churches with spires, on one of which is a clock, made by a settler, which strikes, even the quarters, upon some large bells that were imported on purpose. I had been so long without hearing anything of the kind, that during the week I remained there, the lively tones of these bells gave me great delight.

Mr. Rapp, the founder of the Society, was a dissenter from the Lutheran church, and finding himself persecuted by the clergy and the nobles, for the tenets he promulgated, came in 1803, from near Stutgard in Wurtemburg, to the United States, with nearly 400 adherents. They first settled at a place they called Harmony, in Butler county Pennsylvania, 25 miles from Pittsburg. Here their number was soon increased by emigration to near 800 souls, but not finding Pennsylvania in all respects suited to their views, they sent in 1814, three of their head men to choose another place. Accordingly, they have now fixed their residence 55 miles from Vincennes, 40 from Shawnee town, 24 from Birkbeck's Settlement, and 100 by water from the mouth of the Wabash.

By the sale of their houses, their improvements, &c. in Pennsylvania, they obtained a very large sum of money, and with this they purchased several thousand acres of the best land in Indiana. Upon arriving at their present abode, they erected log-cabins; but as they intended from the first to built brick houses, they marked out very carefully and with much regularity the intended streets of their town, and by placing the log-cabins at the back part of the different lots, left themselves sufficient space to erect their future habitations, without being obliged to move out of their old ones.

They have indeed proceeded in every thing with the greatest order and regularity. They possessed when I was there 100 brick buildings, had planted an extensive vineyard, and made considerable quantitities of pleasant tasted wine. They carried on a very extensive system of agriculture, and their flocks and herds were uncommonly numerous. There is a blacksmith's shop with two furnaces, a thrashing machine, a distillery, brewery, tannery, &c. There is also a large woolen and cotton-factory, the spindles and machinery of which are worked by steam, as is also their mill for grinding flour. Indeed they carry on almost every kind of useful manufacture, and make hats, shoes, sadlery, linen, cotton and woolen cloths, &c. Their broad cloth is very good; and their flannel of so excellent a quality, many of the English settlers at Albion say, that it is superior to the best Welsh flannel they brought out with them. Every one belongs to some particular trade or employment, and never interferes with the others, or even indeed knows what they are about. The only occasion on which they are all called out, is in the event of sudden bad weather, when the hay or corn is cut, but not carried. In such a case, Rapp blows a horn, and the whole community, both men and women, leave their occupations, run out to the fields, and the crop is soon gathered in, or placed in safety. There is a party of blacksmiths, shoemakers, weavers, shepherds, ploughmen or agriculturists, &c. Over every one of these trades there is a head man, who acts as an overseer, and who, in particular cases, as with the blacksmith, shoemaker, &c., receives payment for any work done for strangers. None of the inferiors of each occupation will receive the money. The head man, or foreman, always gives a receipt for the money he receives, which receipt is signed by Rapp, who thus knows every cent that is taken, and to whom all the money collected is transferred. When any one of their number wants a hat, coat, or any thing else, he applies to the head man of his trade or employment, who gives him an order, which is also signed by Rapp, after which he goes to the store and gets what he wants.

They have one large store, in which is deposited all the articles they manufacture. The neighbouring settlers for many miles round, resort to this, not only on account of the excellence, but also the cheapness of the goods. This store is managed by Mr. Baker, who holds the next rank to Rapp himself. The Harmonites have also branch stores in Shawnee town, and elsewhere, which they supply with goods, and which are managed by their agents.

An excellent house of private entertainment is kept by one of their number, named Ekensperker. Every thing here was so clean, comfortable, and well arranged, that I was quite delighted.

The house they have built for their founder Rapp, is very large and handsome, and would be esteemed a good house in any part of Europe. In the court-yard, Rapp has placed a great curiosity, which he brought from the shore of the Mississippi, near St. Louis. It is a block of marble of the size of a large tombstone, on which are two impressions of the human foot, so uncommonly well defined, perfect, and natural as to be worthy even of Canova.

The Indians certainly could not have executed anything of the kind; and the general opinion is, that some human being must have passed over the marble when it was of the consistency of clay, and thus have left the impression of his feet. The impressions indeed appear to have been made by some one who was running, or else stooping forward to pick up something. But I can hardly myself imagine, how or where a piece of marble could ever have been in so soft a state, as to receive the impression of a human foot. I hope that the marble will soon be inspected by some one competent to give an opinion, particularly as the impressions may at no great length of time be effaced, from being always left exposed to the weather.

The religious tenets of the Harmonites are not very well known; but it is at any rate certain that they profess equality and the community of possessions. The most extraordinary part of their system is their celibacy; for the men and women live separate, and are not allowed any intercourse. In order to keep up their numbers they have once or twice sent agents to Germany to bring over proselytes, for they admit no Americans. Among those that last came over, were great many children of both sexes.

Very few of the inhabitants of Harmony could speak English, and indeed the young boys and girls are chiefly educated in the German tongue. The policy of the head men appears to be, that of preventing, as much as possible, any of their inferiors from communicating with the Americans, fearing no doubt, that they would see the folly of their system.

What struck me as very singular was, that no one would answer any questions. Even my host Ekensperker, when I asked if they were permitted to marry, what became of all the money they collected, &c., invariably replied, "We never answer these questions." Some few persons have seceded from this society. These have generally been young men, who sacrificing fanaticism to nature, have gone off with young women and married them. By good fortune I chanced to meet one of these men, and learned from him a few particulars of the sect; but even he did not appear to be very willing to communicate what he knew. He told me that marriage was interdicted; but could give me no reason why it was. Moreover he told me, that it is unknown what becomes of all the money Rapp receives. Now this must be a very considerable sum, as the Harmonites neglect no means of amassing money. For instance, they send every year boats laden with produce to New Orleans; and the little settlement of Albion has paid them altogether nearly 60,000 dollars, though at present it is rapidly becoming independent of them.

The Harmonites will receive in payment no other money but specie or United States Bank notes. At the same time they expend nothing; and indeed money appears to be of no use to men, producing food, and manufacturing all necessaries within their own settlement. Every thing is sold in Rapp's name, and all the money is transmitted to him, even the proceeds of the house of entertainment and the doctor's shop.

This secrecy about the great sums that must be collected annually by the united labour of seven or eight hundred industrious individuals, possessed of a great deal of skill, and having the entire monopoly of the neighbouring country, has, I must confess, a very suspicious appearance, especially as Rapp holds a correspondence with Germany. At the same time, as he is an old man, and never intends to leave Harmony, I do not see any thing he could gain by sending away the money.

The Harmonites all dress very plainly and wear nearly the same clothes; but Rapp and the head men live in better houses. and have plenty of wine, beer, groceries, &c.; while the rest of their brethren are limited to coarse, though wholesome food, are debarred the use of groceries, &c., have a less quantity of meat, and are even obliged to make use of an inferior kind of flour.

In their celibacy, and in some other points, they resemble the Shakers, though they differ from them in refusing to admit proselytes. They are in fact only a somewhat improved order of industrious monks and nuns, except that they are very unwilling to have any thing known about themselves, and are by no means anxious to make converts. If they spoke English, and were allowed a free intercourse with the Americans, they would soon learn, that with the same habits of temperance, industry, and economy, they could in that rich and fertile district have every comfort they at present enjoy, with the additional satisfaction of amassing money for themselves, and of having children who would doubtless rise to opulence and consideration.

At present however Rapp points out to them the difference between their situation and that of the Backwoodsmen in the neighbourhood, leaving them to suppose, that this superiority is owing to their peculiar tenets and mode of life. Moreover, as I am informed, Rapp, like all other Priests, holds out eternal punishment in the next world to those who secede. Like the Virgilian "Rex Anius, rex idem hominum, Phoebique Sacerdos," he is both Governor and Priest, preaching to them in church and managing when out of it their pecuniary affairs. Hence this society presents the extraordinary spectacle of a most complete despotism in the midst of a great republic: for with the exception perhaps of being a little better clothed and fed, the lower orders of the Harmonites are as much vassals, or more so, than they were in Germany.

The settlement was once a benefit to the neighbourhood; but at present most of the Americans consider it as injurious. At first the people, for a great distance around the Settlement, being supplied with goods that they could not easily procure elsewhere, considered it advantageous to them; but they now think precisely the contrary; for the Harmonites, not having to pay their workmen, are enabled to under-sell every one who would wish to set up a store, and thus prevent competition. Moreover, as in exchange for their cloths, linens, hats, whiskey, &c., they receive vast sums of money which they never spend, and thus diminish the circulating medium of the country.

"If," say the Americans, "an ordinary merchant could come among us, and set up a store, as he grew rich he would increase his expenditure, and the money would circulate and enrich those who supplied him with meat, bread, &c.; but these people spend nothing, and therefore we should be very glad to see their society destroyed."

Old Rapp has transferred most of the active superintendence of the temporal concerns of the society to his adopted son Frederic Rapp, thus accustoming the people to a sort of hereditary despotism. We may however very much doubt, whether the society will hold together after the old man's death, an event which in the course of nature must soon take place.

The people, under the present system, are a set of well-fed, well-clothed, hard-working vassals. They are very grave and serious. During the whole time I was at Harmony, I never saw one of them laugh; indeed they appeared to me to enjoy only a sort of melancholy contentment, which makes a decided difference between them and the inhabitants of the other parts of the country, who without fanaticism or celibacy, find themselves well off and comfortable.

From *Memorable days in America; being a journal of a tour to the United States*, by W. Faux [1823], pp. 203-268.

FAUX, WILLIAM.

Chief among those Englishmen who scorned everything American after the second war with Great Britain was one William Faux, author of *Memorable days in America.*

He calls himself an English Farmer, whose tour to the United States was principally undertaken "to ascertain, by positive evidence, the condition and probable prospects of British emigrants; including accounts of Mr. Birkbeck's settlement in Illinois; and intended to shew Men and Things as they are in America."

His accounts were simply one line of ridicule after another, and in the language of one of his fellow reviewers bore the earmarks of a "simpleton of the first water, a capital specimen of a village John Bull, for the first time roaming far away from his native valley— staring at everything and grumbling at most."

His accounts therefore while both interesting and amusing are of little real value.

October 27th, 1819.—At sun-rise I left Louisville, in Colonel Johnson's carriage and pair, for Vincennes, in Indiana, well pleased to turn my back on all the spitting, gouging, dirking, duelling, swearing, and staring, of old Kentucky.

I crossed the Ohio at Portland, and landed at New Albion, a young rising village, to breakfast, where, for the first time in America, I found fine, *sweet*, white, home-baked bread. The staff of life is generally sour, and, though light and spongy, very ill-flavoured, either from bad leaven, or the flour sweating and turning sour in the barrel.

At eleven, a. m., I rested, and baited at a farm log-house, having one room only; the farmer came to it ten years ago, and has settled on two quarter sections of land. He has a good horsemill at work, night and day, to which people come with grist, from 10 to 15 miles, working it with their own horses, four in number, and leaving him (the miller) an eighth for his toll. "My land" (says he) "is good, but not like that of old Kentuck. I get from 40 to 60 bushels of corn, and wheat, 25 to 30 bushels per acre, and a market, at my door, in supplying gentlemen-travellers, and emigrants." The first house is, for five or six years, a miserable hole, with one room only, after which, rises a better, and the old one remains for a kitchen. This man seems full of money, and knows all things; he damns the state government for denying him the privilege of slavery, and of using his Kentucky negroes, who, in consequence, (he says) are hired and exposed to cruelty. "I was raised under a monarchy government, in Virginia, where every man did as he pleased. This Indiana a free state, and yet not at liberty to use its own property! You tell me to quit it, I guess, if I do not like it." "Yes, I do." "Well then, the government, d—n it, has the power, it seems to drive me out." This strange man was very civil and coarsely kind to me, and whispered aside to my driver, that he knew I was a very large proprietor in this state.

I travelled till sun-set, 32 miles from the Ohio, and slept at Mrs. Moore's farm-log-house tavern, with three rooms, and a broken window in each; all moderately comfortable, until the pitiless, pelting storms of winter come, when it will snow and blow upon the beds. My hostess would, in England, pass for a witch, having a singularly long, yellow, haggish, dirty, face and complexion. She has three fine sons, but no servants. They do all the household work, and that on the farm, themselves, hiring none. They clear five or six acres every year, have cleared 60 acres, and mean that the other 60 of their quarter section should remain in wood. They located themselves here eight years since, and find good land, good crops, and a market at the door. Two of the young Moores mounted their horses, and, with five dogs, set off hunting at bed-time, until midnight, after racoons, foxes, wolves, bears, and wild cats. I saw a skin of the latter animal, much like a tame cat, only bigger, and its tail shorter; they live on partridges and young pigs, and poultry when they can get them; they never mew and call out like the domestic cat. Here is a pet bear, which took an ear of Indian corn out of my hand. One of these pets recently broke its chain, and came into the house, where lay a sick and bedridden man, and an infant child on the floor, with which the bear, much pleased, marched off. The poor old man, not knowing, till then, that he was able to turn himself in bed, suddenly acquired supernatural strength, sprung out, and running after the bear, threw him down, rescued the screaming babe, unhugged and unhurt, and then jumped into bed again.

28*th.*—Now quite out of society; every thing and every body, with some few exceptions, looks wild, and half savage. To his honor Judge Chambers's, to breakfast. His log-tavern is comfortable; he farms two and a half quarter sections, and raises from 40 to 60 bushels of corn an acre. Nearly all the good land on this road is *entered.* "I had," says he, "hard work for the first two or three years." The judge is a smart man of about 40, and not only a judge, but a senator also, and what is more, the best horse-jockey in the state. He seems very active, prudent, cautious, and industrious, and, like all the rest of the people on this road, kind-hearted. He fills the two-fold station of waiter and ostler in part; I say in part, for, as he has no servant, the drudgery must be done by the traveller himself, if he have a horse or horses. His honor left my driver to do all, and hastily rode off to a distant mill for his grist, now much wanted, and with which he returned in about two hours, while her honor, Mrs. Judge, and the six Miss Judges, prepared my good breakfast. These ladies do all the work of the house, and some of the field, every thing seems comfortable and easy to them, although the blue sky and the broad sun stare and peep through cracks and crevices in the roof of their house. While I sat at breakfast, his honor's mother, a fine smart young woman of four-score, came briskly riding up, and alighted at the door; as good a horsewoman as ever mounted a side-saddle. She had been to pay a distant visit, and seemed as though her strength and youth were renewed, like the eagle's. She reminded me of Moses, "with his eye not dim, nor his natural force abated."

At noon, I stopped at another log-house, quarter-section farmer's, with two fine healthy boys, much civilized, who, of themselves, have cleared forty acres of heavily timbered land, such as is seldom seen, and cropped it twice in eighteen months. What prodigious industry! It is, they say, worth ten dollars an acre clearing. It is; and an Englishmen would, indeed, think so, and demand double and treble that sum, for that quantity of excessive labour. They, however, now wish to sell out their improved quarter section, and remove further from the road. These young men drink spring water, and like it better than whiskey, and look heartier and healthier than any settlers I have yet seen in the wilds.

I rested all night at another quarter-section farmer's, who, together with his brother and wife, has cleared thirty acres in eighteen months, without hired hands, and is now rearing a second log-house. They find a market at their door for all they can raise, and ten times as much, if they could raise it. They burn all the logs and trees rolled together in immense heaps, and prefer the wood-land to the barrens, the latter being thinly timbered with dwarfish trees and shrubs. The wife, husband, brother, and three wild children, sleep in one room, together with three or four travellers, all on the floor, bedless, but wrapt up in blankets. I, being a mighty fine man, was put into the new house, which, though without either doors or windows, was distinguished by one bed on a bedstead, both home-made, and as soft as straw and wood could be. Into this bed was I honourably put, and at midnight favoured with a bed-fellow, a stranger Yankee man whom I had seen on the mountains; and at my feet, on the floor, slept two Irish, and one poor sick American, all pedestrians, who had wandered here in quest of employment. Thus housed and bedded, we were faithfully watched and guarded by several huge hunting dogs, lying around the entrance of our bed-room, barking and growling to the howling wolves, bears, foxes, and wild cats, now roaming around, and seeming ready to devour us. Our hostess hung on the cook-all, and gave us fowls, ill-flavoured bacon, and wild beef, all stewed down to rags like hotch-potch, together with coffee and home-made sugar, for supper and breakfast. All was coarse, wild, and ill-flavoured.

29th.—At sunrise I passed two waggons and herds of cattle and people, very wild-looking and Indian-like, rising from camp, having *camped* out all night after the fashion of English gypsies. Stopped at a wretched cabin, having only one room, and that brimful of great dirty boys and girls, all very ragged and half naked; and again at the house of a Mr. Lewis, from Virginia, where every thing presented a fine contrast; clean, healthy, civilized children.

Breakfasted at an infant ville, Hindostan, on the falls of the White River, a broad crystal stream, running navigable to the Ohio, over a bed of sand and stone, smooth and white as a floor of marble. This baby ville is flourishing; much building is in progress and it promises to become a pleasant, healthy, large town, before I see it again. The land, too, is rich and inviting. I now crossed, in my chariot, White River, and in two hours after stopped at a quarter-section farmer's, who has never cleared nor inclosed any of his land, because sick or idle; being, however, well enough to hunt daily, a sport which, as he can live by it, he likes better than farming; "and besides," says he, "we had at first so many wild beasts about us, that we could not keep pigs, poultry, sheep, nor anything else." Called on another quarter-section man, sick, and who therefore has done but little himself; two young boys have cleared five or six acres. The tavern keeps them all; a tavern, with one miserable hole of a room.

I stopped again at a two quarter-section farmer's, who said;

"I am an old man, and have only my boys; we cannot hire, but we do all the labour, and get 60 bushels of corn per acre, but no wheat of any consequence yet. We can always sell all the produce we raise from the land to travellers like you, and others, new comers." "But," said I, "what will you do when your said new comers and neighbours have as much to spare and sell as you have?" "O, then we'll give it to cattle and pigs, which can travel to a market somewhere. I see no fear of a market in some shape or other." This was a shrewd old fellow.

I met and passed five or six huge waggons laden with goods, chattels, and children, and families, attended by horsemen, cattle, and footmen, and many negroes, all returning from the Missouri territory to their native home and state of Kentucky, which they had rashly left only two months since. Having sold out there in good times at 30 dollars an acre, and being now scared out of Missouri by sickness, they are returning to repurchase their former homes in Kentucky at 15 dollars an acre; or perhaps, says my informant, they may return to the Missouri, when the fear of sickness subsides. They have left their father behind, as a pledge of returning; but still 100 acres in Old Kentuck are worth 300 in Missouri, except in river-bottoms, that is, valleys of rivers.

Passed another Washington, a young county seat (or town) and several fine neighbourhoods of rich land, full of ironweed, but not so rank as in Kentucky, yet bearing plenty of huge sugar-trees. Every state in this mighty Union seems emulous of building towns, monumental piles of immortality to General Washington.

Rested for the night at a good bricked house tavern on the White-river ferry, but without one glass window in it. It is getting old and wearing out before it is finished. Here I found a good supper of buck venison, fowls, whiskey, and coffee. My hostess, the owner, was lately a rich widow, and might have remained so, but for a Yankee soldier with a knapsack at his back, whose lot it was to call at her house. They are now married, and he is lord of the tavern, land and all. My host had a large party of distant neighbours assembled to effect a corn shucking, something like an English hawkey, or harvest home. All, gentle, and simple, here work hard till eleven at night. Corn shucking means plucking the ears of Indian corn from the stalk, and then housing it in cribs, purposely made to keep it in, for winter use. The stalk is left in the field; the leaves, while half green, are stripped off, and tied up in bundles, as hay for horses and cattle, and good food it is, much resembling in form the flags in English marshes. After I had retired to bed the hawkey supper commenced; all seemed fun, created by omnipotent whiskey, with which they plentifully supplied me, although in bed. "The Doctor, the Squire, the Colonel," said they, "shall drink and lack no good thing." I was consequently pressed to rise and join them, about one o'clock. I refused. "Then," said they, "Doctor, you shall drink in bed." My charioteer had foolishly called me Doctor, Squire, Colonel, and what not, during the whole of this wilderness journey; hence, I was here applied to as an eminent physician.

30*th.*—Travelled 12 miles to breakfast on fine buck venison at three farthings per pound, or one dollar for the buck, at the house of a shrewd old kind-hearted Pennsylvanian, now nearly worn out and ready to sleep, either with or without, his fathers. "I have," says he, "lately lost my son, and my farms are running fast to ruin. I have 200 acres, some of which I hire out, and I have just finished what my son began, a good new log-house. This Indiana is the best country in the world for young men. Were I a young man I would live no where else in all the universal world." "Although," says he, "many hundreds of waggons, with droves of men and beasts, four or five hundred in a drove, and at least 5,000 souls from Kentucky have passed my house since last harvest, all bound for the Missouri."

At eleven, p. m., I reached Old Vincennes, the first and oldest town in this state, situated in a fine woodless *Prairie* on the banks of the big Wabash, a fine broad, clear, and generally deep stream, running to the Ohio by Shawneese town, but when its waters are low, weeds rise from the bottom, and grow, and rot, and impregnate the air with pestilence. On passing through this place, a farmer said that last spring he lost seven cows, and that hundreds were poisoned by some unknown herb found growing in their pastures on river-bottom land. A medical botanist was here much wanted. An immense quantity of land in the neighbouring state of Illinois, is here, I see, posted up in this town for sale or lease, for a term of years, at one peck of corn per acre, per annum. But who will hire, when nearly all can buy? I passed away my 20 dollar note of the rotten bank of Harmony, Pennsylvania, for five dollars only! so losing 3l. 7s. 6d. sterling. I was indebted five dollars to my faithful driver, who was now to leave me behind and press on to St. Louis, Missouri. I said, "Now, driver, which will you have; five silver dollars, or the 20 dollar note; or what more than your demand will you give for the said note?" "Nothing." "Then take it, and bless banks and banking for ever." Bank paper is here an especial nuisance, and ever fruitful source of evil, and ever very unfriendly to honesty, peace, and good will amongst hosts and travellers, who meet and part, cheating and cheated, cursed and cursing, continually. My landlord here is very obliging, and puts me into the best room and bed in the Vincennes hotel, where I am sleeping with a sick traveller from St. Louis, who states that many die daily, and his doctor there had 150 patients to visit every day, or oftener. So much for the healthiness of the ever-tempting Missouri.

Sunday, 31st.—The town of Vincennes is more than 200 years old; older than Philadelphia; but being of French origin, and in the neighbourhood of the Indians, ever hostile to the inhabitants and settlers round it, has grown but slowly, and is an antique lump of deformity. Although long the capital and mother town of the state, it looks like an old, worn out, dirty village of wooden frame houses, which a fire might much improve, for improvement generally has to travel through flames. Here is no church, save the Catholic church, the inhabitants being principally French Canadians, and the rest the refuse of the east, whose crimes have driven them hither, or dissipated young men unable to live at home. Hence Sunday is only a day of frolic and recreation, which commences on the Saturday evening, when every preparation is devoutly made for the Sabbath, and off they start in large parties on foot and on horseback, all riflemen, and cunning hunters, into the deep recesses of the forest, camping out all night in readiness for sabbath sacrifices, the bucks, the bears, the squirrels, and the turkeys, ready to be offered up by peep of day. This holy day is consequently ushered in by guns, which continue to roar in and around the town all day until sunset. The stranger might think it was closely besieged, or that an enemy was approaching. The steam flour-mill, a large grinding establishment of extortion, giving only 30 lbs. of flour for one bushel of wheat, weighing 60 lbs. is in operation all this day, and on other days, day and night, and blacksmiths' shops are in high bustle, blazing, blowing, and hammering in direct opposition to a law against Sunday business and pleasure, but which is never feared, because never enforced. The refuse, rather than the flower of the east, seems, with some exceptions, to be here. But still good is coming out of evil. The east is thus disencumbered, and the west is peopled. Posterity will shew a better face. Such is the process of empire.

I rambled round the town to the court-house, or shire-hall, really externally an elegant building, but decaying before finished, as though the state were unable to finish what it had so well begun before counting the cost. The State Seminary, a very respectable edifice, but in little better plight, was built by *Uncle Sam*, and endowed with an ample township in the state. It is, however, only a nominal seminary, because the trustees are not empowered to sell any of its land for raising funds, but must derive them from hiring and leasing it out in farms. But while plenty of uncleared or cleared farms can be bought at two dollars an acre, who will ever think of hiring?

I saw two Indian graves on the eastern banks of the Wabash. Each hillock is carefully arched over with broad stripes of bark, each three feet wide, with logs and sticks, or bands across. The bodies are buried from one to two feet deep only. Visited the house of J. Lowndes, Esq., the prison philanthropist and Howard of America, but did not see him. He was gone, as an Indian ambassador, to the government in Washington city assembled, and I passed him unconsciously on Thursday last, when I saw and noted in a handsome chariot, a venerable gentlemanly, dignified countenance. It was that of this good and honourable man. I presented his lady, once the widow of the late Judge Vanderburgh, with my introductory letter to her husband, which I had brought from one of my friends at Washington city. She regretted the absence of her spouse, and received me graciously. This generous man is gone a third time to the President on behalf of the Indian chiefs who call him their father, having appointed and chosen him as the only honest American whom they have ever known; all with whom they before had dealt or treated, tricked them out of their lands. Mr. Lowndes knows their language, and has a speech always put into his mouth by these barbarian grandees. "Go," said they, "go, father, and tell our great father, the President, how we are deviled and cheated, and if he does not do us justice, go, tell him he is a hog, and that we would burn up the land if we could." Mr. L. replied, "that this was an undutiful speech for children to send to their father;" but in great rage they rejoined in their own tongue, "He is only a man." The chiefs, whom Mr. Lowndes represents, are of the Delaware tribe, the posterity of those from whom William Penn so honourably bought

Pennsylvania, and who traditionally revere his memory down to this day.

November 1st.—During the last month the weather has been cold and dry, but generally clear and without fogs, and in the night frosty, shewing ice half an inch thick. Summer and I parted on the last of September, at Washington city, where she lingers until Christmas. Late last evening my host returned from his Sunday hunt, heavily laden with his share of the game, namely, two wild ducks, one wild turkey, seven squirrels, and one fine fat buck of 130 lbs. weight. Hunting seems the everlasting delight of this town. When I went to bed last night the prairie and forest were both enveloped in a wide-spreading, sky-reddening blaze, which the hunters had kindled to drive out and start the game.

I met this morning Mr. Baker of Philadelphia, an intelligent traveller, who knows my friend J. Ingle, living eighty miles further west of this place, and who has kindly borrowed a horse for me, and agrees to pilot me thither tomorrow. I saw a large party of Miami Indian hunters, accompanied by their ugly squaws, all on horseback, and all astride, with their tomahawks and frightful knives girdled round them, dressed in blankets and turbans, and painted red, green, black, and white; every feature having a different shade of colour, and all, save the squaws, apparently half drunk, having their bottle of fire-water, or whiskey, with them, which, after drinking from it themselves, they stopped and handed to me and my friend Baker. We took it and applied it to our lips, it being considered the perfection of rudeness and barbarism, and little short of enmity, to refuse any thing so kindly offered. This tribe had approached the town for the purpose of selling their venison. Each horse carried two or three quarters, fat and fine, ready skinned, and hanging down its sides. The price was only a quarter dollar for 30 lbs., not an English half-penny per pound.

Although Vincennes is an old mother town, abounding in rich land, it is uncultivated, and there is occasionally a scarcity of necessaries, particularly of milk and butter, which, with the worst tea, are dealt out very sparingly; no lump sugar, no brandy, no segars, no spitoons are seen at this hotel.

All persons here, and all whom I have met, hitherto, during this western pilgrimage, whether they have or have not visited Birkbeck, think very meanly of both him and his settlement. The English emigrants particularly, (says Mr.——) deem themselves deceived and injured by his books and mis-statements.

2nd.—Yesterday at noon came on a heavy gale, which filled the atmosphere for the remainder of the day and night, with a strange mixture of hot smoke, ashes, and dusty sand, to the density and hue of a London fog in December. The sun was completely shorn of his beams, and the whole horizon, for unknown miles in circumference, filled with a blinding commotion, like a gale in the great desert; and at night to the N. W. the sky blazed and reddened over a great extent, while the big Wabash blushed, and the whole atmosphere became illuminated, as though it was the kindling up of the last universal conflagration.

At ten this morning I left old Vincennes for Princetown. The horse which my friend Baker had borrowed for me was mean and mis-shapen, but covered with buffalo skins, which hide all defects. The horses here are nearly all mean, wild, deformed, half grown, dwarfish things, and much in taste and tune with their riders. The pigs, every where in great abundance, seem more than half wild, and at the approach of man fly, or run like deer at the sight of an Indian rifle. Throughout the western regions they look starved to death. This, however, is a bad season for them, there being little mast, that is, acorns, nuts, and other wild fruit and herbage. I passed over an extensive, sandy, black, burning prairie, the cause of yesterday's and today's thick hazy atmosphere, the sun looking more like the moon, and as if turned into blood. At noon, I rode through a large rich river-bottom valley, on the banks of the White River, and which, in winter, is as yet overflowed, from six to ten feet of water above the surface, as the trees prove by circles round their trunks, and by their boughs dipping and catching the scum of the surf. This land, of course, is the finest for meadow, if it were wanted, but as the prairies are all meadow, it is of no value. In it stand such enormous trees as are seldom seen elsewhere, having trunks like towers. Here, too, flourishes, the long and far-famed, ever-green mistletoe, planted by birds, or propogated only by seed or berries, which are sown or deposited on decayed branches and arms of oak and other trees, to beautify the desolation of the winter forest. Excessive drinking seems the all-prevading, easily-besetting sin of this wild hunting country. Plenty of coal is found on the Wabash banks, and there are salt-springs in this state, but sad Yankee tricks are played off in the working and making salt from them. Grease and fat are used, to make it retain a large portion of water, which asists in filling the bushel with deception. Although fat is so abundant, yet it is sold at 20 cents, or 10*d.* per lb. and candles at 37½ cents, or 19*d.* per lb. Milk, too, in a land which might flow with milk and honey, is 12½ cents, or 6*d.* per quart, and not a constant supply at that price, nor at any other price, unless a cow is kept. Butter, bad, at 25 cents per lb. Beef, six cents per lb. by the quarter, which lies on the ground all day at the tavern doors, as if brought for dog's meat. Tavern doors are here never closed.

Saving two comfortable plantations, with neat log-houses and flourishing orchards, just planted, and which sprout and grow like osiers in England, I saw nothing between Vincennes and Princeton, a ride of forty miles, but miserable log holes, and a mean ville of eight or ten huts or cabins, sad neglected farms, and indolent, dirty, sickly, wild-looking inhabitants. Soap is no where seen or found in any of the taverns, east or west. Hence dirty hands, heads, and faces every where. Here is nothing clean but wild beasts and birds, nothing industrious generally, except pigs, which are so of necessity. Work or starve is the order of the day with them. Nothing happy but squirrels; their life seems all play, and that of the hogs all work. I reached Princeton at sun-set.

3*rd.*—I looked round Princeton, a four-year old town and county-seat. Here I found and called on my countryman Mr. Phillips, who came a visitor from Somersetshire, but fixed on a pleasant good farm of 300 acres close to the town, which he bought with some improvements, such as a small log-house, and a few acres cleared by art and nature, at 20 dollars an acre; "the only farm (says he) which I would have in this state of Indiana, but which I mean to improve and resell, and then return to England. I hate the prairies, all of them; insomuch that I would not have any of them of a gift, if I must be compelled to live on them. They are all without water, except what is too muddy and distant for use. I am much perplexed with labourers; both the English and natives are good for nothing; they know nothing, and it is impossible to get any kind of business well done, either with or without money. Money cannot be gained by cultivation. There is no certain good market; farm produce may, perhaps, be sold at some price, but you cannot get your money of the cheats and scum of society who live here. I think that Birkbeck is right in not cultivating his land, though wrong and mortified in having written so hastily and prematurely. He and Flower are both sinking and scattering money, which they will never see more or gather again. They cannot even hope to gain or increase their capital, but by the contingent increase in the value of their land, which is not the best of its kind. With hired labour and a market, I should prefer the western country, but here, though there is no visible want, yet is there proverty indeed, and but little or no friendship. No sharing things in common; idleness poverty, and cheating, are the order and temper of the day."

Mr. Phillips and his wife both looked very shabby, wild and dirty. He apologized to me for his dishabille, and said, "Sir, if a stranger like you had found me in this plight in England, and I could have seen you coming up to my door, I should have hid myself. Here, however, no shame is felt, but pleasure, at a visit from one of my countrymen, whom I shall be happy to meet again." He keeps a housemaid only, his wife doing nearly all the drudgery herself, although in England, a lady, unaccustomed to soil her hands, or let her feet stray from the parlour carpet.

I had a long and interesting conversation with a young lawyer, the supreme Judge Hart, living in this town, but proscribed and suspended for sending a challenge to three agents of his estates in Kentucky, who, after, injuring him, caricatured him, and then refused to fight. The judge says that English labourers know nothing, and are worth nothing in agriculture here; hewing, splitting, clearing, grubbing, and ploughing among roots, being a business which they do not, and wish not, to understand. It is true that they are handy with the spade, and that only. They feel too free to work in earnest, or at all, above two or three days in a week. Every English body here is above work, except the good little farmer, like your friend, John Ingle, and old Phillips, the former of whom is likely to kill himself with hard work. He was sick twice in consequence, and once nearly unto death. Mrs. Ingle and her husband gain and deserve a good name, and feel happy and contented on a good farm, which is too near the road. They bought a log-house, town lot, pro tempore, at Princeton, at a forced sale, for 300 dollars; which they now let for forty dollars a year, to Mr. and Miss Fordham, Flower's nephew and niece, who were sick of the prairie of Illinois, where health could not attend them. Your friend, J. Ingle, lost his horses for three weeks. He is expecting more of his English friends to follow him. Mr. Birkbeck is disappointed and unhappy; I know him well. He has not cultivated nor raised, as yet, any thing from his land, although the Harmonites refused to sell him produce, because they thought it was his duty to raise it himself, and plainly told him so. He will never make a farmer, nor money by farming there. It is idle to attempt to import English labourers for the use of yourselves exclusively, for Birkbeck and Flower lost all. The same, says Mr. Pittiss, late of the Isle of Wight. Women and girls, too, are here above assisting in the house, at a price per day or week. Wives and daughters must do all themselves. The girl, or white servant, if one can now and then be had, at one dollar per week and board, is pert and proud as her mistress, and has her parasol at six dollars, and bonnet at ten or twelve dollars, and other articles in character, which, as dress generally does with all grades, seduces them from a virtuous regard of their duties, says this young and sprightly lawyer. People here, though poor and idle, feel above thieving, the facility of living without, and the certainty of exposure and summary punishment, seem to conquer the propensity, where it may happen to exist.

I feel convinced that none but working farmers, like John Ingle, ought to come to this western land. Water is bad, white, or milky, at Princeton; but beds are good, with the bed-room doors next the street, unlocked all night, in order that ingress and egress may be free, which is the more necessary, as there are, as is very generally the case here, none of those accommodations, either within or without doors, which an Englishmen looks upon as quite indispensable.

I met and talked with old Squire M'Intosh, who, although he has lived 35 years here, away from his dear native Scotland, still regrets it. "I now live," says the squire, "on the grand rapids of the big Wabash, a mile above the White River ferry; call and spend a night with me on your way to Birkbeck's settlement, which is the reverse of every thing which he has written of it, and described it to be. The neighbourhood, however, do not think he intended to misrepresent and deceive, but that he wrote too soon, and without knowing the real state of things, and understanding his subject, or knowing where to find the best land. He ought to have examined, in company with one of *Uncle Sam's* surveyors; he would not then have entered land in the lump, or mass, a great deal of which is not good, nor ever can be, being wet, swampy, cold prairies, something like undrained marshes in England. Mr. Birkbeck entered much at the land-office, but sold little, only such half sections as he ought to have bought and kept for himself and friends. Mr. Phillips, on whom you have just called, say the gentlemen round me, is the slave of his own English notions and passions; he is, therefore, always hesitating and undecided; sometimes, when things run crossly and crooked, he is seen and heard heartily execrating this country and people; and, at other times, he is well pleased. He is an odd man, surrounded with eight fierce dogs, and has a fine, never-failing mill spring, running a mile through his farm, which, one year ago, cost 20 dollars, but is now worth only ten dollars an acre, with all improvements. This is turning a penny quickly! Despatch is the life and soul of business."

4th.—The Supreme Judge, Hart, is a gay young man of twenty-five, full of wit and humorous eloquence, mixing with all companies at this tavern, where he seems neither above nor below any, dressed in an old white beaver hat, coarse threadbare coat and trowsers of the same cloth (domestic,) and yellow striped waistcoat, with his coat out at the elbows; yet very cleanly in his person, and refined in his language. What can be the inducement for a young man, like him, equal to all things, to live thus, and here?

Judge Hart deems merchandizing to be the most profitable pursuit in the west, and the liberal professions the last and worst.

Mr. Nicholls, a cunning Caledonian, says, that farming, except near the rivers, cannot answer; but raising and feeding cattle and pigs may. Store-keeping is here evidently the best of all employments, if cents and dollars enter into the estimate. Money spent in improving land is seldom more than returned with interest, and often lost by reselling or selling out, especially if the labour is not all done by the farmer; and if it is done by his own instead of hired hands, he is not more than fairly paid for his time and labour, which are both money. It is therefore best for the mere capitalist to buy rather than make all the improvements, as he certainly buys them much cheaper than he can create them. He should confine himself to the east.

Mr. Phillips, the English gentleman on whom I called yesterday, returned my call this evening. He seems a mass of contradiction, and states that this western country is the best he knows, but that it costs more to live in it than in London; that it is idle for a farmer to raise more produce than he can use himself; but that there are farmers making money as fast as they can count it, by raising large quantities of farm produce in this and the neighbouring state of Illinois; that others might do the same; that there is now a market better than in the east, and that in five or seven years the market at New Orleans down the river will be good and great; yet that the parties to whom you must sell are all d——d rogues. Feeding beef and pork he deems a good trade, especially when the land shall come to be clovered and sown with other grass seeds. He thinks there is little or no good beef in the wilderness, because it is raised and fed on natural wild vegetables, many of which are ill-flavoured and poisonous. Beasts often die suddenly in the fall of the year in consequence of being confined to such food. The natural white clover, in the month of June, salivates cattle and horses, which, however, still devour it greedily, and seem to thrive thereon.

Our party this evening were all agreed in this particular; that the western country is only fit for the little hard-working farmer with a small capital. He must live, and better than he could elsewhere, on and from the productions of his own hands and lands. He can retail his produce, and be gardener and farmer both; vegetables every where being scarce and dear, because people are too idle to raise them. Wholesale farmers from England expecting to cultivate from 300 to 1,000 acres, and sell the farm produce in lumps, will come here only to be disappointed. Small retailing farmers only are wanted here. Mr. Phillips deems that Birkbeck, Flower, and Mr. Dunlop of London, who have bought so many thousands of acres, and the latter of whom pays *treble* tax as a non-resident, will greatly benefit at some future time by capital so employed, although they may never cultivate an acre, or touch the land. The capital seems to be idle and sleeps, but it will one day, he thinks, awake, and find itself gigantically augmented. Mr. Phillips, whose opinion is not respected here, was never a farmer until he came here. His improvements do honour to his intuition.

General Evans, who this day formed one of our circle, is in part the owner of this town of Princeton, and of Evansville, which bears his name. He is a pleasant, rustic, middle-aged man, living here in a little log-house, together with his lady and daughter, who, having no servant, do all the work of their establishment themselves. Servants are not to be had. The same may be said of all the rest of the inhabitants. Envy and invidious comparisons have, therefore, no place at Princeton.

General Boon, during the last war, (says the General) lost two sons killed; and his favourite daughter and her friend were stolen by the Indians, who marched the fair captives two days without resting, and intended marrying them, but were overtaken by the colonel and his son, and a lover of the lady. The young couple, previous to this event, were on the point of marriage, and are now living as husband and wife in Kentucky. The captives cunningly indented the ground all the way from the Colonel's house with their high-heeled shoes, so that they might be tracked; and when they saw their brave deliverers coming up full speed, they fell flat on the earth, while the firing of rifles commenced on the Indians, who tried in vain to kill their fair prisoners by throwing their knives and tomahawks at them; but the pursuers triumphed, and all were recovered and restored unhurt. General Boon now lives in solitude 600 miles up the remote Missouri. He is 80 years old, very active, very poor, a hunter and a recluse by choice, and trains up his sons in the same path, feeling more happiness than he possibly could in society, where he would have lived and died, if he had willed it, full of scars, and honours, and days. His parents were always poor; his disposition is kind and hospitable; his manners simple and gentle; preferring to live meanly and rudely as a hardy hunter and squatter, wanting nothing but what nature gives him, and his own hands get him. He sleeps on a bear-skin, and clothes himself in dressed deer-skin, and though shy, is kind to intruding strangers. The western country is indebted to him, as he leads the way into the best spots of the wilderness. He was the first white man in Old Kentucky, and the wide, wild west is full of his licks. A flourishing settlement always rises wherever he has once squatted, and whenever any settlers begin to approach near his location, he quits it for ever, and moves on further west; and the place, which he thus abandons, is called Boon's Lick. He never wants much land; only a spot sufficient for the supply of his household.

I saw a man this day with his face sadly disfigured. He had lost his nose, bitten off close down to its root, in a fight with a nose-loving neighbour.

Judge Hart deems it foolish policy in English-men wishing to form English settlements and neighbourhoods, and thereby to perpetuate English distinctions and prejudices, so offensive to their adopted country, and so unprofitable to themselves. Nothing is good with them but what is English, whereas they should rather endeavor to forget the name, which ever kindles unfriendly feelings.

I saw a fine fat buck, fat as a Lincolnshire wether sheep, and weighing, when dressed and with the head off, 140 lbs. It sold for two dollars, less than three farthings per pound.

Politeness, in manner and address, is more necessary here than in Bond-street, for here you invariably receive it, and to give it in return is justly due. The titles, "Sir" and "Madam," (not Ma'am) are pleasant to and expected by all; for however mean may be the exterior of a citizen of this free, equal country, there is a spirit and an intelligence, and often sprightliness about him, which decorate any thing and make even rags respectable.

Two months ago the High Sheriff of Chilicothè, Ohio, went to jail for want of bail. He had siezed, personally, on the funds of the United States' branch bank. This was hard!

Birkbeck, (say my companions) complained at first of our slovenly state of things, and the indolence of farmers and labourers, and boasted of what might be done, and what he should do, but has, at the end of four years, done nothing but talk of doing. The facility of a living for all, and the consequent difficulty of procuring labour, even for money, together with the sickly, relaxing warmth of the climate, are obstacles which overwhelm all industry. The principal care is how to live easy. Time, and not man, effectually clears and improves land in this country. Time here changes his character, and preserves and replenishés, while man destroys and wears out what he can.

The reason (says Judge Hart) why Scotchmen always get money, in this and all other lands to which they wander, is, because they leave no means untried.

The season, called *the Indian summer*, which here commences in October, by a dark blue hazy atmosphere, is caused by millions of acres, for thousands of miles round, being in a wide-spreading, flaming, blazing, smoking fire, rising up through wood and prairie, hill and dale, to the tops of low shrubs and high trees, which are kindled by the coarse, thick, long, prairie grass, and dying leaves, at every point of the compass, and far beyond the foot of civilization, darkening the air, heavens and earth, over the whole extent of the northern and part of the southern continent, from the Atlantic to the Pacific, and in neighbourhoods contiguous to the all-devouring conflagration, filling the whole horizon with yellow, palpable, tangible smoke, ashes, and vapour, which affect the eyes of man and beast, and obscure the sun, moon, and stars, for many days, or until the winter rains descent to quench the fire and purge the thick ropy air, which is seen, tasted, handled, and felt.

So much for an Indian summer, which partakes of the vulgar idea of the infernal. Why called Indian? Because these fires seem to have originated with the native tribes, and are now perpetuated by the White Hunters, who by these means start, disturb, and pen up the game, and destroy the dens of both man and beast, and all this with impunity.

To-morrow, through floods and flames, I shall endeavour to make good my desperate way to the retreat of my good friend, John Ingle, in Indiana.

6th.—At nine, a. m. I left Princeton on a horse carrying double, me and my guide, through the wilderness, to my friend John Ingle's, who had sent the said horse and boy twenty-five miles for my accommodation. The little town just quitted, and at which I paid the extravagant price of two dollars a day for board, has nineteen streets, and about one hundred and five houses, one prison, and one meeting-house, or church, all of wood; one supreme judge, and four other judges; and in the unpeopled county are another quorum of judges, and three generals. It is called Princeton, in honour of its living founder, Judge Prince.

We rode all day through thick smoke and fire, which sometimes met in pillar-like arches across the road, and compelled us to wait awhile, or turn aside. We passed only one comfortable abode, and three or four filthy one-room log-holes, surrounded by small patches, cleared samples of the bulk, which seems good land. I called at one of the three, a tavern, to beg for bread, but got none; only some whiskey. I saw a deer-lick, at which I dismounted and took a lick. The earth thus licked and excavated by many tongues, is of the colour of *fuller's earth,* not ill-flavoured, but a little salt and saponaceous, always attractive to the beasts of the forest.

At five o'clock, p. m., I reached the welcome abode of my Huntingdonshire friends, Mr. and Mrs. John Ingle, who, together with their English maid-servant, Rebecca, and six children, rushed out to embrace and welcome their old friend, school-fellow, neighbour, and fellow-countryman, and great was the joy of our meeting.

Here I found good sweet bread, like the English, and hot corn-cake, and supped, on what I supposed fine pork steaks. "This meat (said I to Mr. Ingle) is most delicious." "Well then, you like it, do you?" "I do indeed." "What do you think it is?" "Why, pork to be sure." "Well, we thought we would not tell you until after supper, lest you should fancy it was not good and refuse to eat *Bear*." "Oh," said I, "if this be bear, give me bear for ever."

My friend's log-house, as a first, is one of the best I have seen, having one large room and a chamber over it, to which you climb by a ladder. It has, at present, no windows, but when the doors are shut the crevices between the rough logs admit light and air enough, above and below. It is five yards square and twenty feet high. At a little distance stand a stable for two horses, a corn crib, a pig-stye, and a store; for storekeeping is his intention, and it is a good one. Two beds in the room below, and one above, lodge us in the following manner; myself and Mr. Ingle in one bed; in the second, by our side, sleep six fine but dirty children; and in the chamber, Mrs. Ingle and a valuable English maid. Thus on my account, husband and wife were divided. It is not unusual for a male and female to sleep in the same room uncurtained, holding conversation while in bed. In a yard adjoining the house are three sows and pigs half starved, and several cows, calves, and horses, very poor, having no grass, no pasture, but with bells about their necks, eternally ringing. Shame, or rather what is called false shame, or delicacy, does not exist here. Males dress and undress before the females, and nothing is thought of it. Here is no servant. The maid is equal to the master. No boy, or man-servant. No water, but at half a mile distant. Mr. Ingle does all the jobs, and more than half the hewing, splitting, and ploughing. He is all economy, all dirty-handed industry. No wood is cut in readiness for morning fires. He and the axe procure it, and provender for the poor hungry cattle, pigs, and horses. His time is continually occupied, and the young boys just breeched are made useful in every possible way.

Nothing is English here but friendship and good-will. American labourers here, as usual, are very villainous; one, a preacher, took a piece of land to clear for my friend, and received, before he began, forty dollars on account, but refused to perform his contract. To sue him was idle. My friend, in the presence of the fellow's son, called him a right reverend rascal and thief. "Call him so again," said the son, doubling his fist ready to strike. My friend repeated it, and taking up an axe, said. "Now strike, but if you do, as I was never yet afraid of a man, I'll chop you into rails." Money rarely procures its value in labour. He deems that as much money is to be made from 200 acres of land here, as in England, while here the land is made your own. To do that in England, is the top of a farmer's ambition. Here, a man can make all that he cultivates his own. He says that he shall live and gain money this first year, though only sixteen acres are in cultivation. Mrs. Ingle, maid, and children, suffered much in crossing the sea and mountains. They slept on the floor, in a hole, with waggoners, and other male blackguards, where the stench, both by sea and land, was little short of pestilential.

Sunday, 7th.—More than half last night, Mr. and Mrs. Ingle, and maid, were out in the woods extinguishing the wide spreading fires, which threatened to consume their fences, houses, and cornfields. The whole horizon was brilliantly illuminated. These fires, if not arrested, or watched, sweep away houses, stacks of corn and hay, and every thing within reach. So fared Mr. Grant, late of Chatteris, who is now dead. The sound of the axe, splitting fire-wood, salutes the ear every morning, instead of the birds' song. I was smoked to death all night; our friends rested all day absent from meeting, but still the knees of all present were bent to the God of their good fathers. Sunday passes unnoticed in the English prairie, except by hunting and cricket matches.

The bears, during the summer, are lean and hungry, and seize the hogs and eat them alive. It is no uncommon thing to see hogs escape home with the loss of a pound or two of living flesh. These creatures sleep all the winter quite fat. Rattle-snakes abound here. Mr. Ingle killed four or five beautiful snakes of this species this summer, and one or two vipers.

8th.—I accompanied J. Ingle, and water-cart, to the spring, half a mile off, on the farm of Major Hooker, a hunter, who sold us half a fat buck at three cents a pound; thus killing and selling from four to six per week, besides turkeys, pheasants, rabbits, racoons, squirrels, and bears. This half buck, weighing 70 pounds, Mr. Indle carried home on a shoulder-stick. The major's, and other families here, raise cotton for domestic uses, which, in warm and dry seasons, flourishes well. What I saw in pods, and that which the women were spinning, seemed of excellent quality. The seed of this plant was, in slave states, thought nutritious enough, when boiled, for the support of negroes; but as many died in using it, it was abandoned

The China leaf, or tea-plant, has been propagated at Princeton, in Mr. Devan's garden, and at Harmony, from seed brought from China. It is said to grow luxuriantly, yielding more leaf than is used, and making a useful decoction, similar in flavour, though not so pleasant, as that procured from the imported plant. It is manufactured by sweating it in an oven, and when taken out, it cools and curls up, and becomes fit for use. The indigo also is a little cultivated. The woods abound with medical herbs. The Ching Sang and Ipecacuanha are found, for emetics. The vine is very luxuriant, and cultivated at Harmony with success; while the trees are full of gum. The Dogwood Bark is also found as efficient as the Peruvian, and the Sassafras tea is in general use for two or three months.

Great idleness prevails in the Illinois; little or no produce is yet raised. G. Flower had contracted with the American hunters, to raise and cultivate 500 acres of corn and grain; he finding land and seed, and they all the labour of raising and getting it fit for market, at nine dollars an acre. This bargain became void.

9th.—A doctor, of little or no skill, lives twelve miles distant, and this little settlement of Sandersville has no school for the children, who remain at home pestering their parents, and retrograding into barbarism. Mrs. Ingle dreads their mixing and associating with the race of children who surround them. A schoolmaster here would be welcomed with a salary of from 400 to 500 dollars a year, although not one of the first grade, but he must be content to live in a wilderness.

I feel, every day, more and more convinced that the western country is suited only to working families, like those of J. Ingle; where Mrs. Ingle, (delicately bred) and all turn out to work, as today, and the other night to put out the approaching fires.

The bears and wolves have devoured several sows while farrowing; they are then weak and defenceless, and therefore an easy prey. Never did I behold such ghostly pigs as here. Soap, candles, sugar, cotton, leather, and woolen clothes, of a good quality, are here all made from the land, but not without the most formidable, unremitting industry on the part of the females. Filth and rags, however, are often preferred. Imperious necessity alone commands extraordinary exertion. Yesterday, a settler passed our door with a bushel of corn-meal on his back, for which he had travelled twenty miles, on foot, to the nearest horse-mill, and carried it ten miles, paying 75 cents for it. This said corn is invaluable to both man and beast; black and white men both profess to think they should starve on wheat meal without corn.

The everlasting sound of falling trees, which, being undermined by the fires, are falling around almost every hour, night and day, produces a sound loud and jarring as the discharge of ordnance, and is a relief to the dreary silence of these wilds, only broken by the axe, the gun, or the howlings of wild beasts.

Retrograding and barbarizing is an easy process. Far from the laws and restraints of society, and having no servants to do that for us which was once daily done, we become too idle in time to do any thing, but that which nature and necessity require; pride and all stimuli forsake us, for we find ourselves surrounded only by men of similar manners; hence, the face is seldom shaved, or washed, or the linen changed except on washing-days. The shoes are cleaned, perhaps, never; for if, indeed, a servant, from England, is kept, he, or she, is on a happy equality, rising up last and lying down first, and eating freely at the same time and table. None here permit themselves to have a master, but negroes.

A voyage in the stinking steerage of a ship, and then a journey over the mountains in waggons, sometimes camping out all night, or sleeping, like pigs, as did Mrs. Ingle and six children and maid, on the dirty floor of a bar-room, amongst blackguards, and then floating in a little stinking ark, full of unclean things, will prepare the mind and body for barbarizing in a little log-hole, like that in which I dined yesterday, belonging to Mr. Ferrel, who, with his family, some adults, male and female, in all ten souls, sleep in one room, fifteen feet by ten, only half floored, and in three beds, standing on a dirt floor. The table, or thing so called, is formed by two blocks and a broad board laid on them, and covered with a cloth, and seats or forms, in like manner, on each side of the table, which is only knee-high. Proper chairs and tables, they have none. When it rains, boards are laid over the chimney top, (which I can reach with my hand) to prevent the rain putting the fires out. This good-natured man has thus settled and removed, eight times, from one degree of barbarism to another. The victuals are served up in a hand-bason; and thus one room serves for parlour, kitchen, hall, bed-room, and pantry. The settlers, too, here, are without implements, but such as they can patch and form together of themselves; they are too distant and expensive to buy. What they have must cost nothing, like their houses, which are raised in a day by the neighbours all meeting together, so going in turn to serve each other, as we did yesterday.

10*th*.—Mr. Peck, late of Chatteris, introduced himself to me this day. Born and bred a labourer, he at length became a little farmer, on the dearest land in Chatteris, from which he brought a wife, four daughters, one son, a man, and 500*l*.; all, the perfection of British industry. Feeling themselves likely to lose all, they came here to two quarter sections, costing 145*l*. to be paid, in three years, by instalments; so leaving 355*l*. for stock, seed corn, and housekeeping, until they shall have cleared twenty acres, and raised produce. He begged I would come and dine with him, so that I might hear particulars of his former state, present condition and prospects, and be able to tell his old neighbours of his comforts and satisfaction. "Now," says he, "I feel I can live, and live well, by working, and without fretting and working, seventeen, out of the twenty-four hours, all the year round, as I used to do at Chatteris. And what is sweeter than all, I feel I am now the owner of 300 acres of land, all paid for, and free from all poor-rates, parsons, and tax-gathers, and that I shall be able to give and leave each of my children, 100 acres of good land to work upon, instead of the highway, or Chatteris work-house. No fear of their committees now, nor of Ely jail."

It was pleasant to witness the boasting satisfaction of this good, honest fellow, and his family of young Pecks.

I saw an old, dirty, stinking Irishman, very well to do, settled on a quarter section here, but who says, were it not for his family, he could do better in Ireland; and therefore, for the sake of his family, the is content to live a little longer, and die here. They will be better off. He came to breakfast with us, and borrowed a razor to shave his beard, for once, instead of clipping it off.

Meeting Mr. Hornbrook, the first settler here, I said to him, "How is it, that you, and others, can do with such houses here, when you had such comfortable ones in England." "Oh," said he, "after our voyage and journey, we are glad to get into any hole, although we know, that in England, they would think them not good enough for stables."

On the eve of this day, a heavy battering rain came, and put out the fires, and cleared the air, and poured water down upon our beds. Great lumps of the clay, or daubing, stuffed between the logs, also kept falling on our heads, and into our beds, while it rained. We needed an umbrella.

Mrs. Ingle, a woman of superior sense and feeling, states that the prospect of seeing herself, husband, and children dependent on grandfathers and grandmothers, and uncles and aunts, and thereby lessening the resources of two distinct and worthy families, impelled them to emigrate. It ceased almost to be matter of choice. Still, love of country, former friends and comforts, from which they tore themselves, is inextinguishable, and frequently a source of painful thought. Such a good, proud feeling is very honourable, for with fair play in England, it would have kept them there, and increased rather than diminished the resources of grandfathers, &c.

11*th.*—By a conversation with old Ferrel, I find he began,

thirty years ago, with nothing but his own hands. Striking each hand, he said, "This is all I had to begin with;" and it seems, that excepting his children, he has little more now, merely a quarter section just entered, and a log raised on it. All seem very improvident and extravagant, the family sometimes eating four or five pounds of butter a day, the produce of all their cows. Thus, with the corn-cake and bacon, a part of the year, (for they are almost always destitute for fresh meat, tea and sugar) is their table supplied.

Ferrel is a man of experience and discernment, and states that he would not fetch corn from Princeton, twenty miles off, of a gift, if he could grow it, nor would he carry it to the Ohio for sale, because it would not pay carriage and expenses. When (if ever) they shall have surplus produce, he will give it to pigs and cattle, which will walk to market. He always, and every where, had a market at the door, and he always expects it, because of the number of idle people who do not, or cannot raise produce. He says, that as Mr. Ingle was no judge of the quality of land here, he has chosen that which is not lasting, namely black oak land. It is kind and useful, but after three crops, he will see and believe, though he does not now, that his old American neighbours know and have got the best land. He thinks that a slave state, with negroes, well chosen, is the best for capitalists, who need not, or cannot work themselves. He still thinks that hiring when you can, is a free state in the west, may sometimes pay, but as nearly all feel themselves masters instead of labourers, it is impossible to be regularly supplied with hands. Kindness, equality, persuasion, and good pay will sometimes effect it. He says, that a man is seldom more than paid for improvements.

Supped with a Mr. Maidlow, a most intelligent and respectable Hampshire farmer, a neighbour of Cobbett's, who left England and his large farm, at about 16*s.* an acre, because, from a fair trial, he found it impossible to farm without losing money, although his wheat-land averaged six quarters an acre, and his landlord,— Jervis, Esq., had lowered the rent 20 per cent. He brought a considerable capital and English habits and feelings, the best in the world, into the neatest and cleanest log-cabin that I have seen, and is building already a second, larger and better, for the preservation of all that is comfortable and respectable in the English character, being determined that neither himself nor family shall barbarize. This is impossible: all barbarize here. He has bought six quarter sections, and hopes not to do more than keep his property, get land for his family, and live and die comfortably. Riches he thinks out of the question, and it is his wish that the settlement should feel and act towards each other as one family; the reverse of Illinois, in which he intended to settle, and to which he was attracted by the books of Mr. Birkbeck, who refused him land, except at an advanced price, although he had 30,000 acres retained for people in England, who never came; while those who applied, many and respectable practical farmers, were denied.

The settlers here being all out of wheat-flour and Indian corn-meal, Mr. Ingle, self, a boy, and two children began, at noon, to gather and shell ears of corn for grinding into meal, and finished two bushels by night, ready for the mill, ten miles off, next day; when a boy on a horse started with it early, expecting to return the following Sunday morning, if not lost in the woods.

12*th*.—Visited Mr. Potts's cabin and farm, 400 acres of good land, on which he lives, without a woman, but has a good man from Stockport in Cheshire, where they both came from, and thus they alone manage both the house and the field. They have dug a well, many feet through the solid rock, without finding water. I saw here an experiment which I little expected to see; the eighth of an acre of upland rice; three quarts were sown on it in May, in drills, eighteen inches asunder, and the increase is three bushels. The straw is like barley straw, and the stubble rank and stout, and not to be known from oat stubble, on rich fen land, only brighter.

Saw a poor Englishman, who some time since broke his leg, which from want of skill in the doctor, was not properly set; he is therefore now a cripple for life. This is an evil to which all are exposed. Many are now dying at Evansville of a bilious disorder; the doctor employed has lost nearly all who applied.

River banks are here always unhealthy. A family from Lincolnshire, attracted by fine land, on one of the prairie creeks, where no American would live on any terms, all fell sick, one died, and the farmer and his wife both lay unable to help themselves, or get help, except from one of their little boys, who escaped the contagion. Birkbeck strongly remonstrated with them against settling there.

The farmers (Americans) indebted to the store-keepers, are now forced to sell all their corn at one dollar a barrel, and buy it again for their spring and summer use at five dollars, a fine profit for the monied merchant. Forty bushels per acre of corn pays better (says the old farmer) than wheat, with only twenty to twenty-five. The land here, though good, is not first rate, or of the most durable quality.

A pigeon roost is a singular sight in thinly settled states, particularly in Tennessee in the fall of the year, when the roost extends over either a portion of woodland or barrens, from four to six miles in circumference. The screaming noise they make when thus roosting is heard at a distance of six miles; and when the beechnuts are ripe, they fly 200 miles to dinner, in immense flocks, hiding the sun and darkening the air like a thick passing cloud. They thus travel 400 miles daily. They roost on the high forest trees, which they cover in the same manner as bees in swarms cover a bush, being piled one on the other, from the lowest to the topmost boughs, which so laden, are seen continually bending and falling with their crashing weight, and presenting a scene of confusion and destruction, too strange to describe, and too dangerous to be approached by either man or beast. While the living birds are gone to their distant dinner, it is common for man and animals to gather up or devour the dead, then found in cartloads. When the roost is among the saplings, on which the pigeons alight without breaking them down, only bending them to the ground, the self-slaughter is not so great; and at night, men, with lanterns and poles, approach and beat them to death without much personal danger. But the grand mode of taking them is by setting fire to the high dead grass, leaves, and shrubs underneath, in a wide blazing circle, fired at different parts, at the same time, so as soon to meet. Then down rush the pigeons in immense numbers, and indescribable confusion, to be roasted alive, and gathered up dead next day from heaps two feet deep.

13*th*.—Major Hooker frequently shoots, and then cooks and eats the huge wild cats, while Mr. Birkbeck and his family eat the rattle-snake, the flesh of which, says Mr. Ingle, is fine, sweet, and white, as an eel. Pigs also eat them voraciously. Armstrong, a hunting farmer, this day shot four deer, while he is too idle to inclose his cornfield, which is devoured by cattle and horses, save when a boy watches it to keep them off. This man and family then, though with plenty of land, must buy corn, and depend upon wild meat for the support of his idle family, who have either a feast or a famine. They keep several cows, but as calves are constantly with them (having no separate inclosure) and as the family eat 5 lbs. of butter a day, for three days in the week, which consumes all the dairy at once, they go without during the remainder of the week. They never sell any, though it is 25 cents per pound. No fear of surplus produce from such farmers.

The hope, it seemed, of preserving and increasing his property, was amongst Mr. Birkbeck's ruling motives for emigration. To those to whom he is known, he is very hearty and sociable. To J. Ingle he said, "There are so many thousand dollars in that drawer; they are of no use to me: go, and take what you like." He is very careless and improvident, like the rest of his literary fraternity, and unconscious of what his powerful pen and high reputation were effecting by exciting a strong feeling in favour of emigration, at a moment when the people of England were despairing; so strong, indeed, that what he did and wrote, burst in upon them like a discovery. Unconscious of all this, he left undone all which he ought in common policy to have done. The weakest head could see that after purchasing land and alluring settlers, he ought to have guarded against a famine by providing for their accommodation, building a few log-houses, store-houses, and a tavern, and cultivating corn, so that the numerous callers in this inhospitable waste might have found food, and a shelter, and a person to shew the land, which he had to resell. Whereas a stable, a covered waggon, and prairie-grass, formed their only shelter and bed; and not having food sufficient for himself, there was little or none for strangers, and no person to shew the land, nor did he know himself where it lay. He idly thought that if they wished land they would find it themselves; and being in expectation of many such families from England, he thought he had no land to spare, so that the real practical farmers of both worlds who called, turned away disgusted to other and better neighbourhoods, the Kaskasky, and Missouri, and Red River, where more important settlements are rising. He therefore, as the rich families did not come, has no real farmers in his settlement, and hoped J. Ingle, being one, would come and make one solitary farmer amongst them. Trusting too, to his own judgment, he has settled down on and entered indiscriminately good and bad land, much of which will never be worth any thing, being wet, marshy, spongy, on a stratum of unporous clay, over which pestilential fogs rise and hang continually. A United States' surveyor would, for a few dollars, have prevented such a choice. Common policy and prudence, too, ought to have induced him to reduce his fine farming theory into practice, otherwise it seemed as if intended merely to deceive others. Even if he should, (as he now says) lose by it, or could buy produce cheaper than he could raise it, he still ought not so to buy it, but set an example of farming. For of what use is land, if it is not worth culativating?

As a proof of his improvident conduct, and bad management, his thirteen horses were all miserably poor and unfit for use, and when any were wanted, he would say to a hunter, "Here's five dollars for you, if you find and drive up the horses;" for he had no inclosure. The man knew where they were, and soon found them and received the fee; none then were fit for use. "Oh! don't tease me about horses."

This evening, J. Ingle sat down by the fire, and cleaned the shoes of all the family, which he does every week.

Sunday, 14th.—Called on a Caledonian Yankee farmer, busy at work in his garden, who said he had no Sunday in his week, but would buy one if he could. He is a quarter-section man, without wife or child, shoes or hose.

After a meeting of 16 persons of this little settlement, in the log-house of my friend, who read a sermon and prayed for all present, I visited Mr. Hornbrook's, a respectable English family from Devonshire, on a good quantity of land, living in two or three log-cabins.

Amongst the inducements of the Flower family to emigratte may be reckoned the probability of their wasting all their proper,y by farming their own estate, about 500 or 600 acres at Marsden. It was badly farmed, and the Merino trade failed, which was Mr. Flower's hobby-horse; and seeing his favourite son was determined to live in America, emigration now ceased to be a matter of choice. They intended to settle in the east. G. Flower, who brought a letter from the celebrated Marquis de la Fayette to Mr. Jefferson, who he visited, bought an estate of 500 acres at 10 dollars an acre, near Jefferson's, where they were to have lived; but, as Mr. Birkbeck could not approve it, on account of slavery, it was abandoned.

15*th.*—*The English settlement in Indiana*, up to this time, contains 12,800 acres entered, and in possession of actual settlers, 53 families having capital to the amount of 80,000 dollars.

Expenses of clearing and inclosing an acre of land, ready for planting, $6\frac{1}{2}$ dollars; ditto of planting, with four ploughings and four hoeings, and harvesting, and stacking for market, at your own door, six dollars an acre; so making the first year, an acre cost...		$12.50
Second year, wheat $1\frac{1}{2}$ bushel seed	$1.50	
Ploughing once, 75 cents; clearing dead timber, breaking up stumps, and hoeing sprouts, one dollar and 50 cents	2.25	
Reaping $1\frac{1}{2}$ bushel an acre, or in cash	1.00	
Carting, threshing, etc.	3.50	
		$8.25
Cost of one acre in two years		$20.75
Produce of an acre of Indian corn, 35 bushels, at 50 cents the first year		17.50
Ditto, wheat, 25 bushels, at 75 cents the second year		18.75
Value of the acre, in two years		$36.25
Deduct cost		20.75
Profit		$15.50

In the next two years, the two acres will cost less by 8 dollars 75 cents, which, added to 15 dollars 50 cents, makes the net profit on two acres 24 dollars 25 cents, besides the increased value of the land.

The proper expenses of a farmer, arriving with a capital of 2,000 dollars, that is to say, his necessary expenses in establishing himself and family the first year:

First year—Entry of half section, or 320 acres of land	$160.00
House and stable, 80 dollars; smoke house, pigstye and hen house, 40 dollars	120.00
Two horses, good, 160 dollars; two ploughs and harness, 40 dollars.	200.00
Four axes, four hoes, 16 dollars; waggon, 100 dollars; harrows, 12 dollars	128 00
Spades, shovels, six dollars; two cows, 36 dollars; four sows in pig, 20 dollars..	62.00
Corn crib and barn	60.00
Clearing 20 acres of land first year, foot and under, and fenced well	130.00
Ploughing, planting, hoeing and turning	130.00
	$990.00
Twelve month's maintenance of family	250.00
	$1,240.00

So leaving him at harvest 800 dollars of his 2,000 dollars for the uses of the coming year; but still, this money will not be wanted, as the farm will now maintain itself and family; the money then should be at use.

"The foregoing statements," says Mr. Ingle, "I will swear are correct, and they are in part reduced to practice this year." I think, however, that the money should be at command for his own use, as twenty acres more clearing, &c. unless he does most of it himself, (which he ought to do) wants 260 dollars the second year. All the labour, however, is to be done the first year by hired hands, if they can be found, and, if possible, to be done at a price per acre, not by the day.

Mr. Ingle insists on it that none of the old funds will be wanted the second year, but that the farm will maintain itself and family; as the pigs will supply plenty of bacon to eat and some to sell, besides the surplus of the first crop of corn, which will supply some money; but the second year, the work upon the farm must be principally done by himself and family.

He thinks that no more land should be under cultivation and fence, (say about forty or fifty, and thirty acres of grass) than the farmer can manage without hiring, which, at present, it is impossible to do with any thing like comfortable benefit and English regularity. He will not be so grasping as in England. A little will satisfy him; he is not so disposed to disquiet himself in vain. The habits and examples of the country will at length be imperceptibly followed.

New settlers in this state, men, women, and children, seem all exposed to an eruption, ten times worse than the itch, inasmuch as it itches more, runs all over the body, crusting and festering the hands and other parts, and is not to be cured by the common treatment for the itch, which has been tried without effect, and one instance has been known, where the sulphur and grease killed the patient by obstructing perspiration, and driving in the eruption. The doctors know of no remedy, and suffer it to take its tedious course. It comes in the spring and fall, but not to the same person, it is hoped, more than once. It is attributed to the air, soil, and climate. Mr. Ingle's family are all suffering severely under it. Although the climate seems finer here than in the east, more humid and temperate, yet the bite of every insect and reptile, however insignificant, is highly poisonous; an evil not to be remedied at present. New comers and fresh flesh suffer most, and sometimes much inflammation is caused; but when the land becomes more cleared, it is hoped this scourge will be less afflictive.

Fine yeast: Take a small handful, or a good nip of hops, and boil them ten minutes, in one quart of water, then strain away the hops, and pour the liquor into a quantity of flour, sufficient to give the consistency of batter well beaten; a tea-cup full, or something less than the usual quantity of brewer's yeast, is sufficient for a half-stone loaf; two spoonfuls of brewer's yeast to work the first making; then, even after, a little of the last made; the yeast to be put to it while milk-warm, and kept so until it ferments, which it generally does in summer very soon, and in winter in a day, but it must not be used until it does ferment. In winter it keeps one month, in summer (America) one week, two in England, and is a fine saving and a great convenience.

16*th.*—A poor emigrant farmer from Devonshire, called here in search of a home. His family, yet on the river, had been nine weeks in a stinking ark, coming from Pittsburgh, and ever since April last in getting from England, by way of Canada, hither. I asked him if he repented leaving England. "I do," said he, "a good deal, and so does my poor wife;" and then he burst into tears. The tears of a man are hard-wrung drops. "You were getting, I suppose, a comfortable living in England?" "Oh no! taxes, tithes, rates, &c." "What money did you bring away?" "But a little, and besides my passage to Canada, where I could have had 100 acres for nothing, I have spent 50 *l.* in getting to this western country. The captain told me that Canada was my best way, and I have now but little left." He thought of going to the Prairie. I told him he had better settle here. They of the Prairie are proud, and wanted only high-bred English. I encouraged this poor, desponding, ill-advised, weak man to hope for better times in this good land, where he said he was willing to labour.

Taverns are always charitable to moneyless travellers, if they are sure of their poverty, feeding them gratis as they pass along, as instanced in a moneyless female, and a sick man whom I met in the stage coming here. The Scots frequently plead poverty, and get fed gratis, while their pockets are full of dollars.

Mr. J. Ingle and maid started this morning, with a waggon, to Princeton, for boards, though living in a forest full of boards when sawn. He drove the waggon himself, and she was to get groceries and butter, if she could get it under twenty-five cents per lb. Thus, for two days, we were left without water, or an axe to hew firewood, or any person to milk and feed a kicking cow and pigs.

17*th.*—A stranger called and brushed out of the rain. He said he was short of money, and came ten miles to sell two pigs, fat, weighing 400 lbs. the two, but was not able to sell them at more than four dollars a cwt.; he could not afford to make pork at that price. No pigs fat this year at *mast*, only passable pork; but when quite fat they must have corn for two or three weeks to harden them, though they get no fatter, or else the bacon would drip all summer, and when boiled, the fat become oil and run out into the water. He has seventeen acres of corn; a bad crop, not enough for his own use. Few farmers are ever able to hire labourers, though he thinks it would answer if they could; still it is best to do all the work by one's-self or family. I went to turn the grindstone for J. Ingle's carpenter, at Mr. Maidlow's, one mile and a half off. Went over his fine farm, that is to be. I think it is the best I have been in this settlement. On it I saw a lick of singular size, extending over nearly half an acre of land, all excavated three feet, that is to say, licked away, and eaten by buffaloes, deer, and other wild animals. It has the appearance of a large pond dried. The earth is soft, salt, and sulphurous, and they still resort to it. Mr. Maidlow thinks that Cobbett is much nearer the truth than Birkbeck, in his account of the west. Had he now the chance of choosing, he would purchase, in the east, improvements at eighteen dollars an acre, like the farm of Mr. Long, as he finds that making improvements in the west costs much money. He believes Birkbeck is spending money fast. He does not think that capital employed in farming here will answer, or that cultivation will pay, if done by hired labour. Out of 900 acres, (all he intends buying) he means to cultivate and graze only about 100 acres; no more than they can manage of themselves. He does not expect to increase his capital, but by the increase in value of land. He means to build a mill, and plant a large orchard; is digging a well, and finds some fine good burning coal in it, and a vast mine of rich blue marl. The Missouri, says he, is full of all the rich resources of nature; land, very fine. Here is a large family of men, and Mrs. Maidlow and daughter are drudges to the house, cooking, scouring, and scrubbing, continually. A young lady cleaning knives! How horrid!!

18*th*.—A few months since, J. Ingle agreed with a neighbouring Kentuckyan hunter, to build him a log-house, to be begun and finished in a given time. The fellow was procrastinating, and too idle to begin, yet for ever promising. At length Mr. Ingle told him, that unless he began on a certain day, at noon, at latest, the contract should be void, and others should begin it. He came on the day mentioned, but not until six in the evening, when other had begun the job. Greatly enraged, he said, he had come, and would begin in spite of any body. Mr. Ingle said he should never touch it. He said he would, or have Mr. Ingle's blood; "and to-morrow morn, I will come with men, and twenty rifles, and I will have your life, or you shall have mine." Mr. Ingle thought of having recourse to the civil power, which is very distant, insomuch that the people speak and seem as if they were without a government, and name it only as a bugbear.

J. Ingle returned this evening with his poplar boards, not worth carriage, and without being able to buy any tea, sugar, butter, cheese, or apples, for his use, at Princeton, though a county town, having a fine store out of stock, which it receives only once a-year.

19*th.*—A parson, with his wife, and sixty others, about eighteen months ago, came from the east, as settlers, to the big prairie of Illinois; in which, during the sickly season, last fall, an eighth of their number died in six weeks. Having lost his wife amongst the rest, he has cleared out, and lives by his itinerant ministrations.

It is useless to fence much more land than is cleared, because, until the country is cleared round about, the autumnal fires would destroy the fences. The cattle, therefore, must range in the woods, until some small inclosures, for pasture, can be made. Through the summer, both night and day, but mostly in the night, the mosquitoes, both in Indiana and Illinois, but chiefly in the latter, were, in their attacks, almost sufficient to drive English settlers out. If a man had been lashed naked to a post, he must have been stung to death, or unto madness. At Sandersville, says J. Ingle, they blinded several persons.

The Cherokee nation once wishing to war against the United States, sent their favourite chief, *old Double-head*, to Philadelphia, to sound parties, and return with his opinion either for or against it. "Oh," said he, on his return, "we must not war; I have seen more white men in one town, than would be sufficient to eat all the Indians, if made into a pie." They have never since thought of war, but what few remain, are friendly and civilized, and fight for *Uncle Sam.* Some cultivate their land, and possess negroes.

20*th.*—At nine this morning, after a fortnight's stay at Sandersville, I mounted the neck of an ill mis-shapen, dull, stumbling beast, called a horse, the best that friendship and good-will could procure, for conveying me, in company with J. Ingle, to the state of Illinois, by way of the far-famed Harmony. I rode, in fear, all day, through woods and wilds; sometimes almost trackless. We were lost twice. The people seem to know nothing of time, and distance of places from each other; some telling us it was ten, when it was two, and three, when it was twelve o'clock; and as to distance, twenty when it was twenty-seven, and fifteen, when it was ten miles to Harmony. I expected to camp out all night, with no means of getting a fire. I saw nothing but good land, and (where any) fine corn; but no comfortable dwellings; all, miserable little log-holes, having neither springs nor mill-streams. We were very courteously shewn our way by a worshipful magistrate of Indiana, at work by the road side, hewing and splitting wood.

We rested, twenty minutes, at a log of one of Cobbett's Yankee farmers, with a fine family of boys, big enough for men, and handsome, sprightly, and free-looking, as ever walked the earth. I would have given something for a picture of them, being self-taught shoemakers, butchers, wheelwrights, carpenters, and what not, and having cleared, from 320 acres, 60 acres, and cropped them twice in two years. The mother sat, smoking her pipe, fat and easy. The father is ready to sell out at 1,200 dollars; a fair price, says Mr. Ingle. They think well of this country, but were able to grow more wheat per acre in Pennsylvania; there, thirty-four, here, twenty to twenty-four bushels an acre; they can have seventy-five cents at home, or carrying it twenty miles or less, one dollar a bushel, for wheat. The old fellow says that the Harmonites do their business of all kinds better than any body else.

I saw, on the Harmony lands and fields, of great size, wheat, finer and thicker, planted with two bushels, than in England with three and a half bushels per acre. The fields, however, lie in a vale of prodigious richness.

I reached Harmony at dusk, and found a large and comfortable brick tavern, the best and cleanest which I have seen in Indiana, and slept in a good, clean bed-room, four beds in a room, one in each corner; but found bad beef, though good bread, and high charges, one dollar, five cents, each.

A stranger present, asked our landlord of what religion were the community of Harmony. In broken English, and rather crossly, he replied, "Dat's no matter; they are all a satisfied people." The spell, or secret, by which these people are held in voluntary slavery, is not to be known or fathomed by inquiry. We asked if strangers were permitted to go to their church to-morrow. "No," was the answer. This is unprecedented in the civilized world.

Sunday, 21*st*.—At Harmony till ten o'clock, when we were told, "we must then depart, or stay until after the morning service," which commences at ten o'clock. At the moment the bells began chiming, the people, one and all, from every quarter, hurry into their fine church like frighted doves to their windows; the street leading to the temple seems filled in a minute, and in less than ten minutes, all this large congregation, 1,000 men, women, and children, all who can walk or ride, are in the church, the males entering in at the side, the females at the tower, and separately seated. Then enters the old High Priest, Mr. Rapp, of about eighty, straight and active as his adopted son, Frederick, who walks behind him. The old man's wife and daughters enter with the crowd, from his fine house, which looks as if the people who built it for him, thought nothing too good for him. This people are never seen in idle groups; all is moving industry; no kind of idling; no time for it. Religious service takes place three times *every day*. They must be in the chains of superstition, though Rapp professes to govern them only by the Bible, and they certainly seem the perfection of obedience and morality. People who have left them say, that Rapp preaches, that if they quit the society, they will be damned, for his way is the only way to Heaven. He does much by signs, and by an impressive manner, stretching out his arm, which, he says, is the arm of God, and that they must obey it; and that when he dies, his spirit will descend unto his son Fred. The people appear saturnine, and neither very cleanly nor very dirty. They are dressed much alike, and look rather shabby, just as working folk in general look. None are genteel. The women are intentionally disfigured and made as ugly as it is possible for art to make them, having their hair combed straight up behind and before, so that the temples are bared, and a little skull-cap, or black crape bandage, across the crown, and tied under the chin. This forms their only headdress.

I rode round the town, which will soon be the best and first in the Western country. At present, the dwellings, with the exception of Rapp's, and the stores and taverns, are all log-houses, with a cow-house and other conveniences. One is given to each family, and a fine cow, and nice garden; other necessaries are shared in common. Their horses, cattle, and sheep, are all in one stable; herds and flocks are folded every night, in comfortable sheds, particularly an immensely large flock of Merino sheep; and so secured from the wolves. They have a fine vineyard in the vale, and on the hills around, which are as beautiful as if formed by art to adorn the town. Not a spot but bears the most luxuriant vines, from which they make excellent wine. Their orchards, too, are of uncommon size and fertility; and in a large pleasure garden is a curious labyrinth, out of which none but those who formed it, or are well acquainted with it, can find their way.

Their granary is superb and large, and the barns and farm-yards are singularly capacious, as well as their cloth and other manufactories. It is the wise policy of this people to buy nothing which it is possible for them to make or raise, and their industry and ingenuity are irresistible. They have much to sell, at their own price, of almost every thing domestic and foreign. They can not make shoes half so fast as they could sell them. It is not doubted but they are immensely rich, beginning in Pennsylvania with only 4,000 *l.*, and being now worth 500,000 *l.* They keep no accounts, and all business is done and every thing possessed in Frederick Rapp's name. They have been in this Harmony five years only; they bought a huge territory of the richest land, which is all paid for, and keep an immense quantity in high cultivation, and continue to buy out bordering settlers, thus ever enlarging their boundaries. An American widower, with ten children, joined them some time ago, in distress for his children; all are well off now.

They work very gently, but constantly. At eleven I left Harmony, wishing to see more of this singular community. Rapp came hither a poor, unlettered weaver from Germany.

I entered the woods again, on the banks of the fine river, the Big Wabash, wider than the Thames at London. There are no regular roads; but, over creeks and swamps, and the Black River, now dry, we took our way, and met six bastard Indian-like horse-men, drinking whiskey in the woods, looking wild and jovial, dressed in sky-blue and scarlet. Crossed the Big river into Illinois, after being lost one hour.

From *A visit to the colony of Harmony in Indiana*, by William Hebert [1825.]

HEBERT, WILLIAM.

One of the many curious visitors who flocked to New Harmony, Indiana, during the days of the Rappite Colony was one William Hebert of London. He made his visit during the last half of the year 1823. The chief value of his notes lies in the full discussion given of the purely religious and social conditions that prevailed in the colony.

The State Library has a typewritten copy made from the original edition, a copy of which is in the library of the Workingmen's Institute, New Harmony, Indiana.

A

VISIT TO THE COLONY

of

HARMONY,

In Indiana,

In the United States of America,

Recently purchased by Mr. Owen for the establishment of a

SOCIETY OF MUTUAL CO-OPERATION

and

COMMUNITY OF PROPERTY,

In a letter to a friend;

To which are added,

Some observations on that mode of society, and on political society at large:

also,

A sketch of the formation of

A CO-OPERATIVE SOCIETY.

"Many schemes ridiculed as Utopian, decried as visionary, and declaimed against as impracticable, will be realized the moment the march of sound knowledge has effected this for our species; that of making men wise enough to see their true interests, and disinterested enough to pursue them."—Lacon.

By WILLIAM HEBERT.

LONDON:

Printed for George Mann, 39, Cornhill.

1825

A VISIT,

&c.

Albion, Edward's County, Illinois,
6th February, 1823.

Dear Sir,

In the month of September last I made an excursion with a friend to the celebrated German Colony in our neighborhood at Harmony, the name of the place being characteristic of the society that is settled there. It is situated in a thickly wooded country on the banks of the Wabash, on the Indiana side, at about thirty miles from the mouth of that river. The site of ground upon which the town stands is generally flat for about a mile and a half from the river, when the surface of the country becomes hilly and pleasingly undulating. This singular community consists of about seven hundred individuals, chiefly from Wirtemburg and its neighborhood. They have occupied their present situation about seven years, having been induced to relinquish a former establishment in a back situation of Pennsylvania, near Pittsburg, from its beginning, [becoming] as it is supposed, too thickly settled to suit the peculiar tenets or policy of their society. The progress which this religious community made in agriculture and every other kind of industry when settled in Pennsylvania, was a subject of astonishment to their neighbors for many miles around, but I apprehend that their present advanced state of improvement and accumulating wealth, justly excite the admiration of all acquainted with them here to a yet greater degree. It is presumable that they have made far greater progress here than they did in Pennsylvania, from their having been much longer established, and from a consideration of the sum of money for which they sold their former establishment, compared with the vast value of their present possessions. These good people have literally made the "barren wilderness to smile" with corn fields, meadows, and gardens upon a most extensive scale. Their little town, seen from the neighboring hills, which are covered with their vineyards and orchards, has an exceedingly pleasing appearance, the Wabash, which is here an ample stream, being seen to wind its course in front of it, and beneath the luxuriant and lofty woods on the opposite banks of Illinois. The town is regularly laid out into straight and spacious streets, crossing each other at right angles, in common with modern American towns. The log cabins are giving place as fast as possible to neat and commodious brick and framed houses, which are extremely well built, the uniform redness of the brick of which the majority of them is composed giving to the place a brightness of appearance which the towns of England are quite destitute of. Nothing, I think, detracts so much from the beauty of London, next to the irregularity with which it is built, as the earthy or mud-coloured appearance of the houses, forming so great a contrast to the wealth and splendour within a considerable portion of them. The house of Mr. Rapp, the pastor of the community, is a large square mansion of brick, having a good garden and suitable outhouses attached. The streets of the little town of Harmony are planted on each side with Lombardy poplars, but as these are found to die as soon as their roots come in contact with the substratum of sand, they are replaced with mulberry trees. A town being thus planted with trees, has a very picturesque effect from a distance, it appearing to stand in a grove, beside the pleasant use of affording shade and shelter when walking about it. The town is amply supplied with excellent wells, as also with public ovens, which are placed at regular and convenient distances from each other. Their granaries, barns, factories, &c. are generally built in an exceedingly handsome and durable manner. Here too, in token of Christianity being planted, (though in its most rigid character) amongst Indian woods which had but lately resounded with the yells of their untutored inhabitants, rises the pretty village church, the white steeple of which, seen from afar through the widely extended clearings and forests of girdled trees, seems to invite the traveller onward to a peaceful resting place. And such it is, Harmony is truly the abode of peace and industry. The society, however, possesses one principle of so unsocial and dispiriting a character, as to throw a shade over the whole scene in a moral sense, and to fill the mind with commiseration for men who can so construe any of the precepts of Christianity into a virtual prohibition of the sacred ties of the married state. The Harmonians are a class of Lutherans, who, though they do not expressly prohibit marriage, discountenance it to an extent that nearly amounts to a prohibition in effect. They profess to adhere to the advice of St. Paul, in regard to this point of morality. Upon my enquiring of one of them, a candid and amiable person, how long it had been since a marriage had taken place amongst them, he said, nearly three years, and it was presumable that none was contemplated as about to take place at the time of my inquiry. This in a community which can contain scarcely less than a hundred young persons of suitable ages to enter upon the marriage state, and surrounded with plenty secured to them upon their system of society! The Harmonians consider the single state as higher in a moral estimation than the married one, as the Catholics are said to esteem it.

As you may suppose, the utmost regularity and decorum subsists amongst them. They work easily, but their hours of labour are of the usual length of the labourer's day, being from sunrise to sunset. They are an exceedingly industrious race of people, being occasionally busy long before sunrise in some departments of their establishment, such as their Distillery, Brewery and Mills, which sometimes require their attendance through the night. It is understood that they subsist upon a principle of fellowship, or of united labor and capital, all deriving their food and clothing from the common stock, every individual however being accountable for the application of his time, and the amount of the articles he has from the stores. When any one is remiss or irregular to an extent to become an object of attention, no coercive measures are resorted to, but the idle or offending person is treated with distance or neglect, which, together with verbal reproof, are found to be fully efficacious to reform. The Harmonians are, however, an extremely regular and sober-minded people, whose happiness is certainly the happiness of ignorance, the pursuits of literature being wholly neglected or prohibited amongst them. They appear to do every thing with a mechanical regularity. Their town is consequently very still, the sounds of mirth or conviviality being rarely heard within it, excepting when their American or English neighbors resort there for purposes of trade or to negotiate their money transactions. Being great capitalists, resulting wholly from their industry, they are frequently resorted to by persons in this neighborhood, who receive remittances by bills on the eastern cities, to obtain cash for them. As a society they are extremely wealthy. Having overcome all the difficulties incident to their establishment in a wilderness, they have only to improve their manufactures and extend the sphere of their operations to acquire almost incalculable wealth. This numerous community of men of humble life embraces within it several artisans of nearly all of the most useful occupations of life, to the exclusion or suppression of those which they do not deem essential to their welfare. Amongst the latter, I am sorry to say they include that of a printer, they being wholly without one, and seem fully persuaded that the employment of one, if it would not be detrimental to their peace or their interests, is at least superfluous to them. They are generally averse to communication on the subjects of the tenets and the policy of their society. It may be presumed that they are totally unused to liberal discussion, and may be considered an ignorant and priest-ridden set of people. Mr. Rapp is alike their spiritual teacher and temporal director, who is as much accustomed to superintend their operations in their fields and factories, as to lecture them on their duty, and who will sometimes spend as much time in exploring their woods in search of a particular tree for a specific purpose, as in enforcing his arguments for the peculiar doctrines of their faith. He is their alpha and omega, without whom they think nothing, do nothing, and perhaps would have been nothing. Mr. Frederick Rapp, an adopted son of Mr. Rapp the pastor, a bachelor of about forty years of age, appears to be the sole cashier and ostensible proprietor of all the produce and manufactures of the society, all bills and receipts being made and given in his name only. I am informed however that their land which is of great extent and of the first quality, is entered at the land-office in the form of "Frederick Rapp and his associates," which circumstance I was glad to learn, as it indicates something like joint property on this material point, whatever may be the fact in other respects. The affairs of the community are not regulated by a committee, or court of directors, chosen periodically and in rotation from among its members, which would possible be deemed as "romantic" as the representative system of government is termed by the present emperor of Austria, but by a few of the most influential individuals amongst them. The governing power seems to be composed of Mr. Rapp and his adopted son, with the assistance of the superintendent of the general store, the doctor, the sadler, the smith, and the keeper of the house of "private entertainment," (the designation of the tavern,) and perhaps a few other persons; but those enumerated are the ostensible managers, each of whom receives money in his particular department. Further than this, nothing is known respecting the pecuniary arrangements of the society. Whether the governing power of the Harmonians has any constitutional shape is unknown, but its efficiency is matter of astonishment to all who have surveyed the scene of its operation. If justice prevail in the society it is well, and they are a peculiarly respectable body of people, to be compassionated only for the gloomy character of their religious opinions and their general ignorance. And if equity do not subsist amongst them, and the majority are duped by the wary and powerful few, they still appear a contented people, and to entertain an *opinion* of mutuality of possession, though they may not possibly have any very correct ideas or information upon the subject. It is known that books of account are kept, in which are entered the amount of every labourer and mechanic's daily earnings, together with the daily amount of the articles each has from the stores; but it is not known that there is any general account kept of the external transactions of the society, or of the value of grain, beef, pork, whiskey, beer, wine, and of various manufactures that are exported from Harmony to New Orleans and elsewhere, besides an immense amount of goods sold by retail at their general store, the return for all which is chiefly in specie. The Harmonians have commercial agents in several of the principal cities of the Union, whose purchases of merchandise being sent to Harmony, are dispersed through the surrounding country by means of their store at home, and others which it appears they think it worth while to possess in different towns in the neighborhood, which latter are superintended on commission by persons not of their society. They have it already in their power to say that they raise or produce every thing necessary to comfort, with an exception only to groceries, which last however they procure in exchange for their own commodities, chiefly for sale, as it is said the people in general are not allowed the use of tea or coffee, although the heads of the community indulge in those agreeable and exhilarating beverages. The Harmonians are upon the whole an interesting body of people, but it is impossible to regard their commercial spirit without a sentiment of fear or suspicion that it militates against that purity and austerity of character which they are in other respects so scrupulous of maintaining. One might enquire what is the probable destination of this community at the distance of half a century? The principle of celibacy upon which it is governed tends nearly to its extinction within this period. Upon enquiring of the good man, the keeper of the house of "private entertainment," who showed us about the town, if they were not desirous of increasing the number of their society, he replied, "not by strangers," and upon my friend's enquiry whether they were not desirous of receiving an accession of numbers from amongst their own countrymen, he said, that they considered their own countrymen, who were not of their faith, equally strangers to them with Americans or English; and having repeated that they were not desirous of increasing their number "by strangers," he added, "*that is the answer*," implying that the answer he had given us, was "*the answer*" to all enquiries of that nature. Our guide informed us that their number was a little above seven hundred, but that he did not recollect the exact number, which last part of his communication I thought somewhat strange in an elderly and influential associate. With respect to the Messieurs Rapp and their coadjutors keeping books of account of the amount of their annual income by exports and sales at home, and of the value of the disposable property on hand, for the information and satisfaction of the whole of the community, I never heard that there were any kept here, but I have been given to understand that a great book of accounts which had been kept at their establishment in Pennsylvania, was lost at the time of their removal, or shortly after it; and this story is accompanied by another, which, though not surprising in itself, becomes *measureable* so, when connected with the loss of the book of accounts. The second story is, that the heads of the society never received but a small portion of the sum for which they sold their former establishment. These circumstances would be little worthy notice, did the heads of the Harmonians evince an independence of pecuniary or commercial pursuits, whereas they are notoriously keen in dealing, and appear to be arrant money-lovers. The Harmonians seem in a measure to have adopted the policy of the Roman priesthood during the ages of their greatest power, which by forbidding their fraternity to marry, preserved the power and possessions of the church wholly within itself, and prevented that relaxation of interest and opposition of sentiment in its concerns, which would have resulted from a matrimonial connection of the reverend order with the laity, and these humble sectarians preserve an insular policy to the utmost extent of their power. Their children few as they are, have but the common rudiments of an education given to them, and are prevented as much as possible from learning the English language. Mr. Rapp, the pastor, it is said, does not speak a word of English, although he has lived in America nine or ten years; and notwithstanding that his son and the other leading members of the community speak it very well. That an arch craft rules the society I would not insinuate, and am indeed far from concluding upon, but that several circumstances exist, strong enough altogether to induce a fear of wrong, or to keep alive speculation, must I think, be obvious to every person who has any knowledge of the outrageous impositions which avarice and ambition, under the garb of priestly sanctity, have practiced upon the simplicity, the credulity, and pliancy of mankind. As great events sometimes spring from little causes, so small matters sometimes elucidate large ones. On the door of the house of "private entertainment" was written "grapes 12½ cents per lb." Now I would enquire, who were to buy these grapes at 12½ cents, per lb.? Surely not the poor vine dressers or working people themselves, though I doubt whether any of them could obtain any without allowing for them out of their earnings; and if the bill were put up to invite the purchases of American travellers, the proceeds from this source of sale must have been trifling in the extreme. I was struck with the paltry purport of this paper at the moment I saw it, and however it happened, it was taken down a short time after our arrival. It is this excessive spirit of trade in the Harmonians that forms the great defect, and I may say the anomaly of their character, considered as a society of rigid and puritanical christians, living remote from the political world, as one would have supposed, with a view to independence of its cares and pursuits. These people exhibit considerable taste as well as boldness of design in some of their works. They are erecting a noble church, the roof of which is supported in the interior by a great number of stately columns, which have been turned from trees of their own forests. The kinds of wood made use of for this purpose are, I am informed, black walnut, cherry, and sassafras. Nothing I think can exceed the grandeur of the joinery, and the masonry and brick-work seem to be of the first order. The form of this church is that of a cross, the limbs being short and equal; and as the doors, of which there are four, are placed at the ends of the limbs, the interior of the building as seen from the entrances, has a most ample and spacious effect. A quadrangular story or compartment containing several rooms, is raised on the body of the church, the sides of which inclining inwards towards the top, are terminated by a square gallery, in the centre of which is a small circular tower of about ten feet in height, which is surmounted with a silvered globe. The reason assigned by our guide for the erection of this fine edifice was, that the first church being built wholly of wood, is found to be so hot during the summer, when the whole of the society are assembled within it, as to be scarcely supportable, in consequence of which it was resolved to delay the building of their houses for a time, and raise a more spacious and substantial place of worship, and the one they are employed upon bids fairly to do them honor, both in the design and execution. It is much more spacious than the number of their society requires. I could scarçely imagine myself to be in the woods of Indiana, on the borders of the Wabash, while pacing the long resounding aisles, and surveying the stately colonades of this church. Here too the Englishman is once more gratified with the sound of a church bell, which however harsh it may sometimes be thought by those who have never strayed beyond the sound of one, imparts a gratification after a period of estrangement from it, as connected with early associations, infinitely more soothing than could the most delicate strains of music. As if, however the good Harmonians could not lose sight of a gainful utility in any thing, the vaults of their new church are appropriated to the reception of stores of various kinds. In descending from the steeple of the old church (from which a beautiful scene presents itself of the wonderful effects of united industry) we perceived that the upper compartment of that building was also used as a store for grain, earthenware, cotton, &c. The Harmonians are said to be excellent musicians, and to make a great use of instrumental music in their worship, maintaining by the cultivation of this exquisite science and their unanimity, a twofold claim to their designation as a society. The shortness of our stay did not afford us an opportunity of attending their religious service. I am informed that during the harvest season, the troops of reapers, male and female, leave the field preceded by music. To this I would merely say, that I wish them every happiness compatible with the repression of the all-ennobling passion of love. They seem to me however to have struck at the root of earthly joy, and I earnestly wish them every success in devising substitutes, or any means of alleviation of their cheerless situation. These good people retain their German style of dress. There is nothing remarkable in that of the men. The women wear close and long-bodied jackets, or spencers, and gipsey bonnets. They are said to be a healthy looking people, and I imagine they are so, although this was not the case at the time of our visit, which was at the latter end of September, that being generally the most trying time of the year, and a considerable number of them were sick. I must mention, that in addition to their vineyards and orchards covering many of the neighboring hills the Harmonians have formed an extensive garden in the form of a labyrinth, having a pretty rustic building in the centre. The mazy walks toward this hermitage are formed by espalier fruit trees, and currant and hazel bushes in almost interminable rounds. It does not appear that the people enjoy any periods of relaxation, excepting on Sundays, when they are allowed to walk about the garden, the orchards and vineyards, in some situations of which tables and benches are placed for the purpose of taking refreshment. My friend and I were shown their cotton and woolen factories, with which we were much pleased. The products of these establishments are much esteemed by the country around. I saw some very good blue cloth from the wool of their own flocks, and good cotton fabrics, such as are generally worn in the western country. A great number of men, women, and children are employed in these departments. They have a fine steam engine in use in their factories. The morning on which we were shown about the town happened to be somewhat cool after rain, our guide who would be as cheerful as his habits of thinking permitted, observed that the air was "*entirely pleasant*," upon which I took occasion to ask him, if he considered the climate and country of Indiana equal to those of the part of Germany he had quitted. Here however nature was true to herself, for he replied with great feeling, that the climate and beauty of Germany were so superior to those of Indiana, that the latter was not to be brought into comparison with the former. But maintaining his consistency of character, be observed "we are happier here than we could have been in Germany, we could not have done there what we have here". I could perceive however, that his native country had charms for him that he could not do justice to, and that in "expressive silence," he mused its praise. He informed us that the severity of the winter in their part of Indiana, (in about latitude 38,) is such, as to render it necessary to bury one kind of their vines, (the Portugal or red Lisbon,) by bending them to the ground, and covering them with earth; the only method of preserving potatoes and turnips here during the winter being by burying them. The severity of the winters of this part of the world forms an astonishing contrast to the great and long continued heat of its summers, uniting in this respect the cold of much higher latitudes with a heat little inferior to that of the tropics.

During our stay at Harmony we witnessed some very astonishing flights of pigeons. Such were their numbers, that they literally formed clouds, and floated through the air in a frequent succession of these as far as the eye could reach, sometimes causing a sensible gust of wind, and a considerable motion of the trees over which they flew. At that time of the year these birds congregate in the woods of this part of America by millions. Parties are sometimes formed to go to their roosts by night, when by knocking them off the trees with poles, any quantity of them may be taken. In case you may have thought me too severe upon the Harmonians in regard to their trading spirit, an *excess* of which I think derogatory to the christian character, and more especially in a society of christians who profess to live in a state of seclusion from the world and more conformably to the precepts of the gospel, I would say, I have perhaps been the more strict with them from a consideration of the consistent and dignified conduct of a society of friends situated also in Indiana, near the same river, and about a hundred miles to the north of Harmony, who are commonly known here by the name of the "Shakers" or "Shaking Quakers." There is also, I am informed, another society of these friends in the state of Ohio. These societies are constituted upon a principle of reciprocal assistance and common property, and like the Harmonians refrain from marriage, but with a strictness that amounts to an absolute prohibition of it. These good people however consistently disclaim an attention to mercantile or pecuniary concerns beyond the demands of their necessities or personal comfort. They also have effected great things by united exertion, but they have no traffic with the surrounding country beyond the limits I have mentioned. They have their capacious granaries, fine mills, and machinery of various kinds, but they adhere to their object of living in christian fellowship, in a state of plenty and independence of the world. They are not merchants or money-changers, and when visited by strangers, entertain them gratis. This you will allow to be really respectable.

Having mentioned all the particulars of these interesting communities that I think worthy notice,

I remain,
Dear Sir,
Your's sincerely,
W. H.

OBSERVATIONS, &c.

From the foregoing circumstances relative to the Harmonians and Friends, it is but fair to conclude that if a society could be formed of any convenient number of families, each contributing only one hundred pounds towards a common fund, and were with this to seek an agricultural and manufacturing establishment in some convenient situation of Great Britain, Ireland, Hanover, or any part of protestant Europe, they might by the formation of an equitable constitution, and the enactment of a suitable code of laws which should always preserve the door of regress open for insubordinate or discontented members, and by the encouragement of literary and scientific pursuits for the occupation of their leisure time, attain to a degree of earthly comfort, not unassociated with refinement, hitherto unknown. Such a society would of course embrace within it several individuals of all the most useful occupations of life, and every thing would necessarily be effected for the benefit of the community upon an entire system of reciprocation; and might be conducted similarly to the manner in which public societies are generally managed. No one need doubt the practicability of this. No one indeed could doubt it, who had visited Harmony, and seen the astonishing effects of the united and systematic industry of numbers, and the numerous comforts, as well as the security derived from this enlarged system of social intercourse. The greatest internal obstacle to the welfare of a society of this kind in Europe might be the want of a religious bond of union, but surely the spirit of christianity, with all its variety of sects, ought to be equal to this. To obviate or lessen any difficulty that might arise from difference of religious opinion, a general spirit of forbearance and liberality would be necessary, and the erection of places of worship convenient for every denomination of which the community was composed, desirable; the officiating members of which should be prohibited by the constitution, under the penalty of expulsion, from preaching in terms offensive to, or abusive of the tenets of christians of other sects, or laying any stigma on any system or kind of belief whatever; on the principle that differences of religious opinion are within the decision of the Deity alone, on whose favour and approbation all have an equal right of reliance. The objects of such a community would be industry, society, independence or self-subsistence, leisure for mental culture, and rational amusements; and freedom from the solicitude, anxieties, and incertitude of pecuniary pursuits and possessions. The principal obstacles to an establishment of this kind in Europe, would arise from rent, or the high rate of the purchase of the land, the exaction of taxes and military service. From the last of these however exemption might generally perhaps be purchased, and the first and second, if not too heavy, might be defrayed from the funds, or by the sale of a portion of the produce or manufactures of the society. America however has every civil advantage and natural facility for such a society to Europe.

To some it might appear irksome, and perhaps slavish, to be obliged to regulate their conduct as members of a community, by the sound of a bell or the notes of a horn, but this feeling could arise only in the absence of a due apprehension of the situation, and of the circumstances of the case. Those persons who have not property to live independently of industry must exert themselves for their support in some way or other, and industry is pleasant in proportion to its regularity and moderation, and the prospect it affords of being effective of comfortable subsistence. Every person entering an association of the kind contemplated, would be sensible that it could exist only by the industry of all its members; that by the exertion of this, every one would be pursuing his own true interests *as a proprietor*, by contributing to the utmost of his ability to the welfare of the society; that as his entrance into it was voluntary, so would his continuance in it be, consistently with its constitution, and the experience of two or three years would convince its members that the daily quantity of labour and attention requisite to its concerns would be very far less than is given by tradesmen and mechanics in Europe, and in Great Britain especially, to procure their comparatively precarious subsistence. On the other hand, one might suppose a due appreciation of his situation would be calculated to make every individual cheerfully alert in the performance of his portion of assistance in a compact based on the sacred principle of equity, and that of mutuality of possession and enjoyment.

An agricultural and manufacturing community, subsisting its members in plenty and respectability upon the plan of that benefactor of his race, Mr. Robert Owen, and somewhat similar to those of the Friends and Harmonians, would be but carrying the principle of Benefit societies as far as it would go, resting it upon that of an equitable reciprocation of services amongst all its members, which, could the industry and concord of them be established, might be rendered a secure and pleasant mode of subsistence to hundreds, and in different communities perhaps to thousands.

Although this plan of society should appear to be not without objection, or even objectionable on several accounts, it may be asked, whether the evils of insolvency or bankrupcy, of dependence and poverty, or of prisons and workhouses are not greater and more numerous than those of the plan contemplated could be? Supposing such a compact to be practicable, (and with the societies of the Harmonians and Friends of America before our eyes who can doubt it?) he that was hostile to it, merely on account of its being an innovation, would be hostile to his own nature and fellow men. Such a system of society could not indeed hold together, unless a large majority of its members were persons of established principles of virtue and of matured knowledge, combined with habits of activity and industry; who surveying its objects and appreciating its advantages, were inflexibly devoted to its welfare; and who could regulate their conduct on a perfect conviction of the tractableness of mankind in all cases and situations, consistently with their knowledge or apprehension of fitness, propriety and real utility.*

*"On the experience of a life devoted to the subject, I hesitate not to say, that the members of any community may by degrees be trained to live without idleness, without poverty, without crime, and without punishment."

"Any general character, from the best to the worst, from the most ignorant to the most enlightened, may be given to any community, even to the world at large, by the application of proper means."

"Human nature, save the minute differences which are ever found in all the compounds of the creation, is one and the same in all; it is without exception universally plastic, and by judicious training the infants of any one class in the world may be readily formed into men of any other class; even to believe and declare that conduct to be right and virtuous, and to die in its defence, which their parents had been taught to believe and say was wrong and vicious, and to oppose which, those parents would also have willingly sacrificed their lives."

"All men may, by judicious and proper laws and training, readily acquire knowledge and habits which will enable them, if they be permitted, to produce far more than they need for their support and enjoyment; and thus any population in the fertile parts of the earth, may be taught to live in plenty and in happiness, without the checks of vice and misery."

"Train any population rationally and they will be rational."

"In those characters which now exhibit crime, the fault is obviously not in the individual, but the defect proceeds from the system in which the individual has been

Some persons might object that the leisure and security attending such a plan of society would be productive of idleness, insubordination and vice; to which it might be answered that this result would depend on the previous education and habits of its members, and exclusively of the influence of their new social compact; but if there were those who acted so injuriously to themselves and the society to which they belonged, the door of withdrawment from it would be opened to them, however reluctantly, by a vote of the members, through which it would be necessary for such unwise persons to pass, before their evil example had had time to be extensively productive of mischief, but not before they had proved themselves irreclaimable to virtue and social obligation.

Some persons might also object that a community of the kind contemplated would in the course of years by the natural progress of population become too numerous for the means of support contained within it; to which it is answered, that it is not pretended that this plan of society would be wholly without its difficulties, as it is probable no human arrangement of society could be. Difficulty however, like danger and misfortune, is generally greatest in apprehension, and regulating our conduct upon right principles, we may always trust to events. In a society in which every thing was previously established on the simple and natural law of justice and reciprocation, and in which every head of a family would be equally interested in the adjustment of any difficulty that arose, the unanimity of sentiment that would exist in regard to previous circumstances would form more than half the conquest of every source of embarrassment that occurred; and the one contemplated being of very gradual approach, and anticipated by the sagacity of the senior associates, would be met in good season, and perhaps adjusted to the satisfaction and welfare of the community.

trained. Withdraw those circumstances which tend to create crime in the human character, and crime will not be created."

"The worst formed disposition . . . . will not long resist a firm, determined, well-directed, persevering kindness."

"The character of man is, without a single exception, always formed for him."

"Man never did, nor is it possible he ever can, form his own character."

"The kind and degree of misery or happiness experienced by the members of any community, depends on the characters which have been formed in the individuals which constitute the community."

"Hitherto indeed, in all ages, and in all countries, man seems to have blindly conspired against the happiness of man, and to have remained as ignorant of himself as he was of the solar system prior to the days of Copernicus and Galileo."

Vide "Owen's new view of Society."

A work which for correctness of views of human nature and society, and benevolence of design, is calculated to form the basis of a vast improvement of the condition of mankind.

The minds of men being at ease, and satisfied with the previous circumstances of their situation, it is impossible to say what sacrifices would not be offered by individuals for the good of the community, upon the occurrence of a natural inconvenience of the kind supposed, or how far a generous spirit of accommodation might be carried. If men can be found in the wide and tumultuous world to sacrifice themselves for their country, surely the associates of a happy christian and philosophic community would not be found inferior in disinterestedness. The means of support to a community of this kind would of course have a limit, and when the number of its members approached its maximum, if no other remedy could be devised, a resolution might be passed providing, under circumstances, for the withdrawment of a certain number of its members, or providing for the formation of another community in a convenient situation, toward which every facility would of course be afforded; but it is impossible to conjecture what would be the resources of a society that was animated by a sentiment of unanimity, approaching to that of obligation or friendship towards each other. There can be little doubt that human virtue would shine as brightly in this situation as in any recorded in history, and in all probability with this difference, that it would be *general* and not *isolated*. The condition being new, consequently the character of the individuals composing such a community would become altogether altered and raised, as is the case in a limited degree with respect to the working citizens of the United States of America in comparison with those other countries. My imagination is warm enough to believe that in a society properly constituted and regulated, besides being productive of a secure and pleasant subsistence, every scientific pursuit, and every elegant amusement might be participated, not only without injury, but to the happiness of its members. It would of course possess a good library, a well supplied reading room, and apparatus for philosophical research, and secure a liberal education for the children.

I can imagine evening field sports, and sometimes fetes-champetres, in which recourse might be had, according to the taste of the parties, to various juvenile recreations, in which the grave and the elderly might occasionally join without dimunition of the respect and veneration due to them. If industry were supported by virtue, it could not be rendered too cheerful, never losing sight of moderation, which is the standard of wisdom and enjoyment. There can indeed be no doubt that the Deity is most acceptably worshipped when man is most rationally or morally happy, and that he then best answers the object of his creation.

In the case of ladies and gentlemen becoming members of a community of this kind, who might not be used to manual employment of any very necessary or useful kinds, and who could not be rendered immediately or wholly serviceable to the society, such persons might be allowed to avail themselves externally to the society of any acquirements they possessed that were not required by it, upon their paying into the general fund an equivolent for their personal services, or such portion of these as were not afforded to the society. If this adjustment could not in all cases be rendered so precisely exact as some persons might require, it should never be forgotten that the community was one of reciprocal benefit, and that if a little room were left open in regard to the admission of some of its members, for the exercise of liberality or benevolence, it would be of no disadvantage to the society, but probably contribute to its prosperity, as it would certainly augment its respectability and its happiness. All could not be equally useful members perhaps at first, and none could contribute more than the talents they possessed; but general application and industry would soon equalize the services of the members, and a scale of compensation to the society on a valuation of time, might be enacted more particularly for those members whose talents were deemed of inferior value, and whose circumstances required their occasional absence.

Not to anticipate any speedy or general adoption of this plan of society, it would yet be a libel equally upon human virtue and human genius to say that society can never be modelled *locally or in small detached portions*, upon principles of equity and reciprocation. It needs but a conviction of its propriety and desirableness to be attempted; and perhaps it need but be attempted perseveringly and consistently to be brought to success. It would materially lessen the chance of failure if a community were composed wholly of persons of one denomination or class of christians, as they would thereby possess the strongest incentive to agreement, notwithstanding that a religion whose bond is love ought to unite all denominations. The plan of society under consideration seems particularly applicable to persons of small property and of contracted connections; to persons who have been unfortunate in business, but who have retained their integrity; and those whose businesses may be said to be nearly superseded or dissipated in the fluctuations of trade. It is adapted to the relief of those who are unable to withstand the excessive competition, the redundancy of talent, or the pressure of the times singly; and to those who prefer tranquillity and security to turmoil and uncertainty.

Looking at the principle of trade and commerce *morally and independently of its present general or universal necessity*, what is it but petty craft from the merchant to the pedler? The taking advantage of the ignorance or the unfavorable situation of others for the procurement or production of an article, and by the disposal of it at a profit to ourselves to draw by this means a source of subsistence or of wealth at a great expense of every feeling of fellowship, of honor and generosity. Is not, *philosophically speaking*, the toil of producing the elements of subsistence and the conveniences of life, sufficient, without the addition of art or craft in the dealings of mankind with each other? It has been said of old that, "*as mortar sticketh between the stones so sticketh fraud between buying and selling*," and it cannot be supposed that the Deity designed that mankind should be petty tricksters upon one another rather than equal and just helpmates. Why could not the intercourse of mankind be founded on just and reciprocal principles, were it not for the monopoly of the earth, and the various corrupt circumstances and tyrannies of ancient political society? At any rate there is no natural impossibility that mankind should at a future period associate in detached portions upon a principle of reciprocal justice. They are the extremes of society as it exists that chiefly require reconciling, and being brought nearer to each other. The wealth and idleness of the one being brought to the relief of the poverty and slavery of the other. The extremes of society form its greatest deformity and infelicity. Society as it exists may be compared to a connected mass of building, the greater portion of which exhibits poverty and wretchedness of construction, a second portion of which indicates considerable convenience and comfort, and the third portion, though occupying much less space than either of the others, and especially than the first, is composed of erections of such lofty and commanding sizes as to cause the whole to appear an unsightly assemblage of irregularity and disproportion. There is no continuity of design or proportion of parts as yet in society. Society is doubtlessly susceptible of vast improvement, and when the laboring classes shall have become as well-informed as the middle classes are, great alterations it may be hoped will be effected *as the simple result of discussion*, and a more equal balance of possession and enjoyment established through the whole. It is not to be supposed that the present fortuitous jumble of dependance, and unjust and partial possession of the earth, the mere result of conquest and subjection, is the best possible economy of things. Every link in the chain of society as it exists is dependance, which is riveted throughout by the fear of destitution. How inferior this, to what would be a rational fellowship of industry and possession, to an exclusion of want, and of apprehension for the future! Men being by nature equal, physically and morally considered, having the same wants and the same capacities for enjoyment, wherefore, it might be enquired of those who *profess* to believe in a future state, is not the intercourse of mankind founded on principles of reciprocation and justice, analagous to their nature and destination? It is not to be believed that the Deity can view with perfect complacency a state of things that sets a small portion of mankind at an immense distance from the majority; that gives to a comparatively few individuals almost boundless means of gratification, by which the mass are impoverished; whilst many can scarcely obtain the elements of subsistence; and numbers are impressed into the service of vice till they become as depraved as human nature will admit, inflicting on the whole body of society, with a knowledge of their crimes, a portion of their infelicity. Nine tenths of the miseries and the crimes of mankind result from this unequal and unjust state of things. If injustice and its consequent evils exist extensively in society, and human reason can devise the means of their correction or material abatement, wherefore should not this be attempted, *as far as it is seen and acknowledged,* upon the eternal bases of equity and reciprocation? The constant pursuit of individual gain is at variance with the duties and affections of man, considered as a social and generous being. The opulent dealer who extracts a large profit from the poor man; the wealthy manufacturer who holds the mechanic to his machinery at a price just commensurate with his individual subsistence, to say nothing of that of his wretched family; and the rich landed proprietor who retains those who till his fields in a state of penury and pauperism, are excrescences on God's earth, which he gave to all mankind. Individual condition in humble life in Europe, and especially in Great Britain, has constantly to withstand what is to it the two-fold evils of advancing machinery and increasing population, rendering it daily more precarious and more scanty. Witness the frequency and increasing extent of the combinations and strikings of the operative classes. And what could be more rational and honorable than an attempt to construct society, *though locally and upon a small scale*, upon a plan of common property and benefit, aloof from the petty concealments and intricacies, the selfishness, the jealousies, the proverbial absence of friendship, the casualties and opposing interests of ordinary commercial life, which in proportion to its success would be productive of peace, goodwill, security and contentment. Such a plan of society would tend most materially and directly to soften the passions, and consequently to encrease the enjoyment of life; would remove the evils of dependence, also those vast sources of distress insolvency and bankruptcy and family dissensions arising from the unequal distribution of property; and would have a powerful tendency to check the ravages of insanity and suicide, which more frequently result from pecuniary embarrassment than any other cause. As society exists, the journeyman shoe maker or taylor has infinitely the advantage of the man of education and refinement, who through misfortune is reduced to poverty; and the cook or housemaid has infinitely the advantage of her mistress, if the latter is through any calamity brought to indigence. How many respectable females are rendered pennyless through the commercial misfortune, imprudence, or dissipation of male relatives, to whom their property was entrusted! And how many men are from the fluctuations and vicissitudes of the commercial world reduced to a situation in comparison with which that of the journeyman artisan *in employment* is enviable! The distress of the humble poor is frequently obvious to the sight, besides being rendered so to the ear, but the difficulties and sufferings experienced in middle and genteel life are silent and unseen. Misfortune however may be said to be proportionate to the sensibility of the unfortunate; and the utmost splendour of commercial life is but splendid dependance, which is far inferior in real dignity to moderate competence or self-subsistence, however humble. That which is wanting to society is a foundation in equity to which all might appeal, and from which all might derive support by the performance of an equitable quantity of labour. As society exists, the condition of every individual not born to hereditary property is perfectly fortuitous. Cannot this defect be remedied? Shall it never be remedied? The statesman says no; the philanthropist, that it ought to be, *if it be practicable.* As society exists mankind subsists by individual ingenuity and address, and by the advantages which one individual obtains over another by whatever means, instead of associating upon a principle of natural equity befitting rational beings, which would put vicissitude and want and distress at defiance. If Christendom were truly christian, there would exist this spirit of justice and of concord. The christian world however will never fully deserve that name until society be modelled upon and governed by its precepts, to the neglect or non-effectiveness of civil and military government, to which latter powers christianity has hitherto been considered merely as an adjunct, and not as that divine code of laws which should supersede all others that are opposed to it, as the products only of human weakness or depravity. When the christian world becomes really christian, armies will cease to be marshalled to settle its disputes, to check the progress of knowledge or crush its efforts of improvement. Literature will not be curtailed and fashioned by censorships, like trees by the shears of a whimsical gardener. A congress of wise and good men from all its parts, (not of belted chieftains,) will settle the first in peace and welcome and foster the last.

Human nature being not merely ductile, but its ductility being almost without limit, the basis of an improved system of society would be the effect of a general perception of error in the common estimation of wealth and power. True wealth is self-enjoyment; true power, the command over one's-self; and no perception of individual property and power as they exist, (which generally afflict by the weight of anxiety they entail,) could equal the enjoyment that would result from the consciousness of being the free and equal member of an equitably constituted society, which would be proportionably relieved of vice and the numerous infelicities attending the existing intercourse of mankind. History is decidedly hostile to the opinion that individual enjoyment is the general concomitant of power, notwithstanding that the love, and consequent pursuit of power is the general foible of mankind. "Uneasy lies the head that wears a crown," and arduous are its duties if faithfully and honourably performed. The eminences of power and wealth are doubtlessly like other objects of human pursuit that have merely personal gratification or aggrandizement for their end, being more attractive and promising at a distance than satisfactory or pleasurable in the possession. A period may indeed arrive when the resources of ingenuity in manufactures and commerce may fail to such an extent as to render an adjustment of the condition of mankind locally or nationally, upon principles of equity imperiously necessary, as those resources have long failed to the purpose of general subsistence without the vast aid of the poor laws, those wretched supports of indigence which just enable it to limp along or to prolong its sufferings. A period may arrive when from the increased numbers of mankind manual labor shall of necessity supersede the use of machinery, as the latter is now permitted or rather stimulated for purposes of revenue and commerce to operate to the injury and deprivation of millions. When manufactures may be so diffused, improved and simplified in their production throughout the commercial world as to render the shiftings and refinements of commercial treaties, and of import and of export regulations, of little or no avail; when national independence or self-subsistence shall be deemed the standard of security and respectability; and when human knowledge may have attained that maturity of growth as no longer to tolerate the existing crudities of the commercial and political world. That human society is in a state of great immaturity is evident, or mankind would not be subject to all the evils attendant on the vicissitudes and fluctuations of the political and commercial world. Nor would the vast majority of mankind be miserably dependent on the minority. This cannot exist when the former shall be as well informed as the latter, when knowledge shall shed its rays like the meridian sun. It does not indeed exist in the United States of America which seem destined to reform both the political and social system of Europe. Nearly the whole continent of America now invites to a better order of things. Its desert regions from nearly one end of it to the other inviting the philosopher and the philanthropist to aim at a better construction of human society; a construction less opposed to the equality of natural right and of natural wants, and better adapted to moral improvement and social enjoyment.

In regard to the different degrees of enjoyment experienced in two situations of the established form of society, it may be enquired which generally appear to possess the greatest share of enjoyment, those persons who are immersed in business to the whole extent of their property, or those whose competence is ascertained, and who live a retired life? I imagine that in nineteen cases out of twenty, the latter situation is by far the preferable one, and that most persons would allow this. If so, then would that be the best system of society that should the most nearly assimilate to this preferable situation, consistently with the welfare of all its members. If man be a social being, society should be universally a source of support, of improvement and happiness, instead of being as it is in innumerable cases, a source of destitution, of depravity, and consequent misery; and that would be the best plan of society that was the most equal and reciprocal, and consequently the most rational and virtuous. It has however been the lamentable conduct of statesmen, (though in some cases no doubt unintentionally) to degrade and brutalize human nature to the utmost, to render it familiar with privation and suffering, and every moral corruption. If revenue have been collected and armies kept on foot, private condition with the artisan and the labourer has been too generally a matter of little moment. A certain extent of destitution has indeed been considered by eminent statesmen as an essential circumstance of political government, seeing that without that source of impressment into its service its strongest arm of power could not be maintained. But if society be a good in its natural tendency, it may be enquired, whether it be sufficiently perfect; whether it cannot be rendered more perfect, more equitable, and consequently less productive of misery? If society be susceptible of improvement upon natural and equitable principles, then would that be the preferable system of intercourse in which the selfish, the violent, and malignant passions would be least liable to be agitated; in which the turmoil of pecuniary and political pursuits would be quashed; in which the elation and depression of mind attending the vicissitudes of fortune would be subdued into a moderate and even pleasurable quantity of beneficial employment; in which the acquisition of knowledge, and the various enjoyments of society would have the freest scope; in which the sacred tie of marriage would be allowed to take place at suitable ages unobstructed by considerations of property and the frequent averice of parents; in which the most deplorable circumstances of society as it exists would not have place; and in which the education of youth would all form primary and essential objects of the care of its members. If there be reason in this, both virtue and humanity bid us hope that a gradual improvement in society, commensurate with the progress of knowledge and of the true economy of life, may take place. Nothing further is wished or contemplated, as it would not be reasonable to set a man or a number of men to grope for a treasure in the dark, or to make experiments that might result in their injury or destruction. But if the foregoing observations are warranted by truth and the real nature of things, then may one day the restless votaries of ambition and of wealth in Europe borrow valuable instruction from the Societies of Harmonians and Friends in America, or from societies constituted upon similar but improved and equitable principles, adapted to all the purposes of moral and refined society and every human relationship. All persons of habits of business must be sensible that it is a desirable thing to abridge the hours devoted to it within a space to allow of a due attention to domestic concerns, to personal comfort, to the instruction of children, to reading, to scientific pursuit, recreation and the enjoyment of society, all which objects are greatly obstructed by the enormous portion of time devoted by tradesmen to their businesses in order to support their numerous responsibilities; and journeymen, artisans and labourers in employment have no time whatever for these desirable and necessary objects, except on Sundays; all which circumstances however would be most materially and beneficially attained upon the equitable and rational plan of society contemplated, which would also as naturally tend to check the selfish and sordid affections as the existing form of society contributes to excite them. What could be more proper than for various artisans and agriculturists after the work of the day was over, and they had had time to refresh themselves at home, and to attend to various matters, to meet as inclination prompted in a reading room or library, for the purpose of reading or conversation on subjects of physical science or any other more interesting to them, instead of living in ignorance and poverty, neglecting their families from necessity, and from bad habits and associations, wasting their little leisure time, their money and health at public houses? The plan of society under consideration is simply an extensive and equitable partnership in all the essentials of life, or a complete and perfect Benefit Society, based in the equal or proportionate stake of all its members, in which the social feelings would be more freely and constantly exercised than in the present form of society. Though it be allowed that the present state of society in Europe is commensurate with its progress in knowledge, and that it is a great amelioration of that of the Gothic or Feudal ages, it does not follow that a still better order of things shall not take place when that highest of all the sciences, *the science of human life in society,* shall be better understood and more justly appreciated in its enjoyments and object. The present form of society in Europe is merely a modification or amelioration of Feudalism, be that modification or amelioration great or little, and the problem for the philosopher and the philanthropist of the present day is, whether society be susceptible of a basis and super-structure in equity, consistently with the natural equality and dignity of mankind.

If then reason, equity and humanity be allied against ancient political society with all its tyrannies and usurpations, the question is whether the former shall always be overborne by the crude assemblage of circumstances derived from the infancy and pristine ignorance of mankind; or whether that form of society or settling of things which conquest or brute force, aided by superstition, impressed on the weakness and ignorance of mankind, shall always prevail over that which reason would dictate, which equity and humanity demand, or which a council of philosophic friends of mankind would prescribe, acting upon the present or future knowledge of mankind? Shall improvements and discoveries be constantly going forward in physics, and none be made in society, or the art of living in society? And notwithstanding that prejudiced persons are apt to scoff at all plans for the amelioration of the condition of mankind as merely visionary or Utopian schemes, it is consolatory to reflect, that the opposition alluded to is, in some instances, no purer in its source than was that of the Roman clergy against the reforming doctrines of Erasmus and Luther; and no more founded in nature or truth than that of the Spanish nobles against the geographical principles of Christopher Columbus.

It may remain for the writer of the foregoing to assure his readers that no part of it is intended in any manner to wound the feelings of individuals of any class or station of life whatever. Individual excellence is to be found in every rank and walk of life, and is perfectly compatible with great imperfection in the frame of government and that of society generally, which imperfection is deducible from the circumstances of their origin and progress. It is incumbent on the privileged orders of society only to bear their ascendency with meekness and liberality, it not being the fault of any individual belonging to them that he was born to a title not known in moral estimation, or to the possession of thousands of acres of the earth under a system of things which denies to the vast majority a square foot. Although the iron sword of an ancestor or the lavish gift of a conqueror includes but a slender *moral* title to the possession of an estate which would afford thousands of fellow-beings subsistence, it is not to be expected that the hereditary possessors of the earth will yield their monopoly of it until they shall all be presented with what they may deem an equivalent in a greater degree of moral and social happiness, resulting from equity being established as the foundation of society. The privileged orders of the present generation and those for some ages past are altogether innocent of the monstrous disparity of circumstances deducible from conquest and priestcraft acting upon the ignorance and weakness of mankind. The error or crime of the case is attributable only to the system, and not to any class of individuals who are the subjects of it. It is for the present generation only to take care that the "*march of sound knowledge*" be facilitated to the utmost. That improvement be not confined to physical science merely; but that it be admitted to modify, or remodel society, as the pressure of political circumstances on individual condition, or more correct views of human nature or of the economy of life may suggest.

The writer when in Philadelphia, in June, 1823, had put into his hand by an acquaintance, (an opulant farmer and grazier from the west of England, who was then seeking an establishment for himself and an extensive connection in the United States), a pamphlet written by a Mr. Brayshaw from Scotland, who had then recently arrived in America for the purpose of making a tour of the western states, with the view to ascertain a situation for the establishment of a society upon the principle of an equitable participation of labour and capital, from which the following is an extract:

"According to the present form or construction of society, the interest of every individual is placed in opposition to the interests of other individuals, and in opposition to the interests of society at large. In my own opinion,by carefully tracing effects to their causes, I shall be able to prove that this opposition of interests is the fundamental cause of the greatest part of the evils which now afflict or ever have afflicted the human species; and I think if I succeed in this point, I shall be warranted in concluding that if it be possible to give such a construction to human society as shall have the effect of uniting the common interests of mankind, by making the interest of the whole the interest of every individual, and the interest of every individual the interest of the whole body, such a state of things would remove the causes of the evil, and banish the greatest part of the miseries which at present afflict mankind."

A SKETCH

for the formation of a

SOCIETY OF MUTUAL CO-OPERATION

and

COMMUNITY of PROPERTY,

To be composed of tradesmen, farmers, clerks, mechanics, &c. intended to be established in the state of New York.

———

Art. 1. It is proposed that the Society shall in the first instance consist of about a hundred families, exclusively of single members.

2. That the capital to be introduced by every adult male member be not less when arrived in America and at the settlement, than £11. 5s. (50 dollars,) nor more than £900. (4000 dollars.)

3. That the whole of the property of the Society be divided into shares, and that a share be equal to the smallest subscription, viz. £11. 5s.

4. That the less opulent members shall have the opportunity by their industry of increasing their property in the society in proportion to that of the other members, and that an equitable adjustment of the value of time be made for the whole of the members.

5. That the affairs of the Society be conducted by a rotary committee, or board of management, of all its members in succession, which committee or board of management to be chosen monthly, quarterly, or half yearly. To consist of ——— members.

6. That the capital of the Society, after the purchase of the land, the expense of the *first* clearing, fencing and building,

(This outline of a self-subsistent community was made by the author of the foregoing pages at the suggestion of a friend from New York, where a few gentlemen contemplated the formation of a society of this kind, toward which it was proposed that every one designing to become a member should contribute a plan or certain articles; since which time, and within a few days, he has been fortunate enough to meet with Mr. Owen's "AMERICAN DISCOURSES, &c." and the "ARTICLES OF AGREEMENT OF THE LONDON CO-OPERATIVE SOCIETY," in which publications the principles of this plan of society are detailed, and its advantages and general attractiveness rendered apparent.)

(this to be done by natives) the purchase of cattle and other live stock, implements, machinery, &c., be vested in the United States Bank, in the names of all the members of the Society.

7. That every male member of the Society shall engage to employ himself in any and every manner that shall at any time be determined by the existing board of management; that there shall be no exclusive employments; and that every male member be eligible to every employment or office to which he is nominated by the managing board or committee for the time being, or by the election of not less than two-thirds of the members of the Society.

8. That it is a radical principle of this society that labour of every necessary or useful description is honourable; that true respectability consists in integrity of character and utility of conduct. That what must be done by some may be done by all. That idleness, as opposed to usefulness and to honesty is despicable, and to be abhorred.

9. That the constitution of this society be enacted in every article by at least three-fourths of all the members, and that not less than three-fourths of all the members be at all times competent to alter or amend it.

10. That it shall be allowable for any number of the members to practice or follow any trade or calling required for the benefit of the society; and that the artisans of any particular trade do instruct as many of the other members as may be desired by the existing board of management; in return for which the members so teaching, will themselves receive instruction as the wants or circumstances of the society require; reciprocal service for the benefit of the whole being the principle of action throughout the community. In some cases the thanks of the society may be voted to an individual who evinces a particular readiness, activity, or perseverance in this respect.

11. That the value of time devoted to the concerns of the society in whatever trade, calling, or office, be considered uniform and equal amongst all its male members; and that the average length of a day's work required by the society, exclusively of time for meals or refreshment, throughout the year be eight hours, excepting on particular emergencies when it may be extended to any length required. That it be considered at a subsequent period of the establishment whether the term of eight hours' labour per day may not be reduced to six.

12. That every male member do learn to practice some

one necessary or useful trade or calling, in addition to the performance of his duty as an agriculturist or other labourer; that domestic manufactures in as great a variety as possible may be constantly going forward.

13. That no exception whatever shall be taken, or objection made, on account of the religious persuasions or opinions of any member of this society. That the expression of opinion be as free as air. That moral character be solely looked to, this being indispensable to the welfare and happiness of the society collectively and individually.

14. That the wives and children of members be allowed to work at any business or calling that they may be desirous of, at regulated prices and on regulated terms. That the wives of members have the right of voting and of expressing their opinions at all general meetings of the society, and that the females elect each other to all the departments of female employment of the society.

15. That the children of the members be educated upon the Lancastrian plan, and that their education be rendered as liberal and philosophic as possible; to the exclusion however of the retarding and profitless burthen of the dead languages. That every arrangement be made to facilitate the society, recreation, and instruction of the infant children of the members.

16. That the principles of the society be in the strictest sense equal and democratic; that equity and wisdom, and not property may govern. That to this end, as the interest of the proprietor of one share will be equal to that of the proprietor of five or ten, considered as the whole of their vested property respectively, and in a regard to the welfare of their families in the society, that the rights of the members be in all respects equal, that all votes be equal, and that no member have more than one vote upon any question or occasion whatever.

17. That all disputes, misunderstandings, or dissatisfaction arising between members, be settled by arbitration, the arbitrators to be chosen by ballott, either from the existing board of management or from the members in general.

18. That the society have the power of expelling any member for continued idleness, misconduct, or immorality, by a vote of not less than three-fourths of the whole of the members; and that the property of such individual be valued and paid to him at the time of his quitting the society.

19. That no member of the society shall go to law with, or sue another member for debt, or upon any account whatever;

the doing which, shall be deemed on the part of the individual an act of self-expulsion from this society, which, if necessary, shall maintain the defendant's cause.

20. That the society, collectively, may purchase the property of any member that may be desirous of withdrawing from it, but that members can not sell or transfer their shares to each other, the whole of the property, with the exception of household furniture, clothing, books, plate, &c., being the property of the society. That the property in shares of every member being vested in the society, be disposable only by the society at a general meeting; and that a majority of not less than two-thirds of the whole of the members be requisite in all cases of the sale of shares. This restriction is enacted solely to prevent partial interests and obligations; the servitude of the less opulent or poorer members upon the others; and all doubtfulness, perplexity, or confusion in respect to immoveable property, and its consequent disputes.

21. That as a true and equal economy should govern every circumstance of the society, it be enacted, that no more horses or cattle shall be kept by the society than are necessary or useful. That no member shall keep any horse, cow, sheep or pigs for his private use without making a fair allowance to the society for such part of their keep as is derived from the society's property.

22. That the horses, cattle, sheep, pigs, fowls, ducks, geese, &c., the property of the society, be equitably used and participated by all the members; and every article of consumption, when necessary, rated at the time's market price, and every family debited with the quantity or amount of its demands or consumption; which debit, together with that on account of wearing apparel, &c., be regularly placed against the amount of its earnings, and the balance placed to the account of capital in the society's stock of every family once in every year.

23. That regular and correct accounts be kept of the society's property, and of all its transactions, both internal and external.

24. That convenient stores be kept of all the society's property for disposal to its members, or for sale to the public; and that the primitive and fair principle of barter upon a valuation by the quantity of time and labour employed in production, be acted upon to the utmost extent, both within, and without the society.

25. That every member shall devote his time as regu-

lated by the society to its concerns and interests, and be resident on its land.

26. That after the daily employment of eight hours in the service of the society, every member be wholly at his own disposal, and may employ himself for the remainder of his time in any manner that his inclination may prompt. That the products of the private and extra industry of the members be offered to the society at fair prices, and if purchased by it, that the parties be credited by the amount, or should the society not purchase such produce of the extra industry of its members, that the latter be at liberty, after having offered it to the society, to dispose of it out of the society for their own private benefit.

27. That any member wishing to quit the society may at Christmas in each year give written notice of such wish, upon receiving which, the society must within a month after, make an election of either purchasing the share in the society's stock of such individual and family, or of accepting a substitute for him, subject in either case to the approval of not less than two-thirds of the whole of the members.

28. That a law be enacted to settle and determine the mode in which the widows and children of deceased members shall succeed to their property and be retained in the society, rendering to the widows and children of worthy members the utmost protection, sympathy and kindness; as also the manner of payment to such widows and children as may be desirous of withdrawing from the society.

29. That a piece of ground be enclosed and kept sacred as a burial ground, for such of the members as may prefer being interred within the society's land. That grave stones be erected, and the ground kept in the utmost order. That all funerals be performed by the society and without expense to the afflicted family.

30. That every member of the society do occupy for himself and family in permanency, a cottage and garden, comprised within about a quarter of an acre of ground. That the cottages of the society be built detached, (or two together, if deemed preferable,) all of the same size, and upon the same plan, convenient for a family.

31. That the cottages of the society be built so as to form a spacious square, open at the angles, and open also in the centre of each side, of sufficient width to form streets, in order to provide for the increase of its members without crowding the

square. That the square forming the village have a circular enclosure within it, in the centre of which, to be erected with all possible neatness, a Building for Public Worship, and the various purposes of the society. That the enclosure be laid out into walks, planted with fruit and other trees, furnished with benches, and kept with all the neatness of a London square. The enclosure to serve as a play-ground for the children, and for the evening walks and recreations of the members. That the storehouses, granaries, factories, workshops, tannery, brewhouse, barns, stables, cattle-sheds, stack yards, &c., &c., be arranged in the outer square beyond the gardens of the village, and having a good road all round between these and the front of those buildings and appurtenances; which road to be connected with the inner square by streets formed from the angles of both squares, and others from the centre of the sides of each. It is presumed that this plan would embrace contiguity and general convenience, at the same time that offensiveness of all kinds would be removed to a desirable distance. It would perhaps be desirable that the central building were divided on the ground floor into two compartments, and that one of these were exclusively appropriated to religious purposes, the different denominations into which the society might divide itself, occupying it alternately, or by a wise expansion of christian fellowship, or of a sentiment of unanimity, resolve to know no differences of sect, but to use it in common, to read the scriptures in common, and to allow every reader or officiating member to expound, and to express his opinions, without controversy. An upper spacious room might be made to answer the purpose of a library, a reading, lecture, and school room; and be used for the evening amusement of the members. A small tower furnished with a clock with four faces and a bell, would be a desirable addition to the village Hall, and if the roof or tower were railed round it would form a pleasant observatory.

32. That no member be admitted into, or retained in the society in the separate or exclusive character of a minister of the gospel. That this office be free to all the members, and that it confer no privileges whatever.

33. That the growth of the most useful kinds of roots and vegetables be as much an object with the society as the cultivation of grain, by which the time and labour of the members in raising vegetables in their gardens will be materially lessened, and as by this means a more abundant supply of food for the cattle and live stock will be provided, particularly for winter use.

That the cultivation of fruit trees be also an object of attention with the society.

34. That the society's stock be valued, and all accounts appertaining to the society and to individuals be settled and balanced once in every year, and all surplus capital invested in the stock of the United States Bank in the names of all the members.

35. That in order to adopt and preserve the best economy in the society, agricultural, manufacturing and domestic, a friendly correspondence be maintained with all other similar communities as far as circumstances will allow, and that a deputation of two members be occasionally made to visit Harmony or any other community, for the purpose of obtaining any particular information that the society may require.

The author of the foregoing sketch would be permitted to explain that he does not suppose that a society formed upon its principles would constitute a perfect ELYSIUM, he being fully aware that troubles, vexation and imperfection rest upon every thing human; but he would express it as his decided opinion that a society of honorable individuals, of regular business habits, each having the welfare of his family and that of the society at heart, could not fail of being productive of immense security, comfort and advantage to its members. The compact would be simply an equitable partnership in all the essentials of life and means of happiness. The foregoing is designed merely as an outline to be corrected and perfected by the joint labour of the associates and the results of experience.

From *Letters of William Pelham, written in 1825 and 1826.*

These letters were written by William Pelham to his son, William Creese Pelham of Zanesville, Ohio, in 1825 and 1826. The original letters are in the possession of the children of the late Louis Pelham at New Harmony, Indiana. The letters describe William Pelham's journey down the Ohio, stopping at Maysville, Cincinnati, Louisville and Mt. Vernon, with the arrival at New Harmony, where " a new society was about to be formed." They tell of the appearance of the town and mention some of the people gathering there, express unbounded enthusiasm for Robert Owen and his plans for improving the condition of society and describes many of the pleasures and hardships and daily life experienced during some months of the preliminary Society.

William Pelham was born in Williamsburg, Virginia, in 1759, a younger son of Peter Pelham and Ann Creese of Boston, and grand-son of Peter Pelham, of the Pelhams of Chichester, Sussex, England, who was the first mezzotint engraver in America. The family of this elder Pelham is described in the life of John Singleton Copley, the artist, whose mother married Mr. Pelham, as a household of unusual culture and congeniality, and the only one in New England at that time where painting and engraving were the predominant pursuits.

William Pelham when just grown to manhood, was for three years a surgeon in the American Revolution, the older brother whom he met at Maysville being Maj. Gen. Charles Pelham of Virginia. From his journals and account books, he seems to have taken passage more than once for England and at one time to have spent several years there. In a letter written in French, dated London, 1793, he says that the climate of London would break down the constitution of a man of iron and that he will return to his native land as it does not take an iron constitution to live in the climate of Virginia.

He evidently left England determined to change his profession as well as climate for about the year 1800 he opened a book shop and publishing house in Boston, selling out in 1811 and removing to Newark, New Jersey, and the following year to Philadelphia. At this time his young son, William Creese Pelham, was a pupil in the Neef school at the Falls of the Schuylkill and from this time a close friendship with the Neef family continued through their lives.

Having secured some land in Ohio through the Virginia Grant of 1812, William Pelham brought his family west in 1816 and began editing the Ohio Republic at Zanesville. In 1818 he was appointed postmaster and these pursuits he continued until he resigned to come to New Harmony in 1825.

Mr. Pelham was a scholarly man, a deep thinker, delicate in mind and constitution, and his long life as a servant of the public had wearied him of the grasping ways of the world and Robert Owen's communistic plans seemed to him a Utopia of peace for his declining years. So after much reading and some correspondence[1] relative to the matter, he came to New

---

1. A letter from William Owen, son of Robert Owen, will be found following the Pelham letters.

Harmony as described in these letters. From the letters we learn he found occupation at once in the accounting department of the store and when the Gazette was published he became one of the first editors. His son joined him in the spring of 1826 and the following year William Pelham purchased a farm near Mt. Vernon and died very suddenly at his home there on February third, 1827. He passed away just two months before the final dissolution of the society which had filled his last years with a great enthusiasm and interest.

CAROLINE CREESE PELHAM.

Opposite Buffington's Island,
Ohio River, Monday,
1st Aug., 1825,
3 o'clock, P. M.

My Dear Son:—

I have concluded to commence a letter at this place which, you will probably receive from Cincinnatti. It would give you pleasure to see how commodiously I am situated on board this boat. She is 70 or 75 feet long abt. 9 feet wide, very deeply laden with flour and destined to Florence in Alabama—navigated by six men beside the Capt., Absalom Boyd, who is a mild, quiet character,— in fact I have experienced nothing but civility and kindness from all on board. The following rude sketch will give you some idea of my local position in the vessel, premising that at Point Harmar I had a box or bunk made 6f. by $4\frac{1}{2}$ to contain the whole of my bed & bedding. . . . . [Sketch omitted.]

The right side is boarded up, & the whole covered with a substantial roof except the bow & stern. On the roof stands the caboose & the rowers here exercise themselves with 2 and sometimes 4 sweeps which they ply pretty constantly. At the foot of my bunk is an opening in the side of the vessel about 4 by 5 feet, closed at night by 2 folding shutters.

I am now sitting on the foot of my bed, my feet resting on a footboard placed for my convenience by one of my ship-mates. As my bunk is placed on 2 tier of barrels there is abundant space between my head & the roof of the boat. Capt. Boyd and myself lodge together, my bed being sufficiently large for both.

In the article of diet I do not fare so well, as I cannot relish the provision cooked for the crew; & have therefore lived almost entirely on tea & coffee & cheese. Give my kind compliments to Mrs. Mills and tell her that her friendly piece of cake formed almost the whole of my support from Zanesville to Marietta.

I wrote you a few lines from Marietta, which you will not

receive till Saturday next, (Aug. 6). On carrying it to the P. O. I met with Arius Nye, who informed me that Mr. Morris (whom I have not seen)—is no longer P. M. The fact is, he has been *Hamproned* out of the office by Squire Buell who contrived to convince the P. M. G. [Postmaster General] that he was a fitter person to succeeed Willcox than Morris.—This is the individual system in perfection.

This (Buffington's)—Island is always a troublesome place when the water is low. At some future time I will give you a minute account of the hardship, the labor & fatigue—& the immense, extravagant waste of human strength in navigating this river, &c &c. We have a strong active crew, and they make abundant use of the terms, God—Jesus Christ—Hell-fire & Damnation &c &c. &c., but in a manner somewhat different from the reverend clergy and certainly not with so much worldy profit. The most embarrassing place will be Letart's falls. If anything extraordinary occurs there I will note it, I am greatly at a loss for my Ohio Pilot which unfortunately I left behind, and there is nothing of the sort on board this vessel. I have only Melish's small map of Ohio & Indiana.

I feel greatly indebted to Joel Frazey for his kindness; he left me at N. Ayers Salt works—after a delightful ride. Remember me kindly to him.

Saturday Aug. 5, 11 o'clock A. M. We have just passed Portsmouth & Alexandria at the mouth of the Scioto— the former a neat, and even handsome little town— the latter consisting of 4 or 5 log-houses. We are still abt. 50 miles fr. Maysville, which we shall probably not reach till Monday, for we do not move faster than about 28 or 30 miles a day, & lie by every night. I am told, however, that we shall now get forward much faster than we have done while embarrassed with frequent bars, shoals & ripples. The Capt. & others on board calculate that we shall arrive at Mt. Vernon about the 17th or 18th of this month. By that time, I foresee, that I shall require 5 or 6 days rest on land, in some *quiet* lodging house during which I can refit, & get my clothes and blankets washed. I shall write to you immediately on reaching Mt. Vernon. In the meantime give my most affectionate love to Mary and tell her that her ample provision of tea, coffee, and sugar, will probably last me to the point of my destination.—Present me also my most kindly & affectionately to Mr. Peters. I have seen no newspaper *from any place* since I left Z. [Zanesville] and you would be surprised if you could really estimate the indifference I feel about general or local politics and the contentions of opposite parties. I feel once more free from all this turmoil & shall never engage in it again, whether I return or not. Present my kind respects to Mr. John Peters and Michael—to Mr. Sheward & wife & in general to all friends who may think me worthy of their enquiries.

After leaving Maysville I shall make some additions to this letter and then put into the P. O. at Cincinnati.—Our old friend Jim Marshall (who is one of the hired hands) has just brought me half of a fine, tho small water-melon. I have received much kindness from him.

The *steam* boat Lawrence, worked by *4 horses without steam*, (moving in a circle on her deck) has just passed us on her way up the river.

Direct the Ohio Repub. to W. Pelham, New Harmony, Ind.—on the paper itself—put it in a wrapper in the usual manner & direct the cover to Postmaster New Harmony, Ind. Do not forget to remember me kindly to Messrs. Keightley & Harris & Joel Frezey—& Mr. Mills &c. &c.

Monday 8th Aug. Yesterday afternoon, I had the inexpressable happiness of an affecting and joyful meeting with my brother and sister, after a separation of 39 years and 1 month. At first sight, he did not know me, but immediately recollected me on a nearer approach and for my part, I think I should have recognized him if I had met him in Zanesville—tho' we are both much altered by time. He has an interesting family—his 4 daughters and 2 sons were introduced to me. Chas. & Wm. are gone to Arkansas. Peter & Atkinson also absent—, the former at his station in Florida—the latter in Philad. My stay was necessarily short—& in the evening we passed by Maysville— but the evening was too far advanced for me to gain a distinct view of it. We are now, 11.30 A. M. 22 miles distant from Maysville. My brother's daus. accompanied me to the boat which lay ½ mile from the house. During this walk, the two eldest enquired particularly about you & Mary & expressed an earnest desire to see you both—not unmixed with the hope that you at least wd. make a run in the stage one of these days as far as Maysville.

The weather has been remarkably cool and pleasant on the river, since I left Zanesville—I have not been at all incommoded by heat—I make it a rule not to go on deck in the morning till the sun has dissipated the fog, when there is any—and always to retire to my birth soon after sunset.

We expect to arrive at Cincinn tonight or tomorrow morning. I shall therefore, here close my letter and seal it.

Yr truly affectionate Father,

Wm. Pelham.

On bd Post Boy, Ohio River.
Wednesd, noon, Aug. 10, 1825.
32 miles below Cincinn.

My dear Son—

We reached Cincinnati yesterday abt. 10 A.M. & left it about 6 in the evg. It has been so often and so well described, that it is needless for me to make any remarks on it. In fact I saw but little of the city my attention being almost wholly directed to other objects. What I did see, however, greatly surpassed my expectations. In approaching the city we counted 10 new steam boats on the stocks—besides some under repair. Boats continually passing up and down. It is really a handsome and even elegant town, containing an immense amt. of property.

As soon as we got to the shore I landed, and walking up the Main street I unexpectedly met our old friend Mr. John Scott, who resides there with his family. After the usual salutations, I enquired for, and he directed me to a first rate barber, who shaved me admirably, and cut off my pigtail!—the inconvenience of which I could no longer endure. While these operations were performing, Mr. Scott called in, accompanied by Jas. Taylor, Jr. of Zanesville who intended proceedg.—homewards this morning, and will, doubtless, call on you. I feel much indebted to his attentive kindness during my short stay in Cincinn. We went together to the office of the Literary Gaz. [Gazette] and afterwards to the P. O. where I saw Mr. Burke and Mr. Langdon, his asst. and deposited a letter which you will probably receive next Saty evg. Mr. Langdon accompanied me and introduced me to Mr. Wm. Bosson, a mercht. of Cincinn. who has lately returned from Harmony, where he has a brother—a member of the Community, to whom he gave me an introductory letter, and likewise to 2 merchts. in Louisville. Mr. B. also kindly introduced me to Messrs. Clark & Greene, agents for the Community. They offered me, & I accepted an introductory letter to Wm. Owen & likewise one to the Agents in Louisville. I spent *several hours* very agreeably in Mr. Bosson's store in conversation with him. He is a young man, very intelligent—apparently of an amiable disposition—

and devoted to the System. I learnt that Wm. Owen in the only member of his family now at Harmony—that his age is about 25, that the elder Mr. O. previous to his departure for Europe, called a meeting of all the members, in which mutual confidence was most strongly expressed. Mr. Owen dissolved the Committee appointed by himself, and requested the society to choose whomsoever they pleased—for some time this was declined, as all declared themselves well satisfied with his choice—but on being urged to it—they proceeded to the election; and the first person chosen was Wm. Owen. The greater part, if not all the other members were re-chosen. This is a pleasing mark of mutual confidence—another is, that Mr. Owen made an offer to the society of the whole establishment, land, buildings &c, at *their price own* and *on their own terms,* so well satisfied was he of their disposition and ability to carry the System into full & complete operation. Whether this offer was or was not accepted I did not learn, or have forgotten. It is certain, however, that things are going on well—the society has nearly overcome all the difficulties incident to such a heterogeneous congregation of strangers to each other. To my enquiry whether any new members cd. obtain admission, Mr. Bosson replied, that he thought no new families could as yet—but in *2 years,* the contemplated new village will be ready for the reception of members, as they are rapidly preparing materials. By the last accounts, the number of inhabitants amounted to 1050 or 1100. 370 children are daily taught in the schools—So far you will perceive I have heard nothing that has the least tendency to diminish my confidence in the System, either in principle or practice. On my arrival at Louisville, I shall close this letter, and put it into the Post Office there. At present I will only add that here I am again seated upright on the foot of my bed, my feet as before, resting conveniently on my foot board. I have cut the leather hinges of my provision box and the lid placed on my knees and covered with a towel forms a very convenient table for my meals—& writing. On the bed behind me are scattered my books and papers &c., &c., all very handy.—I write at my ease—without hurry or interuption—but after all—I would rather be seated in a comfortable house on shore, provided I hear not the tiresome question, "Is there any letter here for——". . .

Louisville, Sat. 13, Aug. 12 o'clock-noon.

We have just arrived here. The Capt. Finds it necessary to

unload almost entirely as he cannot pass the falls with more than 16 barrels of Flour—besides the winds ahead—I guess we shall not leave this place till noon tomorrow.

Unless something extraordinary occurs you will not hear from me again till I get to Mt. Vernon.

Ohio River 100 miles below Louisville.
Wed. 17 Aug. 1825.—

My dear William,

We reached Louisville last Saturday about noon, where I put a letter into the P. O. which you will probably receive next Tuesday evening. The Capt. immediately commenced unloading, and the boat passed the falls about sunset to Shippingport. In the meantime, I remained at Louisville & called on Messrs. I. & W. Stewart, agents for the Harmony Community, to whom I had a letter from Cincinnati. They have on hand a complete printing apparatus, (weighing about 2 tons) waiting an oppy. of forwarding it to Harmony. Here I regretted that our boat was so deeply laden that we could not take in on board. Here I also met with Mr. Larkin, a member of the Community, on his way down, with his famy—but excessively embarrassed how to contrive a conveyance. His report of affairs at Harmy [Harmony] which he left four weeks ago (to meet his famy—) corresponds exactly with all our previous information. I called at Dr. Galt's but had not the satisfaction of seeing him—his son (your former schoolfellow at Neef's) enquired particularly abt you. Next morning about Sunrise I set out to walk 2 miles to Shippingport & if the weather had been a little cooler shd have performed it with ease. Here I found them reloading the boat. Then I breakfasted & returned to Louisville to get some clothes I had left to be washed. When I returned to Shipt. the boat was reloaded, but everything so transposed, that I am not so conveniently located as before. However it matters little, for we shall be at Mt. Vernon next Saturday or Sunday. At Louisville I recd the O. R. [Ohio Republic] Aug. 6, the first I have seen since leaving Zanesville. The river is uncommonly low—we have had no rain but once—and that was of little or no service. We have left behind us everything we came in sight of—steamboats excepted.

I am writing this letter on board the boat intending, if possible, to put it into the P. O. at Troy, where we shall probably arrive tomorrow forenoon.

We started from Shippingport on Sunday afternoon abt 4

o'clock, and odd as it may appear to you, I was really glad to be on board again. I suffered excessively by the heat of the weather at Louisville and Shippingport, but here, I am comparatively comfortable—the greatest annoyance I now endure is from musketoes which have *begun* to be troublesome since we left Shippgpt. We no longer see any steamboats, though they were frequently passing and repassing us between Cincinn and Louisville.

The Capt. intends to write to Wm. Thompson from the mouth of the Cumberland river. In the meantime he requests you to say to him that he has ascertained the price of flour at Florence by a gentlemen who lately came from there, and who seemed desirous of buying him out at $5 per barrel which he declined. While at Louisville Mr. Boyd enquired of Wilson and Chambers, and likewise Buchanan, but they had no later accounts than about 4 weeks ago when flour was 6.50 to 7.00—their paper being at 10 per cent discount. He desires that you will apologise to W. T. for his not writing from Cincinn and Louisville, as he had not time, being very anxious to get forward. At Cincinn. he found a boat loaded with flour for Florence, which is left far behind.

From Mt. Vernon you may expect another letter from

Your truly affectionate Father,

Wm. Pelham.

Mt. Vernon, Indiana.
Mond. 22nd Aug. 1825.
11 o'clock A.M.

This letter, my dear son, will apprise you of my arrival at this place, where I shall remain 2 or 3 days to recruit and refit, and then *take a walk* to New Harmony in co. [company] with a young man who resides there, and who will then return there.

The Post Boy landed me yesterday about 10 o'clock and I am lodging with Mr. Welburn, the Postmaster who is likewise agent for the new community. I have gained but little addition to me stock of information on the *interesting subject.* The young man alluded to is a carpenter & joiner—has been 3 months in Harmony—and is very well pleased with it.

The weather has, for the last 3 days been cloudy & *cold* and now threatens rain. I find that the E. [Eastern] mail arrives here every Monday, about noon, & immediately returns, crossing the river from, and recrossing to Kentucky & proceeding on that side to Louisville & Maysville. On Friday a mail is recd. from Vincennes & returns the same day through Harmony. You will hence perceive the most direct communication with this place and Harmony. * * *

After remaining here about an hour yesterday, Capt. Boyd proceeded on his voyage. He charged me $7—for my passage from Z. saying that this was $3 less that he would have charged if the agreement had been made at L. I find after all expenses paid *to this place*, I am just 18 dollars *minus* than when I started—and upon the whole, I am very well satisfied.

Remember me kindly to all friends. My next letter will be from N. Harmony. Your affectionate Father,

Wm. Pelham.

[P. S.] By the bye, I have just learned from Mr. Wilburn that a printing press is actually in operation at Harmony though they have not yet commenced the publication of a newspaper.

New Harmony, Ind.
Th. 25 Aug., 1825.

My Dear William,

I can only write you a few lines to say that I arrived here yesterday afternoon in company with a member of the community whose interesting information and conversation tended greatly to diminish the tediousness and fatigue of the *walk*. In a few days I shall write you again & at large.

Remember me kindly to all enquiring friends,

Yr affectn. father,

Wm. Pelham.

New Harmony, Inda. Sept 7, 1825.

My dear Son,

I feel exceedingly desirous of writing to you, because I know a letter from me will be agreeable to you;—and yet I am loth to begin. Such a multitude of ideas crowd upon me, that I am doubtful whether I shall be able to select such as will be most interesting to you.

I wrote you from Marietta—from Cincinn.—from Louisville—from Mt. Vernon— and lastly on my arrival here. At Mt. V. [Vernon] I settled with Absalom Boyd, the Capt. of the boat, and paid him $7 for my passage, baggage included, somewhat less than one cent per mile, which he assured me was, the usual rate.

After paying for the transportation of my baggage from Mt. Vernon hither $2—I found the $25 I had appropriated to the expenses of my journey almost exhausted. But here I am, without having experiences any disaster or serious inconvenience; having enjoyed uninterrupted health till a few evenings ago when I took cold by incautiously exposing myself to the night air. I am now again as well as before.

At Mt. Vernon I was introduced to Mr. Schnee, a member of the Committee, and Postmaster here, on his return from Shawneetown on business of the Society. We soon became acquainted, and it appears that we were mutually pleased with each other. His countenance and manner indicated good sense, good nature, and firmness of character, and on further acquaintance I find these indications were not fallacious. He is an intelligent, active, viligant, and efficient member of the Committee. He left Mt. Vernon the day before I did and met me at the Tavern in Harmony on my arrival. After I had taken some refreshment, he conducted me to the Committee room, and introduced me to Mr. Wm. Owen, Mr. Secretary Lewis, Mr. T. M. Bosson, Mr. Jennings and Dr. McNamee, all members of the Commee, by whom I was severally greeted with kindness unalloyed by affectation or ostentation. I soon discovered that forms and ceremonies have no place here, and the intercourse being plain, easy and free, is exactly suited to my taste. Plainness of manners and plainness of dress are characteristic of this society.

I lodged two nights at the Tavern, and then removed to the room I now occupy and in which I am now writing. It was offered to me by Mr. Bosson, being an unfinished one immediately above his own, which is scarcely any better, but they will do for the present, and as the cold weather advances we shall have to shift our quarters or be frozen to death. These rooms are in the house where the meetings of the Committee are held, and the only difference is, that the Comee rooms are lathed and plastered. Within two-hundred yards of us stands the Old Harmony church, a large frame building painted white with a steeple containing a clock which strikes the hours and quarters. By this clock are regulated the occupations and amusements of the inhabitants. At five every morning the bell is rung for the commencement of the daily business, at seven it is again rung to signify that breakfast will be ready in all the boarding houses and the Tavern in a qr. [quarter] of an hour. At 12 it is rung again & dinner is ready everywhere in fifteen minutes, the same at six for supper. Every

Tuesday evening such as chuse to dance assemble in the Hall (which is a large brick building near and almost adjoining the church) where they find an excellent band of music, and amuse themselves till nine o'clock. The utmost order, regularity and good humor exist here and I have witnessed these periodical dancing assemblies with approbation and pleasure, the music being excellent.

On Wedy, evg. such of the society as choose to attend in the church are made acquainted with the transactions of the Comee —during the preceding week, and everyone gives his opinion freely respecting the best course to be pursued. On Thursday evg. there is a regular concert, on Friday something else which I do not recollect and Saturday evening is not appropriated to any particular object. On Sunday the Rev. Mr. Jennings commonly delivers a lecture in the forenoon (without any formal text) in which he explains the manner of receiving religious impressions. I have not yet heard one of these Sunday lectures, but from several conversations I have had with him, I can plainly see that he will never try to stupify the understanding of his hearers with unintelligable dogmas, and incomprehensible jargon. What he says is plain, and easy to be understood. On the Thursday, that is, the next day following my arrival, a Baptist preacher came into the town and announced his intention of delivering a discourse in the evening in the Church. Accordingly, a large congregation assembled, and listened to him with great attention. He is certainly one of their first rate preachers, and he managed his matters with much address. The next evening—(Friday) Mr. Jennings delivered a lecture in the same place, and ably demonstrated the sandy foundation of the ingenious gentleman's arguments, without any pointed allusion to him or his arguments. At the close of the lecture my gentleman thought proper to make a rejoinder, tho nothing had been said of him or his doctrines, but he did not seem to be in so good a humor as he was the evening before—although he had previously preformed the marriage ceremony for a young couple—especially when this young couple retired with their friends into the *Hall* to enjoy the pleasures of music and dancing instead of listening to his rejoinder.

I have now been here 2 Sundays. On the first (Mr. Jennings being absent on business) Mr. Wm. Owen read to the congregation some extracts from his fathers publications—and last Sunday, Mr. Jennings being indisposed, another member read several extracts from other portions of Mr. Owen's works. In both instances these extracts were accompanied with appropriate remarks of the reader explaining and connecting the passages. Last Sunday *afternoon* we were regaled with a truly *christian* harangue from a rambling shaking quaker who happened to be here.

You would be surprised to see how punctually I attend these Sunday meetings in the Church, and how frequently I am perambulating the streets, and falling in and conversing familiarly with successive groups *before the door of the Tavern* particularly in the evening when these groups commonly assemble—not to drink and carouse, but for the purpose of rational conversation, here are no brawling braggarts, no idle jesters delighting to wound the feelings of each other—no intemperate buffoons eager to make sport of one another, for no member of the community can obtain any ardent spirit either at the Tavern or the store, without a certificate from the Doctor that it is needed as a medicine—a regulation that would be very useful in Zanesville as well as here. I have mixed much with all descriptions of persons, and I declare I have not heard an offensive word spoken by a single individual. Good humored jokes are undoubtedly frequent but the general tenor of the conversation is of a serious philosophical cast. Those who are incapable of this appear still to take an interest in discussions of this kind, or separate into groups to talk over the occurrances of the day, occasionally introducing some jocular remark, tending to excite mirth without wounding the sensibility of any.

As to dollars & cents, they are words seldom heard any where but in the public store, which is like all other trading shops, differing however in this, that every head of a family, or single unmarried member unconnected with a family, instead of carrying money to the store, is furnished a Pass-book in which he is charged with what he buys, and is credited every week with the amount of his earnings. These pass-books exhibit a curious medley of items, bacon, chickens, eggs, melons, cucumbers, butter, tea, sugar, coffee &c &c with all the varieties of *store goods* on the debit side, while on the other are placed the credits of the individuals. I have been several days employed in overhauling and balancing these pass-books (the clerk whose particular duty it is, being sick) and this has given me the opportunity of making these observations, which indeed anyone may do who will take the trouble of looking over them, for they are open to the inspection of all who choose to examine them. There are about 300 of these pass-books continually in motion.

At the particular request of Mr. Keightly and Mr. Harris, I have obtained the insertion of their names in the register of applicants for admission into the Society, and if they were now here, I have no doubt they would both find immediate employment, the former in the Turners' & machine makers shop appertaining to the Steam mill, the latter in the Pub. [public] store; But they would certainly be puzzled to find comfortable lodgings especially if they did not come prepared with a sufficiency of bedding and utensils for housekeeping. If any other of our friends wish me to have their names also inscribed in the Register, I will make application for them, on their request being made known to me—the notification must contain the name and age of the applicant, the age of his wife, if a married man—the number, ages and sexes of his children—the place of his birth, and his present residence—his trade or occupation—and his motive for wishing to join the society.

The manner in which I became employed in the Pub. [public] store was this. As no one in this community is urged or pressed to perform any work that he pointedly dislikes, it was delicately intimated to me by the Accountant at the store that the young man whose duty it was to attend to the pass-book department being sick his business was running behind and my services wd be acceptable *as long as I liked to continue them.* Notwithstanding my aversion to commercial matters I readily assented and entered the Counting room, where I *at once* found myself *at home,* though among strangers—such is the frankness of manners prevailing here. I would, however, rather be somehow or other connected with the printing establishment, and I think I shall accomplish this as soon as the publication of the paper is commenced. I have frequently conversed with Mr. Palmer the superintendent of the pr. [printing] office who has already in some instances accepted my services as corrector of several proof sheets of a pamphlet he is printing. I have been urging on the Comee. to commence the publication and I think it will commence next week, probably on Saturday the 7th inst. I shall not fail to forward it to you for exchange. You will of course send yours & if the Reformer is *not* printed in Philad. let me know where it is printed.

Mr. Schnee informed me yesterday that the mail route from hence is to Princeton—from thence to Evansville, and so along on the Indiana side of the river to New Albany where it crosses over to Louisville, thence to Cincinn. or Maysville, he is not sure which, but most probably to Cincinn.

And now, my dear Wm. I hope you will give me a letter at least once each week, letting me know how you all go on & especially if you meet with any Post Office difficulties. Never mind John Dillon or his ill-humor abt the newspapers, but make him pay his postage. One thing I particularly recommend & that is *to exact punctual payment* from *all* for fear of the worst. * * *

Yr aff. father,

Wm. Pelham.

N. Harmony, Sept. 8, 1825.

My dear Wm. * * *

You will perceive by my letters to the P. M. G. and to Dr. Bradley that I have become a Harmonite and mean to spend the remainder of my days in this abode of peace and quietness. I have experienced no disappointment. I did not expect to find every thing regular, systematic, convenient—nor have I found them so. I did expect to find myself relieves from a most disagreeable state of life, and be able to mix with my fellow citizens without fear or imposition—without being subject to ill humor and unjust censures and suspicions—and this expectation has been realized—I am at length *free*—my body is at my own command, and I enjoy mental liberty, after having long been deprived of it. I can speak my sentiments without fear of any bad consequences, and others do the same—here are no political or religious quarrels, though there is a great diversity of opinion in matters of religion. Each one says what he thinks, and mutual respect for the sentiments of each other seems to pervade all our intercourse. Mr. Jennings is *our* preacher, and I hear him with approbation and satisfaction. The Methodists have likewise a preacher among them, who sometimes holds forth to the great delight of those who take pleasure in confounding their understanding. I am in habits of intimacy with Mr. Jennings, and Mr. Bosson particularly, who are both men of great powers of mind I am on the best terms with Mr. Schnee, who I may even venture to call my friend, and likewise with the other members of the Committee.

I heartily wish you were here—you would at once find employment in the printing office, and pass your life hapily—You would be associated with a number of young men who form a band of music, and perform a concert every Thursday evg. You would even join in the *dance* which takes place once a week. Your military propensities would be fully gratified in finding a sufficient number of congenial dispositions who are fond of that pursuit and have formed themselves into a Co. of St. Infantry under the direction of Capt. Larkin, who takes pleasure in it. They have just recd. their uniform from Pittsburg, but have not yet appeared in it. Upon the whole, after a full comparison of the advantages and inconveniences of my present situation I am quite satisfied. Let us now attend to other matters. * * *

There has for some time past been a good deal of conversation and consultation about establishing a social, circulating library, but nothing has yet been decided on. Whenever this is determined on I am to be Librarian, which, with my occupation in the printing office will be sufficient employment for me—and of the most agreeable kind—and with agreeable people. You may be sure I am doing all I can to bring it about. In the meantime I spend my time in obtaining a correct knowledge of the local affairs of the place. In due time I will communicate the result of the observations I may be able to make. At present I am boarding with the only baker in the town at 57 cents per week. He is a young married man—no children—and our dinner party consists of himself, his wife—Mr. Bosson and myself. That is, Mr. B. and I have our breakfast—dinner and tea there—and our lodging as before described, so that I may say, upon the whole I am very well situated.

I wish you would write me a long letter,—freely & confidentially, which will not fail to impart great satisfaction to, my dear Wm.

Yr. truly affectionate father,

Wm. Pelham.

New Harmony, Inda. Friday Sept. 9, 1825.

My dear William.

Yesterday evening, after I had written, sealed and put into the P. O. 2 packets directed to the "P. M. Zanesville" * * * , I received your acceptable favor of the 15th of August, accompanied with the O. Rep. of Aug. 13.

Associations on Mr. Owen's principles I find are springing up in the various places. Beside the society at the Yellow Spring, and the one you mention in Allegany Co. Pa. another has been formed at Albion, Illinois, the settlement made by the late Mr. Birkbeck, of which a favorable acct. has been recd. here.

Your information that Mess. Keightly and Harris will not

visit this place till October or November corresponds with what I learnt from themselves, and really I do not know how they will contrive to obtain accomodations when they do come. If they remain at the Tavern while they are not members they will be charged, each, $2 a week, as the Tavern is considered one of the sources of revenue for the society. If they come determined and prepared to join the society immediately, I think Mr. K. may manage to fit up some vacant log-hut for the reception of himself and famy. and Mr. H. might find admission into one of the boarding houses established for the accommodation of members of the community. It was fortunate for me that I had the precaution to bring all my bedding, tho upon opening my packages I was disappointed to find no thin coverlet. I really thought a white quilt had been put into the barrel or the large trunk. Your run was of great service to me. On board the boat it saved my bed and blankets from dirt & here it is tacked on the frame of my cob-bedstead. * * *

While at Mt. Vernon I heard the most unfavorable accounts of this place, but knowing how prone mankind are to speak ill of everything *intended for their benefit,* I paid but little attention to what was said. On my arrival here, the mystery was explained. The most bitter denunciators of the system were precisely those who applied for admission and been refused; because they were *idlers,* whose sole object was to be supported by the industrious part of the community. They were disappointed and hence arose their enmity. This society has certainly commenced under the most unfavorable circumstances. Their predecessors left everything to be *renewed*—before this establishment could be made productive. They settled themselves here in poverty and misery and departed in wealth and comfort, and considering these and other circumstances, it is rather surprising that their successors, coming from all quarters of the world, and unacquainted with one another's habits and dispositions, have been able to effect so much as they have done for their mutual convenience and comfort. Everyone with whom I converse, expresses the utmost confidence in the integrity, wisdom, and benevolence of Mr. Owen, and the day of his return will be a day of rejoicing throughout the settlement. The present Committee is composed of men of first rate ability—but they cannot perform impossibilities—they cannot in a day or a month change long established habits and prejudices, there must be time for this, and three months intercourse has already produced much more harmony of mind and unity of action than any other system is capable of producing. On my way from Mt. Vernon, within three miles of this place, I came to an extensive brick yard on the side of the road where a number of men were busily employed in making bricks for the new village, the location of which will be on the opposite side of the road.

You mention that you have "heard some discouraging news from New Harmony, propagated by an English ropemaker who left Cincinn quite charmed with the system, and has since returned disgusted." I have enquired into this matter and learned that the person alluded to, as soon as he came in sight of the town from the neighboring hills, declared that he was utterly disappointed and disgusted, he, nevertheless, came into the town—had all the talk to himself—tarried one night and departed next morning to enlighten his hearers on the subject of Mr. Owen's System for ameliorating the condition of mankind. How little could this man know of what he could so flippantly *talk about*,—and what sort of hearers must those people be, who could swallow his crudities?

Sunday Sept. 11, 12 o'clock M.

I have just returned from *Meeting;*—and strange as it may appear to you, I am a *constant attendant.* The orator was Mr. Jennings; and the substance, and indeed the whole of his discourse was a *moral lecture,* in the plainest and most intelligible language. He began by reading an extract from Robert Dale Owen's "Outline of the System of Education at Lanark" beginning at the 1st page, in which the author disclaims all necessity for reward or punishment in the education of children. The orator then proceeded to illustrate by familiar examples, the beneficial results of a course in which rewards and punishments are exploded, and the pernicious effects of an opposite course. Mr. Jennings then expatiated on the rights and duties of men in society, clearly showing that equality is the parent of liberty and justice; without a full enjoyment of which, mankind cannot be otherwise than unhappy. The discourse, as far as it could be regarded in a political light, was a truly democratic lecture, exhibiting the ill consequences arising from artificial distinctions, in station, in dress, and appearance and recommended as much uniformity in these particulars as may be practicable in this preliminary society. At the close of the lecture he announced that the publication of the "New Harmony Gazette" would be commenced on next Saty. week—viz. the 24" of Sept.

I learnt today that the Committee determined yesterday that the publication of the paper should commence under the direction of Mr. Jennings and Mr. Owen & that my assistance would be acceptable as Corrector &c &c.

Tuesday evg. 13th.

Yesterday morning Mr. J. conducted me to the *Editorial room* which is a commodius one in the house where he resides. * * * Here I commenced my operations by filing, *at my leisure,* all the newspapers in possession of the establishment, consisting chiefly of the N. Intelln. [Intelligence] & N. Journal and of these not many. Mr.J. has a good, tho small collection of books which he has placed in this room.—

Now while I think of it, I will tell you what would be acceptable to me if Mr. Keightly could make it convenient to take charge of them when he comes in November.

1st. All the books &c on the enclosed list. Of the others, retain what you please, and send me the remainder.

2dly. My bedstead which I left standing in the front room and if accompanied with a sacking bottom—the old curtains and valance—so much the better. I can have a tester made here.

3rd. An old quilt of some sort, and a hammer to drive *small* nails, tacks &c.

4th. Four chairs which I left in the front room.

5. The looking glass which hung in the back parlor in the mahogany frame. If I had been certain of remaining here when I left Z. I should have brought these things with me, for I am daily experiencing the want of some of them.

Wed. 14 Sept.

At 4 o'clock this afternoon I shall have been here 3 weeks, having arrived on the 24th Aug. as stated before, and really I seem already to be an *old inhabitant,* which I can no otherwise account for than by the circumstance of my having become acquainted with so many people and the frank and friendly intercourse subsisting among us. Whatever difference of opinion there may be, (and there is in reality a great difference in religious matters)—I hear no illiberal remarks, I see no overbearing temper exhibited, but each one pursues his own course without meddling with his neighbor. The most numerous sect, I believe, is that of the persons who take delight in wandering with Baron Swedenborg in the regions of fancy, where they are permitted to roam at large without annoyance or molestation. As they experience no persecution, they have nothing to complain of, only that others will not wander with them. The same remark applied to the other sectarians, and hence a kind of tacit agreement has been made to let each other alone. You can scarcely imagine how well satisfied I am with this state of things, so much I assure you, that no temptation could again draw me into the vortex of mental tyranny from which I have escaped. Liberty of speech and action without infringing on the rights of others, has ever been the object of my ardent desire, and here at length, I enjoy it.

Thursday Morning.

As I have nothing new to communicate respecting myself or others, I will endeavor to give you some idea of the buildings and general appearance of this place, premising that the town is laid off in squares, similar to Zanesville, though the houses and gardens are far from being as regular. There is a considerable number of brick houses, some frame buildings, and a great many log-cabins, some of which are built of hewed logs, the others round and rough. In the center stands the Church, near which is an excellent pump, at about an equal distance from the Church and Tavern. Mr. Rapp's large brick dwelling on one side fronts the Church, or rather the square in which the Church stands; and on the other, fronts the main street, having in each front 7 windows below and 7 in the second story. The boarding houses, and the boarding school the new church (now called the Hall) the steam mill, and the public store, are all of brick, and are more or less large, acording to their respective uses. The brick as well as the frame dwelling houses are built on an uniform and very limited scale, and none of them of more than 2 low stories, the ground floor being invariably as follows, with the gable end to the street & a small garden full of fruit trees attached to each. They are commonly placed at the corners of the squares. The workshops are mostly in log huts. The upper story is an exact counterpart of the lower one, if the lower rooms hold all the family the large upper room and the little cell over the kitchen are appropriated to boarders.

The log-cabins are scattered about without the least regard to regularity of location. The *situation* of this helter-skelter village is really beautiful, and since the surrounding land has been cleared and drained, is healthy. The town receives its supply of water for domestic use from a number of wells and pumps dispersed through it, and I understand it is of that kind called limestone. For washing the inhabitants depend on rain and river water.

I have been here three weeks & I have not yet seen the Wabash!! The reason is that I find so many other things attracting my attention that my rambles have been much circumscribed. In fact, my chief object has been to make myself acquainted with the individual character of the human beings by which I am surrounded, and the system of government in operation. I have now reason to believe that the principle care of providing matter for the N. H. [New Harmony] Gazette will devolve upon me and my time will consequently be engaged by that concern. Of the two members of the Committee who were appointed to superintend the press, Mr. Jennings has declined, in order that he may give his whole attention to the superintendence of the Boarding School & Mr. Owen's daily & pressing occupations leave him no time, so I think the paper will be left pretty much to Mr. Palmer and myself, with such *occasional* assistance as we can extort from the literati. Although the day fixed for the commencement of the paper of the 24″ of this month, I do not like that it should be begun on that day, and as it has already been so long delayed I shall endeavor to postpone it *one week* longer that it may commence on the 1st of October. By this arrangement the 1st vol. will comprise 7 months ending on the 1st May, the 2nd 6 months ending on 1st Nov. and every other vol. 6 months ending alternatly on 1st Nov. and 1st May, the latter being the anniversary of the adoption of the New Harmony Constitution. Whether the Comee. will agree to the postponement I know not, but I shall urge it, with due diference. I have not mentioned it yet to Mr. Palmer but I have no doubt of his assent.

Since writing the above, I have conversed with Mr. P. [Palmer] on the subject. He says each year will form one vol. in the manner of the Cincinnati Literary Gaz. and other similar papers. * * *

Most truly yr affectionate father,

Wm. Pelham.

Monday 19 Sept. 1825.

Yesterday at 10 o'clock A. M. Mr. Jennings ascended the pulpit in the old Church (which is now called *The Church*) and continued the reading of Robert Dale Owen's Outline of Education. His auditors were about as numerous as usual. He again expatiated on the indispensable necessity of establishing the principle of equality as the basis of liberty. He showed the absolute necessity of everyone being diligent in the performance of his or her respective duty. He was listened to with profound attention, and the discourse he delivered must produce good effects because it was reasonable and perfectly intelligible to all.

At 2 o'clock P. M. it was announced by the ringing of the bell that something was to be said or done at church. I immediately repaired hither, and found the pulpit occupied by a stranger who thought he could say something that would be useful. Very few persons were present. The gentleman began by giving out a hymn to be sung by the congregation—only one person joined him. After hobbling through one verse, the remainder was laid aside and "Let us pray" pronounced in an audible voice. Some knelt down, some stood, and others remained sitting. The preacher delivered a devout prayer, and seemed much relieved by this effusion of the spirit. He then commenced an attempt to reconcile some contradictions in the holy book—and talked about ¾ of an hour in the usual, incoherent, unintelligible manner. I found afterwards that his remarks made little or no impression on his hearers.

At 8 p. m. the bell again rang and I again attended where I found a considerable number of persons assembled to hear a preacher of the Methodist doctrine whose name I could not learn, though I inquired of several persons. I found, however, that he was one of the Circuit preachers. This man appeared to have learned his lessons very accurately, for his cant phrases flowed from him with remarkable ease and rapidity, and were answered by many *spiritual groans*, and other evidences of entire sympathy. When he gave out a hymn, a considerable number of male and female voices were joined with his, and really the music was delightful, for singing is taught here scientifically. He then named a text, and talked as usual about sin, and the devil, and heaven, and the straight and narrow way leading to salvation, the utter impossibility of being saved but through the merits of our blessed Lord and Savior, Jesus Christ &c &c. I mustered patience to sit and hear him to the end and when the judge pronounces against me "Depart ye wicked &c" I intend to plead this command of myself in mitigation of the sentence. After he had finished, a member of the Community with whom I am acquainted, and who is a sort of a Methodist preacher, took his place in the pulpit, and in a moderate tone and manner related his individual experience as an example to others, he was also attended to though he said nothing but what had been said a thousand times. It seems he is unwilling to exchange his belief in divine revelation for all the joys and pleasures of the world.

So be it, for notwithstanding this whimsical notion, he is really a good member of the Society, and devoted to the system as far as he comprehends it.

You would be amused to come into the church while we are at our devotions. The walls bare—the ceiling lofty—the beams and joists uncovered, the pulpit itself nothing but a raised platform furnished with a bench, and sort of desk, the preacher in his ordinary clothing, a striped roundabout and linen pantaloons—(this is the common appearance of Mr. Jennings, Mr. Owen and some others) benches ranged for the congregation, on one side for the men, on the other for the females, many of the former in their shirt sleeves, among the latter a variety of ornamental drapery, and among the whole the greatest order and decorum. No one troubles himself about his neighbor's appearance unless there be an affectation of finical attention to dress. This however, will wear away gradually.

Tuesday evg. 9 o'clock.

I have just returned from the Hall, where there is music and dancing every Tuesday evening. Every Friday evening there is a concert in the same place. Some biggots are dreadfully scandalized that these parties are held in a building originally intended for divine worship, nevertheless, the fire and brimstone have not yet descended from heaven to destroy us for this wicked perversion.

Yesterday evening there was a drunken frolic among some young men who contrived to procure some whiskey from the country people who came in to make their purchases in the store. The Committee took cognizance of the matter today, and have expelled three of the offenders, who are deemed incorrigible, being not only addicted to drink but likewise gamblers and idlers. What sort of character will these men give us when they return to their homes?

It is now determined that the paper shall be published on the 1st of October, being the day Mr. Owen embarked in England 12 months ago, to come to America. I gave Mr. Palmer all the matter I had prepared for the first paper, and he said there was enough for 3 at least. The paper will be in 4to—the size of the Cincinnati Literary Gazette.

Tell Mr. Keightly that articles of provision will be in demand here in the course of the winter, such as hams, pickled pork, potatoes, and perhaps flour. Vegetables of all kinds are very scarce, for the old Harmonites left the garden fences in a wretched condition, and before they could be repaired by the new comers, the hogs and cows had very materially injured the gardens. Some persons think that Mr. Owen will not be here till the middle of December and I am much of the same opinion.

I have traversed the town to find a suitable editorial room in which I might place my bed, but hitherto without success. Many of the young men are lodging in barns and other out-houses, so that my present *shell* is esteemed a very confortable location, nevertheless I must have better winter quarters, or they will have me on the Doctor's list before Christmas. Of this, however, I have no great apprehension, for every member of the Committee seems disposed to accomodate me as well as circumstances will permit. * * *

Thursday Evg.

At this moment (half past eight) the moon is shining brightly and the light infantry company under Capt. Larkin, dressed in their new uniform (very much like yours) are marching and countermarching in the square and in the streets, accompanied by the boys under the direction of their respective school-masters who teach them to perform the same evolutions which they do with great precision.

This afternoon I attended the funeral of a female member. She was burried out of the town in a corner of a fine apple orchard, and without any of the parade and *cant* that I have formerly seen and heard on such occasions.

I must now quit writing and search 12 or 15 newspapers for matter to be inserted in the 1st number of the New Harmony Gaz. It is always best to take time by the forelock.

Tell Mr. Nims, Mr. Westbrook and Mr. Sheward and all others who may inquire of you that the want of accommodation here at present is so great that I would recommend to them if they seriously contemplate a removal hither to postpone it till they hear further from me. * * * Wm. Pelham.

Monday Evg. Sept. 26, 1825.

On Saturday evening last, the Society was called together by the Committee to decide a case, which, being the only one yet presented to their notice, the Committee did not choose to determine, on their own authority only. The case was this.

The Superintendent of the Steam Mill had at several times complained to the Committee, that his pay was not sufficient for the support of himself and his family. On such occasions, the Committee, conformably to their usual practice, gave him an additional credit at the store. By this means he became a debtor to the Society, under the presumption that he would continue a member, and gradually wipe off the debt. But it seems that this was not his intention; for, a few days ago, having obtained another order on the store to the amount of sixty dollars, and received the goods he wanted, he suddenly gave notice of his intention to withdraw from the society. On settlement of his account, the balance against him, after every allowance, was $77.62½ This balance he refused to liquidate in any manner whatever, and the members of the Society were summoned to determine what steps should be taken on this novel case. After much discussion and ample explanation on both sides, a large majority determined by vote, that the Superintendent restore so much of the property drawn from the store as could be restored, for which he should have credit, and that for the remainder of the debt he should give his note payable at a time to be agreed on, and further, that if he refused to comply with these terms he should be expelled.

I understand that the affair has been adjusted in some way, and that he will, tomorrow, retire from this place. During the meeting he endeavored to excite a spirit of general discontent among the members, but in this he utterly failed, and I have reason to believe that such attempts will always meet with a similar fate. I know not whither he is going, but doubtless, wherever he goes he will spread a doleful account of the injustice and oppression he experienced at New Harmony and advise his hearers to shun this place as they would a pleague or pestilence.

Yesterday at the usual hour, Mr. Wm. Owen ascended the *pulpit* in *the Church*, and read that portion of Robert Dale Owen's "Outline of Education" which treats of the subject of religion, with explanatory remarks and comments of his own. He is a good reader and speaker, except that his voice is not sufficiently strong and firm. His audience was numerous and attentive. His manner is most mild and conciliating, for he is an amiable young man, about twenty five. He only wants experience.

This afternoon, the weather being fine, I treated myself with a view of the Wabash; the distance from my lodging being but little more than a quarter of a mile to the landing. The river is beautiful, and at this place about half the width of the Muskingum at Zanesville. The shore is a sandy beach intermixed with small pebbles. The bank appeared to be about twenty feet high from the level of the water. From the foot of the bank to the edge of the water about the same distance. There were two or three boats lying at a little distance above the landing place.

Tuesday noon.

Last night the weather was so cold as to require a good fire. This coldness of the air silenced the musicians who have so diligently amused the inhabitants of this town every since I have been here. I mean certain little winged insects who take care to indemnify themselves for any trouble they are at to entertain us, by piercing the skin and drawing off the *superfluous* moisture. On my complaining of these troublesome visitors, I was told, "Never mind it,—you will get used to them"—and so indeed I found out; for I begin to be very indifferent about them. In reality, I have become inattentive to many inconveniences which would have worried me excessively in Zanesville. So much depends on the state of the mind.

Afternoon 4 o'clock.

I have just come from the printing office, where Mr. Palmer is working off one side of the paper. He has an elegant new Super-royal press of the kind called the Stansbury press, which requires less than one third of the strength necessary for working the common screw press. It cost $170. Having no knowledge in these matters, I cannot give you a description of it. I can only perceive that the labor of pulling the bar is comparatively nothing. I wish you had such a one, or that you were here to try the difference. * * *

As you have had the opportunity of seeing a great number of newspapers, I wish you would send me a list of such as you recommend in exchange, omitting all that you know to be violent party papers, such as Democratic Press, N. York Advocate, Richmond Enquirer, and others of the same stamp. What do you think of the Athens Mirror in this point of view? I think it is a literary paper and it is such we want. But we want not any of the canting, hypocritical, lying religious papers so called, which tell us everything but the truth and whose sole object is to "Milk the Goats."—If you don't understand this expression ask our friend, Martin Hill to explain it as he found it explained in "Plain Truth."

The superintendent alluded to in the beginning of this letter is gone, having previously restored some of the goods he obtained, and given his note for the balance, with acceptable security. * * *

My thoughts often dwell on you & and always with the feelings of An affectionate father,

Wm. Pelham.

Private and confidential. Sept. 29. [1825]

What I have written to you, since my arrival here is strictly true as far as it goes, though I would not wish anything you receive from me *in manuscript*, to appear in the paper, unless I particularly request it. Many things are in an unsettled state, and will probably remain so till Mr. Owen's return.

As an instance—After Mr. Jenn. & Mr. O. were appointed by the Com. to superintend the press, I applied to them for matter, both original and selected. The former explicity declined, and threw the burden on me—& the latter was so immersed in his daily business that I could scarcely get an opportunity of speaking with him. I went on as well as I could, & prepared the matter, corrected the proof of the first side, & returned it to the printer. The form was worked off yesterday afternoon. This morning Mr. J. found several things which he said must be altered—but it was too late. This brought an explanation, and it is now determined, that an hour shall be appointed when they are jointly to attend to the business. This will be a great relief to me. At 2 o'clock this afternoon they did indeed meet at the Printing Off. accompanied with 2 other members of the Com. to revise the matter prepared for the inside of the paper—and cut down a good deal of the manuscript laid before them—whether for better or worse, I cannot determine. At all events they have done something, and the paper will be published according to appointment.—When once begun, it must go on—Mr. J. wrote a few lines to precede my biograph. sketch of Mr. O.—Mr. Bosson wrote the View of N. H. and the piece relating to the salubrity of this town & adjacent country—I wrote the head introducing the Song No. 1 and they say it ought to have been more full & explicit—but none of them presented this full & explicit statement.—I have mentioned these circumstances to show that we have *not yet* got into a regular train, though it will certainly, in 2 or 3 weeks, be established. I want Niles' Reg. to take his Summary of news. This will save time and trouble.

I have several times been present when Mr. Schnee opened his mail & have sometimes assisted. Tomorrow he is going to make up his quarterly accounts & he wants me to be with him tho' I know he can do it as well without as with me for he is an intelligent man of business. His Acct. of Mails Received will occupy 2½ pages.—Adieu!— [Wm. Pelham]

Monday Oct. 3, 1825.

My dear Wm. * * *

Friday evg. was a bustling time in the printing office. The paper was expected with great impatience by the town subscribers (who flocked in at $1 per ann.) besides whom a number were to be prepared for the E. [Eastern] mail which closes at 9 o'clock P. M. However we got through the business pretty well, as we have a set of people to deal with very different from the Zanesvillians or *Lunarians*, as they ought to be called. * * *

Yesterday morning I was prevented by circumstances from shaving and dressing myself till the second bell rung for meeting. I was unwilling to be absent and *finally* at the instigation of Wm. Owen I, determined to go as I was, viz. with a long beard, dirty shirt and cravat and my little short coat which is the coat I most commonly wear when the weather is warm.

Mr. Jennings began with reading something from a late publication on Political Economy, after which he delivered an excellent discourse on Equality:—shewing that it was essential to the happiness of society, as all arbitrary distinctions and partialities not founded on real merit, and all distinctions arising from extravagance in dress and external appearance have no solid foundation—that every person's worth should be measured by his capacity to be useful to his fellow beings. Many ladies were present, some of whom were fashionably dressed and decorated with ribbons and artificial flowers. I suspect that some of them did not quite approve of his remarks.

On Friday I changed my boarding house that I might be better situated in regard to my connection with the pr[inting] off[ice]. The house in which this office is located is also a boarding house, kept by Mr. Palmer, the printer. On one side of the office which is a large room on the ground floor a long table is placed at which the boarders (about thirty)—receive their meals which are punctually on the table at a quarter past 7 A. M. a qr. past 12 noon, and a qr. past 6 P. M. The price of boarding everywhere in town (except the Tavern) is 57½ cents per week for each person, being a member. This table is better supplied with butcher's meat and vegetables than the one I have just left, but not so well supplied with milk just now. You may easily imagine what a contract there must be between the talk and bustle of so many boarders, and that of the four persons which formed our meal parties at the baker's. The first day or two, I was almost stunned with the noise, but I am getting used to it. Another thing I am getting used to is the shrill note of the cricket in my bed room which I have *no possible means* of getting rid of. There are so many and such important circumstances to counterbalance the inconveniences I suffer that I may say "Upon the whole, I am very well satisfied."

Wednesday 5th.

Yesterday evening being the regular dancing evening a number of ladies appeared at the ball in a new *uniform* dress of cheap American manufacture. I was prevented from seeing this exhibition by having to read a proof-sheet which I did not get till after dark. As soon as I had performed this duty I sallied out with the intention of going to the Hall. As soon as I got out of doors I perceived that the Church also was lighted up, and as it lay in my way I called there first and found about twenty devotees listening to the ranting of a stranger who occupied the pulpit, and who was holding forth with great strength of voice about the "scribes and Pharisees." I did not sit down, and only remained a few minutes. Having heard as much about these gentlemen of the ancient world as I desired, I proceeded to the ball-room, but too late to gratify my curiosity with the sight of the new dresses.—The west door of the Church and the e [ast] door of the Hall are about 10 feet apart.—

My best wishes attend you all. Wm. Pelham.

P. S. The impression of No. 1 consisted of 500 copies of which 300 have been distributed to subscribers and others.

Monday 10″ of Oct. 1825.

Yesterday according to my *new* custom, I went punctually to Church, and heard Mr. Jennings continue the reading of select portions of Thompson's Essay on the distribution of wealth. The author shews distinctly, that a very considerable part of the evils suffered in Society may be traced to the unequal, and unjust division of property, and that this again may be attributed to the principle of individual competition. He then contrasts with this the social system, from whence this principle is banished, with all its train of evils, and the principle of mutual co-operation substituted with all its necessary consequences. After the reading, the male and female children of the society sung the song No. 2. If I can get the music I will send it to you. Mr. J. then expatiated on his favorite topics, equality, economy, and good feelings toward one another. At the close of the discourse, he was requested by one of the members to give notice that at 3 P. M. there would be *preaching* in the Church. This he readily did, and with due respect. Accordingly, as I understand, for I did not attend, the Revd. Mr. Slocum a Methodist preacher delivered a very edifying sermon, that is to say, a sermon full of words and phrases quite unintelligible both to the speaker and his hearers—all of whom have probably persuaded themselves that they fully *understand* as well as profess to *believe* such things. In the evening the weather being warm and clear, many were assembled as usual before the door of the Tavern, (which is a sort of Literary Exchange)— where, seated on chairs and benches, we discussed with mutual respect, and perfect freedom, the various ideas of religion entertained by each—and here we sat and talked of God, the soul, eternity, matter, spirit, &c. &c. (without thinking of anything to drink) till after the Tavern doors were closed, which is always done at 10 o'clock. * * *

Adieu, my dear Wm. and remember me kindly to all friends. I must now close and begin reading the proof of the inside of our No. 3.

Wm. Pelham.

P. S. A letter dated Aug. 7 has just been recd. from Capt. McDonald, a member of the Community who accompanied Mr. Owen, stating their arrival at Liverpool, and the expectation that they will be ready about the first of October to embark on their return.

New Harmony, Ind.
Friday, 21 Oct. 1825.

My dear Son,

My time, during the present week has been so fully occupied, that I had none left to continue my journal, though several little things have occurred which might be interesting to you—for instance the mustering and appearance of our Light Infantry company and their marching out of town 5 miles to the ground appropriated to this object according to law.

Yesterday I had the satisfaction of seeing Messrs. Keightly and Harris in good health and spirits after a journey of 14 days having left Zanesville on the 6th inst. * * * They have this morning been accepted by the Committee as members of the Society and consequently each will have his board at one of the boarding houses (or as they are here called Community houses) at the rate of 57½ cents a week. The wages, or pay, or allowance (call it what you will) is proportionately low so that it amounts to this simple fact, that whoever serves the Society faithfully and diligently whatever his occupation may be, gets his living and no more. If he has children they are also provided for; either by his labor or their own if capable of earning anything, but if not then they are provided for by the Community till they are capable of being useful. This is merely a hasty sketch which I will enlarge upon one of these days when I have more time. I can only add that if any man should come here to board, without doing anything deemed *useful*, he must make an individual agreement with the Committee, for we want no *idlers* of any description, and several persons of this sort have already been dismissed, and many more will find it expedient to retire, leaving behind them the best part of the present population, whom nothing could induce to abandon the pleasing prospects before them. * * *

Your truly affectionate father,

Wm. Pelham

[P. S.] I will again revert to Harris and Keightly. After introducing them to the Committee individually and collectively I went with them in search of board and lodging as they wished to leave the Tavern as soon as possible. After going about a good deal we found an unoccupied garret,—in one of the Community houses—similar to mine, that is to say, no ceiling but the outside roof, but better than mine both in extent and walls, theirs being brick, and mine merely a *shell* of weather boarding. Without actual experience, one cannot realize the difficulty of getting house-room in this place. K [eightly] with his warm zeal is satisfied with his location and all concomitant inconveniences and privations. H [arris] is not quite so well contented, but as soon he begins to experience the beneficial change he has made as respects *Society*, he will be as well satisfied as any of us. A double feather bed has been procured—Keightly will make a bedstead—the store will furnish him with a bed cord—blankets must be had somehow. Keightly will be or is already I believe attached to the carpenter's shop and Harris will on Monday next be employed in the counting room at the store.

[P. S.] This is Tuesday night (Oct. 25th) warm and rainy. After supper, (the time of which is uniformly 6 o'clock) I called at the Tavern to see K [eightly] and H [arris]. They were both gone to the ball * * * . I then came home to my lodging, and here I am in my shell, surrounded by boards, carpenters' tools, shavings, sawdust &c. for the Committee, on my proposing to them the alternative of burying me, or making my room *comfortable* this winter very readily embraced the latter alternative and gave me the command of the carpenter's department so far as this was necessary for wood-work. I am also to have bricks, bricklayers &c. to fill in between the studs, and I have now a certain prospect of being very commodiously situated during the winter exactly in the location which of all others I prefer, for I should very reluctantly quit the quarters I have occupied ever since my arrival here. * * *

Thursday Morning.

Mr. Keightly has just called to inform me that he and Harris have concluded to return immediately to Zanesville. He will take charge of this letter accompanied by a pamphlet just warm from the N. Harmony Press. I beg you will read and study it. They are not yet made up. I shall endeavor to send you more copies in sheets for sale 25 cents each.

November 7″, 1825, Monday.

My dear Son,

* * * You enquired how my postage acct. is settled here, I answer that all unpaid letters are charged in my pass book among other charges. In the same book I have credit for my services at——per week. I have yet said nothing about the rate of allowance, but suppose it will be $1.54 per week, this being the allowance to each member of the Comee. Soon after my arrival I deposited in the store $10 & have this day made an additional deposit of $20—both sums being credited to me in the books of the store as well as in my pass-book. These deposits have left me $7—which I still have in cash. I have taken up articles & pd for work $10.36—The pamphlets I sent you by Keightly are likewise charged in my pass-book and also $1.50 for which I became responsible to Mr. Pearson for work done for Messrs. Harris & Keightly while they were here & which was forgotten in the hurry of their departure. By this sketch you will see that my funds decrease but slowly. * * * Nor do I believe that any temptation *whatever* could induce me to quite this tranquil scene.

If I suffer inconveniences here they are accompanied with such alleviating circumstances as greatly deminish their effect.

I cannot help again reiterating the advice I gave you to come here as soon as possible * * *. There is a great number of young persons here of both sexes in this place, and I plainly see that they enjoy themselves and the society of each other, their labor is moderate and easy, and their recreations frequent and innocent. In short they please themselves, and generally if not always please one another. * * * You are aware, that reading written accounts of the circumstances of any place cannot supply the place of actual inspection. In order to form an accurate judgment you must actually see it, and converse *on the spot* with intelligent residents. K [eightly] & H [arris] have been here, the former is too flighty and his stay too short to form a distinct perception—and the latter is too querulous to be happy any where, for every place has its inconveniences and his temper of mind leads him to *dwell* upon these and overlook the counterbalancing advantages. Besides the poor fellow was tormented with a boil which entirely deprived him of whatever comfort he might otherwise have enjoyed. There is not a shadow of doubt in my mind that after five or six month's residence here it would be an exceeding difficult matter to induce you to remove elsewhere, and more especially to Z [anesville.] You may call this *enthusiasm,* if you please, but the real differences between this place and Z. will still exist in all their force, and certainly you must allow me to be a tolerable judge of them, from my having resided in both. The approaching winter will doubtless bring its additional inconveniences, and so will the spring, and so will the following summer, the chief of which is the want of house room.

I am now sitting (Tuesday night 11 o'clock.) in my room which has lately been filled in with brick and otherwise rendered a comfortable dwelling and my prospects during the ensuing winter are almost wholly agreeable. * * *

Respecting an establishment like this there must necessarily be a great variety of opinions and sentiments, and predictions, but you will find that those who have given the *least* attention to the subject are the *most* confident in prophesying its dissolution. Let them say what they will, you may feel *assured of its permanency,* and it is the unqualifies opinion of every intelliegent man here. For my own part, I have not the least doubt that the present inconveniences will gradually be supplanted by circumstances tending to promote and perpetuate the happiness of those who embrace the System.

Wed. Morn. 11 o'clock.

Smart frost last night. Weather now moderate & pleasant. I have just retd. from printg. O. 218 steps from thence to the door of my lodging * * *. There are no settled preachers of the Gospel here—but traveling preachers very frequently call and refresh the flock with the words of grace.

With regard to the new village all that I can say is that the brickmakers—I know not how many—are constantly employed in preparing that material.

New Harmony, Sunday Nov. 27, 1825.

My dear son.

* * * I shall now endeavor to answer all the questions in your last letter, tho it contains some that I think were anticipated in my last. When I said "whoever serves the society faithfully and diligently, whatever his occupation may be, gets his living and no more" I meant that all ideas of individual wealth are banished from among us. If any chooses to earn more than his individual expenses, the surplus profits remain in common stock to be appropriated by the whole Society in whatever manner they please, for the good of the whole. This community being established on the principle of equal benefits and enjoyments, it is obviously different from our former plans of accumulating *wealth* for *individual* expenditure. Every one will enjoy an equal share with every other member, of the immense benefits produced by mutual cooperation. That this will be the ultimate effect of the System I have not the least doubt, though at present it is not exactly so, because it is impossible in the circumstances of the present establishment. You can hardly expect that in the heterogenous population hastily collected here, there shd be no idlers, no speculators &c, the most effectual measures are however in active operation to make a just discrimination and the certain effect will be the withdrawal or expulsion of those who came here to live upon the labors of others. This *preliminary* society cannot be considered as a fair sample of the perfect community in view, because it consists of persons differing much from each other in their tempers and inclinations, whereas the new community will consist of select characters actuated by feelings of *common interest.*

At present there are many wants that cannot be *immediately* provided for, and the greatest of these is the want of suitable accommodation. For this reason the twenty persons you mention as coming from Pittsburg will have to retrace their steps, there is actually not house room for them. *Keep it in mind, however, that my room is large enough for us both.* All the conversations I heard in Zanesville, and the letters I have recd. since about this place relate to *pay.* In fact, no one here talks about *pay.* The Committee in their endeavor to equalize the members fixed the allowance of credit to each at 80 dollars a year which it was supposed wd be sufficient for his maintenance—but the principle, the main principle is that every grown person is able to earn his living, and if he feels disposed to earn more, the surplus, after every reasonable expenditure for individual comfort to every member is applied to the extension of similar establishments. This is the ultimate view—but the immediate object is for each member to do all he can to provide a fund from which he in common with others will derive all the enjoyments he requires, and it is *calculated* that a very moderate portion of labor will be abundantly sufficient for this.—

You want to know how the acct. stands between Mr. Owen & the Society. It is simply thus: Mr. Owen has advanced his own money for the purchase of this property. Just before his departure he made an offer of it to the Society on *their own terms,* which they declined, preferring that it should still continue to be his. He is therefore evidently sole proprietor of the whole; but it is equally evident that it will ultimately be the property of the whole Society, and that, as soon as the individuals find themselves competent to conduct the concern on the principles which brought them together. They have ever since his departure been endeavoring to make such arrangements as to produce the benefits in contemplation. Most of these plans have succeeded, but some have also failed, for the want of requisite practical knowledge. A general sentiment prevailes that "*things will go on better soon after the return of Mr. Owen*" who, it is expected will be here in a week or ten days. It would surprise you to hear the universal expression of the fullest confidence in the wisdom and integrity of Mr. Owen—he is certainly a most extraordinary man or he could never thus have attached him— to him so great a variety of characters as compose this population without a dissenting voice, as far as I know. This is not blind enthusiasm in me for I know the fact, and I know the greater part of these people have been *personally acquainted* with him. When *I* see him you shall have the result of my cool, candid observation.

"If a person joins, and invests, say $500—when he shd wish to retire can he get his cash again?" This is one of your questions. I read it to Mr. Lewis the Secretary of the Committee. He immediately answered "Yes, certainly!" "Does he draw interest?" "No Mr. Owen does not want to borrow." When a person retires who puts nothing into the common stock whatever balance may be due to him for his time & labor will be paid to him in the products of the establishment—the profits arising from his labor, *if any*, will be merged in the common stock, for the benefit of those who remain. It is not an easy matter to ascertain *profits*, in fact, there is no profit till the article manufactured be sold, and the money actually received. "Is there any chance for another butcher?" Not immediately; unless he could sleep in a hay loft.—"Should John Sockman join, what would he have to do?"—"and what *pay*?" We know nothing about *pay*. It is a term used only among you of the old world, and confined wholly to the selfish, *individual* system. Every one here who employs himself usefully has meat, drink, lodging—(when it can be got)—and is continually increasing his comforts. If sick he receives the necessary attendance. If he has children they are provided for. We have so saddler, nor is there any place for one to lodge in. This is a general answer to all inquiries and will continue so until some houses can be built. * * * "I do not at all like the account you give of your lodging room." My last letter will have informed you that it is not quite comfortable, tho still somewhat inferior to the *front room* &c. Everybody who comes into it exclaims "*How comfortably you are fixed here.*" "How does the new village come on?" Not so fast as we wish, but as well as can be expected. The brickmakers have been at work *on the spot* during the whole summer and have made 240,000.

The dismal story you copied from the Pittsb[urg] Mercury was already known here, and the writer is also known. He is a Baptist preacher I heard him preach just after my arrival, and he went away displeased because Mr. Jennings out-preached him. I wd recommend to you to read in the Gazette if you want to know the truth of things—read the "View of Harmony." The Labyrinth has not been destroyed, but it has been neglected as of little comparative importance. * * * "What are the hours of business, summer and winter?" I am not sure about the working hours. The bell rings at six o'clock in the morning, but I believe few persons go to work till the eight o'clock bell rings. From this hour they continue till the 12 o'clock bell, at 1 the bell again rings and the working hours continue till 6 when the supper bell is rung. There is no job work—i.e. no person is paid by the job. When jobs are done in any department for country people or strangers—the superintendent of the department receives the cash and pays it into the store, and the department (be it the printing, tailoring, shoemaking &c department) is credited for the amount. * * * The "parade ground appropriated by law." This was an inadvertance of mine—the law does not appropriate any parade ground The general muster is held at a place five or six miles from hence, and all our *military* marched to that spot on the day appointed—this was what I ought to have said. Apropos—Our Light Infantry Co. & some other companies in full uniform are now, (Sund[ay] afternoon,) parading in the street under the command of their Major the Revd. Mr. Jennings, who is an active and intelligent military officer—He preached in the forenoon in the Church, and this afternoon appeared on horseback in his military dress to exercise the troops. The L. I. Co. make a good appearance being all properly armed, accoutred, and uniformed, they number about 40 all young men. * * *

You wd probably like to know how we go on with the paper. I therefore add to this long letter a few items on that subject. On the 20th inst. we reconed 116 Subd. in town at $1, the *members* being charged only half price. 4 sent to the Reading Room. 2 to the Tavern and 1 to the Committee, making 123 delivered in town. 175 forwarded by mail to Sub. and Prs. viz.

Pennsylvania	11s.	7 prs.	Conn.	1s.	1 pr.
Indiana	27s.	5 prs.	Ill	20s.	1 pr.
Kent'y	7s.	3 prs.	Maryl'd	1s.	4 prs.
Mass	3s.	1 pr.	Delaware	1s.	1 pr.
Missouri	3s.		Tennessee	4s.	
Maine	1s.				
N. York	7s.	4 prs.	Scotl'd & Eng	6s.	1 pr.
Ohio	15s.	14 prs.	Virg'a	1s.	1 pr.
D. Col	8s.	4 prs.	N. Jersey	2s.	1 pr.
N. Carol		1 pr.	Louisiana	1s.	1 pr.
Mississi	1s.		Alabama	1s.	

2 Reading rooms at Cincinnati, 1 at Louisville, Alegheny and Y. Springs associations 2, total, 298. Since the 20 inst., 15 new subscribers abroad have been added to the list & every mail brings some. Papers recd. last Thursday were:

Reformer, Crisis, Ohio Repub. Nov. 2, Niles Reg. Times, Chillicothe, Ohio; State Jour. Col. Louisville Advertr., Dayton Repub., Vevay Regr., Hamilton Advocate, Marietta Friend, Athens Mirror, Lancaster O. Eagle, with a request fr Mr. Detrich of exch. addressed to me, Cleaveland Herald,

Ind. Repub., Madison, Vincennes W. Sun, Balt. Gazette, Balt. Dutch Paper, Delaw. Watchman, Wilmingtonian, Alb. Patriot, Traveller Boston, these are all addressed to the Gaz.—Cincinn also sends us Lib. Hall & N. Repub., Bloomington, Ind. Gazette, Georgetown Sentinal. These are all directed to the Gaz. besides which the followg. directed to individual: N. Intell., N. Journal, Wash. Metropolitan, Geo. T. Sat. Evg. Post, Globe and Emerald, Boston Cent, U. S. Gaz. daily.

The day of publication is changed to Wednesday which is a more convenient time than Saturday. News is a secondary object, the first being to disseminate a correct knowledge of the principles, practice, and local affairs of this Society. Wm. Owen appears to me to possess a better knowledge of the principles than any other person here, and his pieces are therefore the most interesting. His 2 articles in the 2 papers No. 7 & No. 8 preceding the last on the formation of character are peculiarly so. * * *

I wish you would frequently insert in the O. Rep. some extracts from the N. H. Gaz. particularly the editorial remarks in No. 7 & 8 on the formation of character, with any other selections calculated to excite the minds of your readers to the exercise of their *reasoning* faculties. The world has been long enough and too long under the dominion of passion and prejudice, and it is time that REASON shd have fair play. Perhaps while I think of it, I cannot give you a more striking illustration of the principles and practice of this Society than by citing Mr. Schnee as an example, he is Postmaster, Committee-man, Superintendent of the farms, and principle agent in the *selling* department of the store, and yet his *nominal* allowance in money is $1.54 per week for all his services put together. If he takes a boarder, 64 cents a week (it has lately been a little increased)— is added to his credit, and charged to the boarder. He has a wife and two or three sons, two of whom are capable of earning something which is also added to their joint credit unless they choose to have separate pass-books. They occupy a snug dwelling house, yard and garden, and find their allowance sufficient for their maintenance because they are all frugal and industrious. If they were to determine on a removal, their pass-books would be closely and critically examined in the Committee. If it appeared that they have been prudent and economical and a balance still exists against them further allowance will be made, so as to balance the acct, on the principle that the services of every industrious, prudent man are equal to the necessary expenses of his living. If on the contrary it should appear that they came here to speculate on the industry of others by running in *debt at the store* for articles not necessary but merely to accumulate property or indulge idle fancies, whatever balance there might be against them would be rigidly exacted in money or labor. This is evidently a just and necessary precaution against subjecting the better part of the society to the impositions of scheming speculators who might otherwise come here with the view of staying a few months, accumulating property at the expense of the industrious whom they leave behind them after having unworthily enjoyed all the advantages of membership. Some cases of this kind have occurred and the parties have gone away, highly displeased with the Society, because they were disappointed in their schemes of plunder. Others have withdrawn because their sectarian notions in religion were not *prevalent* here—others again, because their ambition and self-importance were not estimated according to their own ideas—others again to look after their private affairs, which they had hastily abandoned in their eagerness to enjoy advantages which they did not give themselves time to study and understand. Thus you see that the Society is gradually becoming a SELECT one, fitted to the purpose originally contemplated by its founder.

In the case of Mr. Schnee which I have cited as an example of the operation of the system, you must not imagine that he is actuated by any unworthy motives; for his devotion to the system, and high standing among us are unquestionable. He is one of the most active, intelligent, and useful members, and is perfectly happy in his present situation.

Wednesday evening.

Two of the Shakers from Kentucky arrived today to join the Society, I suspect they will not be able to find lodgings, and will therefore be obliged to return, or go somewhere else.

As Mr. S. will not agree to reduce the postage to 18¾ I have endeavored to give you 25 cents in quantity and quality. I am sure you will be satisfied with the former, whatever you may think of the latter.

Friday morning.

* * * The Baltimore Gaz. recd. yesterday evg. contains an acct. of the arrival of Mr. Owen and his son Robert Dale Owen and Capt. McDonald. They are impatiently expected here.—A great military parade yesterday afternoon and a splendid military ball in the evening at the Hall.—A great number of stran-

gers in town. Weather continues fine, though somewhat *sharp* this morning. Yr truly aff father,

Wm. Pelham.

New Harmony,
Dec. 9th, 1825.
Friday Evg. 8 o'clock.

My dear William—

* * * The last mail brought forty six newspapers for the Gazette with 4 or 5 new applications for *exchange*. In some of them I perceive Mr. O'S [Owen's] address to "Americans" written on his passage. Mr. Wm. Owen also recd. a letter from his father dated N. York Nov. 10 in which he says he shall be here as soon as possible. By the tenor of the address, however, I suspect it will not be possible until he has spent 2 or 3 weeks at Washington City in erecting the model, and explaining his System to the Members of Congress. * * *

Your truly affectionate father,

Wm. Pelham.

December 27, 1825.
Tuesday Evening.

My Dear Son.

* * * The weather, for several days, has been so cold and the days so short, that I could scarcely do more than make out a hasty summary for the paper, and keep myself tolerably warm—I long for the return of warm, pleasant weather. My room, now it is filled in, is a very tolerable winter room, it was pleasant enough last summer, but will be more so next season. Mr. Owen has not yet arrived, though expected daily. In the mean time many things continue unsettled, and must remain so until his return.

For the last three weeks we have heard a great deal about a numerous assemblage of Methodists expected in this place on the 24th & 25th inst. These days are passed, but only about fifteen or twenty came, including *one* preacher. On enquiring of one of the brethern how this happened, he informed me that a report was circulated in the country that the Committee had refused them the use of the Church, though it is a notorius fact that the Committee very readily granted them the Church for the exercise of their religious worship. This is a specimen of the means resorted to, in order to injure the reputation of the Harmonians.

Facts are distorted & misrepresented, and when facts are wanting for this purpose, malevolent ingenuity can easily fabricate them.

Since I became a member of this Community I have uniformly experienced every kindness that could reasonably be expected under the circumstances at present existing. No doubt there is much inconvenience, but it is in fact unavoidable, considering the hasty manner in which we have been assembled. Time, patience, and perseverance will gradually remove all difficulties. It is supposed, that on the arrival of Rob. D. Owen (now daily expected) the boarding school will be the first object of attention—that it will be reorganized under the superintendence, with the assistance of Mr. Fiquepal, Madam Fretageot & several other teachers on the Pestalozzian plan & we shall probably have Neef among us.

The routine of duty in preparing the articles for the paper is still unsettled, and will probably continue so, until Mr. Owen's arrival. At present, it is thus; Mr. [Wm.] O[wen] & Mr. J[ennings] prepare all the *editorial* articles & *decide* on the extracts to be made from the papers we receive. I make the Summary of news & submit it to their revision; the greater part of which is *accepted*, & some rejected. Mr. Palmer executes the mechanical part, pretty much in his own way. The summary of news, keeping the accounts of subscribers, and aiding Mr. P. in making up the mails seems to have fallen to my share, and, during the present season, is full as much as I want. But this department, as well as the others will undergo a full examination when Mr. O[wen] arrives, and I have every reason to believe that the management of the *library* will be committed to me, which I should be much better pleased with. It is said that Mr. O[wen] has shipped for New Orleans a large collection of books for the contemplated library.

On Sunday last, our military men as usual were paraded before the door of the Tavern, from whence they marched a little way out of town for the purpose of *drilling*, as *usual*, under the command of Mr. Jennings, who is certainly an excellent disciplinarian, & well acquainted with military tactics. This drill on *Sunday* will no doubt be called a profanation of the Sabbath, as all other Sunday Schools are, whether they be literary, or military. It is at least evident that, if a Sunday School for military instruction is a profanation, the other for clerical purposes are not less so.

Wednesday Evg.—

The regular town meeting is held this evening to hear the weekly proceedings of the Committee read, *according to custom.* I have not attended one of these meetings, or attended the Sunday lecture since the cold weather set in, for in fact I cannot risk my health so far—still, I must contrive someway or other to hear Mr. Owen when he returns. He will have some errors to correct, and many things to adjust. Among others, the affairs of the printing office, I hope I shall then have some *specific* duty assigned to me, for the present, unsettled state of things is very unpleasant to me. It seems to be the unanimous sense of the Comee. that the library shall be my destination, than which nothing cd be more agreeable to me—but as yet we have no books. Mr. Wm. O[wen] told me this evening that his father has shipped at N. York a valuable collection which will be here via New Orleans about the middle of Feb. (he thinks) but I do not expect to see them till April. I shd be glad if the books you have packed up cd be here about the same time.

Thursday Evg. Dec. 29,—6 P. M.

I have just recd. your paper of Decr. 10th with Niles Reg. of the 3rd.—This mail brot 2 letters from Wm. Blagrove, one of which contained a list of 11 subscribers he had obtained in New York. He is delighted with the System and severely regrets that his entanglements with Old Society prevents his enjoying the benefits of it—as yet—Mr. Jennings lately said that he was persuaded, if he were sent as a *Missionary* abroad, he would soon collect 30,000 persons desirous of joining the Society & really, I think he would come near the mark. I have just heard that the Yellow Spring association has "blown out." I am not surprised at this for on its commencement I anticipated a blundering business, as John Sheward will testify. When we talked of that place, I constantly said "I will go to *Head Quarters.*" Sheward will confirm this altho he cd not then coincide with me.

Mr. Owen has not yet arrived, but we have certain accounts of his being *on the road.*—You can hardly conceive the impatience with which he is expected. I just think of mentioning that we have very few *old* men—there is only one man here older than myself, Mr. Lewis, the Secretary, is about fifty, lively and active. Dr. McNamee, about the same age, Mr. Bosson abt 35, Mr. Schnee perhaps the same, Mr. Jennings I should think 30—Judge Wattles 30, Wm. Owen probably 25, but in education, experience & general knowledge not less than 35. Still we are much in want of farmers, mechanics and laborers.

New Harmony, Ind. Jan. 6, 1826.
Friday Afternoon

My dear Son,

Yesterday evening I recd your acceptable favor of Dec. 18th with the O. Repub. of the 17th. It seems you are puzzles about our mails,—and so am I.—Mr. Schnee told me a few days ago that letters and papers arrive sooner here when they come via Vincennes! than by any other route, altho' Vincennes appears to be abt 55 miles out of the direct way—he told me yesterday eveng that since the P. O. at Lancaster had become a distributing office the packet for Harmony is now made up *there* instead of Louisville as heretofore. * * *

Mails again. Our Eastern mail carries all letters & papers directed to Princeton, Ind. Vincennes—Paoli—& Evansville, all along this side of the river to Albany, where it crosses to Louisville. The E. Package contains also letters to a large portion of Kentucky as well as all places eastward. The western mail goes to Mt. Vernon crosses the Ohio & proceeds to the Western part of Ky. a great part of Illinois, all Tennessee &c.

* * * You tell me Mr. Mills is preparing to go down the river in the spring, I shd be truly gratified to see him on his way, and I do not see any great difficulty—he can take passage in the steam boat from Cincinn. to Louisville, thence to Mt. Vernon, land there & easily get a conveyance to N. Harmony—stay here as long as convenient—return to Mt. Vernon where steamboats are continually passing up & down the river as long as the water is high enough. I pray you to present my kind remembrance to him & Mrs. Mills.

If the Society has been injured by the withdrawing of some who did not know what they were about when they joined it, the injury cannot be very extensive, for the principles supported here are daily becoming more & more known & applications for admission are still more numerous than is desirable for the Committee until better accommodations can be provided. There is no fear of the Society being dissolved for the want of persons heartily disposed to join us—the only difficulty is house room but this I know will be removed in a great measure during the next spring, summer, & autumn. You seem very desirous that Master Hill shd accompany you—will he be contented to lodge on the floor of my little room with you & myself? Danl Ferson will pay us a visit & I must endeavor to find some sort of lodging for him also. However, what is impracticable in this way during the cold season may not even be difficult in warm weather.

I find you have noticed "Pumpkin Vine." He is our Tavern keeper, and a queer chap he is, forever amusing himself and others with odd, biting, cutting remarks on the missionary begging scheme—the Bible & tract speculations of the clergy, &c &c &c—

I might perhaps be able to fill this sheet without fatiguing you, if I had the time, but I must hasten to a close, otherwise it cannot be sent by this mail.

Why does not Mr. Peters send us some subscribers? I am afraid he does not bestir himself as some other of our agents do. Wm. Blagrove lately sent us 12 at a slap—& promised some 20 or 30 more, all for No. 1.—No. 1 however is exhausted & therefore we were obliged to commence with No. 2.—No 7 is also out but there is some talk of reprinting both nos—and the prospectus also for a subscription paper, for which applications are made by every mail.

My dear Son—accept my tender & affectionate embrace.

Wm. Pelham.

Sunday afternoon, Jan. 8 1826.

My dear William.

On Friday last, I wrote you as long a letter as my time & engagements would permit & now I commence another in season, that I may have time to answer every point contained in yours of Decr. 11-18 which I may have overlooked.

You cannot reconcile the apparent contradiction between Mr. Owen's advertising for so many mechanics, and the Committee's rejecting applications for admission for *want of room* I will endeavor to explain it. On Mr. Owen's arrival at New York, the first news he heard of this place was that the settlement was broke up, and the members dispersed. Instead of this discouraging or disheartening him, the first thing he set about was to replenish the settlement with the population of the most useful kind, *cost what it might.* It was obvious, however, that before this could be done, the spring would be far advanced, and shifts might be made for lodging, which would be impracticable during the rigor of winter.

Monday afternoon. When I had got thus far in my letter yesterday, two of my friends called in to see me, and we sat in my little "garrett" without a fire—(the weather now being uncommonly, and unseasonably warm) conversing till nearly dark, when they left me & I repaired to Dr. McNamee's by previous invitation to supper. Here I found Mr. Lewis, Mr. Wm. Owen & a Mr. Atlee from Philadelphia, besides the Dr. & 3 or 4 ladies, besides the good lady of the house & her 2 daughters. The table was covered with a profusion of delicacies, excellent coffee, tea, cream, honey, sweetmeats, ham, sausage, &c &c in abundance—But I would not have you infer that this good cheer is found in every family in New Harmony,—the time has not yet arrived when *all the members* are to fare alike—though I really believe this will be the case in the *new Community.* In the meantime, contentment sweetens the cup of life, whatever it may contain. Now do not run to the other extreme, and imagine we are starved for this is not true, tho our privations are sometimes such as to test the strength of our principles. * * *

After the enjoyment of a pleasant evening I came home about 9 o'clock & soon after went to bed.

I never see the Philadelphia Gaz. but from a humorous extract which will appear in our next gazette, I should judge that it was not decidedly hostile. The Sat. Ev. Post comes regularly to us, According to your suggestion, I shall offer an exchange to the Western Carrier, Ravenna, O. * * *

You make me laugh when you talk about "Pone Bread, & Musquetoes." The good book saith, "better is a crust of bread with contentment of mind, than the most sumptous fare where there is no love." I know I have not quoted exactly, but I have no bible at hand. Apropos; Do not forget to send me our family 4to bible. Pone Bread & Musquetoes! How wonderfully efficient these will be in defeating the most feasible plan for improving the condition of mankind that was ever devised.

Mr. Hill seems uncertain whether he will visit us or not. I hope you are not so, for I shall be truly disappointed, & grieved if you do not come. This expectation has a considerable share in keeping up my spirit—another source of comfort to me has been the uniform kindness of your expressions and the *cheerful tone* of your letters. * * *

On looking over the list of articles (Nov. 7) packed up in the trunk, I perceive "Book for Map of the World— & U. S." I hope you will contrive to send me the large maps to which they refer.—I see also that [you] have already packed up the Family Bible. The map belonging to Lewis & Clark is in a red leather 8to book cover somewhere about the book shelves.—I had scarcely written the last word "shelves" when Mr. Palmer's young man brot me a proof of the outside of our next paper (i. e.—pages 1st, 4, 5 & 8th.) to be corrected. It contains some excellent matter—especially the "Gray Light No. 4" on the *"Origin of evil;"* a subject which has always puzzled the wisest heads in the world. There is likewise a good letter signed "A Christian." I know not who is the writer of the letter, tho' I might know if I thought it worth the trouble of enquiring. The Grey Light is a communication from N. York by mail—I wish you would occasionally make extracts from our Gazette & especially the 2 Nos. of the "Grey Light." * * *

I am at present, as I have been, a boarder (now at 64 cents a week) with my *old friends* the *young* baker, 22 years of age, & his *young* wife, about 20, where I am as comfortably situated with regard to diet as cd reasonably be expected. Their house is situated on the main street, about 200 yards from my lodging. We have no occasion to be governed by the ringing of the bell for meals, but I find it convenient for us all to take our breakfast at 8—our dinner at ½ past 12 & our supper at dark. They have been uniformly kind, & attentive to my convenience, & I believe we are mutually pleased with each other. * * *

We have heard nothing yet from Mr. O[wen]—the word however now is, that the river havg risen considerably we shall hear his voice in the *Steeple house* next Sunday.

The weather continues so warm that I have taken off *two* blankets from my bed. You may tell Mr. Harris that the Doctor's sick list contains about 20 names—and he will observe that is a much greater number than ever were sick at the same time in *Zanesville* or any where else except Harmony.—The force of prejudice is astonishing to those who have never attended to its effect on *mental vision.* I have lately recd. from Neef a curious letter on this subject.—

Wednesday morng. The weather continues uncommonly warm, we have scarcely seen the face of the Sun for the last 6 or 7 days,—the thermometer on Monday morn stood at 61— and judging by my feelings it is about the same now. A good deal of rain has fallen—but the ground is now dry tho' the sky continues cloudy?—If this warm weather continues much longer we may expect to hear some *musqueto* music.

Wed. evg.—The weather has changed, and we have again enjoyed the splendid light of the sun—the evening is clear & the sky again presents a brilliant assemblage of stars. This is the evening on which our town meetings are weekly held, but they ceased to *interest me as soon as the cold weather commenced.* I prefer sitting here in my comfortable little room, and scribbling what may, or perhaps may not interest you. *The report today* was that Mr. Owen was *actually seen* yesterday at Mt. Vernon with a company of 32 persons on their way to Harmony. "A plague on all liars" say I—for if this had been true he would have been here by noon this day. * * *

Upon looking over my pass-book just now I find a balance of $24.29 in my favor.—From this must be deducted the charge against me for washing, at the rate of 16 cents a doz. and for postage, since my franking privilege ceased.

Thursday noon. The weather has again become sharp, cold and clear, and the glorious sun shines out most brilliantly—No news of Mr. O[wen] yet.

Friday morng. Cloudy again with rain & thunder!—I have the pleasure of saying that Mr. O[wen] *is here*—he arrived yesterday evg. accompanied only by a Russian lady whom he accidently found somewhere below Stubenville on her way to New Harmony. An assembly of almost the whole population met in the *Steeple house* about 7 o'clock—Mr. O[wen] entered & taking his stand in the pulpit expressed the pleasure and joy he felt to be among us. I have not time to give you a sketch of his discourse which he soon closed. He earnestly recommended Unity & brotherly love. He said that he had left his company behind proceeding in a boat which contained more *learning* than ever was before contained in a boat. He did not mean Latin & Greek & other languages but real substantial knowledge. It contained some of the ablest instructors of youth that cd be found in the U. S. or perhaps in the world. I was pleased with his manner as well as his matter. I have not yet been introduced to him, preferring to wait till the *bustle* is over. He is to give a lecture next Sunday in the forenoon. In noticing his passing through Z. you do not say (in the O. Republic) that he gave a lecture. I hope, however, you saw and spoke to him.

Your truly affectionate father,

Wm. Pelham.

N. Harmony, Friday Jan. 27, 1826.

My dear Son,

Yesterday evening I recd your acceptable letter of Jan. 8 with 2 Ravenna Papers but no O. Repub. *At the same time* I recd. your long looked for letter of the 31st Oct!! which appears to have been missent to Peoria Ill. and forwarded from thence on the 12th inst. * * *

When I commenced writing this I intended, if possible to fill the sheet but I now begin to suspect it will not be in my power, for I have at this moment 4 visotors in my room, talking to me and to one another about the *New Constitution* which is about to be formed. As soon as this is accomplished this preliminary Society will be dissolved and we shall immediately commence a *Cummunity of Equality* & mutual cooperation. I would willingly give you some account of the proceedings which have already taken place with this view. Since his return Mr. Owen has delivered frequent lectures, and yesterday evening a committee of 7 was chosen by ballot to draw up a Constitution and a set of Rules & Regulations to be submitted to the Members of the present Society, article by article. Some of my friends thought proper to run me for this committee, and I received 44 purely *unsolicited* votes—the highest number for any person was 136—(Mr. Owen himself)— and the lowest *successful* number of votes was 63. In fact I did not know (& cared not at all)— that my name was thought of, till yesterday about noon & I assure you I speak sincerely in saying that I am *glad* that the number of votes in favor of electing me did not reach the point of election. I was by no means desirous of being placed in the Committee. As soon as things are settled I will write you an acct. of them, unless I shall have the supreme satisfaction of seeing you here. Since the rect. of your letters I have had no time to read them attentively, & my chief purpose in writing this is to inform you of their coming to hand.

Wednesday night 10 o'clock.

Since the date of the above I have been so constantly occupied that I have had no opportunity of continuing my *journal* for your information. Besides the weather has been so cold, that a great part of my time has been consumed in protecting myself against its effects. This day however, it has moderated *considerably* & I am now sitting in my room scribbling what I think may be interesting to you.

This evening was appointed to report the draft of the *Constitution* prepared by the Committee appointed for that purpose. It is in print & I shall enclose a copy in the Gazette directed to the Ohio Repub. But you are to consider it as a proposal only not yet acted upon by the Society. A plan of Arrangement of the affairs of the Society was also presented to the meeting and ordered to be printed. If this be done in time I will also enclose that. The more I see of Mr. Owen the more I am convinced of his prudence, wisdom, integrity and enlarged benevolence. The purity of his views is *unquestionable*, whatever may be said by the enemies of the New Social System. Every article of this Constitution is to undergo a thorough investigation in a public assembly of the Society when the utmost freedom of speech is not only *tolerated* but solicited and encouraged. Young and old are equally invited to express their sentiments, and the common sense & common feeling of the Society decide on their propriety. This is a delightful state of society, and such as I have long entertained in *idea*, but never expected to see *realized*. It will yet be some time, perhaps a week or two before the Society will be able *finally* to determine on their constitution & code of laws.

The persons who have lately arrived are Mr. Wm. Maclure of Philad. reputed to be immensely rich, and certainly *devoted* to the principles of this Society. I have had several interviews and conversations with him and his manners and sentiments are in direct opposition to those of all other *wealthy* men of whom I have any knowledge, excepting only Mr. Owen himself. Besides him we have Mr. Fiquepal & Madam Fretageot, both Pezzalozzian teachers,—Mr. LeSueur an eminent designer, Mr. Say, Dr. Troost, a distinguished mineralogist—and several other men of Science. Mr. MaClure has put into my hands a catalogue of French books and philosophical apparatus now at New Orleans on their way to this place amounting in value to 100,000 francs and weighing abt 50 tons. He wished me to make a fair transcript of the invoice in a book he had provided for the purpose. I shall find some difficulty in doing this for want of a good French dictionary—but I will accomplish it.

Thursday Forenoon.

By the last mail I recd. a letter from Neef,—he is anxious to be among us, but cannot yet bring matters to bear—Mr. MaClure told me yesterday that he wrote to him by the last mail, urging him to come on immediately whether he brings his family and movable property or not, and in the latter case to make arrangements for their following him, for that he was already a Member. This letter of Mr. MaClure's I expect will settle his mind, and we shall probably see him in a week or two.

The plan of the proposed Constitution is in the hands of all the members, and will undergo a thorough investigation. My mind during the last two weeks has been in a state of such constant excitement, as to be painful, and this you will easily conceive when you consider how inactive both in mind and body I have long been previous to my coming hither. I feel now that I want quietness and rest, and I scarcely expect any, until I am appointed *Librarian* which will in all probability be my permanent occupation. Mr. Owen and all the members of the Committee, besides a considerable part of the population appear to think me most fitted for such employment, and it exactly squares with my own inclination.

The bell is now ringing for dinner, immediately after which I must go the Printing Office & assist Mr. Palmer in making up at least 300 papers to be sent by mail. If I have the oppy. of making any addition to this letter I will embrace it, but I rather think it will not be in my power. The warm weather will soon return & I anxiously hope it will bring you along.—

Thursday night. I have just inclosed in a wrapper seperate from the usual inclosure which Mr. Palmer directed to the "Ohio Repub. Zanesville, O." a duplicate No. 19 of the Gazette with the proposed Constitution & Plan of Arrangement.

These are busy times. Meetings are held almost every night in the *Steeple House;* and at the farthest every second night the bell is rung at ½ past 6 and at 7 no vacant seat can be found.—I have hitherto attended them all— but this evening I shall *take my rest,* as I expect the business will chiefly be some verbal criticisms on the Constitution and proposals to amend the phraseology—Everyone gives his sentiments freely, and it is really remarkable that so little uninteresting matter is brought forward. Some of our mechanics are truly eloquent, and none absurd. It would be no amusement to you if I were to give you my crude remarks on the proposed constitution, for I have not had time to read it attentively,—but I certainly do anticipate some considerable alterations in the style of it.—Several other drafts will be offered to the consideration of the Society and which of them will ultimately be preferred, it is impossible at present to say.

It is now between 8 & 9 & I shall go directly to bed—so, good night, my dear boy, & let me still cherish the hope of seeing you here when the season is favorable.

Wednesday Feb. 8″, 1826.

My dear Son,

The Constitution, of which I sent you a printed sketch, has

undergone a thorough examination and discussion; and was recommitted to the Constitutional Committee who again reported it, with considerable alterations and amendments. After these were fully discussed, and some further amendments made the Society finally adopted a Constitution, which would have appeared in this day's paper, if it could have been prepared in season. There being no printed copy, I cannot present you with the articles. It has been transcribed into a book, and 300 names have already been subscribed to it. There will be very few, if any dissentients among the members of the Preliminary Society.

This evening is appointed for the election of three important officers, viz. Secretary, Treasurer & Commissary, and it is expected that the organization of the Community will be completed next week. Every department will be arranged so as to produce a united effort to furnish every practicable means of comfortable subsistence to every individual. Hitherto, there has been much irregularity of effort, the consequence of which nearly paralyzed the energies of the population, but at length I see the way clear, and I see the utter impossibility of such a state of things again recurring. The several parts of the *great machine* will be so admirably adapted to each other, as to effect the most valuable purposes. The experience I have gained convinces me I was right in coming here, in preference to going to any of the *Communities* professedly formed on Mr. Owen's principles in other parts of the country. During the last 8 months the want of organization and arrangement has caused much perplexity and difficulty, and the introduction now of order and regularity into the several departments will be comparatively easy. I anticipate that in 6 months the New Harmony machine will go like a piece of clock work. The preceeding errors are noted and will be avoided. In consequence of the great change which has been just made, I should not be surprised to see it announced in some of the Eastern papers, with *great glee* that Mr. Owen's visionary project on the banks of the Wabash has utterly failed, &c &c. tho nothing can be further from the truth—for in reality one third of it is accomplished— and we are just entering on the second 3d and the next step—(when we are prepared for it) will be into the Village of Equality and Independence. He is an extraordinary man—a wonderful man—such a one indeed as the world has never before seen. His wisdom, his comprehensive mind, his practical knowledge, but above all, his openness, candor & sincerity, have no parallel in ancient or modern history. Do not think I am dreaming, for in fact, I have closely attended to his language and movements since his return.

I earnestly expect to see you here early in the spring when you will have opportunity of seeing, of hearing & judging for yourself. There is now here a young married man from a distant part of this State. He came about a month ago and has resided at the Tavern at the expense of 3 dollars a week for himself and his horse. He has felt so deeply interested in the measures preparatory to the formation of the New Community that he could quit us until he saw its accomplishment. We have spent a good deal of time together & I expect he will shortly set out on his return for the purpose of bringing his wife & child & 4 other families who will accompany him, if he can obtain a previous assurance that they will be received.

Thursday afternoon.—The election was not held yesterday evening, as I had expected it would be. It will probably take place this evening. It is generally thought that Mr. Lewis will be *Secretary*, and Wm. Owen *Treasurer*, the Commissary is rather more doubtful.

There is—Thursday night—I have been to the P. O. and got the O. Repub. of Jany. 21, with letters from Col. Chambers, Mr. Harris and Mr. Neef & none from yourself. There seems to be a great improvement in the expedition of the mail. Col. C's letter is dated Jan. 22d & Mr. Harris' is dated 24th. Tho after all it seems to require 12 or 14 days to come fr. Z. to H. Neef's letter bears the postmark of Louisville Jan. 30″. By the bye, do not omit to call at the P. O. in Louisville on your way hither. You will *probably* find a letter there tho I am not certain. If you can contrive to see Mr. Neef he would be most happy to meet with you. He has a daughter in Louisville whom you may find by enquiring of my friend Mr. Taylor, the Post Office Clerk. Tell Col. Chambers I will not fail to answer all his inquiries as soon as possible, but he must not be impatient, for these are *busy times* for every one in New Harmony. If he will have patience till *warm weather* I shall better be able to satisfy him. The proceedings of the Convention in forming the *Community Constitution* with the Constitution itself will be in the next paper and I will send him a copy. I think I informed you, and I wish you would mention to Col. Chambers & Mr. Harris that soon after Mr. Owen's return he was followed by his son Robert Dale Owen, Dr. Price & Mr. Wm. MaClure of Philadelphia, Mr. Whitwell, Mr. LeSueur, Mr. Say, all men of extensive scientific knowledge,

Mr. Fiquepal and Madam Fretageot first rate teachers on the Pestalozzian plan. There are now at New Orleans on their way hither a vast collection of books, philosophical apparatus & musical instruments weighing upwards of 50 tons & the freight of which will cost 10 to 1200 dollars. In Harmony there will be the best Library & the best School in the United States.

10 O'clock P. M.—The election is again postponed till tomorrow evening, to give further time for the members to form their judgment. My own, indeed, is already formed, and I earnestly hope the election may fall on Mr. Lewis, Wm. Owen, and Richardson Whitby, who came here from a society of shakers in Kentucky, and brought with him a practical knowledge of the order and regularity, and system, by which that society has distinguished itself. This is an anxious time,—(not with a view to a *final* success and of our principles, which must infalliably succeed sooner or later) but with a view to the *speedy* accomplishment of the purposes for which we are associated. It is therefore important that our first selection of agents be made with the greatest circumspection, and due appreciation of the qualifications of the persons choosen to carry into effect the principles which we advocate and support. Forseeing that I shall have no opportunity of continuing this letter tomorrow, and unwilling to send you any *blank* paper, I may as well endeavor to fill the remainder of my sheet with such matters as occur to me now.

You will easily conceive the effect produced on the minds of our citizens when Mr. Owen, after some days examination of the State of things here, proposed the immediate formation of a Community of Equality and mutual cooperation. The subject was debated with the utmost freedom, which he encouraged by constant efforts to make every one speak his *real* sentiments wheather favorable or unfavorable to his proposal. After a full and *verily,* a *free* discussion the proposal was accepted, and we have since been constantly engaged in devising the means by which it can be effected. Next week after your receiving this you will see the constitution and plan of arrangement, and you will perceive that every feature bears the stamp of *genuine* democracy, not the false democracy of the office seekers of Zanesville.

½ past ten. Mr. Bosson has just come in and brought me Mr. Peters' kind & affectionate letter of Jan. 16th. * * * Good-night, Dr William. Wm. Pelham.

Feb. 23, 1826.—Friday.

My Dear William—

I have snatched up the first sheet of paper I could lay my hands on (for want of time to seek a better one) to acknowledge the receipt of yours of Feb. 5—7, postmarked Feb. 7 which came to hand yesterday evening. I cannot at present enter into particulars, but I have enquired about the Steamboat charges. The result is that from Cincinnati to Louisville the charge is probably 4 dollars & from Louisville to Mt. Vernon 8 dollars—perhaps something less.

Our affairs still remain in an unsettled state, the consequence of which is much inconvenience in a variety of ways. There is more to be done at once than can be to place things on the right footing. Three days ago Mr. Owen informed me that Mr. Jennings had declined the editorship of the paper any longer, and he, (Mr. Owen) wished me to undertake it. I answered him that I considered that duty a very important one, and I did not conceive myself by any means adequate to the task. He said that I should have assistance when I required it. But I know full well the difference between promising & performing, however as he seemed to expect it of me, I prepared the 2 editorial articles in the last Gazette, and shewed them to him, before they were inserted.

Your suggestion concerning a direct rout to Indianapolis, is well worthy of attention. It shall be communicated to Mr. Owen, and measures, shall, if possible be put in train to effect the object in view. * * *

I have not time to write more, but will endeavor to send you another letter next week.

Your truly affectionate Father,

Wm. Pelham.

I have had a smart touch of the prevailing Influenza but am now recovering—it has pulled me down considerably.—My face is thin and pale—I believe I have lost 10 pounds of flesh within the last 4 or 5 weeks—but I expect the approach of warm weather will restore me.

Thursday Afternoon, Mar. 16'', 1826.

My dear William.

I have just finished helping Mr. Palmer, (according to custom) to make up our mails and I have a few minutes left before I shall be called upon to open the mail, Mr. Schnee being absent. About 3 or 4 weeks ago Mr. Owen accosted me with a *wish* that I would undertake to conduct the Gazette as Mr. Jennings had declined it on *account of his health.* I answered that I considered it an important concern, and that I was not competent to the task. To make a long story short, he urged it and I merely acquiested. In this new capacity I have done as well as I could, though not so well as I wished. How long this will continue to be my occupation is uncertain. Dr. Buchanan of Shelbyville, Ky. has *at last* been written to, to be the editor, but our hopes of his coming are very slim. I shall be heartily glad to get rid of this burden as soon as possible.

Since I last wrote to you very considerable changes have taken place in our affairs, and the prospect is now daily improving. Mr. Owen is indefatigable in his endeavors to introduce economy, frugality, industry, equality, and other practices essential to the success of his principles. In the meantime I do not doubt you very frequently hear the most unfavorable accounts of this place; but you need not fear a dissolution of this Society, for *it cannot happen.* Various modifications have been, and probably will be made, without touching the foundation, which stands on a rock, not to be shaken by priestcraft or any other worldly craft.

You will perceive that I have given a new complexion to the Gaz. in discouraging those long-winded metaphysical disquisitions with which Mr. J. was wont to fill its columns. There are some able pens employed in the service of the Gaz. and when we *get in order* I am in hopes the paper will become more useful than it has hitherto heen. You will understand that my criticisms on the paper are entirely confidential. I just hear the Mail Stage horn at a distance.

Friday Afternoon.—*Miscellany.* The mail yesterday was unusually small. I recd. neither a letter nor an Ohio Repub. I shall anxiously look for you during the whole of next month. I would wish you to *deposite in your memory* all you hear of us either *good* or *bad,* though I am aware your mind will not be overlooked with reports of the former description. It might not be amiss to make notes, to assist yr memory. The fare from Cincinn to Louisville is about 4 dollars, from L. to Mt. Vernon about 6. Mr. Neef is expected to be here this evening or tomorrow.

I would willing communicate with you further, if I did not feel too cold & uncomfortable & moreover had a convenient situation for writing. I should like you to come alone if you do not accompany Daniel Ferson.

Farewell my dear Son—Let me have the supreme satisfaction

of seeing you in April at furthest. In the meantime present me most kindly to Mr. Peters & Mary and all other friends.

Wm. Pelham.

The following letter from Wm. Creese Pelham written a few weeks before his Father's death, gives some information in connection with the schools and Educational Society of New Harmony.

New Harmony, Wednesday 10 January 1827.

My Dear Father

I was unavoidably detained in school longer this evening than I wished and cannot write you as much as I wished. Bolton and myself have several times agreed to come out to you but have been detained by "counteracting circumstances" such as rainy days and cold days &c but we shall be with you next Sunday or the Sunday following I think.—

We go on in the same old way, changing every thing, somethimes before we have an opportunity to find out its benefits. In the internal arrangements of our society no very considerable changes have been made. Dunn & Johnson have left us. We have received between 30 & 40 children from Mr. Owen's Community as day scholars at No. 2. Mr. McCall has a class and Mr. Brown, they come as day scholars at eight dollars per year. All the other children attend at Madam's at No. 5, where some are well satisfied with their progress and others the contrary as usual. Dr. Embree, a young man from Cincinnati delivers lectures to them on physiology and dissects pigs and dogs &c for their information.

Phiquepal has taken his boys entirely to himself and lives in the Church and hall. Jones and his wife are part of his community and Simms &c. The Carpenters, Shoemakers and all persons not employed in teaching the children have removed from the Church. Thirwell has taken all his tools &c home. Phiquepal has stopped his boys from making shoes for the community, which created some dissatisfaction.

A resolution was passed a short time since by our society forbiding the use of the Hall for dancing &c, without special permission of the society. This week, on the application of Miss Caroline Tiebout, one of our members, a resolution was passed for a ball this evening, but on the earnest representation of Phiquepal that it was impossible to use the Hall for dancing without interfering with his arrangements, the resolution was repealed, and we need expect no more balls in the Hall unless they be on Sunday afternoon as proposed by Mr. Owen, but which meets with great opposition.

Phiquepal's boys sleep in the rooms formerly Lesueur and Troost's in the Hall and go to bed at eight and rise at four when they receive one of their lessons, a lecture I believe from Phiquepal. He has his school room which is likewise his eating room &c covered with skeletons, bones, arithmometers &c &c so that it looks more like a museum than a schoolroom.

The prospect of our leaving here in the spring brightens. I earnestly hope we may not be disappointed. Dr. Price writes from Cincinnati that Neville can be purchased of Gen. Neville with 2600 acres of excellent land for $15000. The Gen. wishes to become a member of the community. A part of the property which is rented produced to the Gen. on an average of 35 bush. of corn per acre being one third of the actual produce. A new steam engine which cost $2600 was put in the mill last year. (a saw and grist mill) there are several good brick houses &c &c. The improvements put on the place by Piate cost $24000, since which Gen. Neville has expended several thousand,—but all this is not talked of publicly yet,—a meeting was held at Thirwell's last evening on the subject and mem. furnished Lees who is going up the river shortly. Dr. Price writes he has no doubt but the money can be raised at any time in Cincinnati and considered as a speculation it is the greatest one ever offered and nothing but the General being such a devoted community man could ever induce him to make the offer &c.

I believe our Rope factory burned down before you were here last, and No. 4 was on fire yesterday but little damage was done. Our Society is still tearing down the log buildings for firewood, and the women sometimes cannot agree among themselves who is the cook. Burton and Beal were the cooks at the Granary last week. The dining tables have all been removed from the Granary into the sitting room at the Green House. Three tables accomodate all who eat there. The reason for this was that the Granary was cold and Phiquepal having taken his boys &c away left but few who might be more comfortably accomodated in the sitting room—the room East of that now used for our meetings. Tiebout has resigned his office of storekeeper.

Our Scientific Journal has not yet been commenced but the plates for it are engraving and preparations making. The Printing press &c have been removed to the Infirmary or old carpenter shop.

Say was married the other day to Lucy Sistare, they went off to a place beyond Springfield. * * *

Your aff. Son

Wm. Creese Pelham.

A letter from William Owen to William Pelham of Zanesville, O.

Harmonie, Indiana

22—January 1825

Sir—

In my Father's absence I have received your letters dated the 1—& 24—of last month.

My father sailed up the river from Mount Vernon about 10 days ago, in company with Mr. Rapp and 70 or 80 Harmonians who were on their way to Economy, a property lately purchased by them near Pittsburg. My Father intends proceeding to the City of Washington without delay, hoping to come into communication there, with most of the leading minds in the States. As soon as he has made known, as far as he considers necessary, the leading features of his plans, he will then return to this place as quickly as possible, in order to complete the arrangements necessary to the formation of a Society here, founded on the Principles, which he has so long advocated; for which purpose he purchased this estate from Mr. Rapp, a few days before his departure.

I am highly gratified to learn that you have been pleased by the perusal of the Dublin Journal, containing an account of my Fathers proceedings while in that City.

At present we have no further publication here; but we are in expectation of receiving several shortly from Europe. When they arrive I am sure my Father will have much pleasure in giving you every information on the subject.

As it is intended to form an establishment here with the least possible loss of time, I fear my Father will be prevented from seeing you at Zanesville, before his return to this town; but I am sure he will take the earliest opportunity of cultivating a personal acquaintance with you.

It is proposed that a Society be formed here, on the Principle of united production and consumption, to be composed of persons practicing all the most useful occupations necessary to the well being of a complete establishment, to whom lodgings, food clothing, attendance during sickness and a good education for their children will be secured. The profits to accumulate in order to form a new Community on the Principle of complete equality, as soon as a sufficient sum shall be realized. In case of expulsion or Voluntary Departure each family to be entitled to draw out all the property they may have brought in with them, and to receive in addition whatever the Directors of the establishment may consider reasonable.

We expect a number of useful tradesmen to come out from Europe in November or December and that we shall be joined by many others both from the Eastern States and from this neighborhood.

I shall forward your letter to Washington City by tomorrow's post. My Father, I think, will be with us again early in March. We shall be happy to see you here whenever you cam make it convenient to leave home and I have no doubt, my Father will endeavor to make his arrangements to visit you if possible, on his return Westward.

With best thanks for your good wishes, believe me

Your Obt. Servt.

Wm. Owen.

From *Travels through North America, during the year 1825 and 1826*, by His Highness, Bernhard, Duke of Saxe-Weimer Eisenach [1828], Vol. II., pp. 105-124.

BERNHARD, KARL, *Duke of Saxe-Weimer*.

Duke Bernhard tells us that the idea of visiting America occupied his mind almost from the earliest years, the chief reason being "I wished to see the new world; the country; the people; their conditions and institutions; their customs and manners." But due to the exactions of the military life, this desire was not granted until rather late in years. Finally in 1825 the opportunity came, and due to the friendship that existed between himself and the king of the Netherlands, the latter provided passage for him on a royal sloop of war—The Pallas.

Duke Bernhard spent fifteen months in this country. By training he was a keen observer, and his accounts therefore are of more than usual interest.

The Wabash, a very beautiful river, rises not far from the sources of the Miami of the Lakes, and meanders through one of the most fertile districts of the west. At its mouth, it is about two hundred and fifty yards broad, and is navigable about four hundred miles. The Wabash forms the boundary between the states of Illinois and Indiana, the right bank belongs to the former, the left to the latter state. About evening, the steam-boat landed Mr. Huygens and myself on the right bank at Mount Vernon, a place established about two years ago, whence we proposed to go by land to New Harmony. Mr. Hottinguer left us, as he pursued his voyage in the steam-boat; I parted very reluctantly from this esteemed fellow traveller, who possessed many good qualities, above all others, one seldom found in his countrymen, great modesty.

Mount Vernon lies upon a high bank, one hundred and twenty-six miles from New Orleans, and eight hundred and three from Pittsburgh. It is a favourable situation for trade, laid out on an extensive plan, but has only frame houses, and at most three hundred inhabitants. It is the new capital of Posey county. A prison was finished for the use of the county; a court-house was about to be built. We formed an acquaintance with a physician established here, and a travelling merchant. The roots of the felled trees remained yet in the streets of the town, the woods began close behind the houses; nay, the latest built were encircled by them.

On the following morning, 15th of April, we hired a two-horse wagon, to carry us to the village of New Harmony, which is sixteen miles distant from Mount Vernon, and lies on the left shore of the Wabash. The road passed through a hilly country, thickly grown with green-leaved trees. The way was made very bad by former rains, and the most miry places were mended with logs, forming a grievous causeway;* over a little stream, called Big creek, we crossed a tolerable wooden bridge. About half way is Springfield, at first made the capital of Posey county, which, however, afterwards was changed to Mount Vernon, as I have mentioned before. In Springfield the county gaol still remains, also a brick court-house, and about ten wooden houses, two of them are taverns. As the road was very bad, and the horses went very slow, I walked at least ten miles, and arrived at New Harmony, before the carriage. As soon as you clear the woods, you have a very handsome view of the place. It lies in a valley, not far from the Wabash. The woody and low banks of this river, were at present, in the neighbourhood of New Harmony, overflowed. From the roots of trees still remaining, it was visible, that this country had been covered with wood but a short time back.

In fact, it is but eleven years since Mr. Rapp with his society, after they had disposed of Harmony in Pennsylvania, moved here, and felled the first tree to found New Harmony in a country inhabited only by wolves, Indians, bears, rattlesnakes, &c.

The hills immediately next to the place, are already cleared of timber of the larger kind; they are converted into vineyards, and partly into orchards. Farther off are meadows and fields to the right, and to the left fruit and vegetable gardens, carefully enclosed by palisades. New Harmony itself, has broad unpaved streets, in which good brick houses appear alternately, with framed cabins and log houses: the streets are regular, running at right angles. We took up our quarters in the only tavern there, belonging to the community; it was passable.

Rapp's society, called from their former residence, the Harmonites, consisted of Wurtemburgers. Their early history is known, and perhaps, when I visit this society from Pittsburgh in their new establishment, "Economy," I may find an opportunity

*["These log turnpikes are better known by the name of "corduroy roads."]
TRANS.

to say more concerning them. Rapp sold New Harmony in the year, 1825, to the Englishman, Robert Owen, and left there with his people on the 5th of May, to go up the Ohio to Economy. Mr. Owen was originally engaged in manufactures, and possessed a large cotton factory at New Lanark, on the Falls of Clyde, ten miles from Glasgow in Scotland, where he had, by the adoption of a new system of education and formation of character, changed a collection of one thousand rude labourers into a community of industrious beings. His system, and his ideas upon the situation of human society, as well as the improvements that are capable of being made, he has divulged in a series of essays, which are collected, and appear in print under the name of a new view of society. They conclude with the project of a constitution for a community formed on his system.

Mr. Owen is an enemy to all sects, the spirit of which has generated so much evil under the imposing name of religion. He allows each person liberty to believe in what he may consider to be good; so that a pure Deism is the peculiar religion of his adherents. On this account he was very obnoxious to the prevailing sects in Great Britain, and accordingly his system could not extend itself there. He was therefore induced to turn this attention to the United States, and particularly to the western part of the Union, where, as he says, there is less hypocrisy of religion prevailing than to the east. He then purchased New Harmony from Mr. Rapp, and commenced his establishment in the month of May last. As he laid the foundation of it entirely on perfect equality and community of property, many enthusiasts in these principles from various parts of the Union joined themselves to him; and also a number of vagabonds and lazy worthless persons, from all parts of the worlds, that would willingly live well at the public expense, who had drank away the little money, if they brought any at all, at the tavern, and who would not work, but desired to say a great deal. Mr. Owen had gone to England on account of business in the month of July, and during his absence, a complete anarchy had been introduced into the new community. At the end of October he arrived from England at New York on his return, gave lectures there, in Philadelphia, and in Washington, upon his system, made some proselytes in Philadelphia, and came back to New Harmony. He lamented over his people, and brought the situation of anarchy in which they had fallen before their eyes so plainly, with the consequences resulting therefrom, that they invested him with dictatorial authority for one year.

In the eastern states there is a general dislike to him. It was thought unadvised that he issued a proclamation to the Americans on his last arrival in New York, in which he told them, that among many virtues they possessed great faults, among which he alluded to an ill-directed propensity to religious feelings, and proposed himself as their reformer in this respect. I heard at that time unfavourable expressions from persons in the highest public offices against him; and one of them gave Mr. Owen to understand very plainly that he considered his intellects rather deranged.* In one family alone, where theory took place of experimental knowledge, did I hear conversation turn to his advantage.

After all this, I came with the utmost expectation to New Harmony, curious to become acquainted with a man of such extraordinary sentiments. In the tavern, I accosted a man very plainly dressed, about fifty years of age, rather of low stature, who entered into a conversation with me, concerning the situation of the place, and the disordered state in which I would find every thing, where all was newly established, &c. When I asked this man how long before Mr. Owen would be there, he announced himself, to my no small surprize, as Mr. Owen, was glad at my visit, and offered himself to show every thing, and explain to me whatever remained without explanation. As the arrangement calculated for Rapp's society was not adapted to his, of course many alterations would naturally be made. All the log houses still standing in the place, he intended to remove, and only brick and framed edifices should be permitted to remain. Also all enclosures about particular gardens, as well as all the enclosures within the place itself, he would take away, and only allow the public highways leading through the settlement to be enclosed. The whole should bear a resemblance to a park, in which the separate houses should be scattered about.

In the first place, Mr. Owen carried me to the quondam church of Rapp's society; a simple wooden building, with a steeple of the same materials, provided with a clock. This church was at present appropriated to joiner's and shoemaker's shops, in which the boys are instructed in these mechanic arts.

Behind the church stands a large brick edifice, built in the form of a cross, and furnished with a species of cupola, the purpose

*[This is perhaps, the most charitable idea that can be formed of the actions of such reformers, as well as of a "lady heretofore mentioned, who has unsexed herself, and become so intoxicated with vanity, as enthusiastically to preach up a "réformation" in favour of the promiscuous intercourse of sexes and colours, the downfall of all religion, and the removal of all restraints imposed by virtue and morality!]—TRANS.

of which is unknown. Rapp, they say, had dreamed three times that this building should be erected, and therefore he had it done; but it is thought, and I believe correctly, that he only did this to keep his society in constant employment, so that they could have no leisure to reflect upon their situation, and dependence upon him. His power over them actually extended so far, that to prevent his society from too great an increase, he forbid the husbands from associating with their wives. I also heard here a report which I had already been apprised of in Germany, that he had himself castrated a son who had transgressed this law, for the sake of an example, and that the son had died under the operation. Over one of the entrances of this problematical edifice, stands the date of the year 1822, hewed in stone; under it is a gilt rose, and under this is placed the inscription Micah. 4 v. 8. The interior of the house forms a large hall, in form of a cross, the ceiling is supported by wooden pillars. Mr. Owen has devoted the hall to the purposes of dancing, music, and meetings for philosophical discussions. He told me that he intended to have the ends of the cross, both of the grand saloon as well as those of the hall under the roof, divided off by partitions, so as to use them for school-rooms, for a library, for a cabinet of natural history, of physical objects, &c.

Mr. Owen then conducted me to Rapp's former dwelling, a large, well-built brick house, with two lightning rods. The man of God, it appeared, took especial good care of himself; his house was by far the best in the place, surrounded by a garden with a flight of stone steps, and the only one furnished with lightning rods. Mr. Owen, on the contrary, contented himself with a small apartment in the same tavern where I lodged. At present, the offices, and the residence of Mr. M'Clure, the associate of Mr. Owen, are in Rapp's house.*

Mr. M'Clure is a man distinguished for learning, who has published a geological chart of the United States. He told me that he was in Germany in the year 1802, and also at Weimar, where he had become acquainted with the literati residing there. I was introduced by him to a native of Alsace, of the name of Neef, a rather aged man, who had the superintendence of the boys. Mr. Owen's two eldest sons were also here shown to me, pupils of Fellenberg, who is greatly respected. Afterwards Mr. Owen made me acquainted with Mr. Lewis, secretary of the society

*[It is understood that Mr. M'Clure has long since given up all connexion with the New Harmony bubble.]—TRANS.

from Virginia, and a relation of the great Washington. He was already pretty far advanced in years, and appeared to have united himself to the society from liberal principles, as far as I could judge from our short conversation. Another acquaintance that I made, was with a Mr. Jennings, from Philadelphia, a young man, who was educated as a clergyman, but had quitted that profession to follow this course of life, and had united himself to Mr. Owen. He intended, nevertheless, to leave this place again, and return back to Philadelphia. Many other members have the same design, and I can hardly believe that this society will have a long duration.* Enthusiasm, which abandons its subjects but too soon, as well as the itch for novelty, had contributed much to the formation of this society. In spite of the principles of equality which they recognize, it shocks the feelings of people of education, to live on the same footing with every one indiscriminately, and eat with them at the same table.

The society consisted, as I was informed, of about one thousand members; at a distance of two miles are founded two new communities. Till a general table shall be instituted, according to the fundamental constitution of the society, the members are placed in four boarding-houses, where they must live very frugally. Several of the most turbulent, with an Irishman who wore a long beard, at their head, wished to leave the society immediately to go to Mexico, there to settle themselves, but where their subsistence will be procured with as much difficulty.

In the evening Mr. Owen conducted me to a concert in the non-descript building. Most of the members of the society were present. The orchestra was not numerous, it consisted at first only of one violin, one violoncello, one clarionet and two flutes. Nevertheless the concert was surprisingly good, especially as the musicians have not been together a year. The clarionet player performed particularly well, and afterwards let us hear him on the bugle. Several good male and female vocalists then took a part, they sang among other things a trio accompanied by the clarionet only. Declamation was interspersed among the musical performances, Lord Byron's stanzas to his wife after their separation were extremely well recited. Between the two parts of the concert the music played a march, each gentleman gave a lady his arm, and a promenade took place, resembling a Polonaise with pretty figures, sometimes in two couples, sometimes in four; two ladies

*By late newspapers it appears that the society actually dissolved itself, in the beginning of the year 1827.

in the middle, the gentlemen separated from the ladies, then again all together. The concert closed with a lively cotillion. I was, on the whole, much amused; and Mr. Huygens took an active share in the dancing. This general evening amusement takes place often in the week; besides, on Tuesday, there is a general ball. There is a particular costume adopted for the society. That for the men consists of wide pantaloons buttoned over a boy's jacket, made of light material, without a collar; that of the women of a coat reaching to the knee and pantaloons, such as little girls wear among us. These dresses are not universally adopted, but they have a good appearance. An elderly French lady, who presides over the department of young mothers, and the nursing of all the very small children, stuck by my side during a large portion of the evening, and tormented me with her philosophical views. All the men did not take a share in the dance, i. e. the lower class, but read newspapers, which were scattered over the side-tables.

The public house in which we lived was conducted on account of the society. General Evans was looked for, who was to keep the house; in the mean time it was directed by the physician of the society, Dr. M'Namee, from Vincennes. Among the public buildings I remarked two of which the lower part was strongly built with rough stone, and provided with loop-holes. The larger of these was the granary, and it was reasonably thought that Rapp had this built as a defensive redoubt for his own people. At the first period of his establishment in this country he had not only had the Indians, but also the rude people known under the general title of backwoodsmen, who not only saw the establishment of such a society with jealous eyes, which they knew would be wealthy in a short time, but also entertained a grudge against Rapp's unnatural rules of chastity.

On the morning of the 14th of April, I strolled about the place to look round me. I visited Mr. Neef, but found his wife only at home, a native of Memmingen, in Swabia. Her husband was in the act of leading the boys out to labour. Military exercises form a part of the instruction of the children. I saw the boys divided into two ranks, and parted into detachments marching to labour, and on the way they performed various wheelings and evolutions. All the boys and girls have a very healthy look, are cheerful and lively, and by no means bashful. The boys labour in the field and garden, and were now occupied with new fencing. The girls learn female employments; they were as little oppressed as the boys with labour and teaching; these happy and interesting children were much more employed in making their youth pass as pleasantly as possible. Madam Neef showed the school-house, in which she dwelt, and in which the places for sleeping were arranged for the boys. Each boy slept on a cot frame, upon a straw bed.

We went next to Rapp's distillery: it will be removed altogether. Mr. Owen has forbidden distilling also, as well as the use of ardent spirits. Nothwithstanding this, the Irishmen here find opportunities of getting whiskey and fuddling themselves from the flat boats that stop here, &c. We saw also a dye-house and a mill set in motion by a steam-engine of ten horse-power. The engine was old and not in good order, Mr. Owen said however, he hoped to introduce steam-mills here in time from England. From the mills we went to the vineyard, which was enclosed and kept in very good order. I spoke to an old French vine-dresser here. He assured me that Rapp's people had not understood the art of making wine; that he would in time make more and much better wine, than had been done heretofore. The wine stocks are imported from the Cape of Good Hope, and the wine has an entirely and singular and strange taste, which reminds one of the common Spanish wines.

We went again to the quondam church, or workshop for the boys, who are intended for joiners and shoemakers. These boys sleep upon the floor above the church in cribs, three in a row, and thus have their sleeping place and place of instruction close together. We also saw the shops of the shoemakers, tailors and saddlers, also the smiths, of which six were under one roof, and the pottery, in which were two rather large furnaces. A porcelain earth has been discovered on the banks of the Mississippi, in the state of Illinois, not far from St. Louis. Two experienced members of the society, went in that direction, to bring some of the earth to try experiments with, in burning. The greater part of the young girls, whom we chanced to meet at home, we found employed in plaiting straw hats. I became acquainted with a Madam F—, a native of St. Petersburg. She married an American merchant, settled there, and had the misfortune to lose her husband three days after marriage. She then joined her husband's family at Philadelphia, and as she was somewhat eccentric and sentimental, quickly became enthusiastically attached to Mr. Owen's system. She told, me however, in German, that she found herself egregiously deceived; that the highly vaunted equality was not altogether to her taste; that some of the society were too low, and the table was below all criticism. The good lady appeared to be about to run from one extreme to the other for she added, that in the summer, she would enter a Shaker establishment near Vincennes.*

I renewed acquaintance here with Mr. Say, a distinguished naturalist from Philadelphia, whom I had been introduced to, at the Wistar Party there; unfortunately he had found himself embarrassed in his fortune, and was obliged to come here as a friend of Mr. M'Clure. This gentleman appeared quite comical in the costume of the society, before described, with his hands full of hard lumps and blisters, occasioned by the unusual labour he was obliged to undertake in the garden.

In the evening I went to walk in the streets, and met with several of the ladies of the society, who rested from the labours of the day. Madam F— was among them, whose complaints of disappointed expectations I had listened to. I feared still more from all that I saw and heard, that the society would have but a brief existence. I accompanied the ladies to a dancing assembly, which was held in the kitchen of one of the boarding-houses. I observed that this was only an hour of instruction to the unpractised in dancing, and that there was some restraint on account of my presence, from politeness I went away, and remained at home the remainder of the evening. About ten o'clock, an alarm of fire was suddenly raised. An old log building used as a wash-house was in flames, immediately the fire-engine kept in a distinct house, was brought and served by persons appointed to that duty. They threw the stream of water through the many apertures of the log-house, and quickly put a stop to the fire. In a quarter of an hour, all was over. Since the houses in the place all stand separately, there is nothing to fear from the extension of fire, unless in a strong wind. The houses, however, are all covered with shingles.

On the 15th of April, I went into the garden back of Rapp's house to see a plate or block of stone, which is remarkable as it bears the impression of two human feet. This piece of stone was hewed out of a rock near St. Louis, and sold to Mr. Rapp. Schoolcraft speaks of it in his travels, and I insert his remarks, as I have found them correct. "The impressions are to all appearance

*[According to the report of some females, who were induced to visit New Harmony, and remained there for some time, any situation much above abject wretchedness, was preferable to this vaunted terrestrial paradise.]—TRANS.

those of a man standing upright, the left foot a little forwards, the heels turned inwards. The distance between the heels by an exact measurement was six and a quarter inches, and thirteen and a half between the extremities of the great toes. By an accurate examination, it will however be ascertained, that they are not the impression of feet, accustomed to the use of European shoes, for the toes are pressed out, and the foot is flat, as is observed in persons who walk barefoot. The probability that they were caused by the pressure of an individual, that belonged to an unknown race of men, ignorant of the art of tanning hides, and that this took place in a much earlier age than the traditions of the present Indians extend to, this probability I say, is strengthened by the extraordinary size of the feet here given. In another respect, the impressions are strikingly natural, since the muscles of the feet are represented with the greatest exactness and truth. This circumstance weakens very much the hypothesis, that they are possibly evidences of the ancient sculpture of a race of men living in the remote ages of this continent. Neither history nor tradition, gives us the slightest information of such a people. For it must be kept in mind, that we have no proof that the people who erected our surprising western tumuli, ever had a knowledge of masonry, even much less of sculpture, or that they had invented the chisel, the knife, or the axe, those excepted made from porphyry, hornstone or obsidian. The medium length of the human male foot can be taken at ten inches. The length of the foot stamp here described, amounts to ten and a quarter inches, the breadth measured over the toes, in a right angle with the first line is four inches, but the greatest spread of the toes is four and a half inches, which breadth diminished at the heels to two and a half inches. Directly before these impressions is a well inserted and deep mark, similar to a scroll of which the greatest length is two feet seven inches, and the greatest breadth twelve and a half inches. The rock which contains these interesting traces, is a compact limestone of a bluish-gray colour."

This rock with the unknown impressions are remembered as long as the country about St. Louis has been known, this table is hewn out of a rock, and indeed out of a perpendicular wall of rock.

The garden of Rapp's house was the usual flower-garden of a rich German farmer. In it was a green-house, in which several large fig trees, an orange, and lemon tree stood in the earth. Mr. Owen took me into one of the newly-built houses, in which the married members of the society are to dwell. It consisted of two stories, in each two chambers and two alcoves, with the requisite ventilators. The cellar of the house is to contain a heating apparatus, to heat the whole with warm air. When all shall be thoroughly organized, the members will alternately have the charge of heating the apparatus. Each family will have a chamber and an alcove, which will be sufficient, as the little children will be in the nursery, and the larger at school. They will not require kitchens, as all are to eat in common. The unmarried women will live together, as will also the unmarried men, in the manner of the Moravian brethern.

I had an ample conversation with Mr. Owen, relating to his system, and his expectations. He looks forward to nothing less than to remodel the world entirely; to root out all crime; to abolish all punishments; to create similar views and similar wants, and in this manner to avoid all dissension and warfare. When his system of education shall be brought into connection with the great progress made by mechanics, and which is daily increasing every man can then, as he thought, provide his smaller necessaries for himself, and trade would cease entirely! I expressed a doubt of the practicability of his system in Europe, and even in the United States. He was too unalterably convinced of the results, to admit the slightest room for doubt. It grieved me to see that Mr. Owen should allow himself to be so infatuated by his passion for universal improvement, as to believe and to say that he is about to reform the whole world; and yet that almost every member of his society, with whom I have conversed apart, acknowledged that he was deceived in his expectations, and expressed their opinion that Mr. Owen had commenced on too grand a scale, and had admitted too many members, without the requisite selection! The territory of the society may contain twenty five thousand acres. The sum of one hundred and twenty thousand dollars was paid to Rapp for this purchase, and for that consideration he also left both his cattle, and a considerable flock of sheep behind.

I went with the elder Doctor M'Namee, to the two new established communities, one of which is called No. 2, or Macluria; the other lately founded, No. 3. No. 2, lies two miles distant from New Harmony, at the entrance of the forest, which will be cleared to make the land fit for cultivation, and consists of nine log houses, first tenanted about four weeks since, by about eighty persons. They are mostly backwoodsmen with their families, who have separated themselves from the community No. 1, in New Harmony, because *no religion* is acknowledged there, and these people wish to hold their prayer meetings undisturbed. The fields in the neighbourhood of this community were of course very new. The community No. 3, consisted of English country people, who formed a new association, as the mixture, or perhaps the cosmopolitism of New Harmony did not suit them; they left the colony planted by Mr. Birkbeck, at English Prairie, about twenty miles hence, on the right bank of the Wabash, after the unfortunate death of that gentleman,* and came here. This is a proof that there are two evils that strike at the root of the young societies; one is a sectarian or intolerant spirit; the other, national prejudice. No. 3, is to be built on a very pretty eminence, as yet there is only a frame building for three families begun.

After we had returned to New Harmony, I went to the orchard on the Mount Vernon road to walk, and beheld, to my great concern, what ravages the frost had committed on the fruit blossoms, the vines must have been completely killed. The orchards planted by Rapp and his society are large and very handsome, containing mostly apple and peach trees, also some pear and cherry trees. One of the gardens is exclusively devoted to flowers, where, in Rapp's time, a labyrinth was constructed of beech tree hedges and flowers, in the middle of which stood a pavilion, covered with the tops of trees.

I afterwards visited Mr. Neef, who is still full of the maxims and principles of the French revolution; captivated with the system of equality; talks of the emancipation of the negroes, and openly proclaims himself an ATHEIST. Such people stand by themselves, and fortunately are so very few in number, that they can do little or no injury.

In the evening there was a general meeting in the large hall, it opened with music. Then one of the members, an English architect of talent, who came to the United States, with Mr. Owen whose confidence he appeared to possess, and was here at the head of the arranging and architectural department, read some extracts from the newspapers, upon which Mr. Owen made a very good commentary; for example, upon the extension and improvement of steam-engines, upon their adaptation to navigation, and the advantages resulting therefrom. He lost himself, however, in his theories, when he expatiated on an article which related to

*He was drowned in the Wabash, which he attempted to swim over on horseback.

the experiments which had been made with Perkins's steam-gun. During these lectures, I made my observations on the much vaunted equality, as some tatterdemalions stretched themselves on the platform close by Mr. Owen. The better educated members kept themselves together, and took no notice of the others. I remarked also, that the members belonging to the higher class of society had put on the new costume, and made a party by themselves. After the lecture the band played a march, each gentleman took a lady, and marched with her round the room. Lastly, a cotillion was danced: the ladies were then escorted home, and each retired to his own quarters.

I went early on the following morning, (Sunday,) to the assembly room. The meeting was opened by music. After this Mr. Owen stated a proposition, in the discussion of which he spoke of the advance made by the society, and of the location of a new community at Valley Forge, in Pennsylvania, and another in the state of New York. A classification of the members was spoken of afterwards. They were separated into three classes, first, of such as undertook to be security for the sums due Mr. Owen and Mr. M'Clure, (that is, for the amount paid to Rapp, and so expended as a pledge to be redeemed by the society,) and who, if desirous to leave the society, must give six months previous notice; secondly, of such as after a notice of fourteen days can depart; and, lastly, of those who are received only on trial.

After this meeting, I paid Mr. M'Clure a visit, and received from him the French papers. Mr. M'Clure is old, childless, was never married, and intends, as is reported, to leave his property to the society. Afterwards I went with Mr. Owen, and some ladies of the society, to walk to the cut-off, as it is called, of the Wabash, where this river has formed a new channel, and an island, which contains more than a hundred acres of the best land; at present, however, inundated by water. There is here a substantial grist-mill, erected by Rapp, which was said to contain a very good set of machinery, but where we could not reach it on account of the water. We went some distance along the river, and then returned through the woods over the hills, which, as it was rather warm, and we could discover no pathway, was very laborious to the ladies, who were uncommonly alarmed at the different snakes we chanced to meet. Most of the serpent species here are harmless, and the children catch them for playthings. The poisonous snakes harbouring about here, are rattlesnakes and copperheads; these, however, diminish rapidly in numbers, for it is a common observation, that the poisonous serpents, like the Indians and bears, fly before civilization. The rattlesnakes have a powerful enemy in the numerous hogs, belonging to the settlers, running about the woods, which are very well skilled in catching them by the neck and devouring them.

In the evening I paid visits to some ladies, and witnessed philosophy and the love of equality put to the severest trial with one of them. She is named Virginia, from Philadelphia; is very young and pretty, was delicately brought up, and appears to have taken refuge here on account of an unhappy attachment. While she was singing and playing very well on the piano-forte, she was told that the milking of the cows was her duty, and that they were waiting unmilked. Almost in tears, she betook herself to this servile employment, deprecating the new social system, and its so much prized equality.

After the cows were milked, in doing which the poor girl was trod on by one, and daubed by another, I joined an aquatic party with the young ladies and some young philosophers, in a very good boat upon the inundated meadows of the Wabash. The evening was beautiful moonlight, and the air very mild; the beautiful Miss Virginia forgot her *stable* sufferings, and regaled us with her sweet voice. Somewhat later we collected together in the house No. 2, appointed for a school-house, where all the young ladies and gentlemen of *quality* assembled. In spite of the equality so much recommended, this class of persons will not mix with the common sort, and I believe that all the well brought up members are disgusted, and will soon abandon the society. We amused ourselves exceedingly during the whole remainder of the evening, dancing cotillions, reels and waltzes, and with such animation as rendered it quite lively. New figures had been introduced among the cotillions, among which is one called the *new social system*. Several of the ladies made objections to dancing on Sunday; we thought however, that in this sanctuary of philosophy, such prejudices should be utterly discarded, and our arguments, as well as the inclination of the ladies, gained the victory.

On the 17th April, a violent storm arose, which collected such clouds of dust together that it was hardly possible to remain in the streets, and I remained at home almost all day. I received a visit from a Mr. Von Schott. This person, a Wurtemburger by birth, and brother of lady Von Mareuil, in Washington, has settled himself seven or eight miles from New Harmony, and lives a real hermit's life, without a servant or assistant of any kind. He was formerly an officer in the Wurtemberg cavalry, took his discharge, and went, from pure enthusiasm, and over-wrought fanaticism, to Greece, to defend their rights. As he there discovered himself to be deceived in his anticipations, he returned to his native country, and delivered himself up to religious superstition. To extricate himself, in his opinion, from this world plunged in wretchedness, he accompanied his sister to the United States, came to Indiana, bought a piece of land from Rapp, by whom he asserted he was imposed upon, and had difficulties to undergo, since he knew nothing of agriculture. He lived in this manner in the midst of the forest with a solitary horse. A cruel accident had befallen him the week before, his stable with his trusty horse was burnt. He appeared to be a well-informed man, and spoke well and rationally, only when he touched upon religious topics, his mind appeared to be somewhat deranged. He declared that he supported all possible privations with the greatest patience, only he felt the want of intercourse with a friend in his solitude.

To-day two companies of the New Harmony militia, paraded with drums beating, and exercised morning and afternoon. They were all in uniform, well armed, and presented an imposing front.

I was invited to dinner in the house, No. 4. Some gentlemen had been out hunting, and had brought home a wild turkey, which must be consumed. This turkey formed the whole dinner. Upon the whole I cannot complain either of an overloaded stomach or a head-ache from the wine affecting it, in any way. The living was frugal in the strictest sense, and in nowise pleased the elegant ladies with whom I dined. In the evening I visited Mr. M'Clure and Madam Fretageot, living in the same house. She is a Frenchwoman, who formerly kept a boarding-school in Philadelphia, and is called *mother* by all the young girls here. The handsomest and most polished of the female world here, Miss Lucia Saistare and Miss Virginia, were under her care. The cows were milked this evening when I came in, and therefore we could hear their performance on the piano forte, and their charming voices in peace and quiet. Later in the evening we went to the kitchen of No. 3, where there was a ball. The young ladies of the better class kept themselves in a corner under Madam Fretageot's protection, and formed a little aristocratical club. To prevent all possible partialities, the gentlemen as well as the ladies, drew numbers for the cotillion, and thus apportioned them equitably. Our young ladies turned up their noses apart at the democratic dancers, who often in this way fell to their lot. Although every one was pleased upon the whole, yet they separated at ten o'clock, as it is necessary to rise early here. I accompanied Madam Fretageot and her two pupils home, and passed some time in conversation with Mr. M'Clure on his travels in Europe, which were undertaken with mineralogical views. The architect, Mr. Whitwell, besides showed me to-day the plan of this establishment. I admired particularly the judicious and economical arrangements for warming and ventilating the buildings, as well as the kitchens and laundries. It would indeed be a desirable thing could a building on this plan once be completed, and Mr. Owen hopes that the whole of New Harmony will thus be arranged.

On the following day I received a visit from one of the German patriots who had entered the society, of the name of Schmidt, who wished to have been considered as first lieutenant in the Prussian artillery, at Erfurt. He appeared to have engaged in one of the political conspiracies there, and to have deserted. Mr. Owen brought him from England last autumn as a servant. He was now a member of the society, and had charge of the cattle. His fine visions of freedom seemed to be very much lowered, for he presented himself to me, and his father to Mr. Huygens, to be employed as servants.

Towards evening, an Englishman, a friend of Mr. Owen, Mr. Applegarth, arrived, who had presided over the school in New Lanark, and was to organize one here in all probability. After dinner I went to walk with him in the vineyard and woods. We conversed much concerning the new system, and the consequences which he had reason to expect would result, &c. and we discovered amongst other things, that Mr. Owen must have conceived the rough features of his general system from considering forced services or statutory labour; for the labour imposed upon persons for which they receive no compensation, would apply and operate much more upon them for their lodging, clothing, food, the education and care of their children, &c. so that they would consider their labour in the light of a corvèe. We observed several labourers employed in loading bricks upon a cart, and they performed this so tedious and disagreeable task, as a statutory labour imposed on them by circumstances, and his observation led us to the above reflection. I afterwards visited Mr. M'Clure, and entertained myself for an hour with the instructive conversation of this interesting old gentleman. Madam Fretageot, who appears to have considerable influence over Mr. M'Clure took an animated share in our discourse. In the evening there was a ball in the large assembly room, at which most of the members were present. It lasted only until ten o'clock, in dancing cotillions, and closed with a grand promenade, as before described. There was a particular place marked off by benches for the children to dance on, in the centre of the hall, where they could gambol about without running between the legs of the grown persons.

On the 19th of April, a steam-boat came down the Wabash, bound for Louisville on the Ohio. It stopt opposite Harmony, and sent a boat through the overflow of water to receive passengers. I was at first disposed to embrace the opportunity of leaving this place, but as I heard that the boat was none of the best, I determined rather to remain and go by land to Mount Vernon, to wait for a better steam-boat there. We took a walk to the community No. 3. The work on the house had made but little progress; we found but one workman there, and he was sleeping quite at his ease. This circumstance recalled the observation before mentioned, concerning gratis-labour, to my mind. We advanced beyond into the woods, commencing behind No. 3: there was still little verdure to be seen.

On the succeeding day, I intended to leave New Harmony early; but as it was impossible to procure a carriage, I was obliged to content myself. I walked to the community No. 2, or Macluria, and farther into the woods. They were employed in hewing down trees to build log houses. The wood used in the brick and frame houses here is of the tulip tree, which is abundant, worked easily, and lasts long. After dinner I walked with Mr. Owen and Madam Fretageot, to community No. 3. There a new vegetable garden was opened; farther on they were employed in preparing a field in which Indian corn was to be sown. This answers the best purpose here, as the soil is too rich for wheat; the stalks grow too long, the heads contain too few grains, and the stalks on account of their length soon break down, so that the crop is not very productive. The chief complaint here is on account of the too great luxuriancy of the soil. The trees are all very large, shoot up quickly to a great height, but have so few, and such weak roots, that they are easily prostrated by a violent storm; they also rot very easily, and I met with a great number of hollow trees, in proportion. I saw them sow maize or Indian corn, for the first time. There were furrows drawn diagonally across the field with the plough, each at a distance of two feet from the other;

then other furrows at the same distance apart, at right angles with the first. A person goes behind the plough with a bag of corn, and in each crossing of the furrows he drops six grains. Another person with a shovel follows, and covers these grains with earth. When the young plants are half a foot high, they are ploughed between and the earth thrown up on both sides of the plants; and when they are two feet high this operation is repeated, to give them more firmness and to destroy the weeds. There is a want of experienced farmers here; the furrows were badly made, and the whole was attended to rather too much *en amateur*.

After we returned to Madam Fretageot's, Mr. Owen showed me two interesting objects of his invention; one of them consisted of cubes of different sizes, representing the different classes of the British population in the year 1811, and showed what a powerful burden rested on the labouring class, and how desirable an equal division of property would be in that kingdom. The other was a plate, according to which, as Mr. Owen asserted, each child could be shown his capabilities, and upon which, after a mature self-examination, he can himself discover what progress he has made. The plate has this superscription: scale of human faculties and qualities at birth. It has ten scales with the following titles: from the left to the right, self-attachment; affections; judgment; imagination; memory; reflection; perception; excitability; courage; strength. Each scale is divided into one hundred parts, which are marked from five to five. A slide that can be moved up or down, shows the measure of the qualities therein specified each one possesses, or believes himself to possess.

I add but a few remarks more. Mr. Owen considers it as an absurdity to promise never-ending love on marriage. For this reason he has introduced the civil contract of marriage, after the manner of the Quakers, and the French laws into his community, and declares that the bond of matrimony is in no way indissoluble. The children indeed, cause no impediment in case of a separation, for they belong to the community from their second year, and are all brought up together.

Mr. M'Clure has shown himself a great adherent of the Pestalozzian system of education. He had cultivated Pestalozzi's acquaintance when upon his travels, and upon this recommendation brought Mr. Neef with him to Philadelphia, to carry this system into operation. At first it appeared to succeed perfectly, soon however, Mr. Neef found so many opposers, apparently on account of his anti-religious principles, that he gave up the business, and settled himself on a farm in the woods of Kentucky. He had just abandoned the farm to take the head of a boarding-school, which Mr. M'Clure intended to establish in New Harmony. Mr. Jennings, formerly mentioned, was likewise to co-operate in this school; his reserved and haughty character was ill suited for such a situation, and Messrs. Owen and M'Clure willingly consented to his withdrawing, as he would have done the boarding-school more injury, from the bad reputation in which he stood, than he could have assisted it by his acquirements. An Englishman by birth, he was brought up for a military life; this he had forsaken to devote himself to clerical pursuits, had arrived in the United States as a Universalist preacher, and had been received with much attention in that capacity in Cincinnati, till he abandoned himself with enthusiasm to the *new social system*, and made himself openly and publicly known as an ATHEIST.*

I passed the evening with the amiable Mr. M'Clure and Madam Fretageot, and became acquainted through them, with a French artist, Mons. Lesueur, calling himself uncle of Miss Virginia, as also a Dutch physician from Herzogenbusch, Dr. Troost, an eminent naturalist. Both are members of the community, and have just arrived from a scientific pedestrian tour to Illinois and the southern part of Missouri, where they have examined the iron, and particularly the lead-mine works, as well as the peculiarities of the different mountains. Mr. Lesueur has besides discovered several species of fish, as yet undescribed. He was there too early in the season to catch many snakes. Both gentlemen had together collected thirteen chests of natural curiosities, which are expected here immediately. Mr. Lesueur accompanied the naturalist Perron, as draftsman in his tour to New South Wales, under Captain Baudin, and possessed all the illuminated designs of the animals which were discovered for the first time on this voyage, upon vellum. This collection is unique of its kind, either as regards the interest of the objects represented, or in respect to their execution; and I account myself fortunate to have seen them through Mr. Lesueur's politeness. He showed me also the sketches he made while on his last pedestrian tour, as well as those during the voyage of several members of the society to Mount Vernon, down the Ohio from Pittsburgh. On this voyage, the society had many difficulties to contend with, and

*[He is at this time advertising a boarding school in the western country, on his own account, which is to be under his immediate superintendence.]—TRANS.

were obliged often to cut a path for the boat through the ice. The sketches exhibit the originality of talent of the artist. He had come with Mr. M'Clure in 1815, from France to Philadelphia, where he devoted himself to the arts and sciences. Whether he will remain long in this society or not, I cannot venture to decide.*

* * * From the want of a church in Mount Vernon, the meeting was held in the court-house. It was a temporary log-house, which formed but one room. The chimney fire, and two tallow candles formed the whole illumination of it, and the seats were constructed of some blocks and boards, upon which upwards of twenty people sat. The singing was conducted by a couple of old folks, with rather discordant voices. The preacher then rose, and delivered us a sermon. I could not follow his discourse well, and was very much fatigued by my day's walk. In his prayer, however, the minister alluded to those who despise the word of the Lord, and prayed for their conviction and conversion. This hint was evidently aimed at the community in New Harmony and the new social system. In the sermon there was no such allusion. Probably the discourse was one of those, which he knew by heart; which he delivered in various places, and admitted of no interpolations. The service lasted till ten o'clock at night.

* * * Eleven miles and a half higher, we saw Evansville upon an eminence upon the right shore, still an inconsiderable place, but busy; it being the principal place in the county of Vandeburg, in the state of Indiana, lying in the neighbourhood of a body of fertile land, and is a convenient landing place for emigrants, who go to the Wabash country. Upon the same shore are seen several dwellings upon the fresh turf, shaded by high green trees. Close below Evansville, a small river called Big Pigeon creek falls into the Ohio. In its mouth we saw several flat boats, with apparatus similar to pile-driving machines. These vessels belong to a contractor, who has entered into an engagement with the government, to make the Ohio free and clear of the snags and sawyers lying in its current. This work was discharged in a negligent manner, and the officer to whom the superintendence was committed, is censured for having suffered himself to be imposed upon.

*[He has left it some time since, as well as Dr. Troost.]—TRANS.

From *Recollections of the last ten years, passed in occasional residences and journeyings in the valley of the Mississippi*, by Timothy Flint [1826], pp. 54-60.

FLINT, TIMOTHY.

Perhaps the foremost authority on the early life and history in the Mississippi Valley was Timothy Flint. He was born in Massachusetts, in 1780. Graduating from Harvard, he entered the ministry, but later resigned—1814—and entered upon missionary work. His territory was extensive, covering the greater part of the Mississippi valley. At different times, his headquarters were at Cincinnati, St. Louis and New Orleans. His extensive travel brought him in contact with all classes of people, in all aspects of society. He saw the first steamboat that descended the Mississippi river. He witnessed the rapid changes occurring in the West following the close of the second war with England. When his "Recollections" were published, they were read with keen interest. His efforts were directed toward bringing the people of the west together and acquainting them with each other. The important feature of his work was that most of it was *original.* This made it one of the most dearly prized accounts of the early western life.

Having exhausted the immediate interest of the most prominent objects of curiosity in Cincinnati and its vicinity, at the commencement of March, I set out on a proposed tour through the state of Indiana, on its front upon Ohio, and then crossing the Ohio, to return to my family, through the state of Kentucky. The weather was mild, and the buds of the trees and shrubs were beginning to swell. The previous weather, from the tenth of December, had been more than usually severe. The mercury had frequently fallen below cypher. The people had a way of accounting for this as they had for many other calamities, by saying, that the hard winter had been imported by the Yankees, of whom unusual numbers had arrived the preceding autumn and winter. The Big Miami was the limit on the front, between the state of Ohio, and the then territory of Indiana. General Harrison's fine plantation is in the delta, which this river makes with the Ohio. Having crossed this river into Indiana, I found myself on the vast and fertile bottom made by the two rivers. I descended this bottom to Lawrenceburg, at this time one of the principal villages in the territory. The soil here, and for a considerable distance on all sides, is highly fertile, but exposed to inundation, which, together with its having a character for unhealthiness, has hitherto kept this place in the back ground. The position evidently calls for a considerable town.

I here obtained letters of introduction through the territory, and the next morning I plunged into the deep forest below this town. I remember well the brightness and beauty of the morning. A white frost had covered the earth the preceding night. Dense white banks of fog, brilliantly illuminated by a cloudless sun, hung over the Ohio. The beautiful red-bird, that raises its finest song on a morning like this, was raising its mellow whistle among the copses. Columns of smoke rose from the cabins amidst the trees into the higher regions of the atmosphere, a cheerful accompaniment to all similar scenery, and which has impressed me, in its echoes ringing and dying away in the distant forests, as having a very peculiar effect in the deep bottoms of the Ohio and Mississippi, is the loud and continued barking of the numerous packs of dogs that are kept there. They evidently feel animated by the cheering influence of such a morning, feel that these vast forests are their proper range; and by these continued barkings that echo through the woods, they seem to invite their masters to the hunt and the chase.

On the margin of a considerable stream, whose name, I think, is the Hogan, a sufficiently barbarous name, I encountered the first bear that I had met in the woods. He seemed as little disposed to make acquaintance with me, as I with him.

In this whole day's ride, I was continually coming in view of new cabins, or wagons, the inmates of which had not yet sheltered themselves in cabins. Whenever my course led me from the bottoms of the Ohio, I found the bluffs, which invariably skirt the bottoms, very ridgy, and the soil but indifferent, and of what is here classed as second rate, and covered generally with a species of oak, called post oak, indicating a cold, spungy, and wet soil; into which, softened as it was by the frost coming out of it, my horse sunk at every step up to the fetlocks; yet in this comparatively poor and ridgy soil, I could hear on all sides the settler's axe resounding, and the dogs barking,—sure indications, that the land had been, as the phrase is, "taken up."

Few incidents, that occur to me as matters of interest, remain on my memory of this long trip on the Indiana shore. Most of the newly arrived settlers that I addressed, were from Yankee land. As usual, I refer you to books, that treat professedly upon that subject for precise geographical information. The inhabitants tell me, that, nothwithstanding I see so much ordinary land in this extent upon the Ohio, there are vast bodies of the richest land in it, particularly up the Wabash and its waters, where the prairies in the vicinity of Fort Harrison are said to vie with the richest and most beautiful of the Illinois and Missouri. The greater portion of the fertile lands was as yet unredeemed from the Indians. The country was evidently settling with great rapidity. The tide of emigration from the northeast was setting farther west. Ohio had already received its first tide and the wave was rolling onward. The southern portion of the emigration seemed to entertain no small apprehension, that this also would be a Yankee state. Indeed the population was very far from being in a state of mind, of sentiment, and affectionate mutual confidence, favourable to commencing their lonely condition in the woods in harmonious intercourse. They were forming a state government. The question in all its magnitude, whether it should be a slave-holding state or not, was just now agitating. I was often compelled to hear the question debated by those in opposite interests, with no small degree of asperity. Many fierce spirits talked, as the clamorous and passionate are accustomed to talk in such cases, about opposition and "resistance unto blood." But the preponderance of more sober and reflecting views, those habits of order and quietness that aversion to shedding blood, which so generally and so honorably appertain to the American character and institutions, operated in these wildernesses, among these inflamed and bitter spirits, with all their positiveness, ignorance, and clashing feeling , and with all their destitution of courts, and the regular course of settled laws to keep them from open violence. The question was not long after finally settled in peace.

From the observations, which I made, which were however partial, and confined to the southern front of the state, I should have placed this state, in point of qualities of soil, behind Ohio, Illinois or Missouri. But it is here a general impression, that this state had large districts of the most fertile character. These tracts are admitted, as a melancholy drawback, appended to this great advantage, to be sickly. At the time I am writing, this state is supposed to contain nearly three hundred thousand inhabitants, a rate of increase considerably more rapid, than that of the states still farther west. It has a very extended front on the Ohio, extends back to the lakes, and its central outlet is the Wabash, a river highly favourable to boat navigation. At a considerable distance up this river is Vincennes, which, when I was there was the principal village in the state. It is situated pleasantly on the Wabash, surrounded by a beautiful and extensive prairie. This place is now surpassed by Vevay, which has grown to be a considerable town. It possesses circumstances of peculiar interest. When I was there, the village had just commenced. I was lodged in the house of a respectable Swiss gentleman, who had married a wife from Kentucky. Such are the unions that result from bringing together the mountaineers of Switzerland, and the native daughters of the west. The people were prompt and general in attending divine service. The next evening, there was a warned meeting of the inhabitants, and the object was to locate the town-house, a market, and first, second and third streets. I attended the meeting. The night was dark and rainy. The deep and rich bottom, the trees of which had but just been cut down, was so muddy, that my feet sunk at every step in the mud. Huge beech and sycamore trunks of trees so impeded these avenues and streets, that were to be, that I doubt if a chaise could have made its way, by day light and the most careful driving, amidst the logs, when you hear about market-houses, and seminaries, and streets No. 1, 2, and 3, in the midst of a wilderness of fallen logs, you will have some idea of the language appropriate to a kind of speculation, almost peculiar to this country, that is to say, town-making. You will infer from this, too, what magnificent ideas these people have with respect to the future. I learned in recently ascending the Ohio, that these splendid anticipations are now realized, that the town-house, market, and streets actually exist, and that instead of huge sycamore trunks, they have now blocks of brick buildings. Its relative position, with respect to the state, and to Cincinnati and Louisville, is favourable to its future advancement.

But what gave peculiar interest to this place was, that it was the resort of a flourishing colony from Vevay in Switzerland. Although this people could not bring here their glaciers and their Alps, in affectionate remembrance of their ancient home, they have brought hither their vines, their "simulatam Trojam," their Vevay on the Ohio in the midst of American forests. I had seen vineyards in Kentucky on a small scale. But this experiment on such a noble scale, so novel in America, was to me a most interesting spectacle. I was delighted with the frank and amiable character of the inhabitants, giving me back the images and recollections of them, from early reading. At that time they principally cultivated a blue grape, which, I think, they called the "cape grape." The wine from that grape was not pleasant to me, though connoisseurs assured me, that it only wanted age to be a rich wine. A position more unlike that, in which they had cultivated the wine in their own country, could scarcely be found. There they reared it on sharp declivities of gravelly soil, levelled in terraces. It was here on a bottom of a loamy and extremely rich soil, on a surface perfectly level, and at the foot of a high bluff. The vine grows here, indeed, in the rankest luxuriance, and needs severe pruning. It overloads itself with an exuberance of clusters, which still want the high and racy flavour of the grape of the hills of Switzerland. But they are introducing other vines, particularly the sweet water-grape of Madeira. The cultivation is understood at this time to be in a very prosperous state. From what I have seen, I believe it would prosper still more, if they should cultivate a grape, more indigenous to the soil; the "pine woods" grape of Louisiana, or the rich grape of Texas.

At a small town at the mouth of Kentucky river, I crossed into that state.

From *A condensed geography and history of the western states, or the Mississippi valley*, by Timothy Flint [1828], Vol. II., pp. 136-172.

INDIANA.

LENGTH, 250.—Breadth, 150 miles. Between 37° 47′ and 41° 50′ N. Latitude; and 7° 45′ and 11° W. longitude. Bounded north by Michigan territory and lake. West by the state of Illinois. South by the Ohio, which divides it from Kentucky; East by the state of Ohio.

The whole of this state belongs to the valley of the Ohio, or lake Michigan. It is the first of the states, in advancing towards the east, and the north, where nature seems to have divided her surface between prairie and wood land. The greater proportion of this state is clearly timbered country. Here, too, we first find the number and manners of northern people predominating among the immigrants. Here we first discover, in many places, a clear ascendency of New England dialect, manners and population. Here, too, we discover the natural tendency of this order of things, and this class of immigrants rapidly, and yet silently to fill the country with inhabitants. Missouri and Illinois have occupied a greater space in public estimation, in newspaper description, and in general notoriety. The immigration to those states has been with four or six horse wagons, with large droves of cattle, with considerable numbers of negroes, and composed of immigrants, who had name and standing, who were heads of families, when they removed, and whose immigration was accompanied with a certain degree of eclat. Of course the immigration of a few families was attended with circumstances, which gave it public notoriety. The immigration to this state has been generally of a different character. It has been for the most part composed of young men, either unmarried or without families. It has been noiseless, and unnoticed. But the difference of the result strikes us with surprize. While the population of neither of these states exceeds 80,000, the population of this state, at this time, is supposed to exceed 200,000.

Face of the country, soil, &c. The South front of this state is skirted with the usual belt of river hills, bluffs and knobs, known here by the name of "Ohio hills." They occupy a greater or less distance from the river; sometimes leaving between their base and the river, a bottom of two or three miles in width; and sometimes, and for no inconsiderable part of the whole length of the southern boundary, they tower directly from the waters of the Ohio. They have a thousand aspects of grandeur and beauty, often rising higher, than 300 feet above the level of the river; and the eye of the southern traveller, ascending the Ohio, which has been used to rest on bottoms boundless to vision, on swamps and plains, and regions without a rock or a hill in the scenery, never tires, in surveying these beautiful bluffs, especially in the spring, when their declivities are crimsoned with the red bud, or whitened with the brilliant blossoms of the dog wood, or rendered verdant with the beautiful May apple.

A range of knobs, stretching from the Ohio to White river of the Wabash, forms the limits of the table lands, that separate the waters of the Ohio from those of White river. North of the Wabash, between Tippicanoe and Ouitanon, the Wabash hills are precipitous, and a considerable extent of country is rough and broken. There are, in different parts of the state, considerable extents of country that may be pronounced hilly. Such is the south front of the state to a considerable distance from the Ohio. There are not such extensive plains in this state, as in Illinois. Nor are there any hills to vie in height with those back of Shawneetown. But, with some few exceptions, the greater proportion of this state may be pronounced one vast level. To particularize the level tracts would be to describe three fifths of the state. The prairies here, as elsewhere, are uniformly level. The wide extent of country, watered by White river, is generally level. The prairies have the usual distinction of being high, and low, swampy and alluvial. For a wide extent on the north front of the state, between the Wabash and lake Michigan the country is generally an extended plain, alternately prairie and timbered land; with a great proportion of swampy lands, and small lakes and ponds. The prairies are no ways different from those of Illinois. They are alike, rich, level, and covered with grass and flowering plants. Some of them, like those of Illinois and Missouri, are broader than can be measured by the eye. Their divisions are marked off, wherever streams cross them, by belts of timbered land. All the rivers of this state have remarkably wide alluvions. Every traveller has spoken with admiration of the beauty and fertility of the prairies along the course of the Wabash, particularly of those in the vicinity of Fort Harrison. We have heard competent judges, who have had opportunities of comparison, prefer the prairies on this part of the river, both for beauty and fertility to those of the Illinois, and the upper Mississippi. Perhaps no part of the western world can show greater extents of rich lands in one body, than that extent of the White river country, of which Indianapolis is the centre.—Judging of Indiana, from travelling through the south front, from twelve to twenty miles from the Ohio, we should not, probably, compare it with Ohio or Illinois. But now, that the greater part of the territory is purchased of the Indians, and that all is surveyed, and well understood, it is found, that this state possesses as large a proportion of first rate lands, as any in the western country. With some few exceptions of wide and naked prairies, the divisions of timbered and prairie lands are more happily balanced, than in other parts of the western country. Many rich prairies are long and narrow, so that the whole can be taken up, and yet timber be easily accessible by all the settlers.—There are hundreds of prairies only large enough for a few farms. Even in the large prairies there are those beautiful islands of timbered land, which form such a striking feature in the western prairies. The great extents of fertile land, the happy distribution of rivers and springs may be one reason for the unexampled rapidity, with which this state has peopled. Another reason may be, that being a non-slaveholding state, and next in position beyond Ohio, it was happily situated to arrest the tide of immigration, that set beyond Ohio, after that state was filled.

But as one of the chief objects, in such a work as this, must necessarily be, to point out the relative position and quality of the first rate lands, we shall, perhaps, be least likely to confuse the reader, by adding a few remarks in a single view, upon the qualities of the soil, upon the several rivers, and near the several towns, which we shall describe in the progress of our remarks. The forest trees, shrubs, plants and grasses do not materially differ from those of Illinois and Missouri. There is one specific difference that should be noted. There is a much greater proportion of beech timber, which increases so much, as we advance east that in Ohio, it is clearly the principal kind of timber. This state is equally fertile in corn, rye, oats, barley, wheat and the cereal gramina in general. Vast quantities of the richer prairies and bottoms are too rich for wheat, until the natural wild luxuriance of tendency in the soil has been reduced by cropping. Upland rice has been attempted with success. Some of the warm and sheltered valleys have yielded, in favorable years, considerable crops of cotton. No country can exceed this in its adaptedness for rearing the finest fruits and fruit bearing shrubs. Wild berries, in many places are abundant; and on some of the prairies, the strawberries are large, rich and abundant. It is affirmed, that in the northern parts of this state in the low prairies, whole tracts are covered with the beautiful fowl-meadow grass, *poa pratensis*, of the north. It is a certain and admitted fact, that wherever the Indians, or the French have inhabited, long enough to destroy the natural prairie grass, which, it is well known, is soon eradicated, by being pastured by the domestic animals, that surround a farmer's barn, this grass is replaced by the blue grass of the western country, which furnishes not only a verdant and beautiful sward, but covers the earth with a perfect mat of rich fodder, not unlike the second crop, which is cut in the northern states, as the most valuable kind of fodder. For all the objects of farming, and raising grain, flour, hemp, tobacco, cattle, sheep, swine, horses, and generally the articles of the northern and middle states, immigrants could not desire a better country, than may be found in Indiana. In the rich bottoms in the southern parts, the reed cane, and uncommonly large ginseng are abundant.

Climate, &c. Little need be said upon this head; for this state, situated in nearly the same parallels with Illinois and Missouri, has much the same temperature. That part of it, which is contiguous to lake Michigan, is more subject to copious and frequent rains; and being otherwise low and marshy, much of the land becomes too wet for cultivation. Some have described the country and climate, near lake Michigan, as productive and delightful.—Neither the soil, timber, nor the experiments of the inhabitants, that have attempted cultivation here, justify these descriptions. For a considerable distance from the lake, sand heaps covered with a few stinted junipers, and swept by the cold, dreary and desolating gales of the lake, give no promise of a fine country or climate. 'But beyond the influence of the lake breeze, the climate is cool, mild and temperate. The state in general is somewhat less exposed to the extremes of heat and cold, than Illinois.

In point of salubrity, we can do no more than repeat the remarks, which have so often been found applicable to the western country in general, and which from the nature of things must apply to all countries. The high and rolling regions of this state are as healthy, as the same kind of lands is found to be in the other parts of the United States. The wet prairies, the swampy lands, the tracts that are contiguous to the small lakes and ponds, deep and inundated bottoms, intersected by bayous, generate fever and ague, and autumnal fevers, and create a bilious tendency in all the disorders of the country. The beautiful prairies above Vincennes, on the Wabash, in the neighborhood of fort Harrison and Tippicanoe, are found to have an unfavorable balance against their fertility, the beauty of their appearance, and the ease, with which they are cultivated, in their insalubrity. That the settlers in general have found this state, taken as a whole, favorable to health, the astonishing increase of the population bears ample testimony.

The winters are mild, compared with those of New England, or even Pennsylvania. Winter commences, in its severity about Christmas, and lasts seldom more than six weeks. During this time in most seasons, the rivers, that have not very rapid currents, are frozen. Though winters occur, in which the Wabash can not be crossed upon the ice. About the middle of February, the severity of winter is past. In the northern parts of the state snow sometimes, though rarely, falls a foot and a half in depth. In the middle and southern parts, it seldom falls more than six inches. Peach trees are generally in blossom early in March. The forests begin to be green from the 5th to the 15th of April. Vast numbers of flowering shrubs are in full flower, before they are in leaf, which gives an inexpressible charm to the early appearance of spring. Vegetation is liable to be injured both by early and late frosts.

Chief towns. Character of the country, in which they are situated, &c. None of the western states have shown, a greater propensity for town making, than this.—Nature has furnished it with so many delightful sites for towns, that their very frequency subtract from the importance of any individual position. In no part of the world has the art of trumpeting, and lauding the advantages, conveniences and future prospects, of the town to be sold, been carried to greater perfection. To mention, in detail, all the villages, that have really attained some degree of consequence, would only furnish a barren catalogue of names. We will mention the chief of these on the Ohio, in descending order, beginning with Lawrenceburg on the southeastern angle of the state.

This town is the seat of justice for the county of Dearborn. It stands on the north bank of the Ohio, twenty-three miles below,

Cincinnati, and two below the Big Miami, which is the eastern limit of the state. This town is in the centre of a rich and deep bottom. The ancient village was built on the first bottom, which was frequently exposed to inundation. It is not uncommon for the water to rise four or five feet above the foundations of the houses and stores, in which case the inhabitants remove to the upper story, and drive their domestic animals to the hills. Visits and tea parties are projected in the inundated town; and the vehicles of transport are skiffs and periogues.—The period of the flood, from ancient custom, and from the suspension of all the customary pursuits, has become a time of carnival. The floods, instead of creating disease, wash the surface of the earth, carry off vegetable and animal matter, that would otherwise putrify, and are supposed to be rather conducive to health than otherwise. The old town, built on the first bank, had been stationary for many years. New Lawrenceburg has been recently built on the second bank, and on elevated ground, formed by the bank of Tanner's creek. Since the commencement of this town, few places have made more rapid progress.—Many of the new houses are handsome; and some of them make a splendid show from the river. . Its position, in relation to the river, and the rich adjacent country, and the Big Miami is highly eligible. It has a number of respectable commencing manufactories, and promises to be a large town.

Aurora is a new village, at the mouth of Hogan creek, four miles below, on the Ohio. It contains between sixty and seventy dwellings. Rising Sun, thirteen miles below Lawrenceburg, occupies a beautiful position on the Ohio, and is a village something larger, than Aurora.

Vevay is the seat of justice for Switzerland county, and is situated eight miles above the point, opposite the mouth of Kentucky river, and forty-five miles below Cincinnati. It contains between two and three hundred houses, a court house, jail, academy, a printing office, from which issues a weekly journal, a branch of the bank of Indiana, and some other public buildings. This interesting town was commenced in 1804, by thirty Swiss families, to whom the United States made a grant, under particular and favorable stipulations, of a considerable tract of land, to patronize the cultivation of the vine. The patriarch of this colony was a Swiss gentleman of the name of J. J. Dufour, who has continued an active and intelligent friend to the town ever since. The colony soon received considerable accessions from the mountains of Switzerland. In grateful remembrance of their native hills, and to create in the bosom of their adopted country tender associations with their ancient country, they named their stream Venoge, and their town Vevay. Messrs. Dufour, Morerod, Bettens, Siebenthal, and others, commenced the cultivation of the grape on a large scale. This cultivation has gone on steadily increasing. An hundred experiments have been since commenced, in different points of the West. But this still remains the largest vineyard in the United States.—We have witnessed nothing in our country, in the department of gardening and cultivation, which can compare with the richness of this vineyard, in the autumn, when the clusters are in maturity. Words feebly paint such a spectacle. The horn of plenty seems to have been emptied in the production of this rich fruit. We principally remarked the blue or Cape grape and the Madiera grape. The wine of the former has been preferred to the Claret of Bordeaux. The fruit seems to have a tendency to become too succulent, and abundant. It is now supposed that some of our native grapes will more easily acclimate to the country and soil, and make a better wine. These amiable, industrious and intelligent people are constantly profiting by the benefit of experience. This species of agriculture already yields them a better profit than any other practised in our country. They are every year improving on the vintage of the past. They are the simple, amiable, and intelligent people that we might expect from the prepossessions of early reading, from the vine clad hills of Switzerland. They are mostly protestants in their worship. They happily compound the vivacity of the French with the industry of the Germans. Like the former, they love gaiety and dancing. Like the latter, they easily fall in with the spirit of our institutions, love our country and its laws; intermarry with our people, and are in all respects a most amiable people. They have a considerable number of professional men in Vevay; a public library, a literary society, and many of the comforts and improvements of a town. Mr. Dufour has distinguished himself by agricultural publications, particularly upon the culture of the vine. This industrious people have created some manufactures peculiar to themselves, particularly that of straw bonnets. The position of the town is extremely fortunate, in relation to the back country, and the other interior large towns. It is equi-distant from Lexington, Louisville and Cincinnati, being forty-five miles from each.

Madison, still lower on the Ohio, is considered to be nearly equi-distant between Louisville and Cincinnati. It was commenced in 1811, and is about the size of Vevay; and is perhaps still better built, than that town. It is central to a great extent of flourishing back country; and is one of the most pleasant and thriving towns in the state.

New London, ten miles lower on the river, and Charlestown, twenty-nine miles lower, and two miles back from the Ohio, are small villages. The land about the latter town was a grant of gratitude from Virginia to the brave general Clark, and his soldiers, for their achievements at the close of the revolutionary war.

Jeffersonville is situated just above the falls of Ohio.—The town of Louisville on the opposite shore, and the beautiful and rich country beyond, together with the broad and rapid river, forming whitening sheets and cascades from shore to shore, the display of steam boats, added to the high banks, the neat village, and the noble woods on the north bank, unite to render the scenery of this village uncommonly rich and diversified. It is a considerable and handsome village with some houses, that have a show of magnificence. It has a land office, a post office, a printing office, and some other public buildings. It was contemplated to canal the falls on this side of the river; and a company with a large capital was incorporated by the legislature. In 1819, the work was commenced, but has not been prosecuted with the success, that was hoped.—The completion of the canal on the opposite side, will, probably, merge this project, by rendering it useless.—One of the principal *chutes* of the river, in low water, is near this shore; and experienced pilots, appointed by the state, are always in readiness, to conduct boats over the falls. Clarksville is a small village just below this place.

New Albany is the seat of justice for Floyd county; and is four and a half miles below Jeffersonville. The front street is three quarters of a mile in length, and makes a respectable appearance from the river. Many steam boats, that can not pass the falls, are laid up for repair at this place, during the summer. It has a convenient ship yard for building steam boats. It is a thriving and busy village.

Fredonia, Leavenworth, Rockport, and Evansville occur, as we descend the Ohio. The last, is a village of some consequence. It is the landing place for immigrants, descending the Ohio, for the Wabash. It is at the mouth of Big Pigeon creek, fifty-four miles south of Vincennes, and forty-five above the mouth of the

Wabash.—Being about half way between the falls of Ohio and the mouth, it is a noted stopping place for steam boats.

Corydon, the seat of justice for the county of Harrison, was for a considerable time the political metropolis of the state. It is distant twenty-three miles from Jeffersonville, and thirteen from the Ohio. It is situated in the forks of Indian creek. North of the town, spreads an extensive region of barrens full of sink holes, and lime stone caves.

Salem is on a small branch of Blue river, thirty-four miles north of Corydon. It is a very flourishing county town, and contains more than 100 houses. Brownstown, Paoli, and Washington are interior county towns. The following towns are on the Wabash, as we descend the river. Above Tippicanoe is the old French post of Ouitanon. It is at the head of boatable navigation on the river, in the centre of what was recently the country of the savages. Its origin dates back nearly 100 years.—The inhabitants are a mixture of French and Indian blood. Merom is on a high bluff of the Wabash, opposite La Motte prairie, in Illinois. It is in the centre of rich and beautiful prairies. It has peopled with great rapidity. *Terre Haute* is situated two miles below fort Harrison, as its name imports, on a high bank of the Wabash. It is a growing and important village. Shakertown, fifteen miles above Vincennes, contains a community of the industrious people, called, Shakers, and exhibits the marks of order and neatness, that are so characteristic of those people everywhere.

Vincennes is, after Kaskaskia, the oldest place in the western world. It was settled in 1735, by French emigrants from Canada. They fixed themselves here in a beautiful, rich and isolated spot, in the midst of the deserts of the new world. For an age they had little intercourse with any other people, than savages. Their interests, pursuits and feelings were identified with them. Their descendants are reclaimed from their savage propensities; and have the characteristic vivacity, amiableness, and politeness of the French people everywhere. It is distant 150 miles above the mouth of the Wabash; and fifty-four from the nearest point of the Ohio. It has improved rapidly of late; and is said to contain more than 300 houses, a brick court house and hotel, a jail, a respectable building for an academy, a Roman catholic and a presbyterian church, a land office, a post office, two printing offices, from one of which is issued a respectable gazette, a bank, and some other public buildings. It is situated contiguous to a beautiful and extensive prairie, 5,000 acres of which are cultivated as a common field, after the ancient French customs. It was for a long time the seat of the territorial government, and still has more trade, than any other place in the state. The plat of the town is level, and laid off with great regularity. The houses have extensive gardens back of them, filled, after the French fashion, with crowded fruit trees. It is accessible, for the greater part of the year, by steam boats; and is a place of extensive supply of merchandize to the interior of the state. Volney, who visited this place not long after the setting up of the Federal government here, gives a very graphic and faithful account of the appearance of this place, and the adjoining country, of the French inhabitants and their manners. At the same time, he presents a revolting picture of the manner, in which the Americans had treated them. He represents them to have been plundered, and insulted by the Kentuckians, soon after the close of the revolutionary war. Perhaps he had not learned, that Vincennes had been, for a long time, a nest of savages, from which they fitted out their murderous expeditions; and that it was natural, that the Kentuckians, who had suffered so much from them, should be disposed to retaliate upon the people, who had harbored them. He represents them, subsequently, to have been cheated out of their lands by the Americans. Their ignorance, he says, at this time was profound. But little more than half their number could read, or write; and he avers, that he could instantly distinguish them, when mixed with the Americans, by their meagre and tanned faces, and their look of poverty and desolation. However just this picture may have been in 1796, it is all reversed now.—Most of the inhabitants have an air of ease and affluence; and Vincennes furnishes a pleasant and respectable society.

Harmony, fifty-four miles below Vincennes, and something more than 100 by water above the mouth of the Wabash, is the seat of justice for the county of Posey. It is situated on the east bank of the river, sixteen miles from the nearest point of the Ohio, on a wide, rich, and heavily timbered plateau, or second bottom. It is high, healthy, has a fertile soil, and is in the vicinity of small and rich prairies; and is, on the whole, a pleasant and well chosen position. It was first settled, in 1814, by a religious sect of Germans, denominated Harmonites. They were emigrants from Germany, and settled first on Beaver creek in Pennsylvania. They moved in a body, consisting of 800 souls, to this place. Their spiritual and temporal leader was George Rapp; and all the lands and possesions were held in his name. Their society seems to have been a kind of intermediate sect between the Shakers and Moravians. They held their property in common. Their regulations were extremely strict and severe. In their order, industry, neatness, and perfect subordination, they resembled the Shakers. They soon erected from eighty to one hundred large and substantial buildings. Their lands were laid off with the most perfect regularity, and were as right angled, and square as compass could make them. They were wonderfully successful here, as they had been in other places, in converting a wilderness into a garden in a short time. They had even the luxury of a botanic garden and a green house. Their great house of assembly, with its wings and appendages, was nearly an hundred feet square. Here they lived, and labored in common, and in profound peace. But from some cause, their eyes were turned from the rich fields, and the wide prairies, and the more southern and temperate climate of the Wabash towards Beaver creek, the place, where they had first settled. While they were under the influence of these yearnings, the leader of a new sect came upon them.—This was no other than Robert Owen of New Lanark, in Scotland; a professed philosopher of a new school, who advocated new principles, and took new views of society. He calls his views upon this subject "the social system." He was opulent, and disposed to make a grand experiment of his principles on the prairies of the Wabash. He purchased the lands and the village of Mr. Rapp, at an expense, it is said, of 190,000 dollars. In a short time there were admitted to the new establishment from seven to eight hundred persons. They danced, all together, one night in every week, and had a concert of music in another. The Sabbath was occupied in the delivery and hearing of philosophical lectures. Two of Mr. Owen's sons and Mr. M'Clure, joined him from Scotland. The society at New Harmony, as the place was called, excited a great deal of interest and remark in every part of the United States. Great numbers of distinguished men in all the walks of life wrote to the society, making enquiries, respecting its prospects, and rules; and expressing a desire, at some future time, to join it. Mr. Owen remained at New Harmony, but little more than a year; in which time he made a voyage to Europe. The fourth of July, 1826, he promulgated his famous declaration of "mental independence." The society had began to moulder before this time. He has left New Harmony, and "the social system" seems to be abandoned. It is to be hoped, that this beautiful village, which has been the theatre of such singular and opposite experiments, will again flourish.

Brookville is a pleasant and a very considerable village, in the forks of the beautiful river White water. It is noted for the number and enterprize of its mechanics and manufacturers. A number of its public and private buildings are of brick, and are respectable. It has grist mills, saw mills, carding machines, a printing office, and numbers of the common mechanic shops, where the usual articles of city manufacture are made for exportation. The town and the public square are on a fine and commanding level.—The streets are so situated, that they are easily kept clean. The position of the town, its salubrity, the clearness and coldness of its waters, and the adjoining scenery give this place uncommon advantages for manufactures. The enterprising inhabitants have not failed to avail themselves of these advantages. The surrounding country is finely timbered, and watered. The soil is rich and productive; and has acquired reputation for the excellence of its tobacco. It is at once extensive and populous. This village can not fail to become a considerable town. The number of houses exceeds one hundred.

Harrison is situated on the north shore of White water, eight miles from its mouth, eighteen north-east [south-east] of Brookville, and in the centre of an excellent body of land.—The village is divided between the jurisdiction of Ohio and Indiana. In the very rich and extensive bottoms, that surround this village, are found great numbers of Indian mounds. They contain large quantities of human bones, in all stages of decay. Indian axes, vases, and implements of war and domestic use, abound in them. In the bottom of most of them are found brands, coal and ashes; indications, from which antiquarians have inferred, that they were places of sacrifice, and that the victims were probably human.

Paoli, Mount Sterling, Washington, Princeton, Salisbury, New Lexington, Charleston, Salem, Brownston, &c. are seats of justice to their several counties, and are places of greater or less importance. In a country, where every year produces new towns, some of them of considerable importance, and where the scene of cultivation, population and improvement, is shifting under the eye of the surveyor and traveller, it can not be supposed, that this is, by any means, a complete list of the towns, that have arisen, and are continually springing up, in this rapidly populating state. It is as complete, as is attainable by our means at present. We close the list with the political metropolis of the state.

Indianapolis. This town, situated on the west [east] bank of White river, has had as rapid a growth, as any one that has arisen in the western country. It is in the centre of one of the most extensive and fertile bodies of land in the western world; nearly central to the state, on White river, and at a point accessible by steam boats, in common stages of the Wabash. No river in America, according to its size and extent, has greater bodies of fertile land, than White river. The country is populating about this town with unexampled rapidity. The town itself has grown up like the prophet's gourd. But a few years since, and it was a solid and deep forest, where the surprised traveller now sees compact streets and squares of brick buildings, respectable public buildings, manufactories, mechanic shops, printing offices, business and bustle. Such is the present aspect of Indianapolis, which is supposed to contain between two and three hundred houses. It will, probably, become one the largest towns between Cincinnati and the Mississippi.

The river Chicago empties into lake Michigan, near the territorial limits of Indiana and Illinois. Its harbor is the south-western extremity of that lake. Fort Dearborn, where the bloody tragedy of September, 1815, was enacted by the Indians, in the massacre of its garrison, was, until recently, a military post of the United States. It has lately been abandoned. At the mouth of this river is the only harbor on the lake for a great distance; and when ever a canal shall unite the Illinois with the lake, it will become a place of great commercial importance.

Indians. Until recently, they owned the greater part of the fertile lands in this state. Most of these lands have lately been purchased of them by treaty. The names of the tribes, as they used to be, convey little idea of their present position and numbers. Great numbers of them have emigrated far to the west, on White river and Arkansas. Others have strayed into Canada, or towards the sources of the Mississippi, and their deserted place are rapidly filling with the habitations of white men. Their names, as they used to be, are Mascontins, Piankashaws, Kickapoos, Delawares, Miamies, Shawnees, Weeas, Ouitanons, Eel rivers and Pottawattomies. Their present numbers can not exceed four or five thousand souls. It is an unquestionable evidence of the fertility of the country in the interior of Indiana, that it was once the seat of the most dense Indian population in the western country.—The Indians invariably fixed in greatest numbers, where the soil was fertile, the country healthy, and the means of transport on water courses easy and extensive. Such countries abounded in fish and game, and such was the country in question. The Indians in this country were invaded, in 1791, by general Wilkinson. He destroyed their principal town. It contained 120 houses, eighty of which were roofed with shingles. The gardens and improvements about it were delightful. There was a tavern with cellars, bar, public and private rooms; and the whole indicated no small degree of order and civilization. The prophet's town, destroyed by general Harrison in November, 1811, was a considerable place.

Game and Fish. The interior and northern parts of this state are abundantly stocked with game. Bears, and especially deer, abound. Wild turkeys have been supposed by some to abound as much on the waters of White river, as they do in the settled regions. Hundreds are sometimes driven from one corn field. Prairie hens, partridges and grouse abound on the prairies, and in some seasons, wild pigeons are seen here in countless numbers. Where they roost, the limbs of the trees are broken off in all directions by their numbers. Venomous snakes and noxious reptiles are sometimes seen, especially in the vicinity of ledges of rocks. The rattle snake and the copper head are the most numerous and dangerous. The streams, and especially those that communicate with lake Michigan, are abundant in fish of the best qualities. The number and excellence of the fish, and the ease, with which they are taken, are circumstances of real importance and advantage to the first settlers, and help to sustain them, until they are enabled to subsist by the avails of cultivation.

Minerals and Fossils. There are salt springs in different parts of the state. We do not know, that any of them are worked to much extent. The salt has hitherto been chiefly brought from the United States' Saline, back of Shawneetown, or from the Salines of Kenhawa.—Stone coal of the best quality is found in various places.—Native copper has been discovered in small masses, in the northern parts of the state. Iron ore is also discovered in some places. But in general it is a country too level to be a mineral one. Although from the first settlement of the country, it has been asserted, that there is a silver mine near Ouitanon.

Antiquities. We have seen, that this state possessed a numerous Indian population. Their mounds, their sepulchres, their runined villages, the sward of blue grass, which indicates in times nearer, or remote, the position of an Indian village, their implements of war and agriculture, dug up by the spade, or turned up by the plough, strike us on all sides, as we travel through this state. They can not but excite deep and serious thoughts in a reflecting mind.—French traditions relate, that an exterminating battle took place in a spot, which is now designated by two or three small mounds, near where fort Harrison now stands. The battle was fought between the Indians of the Mississippi, and of the Wabash. The prize of conquest was the lands, which were adjacent to the field of battle. A thousand warriors fought on each side. The contest commenced with the sun, and was fought with all the barbarity and desperation of Indian bravery. The Wabash warriors were victorious with seven survivors; and the vanquished came off with only five.

Curiosities. Like Alabama and Tennessee, this state abounds with subterranean wonders, in the form of caves. Many have been explored, and some of them have been described. One of them, extensively known in the western country by the name of '*the Epsom salts cave*,' merits a particular description. We shall give it in the words of a letter communicated to the American Antiquarian Society, by John H. Farnham, Esq.

'Your letter, requesting a description of my *Epsom salts cave* has come to hand. From the particulars enumerated in your request, the information on each point must necessarily be very limited.

'The cave is situated in the north-west quarter of section 27, in township No. 3, of the second easterly range in the district of lands offered for sale at Jeffersonville.—The precise time of its discovery is difficult to ascertain. I have conversed with several men who had made several transient visits to the interior of the cave about eleven years ago, at which time it must have exhibited a very interesting appearance, being, to use their own phraseology, *covered like snow* with the salts. At this period, some describe the salts to have been from six to nine inches deep, on the bottom of the cave, on which lumps of an enormous size were interspersed, while the sides presented the same impressive spectacle with the bottom, being covered with the same production. Making liberal allowances for the hyperbole of discoverers and visitors, I can not help thinking that the scenery of the interior at this time was highly interesting, and extremely picturesque. I found this opinion upon conversations with general Harrison and major Floyd, who visited the cave at an early period, and whose intelligence would render them less liable to be deceived by novel appearances.

'The hill, in which the cave is situated, is about 400 feet high from the base to the most elevated point; and the prospect to the south-east, in a clear day, is exceedingly fine, commanding an extensive view of the hills and valleys bordering on Big Blue river. The top of the hill is covered principally with oak and chestnut. The side to the south-east is mantled with cedar. The entrance is about midway from the base to the summit, and the surface of the cave preserves in general, about that elevation; although I must acknowledge this to be conjectural, as no experiments have been made with a view to ascertain the fact. It is, probably, owing to this middle situation of the cave, that it is much drier than is common.

'After entering the cave by an aperture of twelve or fifteen feet wide, and in height, in one place, three or four feet, you descend with easy and gradual steps into a large and spacious room, which continues about a quarter of a mile, pretty nearly the same appearance, varying in height from eight to thirty feet, and in breadth from ten to twenty. In this distance the roof is, in some places, arched; in others a plane; and in one place, particularly, it resembles an inside view of the roof of a house. At the distance above named, the cave forks; but the right hand fork soon terminates, while the left rises by a flight of rocky stairs, nearly ten feet high, into another story, and pursues a course at this place nearly south-east. Here the roof commences a regular arch, the height of which from the floor, varies from five to eight feet, and the width of the cave from six to twelve feet; which continues to what is called the *creeping place*, from the circumstance of having to crawl ten or twelve feet into the next large room. From this place to the '*Pillar*,' a distance of about one mile and a quarter, the visitor finds an alternate succession of large and small rooms, variously decorated; sometimes mounting elevated points by gradual or difficult ascents, and again descending as far below; sometimes travelling on a pavement, or climbing over huge piles of rocks, detached from the roof by some convulsion of nature; and thus continues his route, until he arrives at the pillar.

'The aspect of this large and stately white column, as it comes in sight from the dim reflection of the torches, is grand and impressive. Visitors have seldom pushed their enquiries farther than two or three hundred yards beyond this pillar. This column is about fifteen feet in diameter, from twenty to thirty in height, and regularly reeded from the top to the bottom. In the vicinity of this spot are some inferior pillars of the same appearance and texture. Chemically speaking, it is difficult for me to say what are the constituent parts of these columns, but lime appears to be the base. Major Warren, who is certainly a competent judge, is of opinion that they are satin spar.

'I have thus given you an imperfect sketch of the mechanical structure and appearance of the cave. It only remains to mention its productions.

'The first in importance is the sulphat of magnesia, or Epsom salts, which, as has been previously remarked, abounds throughout this cave in almost its whole extent, and which, I believe, has no parallel in the history of that article. This neutral salt is found in a great variety of forms, and in many different stages of formation. Sometimes in lumps, varying from one to ten pounds in weight. The earth exhibits a shining appearance, from the numerous particles interspersed throughout the huge piles of dirt collected in different parts of the cave. The walls are covered in different places with the same article, and re-production goes on rapidly. With a view to ascertain this fact, I removed from a particular place every vestige of salt, and in four or five weeks the place was covered with small needle-shaped crystals, exhibiting the appearance of frost.

'The quality of the salt in this cave is inferior to none; and when it takes its proper stand in regular and domestic practice, must be of national utility. With respect to the resources of this cave, I will venture to say, that every competent judge must pronounce it inexhaustible. The worst earth that has been tried, will yield four pounds of salt to the bushel; and the best, from twenty to twenty-five pounds.

'The next production is the nitrate of lime, or salt-petre earth. There are vast quantities of this earth, and equal in strength to any that I have ever seen. There are also large quantities of the nitrate of allumine, or nitrate of argil, which will yield as much nitrate of potash, or saltpetre, in proportion to the quantities of earth, as the nitrate of lime.

'The three articles above enumerated, are first in quantity and importance; but there are several others, which deserve notice as subjects of philosophical curiosity. The sulphat of lime, or plaster of Paris, is to be seen variously formed; ponderous, crystalized and impalpable or soft, light, and rather spongy.

Vestiges of the sulphat of iron are also to be seen in one or two places. Small specimens of the carbonate, and also the nitrate of magnesia, have been found. The rocks in the cave principally consist of carbonate of lime, or common lime stone.

'I had almost forgotten to state, that near the forks of the cave are two specimens of painting, probably of Indian origin. The one appears to be a savage, with something like a bow in his hand, and furnishes the hint, that it was done when that instrument of death was in use. The other is so much defaced, that it is impossible to say what it was intended to represent.

'BENJAMIN ADAMS.'

Roads, Canals, Improvements, &c. The same provisions are made here, as in most of the other western states for the improvement of roads and the making of bridges. In the summer and autumn, the passing in this state is tolerable, from the circumstance of the levelness of the lands. Few of the roads are much wrought, or kept in good repair. There are ferries on all the great waters of passing. The roads, during the winter and spring, are excessively deep and heavy. The national road will pass through the centre of this state touching at Indianapolis. None of the western states afford greater facilities for canals. We have seen, that great numbers of ponds and lakes here connect both with the waters of the Mississippi and the lakes; and afford the spectacle of canals, commenced by nature. A canal, beside that mentioned, as having been commenced at Jeffersonville, has been proposed to connect the waters of the Wabash with those of the Miami of the lake, uniting that river with the lakes; and 100,000 acres of land have been appropriated by congress for that object.

That spirit of regard for schools, religious societies and institutions, connected with them, which has so honorably distinguished the commencing institutions of Ohio, has displayed itself also in this state. There are districts, no doubt, where people have but just made beginnings; and where they are more anxious about carrying on the first operations of making a new establishment, than about educating their children. But it ought to be recorded to the honor of the people in this state, that among the first public works in an incipient village, is a school house, and among the first associations, that for establishing a school. Schools are of course established in all the considerable towns and villages in the state. In many of the compact villages, there is a reading room, and a social library.—The spirit of enquiry, resulting from our free institutions, is pervading the country, and a thirst for all kinds of information is universal. Highei schools, as academies and colleges, are in operation or contemplation. This state will soon take a high place among her sister states, in point of population. It is hoped and believed, that her advance in intellectual improvement, and in the social and religious institutions will be in corresponding proportion. The only endowed college, with which we are acquainted, is fixed at Vincennes.

Constitution and Government. This state was admitted into the Union in 1816. The constitution does not differ essentially from that of the other western states.—Where it does differ, it is in having a more popular form, than the rest. The governor is elected for three years; and is eligible six years out of nine. The judiciary is composed of a supreme and circuit courts.

The judges of the supreme court are appointed by the governor, and have appellate jurisdiction. The circuit courts are to be held by one judge and two associates—the former to be appointed by the legislature, and the latter by the people; all to be held for the term of seven years. All free white males, of twenty-one years and upwards, that are citizens of the United States, are admitted to the elective franchise.

History. All the striking historical events, that relate to the country, which is now the state of Indiana, have either been related in the general history of the Mississippi valley, or remain to be more properly related under the history of Ohio, in which country, under the name of the North Western Territory, it was originally included.—It has been the scene of a number of bloody contests at different periods. The country on the Wabash was early visited by French traders, or hunters from Canada. The settlement of Vincennes, dates back as far as 1702. The first settlement was composed of soldiers of Louis XIV. They were, for more than an age, almost separated from the rest of mankind; and had, in many respects, assimilated with the savages, with whom they intermarried. In the time of the American revolution, they manifested a disposition so unequivocally favorable to it, that the general government ceded to them a tract of land about Vincennes, at the close of that war.—The sparse population in this then wilderness, suffered severely from the savages, until the peace, which was restored by the treaty at Greenville. The Indians still owned the greater portion of the territorial surface. In the year 1811, in consequence of their depredations and murders, a military force was sent against them; and they were defeated, and compelled to sue for peace. The bloody battle of Tippicanoe has already been related. Since the peace they have been quiet, and have ceded the greater part of their lands to the United States. In 1801, Indiana was erected into a territorial government. During the late war the tide of immigration was almost completely arrested. Many of the settlements were broken up by the savages. Immediately on the termination of that war, the tide set strongly again, through Ohio, to this state; and population poured in upon the woods and prairies. It has been filling up with almost unexampled rapidity, since that time. It suffered severely along with the other western states by the change of times, that occurred after the close of the war. The same foolish, or iniquitous system of spurious banks, or *relief laws*, was adopted here as in the states farther west; and with the same results. The bank of New Lexington was a notorious scheme of iniquity; and was one of the first bubbles, that burst in this young community. Though the people did not immediately take warning, they were among the first, that discarded all the rediculous temporizing expedients of relief, and restored a sound circulation.

The progress of the state in population and prosperity, some years past, has been uniform. It will now, probably, have 250,000 inhabitants; and in 1830, 300,000. If we could present a scenic map of this state, exhibiting its present condition, it would present us a grand and very interesting landscape of deep forests, wide and flowering prairies, thousands of log cabins, and in the villages, brick houses rising beside them. We should see chasms cut out of the forests in all directions. We should see thousands of dead trees surrounding the incipient establishments.—On the edges of the prairies, we should see cabins, or houses, sending up their smokes. We should see vast droves of cattle, ruminating in the vicinity of these establishments, in the shade. There would be a singular *melange* of nature and art; and to give interest to the scene, the bark hovels of the Indians, in many places, would remain intermixed with the habitations of the whites. But the most pleasing part of the picture would be to see independent and respectable yeomen presiding over these great changes. The young children would be seen playing about the rustic establishments; full fed and happy, sure presages of the numbers, healthfulness and independence of the coming generation.

From *The Christian Traveler*, by Isaac Reed [1828], pp. 70-94, 96-97, 120-22, 131-34, 137-41, 144-49, 177-84, 211-15, 216-30.

Reed, Isaac.

It is a pleasure to turn from the more or less critical accounts given by foreigners who travelled in our midst, to the narrative of one who was truly American in birth and sympathy. No traveller had such an opportunity to study the real conditions that existed along the frontier as did the missionary ministers. In 1816 the Presbyterian Societies of New England sent a number of Missionaries to Indiana. The most noted of these were Isaac Reed and William W. Martin. Like the Methodist circuit riders, they travelled all over the state. They therefore were in a position to give a valuable detailed survey of the religious and social conditions then existing. The following observations are from the pen of Mr. Reed.

LETTER XIX.

Madison, Jefferson Co., Indiana, July 29, 1818.

My dear C———,

My last was from the Rev. Mr. Cleland's, of Mercer, Kentucky, where I remained over Sabbath, and on the 22d inst. in company with Mr. C. started for this place. We stopped at noon, at a decent cabin, and found they had a bible. The woman said she was a great sinner, and was very attentive to what we said to her. She seemed willing to learn, but very rarely hears preaching. We put up at night, with a religious family on the north edge of Shelby Co. Leaving it early the next morning, we breakfasted near Newcastle, and soon after passed through the town. This is the seat of justice of Henry Co. It is built on the southern declivity of a hill, contains a population of about 800, and is surrounded by a fertile and populous country. It is wholly destitute of religious society. I thought this field needs culture, and said to my companion, that it ought to receive religious attention, and would be, I thought, a favourable missionary station. In these parts thought I, and wrote it in my journal, "There remains yet very much land to be possessed." We made little stop the rest of the day, being anxious to reach this that night; and just at sun-set we came down to the Ohio river, which is here half a mile wide. Crossing over, we came into Madison, and put up with Mr. D. M'Clure. In my travels in Kentucky, which have included about 700 miles, I have learned much of its religious state. This is truly low, though it is thought better than a few years since. There are many which wear the Baptist's name, but they have neither the knowledge, order, nor the apparent piety of the Baptists in the northern states. The Methodists are not very numerous, and the Presbyterian cause and interest is low. There are some precious people, whom I highly respect: they are walking in the ordinances of God, and sighing over the abominations of the land, in which their lot is cast. And there are some faithful ministers, who are zealous for the cause of the Redeemer. But they are so few,—they are so very few,—more than 30 counties, containing an immense population, are without a single Presbyterian minister. Several of these counties have in them little churches, but they have no pastors. Poor souls, how I pity them. Since I came into the state, most of my time has been spent with such. I hope some good has arisen, and will arise from it.

I am now, for the first time, on the north side of the Ohio. This town lies on its bank. We are come here to preach the glorious Gospel, and Mr. C. is to administer the Sacrament. More at a future time. Your's, &c.

LETTER XX

New-Albany, September 5, 1818.

My dear C———,

In Madison and the country about it, I spent six weeks. Some account of this time, and my labours in it, I am now about to give my friend. My former letter closed with our arrival in Madison, and just at the eve of a sacramental occasion. On that occasion the meeting lasted four days.—I preached three times, and Mr. C——— three. Saturday, it rained profusely; but Sabbath the weather was good, and the attendance very numerous. The attention seemed also fixed and solemn.

During the sacrament, many were in tears. There were five tables, and about 80 communicants. Several addresses at the table were long and affecting. I preached at evening, and Mr. C——— gave an exhortation. It was a very superior one; showing the excellence of Christianity from its effects. He was animated and very pathetic. He is a devout man, and has a great gift in extemporary speaking. The next morning was very rainy, but the people convened at 10 o'clock, and Mr. C———

preached an able and instructive discourse, and the meeting was closed. He set out for home the same day, and I came six miles down the river with W. D. Esq., where, much fatigued, I remained through the next day.

July 29th.—I was this morning at Mr. G. L.'s; who lives on high ground, beautifully overlooking the Ohio. He is an intelligent and pious man of the Associate Reformed Church. After dinner, I started for Graham's Fork, a settlement in Jennings county. The country through which I passed, is new; but the log houses are scattered along near the road. The distance is 13 miles, and I reached there just before sun-set. Put up with Mr. S. Graham, where I am to preach to-morrow. He seems a good man, and was with his wife at the late sacrament inMadison. They have a little church collected here of 17 members. Oh! that their number may soon be increased, and this wilderness blossom as the rose, and become vocal with the praises of God. Oh! that the Rose of Sharon may be known and prized by these new settlers of the western wilds.

July 30th.—The weather was very showery, but a considerable number of people came to meeting, to whom I preached for about an hour, from the text, "Fear not, little flock, for it is your Father's good pleasure to give you the kingdom." They were very attentive, and it looked as though the fields were white, ready to the harvest. O Lord, send forth labourers into thy harvest!

July 31st.—Preached at 9 o'clock this morning, in the same place, and to nearly the same congregation as on yesterday. Their attention was silent and good. It was a pleasure to preach to them, they seemed so highly to prize it. I left them on my return at 11 o'clock. The late rains had raised the rivers, and the waters were very high. Fording was somewhat difficult, but I succeeded in crossing, and returned to the neighbourhood of W. D. Esq., near the Ohio.

Sabbath, Aug. 2d.—I preached for the first time in the open woods. The collection of people was considerable, much greater than could get into the school house,—meeting house they have none. I felt considerable freedom in preaching from the text, "They that be whole need not a physician; but they that are sick." Near evening I held a society, or conference meeting at Mr. D.'s, and it was very well attended.

Aug. 5th.—I rode into Madison, and spent the afternoon with some religious people there, and went home at night with J Ritchie, Esq., an elder in the church, living out of town.

Aug. 6th.—Went to Mr. C.'s, another elder in the church, who is a very sedate and good man. He was raised in Rockbridge, Virginia, and he told me much concerning a revival of religion in that county in the days and ministry of old Parson Graham. The Rev. Dr. Alexander of Princeton, was one of the converts.

Sabbath, Aug. 9th.—Preached again in Madison. The day was warm and pleasant, but the place of preaching bad. It was a little, old log court-house. In the morning it was crowded, and numbers were out of the doors; but in the afternoon, there were not so many.

Aug. 13th.—I felt happy to-day in meeting at W. Dunn's, Esq., the Rev. O. Fowler, Missionary from Connecticut. We had been acquainted there when students of divinity; and were licensed by the same association. It was now very pleasant to meet him in these new settlements. At 5 P.M., we attended meeting together, and found a school-house filled with people, waiting to hear. I preached, and he prayed after sermon. In prayer, he was able, devout, and solemn. The people gave very good attention, and he is to preach to them the next Sabbath; whilst I make another trip to Graham's Fork. We remained together over night. Oh! that many like him may be sent into the harvest in these parts.

Aug. 14th.—I left brother F———, and rode to G.F.K.: stopped by the way at Mr. M'C.'s, and conversed awhile with the family upon religion, and appointed to preach a lecture there as I return on Monday. They had just buried a little son, and the mother seemed serious.

Aug. 15th.—Preached at Mr. S. Graham's, at 2 P.M., and after preaching, rode to Mr. Miller's, five miles up the fork, where I held a conference in the evening with his family and a few neighbours.

Sabbath, Aug. 16th.—There is no house in the neighbourhood large enough to hold the people, which it was expected, would be at preaching today. They had, therefore, some days before, fixed a stand, and made seats in the woods. The place was well chosen, and the arrangement discovered good taste. Time for preaching came, and I went forth into the woods, and preached two sermons to a considerable congregation, who were very still and attentive. The blue arch of heaven was my canopy, and the forest trees were thick on either hand. I was strengthened and encouraged, and in the afternoon spoke more easily than in the morning. Here again, let me say, "Hitherto the Lord hath helped me." I desire to rejoice that ever I came over into this State, and that I came out to see this poor people, who so much loved the preached gospel, but who have had so little, since they settled here. I am the second Presbyterian minister, who has visited them; but Mr. F. is to follow me in two weeks.

Monday morning, took an affectionate leave of these simple-hearted people, where a number of young persons are seriously impressed. May the Lord bring them to know Him, and give them peace in believing. Rode in the rain, and at 11 o'clock preached at Mr. M'C———'s. Next day, with brother Fowler, rode to Madison, and attended the formation of the Madison Bible Society. In this meeting, we both addressed the people. Eighty four members signed the constitution, and $96 were paid into the hand of the treasurer. The occasion was, to most of the people, altogether new; they were attentive, and seemed to take a deep interest in the subject; and when they retired from the meeting, a smile lighted up their countenance, and bespoke good will to fill the breast. The cause is the Lord's.—It is to diffuse more widely his own book, and he seemed to smile on the efforts of his people.

Sabbath, Aug. 23.—A beautiful day; I preached again two sermons in the old log court-house; the attention of the people seemed very good. The sermon in the afternoon was accommodated to encourage the people to build a meeting-house, for which they are making an effort. The text was Neh. ii, 20: "The God of heaven he will prosper us, therefore, we his servants will arise and build."

Aug. 29th.—I have been this week 18 miles into the country, north east of M. and preached two sermons, and visited a few scattered Presbyterian families, and this afternoon met with a few ladies and assisted them to form a religious Tract Society; they have had opposition, but the thing is accomplished; it is a good work, and though few, they are engaged about it. May the Lord bless and prosper them!

Aug. 30th.—This day being Sabbath, I preached again two sermons in Madison. The congregation was small.

Sept. 1st.—Preached a lecture in the school-house, near W. Dunn's, Esq. where the attendance and attention were very good.

Sept. 3d.—Left this settlement and rode 24 miles, through a thinly settled country to Charlestown, the seat of justice of Clark county. Here I called on the Rev. Mr. Todd, and tarried with him over night. Charlestown is a considerable place, and seems fast improving.

Sept. 4th.—Left Mr. Todd's this morning and went to Jeffersonville, 13 miles; this is on the bank of the Ohio, opposite the mouth of Bear-Grass creek. I found there Mr. Webster, a college acquaintance, who was an officer in the late war; he was in the battle of Bridgewater, near the falls of Niagara, where he was wounded, and left for dead on the field of battle. He was shot through the right cheek, and the ball lodged in the back part of the neck; being taken up after the battle, it was extracted, and he recovered; after this he read law, and has been some time in practice. In the afternoon I rode to New Albany, four miles further down the river. To this place I had a letter of introduction, and put up with Mr. J. Scribner, an elder in thePresbyterian church.

LETTER XXI

New Albany, Ind., Oct. 4th, 1818.

My dear C———,

I have been steadily in this place, visiting the people, preaching, and attending to ministerial duties near five weeks. I have preached twice every Sabbath, till the present, when the Rev. Mr. Fowler preached in the morning, and administered the sacrament of the Lord's Supper. I have also attended one evening prayer-meeting each week. I have also attended several funerals. The last has been the most sickly month in the year; many have been ill, and six or seven have died since I came here.

This is a new place, having been laid out into town lots but five years. At that time it was thickly covered with heavy timber. It is now rude in appearance, and has few good houses, but is fast improving, and contains 700 inhabitants; its situation is eligible, being high above the river, and lying along its bank. The surrounding country is of a rich soil, but thinly settled, and little improved. The town is two miles below the Falls of the Ohio; its religious character is low, but gaining. There are two small societies, a Presbyterian and a Methodist. In the Presbyterian the communicants are 13. In looking over my journal, I find the following, written a few days after I first came into the town. "I am here in this new country. I have come to this town; why it is I know not; but Divine Providence has so ordered it. O that I may be submissive! heartily inclined to do my duty whilst I stay. And O that I may daily feel myself the Lord's servant, and be about my master's business! This evening we begin to hold the monthly concert of prayer in this place. O may my heart be engaged, and it be a good time to the Lord's people here! It is a sweet and refreshing consideration, to think how many others, in various parts of the world, are, at the same time, engaged in the same way. Thy kingdom come, O Lord! and may the whole earth be filled with thy glory. Amen."

I have been in this place as long as I intended, at my first coming, and am now ready to depart on the morrow, having to meet the Presbytery of Transylvania, in Mercer, Ky. next Wednesday. Your's, &c.

LETTER XXII.

New Albany, Nov. 5th, 1818.

Mr Dear C———,

After several weeks absence, and travelling through a considerable part of Kentucky, I am again at this place, and at the request of the people, have concluded to settle here, at least for the present; they need help, and I wish to help them. But I will look back awhile, and give some account of my late tour.

October 5th.—It was late this morning before I got away from New Albany, and I was detained an hour at the ferry; before I set out, the trustees put in my hand $30, as a reward for my services. No people in this western country have treated me so generously. Passing through Louisville, and taking the Frankfort road, I put up at an inn, eight miles short of Shelbyville. Here I found a liberally educated and pious young man of Fairfield, Conn. on his way home, after spending ten months in this state, teaching in a private family.

Oct. 6th.—Travelled in company with the young man above mentioned till afternoon, when our roads parted. At night I reached within six miles of the place of the meeting of the Presbytery.

Oct. 7th.—Met the Presbytery at its opening in New Providence meeting-house. The Rev. J. Howe, of Greene co. preached the sermon, after which Presbytery constituted, and adjourned to meet to-morrow. I lodged with the Rev. Thomas Clelland, where I had the company of Messrs. Howe and Nelson.

Oct. 8th.—Presbytery took me under their care, and concluded to grant me an examination, and if approved, to ordain me next Saturday. The examination commenced this P.M.

October 9th.—The examination continued, and I preached my trial sermon; it was on the docrine of justification. The examination is sustained, and public notice given of ordination to-morrow.

Oct. 10th.—My feelings were pleasant, this morning, as I rose from bed, and engaged in morning duties. I was solemn while thinking of what a few hours would bring me to pass through:—the day was warm and the weather fair:—it was a day for which I had long wished,—to which my aims and my hopes had long directed: for it was the day when, by the laying on of the hands of the Presbytery, I was to be fully invested with ministerial office and authority. The morning was now come, and I rejoiced with thanksgiving:—the sermon was preached by the Rev. J. B. Lapsley, from 2 Cor. x. 4,—"For the weapons of our warfare are not carnal, but mighty through God, to the pulling down of strong holds." It was a very able sermon; and in the prayer before it, he was both able and fervent. The ordination prayer was offered by the Rev. J. Howe, presiding bishop; and the right hand of fellowship given, first by him, and then by each of the ministers:—He also gave the charge; it was scriptural and very solemn:—solemn, indeed, was the whole of the transaction, though very weak in health, I was greatly supported in spirit, and my mind kept even through the whole. This was the most momentous day of my life. And now, Lord, I am thine, for ever thine, nor would my purpose move:—so I thought while the ordination lasted:—so I think whilst I record it.

Oct. 11th.—This is a sacramental Sabbath in this place. The congregation was very large; the preaching excellent; and the whole service especially solemn: many were in tears: a goodly number of young people were, I trust, truly convicted. Three young men, brothers, were admitted; one married man and a young woman were baptized.

Oct. 12th.—I preached, and Mr. Cleland, immediately after me, when the meeting closed. On the 13th, we set out for the Synod at Lexington: on our way, the conversation turned on a ministerial facility, of introducing and keeping up religious conversation in company, and on common occasions, as means of doing good. He said, there are three ways, one of which he embraced, according to the time, disposition of persons, or other circumstances; always aiming at the benefit of the person or persons present. One way is, direct and personal address, questioning, exhorting, and reasoning; the next is, whatever be the subject introduced, so to shape the conversation as to make it lead into religion; and then it may be most personal and serious, without difficulty, and generally without offence. The third way is, to converse directly with one person, with a view and aim to interest, impress, and instruct another person present, who takes no other part than to listen to it. He is judged by many to have a happy gift this way, and has been a very popular and successful minister. To this, I might add my own conviction, formed on experience, of the special benefit of the two latter, both in making the desired impression, and securing the good will of the person, whose benefit is sought. He preached at night in the house where we stayed.

Oct. 14th.—The Synod met in Lexington, and the Rev. Mr. Cunningham preached the opening sermon; when Synod constituted, and adjourned to meet next day. Its sessions continued from day to day, and closed on the 19th; there was preaching every evening, and a missionary sermon on Saturday; after which, a free conversation was held on the state of religion within the bounds of the Synod. In this it appeared that there have been special revivals of religion in some congregations. In Harrison county, two hundred communicants have been added to the church, the last year; between ninety and one hundred in Paris; one hundred and thirty in Concord; forty four in New-Providence in Harodsburgh. At this session, Synod resolved to establish, on Christian principles, a new college, to be called the college of Kentucky, and located at Danville.

Oct. 20th.—Left Lexington, and travelled in company with Messrs. J. Lyle and N. H. Hall, to the Rev. Mr. Nelson's, near Danville; and next day to Springfield.

Oct. 22d.—Visited again my much-esteemed friend Mrs. Reed, where I spent the day in a very cheerful and pleasant manner. Next day rode to Lebanon, to attend a sacrament in Hardin's creek congregation: the meeting commenced the day before, and I preached to-day.

Oct. 24th.—This day, being Sabbath, the congregation was too large for the meeting-house, and they retired to a grove, where the Rev. Mr. Lyle preached, and the sacrament was administered: the attention seemed solemn; five new members were added:—I preached again this evening; next day Mr. Cleland preached, and the meeting was closed. I returned the same evening to Springfield, and left there the next day; from this, my journey was very pleasant through Nelson and Jefferson counties, Kentucky, to this town, which I reached the evening of the 29th of October. I was expected by the people, who had raised a salary for a year, by subscription, and sent after me to Lexington, requesting my immediate return, and settlement with them:—to this I have consented; viewing it as the direction of Providence, for my usefulness in the ministry. Here I preached last Sabbath, to a considerable congregation of attentive hearers, and here I expect to reside, at least for a season; using my endeavours to serve my generation, by the will of God, in the ministry of the Gospel. That I may be enabled to do this, and rightly divide the word of truth to this people, I devoutly implore the influence and guidance of the Holy Spirit. O may the Lord bless this little church, and increase it;—bless this town and reform it;—reformation is greatly needed.

Thus, my early and much-esteemed friend, have I been led on from step to step, and from place to place, by Divine Providence. Surely he hath led in a way, which I knew not; and he hath guided me with his eye;—he hath preserved me from dangers seen and unseen;—he hath kept me from death; and, in the midst of sickness, hath given me to speak a word to comfort the distressed:—he hath led me to a people, whom I knew not; and given me favour in their sight;—wherefore, let my heart praise him;—let my pen honour him;—let me take the cup of salvation, and call on the name of the Lord;—the Lord is my helper and my shield;—let me not fear while my trust is in him; neither in the wilderness nor "in the city full;"—but may it be my constant aim to serve, and thus to glorify him, in the Gospel of Jesus Christ, to which, by his Spirit and Providence, he has called me. And you, my friend, you know of his mercies, and will help me to praise him. And let me request that I may even share in your prayers, and that the people of these western regions, who are so destitute of the regular preaching of the Gospel, may also be often in your mind, when you look to the mercy-seat.

May the peace of God fill your heart,—may you be the honoured instrument of winning souls to the blessed Saviour,—and finally, with all the redeemed, that blood-washed throng, rest in his holy kingdom; is the ardent prayer of, dear C———, your early, your constant, and your affectionate friend. Farewell.

ISAAC REED.

PART II.

RESIDENCE AND LABOURS AT NEW-ALBANY.

At New-Albany I became located in October, 1818. The engagement was for one year. The salary was $500. As a place, its morals were low; its general society was rude, and much of it profane. There were some pious persons, but their number was small, and even these were not well known to each other, nor united. There was a small Presbyterian church of fifteen members, and a small Methodist society. The inhabitants were from various parts of the older settled country:—some were from Connecticut—more from New-Jersey, some from Massachusetts, some from Pennsylvania, numbers from Kentucky, and some from Ireland. The place itself was about five years old, but its inhabitants had been very few till within two years: it had now a steam saw-mill, several stores, mechanics' shops, &c., and a boat yard for the building of steam-boats. Over most of the town-plot, lay thickly, the large trunks of trees which had been felled, but were not removed. This plot is upon the bottom lands of the Ohio river, a mile and a half below the falls. The forest trees had been thick and large, and many of the poplars of immense size. There was a little frame covered in for a Methodist meeting-house;—the Presbyterians had none;—and the only school-house was a miserable log one. In this state of things my year commenced with that people. I undertook with this Presbyterian society with an intent to remain with them, if the Lord should so direct, and rear the society from its weak and low condition, till it should become a numerous, respectable, and strong society. And in this review after eight years of absence, I am rather surprised that I succeeded so well, and did so much, than that I did not succeed better and do more. It was a strained effort on the part of the society, which was made to obtain me. One man subscribed $75, another $60, another $30. The church had been but lately formed, and had three elders, neither of them experienced respecting their office. Many of the people were poor: numbers came there with some relics of better condition, to retrieve their fortunes. The place had a sickly character. Numbers were single men just setting out in life;—some as merchants, others as mechanics. The buildings were mostly crude; either logs or frames just capable of being occupied by families. The families were too numerous for the buildings, and were therefore cramped for room. With this people, thus circumstanced, I commenced single handed. There was not an installed minister of the Presbyterian church in the state; and, by God's blessing, I kept the ground, defended and fortified the post, and won some from without, to come into the garrison. This year was one of the most unremitted, intense and painful watchfulness of any year of my life. I often felt the weight and pressure of my situation. My hope was in God, and he sustained me. I set myself to instruct the church—to win the attention of my hearers, and to become acquainted with the people. It was not long before the grocery shops, which were kept open on the Sabbath when I came here, were closed upon that holy day. A respectable number attended meeting on the Sabbath. The meetings were held under great inconveniences: sometimes in the old school-house, and sometimes in private houses. The church members became gradually better known to each other and more united. The church also increased slowly, till September, 1819: then a number of young people became deeply and anxiously impressed with a concern for their salvation: this issued in the hopeful conversion of several in a short time. A few weeks afterwards nine were added to the church in one day. This may seem small in other places, but it was great here. Some others were added to the church from time to time till the number came to be thirty-five before my leaving it. My year of contract was now out, and the society was incompetent to renew the salary. The largest subscriber was dead, and his estates deeply involved with debts. The times seemed changing for the worse. Many of the society were considerably embarrased with debts. My heart was with the people. I had thought, this is my home, and here will I build my house. I delayed with them till December; but found it necessary at that time to remove. It was trying to quit this ground; to leave my plans of improvement; to leave my flock—numbers of which were young and tender lambs, just beginning to be reckoned of the flock of Christ:—but it seemed necessary, and I felt that I must submit. In this year a meeting house was built by my society. A Sabbath school society was formed in the place, and a school of sixty scholars gathered and instructed. This was the first Sabbath school society ever formed in the State. The same year the Methodist society at New-Albany was increased; and just before the close of the year, a Baptist society was commenced.

My travels this year were not extensive. In the fall of 1818, I made a tour to Frankfort, Kentucky, and in my return was well nigh being drowned in attempting to ford a small river, which had been suddenly raised by a great rain the preceding night. It was immensly rapid. After breaking the girth of my saddle, and being carried a little below the ford, I succeeded in getting out on the same side I went in. I then turned back and took another road. Another tour was to attend a meeting of the Louisville Presbytery, held at Livonia, in the interior of the settled parts of Indiana. The others were chiefly of a missionary character. Up to this time I had been a volunteer for the Gospel in the Western states. I now began to be in the commission of the Missionary Society of Connecticut. Their first commission was sent me this year. It was issued in January 1819, and I received it in February of the same year. But I did nothing under it till May, when I spent eight days in the two next counties down the Ohio river from New-Albany. In this tour travelled 95 miles, visited and spent the Sabbath with a little church at Corydon, county seat of Harrison county, and then the place for the residence of the Governor, and the holding the sessions of the State Legislature. This church was gathered the preceding winter by the Rev. John F. Crow, and consisted of seven members. From Corydon, I went down the Ohio river to Leavensworth, and Fredonia, two little towns of Crawford county, just commencing, and lying upon the Ohio river. Neither of these had been visited by any Presbyterian minister before. In this tour I preached seven times—held one meeting of the Corydon church session, and received one new member.

In June, I made a tour to some medicinal springs in Mercer county, Kentucky; and was absent from New-Albany between three and four weeks. In this tour I assisted at two sacramental meetings. The first was held in a grove near Springfield, in Washington county, Kentucky. The attendance was great, and the attention appeared favourable. In this county are two Presbyterian churches supplied by one minister. A large part of the population are Roman Catholics. The other was held in a beautiful little grove near a meeting house, about two miles from Harodsburg. The attendance was great. The ministers were the Rev. Thomas Clelland, the pastor, and the Rev. J. F. Crow, of Shelby county. The state of feeling seemed to be lively. A few persons made a Christian profession. About twenty have done this in the three places which this pastor tends upon, since last October.

From the springs in Mercer, I went to Lancaster, in Garrard county, and spent the next Sabbath; and returned the following week to New-Albany, by way of Frankfort, Shelbyville, and Louisville, having travelled about 240 miles.

At an earlier time the same season, I assisted at a sacramental meeting of three days with the Rev. John F. Crow, at a place called Fox-Run, near Shelbyville, in Shelby county. Here also the Sabbath meeting was held in a grove. The only reason why these meetings were held in groves, was because the meeting houses were not competent to contain the people. This is very generally the case at sacramental meetings in these parts.

In August I attended a second meeting of the Louisville Presbytery. This was held at New-Lexington, Indiana. There I fulfilled an appointment which had been assigned to me at the spring session. This was to preach a sermon at the installation of the Rev. John M. Dickey, now settling at this place, in connection with another eight or nine miles distant. This was the first Presbyterial settlement of a minister in the State. The installation was on Saturday, and the sacrament of the Lord's Supper followed the next day. Meeting on both days, and Monday also, was held in the wood, under the shade of forest trees.

From this place I went on to Madison, about 16 miles further up the Ohio river. There I greeted again the friends which I had made in my labours the preceding year. I also did the same in the settlement of Dunn and Logan, 7 miles below. These people had showed me some acts of religious friendship. They were my first acquaintance in Indiana. Their manners were plain and easy, Christian and friendly; and they were peculiarly dear to me. This is the same place which now embraces the society of my friend, the Rev. J. F. Crow: and they have now a commodious stone meeting house. At that time they were a part of the church at Madison, and had no meeting-house.

On my way from New-Lexington, a young man was my travelling companion, who lived near Madison. He was now a professor of religion, and in the communion of the Madison church. His views were now turned towards qualifications for the gospel ministry. He informed me that his attention had been greatly excited when hearing me preach in that settlement, the preceding year. The first time I ever preached in the woods, he heard me; and was greatly impressed with the text, and the whole sermon.

The text was Matt. ix. 12—*They that be whole need not a physician, but they that are sick.* That young man is now, 1827, a gospel minister in Indiana. At Madison I met with the Rev. Thomas C. Searle. He had just arrived there under the patronage of the Missionary Society of young men in New-York city. The next year he became settled as pastor, and died there, in the autumn of 1821. I returned by way of Charlestown, where I preached at night during the term of the circuit court.

In September, I went into the interior of the State: travelled through several counties, and preached in different places, and made an arrangement to distribute bibles in some. These bibles were the remains of a society, which has been formed at Jeffersonville by the agency of the Rev. Samuel J. Mills and the Rev. Daniel Smith, while what is now the State of Indiana, was a territory; and I think it was while Col. Posey was Governor. In the new and frontier counties of Monroe and Owen, I spent nearly two weeks. In both these counties I found some Presbyterian families. In Monroe county, a church was gathered and constituted at Bloomington, the county seat. This was the first church formed by my ministry. From this I returned by way of Livonia, and saw the Rev. Wm. W. Martin, who had located there.

A slow fever had commenced upon me in this tour, and it rose daily; but when I had reached New-Albany, by medicine and a blessing, it was speedily removed. The fall Session of the Louisville Presbytery followed soon. This was held at Shelbyville in Kentucky: and the Synod soon after at Danville. These were both attended in their time and place: and the attendance of the latter, led to the formation of a new relation of life. There I first saw the companion of my future life. She was a widow's daughter, then resident at that place; but had lately come there. Her family were of the second Presbyterian church in the city of Philadelphia. But having suffered from misfortunes, they had removed to Kentucky. Here, under the name of their mother, the three daughters taught a female boarding school.

When the Synod had closed its sessions, I returned by way of Frankfort and Shelbyville; and was immediately most assiduously employed in my little society till the 20th of December, when I took my final leave of that society as its minister.

This is a year to be remembered in the *history* of my life. It was a year on which much depended. God himself was my teacher. I held a station in which much was needed, and from which much was expected:—it was a station, for which the activity of youth and the wisdom of long experience were requisite. My health was weak, but my mind was active, and my efforts were not intermitted, and they were in many things successful. In this year I also published a piece in the Weekly Recorder, a religious paper of the quarto form, edited by the Rev. John Andrews, at Chillicothe, respecting Indiana, under the title, "The budding of the Wilderness, or a Gospel light dawning in Indiana."

Some Extracts from Correspondents in this year, addressed to the Rev. Isaac Reed.

The first was from the Post Master at New-Albany, and sent to the writer of this narrative, when at Lexington, Kentucky, attending Synod.

New-Albany, Oct. 10th, 1818.

Dear Sir,

With pleasure I inform you, that we have succeeded with our subscription so far, as to enable us to engage with you, and ensure you five hundred dollars a year for the present, and will thank you to make arrangements accordingly, and come as soon as convenient.

I am respectfully, your friend and brother,

JOEL SCRIBNER.

A third extract is taken from a letter of the Rev. Orin Fowler, then a Missionary in Indiana.

Carlisle, Jan. 12th, 1819.

My dear Sir,

I have just returned from a tour up the Wabash, as far as Fort Harrison. Your letter is received, and read with pleasure; and shall now be answered. That you are in usual health—that you have reason to hope you will yet be well at New-Albany; I am rejoiced to hear: but that you have unexpected difficulties, grieves me. May the Lord, the fountain of knowledge and consolation, give you wisdom, which is profitable to direct; and the blessed influences of his Spirit, to comfort you, and make you instrumental of great good, in that part of the vineyard, where you are called to labour. It appears that God, in his righteous providence, has removed from this state of probation, one of your parishioners, Mr. Nathaniel Scribner. May this dispensation be sanctified to his friends and fellow-citizens, that you may all finally have cause to say; 'It was good for me to be afflicted.' Since I left you, my health has been, as usual, very good. I have preached very often; almost every day; and have found the people generally attentive to know the word: though the difficulties and discouragements of a missionary in this part of the State, are much greater than in the eastern and middle parts of it. I have been on a tour to Monroe county (Bloomington county seat) which was very fatiguing;—have been up the Wabash river to Fort Harrison, and preached in nearly every neighborhood in these several directions. After three or four weeks, the Lord willing, I propose to return to my old field of labour, and from thence to my native land. It is my present intention to return to the east, upon the old wilderness route through Virginia. From you, I hope to obtain some information of importance, relative to this route. That the consolations of the Holy Spirit may be ever yours, and the blessings of heaven attend your labours, is the prayer of your brother,

O. FOWLER.

REV. I. REED.

. . . I went through Shelby county, and crossed the Ohio river at the mouth of Harrod's creek, twelve or thirteen miles above Louisville. Left Charlestown a few miles to the right, and passed through Salem, Indiana. Thus far I had the company of one of the elders in my church. Thence I travelled alone. I reached Bloomington Saturday. Rode twenty miles without my breakfast, and then found the family where I stopped to obtain it, without bread, meat, or flour,—they had potatoes, and on these I made a good meal. At Bloomington I spent the Sabbath with the little church, which I had formed in the year 1819, and preached twice. They were still vacant, and but little increased. The Lord's Supper had been twice only dispensed to them since its constitution. Two men had moved in, who were ruling elders in other places, and were chosen such by this church. For the election of the second, the church was together when I arrived.

Monday, Nov. 5th.—I went on from Bloomington to Owen county. Found, after some difficulty, my way to the residence of Mrs. Reed's relations. Most of them were in health, and elated at seeing me; but her uncle, who had made the purchase, and moved the family there, and who was the head of Mrs.

Young's family, had been sick with a fever, and was now slowly recovering. The rest were cheerful, and seemed in good hopes. They seemed in the midst of the woods, and had not a cleared field in sight. In this county a little church had been gathered, and constituted the year before, by the Rev. Mr. Dickey. They held Sabbath meetings about five miles from these our relatives. I preached at Mr. Holmes' the day after my arrival, and for this church the following Sabbath: and that week, in company with my brother-in-law, went through the woods by the forks of the Eel river, to the Land Office of Terre Haute, about fifty miles. There I entered a half quarter section of land joining upon that bought by Mr. Holmes. Returned and preached at Mr. Holmes' Wednesday night, from Philippians iv. 19.—"My God shall supply all your need, according to his riches in glory, by Christ Jesus." A text which was chosen in consequence of the situation of the family, and their many privations here in this wilderness; and it was received like a meal, to go in its strength many days. The next day I forded White river and returned to Bloomington, twenty miles.

I was now ninety miles from New-Albany, where I had sent an appointment by mail, to be the next Sabbath; and I had but two days to ride it in. Left Bloomington Friday morning, and put up for night at Orleans, having travelled forty miles.—Saturday morning I was up and started at daylight, and rode fourteen miles to breakfast, and at eight o'clock in the evening reached New Albany, about fifty miles. As I passed over the height of the Knobbs, about four miles before entering the town, a scene of the strong sublime opened to my view. It was star light, with a clear air, and the sky was brilliant and glowing. Beneath, over the broad vale of the Ohio river, rested thin clouds of a smoky and damp atmosphere. And all this grandeur and beauty were heightened by the stillness and silence of the night, and the solitude of the observer. The writer's mind was filled with adoring admiration, while he gazed in silence and reflection as he descended from these heights. The next day was Sabbath, and was spent at New-Albany in preaching again to that people; but, ah! there had been many and sad changes since I had lived there:—some were removed from the church by death;—some were removed away from the place;—some had turned aside to ungodliness;—a few were steadfast and abiding here; these were mourning over the desolations and the abominations:—I was sad to see the low estate of Zion here. Their meeting-house was burnt; but there was something which was cheering to me still in all this wretchedness; it was this:—a number of the young converts, who had been admitted by my ministry, were still cleaving to the Lord, and following his ways. From New-Albany I made my way to Mercer county, Kentucky, and found my wife and child in health; the night after my arrival there, there fell a deep snow, which kept me from returning to Nicholasville the next day: . . . I omit to send you the particulars of my journal, that I may have room to give you an account of Indiana as a missionary field; I think it an encouraging field, could it be supplied soon: it contains 140,000 inhabitants; these inhabitants are settled along the Ohio river more than three hundred miles, including its windings: up the Wabash river, from its mouth, two hundred miles; and up the west line of the Ohio State, one hundred and thirty or more miles: settlements are contained in all parts between these three boundary-lines. The north part of the State is not yet settled; and but lately purchased of the Indians: the east part of the State from the Ohio line down the Ohio river, to a point directly opposite the mouth of the Kentucky river; and to a line running thence due north is included within the bounds of the Synod of Ohio. I know not how many Presbyterian churches there are in this district; it is among the oldest settled parts of the State; it is about forty miles wide from east to west; but whatever may be the number of churches, there are but two Presbyterian ministers, and neither have a pastoral charge. From this line, proceeding westward, the whole remainder of the State belongs to the Synod of Kentucky; this is a tract of about one hundred miles from east to west; and many parts of it are thickly settled: all this territory is in the bounds of the Louisville Presbytery; and in it all, there are only five Presbyterian ministers of the General Assembly; one of these is nearly superannuated; of this number, three only are settled pastors; one of these has one, another two, and the third three stated places for their preaching: besides these six churches, which are thus partially supplied with preaching, the whole of the rest of the country is missionary ground; and in it there are now fourteen infant Presbyterian churches; several of these have been gathered and planted; and all of them have been watered by missionaries; of these, the missionaries from the Connecticut society, have borne their full share; and if the country could be well supplied with missionaries, who could spend a year or more among the new settlements, or who could be settled in them, after the plan of many in the western reserve part of Ohio; labouring the fourth part or more of his time as the pastor to some church; and the rest of the time as a missionary; there is a fair prospect that new churches would be rapidly forming. I have travelled considerable in new settlements in other parts, besides Indiana; but I have never found so great numbers, who seem to be religiously inclined, and who are professors of some sort, as in Indiana; there are all the kinds, regular and irregular, orthodox and heresy of the older States.

In some parts, these professions are gathered into societies, and have the ordinances; in other parts they are scattered here and there without being so gathered. You therefore see the need there is of missionaries, and of missionaries who are faithful men, *able also to teach others;* and these places must be supplied by missionaries, or they must remain unsupplied: the settlers in general are poor; and the churches have from ten to fifty communicants, male and female; a few have over fifty, and numbers have not over twenty, and some less. These people are without money; and but little stock. They are opening, with their own labour, farms, where the land is heavily timbered; they are living in mud-walled log cabins. What can these people do towards settling ministers, who must be supported by their salaries?—what can they do?—in money they cannot do hardly any thing; the older churches, therefore, must send them missionaries, and help them to creep, till they can stand and go alone: or, ah me! their brethern perish without the gospel; and the neglect of their poor brethern will be upon them.

I wish to raise for the poor inhabitants of Indiana, the Macedonian cry; "Come over and help us." Brethern, I tell you what I know; I speak of what I have seen; and the eagerness of those poor people, to hear the gospel and to attend upon the appointments of your missionary; and the thankful prayers, (which he heard some of them offer,) are still fresh in his recollection; and they plead with him to plead with his older brethren, the trustees of the Connecticut society, to send them help, as they may have ability. Brethern, you have here the map of the country before you; it has only seven Presbyterian ministers; and it has 140,000 inhabitants; these are scattered over an area of country three times as large as Connecticut; and what makes it still more important is this,—a vast tract of first-rate land has been lately brought into market, and is now fast filling up with people, from nearly all the other States. In my late tour, I was within the bounds of this new purchase, and preached two sermons in it; and if it shall please the trustees to continue my appointment, I contemplate removing there in less than a year, to endeavour to build up a little church in Owen county, and to labour as a missionary: I shall then be in the heart of the State, and of the mission ground; and I think I could do more good in the church there than where I now am.

. . . .

RETURN TO INDIANA—DESIGN OF THAT RETURN—LOCATION ON THE FRONTIER—RESIDENCE AND MINISTERIAL LABOURS OF NEAR FOUR YEARS—WITH OBSERVATIONS ON THE COUNTRY—ITS RELIGIOUS CHARACTER, WANTS, ENCOURAGEMENTS, AND PROSPECTS—WITH THE NAMES AND PLACES OF THE CHURCHES FORMED BY HIS MINISTRY.

IT was the 25th of September, 1822, when we departed from Nicholasville in our migration to the frontier settlements of Indiana. This journey was 200 miles; and the way led through Frankfort, Louisville, New-Albany and Bloomington:—Owen county, and the place of location in it, being 20 miles beyond the last named of these places. A four-horse team went with our stuff, and Elinor and myself travelled in my one horse dearborn.

The design of this remove has been partly exhibited in PART THIRD, in the letter to the Rev. Dr. Flint, secretary of the Connecticut Missionary Society.

It was partly to enjoy the society of family relatives; but it was principally, on my part, to take the blessing of the gospel, in its ministry, to the needy and the destitute, and to maintain and preserve them there. In my former travels I had seen, measurably, the condition of the country. I knew that Presbyterian people were thinly scattered in it. I saw the settlements of the country were spreading very rapidly, and that none of our ministers were venturing a location on the frontiers. I saw, that to keep our people and to instruct their children, churches must be formed, and in some measure supplied. I saw also, that some minister must go before in this service; that his example and his influence might induce others to venture out and follow into these needy new settlements. I saw also, that the field needed that some minister of some experience should commence this self-denying and laborious service, for the good of the church and the salvation of souls. And as none others had given themselves up to settle in those new parts of the state, the writer resolved to venture forward and lead in this way.

His scheme for improvement was this:—To locate with a little infant church already formed, to instruct them and encourage them;—to appropriate the one-half of his ministerial labours to their benefit; and to receive from them in return, as much salary as they should be able to raise, paid in their personal labour, or in the produce of their farms. The balance of his time he held, to be devoted to missionary service; and his plan and his practice, was to spend alternately one week at home, and the next abroad; and certain places were selected for these missionary labours, either to strengthen and nourish, and increase some churches, which were already begun, or to prepare the way and establish new ones. And such was the state of the country and the manner of its settlements, that these places were distant from each other, and most of them distant from the writer's residence and charge. The consequence was, that to be punctual in the attendance of his appointments, and to keep up the hopes of the Presbyterian people, subjected him to a vast deal of riding. Respecting this plan and this field of action, before his removal from Kentucky, he wrote to a friend, a student of theology at Princeton, "that it opened to the view of his mind such a field for Christian enterprise and usefulness, as almost raised him above himself."

At this time, this was theory, but theory which had been formed from much observation, and with some knowledge of the country, and it soon became practice.

It was the first week in October when we arrived in Owen county, Indiana.

My place was new and covered with timber.—A tenement was to be prepared; I found much difficulty to obtain labour from the people, they being hurried with their own work. As far as my own personal labour could supply this dificiency, it was supplied. But still, with all my efforts, much was lacking; my building progressed slowly, and to increase my difficulty, the winter closed in early. We entered our house the week before Christmas, and occupied it that winter, without a loft, with no plastering of the chinking, between the logs, above the joice plates, and with a large wooden chimney place cut out of the end of the house, and built up a little above the mantle piece.

Wood was plenty, and well it need to be, for a situation like that. Yet many were the comforts which were mingled with those difficulties, though the trial sat heavily on my Elinor. And indeed, I have often wondered since that time, how I could have ever had resolution enough to have voluntarily brought myself into that situation. But now necessity pushed us on, and hope cheered us with the return of spring, and a better prospect in the future. Nor do I remember that I ever felt a wish that I had not ventured upon this service. It always appeared to me to be worthy of my trials in it. This winter of 1822 and '23 I did not go beyond the bounds of the county, except a few times into Monroe, and to supply at Bloomington.

Before the spring meeting of Presbytery, which was held at Charlestown, 105 miles distant, a call was made out by the Bethany church in Owen county, to obtain my ministerial labours for one half of the time. I attended the Presbytery and accepted the call, when the arrangements were made for an installation in August. Soon after my return from this Presbytery, I began to open regularly upon my plan of missionary labour. About the time of my removal from Kentucky, the Rev. David C. Proctor engaged for a year at Indianapolis, for three-fourths of his time, and soon after he engaged to supply the remaining fourth part of his time at Bloomington. These places are 52 miles apart. In passing from one to the other of these places, he usually came by my house. It was not before July of this year that the way became prepared to constitute a church at Indianapolis. My first visit to that place was through many perils of waters by the way, in company with Mr. Proctor, the 3d of July. On the afternoon of the 4th I preached to the Presbyterian friends at a cabinet maker's shop; and at the same place on the morning of the 5th, I presided as moderator, in the formation of the church at Indianapolis. The same day two other ministers arrived; the next day was the Sabbath, and there were four ministers with this new-formed church. This was now the second year of the settlement of this town. In the same month I made my first tour through the churches and settlements near the Wabash above Terre Haute, and visited the newly located town of Crawfordsville. In this tour, I passed a night in the woods, without human company, or other light than that made by the lightning.

In August, I went to a sacrament in Knox county, and first saw Vincennes; this was about 85 miles from my residence, nearly south west;—here has been a Presbyterian minister for many years well nigh alone, keeping a Presbyterian post near the old French military post of Vincennes. To this place I was invited by the resident minister to assist him in a sacramental meeting to be given on Friday.—In October, I again attended Presbytery; (this session was held at Shelbyville, Kentucky;) and from Presbytery went on to Synod at Lexington; this was a travel of 150 miles to attend Presbytery, and 200, or very nearly, to attend Synod. After the Synod, I visited Nicholasville, White Oak, and Danville; preached again on the Sabbath to my congregation of Nicholasville, and a number of times in the county; this is the last time of my being in those places. That meeting of Synod divided the Louisville Presbytery, and formed a new one in Indiana; this had been an object greatly desired by the members in Indiana. The new one was, at my suggestion, named "Salem Presbytery." In this name I regarded its Scriptural signification;—its first meeting was not held till the following April.

. . . .

In April, 1824, the Salem Presbytery had its first meeting. This was held in the town of Salem. That meeting I attended, and was one of the committee to form rules for its regulations, and times of meeting. I also drew up the report respecting the state of religion within its bounds. In this I endeavoured to give a brief outline of the country, with its need of increase of ministers. This report was designed for the general assembly at Philadelphia, whither it was sent. A copy was also sent to Hartford, Connecticut, and published in the Connecticut Observer.

Immediately after Presbytery, I spent some days, by special request, in the south part of Washington county, to form a church; this church was formed and named "Bethlehem." I think its members were 14; to this church I administered the sacrament the day after its formation. Early this spring was printed my first little book; this was a tract of twelve pages with this title, "The Christian's Duty;" of this, I published an edition of a thousand copies. Most of these I have either distributed gratuitously or sold, and I have reason to believe they have been useful. This year I also constituted two other Presbyterian churches, and revived, by God's blessing, a third. The first of these was gathered at Crawfordsville in June, and revisited and the sacrament administered in September. The other was over the Wabash river, in Edgar county, Illinois. This was over 70 miles westward from my residence. It was not till after a third application that I was able to go.

At the time of that visit, there seemed a special divine influence on the minds of several. Returning from that place, I came through a relic of a church formed just upon the line of the two states, by the Rev. N. B. Denow. It had now but one ruling elder and nine or ten members; but here the spirit of the Lord seemed to be moving on the minds of numbers. I held a sacrament for them and others on the east side of the Wabash river, in the village of Terre Haute, on Thursday in the week, and five were received into this little church, and from that time it has a blessed season of revival till its numbers were seventy. Its first name had been "Hopewell," but at my suggestion, it was changed to New Hope. Of this tour and these things, a letter was published in the Western Luminary, printed at Lexington, Kentucky, under the title of "Good News from the Frontiers."

In the fall of 1823, the Rev. D. C. Proctor left Indiana, and located in Kentucky. From this time, the particular care of the church at Bloomington and at Indianapolis, fell upon me, till the arrival of the Rev. Mr. Bush at the latter place in the summer of 1824, and the Rev. Mr. Hall at Bloomington near the same time. Neither sacraments nor baptism were performed in either, but by my ministry. My travels in this year, 1824, were 2,480 miles. I attended sixteen sacramental meetings, in which I either had the whole ministerial labours, or assisted with others; examined about forty persons, who were received into the communion of the church; nine of these where I was pastor. Baptised eight adults and sixty-one children.

The fall session of our Presbytery was held at Charlestown. At this was granted the first licensure, which ever took place in the Presbyterian church in Indiana. At this meeting, the writer acted as moderator; as he did also in the first ordination the following March. In the spring session of the Presbytery of 1825, which was held at Washington, the writer preached the opening sermon, and the following week he preached the ordination sermon at Bloomington, when the Rev. B. R. Hall was ordained and installed over the church at Bloomington. In this year there were six ordinations in the Presbyterian church in Indiana. Four of these I attended and took a part;—at the first, which was the Rev. Geo. Bush at Indianapolis, as moderator, I gave out the appointments to the others, and took the address to the congregation on myself. At the second, which was this at Bloomington, I preached the sermon. At the next, which was the Rev. Alexander Williamson as evangelist, I was not present. At the fourth, which was the Rev. T. H. Brown, over the Bethlehem church, I preached the sermon. At the fifth, which was the Rev. Stephen Bliss as evangelist, and which took place at Vincennes, I gave the charge to the evangelist.

This was at a meeting of the Presbytery, held in connexion with the annual meeting of the Indiana Missionary Society; this was a society in which I felt a great interest. It was formed by the brethren in Indiana, in the summer of 1822; whilst I was in Kentucky I became a member of it, at its first anniversary, 1823, and received a commission to perform eight weeks of missionary labours. A part of these weeks of labour were performed. That anniversary I was not able to attend.

The second anniversary, which was held in August, 1824, I attended, and made myself and my wife life members, by the payment of 10 dollars for each. The next year, was this time at Vincennes, when I made my oldest child a life member by the payment of 10 dollars more, and before leaving Indiana, in 1826, I made another child a life member by the payment of 10 dollars more; I also interested myself much in the increase of its funds by others, and with some success; particularly was this the case at Bloomington, Charlestown, Indianapolis, and Terre Haute, and from a female friend in Green county. I looked upon it as a means which promised great good to the needy churches in Indiana, and its meetings were seasons of much satisfaction to my mind. The last of these meetings which I was favoured to attend, was that in August, 1825, where, in connexion with another brother, I drew up its report and prepared it for the press. In the summer also of this year, I published two sermons in one book. One of these was a New-Year's sermon to the young people of Owen county, the other, the ordination sermon at Bloomington. This sermon also the Salem Presbytery had printed, at Lexington, Kentucky. A little book of my preparing, called "Conversations on Infant Baptism, mainly abridged from a work of Charles Jaram, A.M., of England." This abridgment had been first made, when I resided at Nicholasville; it was now revised the last winter, and submitted to our Presbytery in its session at Bloomington in April. By them it was adopted, and a resolution passed to publish it. It was published in an edition of 1000 copies. These were sold, as far as I have known, very readily.

This year my missionary labours were principally bestowed upon certain settlements in Green county, which lay south west of my residence, and upon several settlements in Putnam county, which lay west, and upon three settlements in Johnson county, which lay north east. My effort was, to found a Presbyterian church in each of these counties; and though there were many impediments and few members, and in two of them, these few members lived very distant from each other, yet the Lord blessed my labours. These members were brought together, and a church was constituted in each county. The one in Green was formed in July, with three male and two female members. This is the smallest number of which I have ever formed a church; and it seems that a blessing has been in it, for, before I left the State, in 1826, it had increased to twelve members. This society seemed to form a connecting link between the upper and the lower Presbyterian churches near White river. Before this there was no Presbyterian church between my own in Owen county, and Washington in Davies' county, about 70 miles. This new formed one was in the intervening county, and about the middle way between the others. Upward upon, or near White river, the nearest was Indianapolis, 45 miles above my place. The church formed in Putnam county, formed a connecting link between the Presbyterian churches on White river and those on the Wabash; it being about middle way between them, and the road, from both Indianapolis and Bloomington, pass through the county seat of Putnam.

To form this church required much previous labour in preaching, visiting, and travel. The preparation was commenced the preceding year, and the church was constituted in August of this year, with twelve members; four of these were received by examination.

In September of this year, I visited the churches of Paris and New Hope, west of the Wabash: from the former I had received a Macedonian call, when at Presbytery at Vincennes: and, as said Nehemiah of the king of Persia, *I had set them a time*, and in this time, as the Lord would have it, I came to condole with them in their affliction, at the death of a missionary, who had been with them from the spring till the middle of July, and by whom they had been greatly blessed. The Lord owned his ministry with them, and they loved him. Soon after he left them to return to his friends in New-York state, he was taken sick at Vincennes, and died about the middle of August. His name was John Young, about 28 years old, and he had been about eight months living in the State. To both these congregations, I preached a funeral sermon respecting his death; they requested its publication, and provided the means; it was printed at Indianapolis in October.

. . . .

I have thought my readers would like to have introduced a short specimen of my journal. I begin with my last missionary tour, before my leaving the service and the State, in 1826. The notices are short, and the journal is as follows.

April 11th, 1826.—Left home on a mission tour. Mrs. Reed and Mr. Dayhoff were with me. There was a great freshet in White river. We had to ride about fifteen miles to get nine. Passed the first night at Spencer. This is a little place, which improves but slowly.

April 12th.—Crossed White river by a ferry, and made our way downward upon the East side. The creeks on the west side being impassable from back water out of White river. On this side, too, the low bottoms were under water, and the back water filled the mouths of all the creeks. Often we could not keep the road, but had to make through the woods—to climb the steep points of the hills, and cross over the guts. Two creeks we crossed upon fallen trees. We had first to strip our horses, and drive them through swimming; then to walk the log, and carry over our saddles, great coats, and saddle-bags—catch our horses—remount, and make our way through the woods and brush. Rode about thirty miles, which took up the whole day.

April 13th.—Crossed White river, by another ferry, a distance of three quarters of a mile. When the water is within the river banks the ferry is not above ten rods. The water has been three feet higher with this rise than was the preceding. Got a late breakfast at Mr. Ingersol's, near the river; then crossed the prairie to Mr. Dayhoff's. He was now my travelling companion, and had been to Owen to attend the Presbytery, as a ruling elder from the White river church in Green county. This made a ride of eight miles to-day. Preached at night at his house on Scaffold Prairie: it was a small congregation. The settlement is very small. The attention seemed good. This and surrounding settlements are an encouraging field for missionary labour.

April 14th.—Spent the morning at Mr. Dayhoff's, partly writing in my journal; then rode five miles to Nine Mile Prairie. This settlement has six families—visited two, and catechized one of them. Preached at night; very good attendance, and still attention.

April 15th.—Returned to Scaffold Prairie—visited two families, and preached at night. This is a very needy missionary tract.

April 16th, Sabbath.—Rode seven miles and preached two sermons at a school-house, called "Fairplay" School-house. The attendance and attention were pretty good. In this neighbourhood there are some of the advocates of Robert Owen's new system of society—visited two families.

April 17th.—Returned to Scaffold prairie—was this day very weak, being much overdone.

April 18th.—Copied the records of the White river church, which I had constituted the last summer with five members. It was now increased to twelve members. It has had no supplies but the few visits which I have made. Wrote a man his will to-day.

April 19th.—A very high and strong wind to-day. Started this morning, Elinor with me, and our infant child, and rode about five miles on our way toward Terre Haute, but the wind was so strong, and the way so wet, that we returned to Mr. Dayhoff's. Read in Josephus' History the wars of the Jews.

April 20th.—Mrs. Reed concluded to stay behind, and let me go up the Wabash without her. Travelled thirty-four miles,—most of the way was through wet clay prairies. It was seventeen miles to the first house, then six miles to the next. Spent the night at Terre Haute.

April 21st.—Called to see two young men, merchants, whose younger brother died last night. Saw the corpse: the case was pleurisy;—the disease was violent and rapid—lasted just twenty-five hours. After this, I rode thirty-four miles, and crossed the Wabash river into Vermillion county. On my way to-day, I had to ferry across Raccoon creek. The young man who tended and worked the flat, used considerable profane language. I was silent till we were over, and then, as I handed him the ferriage money, looking him in the face, I said, "I have one request to make of you, Sir; it is, that the next man you ferry over, shall not hear you swear." The man looked confused, and was silent.

April 22d.—Rode eight miles in Vermillion county, and visited one family. Appointed to preach to-morrow at a log school-house, in the central part of the county. I was this day very ill with a severe cold deeply seated in my head. I think the prospect is good of getting a church here. O Lord, strengthen me to the work.

April 23d, Sabbath.—Rode four miles to the school-house, and preached. Then, three miles further, to visit a family and pass the night, the woman being a member of the church in Vigo county. The Lord be praised: I have been supported to-day, and feel much better this evening than I did in the morning. I am now on the bank of the Little Vermillion river.

April 24th.—Rode four or five miles, and visited two families. In one of these were two church members, but no appearance of religion at the other.

April 25th.—Rode three miles and preached in a private house, near the Big Vermillion river; there was only a small attendance.

April 26th.—Rode nine miles and preached at a house on Big Vermillion prairie. It was a very beautiful place, and an attentive congregation. Visited three families.

April 27th.—Visited three families, and rode five miles.

April 28th.—Rode four miles, and visited two families. In one of these I examined four persons for church membership. Two of these were an old couple, who have been 40 years married; they are about 70 years old. Two were young women daughters of this old couple. This family is from Pennsylvania.

April 29.—Preached a sermon on family religion, and baptised an infant child. I then set apart and constituted a new church; called for the river and county, "Vermillion church." It consists of four male and nine female members. Four of them were received by examination, the other nine had been members in other places. I also wrote a subscription paper for this new congregation.

Sabbath, 30th April, 1826.—This was a lovely day in weather and in worship at this place.—Preached at Mr. Thompson's, near the south bank of the Big Vermillion, and near the west bank of the Wabash. After sermon, administered the Lord's supper to the new church of Vermillion. Received one member by letter, making fourteen members in all. Rode 9 miles to lodge that night.

May 1.—Re-crossed the Wabash, and rode 38 miles down the river in my returning way. Lodged about five miles below Terre Haute, at Mr. Caldwell's. This family is friendly, and Presbyterially attached, but not pious.

May 2.—This was a very rainy day. I had appointed to be back where I had left Mrs. Reed to-day, and to preach there to-morrow.—The first part of the day, the rain was light, but increased. Rode 32 miles without stopping, the last 13 miles in a very fast rain; was thoroughly drenched, but reached my destined place some time before night; found my wife and child well, with all the friends at Mr. Dayhoff's.

May 3.—Clear and pleasant; felt a little dull and sore, from my hard and wet ride; read some in Josephus; preached at 4 o'clock, P. M.; had a small and attentive congregation; went about half a mile to lodge; visited two families to-day.

May 4.—Remained with friends at Scaffold priairie; attended meeting with a Methodist travelling preacher; exhorted and prayed after his sermon, read in Josephus.

May 5.—A clear, but very windy day; rode 32 miles back the same road which I had rode the second. Mrs. Reed was now with me. We had some difficulties from high waters in the wet prairies. We were in some times up to the saddle skirts for several roods; but were mercifully preserved and enabled to reach the house I designed to reach.

May 6.—Rode five miles to Terre Haute; expected to preach there at 12 o'clock, preparatory to the Lord's supper the next day; but no congregation assembled; concluded not to have the sacrament the next day; preached at night to a small congregation in the court house. In the afternoon, ascended into the cupola of the court house, from which is an extensive and beautiful view, embracing the whole of fort Harrison prairie, with the skirting forests, the farms and buildings.

Sabbath, May 7.—A lovely day; preached at 11 o'clock in the court house; a large congregation. I was much pleased to find this town so still on the Sabbath.

Its order is greatly improved in two years. But still it is without any religious society. A Methodist now preaches here two Sabbaths in each month. The professors of religion, whom I expected to meet here, live at a distance from the town.

May 8.—Rode six miles in the morning. It rained a little; then crossed the Wabash about 5 miles; visited and prayed with a sick woman. She was supposed to be dying: she was sensible, patient, and pious:—numbers were there watching to see her expire. Thence I rode to New-Hope meeting house, 5 miles, and preached at 4 o'clock, P. M.; had about forty hearers, who were very attentive; returned across the Wabash 4 miles.—The whole ride to-day, 20 miles. Twice crossed the Wabash by a ferry. It is high, and overflows its banks in many places.

May 9.—Retraced the way to Scaffold prairie, about 33 miles, Mrs. Reed with me. There was a great rain the last night.

And this, so soon after others, made the roads very wet. Much of our way was under water. The course was through low clay prairies. We stopped but once, and then only half an hour.

May 10.—Weak from the fatigue of yesterday. Left Mrs. Reed, and rode about 13 miles: visited three families; returned and preached on Scaffold prairie at night, to a small congregation of attentive hearers; but there was one traveller, who, I have been told, is an avowed and strong deist.

May 11.—Rode 12 miles to-day. Did not preach, but appointed to preach on Nine Mile prairie to-morrow.

May 12.—Rode 10 miles to-day; preached at Mr. A's, at Nine Mile prairie. The meeting was well attended. The settlement is made up of five or six families.

May 13.—Spent the day at Mr. D.'s, and preached at night.

Sabbath, May 14.—Preached at Mr. D.'s on the death of Christ. Had a very attentive congregation. I am encouraged in my labours here. The beginning was very small, but it has grown. After the meeting, I asked the family the questions of the shorter catechism.

May 15.—Started for home. Had to swim our horses over Fish creek, and cross in a canoe; rode 34 miles, make one stop, and reached home just at dusk, and found our friends in our house, and the child we had left with them, well.

In this tour I had been absent 34 days; preached sixteen times; had two seasons of asking the shorter catechism to families; baptised one child; gathered and constituted a church; administered the Lord's supper; visited and prayed with one dying person; made twenty-eight visits in families, and travelled 394 miles.

. . . .

Churches in Indiana.

The following "Sketches of the former history, and present religious state of Indiana," were made by the Rev. Isaac Reed, in the winter of 1826.

My first introduction into Indiana, was in July, 1818. At that time there was a Presbyterian church at Madison, and a minister there; but not its pastor. Indeed, there was no pastor in any Presbyterian church in the State. Down the Ohio river from Madison, was Pisgah church. This was a little church in a country settlement formed by the Rev. James M'Gready. At Charlestown, County seat of Clarke county, was a small church and resident minister. At New-Albany, was a little church of twelve members, formed by the Rev. D. C. Banks. From this down the Ohio river to the State line at the mouth of the Wabash, there was no church, and no minister. In the direction towards Vincennes, there was a little church at Blue river, and another at Livonia, both formed by Mr. M'Gready.—In these two last mentioned, and another at Salem, the Rev. Wm. W. Martin preached at that time. At Washington, Davis county, was a little church, which the Rev. J. M. Dickey had supplied for a time, but was then about to leave it. In Knox county, and near Vincennes, was a small church, supplied by the Rev. S. T. Scott. Thirty miles higher up the Wabash river, was a little church, supplied by the Rev. J. Balch, an aged man. Besides these, the Rev. Nathan B. Derrow was in the State, as a missionary from the Connecticut Missionary Society; and had formed two little churches; one in Jennings, and one in Jackson counties. The Rev. Orin Fowler, another Missionary from Connecticut, came into the State this summer, and remained till the next spring. He organized three churches. He was diligent and popular, and appeared to do much good.

The writer stopped at New-Albany in September, and engaged to supply there for a year, in October. He had come as a volunteer, at his own charges, into Kentucky the preceding year. In December, a little church was formed at Corydon, at that time the seat of government of the State, by the Rev. J. F. Crow. All these places, churches, and ministers, were in the bounds of the Louisville Presbytery, and of the Kentucky Synod. In August, 1819, the Rev. J. M. Dickey was installed pastor over the united congregations of New-Lexington and Pisgah. This was the first installation in the Presbyterian church, ever held in the State. The same summer, the Rev. Thomas O. Searle came to Madison, and the Rev. N. B. Derrow left the State. About this time, the Rev. J. Balch died. The writer also having fulfilled his year at New-Albany, left the State in December, and went into Kentucky. A young man, missionary from the Board of Missions of the General Assembly, was in the State for six months; the last of the former, and the first part of this year: and two others for a like term the following winter and spring. In 1820, Mr. Searle became pastor at Madison, and Mr. Martin was installed pastor at Livonia. A new church, named Hanover, was formed and united with the Madison church. In the Autumn of 1821, Mr. Searle died at Madison. He was pious, active, and eminently useful. In the autumn of 1822, the writer returned to the State, a missionary from the Connecticut Society, with his family, and settled in Owen county, upon White river. The same time the Rev. D. C. Proctor, missionary from the Connecticut Society, engaged for a year at Indianapolis, the new seat of government of the state. The following winter, the Rev. C. C. Beatty performed a mission tour of four months, along the Wabash river; and formed three churches. He was sent by the General Assembly. In the spring of 1823, the Rev. J. F. Crow removed from Kentucky, to the Hanover church.

He and the writer were both installed in their respective congregations this year. The Rev. Ezra H. Day came to New-Albany in the summer of 1822. He preached there a year, and died in September, 1823. The following winter, Joseph Trimble, missionary from the General Assembly, came into the State. He fulfilled a mission of six months, and engaged to become settled at Madison. The Presbytery was called to ordain and install him; but found him, on the day of meeting, on his death-bed. He died the same day which was set for his ordination. He was very diligent, and highly useful. The Salem Presbytery, the first Presbytery in the State, was formed by the Synod of Kentucky, in October, 1823, and held its first meeting in April, 1824.

The first candidate for the ministry licensed in the State, was Mr. T. H. Brown, at Charlestown, October, 1824. The first ordination, was that of the Rev. George Bush, at Indianapolis, March 5, 1825. Since that, five other ministers have been ordained, and three of them installed. The Rev. S. T. Scott has also been installed pastor at Vincennes. The churches have been increased from twelve, the number in 1818, to forty-two, the present number. There was a Missionary Society formed in August, 1822; and in 1824, and part of —25, it employed, for a short time, six missionaries. In October, 1825, the Synod of Kentucky divided the Salem Presbytery, and formed two new ones; viz. the Wabash Presbytery, and the Madison Presbytery. In August, 1825, Mr. John Young, missionary for the General Assembly died, at Vincennes, having just finished a mission of six months: he was very active, and is greatly lamented.—Such have been the trials, such the increase, and such the enlargements of the church in Indiana. And may her Master say to her, INCREASE, INCREASE, and possess the land.

. . . .

INDIANA THE COUNTRY FOR CHRISTIAN EFFORT AND THE FIELD OF HOPE.

No. I.

The State of Indiana lies between the States Ohio on the east, and Illinois on the west; the Ohio river on the south, and Lake Michigan and Michigan territory on the north. It is in one of the happiest latitudes in the Union. Stretching from 37 deg. 50 min. to 41 deg. 48 min. north latitude; and from 7 deg. 40 min. to 11 deg. west longitude from Washington. It is without a mountain, and has scarcely a swamp over which a man cannot ride on horseback. It has much low lands, which at some seasons are wet. Its river banks are low and they overflow widely. It has much high, rolling and dry lands. The writer's residence has been for years in the central part, in Owen county, and his travels have been over almost every part which is either settled or begun to settle. In these rolling lands springs of the very best water are plenty; and many of them are very large. In its flat lands good water is easily obtained by digging. The lands near the Ohio river are in many parts broken; but as you leave the Ohio and advance into the interior, the good tracts become larger and the soil richer; and the same, as you ascend up the Wabash and White rivers. These are elegant streams. The Wabash traces the western part, and the two White rivers the central parts of the State. They furnish a water conveyance for the produce of the country to the Ohio river, and thence to New-Orleans. Steam-boats ascend the Wabash in the spring. In the spring of 1826, some ascended as high as the mouth of Tippecanoe river. The Indians are almost wholly gone from the state, and the white settlements are very rapidly extending up the rivers towards their source. The State has 54 organized counties, containing an average of 20 or 24 miles square. Each of these counties has a seat of justice and county business, called the Town, and the other settlements are called the country. In the Town are the stores, the taverns, the doctors, the lawyers, and numbers of the mechanics of the county. The population is a mixture from almost every quarter; but mainly from south of the Ohio river. Interest has drawn most; to be in new countries has induced others, and to get away from negro slavery, has influenced not a few in their removes from the slave-holding states. There are many from Ohio, and some from the northern states, but their numbers are few.

Their religions are avowedly *Christian*, but of all the different sects in the Union. And a very large part are professors of religion in some society. There are many meetings, and there is much of family prayer. Indeed, I believe there is much of religion—much of experimental Christianity in this new state. There are many assumed *preachers*, but there are but few truly competent gospel preachers; at least they are few in proportion to the population, and the extent of settled country.

My next Number shall be upon its government, and its increase of population, since my going into it, in the summer of 1818, and its character for health. Respectfully yours,

ISAAC REED.

No. II.

The Government.

This, like the other States of the Federal Union is Republican. It became a State government in 1816. Almost all manner of offices are made immediately by the election of the people. Every freeman, except persons of colour, is entitled to vote for the Governor and representation in both branches of the Legislature. Its Senators are chosen for four years. It representatives are chosen for one year. And its Governor is chosen for three years. Its Legislature, in both branches, meets annually. Its Senators in the Congress of the United States—its President Judges of judicial districts: its Judges of the Court of Appeals, and some of its State officers, such as the Secretary of State, Treasurer, and Auditor, are elected by the Legislature. The Judges of the Court of Appeals, or the supreme court of the State, are three. And this court is held twice each year in the seat of government. The judicial districts are five, and there is a president judge to each of these districts. Associated with him, in holding court in each county, are two, chosen by the freemen of the county, and called associate judges of the circuit court. This court has both criminal and civil jurisdiction. And it answers to Oyer and Terminer, and common pleas.

The county court consists of all the magistrates in the county, or rather of all those who attend in the county seat, at the time set, for holding the court. These determine respecting county regulations; such as building court houses and jails, making townships, granting roads, assessing and collecting taxes, granting tavern licenses, &c. Each county has its clerk of the circuit court, and recorder, chosen by the electors in the county. These are two distinct offices, but they are frequently held by the same individual.

From the office of the County Clerk, must be issued the certificates for solemnizing marriage, between the persons therein named. And to the same office must a return certificate be made, by the person who solemnizes a marriage. Ordained and licensed preachers of the gospel, of all denominations, judges of the courts, and county magistrates, are legally authorized to solemnize marriage. In each of the judicial districts, the president judge goes round his circuit, and holds a court in each county, twice a year. His salary is $700 a-year, the Governor's salary is $1000 a-year, and the Secretary of State's salary $400 a-year. The State has three congressional districts, each of which elects one representative to congress. Such is a brief outline of the government of Indiana. Its present and permanent seat of government is Indianapolis;—a fast rising and flourishing town, delightfully situated on the east side of White river, just below the junction of Fall creek. To this place the government was removed from Corydon in the winter of 1826.

Its Increase of Population.

My first entrance into Indiana was from the State of Kentucky, in the character of a VOLUNTEER PREACHER of the GOSPEL, with no patronage but from on high. I then travelled, and had travelled the whole preceding year at my own charges. This entrance was in the month of July. And by turning to my journal for the time, I find that I crossed the Ohio river at Madison, and first put my feet upon the north shore the 23d of July, 1818. At that time, as near as I could learn, the population of the State was about 100,000. When the United States census was taken in 1820, it was between 140,000 and 150,000. Since that time, it has increased very rapidly. At present it equals, and probably exceeds 200,000. Eight years has then given an increase of near 100,000 population, and this in a State which is but ten years old.

Its Health.

Like all large tracts of country, its character for health differs in different parts. It is a State, almost precisely similar to the State of Ohio. There are parts which are sickly: there are parts which are healthy: and there are parts which have a mixed character. It is equally favourable in health, with the State of Ohio; or with the State of New-York, westward from the village of Utica. The hilly and rolling lands, and parts of the State, are healthy. The flat lands, and river bottoms, are sickly. My residence with my family of almost four years, was without once employing a physician; and I would have no more fears of sickness in that settlement, than in Connecticut. But pretty extensively, the inhabitants are prone to bilious diseases, and strangers have to require a seasoning. This, Sir, is its character for health. And I have made these observations from an acquaintance of eight years; and five years entire residence in the State.

ISAAC REED.

Moriah, N. Y., Feb. 18th, 1827.

No. III.

Principal Towns.

Madison is a brick built commercial town. It lies on the north bank of the Ohio river, 80 miles below Cincinnati. It has about 1200 population. It is a point of deposite and trade, for an extensive interior of fertile country. Charlestown is near 30 miles lower down the Ohio river, and is four miles back from it. It is brick built, and nearly the size of Madison. Both places are county seats. They have each a Presbyterian church and minister.—Jeffersonville is 14 miles south-west from Charlestown: it lies on the Ohio river, nearly opposite Louisville. Here is the location of the State Prison. This is a trading village, but not large. New-Albany, 4 miles below Jeffersonville, is the first village below the falls of the Ohio. The population is about 800. On the Ohio, below New-Albany, the only villages of note, are Leavenworth and Evansville; the latter is near the lower corner of the State. They are not large, but increasing.—On the Wabash river, are Vincennes, an old military Post, called "Post Vincent." It was originally settled by the French, and numbers of French are still there. It is situated upon a delightful, small, dry prairie. It is improving. The population is about 1000.—Sixty miles higher, up the Wabash, is Terre Haute, a handsome little village of white buildings. It has a great deal of mercantile business, and about 300 population. In the interior of the State is Salem, county seat of Washington county, 30 miles from the Ohio river.—Bloomington, in Monroe county, about 90 miles from the Ohio river. This is a thriving town of about 400 or

500 population, and the location of the State Seminary.—Indianapolis is about 50 miles northward of Bloomington. This is the permanent seat of the State Government, and has 800 population. The first sale of its lots was in the autumn of 1821; and it was then mainly covered with thick woods. About it is a wide extent of first rate lands, and though so young in settlement, the population is becoming dense. The town has three religious societies; a well finished Presbyterian meeting-house, and settled minister. In May, 1826, there was a Sabbath school of 85 boys and 87 girls. The attention to good order and to religion is favourable.—In the east part of the State is Richmond, a small but neat town, inhabited principally by Friend Quakers. There is held their yearly meeting.—In the south-east part is Brookville, seat of justice of Franklin county, and Lawrenceburg of Dearborn county, and Vevay of Switzerland county. And there are in the State a number more, which are nearly equal to some of these.

Literature.

The State is not districted: and the common schools are generally of a low character, when compared with the schools of the Northern States. Here and there is found a district, where the school is well supported, and well taught. The schools are nearly all taught by men. It is a rare thing to see a woman teaching school. There are a good many men of public education in the State, graduates from different colleges. There are many people of common school education; but there are also many men, and many women, who cannot read at all. In Indianapolis there is a common school, on a fine plan, and well supported. There are a few Academies in different parts, but they are not distinguished. There is one College in its incipient state, located at Bloomington. It is the State Seminary. It is taught by a Presbyterian minister, of superior attainments, and distinguished character. It is richly endowed in lands, which, as yet, are not much productive.

Respectfully, &c.

Moriah, N. Y. March 19, 1827. ISAAC REED.

No. IV.

My last number introduced the state of learning in Indiana. I believe there are more men of public education in the professions of law and medicine, than would be expected abroad, in the State so young. The ministers also of the Presbyterian church are such men, and but few of the other denominations are such. Among the common people, many are found possessing much intelligence, and who, in older States, have been men of active business. The state of learning is also on the advance. But there are many of the people without even a common school education. When I began first to distribute Religious Tracts, in different parts, I found I often gave, or was about to give tracts, to persons who could not read. Afterwards, when I was about to give tracts to strangers, I first asked them whether they could read, before I offered them the tracts.

Its Benevolent Institutions.

The first of these is the Indiana Missionary Society, formed in August, 1822, and designed to aid in supplying the destitute with the preaching of the gospel and Christian sacraments in the bounds of the State. Its funds are small, but it has employed several missionaries for a few months at a time. Of those missionaries the writer is one. While in the State, he perseveringly and successfully endeavoured to advance the Institution. He looks back to it now with satisfaction and intense interest.—The next is the Sabbath School Society. The writer believes the first Sabbath School in the State, was commenced by his efforts at New Albany, in 1819. From that time they increased and commenced in different places. They have become numerous, not merely in the towns and villages, but in country neighbourhoods and in new settlements. The writer has often addressed them in missionary tours, and sometimes in log school houses—sometimes in little cabins, and once in the woods without a house.—In October, 1825, a Constitution was formed and Society constituted, to be called the State Union Society. It was to have its first anniversary at Indianapolis in August, 1826. The writer was one of the committee which formed the constitution.—There are a number of County Bible Societies: of these the Madison Bible Society has, I believe, been the most efficient. The writer made an address at its formation at Madison, in the summer of 1818.—A Presbyterian Education Society was commenced in the Salem Presbytery in its session at Charlestown in October 1824, and made its first report in October, 1825; and then adjourned to meet at Indianapolis in August, 1826, to form a State Society. In the Missionary Society, the Sabbath School Society, and the Education Society, it is but just to say of the Presbyterian ministers, they have led the way; they have been the pioneers and the active agents. Few as they are, besides doing their utmost to preach and to minister in their own congregations, the partial supply of four times as many destitute congregations has come upon him, and the whole weight of the formation and leading support of these Benevolent Institutions. These ministers are a company of men who fear not difficulties—who shrink not from service—and who love as brethren. The writer loves them as his fellow-labourers in the field of Christian enterprise, and the vineyard of the Lord. His heart is with them—his prayers are for them; may they still pursue and overcome in the strength of the Lamb.

Its Religion.

The Methodists and the Baptists are both numerous. There is one or two societies of the Associate Presbytery or Seceders; two or three societies of the Reformed Presbytery or Covenanters; one Roman Catholic; one of the Shakers; a good many societies of Quakers; many of the Cumberland Presbyterians; many of the New Lights, and fifty of the Presbyterian churches in connexion with the General Assembly. Of these churches, the writer has constituted eight, and one in Illinois, nine in all. And he has laboured in, and tried to cherish and strengthen many of the others. Sometimes he has administered the Lord's Supper 14 or 16 times in a year, and not more than 4 of these in his own society. Through summer heat and rains—through winter cold, winds and snows, early and late, he has sought after the wandering sheep of his Saviour's flock. He has found them in the wilderness, gathered them into the fold, and fed them for Christ. For the last four years his travels in this service exceed 2000 miles a year. In one year he baptized 8 adults and 61 children, and received about 50 persons into church-membership by examination. And why has he left this field? Just because the Lord has called him away, and bid him occupy in another. But he loves that field still. And he loves to direct others in the way to it. It is a field, long and broad and goodly. And many may find a place to labour there.

ISAAC REED.

Moriah, N. Y. March 21, 1827.

No. V.

I thought I had done with these numbers, but my last was written in a pressure of other things; and I found I had omitted to say any thing of the hospitality which abounds, and may be considered as characteristical in Indiana. I have seen it in almost all parts of the State, in near a hundred different settlements; and I therefore believe it is general. Travelling expenses at the houses of entertainment, are low. But there is much of *true hospitality;* such hospitality as I have rarely seen in the Northern States. There is much equality among the people, especially in country neighbourhoods. There is less absolute and suffering poverty, than I have ever seen in so large a country; and a man is an idle and lazy fellow, if he does not soon get a farm of his own. There are very few who are rich; and it is not easy to get rich there. It is very easy to lay out money, but very difficult to get it back again. Money is scarce, and prices are low. Provisions for bread and meat are abundant; and the people seem to love the opportunity to have a neighbour or a stranger to be with them at their meals; and also to share with them the safety and the comforts of their house for the night. This hospitality may be found almost any time, but more especially at the times of large meetings—such as "a sacrament," with the Presbyterians—Quarterly and Camp-meetings with the Methodists—Associations with the Baptists, and Camp-meetings with the Cumberland Presbyterians. No one withholds going to any of these meetings, for fear of expense for himself or his horse. If he be not known in the neighbourhood, he is invited to some house as a stranger, and treated as a friend. Frequently five or six go to the same house, and they all seem as welcome as the members of the family.

This leads me to disclose some customs about holding meetings, existing there, which may seem a peculiarity in the northern states. As the Presbyterians there are chiefly from the southern states, they have brought with them the customs of the Presbyterians of Virginia and Carolina; and these have brought them from the mother church in Scotland. One of these customs is, to have a sacramental meeting consist of several successive days, including a Sabbath. At this meeting it is common to have a plurality of ministers. It is in this way that the ministers keep up a system of exchange. You assist me, and I assist you in return. The meeting begins either Friday or Saturday, and closes Monday;—Sabbath is the communion. Preaching each day is at the same place, which is either a meeting-house, or a stand in some piece of woods; and often where there is a meeting-house, the house is so small, and the assembly so large, that they have to go to the woods. The congregation consists of the people of the congregation, where the meeting is held, and numbers, from others round about. One or two sermons is preached each day, and frequently some at night in neighbourhoods. On the Sabbath a sermon is preached before communion, called "the action sermon." Then the other minister rises and introduces the communion service according to the Directory. He then gives out the institution hymn; and as they are singing that, the ministers go to the table, and as many communicants as can sit on each side of it. The table is a long one. The minister who preached the sermon, sits at the table; and the other gives thanks and breaks and gives out the bread, and the cup. The ruling elders serve at the table. When all have received, another hymn is sung; and while singing, these withdraw, and the table fills again. Then the other minister serves, and the first communes. In like manner, if there are more ministers, and if there are more tables, till all are served. I have sometimes seen five settings: I have myself served at three, when no other minister was with me. Monday they assemble early, and dismiss about midday. This practice leads the Christians to know and love one another, all round a large tract of country, and cherishes this spirit and practice of hospitality. When in missionary service, I have held sacramental meetings; I have sometimes seen members from six different Presbyterian churches, and all destitute. Some of these came 25, and others 30 miles, purposely to attend the meeting. In some cases, I have seen women who walked 10 miles, to be at such a meeting; one of these was a young woman, in 1823, who was awakened at the meeting; and the next year, at another similar meeting, I received her to communion. With the Methodists, their sacraments are held at their quarterly meetings, and their camp-meetings. The Cumberland Presbyterians, who are much like the Methodists in doctrines and manners, but who hold to the Presbyterian form of government, have their sacraments at camp-meetings. This is a young, but fast increasing sect. They have had being as denomination, only about sixteen years, and they have now 11 Presbyteries, and are very widely spread. They have lately founded a college in the lower parts of Kentucky. Their preachers travel upon circuits by two and two, like the Methodists. All these large meetings tend to extend the acquaintance of the Christians of the country, and to foster and continue the hospitality of the people.

ISAAC REED.

Moriah, N. Y. March 27, 1827.

From *Travels in North America in the years 1827 and 1828*, by Captain Basil Hall [1829], Vol. III., pp. 386-388.

HALL, BASIL.

Captain Hall, a British naval officer and writer, was recognized as one of the most widely travelled Englishmen of his day. He had not only visited the greater part of the British possessions, but in 1815, accompanied Lord Amherst on an expedition to China. In 1827 he made a tour of Canada and the United States, his object being "to see with my own eyes how far the sentiments prevalent in England with respect to that country (America) are correct or otherwise." The notes of his travels were published in 1829, and occasioned adverse criticism in the United States because of their outspoken and somewhat supercilious comments.

On the 27th of May, we entered the State of Indiana, where we found a very different sort of travelling from that we had met with in the delightful Prairies. The country is hilly nearly all the way, the roads execrable, and the carriages made as rigid as if they had been cast in one piece of metal. This is quite necessary, I admit, considering the duty they have to go through. One other refinement in these vehicles I must mention. In every other part of the Union we found at least one door, though very rarely two, in any stage-coach. But upon this occasion, where so large an opening was a weakness that could not be afforded, the passengers had nothing left for it—females as well as males—but literally to mount the coachman's seat by aid of the wheel, and then scramble in at the front as well as they might. The only one of our party who particularly relished this primitive method of stowage was the child, who was enchanted with the variety of traverses which she was exposed to before reaching the seats within.

During this rugged journey, we were never exposed to those privations as to food that we had met with sometimes in the South, for provisions of all kinds were in abundance. I cannot say, however, that my observations go to confirm the accounts I have read of the intelligence, and highmindedness, as it is affectedly called, of the thinly scattered inhabitants of those new countries. I did not expect, indeed, to find any great polish of manners in the backwoods, but I must say, that although we met with no inhospitality, we encountered so many instances of coldness and gruffness, that I have no wish again to exchange the obligations and entanglements of civilisation for the selfish freedom of the forest.

It is not that the inhabitants of those countries are ill-natured —quite the reverse—they seem always most willing to oblige when prompted so to do. But what I complain of is the want of habitual politeness—the spontaneous desire to be civil and useful. And I strongly suspect, that such is the inevitable consequence of people living far apart, and trusting exclusively to their own exertions for their support. The same class of things which limit the range of their good offices, limit also their means of acquiring knowledge, tend to rivet prejudices, and to augment ideas of self-importance. To talk, therefore, of people so circumstanced, being possessed of any remarkable degree of intelligence, is to declare the existence of a moral or rather a political miracle, of which civil society presents no example.

On the 29th of May, having passed through the State of Indiana, we recrossed the Ohio to Louisville in Kentucky. Next day we embarked in a steam-boat for Cincinnati in the State of Ohio, which we reached on the 31st, having occupied twenty-three hours in a passage of 150 miles, against the current.

From *A years' residence in the United States of America*, by William Cobbett [1828], Part 3, pp. 276-292.

COBBETT, WILLIAM.

Mr. Cobbett was by training a soldier and had spent several years in the English garrisons. But his "heart passion was to possess a farm and cultivate gardens." And in order to see just what could be accomplished in this line, he migrated to America in 1817 and settled on Long Island. There he spent one year, and undertook on a very extensive scale the art of gardening. He apparently achieved success, and found time to take several trips inland. His observations are interesting because they contain accounts of what the farmers and gardeners were actually doing, and not what they hoped to do. Mr. Cobbett was greatly interested in the possibilities he found here, but felt it necessary to return to his native country and re-enter the military service.

June 16th.—Left Cincinnati for Louisville with seven other persons, in a skiff about 20 feet long and 5 feet wide.

June 17th.—Stopped at VEVAY, a very neat and beautiful place, about 70 miles above the falls of the Ohio. Our visit here was principally to see the mode used, as well as what progress was made, in the cultivation of the vine, and I had a double curiosity, never having as yet seen a vineyard. These vineyards are cultivated entirely by a small settlement of Swiss, of about a dozen families, who have been here about ten years. They first settled on the Kentucky river, but did not succeed there. They plant the vines in rows, attached to stakes like espaliers, and they plough between with a one-horse plough. The grapes, which are of the sorts of Claret and Madeira, look very fine and luxuriant and will be ripe in about the middle of September. The soil and climate both appear to be quite congenial to the growth of the vine: the former rich and the latter warm. The north west wind, when it blows, is very cold, but the south, south east, and south west winds, which are always warm, are prevalent. The heat, in the middle of the summer, I understand, is very great, being generally above 85 degrees, and sometimes above 100 degrees. Each of these families has a farm as well as a vineyard, so that they supply themselves with almost every necessary and have their wine all clear profit. Their produce will this year be probably not less than 5000 gallons; we bought 2 gallons of it at a dollar each, as good as I would wish to drink.

Thus it is that the tyrants of Europe create vineyards in this new country!

June 18th.—Arrived at Louisville, Kentucky. The town is situated at the commencement of the falls, or rapids of the Ohio. The river, at this place, is little less than a mile wide, and the falls continue from a ledge of rocks which runs across the river in a sloping direction at this part, to Shippingport, about 2 miles lower down. Perceiving stagnant waters about the town, and an appearance of the house that we stopped at being infested with bugs, we resolved not to make any stay at Louisville, but got into our skiff and floated down the falls to Shippingport. We found it very rough floating, not to say dangerous. The river of very unequal widths and full of islands and rocks along this short distance, and the current very rapid, though the descent is not more than 22 feet. At certain times of the year the water rises so that there is no fall; large boats can then pass.

At Shippingport, stopped at the house of Mr. Berthoud, a very respectable French gentleman, from whom we received the greatest civility during our stay, which was two nights and the day intervening.

Shippingport is situated at a place of very great importance, being the upper extremity of that part of the river which is navigable for heavy steam-boats. All the goods coming from the country are reshipped, and every thing going to it is un-shipped, here. Mr. Berthoud has the store in which the articles exporting or importing are lodged: and is, indeed, a great shipper, though at a thousand miles from the sea.

June 20th.—Left the good and comfortable house of Mr. Berthoud, very much pleased with him and his amible wife and family, though I differed with him a little in politics. Having been taught at church, when a boy, that the Pope was the whore of Babylon, that the Bourbons were tyrants, and that the Priests and privileged orders of France were impostors and petty tyrants under them, I could not agree with him in applauding the Boroughmongers of England for re-subjugating the people of France, and restoring the Bourbons, the Pope, and the Inquisition.

Stop at New Albany, 2 miles below Shippingport, till the evening. A Mr. Paxton, I am told, is the proprietor of a great part of the town, and has the grist and saw-mills, which are worked by steam, and the ferry across the river. Leave this place in company with a couple of young men from the western part of the state of New York, who are on their way to Tennessee in a small ferry boat. Their whole journey will, probably, be about 1,500 miles.

June 21st.—Floating down the river, without any thing in particular occurring.

June 22nd.—Saw a Mr. Johnstone and his wife reaping wheat on the side of the river. They told us they had come to this spot last year, direct from Manchester, Old England, and had bought their little farm of 55 acres of a back-woodsman who had cleared it, and was glad to move further westward, for 3 dollars an acre. They had a fine flock of little children, and pigs and poultry, and were cheerful and happy, being confident that their industry and economy would not be frustrated by visits for tithes or taxes.

June 23rd.—See great quantities of turkey-buzzards and thousands of pigeons. Came to Pigeon Creek, about 230 miles below the Falls, and stopped for the night at Evansville, a town of nine months old, near the mouth of it. We are now frequently met and passed by large, fine steam-boats, plying up and down the river. One went by us as we arrived here which had left Shippingport only the evening before. They go down the river at the rate of 10 miles an hour, and charge passengers 6 cents a mile, boarding and lodging included. The price is great but the time is short.

June 24th.—Left Evansville. This little place is rapidly increasing, and promises to be a town of considerable trade. It is situated at a spot which seems likely to become a port for shipping to Princeton and a pretty large district of Indiana. I find that the land speculators have made entry of the most eligible tracts of land, which will impede the partial, though not the final, progress of population and improvement in this part of the state.

On our way to Princeton, we see large flocks of fine wild turkeys, and whole herds of pigs, apparently very fat. The pigs are wild also, but have become so from neglect. Some of the inhabitants, who prefer sport to work, live by shooting these wild turkeys and pigs, and indeed, sometimes, I understand, they shoot and carry off those of their neighbours before they are wild.

June 25th.—Arrived at Princeton, Indiana, about twenty miles from the river. I was sorry to see very little doing in this town. They cannot *all* keep stores and taverns! One of the storekeepers told me he does not sell more than ten thousand dollars value per annum: he ought, then, to manufacture something and not spend nine tenths of his time in lolling with a segar in his mouth.

June 26th.—At Princeton, endeavouring to purchase horses, as we had now gone far enough down the Ohio. While waiting in our tavern, two men called in armed with rifles, and made enquiries for some horses they suspected to be stolen. They told us they had been almost all the way from Albany, to Shawnee town after them, a distance of about 150 miles. I asked them how they would be able to secure the thieves, if they overtook them, in these wild woods; "O," said they, "shoot them off the horses." This is a summary mode of executing justice, thought I, though probably the most effectual, and, indeed, only one in this state of society. A thief very rarely escapes here; not nearly so often as in more populous districts. The fact was, in this case, however, we discovered afterwards, that the horses, had strayed away, and had returned home by this time. But, if they had been stolen, the stealers would not have escaped. When the loser is tired, another will take up the pursuit, and the whole country is up in arms till he is found.

June 27th.—Still at Princeton. At last we get suited with horses. Mine costs me only 135 dollars with the bridle and saddle, and that I am told is 18 dollars too much.

June 28th.—Left Princeton, and set out to see Mr. Birkbeck's settlement, in Illinois, about 35 miles from Princeton. Before we got to the Wabash we had to cross a swamp of half a mile wide; we were obliged to lead our horses, and walk up to the knees in mud and water. Before we got half across we began to think of going back; but there is a sound bottom under it all, and we waded through it as well as we could. It is, in fact, nothing but a bed of very soft and rich land, and only wants draining to be made productive. We soon after came to the banks of the great Wabash, which is here about half a mile broad, and as the ferry-boat was crossing over with us I amused myself by washing my dirty boots. Before we mounted again we happened to meet with a neighbour of Mr. Birkbeck's, who was returning home; we accompanied him, and soon entered into the prairie lands, up to our horses' bellies in fine grass. These prairies, which are surrounded with lofty woods, put me in mind of immense noblemen's parks in England. Some of those we passed over are called *wet prairies*, but, they are dry at this time of the year; and, as they are none of them flat, they need but very simple draining to carry off the water all the year round. Our horses were very much tormented with flies, some as large as the English horse-fly and some as large as the wasp; these flies infest the prairies that are unimproved about three months in the year, but go away altogether as soon as cultivation begins.

Mr. Birkbeck's settlement is situated between the two Wabashes, and is about ten miles from the nearest navigable water; we arrived there about sunset and met with a welcome which amply repaid us for our day's toil. We found that gentleman with his two sons perfectly healthy and in high spirits: his daughters were at Henderson (a town in Kentucky, on the Ohio) on a visit. At present his habitation is a cabin, the building of which cost only 20 dollars; this little hutch is near the spot where he is about to build his house, which he intends to have in the most eligible situation in the priairie for convenience to fuel and for shelter in winter, as well as for breezes in summer, and will, when that is completed, make one of its appurtenances. I like this plan of keeping the old loghouse; it reminds the grand children and their children's children of what their ancestor has done for their sake.

Few settlers had as yet joined Mr. Birkbeck; that is to say, settlers likely to become "*society*:" he had labourers enough near him, either in his own houses or on land of their own joining his estate. He was in daily expectation of his friends, Mr. Flower's family, however, with a large party besides; they had just landed at Shawnee Town, about 20 miles distant. Mr. Birkbeck informs me he has made entry of a large tract of land, lying, part of it, all the way from his residence to the great Wabash; this he will re-sell again in lots to any of his friends, they taking as much of it and wherever they choose (provided it be no more than they can cultivate), at an advance which I think very fair and liberal.

The whole of his operations had been directed hitherto (and wisely in my opinion) to building, fencing, and other important preparations. He had done nothing in the cultivating way but make a good garden, which supplies him with the only things that he cannot purchase, and, at present, perhaps, with more economy than he could grow them. He is within twenty miles of Harmony; in Indiana, where he gets his flour and all other necessaries (the produce of the country) and therefore employs himself much better in making barns and houses and mills for the reception and disposal of his crops, and fences to preserve them while growing, *before he grows them,* than to *get the crops first.* I have heard it observed that *any* American settler, even without a dollar in his pocket, would have *had something growing by this time.* Very true! I do not question that at all; for, the very first care of a settler without a dollar in his pocket is to get something to eat, and, he would consequently set to work scratching up the earth, fully confident that after a long summering upon wild flesh (without salt, perhaps,) his own belly would stand him for barn, if his jaws would not for mill. But the case is very different with Mr. Birkbeck, and at present he has need for no other provision for winter but about a three hundredth part of his fine grass turned into hay, which will keep his necessary horses and cows: besides which he has nothing that eats but such pigs as live upon the waste, and a couple of fine young deer (which would weigh, they say, when full grown, 200 lb. dead weight) that his youngest son is rearing up as pets.

I very much admire Mr. Birkbeck's mode of *fencing*. He makes a ditch 4 feet wide at top, sloping to 1 foot wide at bottom, and 4 feet deep. With the earth that come out of the ditch he makes a bank on one side, which is turfed towards the ditch. Then a long pole is put up from the bottom of the ditch to 2 feet above the bank; this is crossed by a sort pole from the other side, and then a rail is laid along between the forks. The banks were growing beautifully, and looked altogether very neat as well as formidable; though a live hedge (which he intends to have) instead of dead poles and rails, upon top, would make the fence far more effectual as well as handsomer. I am always surprised, until I reflect how universally and to what a degree, farming is neglected in this country, that this mode of fencing is not adopted in cultivated districts, especially where the land is wet, or lies low; for, there it answers a double purpose, being as effectual a drain as it is a fence.

I was rather disappointed, or sorry, at any rate, not to find near Mr. Birkbeck's any of the means for machinery or of the materials for manufactures, such as the water-falls, and the minerals and mines, which are possessed in such abundance by the states of Ohio and Kentucky, and by some parts of Pennsylvania. Some of these, however, he may yet find. Good water he has, at any rate. He showed me a well 25 feet deep, bored partly through hard substances near the bottom, that was nearly overflowing with water of excellent quality.

July 1st.—Left Mr. Birkbeck's for Harmony, Indiana. The distance by the direct way is about 18 miles, but, there is no road, as yet; indeed, it was often with much difficulty that we could discover the way at all. After we had crossed the Wabash, which we did at a place called Davis's Ferry, we hired a man to conduct us some part of the way through the woods. In about a mile he brought us to a track, which was marked out by slips of bark being stipped off the trees, once in about 40 yards; he then left us and told us we could not mistake if we followed that track. We soon lost all appearance of the track, however, and of the "*blazing*" of the trees, as they call it; but, as it was useless to go back again for another guide, our only way was to keep straight on in the same direction, bring us where it would. Having no compass, this nearly cost us our sight, for it was just midday, and we had to gaze at the sun a long time before we discovered what was our course. After this we soon, to our great joy, found ourselves in a large corn field; rode round it, and came to Johnson's Ferry, a place where a Bayou (*Boyau*) of the Wabash is crossed. This Bayou is a run out of the main river round a flat portion of land, which is sometimes overflowed: it is part of the same river, and the land encompassed by it, an island. Crossed this ferry in a canoe, and got a ferry-man to swim our horses after us. Mounted again and followed a track which brought us to Black River, which we forded without getting wet, by holding our feet up. After crossing the river we found a man who was kind enough to shew us about half a mile through the woods, by which our journey was shortened five or six miles. He put us into a direct track to Harmony, through lands as rich as a dung-hill, and covered with immense timber; we thanked him, and pushed on our horses with eager curiosity to see this far-famed Harmonist Society.

On coming within the precincts of the Harmonites we found ourselves at the side of the Wabash again; the river on our right hand, and their lands on our left. Our road now lay across a field of Indian corn, of, at the very least, a mile in width, and bordering the town on the side we entered; I wanted nothing more than to behold this immense field of most beautiful corn to be at once convinced of all I had heard of the industry of this society of Germans, and I found, on preceeding a little farther, that the progress they had made exceeded all my idea of it.

The town is methodically laid out in a situation well chosen in all respects; the houses are good and clean, and have, each one, a nice garden well stocked with all vegetables and tastily ornamented with flowers. I observe that these people are very fond of flowers, by the bye; the cultivation of them, and musick, are their chief amusements. I am sorry to see this, as it is to me a strong symptom of simplicity and ignorance, if not a badge of their German slavery. Perhaps the pains they take with them is the cause of their flowers being finer than any I have hitherto seen in America, but, most probably, the climate here is more favourable. Having refreshed ourselves at the Tavern, where we found every thing we wanted for ourselves and our horses, and all very clean and nice, besides many good things we did not expect, such as beer, porter, and even wine, all made within the Society, and very good indeed, we then went out to see the people at their harvest, which was just begun. There were 150 men and women all reaping in the same field of wheat. A beautiful sight! The crop was very fine, and the field, extending to about two miles in length, and from half a mile to a mile in width, was all open to one view, the sun shining on it from the West, and the reapers advancing regularly over it.

At sun-set all the people came in, from the fields, work-shops, mills, manufactories, and from all their labours. This being their evening for prayer during the week, the Church bell called them out again in about 15 minutes, to attend a lecture from their High Priest and Law-giver, Mr. George Rapp. We went to hear the lecture, or, rather, to see the performance, for, it being all performed in German, we could understand not a word. The people were all collected in a twinkling, the men at one end of the Church and the women at the other; it looked something like a Quaker Meeting, except that there was not a single little child in the place. Here they were kept by their Pastor a couple of hours, after which they returned home to bed. This is the quantum of Church-service they perform during the week; but on Sundays they are in Church nearly the whole of the time from getting up to going to bed. When it happens that Mr. Rapp cannot attend, either by indisposition or other accident, the Society still meet as usual, and the *elders* (certain of the most trusty and discreet, whom the Pastor selects as a sort of assistants in his divine commission) converse on religious subjects.

Return to the Tavern to sleep; a good comfortable house, well kept by decent people, and the master himself, who is very intelligent and obliging, is one of the very few at Harmony who can speak English. Our beds were as good as those stretched upon by the most highly pensioned and placed Boroughmongers, and our sleep, I hope, much better than the tyrants ever get, in spite of all their dungeons and gags.

July 2nd.—Early in the morning, took a look at the manufacturing establishment, accompanied by our Tavern-keeper. I find great attention is paid to this branch of their affairs. Their principle is, not to be content with the profit upon the manual labour of *raising* the article, but also to have the benefit of the machine in preparing it for *use*. I agree with them perfectly, and only wish the subject was as well understood all over the United States as it is at Harmony. It is to their skill in this way that they owe their great prosperity; if they had been nothing but farmers, they would be now at Harmony in Pennsylvania, poor cultivators, getting a bare subsistence, instead of having doubled their property two or three times over, by which they have been able to move here and select one of the choicest spots in the country.

But in noting down the state of this Society, as it now is, its *origin* should not be forgotten; the curious history of it serves as an explanation to the jumble of sense and absurdity in the association. I will therefore trace the Harmonist Society from its outset in Germany to this place.

The Sect has its origin at Wurtemberg in Germany, about 40 years ago, in the person of its present Pastor and Master, George Rapp, who, by his own account, "Having long seen and felt the decline of the Church, found himself impelled to bear testimony to the fundamental principles of the Christian Religion; and, finding no toleration for his inspired doctrines, or for those who adopted them, he determined with his followers to go to that part of the earth, where they were free to worship God according to the dictates of their conscience." In other words (I suppose), he had long beheld and experienced the slavery and misery of his country, and, feeling in his conscience that he was born more for a ruler than for a slave, found himself imperiously called upon to collect together a body of his poor countrymen and to lead them into a land of liberty and abundance. However allowing him to have had no other than his professed views, he, after he had got a considerable number of proselytes, amounting to seven or eight hundred persons, among whom were a sufficiency of good labourers and artizans in all the essential branches of workmanship and trade, besides farmers, he embodied them into a Society, and then came himself to America (not trusting to Providence to lead the way) to seek out the land destined for these chosen children. Having done so, and laid the plan for his route to the land of peace and Christian love, with a foresight which shows him to have been by no means unmindful to the *temporal* prosperity of the Society, he then landed his followers in separate bodies, and prudently led them in that order to a resting place within Pennsylvania, choosing rather to retard their progress through the wilderness than to hazard the discontent that might arise from want and fatigue in traversing it at once. When they were all arrived, Rapp constituted them into one body, having every thing in common, and called the settlement *Harmony*. This constitution he found authorised by the passage in Acts, iv. 32, "And the multitude of them that believed were of one heart, and of one soul: neither said any of them that aught of the things be possessed was his own, *but that they had all things common*." Being thus associated, the Society went to work, early in 1805, building houses and clearing lands, according to the order and regulations of their leader; but the community of stock, or the regular discipline, or the restraints which he had reduced them to, and which were essential to his project, soon began to thin his followers and principally, too, those of them who had brought most substance into the society; they demanded back their original portions and set out to seek the Lord by themselves. This falling off of the society, though it was but small, comparatively, in point of numbers, was a great reduction from their means; they had calculated what they should want to consume, and had laid the rest out in land; so that the remaining part were subjected to great hardships and difficulties for the first year or two of their settling, which was during the time of their greatest labours. However, it was not long before they began to reap the fruits of their toil, and in the space of six or seven years their settlement became a most flourishing colony. During that short space of time they brought into cultivation 3,000 acres of land (a third of their whole estate), reared a flock of nearly 2,000 sheep, and planted hop-gardens, orchards, and vineyards; built barns and stables to house their crops and their live stock, granaries to keep one year's produce of grain always in advance houses to make their cyder, beer, and wine in, and good brick or stone warehouses for their several species of goods; constructed distilleries, mills for grinding, sawing, making oil, and, indeed for every purpose, and machines for manufacturing their various materials for clothing and other uses; they had, besides, a store for retailing Philadelphia goods to the country, and nearly 100 good dwelling-houses, of wood, a large stone-built tavern, and, as a proof of superabundance, a dwelling-house and a meeting-house (alias the parsonage and church) which they had neatly built of brick. And, besides all these improvements within the society, they did a great deal of business, principally in the way of manufacturing, for the people of the country. They worked for them with their mills and machines, some of which did nothing else, and their blacksmiths, tailors, shoe-makers, &c. when not employed by themselves, were constantly at work for their neighbours. Thus this everlastingly-at-work band of emigrants increased their stock before they quitted their first colony, to upwards of two hundred thousand dollars, from, probably not one fifth of that sum. What will not unceasing perseverance accomplish? But, with judgment and order to direct it, what in the world can stand against it!*

In comparing the state of this society as it now is with what it was in Pennsylvania, it is just the same as to *plan;* the temporal and spiritual affairs are managed in the same way, and upon the same principles, only both are more flourishing. Rapp has here brought his disciples into richer land, and into a situation better in every respect, both for carrying on their trade, and for keeping to their faith; their vast extent of land is, they say, four feet deep of rich mould, nearly the whole of it, and it lies along the banks of a fine navigable river on one side, while the possibility of much interruption from other classes of Christians is effectually guarded against by an endless barricado of woods on the other side. Bringing the means and experience acquired at their first establishment, they have of course gone on improving and increasing (not in *population*) at a much greater rate. One of their greatest improvements, they tell me is the working of their mills and manufacturing machines by steam; they feel the advantage of this more and more every year. They are now preparing to build a steam boat; this is to be employed in their traffick with New Orleans carrying their own surplus produce and returning with tea, coffee, and other commodities for their own consumption, and to retail to the people of the country. I believe they advance, too, in the way of ornaments and superfluities, for the dwelling-house they have now built their pastor, more resembles a Bishop's Palace than what I should figure to myself as the humble abode of a teacher of the "fundamental principles of the Christian Religion."

The government of this society is by bands, each consisting of a distinct trade or calling. They have a foreman to each band, who rules it under the general direction of the society, the

*A more detailed account of this society up to the year 1811, will be found in Mr. Mellishe's Travels, Vol. 2.

law-giving power of which is in the High Priest. He cannot, however make laws without the consent of the parties. The manufacturing establishment, and the mercantile affairs and public accounts are all managed by one person; he, I believe, is one of the sons of Rapp. They have a bank, where a separate account is kept for each person; if any one puts in money, or has put in money, he may on certain conditions as to time, take it out again. They labour and possess in common; that is to say, except where it is not practicable or is immaterial, as with their houses, gardens, cows and poultry, which they have to themselves, each family. They also retain what property each may bring on joining the concern, and he may demand it in case of leaving the society, but *without interest.*

Here is certainly a wonderful example of the effects of skill, industry, and force combined. This congregation of far-seeing, ingenious, crafty, and bold, and of ignorant, simple, superstitious, and obedient, Germans, has shown what may be done. But their example, I believe, will generally only tend to confirm this free people in their suspicion that labour is concomitant to slavery or ignorance. Instead of their improvements, and their success and prosperity altogether, producing admiration, if not envy, they have a social discipline, the thought of which reduces these feelings to ridicule and contempt: that is to say, with regard to the *mass;* with respect to their leaders one's feelings are apt to be stronger. A fundamental of their religious creed (*"restraining clause,"* a Chancery Lawyer would call it) requires restrictions on the propagation of the species; it orders such regulations as are necessary to prevent children coming but once in a certain number of years; and this matter is so arranged that, when they come, they come in little flocks, all within the same month, perhaps, like a farmer's lambs. The Law-giver here made a famously "restraining statute" upon the law of nature! This way of expounding law seems to be a main point of his policy; he by this means keeps his associates from increasing to an unruly number within, while more are sure not to come in from without; and, I really am afraid he will go a good way towards securing a monopoly of many great improvements in agriculture, both as to principle and method. People see the fine fields of the Harmonites, but, the prospect comes damped with the idea of bondage and celibacy. It is a curious society: was one ever heard of before that did not wish to increase! This smells strong of policy; some distinct view in the leaders, no doubt. Who would be surprised if we were to see a still more curious society by and bye? A *Society Sole!* Very far from improbable, if the sons of Rapp (for he has children, nevertheless, as well as Parson Malthus) and the *Elders* were to die, it not being likely that they will renounce or forfeit their right to the common stock. We should then have societies as well as corporations vested in one person! That would be quite a novel kind of benefice! but, not the less fat. I question whether the *associated* person of Mr. Rapp would not be in possession of as fine a domain as many good things as the *incorporated* person of an Archbishop: nay, he would rival the Pope! But, to my journal.

Arrive at Princeton in the evening; a good part of our road lay over the fine lands of the Harmonites. I understand, by the bye, that the title deeds to these lands are taken in the name of *Rapp and of his associates.* Poor associates: if they do but rebel! Find the same store-keepers and tavern-keepers in the same attitudes that we left them in the other day. Their legs *only a little* higher than their heads, and segars in their mouths; a fine position for business! It puts my friend in mind of the Roman posture in dining.

July 3rd.—At Princeton all day. This is a pretty considerable place; very good as to buildings; but is too much inland to be a town of any consequance until the inhabitants do that at home which they employ merchants and foreign manufacturers to do for them. Pay 1 dollar for a set of old shoes to my horse, half the price of new ones.

July 4th.—Leave Princeton; in the evening, reach a place very appropriately called Mud-holes, after riding 46 miles over lands in general very good but very little cultivated, and that little very badly; the latter part of the journey in company with a Mr. Jones from Kentucky. Nature is the agriculturist here; speculation instead of cultivation, is the order of the day amongst men. We feel the ill effects of this in the difficulty of getting oats for our horses. However, the evil is unavoidable, if it can be really called an evil. As well might I grumble that farmers have not taken possession as complain that men of capital have. Labour is the thing wanted, but, to have that money must come first. This Mud-holes was a sort of fort, not 4 years ago, for guarding against Indians, who then committed great depredations, killing whole families often, men, women and children. How changeable are the affairs of this world! I have not met with a single Indian in the whole course of my route.

July 5th.—Come to Judge Chamber's, a good tavern; 35 miles. On our way, pass French Lick, a strong spring of water impregnated with salt and sulphur, and called *Lick* from its being resorted to by cattle for the salt; close by this spring is another still larger, of fine clear lime-stone water, running fast enough to turn a mill. Some of the trees near the Judge's exhibit a curious spectacle; a large piece of wood appears totally dead, all the leaves brown and the branches broken, from being roosted upon lately by an enormous multitude of pigeons. A novel sight for us, unaccustomed to the abundance of the back-woods! No tavern but this, nor house of any description, within many miles.

July 6th.—Leave the Judge's, still in company with Mr. Jones. Ride 25 miles to breakfast, not sooner finding feed for our horses; this was at the dirty log-house of Mr. ——— who has a large farm with a grist mill on it, and keeps his yard and stables ancle deep in mud and water. If this were not one of the healthiest climates in the world, he and his family must have died in all this filth. About 13 miles further, come to New Albany, where we stop at Mr. Jenkins's, the best tavern we have found in Indiana, that at Harmony excepted.

July 7th.—Resting at New Albany. We were amused by hearing a Quaker-lady preach to the natives. Her first words were "*All the nations of the earth are of one blood.*" "So," said I to myself, "this question, which has so long perplexed philosophers, divines and physicians, is now set at rest!" She proceeded to vent her rage with great vehemence against hireling priests and the trade of preaching in general, and closed with dealing out large portions of brimstone to the drunkard and still larger and hotter to those who give the bottle to drink. This part of her discourse pleased me very much and may be a saving to me into the bargain; for, the dread of everlasting roasting added to my love of economy will (I think) prevent me making my friends tipsy. A very efficacious sermon!

July 8th.—Jenkins's is a good tavern, but it entertains at a high price. Our bill was 6 dollars each for a day and two nights; a shameful charge. Leave New Albany, cross the Ohio, and pass through Louisville in Kentucky again, on our way to Lexington, the capital. Stop for the night at Mr. Netherton's, a good tavern. The land hitherto is good, and the country altogether healthy, if I may judge from the people who appear more cheerful and happy than in Indiana, always excepting Harmony. Our landlord is the picture of health and strength: 6 feet 4 inches high, weighs 300 lb. and not fat.

From *The Americans as they are; described in a tour through the valley of the Mississippi*, by the author of "Austria as it is" [1828], pp. 31-42, 58-60, 66-71.

POSTEL, KARL. (*Pseudonym* Charles Sealsfield)

To the political thinkers of Europe, the period of the "twenties" during the last century witnessed a very important transition in our nat on's development. If we are to believe the contemporary accounts, the Europeans were taken by surprise when they read the significant warning couched in the Monroe Doctrine, issued in 1823. And when John Quincy Adams gave it still greater force, a few observers began to inquire into the reason for this sudden evolution of a world power. Many came to study our society and institutions first hand. Among them was one Karl Postel, who had travelled extensively over Central Europe, and had written a creditable work entitled "Austria as it is." His observations in America were confined largely to the region of the Ohio and Mississippi valleys. While his notes are somewhat brief, the reader can feel certain that they are his own, and his conclusions are drawn from actual experience.

VEVAY, in Indiana, became a settlement twenty years ago, by Swiss emigrants, who obtained a grant of land, equal to 200 acres for each family, under the condition of cultivating the vine; they accordingly settled here, and laid out vineyards. The original settlers may have amounted to thirty; others joined them afterwards, and in this manner was founded the county town of New Switzerland, in Indiana, which consists almost exclusively of these French and Swiss settlers. They have their vineyards below the town, on the banks of the river Ohio. The vines, however, have degenerated, and the produce is an indifferent beverage, resembling any thing but claret, as it had been represented. Two of them have attempted to cultivate the river hills, and the vineyards laid out there are rather of a better sort. The town is on the decline; it has a court-house, and two stores very ill supplied. The condition of these, and the absence of lawyers, are sure indications of the poverty of the inhabitants, if broken windows, and doors falling from their hinges, should leave any doubt on the subject; they are, however, a merry set of people, and balls are held regularly every month. In the evening arrived ten teams laden with fifty emigrants from Kentucky, going to settle in Indiana; their reasons for doing this were numerous. Although they had bought their lands in Kentucky twice over, they had to give them up a third time, their titles having proved invalid; but still they would have remained, had it not been for the insolent behaviour of their more wealthy neighbours, who, in consequence of these emigrants having no slaves, and being thus obliged to work for themselves, not only treated them as slaves, but even encouraged their own blacks to give them every kind of annoyance, and to rob them—for no other reason than their dislike to have paupers for neighbours.

My landlord assured me that at least 200 wagons had passed from the Kentucky side, through Vevay, during the present season, all full of emigrants, discouraged from continuing among these lawless people.

The state of Indiana, which I had now entered, begins below Cincinnati, running down the big Miami westward to the big Wabash, which separates this country from the Illinois. To the south, it is bounded by the Ohio; to the north, by lake Michigan; thus extending from 37° 50″ to 42° 10″, north latitude; and from 7° 40″, to 10° 47″, west longitude. Like the state of Ohio, it belongs to the class coming within the range of the great valley of the Mississippi. It exhibits nearly the same features as the state of Ohio, with the exception, that it approaches nearer to the Mississippi than its eastern neighbour, and is the second slope of the eastern part of the valley of the Mississippi: it declines more than Ohio, being but 250 feet above lake Erie, and 210 feet above lake Michigan, which is one hundred feet less in elevation than the state of Ohio. Two ridges of mountains, or rather hills, traverse the country; the Knobs, or Silver-hills, running ten miles below Louisville, in a north-eastern direction, and the Illinois mountains appearing from the west, and running to the north-east, where they fall to a level with the high plains of lake Michigan. These hills have a perfect sameness. The climate is rather milder than that of Ohio. Cotton and tobacco are raised by the farmers in sufficient quantities for their home consumption. The growth of timber is the same as in Ohio. The vallies are interspersed with sycamores and beeches; and below the falls, with maples, and cotton and walnut-trees. The hills are covered with beech, sassafras, and logwood. This state, though not inferior to Ohio in fertility, and taken in general, perhaps, superior to it, has one great defect. It has no sufficient water communication, and thus the inhabitants have no market for their produce. There is not in this state any river of importance, the Ohio which washes its southern borders excepted. A scarcity of money therefore is more severely felt here, than in any other state of the Union. This want of inter-communication, added to the circumstance that the state of Ohio had already engrossed the whole surplus population from the eastern states, had a prejudicial effect upon Indiana, its original population being in general by no means so respectable as that of Ohio. In the north-west it was peopled by French emigrants, from Canada; in the south, on the banks of the Ohio, and farther up, by Kentuckians, who fled from their country for debt, or similar causes.

The state thus became the refuge of adventurers and idlers of every description. A proof of this may be seen in the character of its towns, as well as in the nature of the improvements that have been carried on in the country. The towns, though some of them had an earlier existence than many in Ohio, are, in point of regularity, style of building, and cleanliness, far inferior to those of the former state. The wandering spirit of the inhabitants seems still to contend with the principle of steadiness in the very construction of their buildings. They are mostly a rude set of people, just emerging from previous bad habits, from whom such friendly assistance as honest neighbours afford, or mutual intercourse and good will, can hardly be expected. The case is rather different in the interior of the country, and on the Wabash, the finest part of the state, where respectable settlements have been formed by Americans from the east. Wherever the latter constitute the majority, every necessary assistance may be expected.

For adventurers of all descriptions, Indiana holds out allurements of every kind. Numbers of Germans, French, and Irish, are scattered in the towns, and over the country, carrying on the business of bakers, grocers, store, grog shops, and tavern keepers. In time, these people will become steady from necessity, and consequently prosperous. The number of the inhabitants of Indiana amounts to 215,000. Its admission into the Union as a sovereign state, dates from the year 1815 to 1816; its constitution differs in some points from that of Ohio, and its governor is elected for the term of three years.

Madisonville, the seat of justice for Jefferson-county, on the second bank of the Ohio, fifty-seven miles above its falls, contains at present 180 dwelling-houses, a court-house, four stores, three inns, a printing office—with 800 inhabitants, most of them Kentuckians. The innkeeper of the tavern at which I alighted, does no credit to the character of this people. He was engaged for some time in certain bank-note affairs, which qualified him for an imprisonment of ten years; he escaped, however, by the assistance of his legal friends, and of 1000 dollars. The opportunity of testifying his gratitude to these gentlemen soon presented itself. One of his neighbours, a boatman, had the misfortune to possess a wife who attracted his attention. Her husband knowing the temper of the man, resolved to sell all he had, and to move down to Louisville. Some days before his intended departure, he met Sheets in the street, and addressed him in these words: "Mr. Sheets, I ought to chastise you for making such shameful proposals to my wife:" so saying, he gently touched him with his cane. Sheets, without uttering a syllable, drew his poniard, and stabbed him in the breast. The unfortunate husband fell, exclaiming, "Oh, God! I am a dead man!"—"Not yet," said Sheets, drawing his poniard out of the wound, and running it a second time through his heart; "Now, my dear fellow, I guess we have done." This monster was seized and imprisoned, and his trial took place. *His* countrymen took, as might be expected, a great interest in his fate. With the assistance of 3000 dollars, he even this time escaped the gallows. I read the issue of the trial, and the summons of the jury, in the county paper of 1823, which was actually handed to me in the evening by one of the guests. But a more remarkable circumstance is, that the inhabitants continue to frequent his tavern. At first they stayed away for some weeks; but in less than a month the affair was forgotten, and his house is now visited as before.

The road from Madison to Charleston, leads through a fertile country, in some parts well cultivated. The distance from Madison is twenty-eight miles. It is the chief town of Clark county, and seems to advance more rapidly than Madison, the country about being prety well peopled, and agriculture having made more progress than in any part of the state through which I had travelled. I found it to contain 170 houses and 750 inhabitants, five well stored tradesmen's shops, a printing office, and four inns. The town is about a mile distant from the river, on a high plain. When I arrived, the court was going to adjourn, and I hastened to the court-house. The presiding judge and his two associate judges were in their tribune, and the parties seated on boards laid across the stumps of trees. One of the lawyers having concluded his speech, the defendant was called upon. The gentleman in question, whom I took for a pedlar, stood close by my side in conversation with his party, holding in his hand half an apple, his teeth having taken a firm bite of the other half. At the moment his name was called, he walked with his mouth full, up to the rostrum, and kept eating his apple with perfect indifference. "Well," interrupted the judge impatient of the delay; "what have you to say against the charge? You know it is high time to break up the court, and I must go home." The gentleman at the bar now pocketted his apple, and having thus augmented the store of provision which he probably kept by him, looked as if he carried two knapsacks behind his coat. "It strikes me mightily"—was the exordium of this speech, which in point of elegance and conciseness was a true sample of back-wood eloquence. Fortunately the speaker took the judge's hint; in less than half an hour he had done—in less than one hour the jurymen returned a verdict, the county transactions were finished, and the court broke up.

From Charleston to Louisville, the distance is fourteen miles. The lands are fertile. Several very well looking farms shew a higher degree of cultivation, especially near Jeffersonville. There the road turns into an extensive valley formed by the alluvions of the Ohio. Jeffersonville, the seat of justice for Floyd-county, three quarters of a mile above the falls of the Ohio, was laid out in 1802, and has since increased to 160 houses, among which are a bank, a Presbyterian church, a warehouse, a cotton manufactory, a court-house, and an academy, with a land office, for the disposal of the United States' lands. The commerce of the inhabitants, 800 in number, is of some importance, though checked by the vicinity of Louisville, and by the circumstance, that the falls on the Indiana side are not to be approached, except at the highest rise. Two miles below this town, is the village of Clarksville, laid out in 1783, and forming part of the grant made to officers and soldiers of the Illinois regiment. It contains sixty houses and 300 inhabitants. New Albany, a mile below Clarksville; has a thousand inhabitants, and a great deal of activity, owing to its manufactory of steam engines, its saw mills and the steam boats lying at anchor and generally repairing there. It is a place of importance, and though hitherto the resort of sailors, boatmen, and travellers, who go down the river in their own boats, it is annually on the increase.

The Ohio is generally crossed above the falls at Jeffersonville. The sheet of water dammed up here by the natural ledge of rocks which forms the falls, expands to 5,230 feet in breadth. The falls of the Ohio, though they should not properly be called falls, cannot be seen when crossing the river, and the waters do not pour like the falls of Niagara over an horizontal rock down a considerable depth, but press through a rocky bed, about a mile long, which spreads across the river, and causes a decline of twenty-two feet in the course of two miles. When the waters are high, the rocks and the falls disappear entirely. Seen from Louisville at low water, they have by no means an imposing appearance. The majestic and broad river branches off into several small creeks, and assumes the form of mountain torrents forcing their way through the ledge of rocks. When the river rises, and only three islands are to be seen, the immense sheet of water rushing down the declivity at the rate of thirteen miles an hour, must afford a magnificent spectacle. At the time I saw it, the river was lower than it had been for a series of years. . . .

Troy, the seat of justice for Crawford county, in Indiana, was the first place we visited. It has a court-house, a printing-office, and about sixty houses. The inhabitants seem rather indolent. On our asking for apples, they demanded ten dollars for half a barrel; the price for a whole one in Louisville being no more than three dollars. We advised them to keep their apples, and to plant trees, which would enable them to raise some for themselves; and to put panes of glass in their windows, instead of old newspapers. The surrounding country is beautiful and fertile. Farms, however, become more scarce, and are in a state of more primitive simplicity. A block cabin not unlike a stable, with as many holes as there are logs in it, patches of ground planted with tobacco, sweet potatoes, and some corn, are the sole ornaments of these back-wood mansions. We purchased, below Troy, half a young bear, at the rate of five cents per pound. Two others which were skinned, indicated an abundance of these animals, and more application to the sport than seems compatible with the proper cultivation of these regions. The settlers have something of a savage appearance: their features are hard, and the tone of their voice denotes a violent disposition. Our Frenchman was bargaining for a turkey, with the farmer's son, an athletic youth. On being asked three dollars for it, the Frenchman turned round to Mr. B., saying: "I suppose the Kentuckians take us for fools." "What do you say, stranger," replied the youth, at the same time laying his heavy hand across the shoulders of the poor Frenchman, in rather a rough manner. The latter looked as if thunderstruck, and retired in the true style of the Great Nation, when they get a sound drubbing. We remarked on his return, the pains he took to repress his feelings at the coarseness of the Kentuckians. He was, however, discreet enough to keep his peace, and he did very well; but his spirit was gone, and he never afterwards undertook to make a bargain, except with old women, for a pot of milk, or a dozen of eggs, &c. . . .

ABOUT a hundred and fifty houses, built on the Swabian plan, with the exception of Mr. Rapp's former residence—a handsome brick house—presented themselves to our view. We were introduced to one of the managers, a Mr. Shnee, formerly a Lutheran minister, who entered very soon into perticulars respecting Mr. Owen's ulterior views, in rather a pompous manner. This settlement, which is about thirty miles above the mouth of the big Wabash, in Indiana, was first established by Rapp, in the year 1817, and was now (in the year 1823), purchased by Mr. Owen, of Lanark, for the sum of 150,000 dollars. The society is to be established on a plan rather different from the one he has pursued in Scotland, and on a larger scale. Mr. Owen has, it is said, the pecuniary means as well as the ability to effect something of importance. A plan was shown and sold to us, according to which a new building of colossal dimensions is projected; and if Mr. Owen's means should not fall short of his good will, this edifice would certainly exhibit the most magnificent piece of architecture in the Union, the capitol at Washington excepted. This palace, when finished, is to receive his community. According to his views, as laid down in his publications, in the lectures held by him at Washington and at New York, and as stated in the verbal communications of the persons who represent him, he is about to form a society, unshackled by all those fetters which religion, education, prejudices, and manners have imposed upon the human species; and his followers will exhibit to the world the novel and interesting example of a community, which, laying aside every form of worship and all religious belief in a supreme being, shall be capable of enjoying the highest social happiness by no other means than the impulse of innate egotism. It has been the object of Mr. Owen's study to improve this egotism in the most rational manner, and to bring it to the highest degree of perfection; and in this sense he has published the Constitution, which is to be adopted by the community. It is distributed, if I recollect rightly, into three subdivisions, with seventy or more articles.—Mechanics of every description—people who have learned any useful art,—are admitted into this community. Those who pay 500 dollars, are free from any obligation to work. The time of the members is divided between working, reading, and dancing. A ball is given every day, and is regularly attended by the community. Divine service, or worship of any kind, is entirely excluded; in lieu of it, moreover, a ball is given on Sunday. The children are summoned to school by beat of drum. A newspaper is published, chiefly treating of their own affairs, and of the entertainments and the social regulations of the community, amounting to about 500 members, of both sexes, composed almost exclusively of adventurers of every nation, who expect joyful days. The settlement has not improved since the purchase, and there appeared to exist the greatest disorder and uncleanliness. This community has since been dissolved as was to have been expected. The Scotchman seems to have a very high notion of the power of egotism. He is certainly not wrong in this point; but if he intends to give still greater strength to a spirit which already works with too much effect in the Union, it may be feared that he will soon snap the cords of society asunder. According to his notions, and those of his people, all the legislators of ancient and modern times, religious as well as political, were either fools or impostors, who went in quest of prosperity on a mistaken principle, which he is now about to correct. Scotchmen, it is known, are sometimes liable to adopt strange notions, in which they always deem themselves infallible. I am acquainted with an honorable president of the quarter-sessions, who, as a true Swedenborghian, is fully convinced that he will preside again as judge in the other world, and that the German farmers will be there the same fools they are here, who he may continue to cheat out of their property. Great Britain has no cause to envy the United States this acquisition. We stayed at this place about two hours, crossed the Wabash, and took the road to Shawneetown, through part of Mr. Birkbeck's settlement. The country is highly cultivated, and the difference between the steady Englishman of the Illinois side, and the rabble of Owen's settlement, is clearly seen in the style and character of the improvements carried on.

From *Remarks made on a tour to Prairie du Chien, 1829*, by Caleb Atwater [1831], p. 205.

Atwater, Caleb.

Caleb Atwater is best known as Ohio's First Historian. He was one of the most versatile men produced in the old northwest: minister, lawyer, educator, legislator and antiquarian. He was born in Massachusetts in 1778, graduated from Williams College, came west when thirty-seven years old, and settled in Circleville, Ohio. Always public spirited, he supported improvements of every nature, and personally urged a system of public education.

He was the best informed man of his age on western antiquities and archeology. His knowledge extended over many years of investigation made from New York to the Mississippi River.

In May 1829, President Jackson appointed Atwater as one of the three commissioners to treat with the Winnebago Indiana on the upper Mississippi. While on this trip, Mr. Atwater kept a personal diary of all his observations, and from these, the following extracts are taken.

VINCENNES

Stands on the east bank of the Wabash, surrounded by fertile lands. It is an old town, for the western country, having been settled about the same time with St. Louis, Rock Island, Prairie du Chien, and Kaskaskia, as I have already stated in a former page. Vincennes contains more than fifteen hundred people, who certainly appear very well to a stranger. The houses were mostly new ones, and everything I saw here made a very favorable impression. I tarried at Clark's Hotel, and take a pleasure in recommending the house to other travellers.

Leaving this beautiful town in the stage for Louisville, I reached that town in two days. The first twenty miles from Vincennes, was over a good road and through a delightful country —the remainder of the rout was over as undulating a surface as I ever saw.

Indiana is rapidly setling with an excellent population. The face of the country is undergoing a change in its external appearance—the forest is disappearing before the industrious husbandman—the state of society, considering the newness of the country, is good, and in numbers, wealth and improvements of all kinds, Indiana is only ten, or at most, only about twelve years behind Ohio. Next to the latter, Indiana is most rapidly improving of any western state, at this moment. To any one emigrating from the Atlantic states westwardly, though Ohio would best suit him, in all respects, yet Indiana is decidedly next in advantages of all sorts. The soil and climate are about the same in both states—the people nearly the same, and their interests, feelings and views, precisely the same. These states may be considered as Pennsylvania and Maryland, extended from the Atlantic ocean to the Wabash river. They are one and the same people, and so may they ever act and feel towards each other, in Congress—at home and abroad.

From *Personal Reminiscences of Charles F. Coffin, of Wayne County, Indiana, from 1824 to 1833.*

COFFIN, CHARLES F.

Charles F. Coffin was born in North Carolina in 1823. He was brought by his parents to Wayne County, Indiana, in 1824, and resided in that county for sixty years. He died in Chicago, Illinois, August 9, 1916.

He was a man of unusual ability. For twenty-seven years he was Clerk of Indiana Yearly Meeting of Friends. He was a prominent banker and was closely associated with his friend, Governor Oliver P. Morton, in the financial affairs of the state during the Civil War. He was offered the position of Commissioner of Indian affairs under President Grant, and afterward Comptroller of Currency, but he declined both. He was a pioneer in prison reform and was one of the originators of the Woman's Prison of Indiana.

He possessed a very clear, accurate, historical mind, and wrote a number of valuable historical articles pertaining to local history.

I was brought by my parents to Wayne County in 1824. As I was only one year old, of course I can give no personal recollections at that early date, but I have a very distinct recollection of the latter part of this period mentioned in this letter.

The County was comparatively new, although settlements had been made in most parts of it and in some places for a good many years. There was a large emigration from North and South Carolina, especially of Friends, who settled in different parts of the County. The main body of them at Richmond and immediate vicinity; others at Fountain City in the north part of the County; others at Economy in the northwest part of the County and others in the neighborhood of Milton in the west part of the County and a few in the vicinity of Centerville in the central part of the County. Large improvements were made at all these places. There was also considerable emigration from Kentucky and Tennessee which settled principally in the southeast and central parts of the county. Very few New England or Eastern people were amongst these early emigrants. The country in my first recollections was still thickly wooded except small clearings around each homestead and the woods were grown up with underbrush and vines of various kinds.

The wild animals had principally been exterminated before my recollection and there were no Indians in the County. Some of them frequently visited the county in the earliest settlements, but it is not known that any of them ever permanently resided within its limits. The houses of the new settlers were of their own build;—at first Cabins, succeeded then by small hewed log houses interspersed occasionally with cheap frame buildings which ultimately took the place of the others. The streams were nearly double the size that they are at present, during most of the year, large reservoirs of water in the woods and swamps furnishing a continued supply to keep their volume up. The clearing up of the country has caused great change in this respect and reduced the size of the streams most of the year, but causes them to swell very largely during freshets and heavy rains. The first settlers had very few comforts and lived in an exceedingly rough and simple way, mostly upon Hog and Hominy and upon corn bread, as corn was raised the first thing after the clearing of a piece of ground. Along all the streams were soon built small mills which supplied the local demands of the community and also saw mills which furnished lumber for improvements. There was a vast amount of fine walnut timber, especially in the bottom of the west fork of Whitewater River, where my father first settled, near what is now the town of Milton. This timber was used lavishly because it was easily split into rails and greatly wasted. In subsequent years it became exceedingly valuable and every remaining tree was carefully protected until a market was found for it. The early settler was generally of the younger and vigorous class of people, but there was much sickness; chills and fever and severe fevers prevailed, especially along the water courses. There are no records of the mortality but there is no doubt that it was very great and in many instances great suffering ensued from the want of proper medical treatment and care and of proper food. I remember well of hearing my Father speak of a severe attack of fever which he had when living in a cabin on the bank of the West Fork of the Whitewater River which came very nearly taking his life, and the great difficulty experienced by my Mother when recovery commenced in getting anything suitable for a fever patient to eat. The difficulty connected with the terrific labor involved in clearing the trees from a new country and opening farms was vigorously and cheerfully met by the settlers. Great personal kindness abounded; they assisted each other in every way possible. There was a great deal of traveling through the community of persons out in search of homes. Hotels were not much known and every private house was opened freely to the traveler. There was no roads except as trees were cut away by the first settlers. The streams were unbridged and often impassable, always during a freshet and as the roads were largely shaded they remained wet a great deal of the years and became almost impassable at times—a large proportion of that time they were muddy and disagreeable to travel over. There were very few, if any carriages in the county in these days. The people rode on horseback mostly, or in their wagons. During the latter part of the time the comforts of the community increased. farms became better opened and roads were somewhat improved though still very bad. Merchants established little stores at various points where they kept a few drygoods and groceries. Some of the towns had commenced growing and improvements were increasing in them. A few brick houses were erected but not many until after the period mentioned. All of the groceries and drygoods used had to be hauled in wagons from Cincinnati, a distance of 60 to 70 miles and large four horse wagons passed over the route frequently occupying three or four four days in the passage. Salt and other necessaries were brought in the same way. Products of the farms were driven to market, such as hogs, cattle etc. Cincinnati was the great commercial point of the whole country. Orchards had been planted and in many places were bearing fine crops of fruit, especially of apples. The fresh virgin soil produced a very fine article of fruit.

There were but few schools and no general public school system. A teacher was employed for three months of the year and such children as could be spared from home were sent to him. They were of a primitive kind and not of the highest type but very useful in their results. In the neighborhood of Friends it was made a special point to open what was called "A Friend's School," and they were kept at all the meeting places in the county. There were different religious denominations which mostly located by a kind of natural affinity near to each other, Methodist, Baptist, Presbyterian etc. The pioneer preachers of the county, however, were Methodists who spread over the whole land. They traveled on horseback and lived with the people in their method of life and were indefatigable in establishing churches and elevating the people. Their influence was exceedingly good. In other places where there were no special religious influences there grew up a class of people who disregarded the Sabbath, attended no place of worship and their children mostly became a very undesirable part of the community.

The mails were carried first on horseback, then in small wagons or carriages, during the muddy season of the year were taken with great difficulty through the land. Postage was from six and one-quarter cents to twenty-five counted in Spanish coin which was the current coin of the country at the time, namely, $6\frac{1}{4}$, $12\frac{1}{2}$ and 25 cents. But money was exceedingly scarce and the settlers managed to do with a great deal less than would be possible at the present time.

From *Diary and Recollections of Victor Colin Duclos.* Copied from the original manuscript by Mrs. Nora C. Fretageot, New Harmony, Ind.

Duclos, Victor Colin.

Mr. Duclos came from France in 1823 at the age of five. In his recollections he describes his attendance at William Maclure's school in Philadelphia, the visit of Lafayette, and his departure for New Harmony to join the Owen colony in 1825. From Pittsburgh to Mt. Vernon, Ind., the trip was made by the Ohio River and the company is known as the "Boat load of knowledge." The passenger list included the names of Thomas Say, Charles A. Lesueur, Robert Dale Owen, Gerald Troost, Joseph Neff and Madame Fretageot. The account of New Harmony life is brought down to the year 1834.

I am a native of France and was born in Paris, May 22, 1818. I left there in the early part of the year 1823 with my aunt, Madam Marie D. Fretageot, to attend a School of Industry established by Mr. William Maclure in Philadelphia, Pa. We started from Havre in a sailing vessel in March, 1823, and were six weeks on the voyage. On board this vessel, who intended to make this school their home, were Madam Fretageot, her son Achilles E. Fretageot, a Swiss named Balthazar, Charles A. Lesueur, two French students, my brother, Peter L. Duclos, myself and several others. We arrived in New York in May, and went to Philadelphia in June. The school house was situated on the Schuylkill road about one mile from the city. It was a large fine brick building with a very large arched door in the centre. Surrounding the school building, were the most beautiful pleasure ground immaginable. This was William Maclure's "School of Industry."

In the year 1824, while at this school in Philadelphia, General Lafayette made his last visit to the United States. He visited our school, and in his review, all of us marched in single file in front of him, and he gently laid his hand on our heads and told us to be good boys. General Lafayette was a man about 5 ft. 9 in. in highth and spare built. His hair was long and very gray. He wore a black broadcloth frock coat. If the Almighty God should have dropped into the city at that time he could not have been more highly worshipped than was General Lafayette. This was about 76 years ago, and I imagine that I can to this day feel the gentle tap on my head from that noble man.

In the year 1824, Mr. Robert Owen, a gentleman from Scotland, purchased all of the interests of the Rapp Society in Posey County, Indiana, including the town of Harmonie where he, in a short time, founded the noted Owen Community. Somewhat later than this, William Maclure bought an interest in the property and concluded to remove his School of Industry to New Harmony from Philadelphia. Therefore the early part of the year 1825 was occupied in building a large keel boat at Pittsburgh, Pa. This boat being well fitted with rooms and otherwise properly arranged for the comfort of the passengers and crew, we moved to Pittsburgh by means of wagons and carriages. The boat contained the leading members of talent of the school, and was therefore styled the Boat load of knowledge, and named the Philanthropist.

In the fall of the year 1825 we started from Pittsburgh down the Ohio River to Mt Vernon, Ind. from thence to New Harmony. As well as I can remember the names of those on the boat, with incidental remarks concerning them, are about as follows:—

Madam Fretageot and son, A. E. Fretageot, Allan Ward, Mark Penrose, Phiquepal d' Arusmont—who afterwards married Francer Wright—Charles A. Lesueur, artist and naturalist, Thomas Say, naturalist, M. Chase, chemist, Mrs Chase, artist and musician, Cornelius Tiebout, artist and engraver, Miss Lucy Sistaire, and two sisters—Miss Lucy afterwards married Thomas Say—Virginia Dupalais and her brother, John Beal, wife and daughter Caroline—baby—William Maclure, Captain McDonald of the Isles, Balthazar, a Swiss, Charles Falque, Amedie Dufour, Peter L. Duclos, Victor C. Duclos, Miss Tiebout, age 10,—last five pupils of Phiquepal—Mr. Speakman and family, Robert Dale Owen, Gerard Troost, chemist and geologist, Robert Owen came part way with them. Mme. Fretageot was employed by Mr. Maclure to superintend the school, while the scientific gentlemen and some of the others were professors in the new School of Industry he was to establish at New Harmony

Cincinnati was the first place of importance at which we landed. There was at that time very few buildings between 3d street and the river. We traveled very slowly for the reason that we did not run the boat nights, and many delays were occasioned by the wind being too high for our boat to be handled.

During the trip while the boat was thus delayed, many of the party would spend their time in hunting, fishing and in scientific investigations. Fish and game abounded, so that a large portion of our subsistance was derived from these sources.

On reaching Louisville the weather was very windy and cold. Here we stopped for some time in order to find a "Falls pilot", to buy provisions, etc. In passing over the Falls we had a narrow escape from wrecking the boat. Soon after leaving Louisville, the ice came rushing down the river and pushed the boat out into the woods. Here we were compelled to stay three or four weeks. One of our party while out hunting broke his leg by falling off a rail fence, and two of the French students broke through the ice while skating and came near drowning. As soon as possible after the ice broke up, we launched our boat and continued our journey.

About the middle of January, 1826, we arrived at Evansville. At that time it was but little more than a flat-boat landing, the settlement consisting of a few small log cabins. On our arrival at Mt Vernon about the last week in January, 1826, we were transferred by wagons. Thus we finally reached our destination on the scene of the former home of the Rapp Society, the home of the new Owen Community, and the location of our new School of Industry.

To give some idea of the value and importance of the property belonging to the Rapp Society previous to the sale of Mr. Robert Owen, it is necessary to describe in detail the territory and the great amount of improvements, in building and in the productive and manufacturing interests of the society in the town and vacinity. During their occupancy, considering the short time in which this vast amount of work was performed the results were remarkable. Coming in 1814 and removing in 1824–5, beginning in the unbroken forest, in the short space of ten years they cleared about 4000 acres of land, built the town, containing comfortable homes of brick and frame, large granaries of wood and stone, oil mills, grist mills, sawmills, distilleries, and factories for the various branches of manufactures they engaged in.

The property consisted of about 3,000 acres of land surrounding and including the town site. This being on what is called the second bottom, a narrow strip of lower land between it and the river and stretching out into a wide low valley to the north, a range of hills on the south and east, and the low land of the Cut-off River to the west. Judging from the location of the principal buildings, the town was laid off in the form of a square, bordered by North, South, East and West Streets. The Main Street extended from the entrance of the Mt. Vernon wagon road to the foot of the hills north to North Street, with a wagon road from thence to the ferry landing on the Wabash River. One square west of Main Street was west Street, and to the east were Brewery and East Streets. The principal street leading east and west was Church Street, connecting on the east with the wagon road leading to Princeton and Evansville. North of Church were Granary and North Streets, to the south, Tavern, Steam Mill, and South Streets. The streets were named from the locations and after the buildings situated thereon. Thus Church St. from the old German Church, the old Fort or granary gave its name to Granary St. Brewery St. from the brewery, and so on.

In the town and surrounding suburbs there were a great many rudely constructed log cabins which were the homes of these industrious people in the first years of the settlement, many without floors and undoubtedly built for temporary use while the more substantial buildings were being erected. In the town limits were constructed about twenty substantial two story brick buildings, which with a few exceptions were built east and west on the corners of the blocks. There were about the same number of frame buildings two stories in heighth. The dwelling houses both frame and brick were built after the same design with the door opening into the yard, the houses being on the line of the streets, making the corners of the blocks. Most of the houses are still in use though the majority have been remodeled.

On the west of Brewery, between Church and Granary Sts. was a one story frame building about 30 x 60 ft. which was used as a hospital, now in use as a warehouse. On the north west corner of Main and Tavern streets was the Rapp Tavern, a two story frame about 30 x 60 ft fronting on Main Street. In the rear of this on Tavern Street was a two story brick of about the same dimensions. On the north of the brick was a large double porch in which was located the stairway for both buildings. In after years this property was used for many purposes and was known as the "White House," the upper and rear parts being used as a tenament house, now known as the Monitor Saloon, but in the early history of the town it was called the "Yellow Tavern". (Burned Aug. 1908)

Within the block east of Main and between Tavern and Church Sts. was a two story brick about 40 x 60 ft. built east and west, and within the block south of this was a building about 30 x 40 (still in use. 1902), the first story of stone, the second of brick. On the corner of Church and Brewery Sts. was a large frame livery stable. On the south east corner of Main and Church Sts. was a pit for whip-sawing the lumber first used in the construction of the buildings. These buildings were mostly used as dwellings for single families.

For school buildings the larger buildings were used. In reference to a class of buildings of special note that were numbered from 1 to 5, it is not definitely known what purpose they were constructed for. A study of position and internal arrangement, surroundings, etc. will offer some suggestions as to their use.

No. 1 stood east of West Street on the corner of West and Steam Mill Streets (N.E.) was a two story brick about 40 x 70 ft. with a hallway on both floors, the whole length of the building. Contained sixteen large rooms.

No. 2, on the east side of Main between Church and Granary Str. was a three story brick 40 x 70 ft. with a kind of mansard roof, two stories of brick and the third formed by the mansard roof. The entrance was on an alley opening into a hall extending from end to end, with rooms on both sides in each story opening into the hallways. East of this was a large building used for a kitchen.

No. 3 was situated about the center of the block on the south side of Church, between Main and Brewery Sts. similar in size and construction to No. 1. It is built off the line of the street about ten feet. Runs north and south, the entrance on Church Street.

No. 4, same as No. 1–3, on Church Street, North side between brewery and East Street.

No. 5 was the home of George Rapp, the founder of the society. It was located on the Northwest corner of Church and Main Streets, about 30 feet back from both streets. It was of brick, two stories in highth, with a one story ell on the west. The foundation was about four feet in highth, of dressed sandstone. A porch or verandah extended the whole length on the south and east sides, with large stone steps to each entrance. On each floor there were large halls leading east and west. This building was destroyed by fire about the year 1842, (1844), supposed to have been the work of an incendiary.

A few feet north of No. 5 was a large oak tree. Tradition tells us that this spot was the camping ground of those members of the society who were the first to spend the night in this locality, and ever after during their residence here, it was a favorite spot for the society band to meet and discourse sweet music.

The place of worship during the last few years of their residence here was a building constructed from plans of George Rapp and conceived by him in a dream. This was a two story brick building constructed in the year 1822, but the internal arrangement was never carried out. It stood on the northwest part of the block on Church Street between Main and West Streets. It was planned so that the interior at the pulpit represented a large cross. The dimensions of the centre square was about 40 feet, and each wing the same. (Mr. Dransfield has written in parenthesis "This is not exact as the wings were 50 feet in width, and the interior square was about 70 feet each way.") The centre roof was supported by four columns about eighteen inches in diameter and twenty-five feet in highth (really two feet in diameter), each turned by hand from one stick of timber, of cherry, poplar, or walnut. These columns stood on a large moulded base of the same wood, about forty feet in highth from the foundation. In the centre of the building was a large dome, encircling which was a balcony at times used as a band stand. The entrances to each wing were large stone foundations with the semi-circular stone steps. The second and third steps were moulded on the edge. The north door, which was the principal entrance, was of cherry. The doorway was of carved stone capped by a cornice terminating in a gable in the panel of which was carved a rose, gilded, with a reference to it taken from the Bible, carved in the stone. The other doorways were also of stone but more simply finished.

The old church built about 1815 stood east of this on the same lot and was a two story frame with six large arched windows on the sides, and two in the end, with round windows in the gables. A belfry 20 x 20 feet and 20 feet above the roof was built on the east end. This had large slatted windows in each side and contained one large and one small bell. A clock room, hexagonal in shape was built above the belfry. On the northeast of this was a clock face about eight feet in diameter, and a similar one on the southeast. Within this room was a clock gearing occupying a space of about six (ft?) square and the same in highth. This was arranged to strike the hours on the large bell and the small bell to note the quarter hours. These bells could be heard a distance of seven miles, and were the two finest ones in the state at that time. (went to Concinnati). The church steeple was built above the belfry.

As a protection against Indians and known as the Fort was a building 40 x 70 feet south of Granary between Main and West Streets. The first story was of rough stone, the walls about two feet in thickness with six port holes on either side and two on each end. The windows were barred with iron. The second and third stories were of brick. The two lower floors were laid with tile about nine inches square, probably with the object of preventing them being fired from the outside. The third story in the attic was floored with wood. The roof was what is known as a hipped roof and was very strongly built and covered with large tiles 7 x 12 inches, with hooks on the under side to lap over the lathing. There were three doorways, one on the north, south and east. The doors were very thick and strong and were securely fastened by enormous locks, and also barred as an additional security. At the south end of this was a kitchen with a subterranean passage way connecting the cellar with the interior of the Fort. But this has never been substantiated. (There was no cellar to this building, but when it was torn down to build the "new laboratory", a small arched chamber about six feet wide and eight feet long was found.)

On the same block, fronting on Church Street was a greenhouse about 20 x 40 feet, supported on rollers with lower foundation timbers twice the width of the house. On these were rails on which the grooved rollers travelled, allowing the building to be moved back and forth. In each side of the house was a liberal supply of glass windows, and the room was heated with the old style of tinplate stoves. Within this house were grown many kinds of tropical fruits, flowers, ferns, etc.

Within the same block and west of this was a press house, a one story frame about 30 x 36 feet. Here was located the cider and wine press, a large wooden screw with a large lever to operate it. The apples were reduced to pulp by a large circular stone pivoted in the centre. This stone was twelve inches in thickness and about six feet in diameter. It was revolved on a shaft and travelled in a circle probably twenty feet in diameter in a stone trough, in this the apples are shovelled and crushed by the revolving stone until in condition for the press.

The brickyard was at about the distance of two blocks south of South Street on the east side of the Mt. Vernon road near where Murphy Park is located.

West of this was the rope walk, west side of the road. This was not enclosed except to protect the machinery. Southwest of this and to the north of the road, leading to the Cutoff River was their Labyrinth. Within a circle of about 140 feet in diameter there were formed concentric circles with growth of hedge plants, presenting an intricate pathway leading to a small block house in the centre. The house was built of blocks of wood about twelve inches long pointed at one end. These were placed with the pointed ends outward to form a circular wall. The arrangement was such that it was almost impossible for anyone not accustomed to the construction to find their way to the building or to its interior.

At the northwest intersection of Brewery and North Streets was a frame building used for a brewery. In connection with this was a tread wheel built on a platform about twelve feet high. Within the wheel a dog or other small animal was used to furnish power to pump water.

On the south side of Steam Mill Street between Brewery and East Streets were two frame buildings about 40 x 45 feet, three stories high. The one to the west was used for a cotton mill, the other as a store house. The cotton mill was driven by steam power and contained a complete outfit of cotton manufacturing machinery. The mill was operated after the Germans left until destroyed by fire in 1826.

East of East Street between Tavern and Steam Mill Streets were two large three story frame hip-roofed granaries about 50 x 80 feet. In the attic of one of them was a large tread wheel about fourteen feet in diameter in which cattle or other heavy animals were used to create power for elevating grain.

Other buildings used for warehouses, etc. were located in different parts of the town. About forty acres of land west and south of the town were planted in orchards (nearer sixty) and vinyards. On the hills east of the Mt Vernon road was a large vinyard of about eighteen acres, and east of this large orchards. The sight of these orchards was enough to impress the mind of anyone of the ability and industry of this remarkable society.

South of the Labyrinth was a large locust grove. East of the Mt Vernon road were a number of log cabins. To the west of the road but on the hills were many black locust trees evidently set out to supply material for fence posts.

On my arrival here the only flouring mill in this locality was the one built by the Germans on the east bank and near the mouth of the Cut-off River about two miles southwest of town. The building was a three story frame. It was run by water power, containing four run of stones. About two miles southeast of town, located on Gresham Creek was an oil mill driven by water power. There was also a distillery on the same stream below and north of the Princeton road. Near this and east of the Creek were many log cabins. This was Community No. 2. No. 3 was west of the Creek at the foot of the hills.

When we arrived the scholars of the Maclore school went to the Neef boarding school in No. 2 until No. 5 was prepared for them. Then Madam Fretageot assumed controll as superintendent. In the No. 5 building painting, drawing, engraving and type-setting along with the common branches were taught. The painting and engraving department was in the assembly hall. In the old German frame church, with its belfry containing the town clock, shoe making was conducted on quite a large scale. In other buildings in the western and northern parts of the town, different branches of manufactures were conducted, so that the scholars could work at any trade they wished.

In No. 5 we would study from an early hour, frequently beginning at three A.M. until eight, and from one P.M. to three P.M. The remainder of the mornings and afternoons would be devoted to work at the various trades.

West of No. 5 was a building in which our meals were served. For breakfast we had an allowance of one and a half pints of milk, one large spoonful of molasses and as much corn meal mush as we wished. At noon we would have meat and vegetables, for supper we would return to mush and milk. At first we had coffee for breakfast but later Mme. Fretageot thought that was too extravagant, so henceforward we were only allowed coffee Sunday mornings. Two Mexican boys attended the school, who were sent from Mexico by William Maclure. James-Louis, aged 10, and Sevalla, 8. They could not speak English and when they wanted to know if the next day was Sunday they would say "Tomorrow coffee?" and if answered in the affirmative their joy would be unbounded. After the close of the school they were sent back to Mexico and a few years later Sevalla was killed by brigands while driving a stage coach near the City of Mexico. Louis was never heard from after his arrival in his native home.

The pupils would alternately assist in the kitchen, stirring the mush, preparing the vegetables, washing dishes, etc. also milk the cows and attend to the horses and other stock. An intermeddling Dutchman, named Kreutz, assisted in the care of the stock, whose overbearing ways made him very obnoxious to the boys who were daily brought in contact with him. One day I was out in the yard milking and was unfortunate enough to be kicked over by the cow who also as a parting act of good friendship, stepped on my foot which I resented by striking her three or four times with the milking stool. The Dutchman saw me tanning the cow and commenced abusing me. He also threatened to thrash me. I told him I would not milk another cow. He though I called him "A d—— old sow." He picked up a clapboard and started after me. I ran for the house yelling for help, as I reached the door the whole school was up greatly excited. They let me in and closed the door on my pursuer. The teacher wanted to know what it was all about. The Dutchman told her what he thought I had called him, but with a full explanation I came out all right.

A Swiss, named Baltazzar, a kind of an artist had a room in the south east corner of No. 2, and had made a large oil painting of the old Rapp church. It was hanging on the wall of his room and some of the boys decided that his lines were not perpendicular, so they drew on one side a number of men with poles against it to push it into position and a number on the opposite side pulling on ropes fastened to the eaves, pulling at it. When he saw what they had done he was so angry that he surely would have killed the guilty parties had he been able to find out who they were. Another trick played on Balthazzar (spelled several ways) was then he and Mike Craddock quarrelled. He sent Mike a challenge to fight a duel which was accepted and it was decided that pistols should be used, distance—five paces. Seconds were appointed who decided that blank cartridges should be used, and that Craddock should fall at the first fire. So early in the morning the parties repaired to a secluded spot in the old orchard and the men took their positions and glared at each other while the seconds carefully loaded the pistols. Tom Cox, one of the seconds, instructed the principals that the signal to fire should be the dropping of a handkerchief, and that the result of this fire should settle the matter. To this the principals agreed. Their weapons were handed them and the signal given. There was scarcely any difference in the reports of the two weapons. Balthazzar was apparently unhurt, but Craddock staggered, dropped his pistol, clapped his hand to his heart, and fell backward apparently dead. It was a most realistic performance. His seconds rushed up, opened his coat and pronounced him dead. Balthazzar was frightened almost to death. He cried "For God's sake, run for a doctor." At this Craddock burst out laughing. Balthazzar saw he was the victim of a practical joke, altho much chagrined, he was well satisfied as to the outcome. He was very sensitive over it when the subject was brought up and finally returned to Europe, and as he said "to the company of gentlemen."

One morning at the breakfast table we were all seated on a row of benches at either side of the table, and the mush placed near one of the rows so the scholars could help themselves. A young man, wishing more mush, lifted his foot over the seat and placed it down in the hot mush that happened to be directly behind him. He jumped about four feet high and yelled like a wild Indian, dancing over the floor he scattered the hot mush in every direction.

One of our teachers, Mr. Lesueur, was a fine artist. He taught drawing and painting, and did a great deal of artistic work outside of the school. He and Thomas Say spent most of their leisure in the woods or in the river searching for shells and catching fish which they painted and described. Mr. Lesueur also devoted some of his time to painting scenes for the Theatre. One notable scene on the south end of the old Hall was for the play of William Tell. It was still in good preservation when the building was torn down in 1874. It is related that one of his scenes represented a forest and the work was so artisticly executed that many of the audience thought they were real trees. The first piece put on the stage was The Maid and the Magpie. One scene represented a church with steeple and belfry. The maid arranged the table on the stage.

Mr. Lesueur constructed a magpie and operated it so that it flew down while the maid was absent and took a spoon from the table, up to its nest in the belfry, then returned and flew back with another spoon. The spoons were missed and the maid accused of the theft. After having been put on trial, she was condemned to death. The day of execution arrived. The executioner, supported by a double file of soldiers, marched in. The belfry man goes up in the belfry to toll the bell and finds the spoons in the magpie's nest. One of our teachers, Mrs Chase, took the part of the maid. About one year afterwards, Mr. Lesueur was called back to France by the French government and on his arrival there he was granted a large pension for valuable services rendered on various exploring expeditions.

One of our teachers was a copper plate engraver named Tiebout, who instructed the scholars in the art. Mrs Tiebout also taught in the schools. They had two children who were pupils, one, a daughter, about twelve years old who in later years married a man named Cologne, the other a son about nine. Mr. Tiebout died here and was buried in the Woods' graveyard.

Mr. Thomas Say was a fine gentleman and the scholars thought a great deal of him, in fact he was beloved by the whole community. I spent a part of almost every day at his home on the northwest corner of Granary and West Streets.

Our clothing was quite an item with us. The costume of the men and boys consisted of a jacket made quite large, pleated back and front with a band at the waist to which the pantaloons were buttoned. These were made to fit loosely and had no pockets. This formed our summer suit.

One summer, while in swimming, at the ford of Gresham Creek, where the old covered bridge spans the stream, with the other boys, I left my suit up on the bank and lingered in the water after the other boys had dressed and gone. When I came out I could not find my clothes. On looking around, a saw a cow about thirty yards off with something hanging from her mouth. I discovered it was a leg of my lost pants which she was trying to dispose of. So I put on my little jacket and chased her around the common until I managed to secure a hold on about six inches of the leg. I pulled them out but they were in a sad condition. I took them to the Creek and washed them out the best I could and put them on and went home. For a long time after that I went by the name of "chawed breeches."

About the year 1830, a young man named Oliver Evans came to town, and about a year later married Miss Louisa Neef, a daughter of one of our principal teachers. Mr Evans built a foundry north of North Street and east of Main. In connection with the foundry was a plow factory. Working on the building of the foundry, was a carpenter, named Chambers. He made a mortise on the wrong side of a stick of timber. He stood with his foot on the timber studying how to remedy the error, his elbow on his knee and his chin resting on his hand. A man coming up from the river noticed his preoccupied situation and asked him if he had the toothache, he said "yes", so the man said he would send Dr. Thompson down to pull it. The Doctor hastened down and found Chambers still resting as the man had found him. The Doctor asked him if he wanted it extracted he said "no" but he would like him to pull out this hole and put it on the other side of the timber. Dr. Thompson was very wrothy.

He said "yes, yes, Chalmers, I will make you pay for this", and sure enough, he did.

The Evans foundry made the first cast plows that were made in the state, but he found he could buy the castings in Pittsburgh for about what the pig iron would cost delivered in New Harmony.

The flouring mill at the Cutt-off was owned by Mr. Maclure and the miller was named Pennypacker. He was a man of great strength, and very proud of showing what he could do. One of his feats was to hang a 56 pound weight on his little finger and write his name with his arm extended full length. He would carry a barrel of flour under each arm. Mr. Pennypacker would come to the school to pay his rent. He frequently had to take two or three yoke of oxen and plow out the head of the Cut-off to get enough water to run the mill.

There was a fire engine left here by the Germans that was used for protection against fire. It was arranged to be worked by eighteen men and was supplied with water by buckets. It was made by Pat Lyon in Philadelphia about 1804 and is still in use by the town.

About 1834, a gentleman, Prince Maximillian, visited the town. He had with him three or four scientific men. He traveled under the name of Baron Brownsburg. While here he had a room in the northwest corner of No. 2, on the second floor. I was with him nearly every day and often accompanied him as a guide in his rambles over the country. Mr. B. asked me one day to get a skift and take him over on Fox Island. I did so, and fired his gun, frequently, but with poor success.

INDEX

A

G

K

L